AFTER STALINGRAD

The Red Army's Winter Offensive 1942–43

David Glantz

Helion & Company

Helion & Company Limited
26 Willow Road
Solihull
West Midlands
B91 1UE
England
Tel. 0121 705 3393
Fax 0121 711 4075
Email: publishing@helion.co.uk
Website: www.helion.co.uk

Published by Helion & Company 2009, reprinted 2009

Designed and typeset by Helion & Company Limited, Solihull, West Midlands
Cover designed by Bookcraft Limited, Stroud, Gloucestershire
Printed in the UK by The Cromwell Press Group

ISBN 978–1–906033–26–2

British Library Cataloguing-in-Publication Data.

A catalogue record for this book is available from the British Library.

For details of other military history titles published by Helion & Company Limited
contact the above address, or visit our website: http://www.helion.co.uk.

We always welcome receiving book proposals from prospective authors.

Contents

PART 1 – SOVIET OFFENSIVE OPERATIONS WITHIN THE CONTEXT OF THE STALINGRAD OFFENSIVE (NOVEMBER 1942-JANUARY 1943)

PART 2 – SOVIET OFFENSIVE OPERATIONS ALONG THE SOUTHWESTERN AXIS (FEBRUARY-MARCH 1943)

PART 3 – SOVIET OFFENSIVE OPERATIONS ALONG THE WESTERN (CENTRAL) AXIS (FEBRUARY-MARCH 1943)

PART 4 – SOVIET OFFENSIVE OPERATIONS ALONG THE NORTHWESTERN AXIS (FEBRUARY-MARCH 1943)

List of Photographs

(the photographs can be found together in a section starting on page 452)

List of maps

List of Figures

Preface

Although over sixty years have passed since the end of World War II in Europe, major gaps continue to exist in the historical record of the so-called Soviet-German War, the war on Germany' Eastern Front which began with Hitler's Barbarossa invasion of the Soviet Union on 22 June 1941 and ended with the defeat and surrender of Hitler's Third Reich on 9 May 1945. These gaps include numerous so-called "forgotten battles," specifically, military engagements and operations which Soviet and German historians alike have either deliberately expunged from the historical record of the war or simply overlooked, as well as important aspects of more famous battles and operations already described in war histories, which proved too controversial or embarrassing to include in these accounts.[i] This flawed mosaic of wartime military operations spans the entire duration of the war, from 1941–45, and, for a variety of reasons, ignores as much as forty percent of the war's operational record.

These "forgotten battles" exist because, on the one hand, the Soviet Union strictly censored the work of its military historians and, on the other, because German historians and many Western historians who have described the war from the German perspective preferred to concentrate on the *Wehrmacht's* victories during the first two years of the war rather than its defeats later in the war. In the case of the Soviet Union and, to a lesser extent, "official" historians writing in the Russian Federation today, the government either denied military historians access to the Red Army's wartime archives or routinely censored their work in an attempt to conceal as many of the Red Army's military failures as possible. They did so, first, to avoid embarrassing the Red Army and to protect its reputation, particularly during the period when it held the strategic initiative (November 1942-May 1945), and, second, to protect the reputations of some of Red Army's most famous wartime generals, who presided over embarrassing wartime defeats before rising to greater prominence during the postwar years.[ii] Likewise, prominent German generals who wrote memoirs after war's end, as well as historians who described the war from primarily a German perspective, preferred to focus on the dramatic victories the *Wehrmacht* achieved during the first two years of the war rather than the many defeats it suffered during the final two years of the war and generally blamed Hitler for Germany's defeat.[iii]

German and Western military historians faced an impossible task when attempting to conceal or ignore the *Wehrmacht's* many wartime defeats, in particular, after the battle for Stalingrad, because their Soviet counterparts, who were able to exploit German archival documents the Red Army captured during the war, described these defeats in vivid detail. Conversely, Soviet historians were able to mask many of the Red Army's wartime failures successfully simply because these defeats occurred within the context of the army's more dramatic victories in the battles for Moscow, Stalingrad, Kursk, Belorussia, Poland, and, finally, Berlin. In fact, most of the Red Army's failed and "forgotten" battles and operations occurred while the *Stavka* was attempting to exploit offensively these more famous victories. In addition, because they were blinded or at least preoccupied by these major Red

Army victories, German and Western historians also either overlooked or utterly ignored these Red Army failures. Together with the Soviet Union's constant refusal to release relevant documents from its military archives and, to a lesser extent, the Russian Federation's continuing reluctance to do so today, the absence of sound and detailed information about these "forgotten battles" makes it difficult if not impossible for military historians to determine Stalin's and his *Stavka's* ultimate strategic intentions or to assess the Red Army's actual combat performance throughout the war.

Prior to the Russian Revolution of 1991, when the ostensibly more democratic Russian Federation replaced the Soviet Union, the Communist regime denied military historians access to archival materials related to the Red Army's combat performance in the Soviet-German War. Despite this lack of access to Soviet military archives, however, diligent historians could identify and sketchily describe many of these "forgotten battles" by scouring German military archives and collating this data with information gleaned from Soviet military studies, formation and unit histories, and memoir literature. However, since this Soviet information was fragmentary and often incomplete, restoring an accurate and detailed historical record of the war was an arduous if not often totally impossible task.

After its creation in 1991, the Russian Federation embarked on an ambitious program to declassify and release archival materials related to the Red Army's performance in the war. Based on the efforts of several "Declassification Commissions" working in the archives of the former Soviet Ministry of Defense (*TsAMO*), the government subsequently released, in chronological order, important collections of key wartime documents, such as the orders and directives of the State Defense Committee (GKO), the *Stavka*, the Peoples' Commissariat of Defense (NKO), and the Red Army General Staff. It also authorized the publication of these documents in book form.[iv] Likewise, but at a far slower pace, these Commissions have also declassified and released (although not yet in published book form) the records of many wartime Red Army *fronts*, armies, and divisions and brigades.

After a promising beginning, however, this process of declassifying and releasing archival documents began to slow in the late 1990s. Specifically, the collections of wartime GKO, *Stavka*, NKO, and General Staff documents which the Russian Federation's Ministry of Defense initially released were far more comprehensive than those subsequently released. For example, as indicated by the sequential numbers of respective *Stavka*, NKO, and General Staff orders and directives, the collections of released documents pertaining to operations during 1941 and 1942, published through 1996, included most if not all of the pertinent documents. Conversely, the collections of documents issued by these same organs in 1943, 1944, and 1945, which have been published since 1998, are more highly selective and far less complete. Likewise, after the Declassification Commissions declassified the records on many military formations and units, at least reportedly, they are now reclassifying many of these documents (generally as secret). Regardless of the state of the declassification process, the fresh Russian archival materials released since 1991 now make it far easier for historians to reconstruct a far more complete and accurate history of the war.

   This book will form part of a series seeking to restore a complete and accurate record of the war by identifying and describing concealed wartime battles and operations. The entire series takes the form of a documentary history, with one volume devoted to each of the Red Army's eight self-identified wartime campaigns. Although the historical record of the war will likely remain incomplete unless and until the Russian Federation fully opens its military archives to public view, this series hopes to increase the accuracy of current and future mosaics of the war from the present sixty percent coverage to an accuracy of well over ninety percent.

Chapter 1

Overview

The famous battle of Stalingrad in the fall of 1942 and the offensive campaign the Red Army conducted in the winter of 1942–43 were indeed critical moments in the Soviet-German War. At Stalingrad, for the second time in the war, the Red Army succeeded in halting a major German offensive and, thereafter, mounted a successful counteroffensive of its own during which, for the first time in the war, multiple Red Army tank and mechanized corps succeeded in exploiting deep into the Germans' rear area, subsequently defeating, encircling, and destroying an entire German army. As a result, the battle of Stalingrad became the most important of three identifiable turning points in the war. The first of these turning points had occurred the year before, at Moscow in December 1941, when, by halting and defeating Hitler's Barbarossa juggernaut, the Red Army proved that Nazi Germany could not win the war on Hitler's original terms. The second turning point, the Red Army's victory at Stalingrad in November 1942, indicated that Hitler could not win the war on any terms favorable to the Third Reich. The war's third turning point, the climactic battle fought at Kursk in July and August 1943, confirmed that Germany would indeed lose the war. After Kursk, the only unanswered question was, "How long would it take for the Red Army to win final victory?"

After achieving victory in the Stalingrad region during late November 1942, in December 1942 and January and February 1943, the Red Army expanded its counteroffensive into a full-fledged offensive campaign, which ultimately encompassed the entire southern wing of the Soviet-German front and endured until late March 1943. As is the case with the war as a whole, the fighting during this period of the war is fraught with stereotypes fashioned and passed on to us by multiple generations of postwar German, Soviet, and other Western historians. Although most of these historians agree on the general chronology of military operations that took place during this period, they sharply disagree over such matters as "Why?" each operation occurred, "How" it was conducted, "What?" were its consequences, and "What if?" it had been fought in a different fashion.

Conventional Wisdom

"Conventional wisdom" contained in existing accounts of the fighting on the Soviet-German front from November 1942 through March 1943 argues that the Red Army seized the strategic initiative from Hitler's *Wehrmacht* in the second half of November 1942, when it unleashed a successful counteroffensive code-named Operation Uranus [*Uran*] against German Army Group B's forces in the Stalingrad region. Instead of attacking in the immediate vicinity of Stalingrad city proper, where the bulk of the formidable German Sixth Army was bogged down in intense and costly fighting, instead the Red Army chose as its targets the Romanian Third and Fourth Armies, which were defending more vulnerable sectors northwest and south of the city. Attacking on 19 November, Red Army forces collapsed the defenses of the two Romanian armies, exploited deeply with armored forces, and within days linked up west of Stalingrad, encircling roughly 300,000 German and Romanian forces in the Stalingrad region (see Map 1).

As the Red Army prepared to liquidate Axis forces encircled in the Stalingrad region by conducting an operation code-named Ring [*Kol'tso*], Hitler appointed Field Marshal Erich von Manstein, the former commander of the German Eleventh Army, to command Army Group Don (the armies on the right wing of Army Group B) and ordered him to restore the situation in southern Russia. Manstein immediately began organizing operations to relieve encircled German Sixth Army, employing to that end his own army group's XXXXVIII Panzer Corps and the LVII Panzer Corps, transferred to his control from Army Group A. Simultaneously, the German Army High Command (OKH – *Oberkommando des Heeres*) ordered Army Group A to withdraw its forces from their overexposed positions deep in the Caucasus region. Ultimately, in mid-December Manstein began two relief operations designed to rescue the encircled Sixth Army. In the first of these operations, the LVII Panzer Corps was to attack northeastward toward Stalingrad via Kotel'nikovskii and the Aksai River, and, in the second, the XXXXVIII Panzer Corps was to attack eastward toward Stalingrad from the Nizhnaia Chirskaia region on the Don River. The first relief effort, however, faltered in heavy and frustrating winter fighting, and the second never materialized. Subsequently, after a long and terrible winter siege, the Sixth Army and its commander, General Friedrich Paulus, surrendered to the Red Army on 2 February 1943.

Historians generally agree that Manstein's relief efforts failed, first, because the Red Army organized fresh offensive operations which disrupted the Germans' plans and, second, due to the weakness of the forces Manstein employed to conduct the relief. The Red Army did indeed orchestrate two offensives designed to thwart the XXXXVIII Panzer Corp's relief operation. The first of these offensives, conducted by the Southwestern Front's 5th Tank Army during the first two weeks of December, dented but failed to collapse the defenses of German and Romanian forces along the lower Chir River. However, the intensity of this assault forced the XXXXVIII Panzer Corps to divert part of its forces (the 11th Panzer Division) to deal with the new threat, by so doing disrupting the panzer corps' planned relief effort toward Stalingrad from the west. The second offensive, so-called Operation "Little Saturn," conducted by the Voronezh Front's 6th Army and the Southwestern Front's 1st and 3rd Guards Armies during the second half of December, smashed the defenses of the Italian Eighth Army along the middle reaches of the Don River, forcing the entire XXXXVIII Panzer Corps to intervene to stave off further disaster. In addition to destroying the bulk of the Italian army and tearing a gaping hole in Army Group Don's defensive front, this offensive forced Manstein to commit the XXXXVIII Panzer Corps' 11th and 6th Panzer Divisions to stem the Red tide, thereby totally aborting the panzer corps' relief attempt and, not coincidentally, also seriously weakening the LVII Panzer Corps' relief effort.

Ultimately, Manstein's LVII Panzer Corps also failed to accomplish its assigned mission. Although the panzer corps' 6th, 23rd, and 17th Panzer Divisions fought their way forward to the Mishkovo River, only about 60 kilometers from

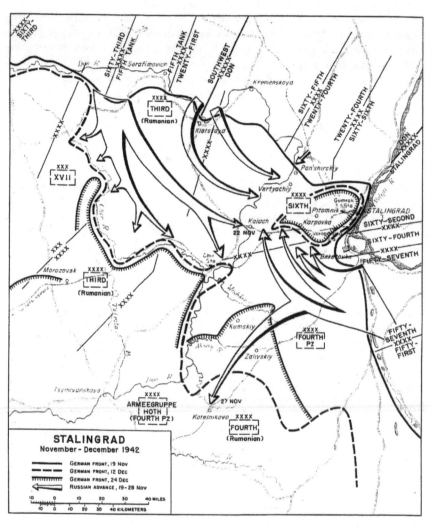

Map 1. Soviet counteroffensive at Stalingrad, 19 November 1942–2 February 1943

the southwestern edge of the Sixth Army's pocket around Stalingrad, stout Soviet resistance halted any further German advance. While many German and Western historians assert that the LVII Panzer Corps' relief effort failed simply because Paulus refused to permit his Sixth Army to conduct a breakout, others admit that combat in such severe winter conditions simply made successful relief impossible. In either case, within weeks the LVII Panzer Corps' relief force itself came under heavy attack and was forced to begin a fighting withdrawal westward toward Rostov.

Conversely, Soviet (Russian) historians assert that, during the first few days of December, Stalin's *Stavka* (High Command) consciously planned an operation code-named Saturn as a logical sequel to Operation Uranus. In addition to disrupting the anticipated efforts by German forces to relieve the encircled Sixth Army, Operation Saturn required the Southwestern Front, now reinforced by the new and powerful 2nd Guards Army from the *Stavka's* reserve, to conduct a full-scale offensive toward Rostov to destroy all Axis forces in the "great bend" of the Don River, capture Rostov, cut off Army Group A's withdrawal from the Caucasus region, and destroy the isolated army group. However, when Soviet forces encountered difficulties in reducing the Sixth Army's pocket around Stalingrad, in early December the *Stavka* diverted the 2nd Guards Army to the Stalingrad region, truncated Operation Saturn into the less ambitious Operation Little Saturn, and assigned the 2nd Guards Army the task of participating in the reduction of the Sixth Army's encirclement at Stalingrad. In mid-December, however, after the LVII Panzer Corps initiated its relief operation toward Stalingrad from the southwest, the *Stavka* quickly diverted its 2nd Guards Army southward to help defeat the panzer corps' relief effort.

Soviet historians claim that, despite frequently altering its plans, the *Stavka* achieved all of its most important objectives. First, the 2nd Guards Army's employment southwest of Stalingrad in mid-December not only defeated the LVII Panzer Corps' relief operation but also permitted the Red Army to conduct its subsequent Kotel'nikovskii offensive, which compelled the LVII Panzer Corps to withdraw westward toward Rostov. Second, the Southwestern Front's victory in Operation Little Saturn destroyed the Italian Eighth Army and forced the Germans to employ the entire XXXXVIII Panzer Corps to prevent their defenses west of the Don and Chir Rivers from totally collapsing. Within the context of these operations, Soviet historians assert the 5th Tank Army's assaults along the Chir River (most notably in the vicinity of State Farm 79) in early December were simply designed to divert German attention from the most important offensive operations elsewhere along the front.

Soviet and German accounts of the fighting in January and February 1943 generally agree. Hard on the heels of Operation Little Saturn and the Kotel'nikovskii offensive, the Southwestern and Stalingrad Fronts continued their offensive operations toward Millerovo, at the western base of the Don River bend, Tormosin, and Rostov. As these offensives developed, on 13 January the Voronezh and Southwestern Fronts' armies demolished the defenses of Army Group B's Hungarian Second Army and Italian Alpine Corps along the Don River in what the Soviets term the Ostrogozhsk-Rossosh' offensive (see Map 2). This offensive tore an immense hole in the army group's defenses, threatening to envelop the

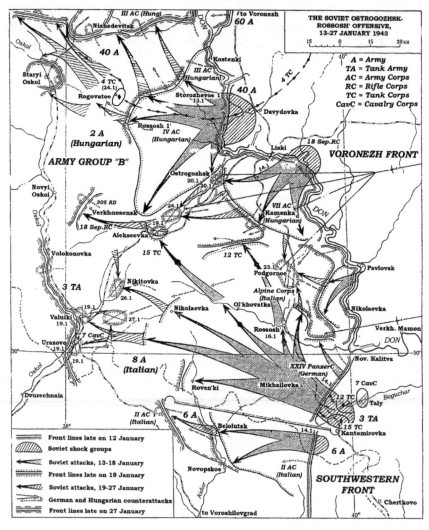

Map 2. The Soviet Ostrogozhsk–Rossosh' offensive, 13–27 January 1943

southern flank of Army Group B's German Second Army, defending a salient in the Voronezh region. Before the army group could restore a coherent front, on 24 January the forces of the Briansk and Voronezh Fronts began the so-called Voronezh-Kastornoe offensive against the German Second Army. Attacking the Second Army's flanks and front, Soviet forces demolished its defenses, forcing the army's remnants to withdraw westward in disorder toward Kursk and Belgorod (see Map 3).

Simultaneously, the forces of the Southwestern and Southern (former Stalingrad) Fronts continued their slow but inexorable advance westward through the Millerovo, Tormosin, and Kotel'nikovskii regions, driving Army Group B's and Don's forces toward the Northern Donets River and Rostov, even further away from Stalingrad. In the Millerovo offensive, the Southwestern Front's 1st and 3rd Guards and 5th Tank Armies and the Stalingrad Front's 5th Shock Army cleared the forces of Army Group B's Army Detachment [*Abteilung*] Fretter-Pico and Army Group Don's Army Detachment Hollidt from the Millerovo and Tormosin regions, pressing them westward toward Starobel'sk on the Aidar River and Voroshilovgrad on the southern bank of the Northern Donets River. South of the Don River, the Southern (former Stalingrad) Front's armies drove the forces of Army Group Don's Fourth Panzer Army westward toward Rostov, capturing the key city on 14 February, and then pursuing the retreating German forces to the Mius River line by 18 February, where, according to Soviet accounts, the front line stabilized for five months. Marring these otherwise successful Soviet offensives, Army Group A's First Panzer Army managed to extract its forces from the Caucasus region through the Rostov "gate" successfully before Soviet troops seized the city.

Exploiting its previous successes, in late January 1943, the *Stavka* ordered its Southwestern and Voronezh Fronts to mount two new offensive operations literally "from the march," even before they completed their previous operations. In an offensive code-named Operation Gallop [*Skachok*], the Southwestern Front's 6th and 1st and 3rd Guards Armies, supported by multiple tank corps operating under Mobile Group Popov, were to advance westward across the Northern Donets River and through the Donbas region to the Dnepr River, capture Voroshilovgrad and Zaporozh'e, and then wheel southward to Mariupol' on the Sea of Azov to encircle and destroy all of Army Group Don's forces in the Donbas, as well as Army Group A's forces attempting to retreat westward through Rostov. Simultaneously, in an offensive code-named Operation Star [*Zvezda*]), the armies of the Voronezh Front's left wing (the 40th Army and 3rd Tank Army) were to advance westward across from the Starobel'sk region, capture Belgorod and Khar'kov, destroy the bulk of Army Group B's forces, and, if possible, advance to the Dnepr River in the Kremenchug and Dnepropetrovsk regions. Because the Voronezh Front's forces had made such spectacular progress in its Voronezh-Kastornoe offensive, on the eve of Operations Gallop and Star, Stalin's Deputy Supreme Commander, Marshal of the Soviet Union G. K. Zhukov, ordered the armies on the Voronezh Front's right wing (the 38th and 60th Armies) to add Kursk to their list of designed objectives.

Attacking from the march, the Southwestern and Voronezh Fronts' armies recorded spectacular gains during the initial stages of their February offensives.

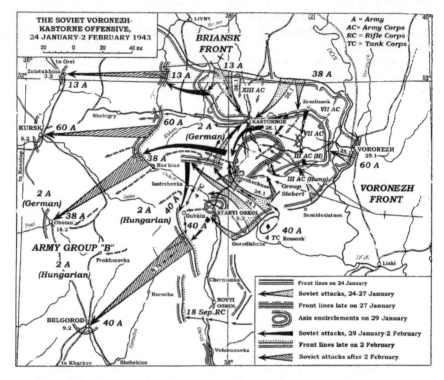

Map 3. The Soviet Voronezh-Kastornoe offensive, 24 January–2 February 1943

Crossing the Northern Donets River with relative ease, the Southwestern Front's 6th and 1st and 3rd Guards Armies penetrated deep into the Donbas region in early February, tearing an immense hole in Army Group Don's defenses, capturing Voroshilovgrad on 14 February and exploiting to Krasnoarmeiskoe and the approaches to Zaporozh'e on the Dnepr River by 18 February. At the same time, after shattering Army Group B's defenses, the Voronezh Front's 38th Army captured Kursk on 8 February, its 40th Army seized Belgorod on the 9th, and its 3rd Tank Army took Khar'kov on the 16th.

Emboldened by the Voronezh and Southwestern Fronts' apparent successes, in early February the *Stavka* began dispatching the armies of General Rokossovsky's Don Front, which had accepted the surrender of Paulus' Sixth Army in Stalingrad on 2 February, forward to reinforce its forces advancing toward Kursk and into the Donbas region. Assuming optimistically that the Germans were about to abandon the entire Donbas region and withdraw westward to the Dnepr river line, the *Stavka* egged its attacking forces on toward ever-deeper objectives, even though its forces were clearly becoming ragged and overextended and were outrunning their logistical support.

At this juncture, Manstein struck back at his tormenters by orchestrating his now famous Donbas and Khar'kov counterstrokes (see Map 4). After the OKH reorganized his Army Group Don into a new Army Group South on 13 February, a week later Manstein skillfully employed his army group's Fourth and First Panzer Armies, the former reinforced by the powerful II SS Panzer Corps recently trans-ferred from the West and the latter just regrouped from the Caucasus region, to mount a dramatic and effective counterstroke against the flanks of the South-western Front's now overextended armies just as they were approaching the Dnepr River at and north of Zaporozh'e. Under assault from three sides, the South-western Front's exploiting forces collapsed within days. Manstein's panzers, encir-cling and destroying the bulk of the *front's* 6th Army, 1st Guards Army, and Mobile Group Popov, forced the remnants of the Southwestern Front's forces to withdraw northward to the Northern Donets River in disorder.

Manstein's Fourth Panzer Army, after pausing briefly to regroup, struck the Voronezh Front's 40th and 69th Armies and 3rd Tank Army in early March, just as they were attempting to exploit their offensive southwest of Khar'kov. Once again employing concentric blows, this time in concert with an assault from the west by newly-formed Army Detachment Kempf, Manstein's Fourth Panzer Army smashed the Voronezh Front's three armies southwest of Khar'kov, encircled and destroyed the 3rd Tank Army, recaptured Khar'kov on 16 March, and seized Belgorod on the 18th. In addition to thwarting the *Stavka's* Donbas and Khar'kov offensives and recapturing considerable lost territory, Manstein's counterstrokes brought the Red Army's winter offensive to an abrupt and unpleasant end. Now fearing that the German counterstroke would continue with even worse conse-quences, during the second half of March, the *Stavka* transferred fresh reserve armies into the Belgorod region from other regions of the front, which, in combi-nation with the onset of the spring thaw [*rasputitsa*], forced the German OKH to call off further attacks.

During the intense fighting in February and March, the OKH acted decisively to restore coherence to its front in the East by abandoning the precarious salients

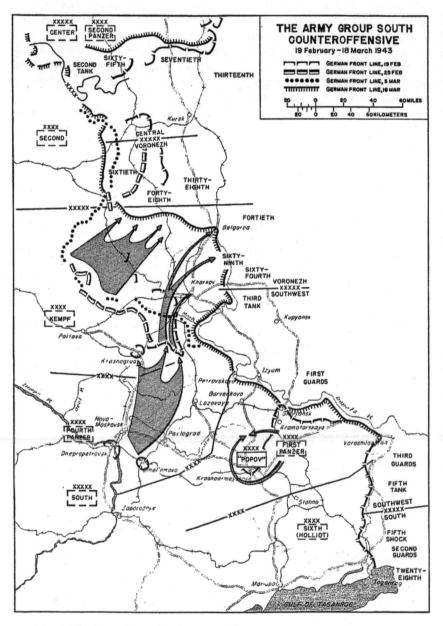

Map 4. The Army Group South counteroffensive, 19 February–18 March 1943

defended by Army Groups North and Center in the Demiansk and Rzhev regions and by forming a new defensive line extending from the Orel region in the north to the Mius River in the south. After the front stabilized in late March, both sides regrouped their forces and improved their defenses as they began preparations to resume active operations in the summer. Quite naturally, all eyes now turned to the infamous Kursk "Bulge," the curious terrain feature dominating the central sector of the front, which represented the most visible legacy of Manstein's successful spring counterstrokes.

German, Soviet, and Western accounts of combat operations during February and March 1943 agree that the *Stavka* chose the southwestern axis, specifically, the Donbas and Khar'kov regions, as its principal strategic objective. Understandably, Soviet historians emphasize the Southwestern and Voronezh Fronts' spectacular initial successes, while German historians focus almost exclusively on the brilliance of Manstein's Donbas and Khar'kov counterstrokes. Many, however, have criticized Hitler for refusing to permit Manstein to continue his counterstrokes, asserting that if he had been permitted to do so, his forces might have defeated Soviet forces in the Kursk bulge during March and April, thereby avoiding the fateful battle of Kursk that followed in July. A few of these historians acknowledge that weather and terrain conditions in the spring were simply not conducive for continuing the counterstroke and, in the instance of at least one former German general, admit that the Red Army's forces available to defeat such an offensive were far more powerful than previously assumed.[5]

Chronologically by strategic axis, major military operations constituting the winter campaign of 1942–43 traditionally include:

THE NORTHWESTERN AXIS

- The Leningrad and Volkhov Fronts offensive to penetrate the blockade of Leningrad (Operation Spark [*Iskra*]) (12–30 January 1943)
- The Northwestern Front's Demiansk offensive (15–28 February 1943)

THE WESTERN AXIS

- The Kalinin Front's Velikie Luki offensive (24 November 1942–20 January 1943)
- The Kalinin and Western Fronts' Rzhev-Viaz'ma offensive (2–31 March 1943)

THE SOUTHWESTERN AXIS

- The Southwestern, Don, and Stalingrad Front's winter offensive (11 November 1942–2 February 1943)
  - The Southwestern, Don, and Stalingrad Fronts' Stalingrad counteroffensive (Operation Uranus) (19–30 November 1942)
  - The Stalingrad Front's Kotel'nikovskii defense (12–23 December 1942)
  - The Southwestern and Voronezh Front's Middle Don offensive (Operation Little Saturn [*Malyi Saturn*]) (16–30 December 1942)

- – The Stalingrad Front's Kotel'nikovskii offensive (24–30 December 1942)
- – The Don Front's liquidation of the Stalingrad encirclement (Operation Ring [*Kol'tso*]) (10 January–2 February 1943)
- The Southwestern Front's Millerovo-Voroshilovgrad offensive (1 January–18 February 1943)
  - – The Southwestern Front's Millerovo offensive (1–28 January 1943)
  - – The Southwestern Front's Voroshilovgrad (Donbas) (Operation Gallop [*Skachok*]) offensive (29 January–18 February 1943)

- The Voronezh, Briansk, and Southwestern Front's Voronezh-Khar'kov offensive (13 January–3 March 1943)
  - – The Southwestern and Voronezh Fronts' Ostrogozhsk-Rossosh' offensive (13–27 January 1943)
  - – The Briansk and Voronezh Fronts' Voronezh-Kastornoe offensive (24 January–2 February 1943)
  - – The Voronezh Front's Khar'kov offensive (Operation Star [*Zvezda*]) (2 February–3 March 1943)
- The Southwestern and Voronezh Front's Khar'kov defensive (19 February–25 March 1943)
  - – The Southwestern Front's Donbas defensive (19 February–3 March 1943)
  - – The Voronezh Front's Khar'kov defensive (4–25 March 1943)

THE SOUTHERN AXIS

- The Trans-Caucasus, Southern, and North Caucasus Front's North Caucasus strategic offensive (Operation Don) (1 January–4 February 1943)
  - – The Southern Front's Rostov offensive (5–18 February 1943)
  - – The Northern Group of Forces' (Trans-Caucasus Front) (North Caucasus Front on 24 January) Mozdok-Stavropol' offensive (1–24 January 1943)
  - – The Trans-Caucasus Front's (Black Sea Group of Forces') Novorossiisk-Maikop offensive (11 January–4 February 1943)
  - – The North Caucasus Front's Tikhoretsk offensive (24 January–4 February 1943)
- The North Caucasus Front's Krasnodar offensive (9 February–24 May 1943)

The Forgotten War

Generally adhering to this traditional construct of the course of combat operations during the winter campaign of 1942–43, Soviet historians have also deliberately concealed many facets of well-known battles and operations and masked the ambitiousness of the *Stavka*'s winter offensive, particularly in regard to the scope and scale of strategic offensive operations the Red Army conducted in November 1942 and in February and March 1943. Until quite recently, Soviet histories of operations during November and December 1942 focused exclusively on the Red Army's dramatic counteroffensive at Stalingrad and, to a lesser extent, on the fighting in the Caucasus region and on combat of a more local nature in the

Demiansk and Velikie Luki regions. Nowhere, however, do these histories mention the heavy fighting that took place around the Rzhev and Viaz'ma salient west of Moscow. As concerns the fighting in February and March 1943, although these histories cover the Red Army's successful offensives in the Khar'kov and Donbas regions in considerable detail, they offer significantly less detail regarding Manstein's successful counterstrokes in these regions. A thorough account of these operations has yet to be written, fragmentary information about these operations can be found buried deep in Soviet military unit histories and memoir literature. Together with German studies and archival materials, these materials provided the basis for the only English-language study of these operations, David M. Glantz, *From the Don to the Dnepr: Soviet Offensive Operations, December 1942-August 1943*.[6] As accurate as this study was, however, even it failed to capture the complete cope of the Donbas offensive or the full context of the *Stavka's* ambitious winter offensive campaign.

Based on the study of newly-available archival materials, it is now possible to sketch out a new construct for the course of combat operations during the Red Army's winter campaign of 1942–43. After enduring the full offensive weight of the *Wehrmacht* for almost five excruciating months, in mid-November 1942, the Red Army struck back at the Germans along virtually every strategic axis on the German Eastern Front. The *Stavka* began its counteroffensive along the vital southwestern axis on 19 November in an operation code-named Uranus, when the armies of its Southwestern and Stalingrad Fronts attacked and demolished the Rumanian Third and Fourth Armies' defenses north and south of Stalingrad. Within a matter of only days, multiple Red Army tank, mechanized, and cavalry corps, exploiting deep into the rear areas of Axis forces for the first time in the war, linked up east of Kalach-on-the-Don, by doing so encircling more than 300,000 German and Rumanian forces in the infamous Stalingrad "cauldron."

As the trap slammed shut around the German Sixth Army in the Stalingrad region, the Red Army's Kalinin and Western Fronts, operating west of Moscow under Marshal Zhukov's direct control, launched multiple simultaneous blows against the defenses of German Army Group Center around the Rzhev salient, the so-called German "dagger" aimed at Moscow. After the Kalinin Front's 3rd Shock Army assaulted the German Third Panzer Army's defenses around Velikie Luki on 24 November, the next day five armies and five mobile (tank, mechanized, and cavalry) corps subordinate to the Kalinin and Western Fronts attacked German Ninth Army's defenses around the entire periphery of Rzhev salient. Expanding this offensive, on 28 November the armies of the Northwestern Front once again assaulted the defenses of Army Group North's Sixteenth Army in the Ramushevo corridor and around the Demiansk salient, south of Lake Il'men'.

The *Stavka* harbored no illusions about its chances for success when it decided to unleash its multiple offensives and counteroffensives in November 1942. On the one hand, it firmly believed these operations would indeed succeed and turn the tide of war in the Red Army's favor, primarily because it had accomplished the same feat the year before when it committed multiple armies from its strategic reserves to save the cities of Leningrad, Moscow, and Rostov. On the other hand, however, the *Stavka* tempered its optimism in late 1942 because it realized that, while the Red Army had indeed saved these cities, during these offensives it had failed to achieve all of its ambitious aims. In spite of the Red Army's dramatic victories at the gates of the three cities, when the winter of 1941–42 ended, Army Group North was still besieging Leningrad, Army Group Center was still lodged in the Rzhev salient, less than 150 kilometers west of Moscow, and German Army Group South was still threatening Rostov and Stalingrad and the Caucasus beyond. Furthermore, while the *Wehrmacht* was conducting its spectacular advance to Stalingrad and into the Caucasus during the late summer and fall of 1942, repeated counteroffensives, counterstrokes, and counterattacks orchestrated by the *Stavka* failed to halt the advance short of Voronezh, Stalingrad, and the crest of the Caucasus Mountains. In short, in November 1942 the *Stavka* well understood how difficult it would be to conduct and sustain multiple strategic offensive operations.

As the *Stavka* planned its offensives and counteroffensives in the late fall of 1942, it consciously hearkened back to its experiences during the winter campaign of 1941–42; in particular, by carefully analyzing the techniques it employed to achieve victory and the shortcomings evident in its conduct of the campaign. Once again, Stalin hoped to achieve victory by judiciously employing forces from his strategic reserves, a sizeable portion of which he had already committed to combat in futile attempts to halt the *Wehrmacht's* summer juggernaut. Since the dictator and his senior military advisers realized that the more mobile and flexible German forces would likely prove able to parry any offensive conducted along a single strategic axis, therefore, they planned to launch strategic offensive along two such axis to deny the Germans this flexibility. Faced with multiple large-scale onslaughts, somewhere, thought Stalin, the German lines were likely to crack and crumble. Based on this assumption, he chose the western and the southwestern axes as venues for the Red Army to launch strategic offensive operations, the Kalinin and Western Fronts conducting Operation Mars against Army Group Center in the Rzhev salient and the Southwestern, Don, and Stalingrad Fronts Operation Uranus against Army Group B in the Stalingrad region. In addition, the *Stavka* orchestrated supporting attacks on an operational scale around Demiansk along the Northwestern axis and in the Mozdok and Ordzhonikidze regions deep in the Caucasus. Thereafter, Stalin and his *Stavka* would consistently adhere to this pattern of operating along multiple axes throughout the entire ensuing winter campaign.

The offensives and counteroffensives the Red Army conducted in November and December 1942 proved successful on three of the four axes along which it operated; however, only one of these operations, its counteroffensive at Stalingrad, proved strategic in terms of its scale and consequences. Along the northwestern axis, the assaults conducted by the Northwestern Front's 11th, 1st Shock, 27th, 34th, and 53rd Armies against the defenses of Army Group North's Sixteenth Army around Demiansk failed. Further south, at the junction between the northwestern and western axes, the Kalinin Front's 3rd Shock Army attacked the defenses of Army Group Center's Third Panzer Army in the vicinity of Velikie Luki. This offensive, which was designed to support both the Northwestern Front's offensive at Demiansk and the Kalinin and Western Fronts' Operation Mars, achieved some local successes by threatening to sever communications between German Army Groups North and Center.

Along the vital western axis, where, under Zhukov's supervision, the Kalinin Front's 41st, 22nd, and 39th Armies and the Western Front's 31st, 20th, and 29th Armies conducted Operation Mars against the defenses of Army Group Center's Ninth Army around the entire periphery of the Rzhev salient, Zhukov's forces achieved temporary but fleeting successes. While the Kalinin Front's armies penetrated the Ninth Army's defenses in several key sectors, the Western Front's penetration operation failed. Although Zhukov insisted his armies continue their fruitless assaults through mid-December, the entire offensive collapsed because Army Group Center was able to launch effective counterstrokes with panzer divisions it hastily regrouped into the region.

Only along the southwestern axis did Red Army forces record genuine strategic success in November and December 1942. Here, conducting Operation Uranus in the Stalingrad region, the Southwestern Front's 5th Tank and 21st Armies penetrated the Romanian Third Army's defenses along the Don River northwest of Stalingrad. Virtually simultaneously, the Stalingrad Front's 57th and 51st Armies did the same to the Romanian Fourth Army's defenses south of Stalin's namesake city. Supported by the Don Front's 65th, 24th, and 66th Armies, multiple mobile corps subordinate to the Southwestern and Stalingrad Fronts succeeded in exploiting well into Army Group B's operational rear, encircling Army Group B's Sixth Army and part of the army group's Fourth Panzer Army in the Stalingrad region. When Manstein tried to marshal forces in early December to conduct a relief of the Sixth Army encircled in the Stalingrad region, Marshal of the Soviet Union A. M. Vasilevsky, the *Stavka* coordinator for operations along the southwestern axis, skillfully expanded the scope of the counteroffensive to thwart any successful German relief attempts. After mounting a new offensive operation by the 5th Tank Army against Axis defenses along the Chir River in early December, at mid-month he unleashed the Voronezh Front's 6th Army and the Southwestern Front's 1st and 3rd Guards Armies in an offensive against the Italian Eighth Army's defenses along the middle reaches of the Don River (Operation Little Saturn). Soon after, the Stalingrad Front's 51st Army conducted an offensive against the LVII Panzer Corps as it attempted to conduct its relief operation along the Kotel'nikovskii and Aksai River axis southwest of the city.

Vasilevsky's offensive operations succeeded. The Southwestern and Stalingrad Fronts' forces, after disrupting Manstein's relief attempts, continued their slow advance during the first half of January 1943, pressing Army Group Don's forces westward from the Don bend toward Millerovo and Rostov. Then, in mid-January, the *Stavka* ordered all of the Red Army's *fronts* operating along the southwestern and southern axes to join battle in a series of simultaneous and consecutive offensives which endured into early March 1943. These operations included the Briansk and Voronezh Fronts' Voronezh-Khar'kov strategic offensive (13 January–3 March 1943), the Southwestern and Southern Fronts' Millerovo-Voroshilovgrad (Donbas) strategic offensive (1 January–22 February 1943), and the Southern (North Caucasus on 24 January) and Trans-Caucasus Fronts' North Caucasus strategic offensive (1 January–4 February 1943), with its continuation from 5 February through 24 May 1943.

Emboldened by the spectacular successes achieved by its *fronts* operating along the southwestern and southern axes during January, the *Stavka* expanded the scope of its winter campaign in early February by ordering its *fronts* operating along the northwestern and western axes to join the offensive. This new series of multiple, simultaneous offensive operations along the northwestern and western axes sought to defeat and destroy major portions of German Army Groups Center and North, recapture the city of Smolensk, and lift the siege of Leningrad. These operations included the Kalinin, Western, Briansk, and Central Fronts' Rzhev, Viaz'ma, Smolensk and Orel, Briansk, Smolensk offensives (25 February–21 March 1943) and the Leningrad, Volkhov, and Northwestern Fronts' Operation Polar Star (10 February–2 April 1943). Collectively, these five strategic offensive operation involved forces from virtually every Red Army *front* operating across the vast expanse of the Eastern Front from the Baltic Sea to the Black Sea.

Chronologically by strategic axis, a complete list of all major military operations the Red Army conducted along the northwestern, western, southwestern, and southern axes during its winter campaign of 1942–43 includes:

THE NORTHWESTERN AXIS

- The Northwestern Front's (11th, 1st Shock, 27th, 34th, and 53rd Armies') Demiansk offensive (28 November 1942–6 January 1943)
- The Leningrad (67th Army's) and Volkhov Front's (2nd Shock and 8th Armies') Operation Spark [*Iskra*] (Siniavino) (12–30 January 1943)
- The Leningrad, Volkhov, and Northwestern Fronts' Operation Polar Star [*Poliarnaia zvezda*] (Demiansk) (10–28 February 1943)
    - The Leningrad Front's (55th Army's) Krasnyi Bor-Tosno offensive (10–23 February 1943)
    - The Volkhov Front's (54th Army's) Chudovo-Tosno offensive (10–23 February 1943)
    - The Volkhov Front's (67th and 2nd Shock Armies') Siniavino offensive (12–23 February 1943)
    - The Northwestern Front's (27th, 11th, 1st Shock, 34th, and 53rd Armies') Demiansk offensive (15–28 February 1943)
- The Leningrad, Volkhov, and Northwestern Fronts' Truncated Operation Polar Star (Staraia Russa) (4 March–2 April 1943)
    - The Northwestern Front's (27th, 11th, 1st Shock, 34th, 53rd, and 68th Armies') Staraia Russa offensive (4–19 March 1943)
    - The Leningrad Front's (55th Army's) Krasnyi Bor-Tosno offensive (19–21 March 1943)
    - The Volkhov Front's (8th Army's) Mga offensive (19 March–2 April 1943)

THE WESTERN AXES

- The Kalinin and Western Fronts' 2nd Rzhev-Sychevka offensive (Operation Mars [*Mars*]) (25 November–20 December 1942)

- The Kalinin (41st, 22nd, and 39th Armies) and Western Fronts' (30th, 31st, 20th, and 29th Armies') 2nd Rzhev-Sychevka offensive (25 November–20 December 1942)
- The Kalinin Front's (3rd Shock Army's) Velikie-Luki offensive (25 November 1942–20 January 1943)
- The Briansk Front's Orel offensive and the Voronezh Front's (60th and 38th Armies') L'gov and Sumy offensives (26 January–12 February 1943)
  - The Briansk Front's (13th and 48th Armies') Orel (Maloarkhangel'sk) offensive (26 January–12 February 1943)
  - The Voronezh Front's (60th Army's) L'gov offensive (3–12 February 1943)
  - The Voronezh Front's (38th Army's) Sumy offensive (3–12 February 1943)
- The Kalinin, Western, Briansk, and Central Fronts' Orel, Briansk, and Smolensk offensives (12 February–21 March 1943)
  - The Briansk Front's Orel offensive (12–21 February 1943)
  - The Voronezh Front's (60th Army's) L'gov-Ryl'sk offensive (12–20 February 1943)
  - The Western Front's (16th Army's) Zhizdra offensive (22–27 February 1943)
  - The Briansk Front's (61st and 3rd Armies') Bolkhov offensive (22–27 February 1943)
  - The Western Front's (5th Army's) Gzhatsk offensive (22–27 February 1943)
  - The Western Front's (33rd Army's) Viaz'ma offensive (22–27 February 1943)
  - The Central Front's (65th, 70th, and 21st Armies' and 2nd Tank Army's) Sevsk-Trubchevsk offensive (25 February–6 March 1943)
  - The Briansk Front's (13th and 48th Armies') Orel offensive (25 February–6 March 1943)
  - The Central Front's (65th, 70th, and 21st Armies' and 2nd Tank Army's) Orel offensive (7–21 March 1943)
  - The Western Front's (16th Army's) Zhizdra-Orel offensive (7–21 March 1943)
- The Kalinin and Western Fronts' Rzhev-Viaz'ma offensive (pursuit) (6 March–1 April 1943)
  - The Kalinin (22nd, 39th, 41st, and 43rd Armies') and Western Fronts' (5th, 20th, 30th, 31st, 33rd, 49th, and 50th Armies') Rzhev-Viaz'ma offensive (pursuit) (6–18 March 1943)
  - The Western Front's (49th and 50th Armies') Spas-Demensk offensive (18 March–1 April 1943)
  - The Western Front's (31st and 5th Armies') Dorogobuzh offensive (18–27 March 1943)

THE SOUTHWESTERN AXIS

- The Southwestern, Don, and Stalingrad Fronts' Stalingrad strategic offensive (19 November 1942–2 February 1943)

- The Southwestern (1st Guards, 5th Tank, and 21st Armies'), Don (65th and 24th Armies'), and Stalingrad Fronts' (62nd, 64th, 57th, 51st, and 28th Armies') Stalingrad counteroffensive (Operation Uranus [*Uran*]) (19–30 November 1942)
- The Southwestern (5th Tank Army's) and Stalingrad Fronts' (5th Shock Army's) Chir offensive (6–23 December 1942)
- The Stalingrad Front's (5th Shock, 51st, and 2nd Guards Armies') Kotel'nikovskii defense (12–23 December 1942)
- The Southwestern (1st Guards and 3rd Guards Armies') and Voronezh Fronts' (6th Army's) Middle Don offensive (Operation Little Saturn [*Malyi Saturn*]) (16–30 December 1942)
- The Stalingrad Front's (5th Shock, 2nd Guards, and 51st Armies') Kotel'nikovskii offensive (24–30 December 1942)
- The Don Front's (21st, 65th, 24th, 66th, 62nd, 64th, and 57th Armies') liquidation of the Stalingrad encirclement (Operation Ring [*Kol'tso*]) (10 January–2 February 1943)
- The Southwestern and Southern Fronts' Millerovo-Voroshilovgrad (Donbas) strategic offensive (1 January–22 February 1943)
  - The Southwestern Front's (6th, 1st Guards, 3rd Guards, and 5th Tank Armies') Millerovo offensive (1–28 January 1943)
  - The Southwestern Front's (6th, 1st Guards, 3rd Guards, and 5th Tank Armies' and Mobile Group Popov's) Voroshilovgrad (Donbas) offensive (Operation Gallop [*Skachok*]) (29 January–18 February 1943)
  - The Southern Front's (5th Shock, 2nd Guards, 51st, 28th, and 44th Armies') Mariupol' (Donbas) offensive (16–22 February 1943)
- The Briansk, Voronezh, and Southwestern Fronts' Voronezh-Khar'kov strategic offensive (13 January–3 March 1943)
  - The Voronezh (40th Army, 18th Sep. Rifle Corps, and 3rd Tank Army's) and Southwestern Fronts' (6th Army's) Ostrogozhsk-Rossosh' offensive (13–27 January 1943)
  - The Briansk (13th Army's) and Voronezh Fronts' (38th, 60th, and 40th Armies') Voronezh-Kastornoe offensive (24 January–2 February 1943)
  - The Voronezh Front's (60th, 38th, 40th, 69th, and 3rd Tank Armies') Khar'kov offensive (Operation (Star [*Zvezda*]) (2 February–3 March 1943)
  - The Voronezh Front's (60th and 38th Armies') Ryl'sk-Sumy (Glukhov) offensive (4–28 March 1943)
- The Southwestern and Voronezh Fronts' Voroshilovgrad-Khar'kov defensive (19 February–25 March 1943)
  - The Southwestern Front's (6th, 1st Guards, 3rd Guards, 5th Tank Armies' and Mobile Group Popov's) Donbas (Voroshilovgrad) defensive (19 February–1 March 1943)
  - The Voronezh Front's (38th, 40th, 69th, 21st, 64th, 1st Tank, and 3rd Tank Armies') Khar'kov defensive (4–25 March 1943)

THE SOUTHERN AXIS

- The Trans-Caucasus, Southern, and North Caucasus (from 24 January) Fronts' North Caucasus (Don) strategic offensive (1 January–4 February 1943)
    - The Southern Front's (5th Shock, 2nd Guards, 51st, and 28th Armies' and, on 6 February, 44th Army's) Rostov-Sal'sk offensive (1 January–18 February 1943)
    - The Northern Group of Forces' (Trans-Caucasus Front) (37th, 9th, 58th, and 44th Armies' and Cavalry-Mechanized Group Kirichenko's) (North Caucasus Front on 24 January) Mozdok-Stavropol' offensive (1–24 January 1943)
    - The Black Sea Group of Forces' (Trans-Caucasus Front) (47th, 56th, 18th, and 46th Armies') Novorossiisk-Maikop offensive (11 January–4 February 1943)
    - The North Caucasus Front's (37th, 9th, 58th, and 44th Armies' and Cavalry-Mechanized Group Kirichenko's) Tikhoretsk-Eisk offensive (24 January–4 February 1943)
- The North Caucasus Front's (58th, 9th, 37th, and 46th Armies') and Black Sea Group of Forces' (Trans-Caucasus Front) (18th, 56th, and 47th Armies') North Caucasus strategic offensive (5 February–24 May 1943)
    - The Black Sea Fleet's and Black Sea Group of Forces' (Trans-Caucasus Front, North Caucasus Front on 5 February) (18th Amphibious and 47th Armies') Novorossiisk amphibious offensive (Operation Little Land [*Malaia Zemlia*]) (4–15 February 1943)
    - The North Caucasus Front's (58th, 9th, 37th, and 46th Armies') and Black Sea Group of Forces' (North Caucasus Front) (18th Amphibious, 56th, and 47th Armies') Krasnodar offensive (9–22 February 1943)
    - The North Caucasus Front's (58th, 9th, 37th, and 46th Armies') and Black Sea Group of Forces' (North Caucasus Front) (18th Amphibious, 47th, and 56th) Slaviansk-Krymskaia offensive (23 February–27 March 1943)
    - The North Caucasus Front's (18th, 56th, 37th, 9th, and 58th Armies') Taman' (Krymskaia-Neberdzhaevskaia) offensive (4 April–24 May 1943) (see *Forgotten Battles, Volume V*)

Although existing histories of the Soviet-German War adequately describe some of these military operations, they provide only sketchy descriptions of or simply ignore many others. Historians, for example, have written detailed studies of the famous battle for Stalingrad, focusing primarily on the fierce fighting in the city, the Red Army's Uranus counteroffensive in late November, and the encirclement and destruction of the German Sixth Army in the city. They have also described, though in far lesser detail, the Red Army's subsequent offensives toward Kursk and Khar'kov and into the Donbas, with Russian historians focusing on the Red Army's dramatic victories in the Middle Don (Operation Little Saturn), Ostrogozhsk-Rossosh', Voronezh-Kastornoe, Khar'kov, Rostov, and Krasnodar offensives and German historians stressing Manstein's successful counterstrokes in the Donbas and Khar'kov regions which brought the Red Army's winter campaign to an abrupt end. All the while, however, historians on both sides have paid little or no attention to the spectacular fighting in the Rzhev region (Operation Mars) during November and December 1942 (other than detailed coverage of the fighting around Velikie Luki), to the fighting along the Chir River in early December 1942 (aside from sketchy German descriptions of the fighting around State Farm 79), and to the dramatic struggle in the Orel region and west of Kursk (the Briansk-Smolensk Offensive) in February and March 1943, which left as a legacy the infamous "Kursk Bulge." In short, whether writing from the German or the Soviet perspective, historians tend, quite naturally, to emphasize their side's victories, while only grudgingly acknowledging or utterly ignoring their army's defeats.[7]

In the case of military operations whose ultimate outcome was difficult to conceal, such as the Red Army's Donbas, Khar'kov, and Orel-Briansk-Smolensk offensives, Soviet (Russian) historians have carefully concealed the full scope of these operations. For example, when describing the Red Army's Donbas offensive in February 1943, they have remained totally silent about the Southern Front's role in the offensive (the failed Mariupol' operation). Likewise, when writing about operations along the western axis in February and March 1943, they have acknowledged the commitment of General K. K. Rokossovsky's newly formed Central Front into the fighting west of Kursk but have provided virtually no detail about this *front's* operations or about the Kalinin, Western, and Briansk Fronts' attacks in support of Rokossovsky's offensive.[8] Similarly, these historians have almost totally ignored Zhukov's Operation Polar Star along the northwestern axis during February and March, aside from occasional references to the heavy fighting in the Staraia Russa region occasioned by the German abandonment of the Demiansk salient.

Therefore, a definitive listing of the totally "forgotten" or partially concealed battles that took place during the Red Army's winter campaign of 1942–43 would include at least the following (see Map 5):

SOVIET OFFENSIVE OPERATIONS WITHIN THE CONTEXT OF THE STALINGRAD COUNTEROFFENSIVE

- The Kalinin and Western Fronts' 2nd Rzhev-Sychevka offensive (Operation Mars [*Mars*]) (25 November–16 December 1942)
- The Northwestern Front's Demiansk offensive (28 November 1942–6 January 1943)

SOVIET OFFENSIVE OPERATIONS ALONG THE SOUTHWESTERN (DONBAS) AXIS

- The Southwestern and Southern Fronts' Millerovo-Voroshilovgrad (Donbas) offensive (1 January–22 February 1943)
  - The Southwestern Front's Voroshilovgrad (Donbas) offensive (Operation Gallop [*Skachok*]) (29 January–18 February 1943)

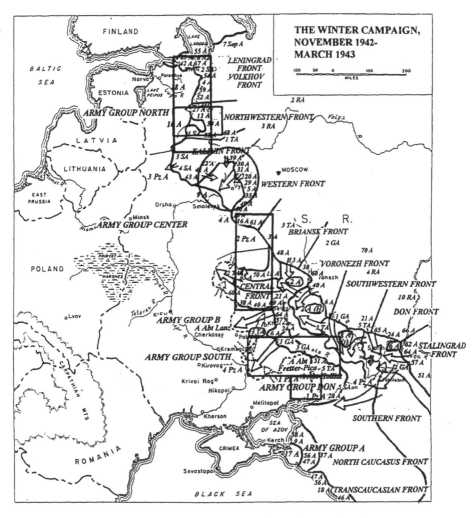

Map 5. The Winter Campaign, November 1942–March 1943

- The Southern Front's Mariupol' (Donbas) offensive (16–22 February 1943)

SOVIET OFFENSIVE OPERATIONS ALONG THE WESTERN (CENTRAL) AXIS

- The Briansk Front's Orel offensive and the Voronezh Front's (60th and 38th Armies') L'gov and Sumy offensives (26 January–12 February 1943)
  - The Briansk Front's (13th and 48th Armies') Orel (Maloarkhangel'sk) offensive (26 January–12 February 1943)
  - The Voronezh Front's (60th Army's) L'gov offensive (3–12 February 1943)
- The Kalinin, Western, Briansk, and Central Fronts' Orel, Briansk, and Smolensk offensive (12 February–21 March 1943)
  - The Briansk Front's Orel offensive (12–21 February 1943)
  - The Voronezh Front's (60th Army's) L'gov-Ryl'sk offensive (12–20 February 1943)
  - The Western Front's (16th Army's) Zhizdra offensive (22–27 February 1943)
  - The Briansk Front's (61st and 3rd Armies') Bolkhov offensive (22–27 February 1943)
  - The Western Front's (5th Army's) Gzhatsk offensive (22–27 February 1943)
  - The Western Front's (33rd Army's) Viaz'ma offensive (22–27 February 1943)
  - The Central Front's (65th, 70th, and 21st Armies' and 2nd Tank Army's) Sevsk-Trubchevsk offensive (25 February–6 March 1943)
  - The Briansk Front's (13th and 48th Armies') Orel offensive (25 February–6 March 1943)
  - The Central Front's (65th, 70th, and 21st Armies' and 2nd Tank Army's) Orel offensive (7–21 March 1943)
  - The Western Front's (16th Army's) Zhizdra-Orel offensive (7–21 March 1943)
- The Kalinin and Western Fronts' Rzhev-Viaz'ma offensive (pursuit) (6 March–1 April 1943
  - The Kalinin (22nd, 39th, 41st, and 43rd Armies') and Western Fronts' (5th, 20th, 30th, 31st, 33rd, 49th, and 50th Armies') Rzhev-Viaz'ma offensive (pursuit) (6–18 March 1943)
  - The Western Front's (49th and 50th Armies') Spas-Demensk offensive (18 March–1 April 1943)
  - The Western Front's (31st and 5th Armies') Dorogobuzh offensive (18–27 March 1943)

SOVIET OFFENSIVE OPERATIONS ALONG THE NORTHWESTERN AXIS AND OPERATION POLAR STAR

- The Leningrad, Volkhov, and Northwestern Fronts' Operation Polar Star [*Poliarnaia zvezda*] (Demiansk) (10–28 February 1943)

- – The Leningrad Front's (55th Army's) Krasnyi Bor-Tosno offensive (10–23 February 1943)
- – The Volkhov Front's (54th Army's) Chudovo-Tosno offensive (10–23 February 1943)
- – The Volkhov Front's (67th and 2nd Shock Armies') Siniavino offensive (12–23 February 1943)
- – The Northwestern Front's (27th, 11th, 1st Shock, 34th, and 53rd Armies') Demiansk offensive (15–28 February 1943)
- The Leningrad, Volkhov, and Northwestern Fronts' Truncated Operation Polar Star (Staraia Russa) (4 March–2 April 1943)
  - – The Northwestern Front's (27th, 11th, 1st Shock, 34th, 53rd, and 68th Armies') Staraia Russa offensive (4–19 March 1943)
  - – The Leningrad Front's (55th Army's) Krasnyi Bor-Tosno offensive (19–21 March 1943)
  - – The Volkhov Front's (8th Army's) Mga offensive (19 March–2 April 1943)

PART 1

SOVIET OFFENSIVE OPERATIONS WITHIN THE CONTEXT OF THE STALINGRAD COUNTEROFFENSIVE (NOVEMBER 1942–JANUARY 1943)

Chapter 2

The Kalinin and Western Fronts' 2nd Rzhev-Sychevka Offensive (Operation Mars) (25 November–16 December 1942)

Introduction

When the *Stavka* determined the strategic objectives it wished the Red Army to accomplish during the offensives and counteroffensives it launched in late November 1942 and conducted during its subsequent campaign in the winter of 1942–43, its attention quite naturally focused on the German-occupied Rzhev salient west of Moscow. Stalin and his senior military advisers in the *Stavka* considered this salient, whose eastern face was situated only 150 kilometers from the Soviet capital, as a virtual "dagger" aimed at the Soviet Union's heart. This salient, which was occupied by the Ninth Army of the Red Army's long-standing nemesis, German Army Group Center, offered the forces lodged within it direct access to the Soviet capital city via the main highway running from Viaz'ma through Gzhatsk to Moscow. Therefore, as long as the salient existed, the forces lodged within it posed a direct, constant, and menacing threat to Stalin's capital. Immediately after the salient formed during the Red Army's winter campaign of 1941–42, its existence compelled the *Stavka* to organize the Moscow Defensive Region, at times numbering as many as 800,000 troops, to defend Moscow against a possible German attack from the Rzhev region. After the winter campaign of 1941–42 ended in April 1942, the elimination of the Rzhev salient and the destruction of its defenders headed the list of the *Stavka's* priority strategic objectives.

Army Group Center's Ninth Army had captured the city of Rzhev and its associated salient on 14 October 1941 during its advance on the city of Kalinin Operation Typhoon. Thereafter, the Red Army launched numerous offensives to recapture the city; the most significant of these during its winter campaign of 1941–42 and, once again, while the Germans were conducting Operation Blau during the summer of 1942. However, all of these offensives failed, and both Rzhev and its salient remained in German hands. The Red Army's first attempt to recapture the city occurred between 5 December 1941 and 7 January 1942, when the Kalinin Front conducted an offensive to capture Kalinin and the region to the south. During this offensive, the Kalinin Front's 39th, 29th, and 31st Armies did indeed seize the Kalinin region but, during the exploitation phase of the operation, failed to overcome the Ninth Army's defenses on the northern bank of the Volga River north of Rzhev. Since Hitler considered the Rzhev region to be a vital launching pad for a future offensive against Moscow, he insisted the Ninth Army's forces dig in and hold on to the city and its bridgehead on the Volga's northern bank at all costs. Its German defenders thus transformed the city and its associated bridgehead on the Volga's northern bank into a fortified bastion.

The *Stavka* also included Rzhev and its nearby bridgehead as premier objectives when the Red Army conducted the second stage its counteroffensive in the Moscow region from mid-January through late April 1942. Accordingly, during the Rzhev-Viaz'ma offensive (8 January–20 April 1942), the Kalinin Front's 29th, 39th, and 30th Armies, in intense winter fighting along the offensive's northern wing, launched assault after assault against the Ninth Army's defenses north and northeast of the city, but once again to no avail. Although the attacking Soviet troops managed to compress the salient somewhat from the east and west and even managed to carve salients of their own in the German rear area, the Ninth Army stubbornly clung to the bulk of the salient and strengthened the fortifications around its periphery. Three months after the winter campaign ended, the Ninth Army consolidated its grip on the Rzhev salient in July 1942 by encircling and destroying the Red Army's forces (the 39th Army) lodged in their rear area.

Later in the summer, when the *Stavka* planned and conducted a series of offensive operations designed to thwart the German advance toward Stalingrad in southern Russia, on Zhukov's recommendation, Stalin once again designated the Rzhev salient as a key Red Army target. As a result, in July and August 1942, Zhukov's Western Front and Colonel General I. S. Konev's Kalinin Front conducted the massive Pogoreloe-Gorodishche (Rzhev-Sychevka) offensive operation and associated Gzhatsk-Viaz'ma offensive operation against German forces defending the salient (see *Forgotten Battles*, volume III). Conducted by Zhukov with characteristic audacity and ferocity, the Western Front's forces collapsed the northeastern part of the salient but failed to capture Sychevka or crush the salient as a whole. In the offensive's aftermath, with an eye to the future, Zhukov lamented, "With one or two more armies at our disposal, we could have combined with the Kalinin Front … and defeated the enemy not only in the Rzhev area but the entire Rzhev-Viaz'ma German force and substantially improved the operational situation in the whole Western strategic direction [axis]. Unfortunately, this real opportunity was missed by the Supreme Command."[9]

In late September 1942, the *Stavka* began planning the offensive and counteroffensive actions it intended to conduct in late fall, as well as its anticipated offensive campaign during the winter of 1942–43. Zhukov, still inspired by the unrequited potential of the offensive he had conducted in the Rzhev region during the late summer, strenuously urged the *Stavka* to conduct major strategic offensive operations along both the western (Moscow) and southwestern (Stalingrad) axes. Stalin, accepting his deputy Supreme Commander's recommendations, then ordered the *Stavka* and its principal planning organ, the Red Army General Staff, to plan two major strategic efforts, the first, a counteroffensive code-named Uranus in the Stalingrad region to encircle and destroy Axis forces in the vicinity of Stalin's namesake city and, the second, a major offensive code-named Mars against the Ninth Army in the Rzhev salient west of Moscow to destroy the army and cripple Army Group Center. Although the *Stavka* initially planned to commence both operations in late October, because of the uncertain situation in the Stalingrad region and difficulties it encountered while raising and fielding its strategic reserves and regrouping and supplying its forward operating forces, ultimately it postponed the two offensive operations until mid- and late November.

When the *Stavka* finally began Operation Mars in late November 1942, it expected the forces of its Kalinin, Northwestern, and Western Fronts to "utterly defeat the enemy in the Rzhev and Novo-Sokol'niki [Velikie Luki] regions."[10] At the same time, the armies of the Northwestern Front were to encircle and destroy German forces in the Demiansk salient. Since a recently-published book covers all aspects of Operation Mars in considerable detail, what follows is an abbreviated overview of the operation, which includes documents released since the book's publication.[11]

Planning

Operation Mars is one of most glaring instances when existing histories of the German-Soviet War have failed us. Together with Operation Uranus, the Red Army's counteroffensive in the Stalingrad region, Mars constituted the focal point of Soviet strategic efforts in the fall of 1942 and the launching pad for the subsequent conduct of a massive offensive campaign during the winter of 1942–42. Originally, the *Stavka* ordered the Kalinin and Western Fronts to commence Operation Mars in mid-October; however, because the local counterstrokes it conducted during early and mid-October in the Stalingrad region failed and it underestimated the amount of time necessary to assemble and prepare the required assault force, it ultimately postponed the offensive's start date to 25 November. By authorizing the Red Army to conduct these two strategic offensive operations virtually simultaneously, Stalin was convinced his forces could regain the strategic initiative along the entire Soviet-German front and, thereafter, begin its march to ultimate victory.

Appropriately named after the Roman God of War, Operation Mars was planned by Zhukov and the commanders of the two *fronts* designated to conduct the offensive, Colonel General I. S. Konev, the commander of the Western Front, and Colonel General M. A. Purkaev, the commander of the Kalinin Front. The offensive was coordinated by Zhukov and conducted by the two *front* commanders and their respective army commanders. In terms of its immense scale and ambitious objectives, Operation Mars was roughly equivalent to Operation Uranus. In its fickleness, however, history "remembered" Uranus, largely because it succeeded, but "forgot" Operation Mars because it failed. Only now can we correct this historical mistake and commemorate properly the sacrifices of the many Red Army soldiers and Germans who fell during the operation.

In late September 1942, the *Stavka* formulated a strategic plan designed to reverse the spectacular gains the German *Wehrmacht* had recorded during the summer and fall of 1942 and restore the strategic initiative into the Red Army's hands.[12] Army General Zhukov, a charter member of the *Stavka* and now a deputy Commissar of Defense of the USSR and, as Stalin's most trusted senior military adviser, a deputy Supreme High Commander to the dictator, played a significant role in planning the offensive.[13] Based on his own strategic analysis and personal experiences he amassed while serving as chief of the Red Army General Staff and as a *Stavka* representative and a *front* commander during 1941 and 1942, Zhukov was convinced the Red Army could best attain strategic victory in 1942 by defeating and destroying German Army Group Center, whose forces posed the most serious threat to Moscow and the Soviet regime.[14] He also believed the *Stavka* had sufficient forces in its operating *fronts* and strategic reserves to conduct two major, mutually supporting, strategic offensive efforts, the first an offensive against Army Group Center's Ninth Army lodged in the Rzhev salient west of Moscow and, the second, a counteroffensive against Army Group B's overextended German Sixth Army in the Stalingrad region.

In support of Zhukov's contention, the *Stavka* had roughly equivalent forces deployed along the western and southwestern axes in the early fall of 1942. Along the western (Moscow) axis, the Red Army's Kalinin and Western Fronts, together with the Moscow Defense Zone to their rear, fielded a force of almost 1,900,000 men, supported by over 24,000 guns and mortars, 3,300 tanks, and 1,100 aircraft along the critical western (Moscow) axis.[15] Along the southwestern axis, the Stalingrad and Don Fronts (which were formed on 28 September from the former Stalingrad and Southeastern Fronts) fielded over 1 million men, supported by a force of about 15,000 guns and mortars, 1,400 tanks, and over 900 aircraft.[16] Although a major Red Army counteroffensive in the Stalingrad region would exploit the presence of Rumanian, Italian, and Hungarian Armies now deployed in large sectors of Army Group "B's" defensive front, Zhukov thought it wiser and more prudent to defeat the large and wholly German force in the Rzhev salient, thereby removing the threat to Moscow once and for all.

Stalin, accepting Zhukov's strategic judgment, approved his deputy's proposals on 26 September 1942 and, soon after, assigned the twin offensive operations their respective codenames, Mars and Uranus and appointed Zhukov to coordinate Operation Mars in the Rzhev region and Colonel General A. M. Vasilevsky, the Chief of the Red Army General Staff., to coordinate Operation Uranus at Stalingrad.[17] Once fully developed, the *Stavka's* strategic plan for offensive action in the fall of 1942 required the Red Army to conduct two major offensive operations, each consisting of two distinct stages, with each of the four stages designated by the code-name of a planet. Operating along the western axis under Zhukov's overall supervision, in Operation Mars the Kalinin Front's 41st, 22nd, and 39th Armies and the Western Front's 31st, 20th, and 29th Armies were to attack to encircle and destroy Army Group Center's Ninth Army in the Rzhev and Sychevka regions. After successfully completing Mars, the same force, joined by the Kalinin Front's 43rd Army and 4th Shock Army attacking southward through Dukhovshchina toward Smolensk and by the Western Front's 5th and 33rd Armies and 3rd Tank Army attacking westward through Viaz'ma toward Smolensk, was to destroy all of Army Group Center's forces east of the Smolensk region in an operation probably code-named either Jupiter or Neptune (see Map 6).[18]

At roughly the same time, operating along the southwestern axis under Vasilevsky's supervision, in Operation Uranus the Don Front's 63rd, 21st, 65th, 24th, and 66th Armies, the Stalingrad Front's 57th and 51st Armies, and, after it was formed on 22 October, the Southwestern Front's 1st Guards, 5th Tank, and 21st Armies, were to attack to encircle and destroy Axis forces in the Stalingrad region.[19] During the second stage of his offensive, Vasilevsky's forces, now joined

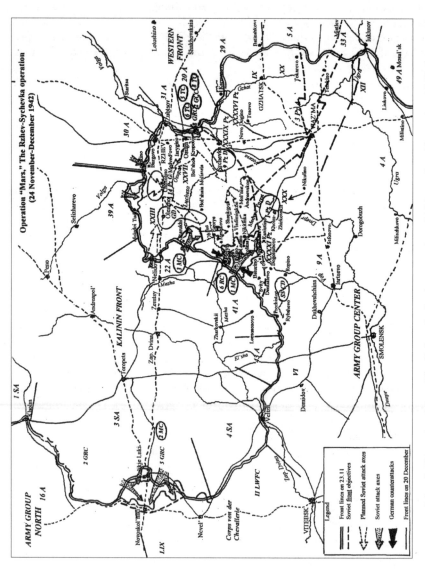

Map 6. Operation Mars, The Rzhev-Sychevka operation, 24 November–December 1942

by the Voronezh Front's 6th Army, were to conduct Operation Saturn to capture Rostov, destroy German Army Group "B," and isolate Army Group "A" in the Caucasus region.[20] In terms of their timing, although the *Stavka* initially ordered the Red Army to launch both offensives in mid-October, ultimately it delayed the start dates of both to mid- and late November.

The *Stavka* ordered the Kalinin and Western Fronts to conduct Operation Mars in a directive it dispatched to the two *fronts* on 28–29 September. In turn, the two *front* commanders, Purkaev and Konev, dispatched orders implementing the *Stavka's* directive to the armies participating in the offensive at 0240 hours on 1 October:[21]

> Western Front Directive No. 0289/OP to the Commanders of the 20th, 29th, and 31st Armies and Subordinate Formations Concerning the Destruction of the Enemy's Sychevka-Rzhev Grouping
>
> Copy to the chief of the Red Army General Staff
>
> To destroy the enemy Sychevka-Rzhev grouping, I order:
>
> 1. The commander of the 31st [Army] Grouping, consisting of the 88th, 239th, 336th, and 20th Guards Rifle Divisions, the 32nd and 145th Tank Brigades, seven *RVK* [*Stavka* reserve] artillery regiments, and six multiple rocket launcher battalions (including four M–30 battalions), will attack in the *front's* sector from Staroselovo to Kriukovo (inclusive) [and advance] along the Osuga, Artemovo, and Ligastaevo axis. The immediate mission is to penetrate the enemy's front, secure the railroad in the sector from KAZ (4 kilometers north of Osuga) through Osuga Station to the Osuga River with the [army's] main force, and the subsequent mission is to attack westward from the railroad line toward Rzhev with its main grouping and, together with the 29th, 30th, and 20th Armies, destroy the enemy's Rzhev grouping.
>
> 2. The commander of the 20th [Army] Grouping, consisting of the 251st, 331st, 415th, 26th Guards, 42nd Guards, 247th and 379th Rifle Divisions, the 148th and 150th Tank Brigades, the 11th, 17th, 25th, 31st, 93rd, 255th, 240th, 18th and 80th Tank Brigades, 18 *RVK* artillery regiments, and 16 multiple rocket launcher battalions (including 10 M–30 battalions), will attack toward Sychevka in the *front's* sector from Vasil'ki to Pechora. The immediate mission is to penetrate the enemy's front and secure Sychevka and the railroad line in the Osuga River and Sychevka sector, with [the army's] main forces, and the subsequent mission is to protect reliably the Podsoson'e, Sychevka, and Marinino sector and [the sector] along the Vazuza against attack from the west and southwest ....
>
> Attack northward and northwestward through Karpovo, Osuiskoe, and Afonasovo from the line extending from Iakovka through Iuratino to Podsoson'e with a main force of no fewer than 4 reinforced divisions and, together with the forces of the 30th and 31st Armies and those of the Kalinin Front, destroy the enemy's Rzhev grouping.
>
> 3. The boundary line between the 31st and 20th Armies extends to Kortnevo, as before, farther along the Osuga River to Kasatino, and still

farther to Kul'nevo and Afonasovo, with all points inclusive for the 20th Army.

4. The armies are to be prepared to attack on 12 October.

5. After penetrating the enemy's front, a mobile group consisting of the 2nd Guards Cavalry Corps and 6th Tank Corps, under the command of the 2nd Guards Cavalry Corps' commander, will be committed along the southern bank of the Osuga River at the boundary between the armies, with the mission of reaching the Nashchekino, Tatarinka, Pribytki, and Aleksandrovka regions, from which one cavalry division will be sent to occupy Andreevskoe and establish communications with Kalinin Front's forces attacking from the Belyi region.

6. Army commanders will submit their plans for conducting Operation "Mars" by 5 October.

[signed] Konev, Bulganin, Sokolovsky[22]

The after-action report of the Western Front's 20th Army later described the order it received from Konev in even greater detail:

On 1 October 1942, the commander of the 20th Army received directive No. 0289/OP of the Western Front commander, which assigned the Western Front the mission of destroying the enemy Sychevka-Rzhev grouping with the 29th, 30th, 31st, and 20th Armies, in cooperation with Kalinin Front units.

In accordance with this directive, the 20th Army received the mission to penetrate the enemy defense in the Vasil'ki-Pechora sector and, while developing the attack on Sychevka with the 8th Guards Rifle Corps and a mobile group, to reach the line of the Rzhev-Sychevka railroad and capture Sychevka by the end of the first day of the offensive.

Subsequently, while reliably protecting the Podsoson'e, Sychevka, and Marino regions along the Vazuza River against an attack from the west and the Viazovka, Iuriatino, and Podsoson'e line against an attack from the southwest, attack northwestward through Karpovo, Osuiskoe, and Afonasovo with your main forces to destroy the enemy's Rzhev grouping in cooperation with the 31st Army.[23]

However, deteriorating weather conditions in the Rzhev region during the first half of October forced the *Stavka* to postpone the start date for Operation Mars.[24] Accordingly, the *Stavka* dispatched a revised directive to Purkaev's and Konev's *fronts* on 10 October, which required the armies on the Western Front's right wing and the Kalinin Front's left wing "to encircle the enemy Rzhev Grouping, capture Rzhev, and free the rail road line from Moscow to Velikie Luki."[25] Specifically, the Western Front's 20th and 31st Armies, supported by its 29th Army, were to conduct the *front*'s main attack along the Osuga and Vazuza Rivers northeast of Sychevka (see Map 7). After the two armies successfully penetrated the Germans' front, a cavalry-mechanized group consisting of the 6th Tank and 2nd Guards Cavalry Corps was to capture Sychevka, roll up the Germans' defenses around Rzhev from the south and link up with the forces of the Kalinin Front's 41st Army advancing eastward across the base of the salient from the Belyi

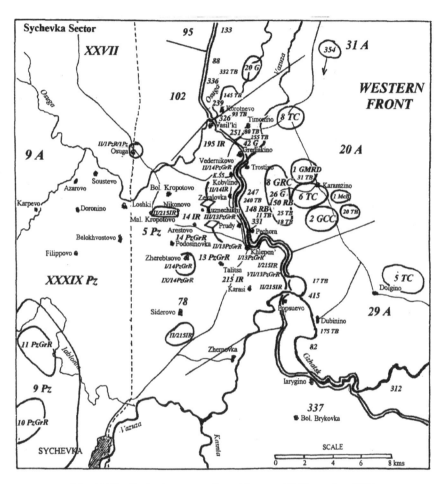

Map 7. The Sychevka sector, dispositions on 24 November 1942

region. Thereafter, the Western Front's 20th and 31st Armies were to "mop up" German forces encircled in the northern half of the salient in conjunction with the Western Front's 30th Army and the Kalinin Front's 39th, 22nd, and 41st Armies and then prepare to attack southward toward Viaz'ma with the *front's* 5th and 6th Tank Corps in their vanguard.

According to amended orders Konev issued at 0230 hours on 11 October 1942, his Western Front's cavalry-mechanized (mobile) group was to play a key role in the operation:

Top secret

Special importance

To the Commanders of the 2nd Guards Cavalry and 6th Tank Corps.

Copy to the Commanders of the 31st and 20th Armies

Copy to the chief of the Red Army General Staff

As an addendum to *front* Directive No. 0289, dated 1 October 1942, I order:

1. After the 31st and 20th Armies have penetrated the enemy's front, a mobile group consisting of the 2nd Guards Cavalry Corps, 6th Tank Corps, and 1st Motorcycle Brigade, under the command of the commander of the 2nd Guards Cavalry Corps, will enter the penetration on the 20th Army's right, with the immediate mission of quickly reaching the Nashchekino, Tatarinka, Pribytka, and Aleksandrovka regions.

The mobile group's subsequent mission is [as follows]:

The 2nd Guards Cavalry Corps —one cavalry division will secure the Andreevsko region (30 kilometers northwest of Sychevka) by a decisive attack and from this region will establish communications with the Kalinin Front forces advancing from the Belyi and Kholm-Zhirkovskii region and prevent enemy reserves from approaching Sychevka from the southwest. While deploying strong reconnaissance detachments toward Shizderevo to protect against attacks from the west, the 2nd Guards Cavalry Corps' main forces will continue resolute operations northward toward Chertolino in the rear of the enemy's Rzhev grouping and conduct reconnaissance operations toward Olenino to establish communications and cooperate with the Kalinin Front's forces advancing on Olenino.

The 6th Tank Corps, with the 1st Motorcycle Brigade — will attack from its designated region toward Viazovka, Barsuki, and Kholodnia, with the mission of attacking from the southwest in cooperation with the 20th Army, capturing the town of Sychevka, and blocking the approach of enemy reserves toward Sychevka from the south.

2. The mobile group will occupy jumping-off positions for its commitment into the penetration in the Karganovo, Krasnovo, Il'inskoe, Rakovo, and Rovnoe regions the day before the penetration, and [its forces] will reach the Vazuza River the night before the attack.

3. To the commanders of the 2nd Guards Cavalry Corps, 6th Tank Corps, and 1st Motorcycle Brigade – you must work out procedures for the commitment of the mobile group into the penetration and for artillery support with the commander of 20th Army in timely fashion.

4. To the commanders of the 31st and 20th Armies — the *front's* chief of artillery will provide artillery support for the commitment of the mobile group into the penetration.

5. To the commander of the 1st Air Army — fighter aviation will protect the mobile group while it is in its jumping-off positions and during the period when the mobile group is being committed into and operating in the penetration, and assault aviation will assist the mobile group in accomplishing its missions.

6. To the commander of the 2nd Guards Cavalry Corps — plan measures for the commitment of the mobile group into the penetration and for its operations in the depths by 14 October, in accordance with the actual directive missions assigned to the [respective] groupings by me at the *front* auxiliary command post (in the forest 0.5 kilometers southeast of Ryl'tsevo).

Confirm receipt.

Konev, Bulganin, Sokolovsky[26]

According to the *Stavka's* revised directive, Purkaev's Kalinin Front was to conduct its main attack with two armies: Major General F. G. Tarasov's 41st Army advancing eastward in the region just south of Belyi, and Major General V. A. Iushkevich's 22nd Army attacking eastward along the Luchesa River north of Belyi (see Maps 8 and 9). To the north, on the Kalinin Front's left wing, Major General A. I. Zygin's 39th Army, which was deployed along the northwestern face of the Rzhev salient, was to conduct a secondary assault southward across the Molodoi Tud River toward Olenino (see Map 10).[27] The 41st Army planned to conduct its main attack south of Belyi with Siberian 6th Stalin Volunteer Rifle Corps, commanded by Major General S. I. Povetkin, and thereafter exploit the attack with the 1st and 2nd Mechanized Corps, commanded by Majors General of Tank Forces M. D. Solomatin and I. P. Korchagin, respectively, which were to advance eastward to link up with 20th Army's cavalry-mechanized group somewhere west of Sychevka. At the same time, the 22nd Army was to advance eastward through rough and heavily wooded terrain along both banks of the Luchesa River valley to outflank the German defenses at Belyi from the north, capture the town, and, cooperating with the 39th Army's forces advancing on Olenino from the north, help encircle German forces in this region by advancing on Olenino from the south. The newly formed 3rd Mechanized Corps, commanded by the experienced tank commander, Major General of Tank Forces M. E Katukov, was to lead the 22nd Army's exploitation operation. Subsequently, the other armies around the flaming circumference of the Rzhev salient, specifically, the Kalinin Front's 39th Army and the Western Front's 30th Army, were to join the offensive, assist in the destruction of the German Ninth Army, and then regroup to participate in the

Map 8. The Belyi sector, planning and dispositions on 24 November 1942

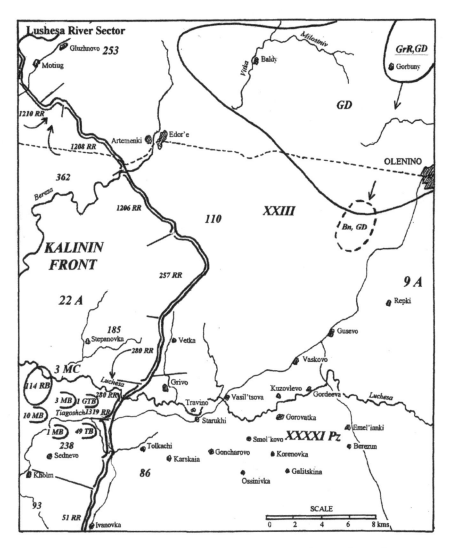

Map 9. The Luchesa River sector, dispositions on 24 November 1942

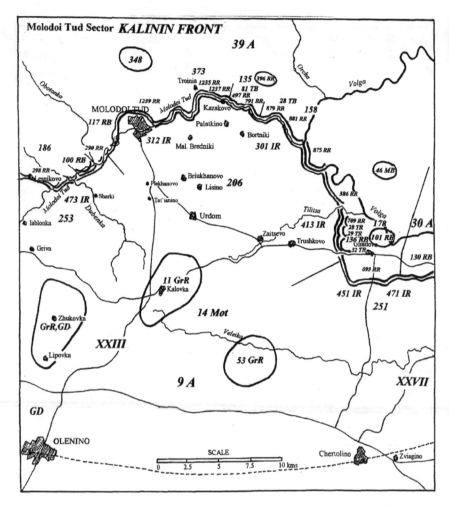

Map 10. The Molodoi Tud sector, dispositions on 24 November 1942

second stage of the offensive against Army Group Center's forces in the Viaz'ma region and east of Smolensk.[28]

During the second phase of the offensive, Operation Neptune or Jupiter, the *Stavka* planned to reinforce its force conducting Operation Mars with the Western Front's 5th and 33rd Armies and the Kalinin Front's 43rd Army and 4th Shock Army, the former attacking toward Viaz'ma and Smolensk from the east and the latter attacking through Dukhovshchina to Smolensk from the north, In this expanded offensive, the Western Front's heavily reinforced 5th and 33rd Armies, which were deployed astride the Moscow-Viaz'ma road, were to penetrate the defenses of Army Group Center's Third Panzer Army east of Viaz'ma. The 9th and 10th Tank Corps, followed by 3rd Guards Tank Army, were to then capture Viaz'ma, link up with the Kalinin Front's forces, and, if possible, continue the attack westward toward Smolensk.[29] To insure success, the *Stavka* provided extraordinary armor, artillery, and engineer support for Zhukov's two attacking *fronts*.[30] In fact, this support exceeded that provided to Vasilevsky's armies earmarked to carry out Operation Uranus.

Several newly-released documents underscore the *Stavka's* intent, at least through 6 November, to employ the Kalinin Front's 43rd Army during the second stage of its offensive against the Rzhev salient. For example, a copy of an order the 43rd Army sent to its subordinate formations in early October 1942, which was later found in the records of the army's 145th Rifle Division, provides further details on the army's mission and organization for combat:

Plans for Offensive Operation Mars in October-November 1942

1. The mission of the army: Destroy the opposing enemy units, reach the Demidov (incl.), Kholm, and Dukhovshchina (incl.) front, and sever enemy communications to Smolensk by an attack with a mechanized corps in the general direction of Smolensk, where it will dig in with its main forces. Be prepared to begin the operation on 12 October 1942.

2. Boundary lines: to the right – Demidov (incl.), Lake Baklanovskoe, Baevo (incl.); and to the left – Dukhovshchina (incl,), Pashkovo (incl.), Smalkovo (incl.), Lake Shchuch'e (incl.), Glinskoe, Western Dvina.

3. Combat composition of the army – see attachment No. 4 [the 145th, 306th, 32nd, 279th Rifle and 21st Guards Rifle Divisions, the 2nd Mechanized Corps, and the 154th and 236th Tank Brigades] ….

7. Decision

a. Deliver your main attack from the Lake Baklanovskoe (incl.) and Lake Sapsho front with three rifle divisions and two tank brigades, reinforced by one gun artillery regiment, two howitzer artillery regiments, three anti-tank artillery regiments, three multiple rocket launcher battalions, and three engineer battalions, with the missions of penetrating the front and destroying the opposing enemy … After the army's forces reach the Demidov (incl.) and Dukhovshchina (incl.) front or when they have approached this line, the mechanized corps will be committed to battle to sever the communications to Smolensk. The nature of the mechanized corps' operation will depend on the existing situation and the degree of enemy fortifications in the Smolensk region ....Do not exclude the possibility of capturing Smolensk in the event of the absence of large enemy forces in Smolensk. The 2nd Mechanized Corps' operations must be reliably protected by air cover and supporting aviation consisting of no fewer than one mixed aviation division, and it is desirable to reinforce the axis along which the mechanized corps is operating with one rifle division from the *front's* reserve ... The initial stage of the artillery offensive before the beginning of the attack will last 25 minutes ...

e. Ammunition expenditure. Allocate for the entire operation: 1 combat load of mines; 76mm shells – 2 combat loads; 45mm – 3.5 combat loads; 122mm and 152mm – 3.5 combat loads ....

f. Communications with the 4th Shock Army and the 41st Army will be by radio, telegraph station 35, and liaison aircraft.

g. Communication with *front* will be by radio, BODO, and aircraft ....

15. Conclusions and Recommendations.

1. Given the period on concentrating the army and the necessity for having 6–7 days for the combat training of forces, it is desirable to begin the operation on 18–20 October.

> The commander of the 43rd Army, Lieutenant General Golubev,
> The member of the Military Council, Division Commissar Shabalov,
> The chief of staff, Major General Bogoliubov[31]

Additionally, a *Stavka* directive dated 0350 hours on 13 October notified Purkaev that it was reinforcing his *front's* 43rd Army with a fresh rifle corps so that it could successfully conduct its climatic advance on Smolensk from the north:

The *Stavka* of the Supreme High Command orders [the following] be transferred to you for the forthcoming Operation "Mars:"

1. To reinforce the 43rd Army – the 5th Guards Rifle Corps, consisting of the corps headquarters, beginning to load at the Western Front's Uvarovo Station on 14 October, the 9th Guards Rifle Division, beginning to load at Riazan' Station on 13 October, the 46th Guards Rifle Division from the Voronezh Front, beginning to load on 14 October, and the 357th Rifle Division, beginning to load at Naro-Fominsk Station on 15 October.

2. In the *front's* reserve in the Soblago region – the 8th Estonian Corps, consisting of the corps headquarters, the 7th and 249th Estonian Rifle Divisions, and the 19th Guards Rifle Division. The corps is beginning to move following the 5th Guards Rifle Corps from the Egor'evska region and the 19th Guards Rifle Division from the Volkhov Front. This corps will not be employed without the *Stavka's* permission.

3. We will inform you later about the movement plan.

> For the Supreme High Commander
> Chief of the General Staff, A. Vasilevsky[32]

Finally, after the *Stavka* delayed the launch of Operation Mars several times, at 0410 hours on 5 November, the commander of the 43rd Army, Lieutenant General K. D. Golubev, sent enciphered telegrams to his subordinate commanders with specific instructions regarding how they were to conduct their offensive and indicating they were to be prepared to attack on or about 9 November. The first telegram was addressed primarily to the army's 145th, 32nd, and 306th Rifle Divisions and the 2nd Mechanized Corps:

[Copies to the deputy commanders of the Artillery, Auto-Tank Directorate and Engineer Forces]

In preparation for "Mars," I order the rifle division commanders in designated offensive sectors:

1. Conduct reconnaissance and coordinate matters of cooperation on the missions of Operation "Mars" with company and battery commanders on 6 and 7 November.

2. Beginning on 5 November, the commanders of the 306th Rifle and 21st Guards Rifle Divisions will commence preparing jumping-off positions for their divisions, including:

a) Open full-profile trenches in their sectors;

b) Prepare covered observation posts for company, battery, and battalion commanders and command posts for regimental and division commanders.

c) Dig trenches in the direction of the enemy … Conduct all work only at night, while observing all of the principals of *maskirovka* [camouflage]. Complete all work by 8 November 1942. The commander of the 2nd Mechanized Corps will organize personal reconnaissance of the forward edge of the enemy's defense with the commanders of rifle and tank companies in the intended movement sector of the mechanized corps. The period [of this activity] is 6 and 7 November. On 6 November the commanders of the [mechanized] brigades, which are assigned to secure the line of the Gobza River, will work out questions of coordination with the 21st Guards Rifle Division commander …

4. Report fulfillment.

Golubev   Shabalov
Bogoliubov

The second telegram to Korchagin, the commander of the 2nd Mechanized Corps, described his corps role in the forthcoming offensive.

[Copies to the commander of the 21st Guards Rifle Division and deputy commander of Auto-Tank Forces]

Since the 236th Tank Brigade unable to return to the army, I order:

1. In plan "Mars" the 2nd Mechanized Corps commander will make provision for the advance of his mechanized brigades to seize the Gobza

River line before the approach of the 2nd Mechanized Corps' main forces. The line must be seized by the end of the first day of the operation.

2. Commit the motor-mechanized brigades in the sector of the 21st Guards Rifle Division.

3. The brigade commanders will work out matters of cooperation with the 21st Guards Rifle Division by 6 November 1942 ...

Golubev   Shabalov
Bogoliubov[33]

Left unsaid in all of these orders was the fact that the 43rd Army was to launch its attack only if the forces conducting Operation Mars were successful.

The Initial Offensive (25–29 November)

The Western Front's (20th and 31st Armies') Assault

The Kalinin and Western Fronts commenced Operation Mars at dawn on 25 November, when the five armies designated to conduct their joint offensive assaulted the eastern, western, and northern flanks of the Ninth Army's defenses around the Rzhev salient simultaneously.[34] Spearheading the Western Front's assaults, the forces of Major General N. I. Kiriukhin's 20th Army and Major General V. S. Polenov's 31st Army struck hard at the defensive positions of the Ninth Army's XXXIX Panzer Corps along and north of the Vazuza and Osuga Rivers, east and northeast of the vital German railhead at Sychevka (see Map 11). Although the Germans expected the attack, it caught the defenders at an extremely awkward moment, the very time when the 5th Panzer Division's two panzer grenadier regiments were in the process of relieving the 78th Infantry Division's three grenadier regiments in their defenses along the Vazuza River.[35] Although the Western Front's preliminary artillery bombardment produced considerable damage and confusion in the Germans' defenses, the heavy snow and dense fog that enveloped the battlefield prevented Soviet aircraft from attacking the Germans' defenses and severely hindered the subsequent Soviet infantry and tank assaults.

Nevertheless, Konev's shock group struck precisely as planned, attacking with Kiriukhin's 20th Army deployed on its left and Polenov's 31st Army on its right. Kiriukhin's army launched its main attack due westward across the Vazuza River proper and a secondary attack in the narrow strip of ground between the Osuga and Vazuza Rivers. Further north, Polenov's army assaulted westward from its shallow bridgehead on the western bank of the Osuga River. Despite the ferocity of his assaults, Konev's forces achieved only limited initial success. On his shock group's right wing north of the Osuga River, where the 31st Army conducted its main attack with a force of three rifle divisions and two tank brigades, the German 102nd Infantry Division successfully fended off repeated infantry and tank attacks for three days, in the process inflicting heavy and indeed crippling casualties on the attackers.[36] Between the Vazuza and Osuga Rivers to the south, where the 20th Army launched its secondary attack with a shock group made up of three rifle divisions and two tank brigades, the 78th Infantry Division's 195th Infantry Regi-

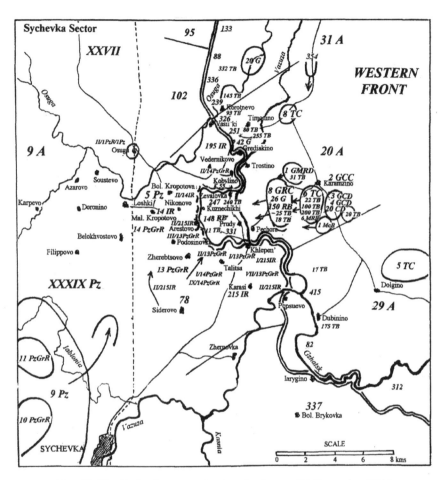

Map 11. The Sychevka sector, the situation late on 25 November 1942

ment, supported by a battalion of panzer grenadiers from the 5th Panzer Division, also succeeded in containing the 20th Army's secondary attack after only limited gains. Thus, despite strong armored support, the attacks by Konev's forces north of the Vazuza River stalled almost immediately and resulted in frightfully high casualties among the attackers.[37] Seemingly oblivious to these failures, Zhukov and Konev insisted these attacks continue, if only to support the more successful operations by the 20th Army's main shock group farther to the south.

Although the assaults by Konev's shock groups operating north of the Vazuza River faltered badly, the 20th Army's main attack across the frozen Vazuza River, which was conducted by a shock group consisting of the 331st and 247th Rifle Divisions, backed up by several tank brigades and the full-strength 8th Guards Rifle Corps, achieved signal, if only limited, success.[38] Exploiting the temporary confusion in German ranks caused by the intense artillery preparation, Major General G. D. Mukhin's 247th Rifle Division lunged across the Vazuza River, seizing a small lodgment on the river's western bank. Reacting quickly to this success, Kiriukhin then ordered Colonel P. F. Berestov's 331st Rifle Division to cross the river and widen the breech. Fierce fighting raged all day as the 20th Army's infantry, but without significant tank support, struggled to expand the bridgehead.[39] It was critical they do so because Konev and Kiriukhin intended to commit, first, the 8th Guards Rifle Corps into the breech to widen the bridgehead and, thereafter, the army's mobile group (the 6th Tank and 2nd Guards Cavalry Corps) into the enlarged bridgehead to commence the exploitation operation toward Sychevka and into the Germans' deep rear area. Throughout the first day of fighting, Zhukov, Konev, and Kiriukhin raged at and cajoled their commanders to accelerate their advance at all cost. Although by day's end the bridgehead was still too small to offer the forces operating within it any freedom of maneuver, nevertheless, overnight Konev, acting boldly but accepting significant risks, ordered Kiriukhin to commit, in succession, his 8th Guards Rifle Corps and cavalry-mechanized group into the small bridgehead the next day.

The desperate but skillful resistance by the defending German troops, however, soon proved that Konev's risky decision was both premature and ill advised. Although the Soviet attacks struck the 5th Panzer and 78th Infantry Divisions' forces while they were in the midst of a complex regrouping and in no way organized well enough to conduct an effective defense, the German soldiers fought with grim determination. Forming small ad hoc battalion-, company-, and even platoon-size *kampfgruppen* [combat groups], the beleaguered Germans formed hedgehog defenses around the numerous villages and farmsteads dotting the partially wooded region west of the Vazuza and converted the stone houses and other buildings within these villages and farms into veritable fortresses to anchor these hedgehog defenses. Attacking with abandon, the Soviet riflemen advanced directly into these strong points, overcoming some, bypassing others, but leaving many as deadly obstacles strewn throughout their rear area. The headquarters of the Ninth Army's XXXIX Panzer Corps, out of contact with most of its subordinate units because of its severe command, control, and communications difficulties, could not appreciate the chaos and confusion their fragmented but desperate resistance was causing in Soviet ranks. Nevertheless, the corps desperately attempted to shore up its sagging defenses by ordering the 9th Panzer Division, then in reserve west of Sychevka, to march to the sounds of the guns and plug the developing breech.

Zhukov and Konev, also understanding the gravity of the situation, reacted accordingly by ordering their forces to press forward at all cost. Therefore, while the riflemen of Mukhin's and Berestov's divisions strained to expand their tenuous bridgehead on the Vazuza's western bank, overnight on 25 November and throughout the morning of the 26th, they urged Kiriukhin to move his second echelon and designated exploitation forces forward to and across the river. Under near constant German artillery, mortar, and machine gun fire, the 8th Guards Rifle, 6th Tank, and 2nd Guards Cavalry Corps, with their combined force of over 200 tanks, 30,000 infantry, and 10,000 cavalrymen, as well as their extensive accompanying logistical trains, moved inexorably toward the river. However, since only two roads led to the river's eastern bank, and German artillery fire had strewn craters along both routes, the results were utterly predictable – chaos reigned supreme. Advancing in the 20th Army's second echelon, the reinforcing infantry and tanks of Major General F. D. Zakharov's 8th Guards Rifle Corps clogged the crossing sites over the Vazuza as harried *front* and army staff officers tried in vain to clear the way for the advancing armor and cavalry of Major General V. V. Kriukov's cavalry-mechanized group. It was an impossible task. Although the rifle corps finally managed to cross the river by dawn on 26 November, the tank and cavalry corps could not. Thus, the 170 tanks of Colonel P. M. Arman's 6th Tank Corps would not be able to begin going into action until mid-day on 26 November, and the 2nd Guards Cavalry Corps, under Kriukov's personal command, would remain on the river's eastern bank until mid-day on 27 November. Utterly frustrated, Zhukov and Konev realized the momentum of their offensive was already flagging.

The defending Germans finally felt the full impact of Kiriukhin's assault on 27 November, when the 6th Tank and 2nd Guards Cavalry Corps finally fully deployed for combat within the bridgehead (see Map 12). By this time, however, regrouping German panzer reserves and the skillful but often desperate forward defense by beleaguered German infantrymen and panzer grenadiers condemned the 20th Army's assault west of the Vazuza River to a disastrous fate. Combined with the 5th Panzer and 78th Infantry Divisions' stubborn defense of countless fortified villages within and adjacent to the 20th Army's bridgehead on the western bank of the Vazuza River, local counterattacks by multiple *kampfgruppen* from the 9th Panzer Division thoroughly disrupted the planned Soviet armor and cavalry exploitation. The tanks and motorized riflemen of Arman's 6th Tank Corps, attacking shortly after midday, lunged through the Germans' hedgehog defenses, followed shortly thereafter by the cavalrymen of Kriukov's 2nd Guards Cavalry Corps, which rode headlong into combat on horseback. Unable to crush the tens of German fortified village strong points in and adjacent to the bridgehead, the attacking Soviet forces shattered into multiple fragments.

Although three of Arman's armored brigades "ran the gauntlet" successfully and managed to cross the vital Rzhev-Sychevka road, one could not.[40] Kriukov's cavalry corps too suffered dreadful losses when, under withering German fire, one of its cavalry divisions, together with portions of three others, also managed to advance across the Sychevka road. Kriukov's corps, however, left parts of three of

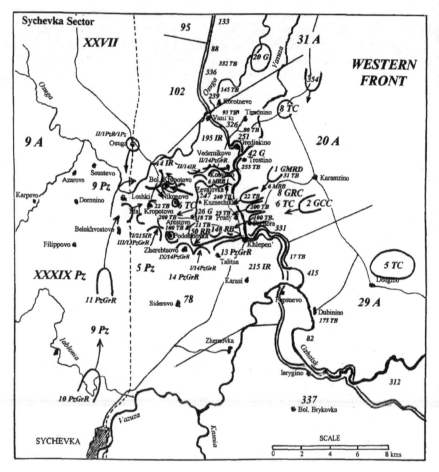

Map 12. The Sychevka sector, the situation late on 27 November 1942

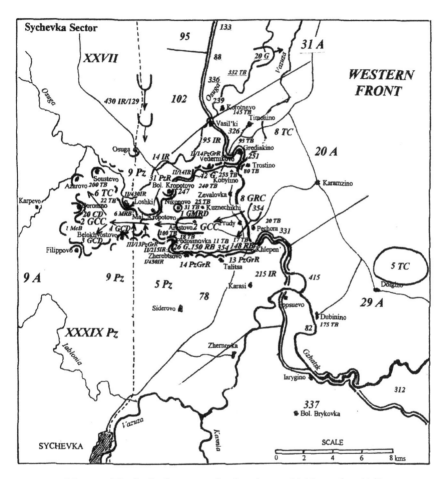

Map 13. The Sychevka sector, the situation on 28 November 1942

its divisions, as well as its headquarters and all of its logistical trains, isolated in the bridgehead far to the rear.[41] Meanwhile, the riflemen and tanks of Zakharov's 8th Guards Rifle Corps, together with those from the divisions subordinate to the 20th Army's main shock group, engaged in a painstakingly slow and costly struggle to expand the bridgehead in the face of undiminished German resistance. Along the periphery of this fight, *kampfgruppen* from the regrouping 9th Panzer Division launched counterattack after counterattack against the northern and southern flanks of Soviet forces exploiting westward across the Sychevka road and the southern flank of the 20th Army's bridgehead defenses.

By nightfall on 28 November, it was abundantly clear to both Zhukov and Konev that their offensive was in serious trouble (see Map 13). Although three quarters of Arman's 6th Tank Corps and the bulk of three cavalry divisions from Kriukov's 2nd Guards Cavalry Corps had made it across the Rzhev-Sychevka road, Arman's corps had lost over half of its tanks, and, by capturing the roads to their rear, counterattacking German forces had ended all opportunities for the two corps to conduct an orderly withdrawal back into the bridgehead. Making matters worse, the 20th Army's exploiting tankers and cavalrymen had outrun the range of their supporting artillery, which, because there was no room to deploy it in the bridgehead, was forced to remain on the Vazuza River's eastern bank.[42] Nevertheless, Zhukov and Konev, undeterred by the multiple misfortunes, ordered Arman's and Kriukov's beleaguered tankers and cavalrymen to exploit westward toward the Belyi region overnight on 28–29 November and the 20th Army's forces to continue widening the bridgehead and, simultaneously, support the westward exploitation by Kriukov's cavalry-mechanized group.

The Kalinin Front's (41st, 22nd, and 39th Armies') Assault

Zhukov's continued optimism in the face of such mounting difficulties was conditioned, at least in part, by his own stubborn refusal to admit defeat and also by the striking successes the shock groups of the Kalinin Front's 41st and 22nd Armies seemed to be achieving along the western face of the Rzhev salient. Indeed, based on their initial combat reports, the shock groups of Tarasov's 41st Army and Iushkevich's 22nd Army did appear to be making spectacular forward progress. Attacking eastward south of Belyi and along the Luchesa River valley, respectively, by late on 28 November, the two armies had successfully penetrated the German defenses and driven deep into the Ninth Army's operational rear along both axes. If they continued to do so, reasoned Zhukov, the Kalinin Front's successes would render temporary and irrelevant the Western Front's difficulties along the Vazuza River axis.

The shock group of Tarasov's 41st Army struck the defenses of the Ninth Army's XXXXI Panzer Corps south of Belyi at 0900 hours on 25 November (see Map 14).[43] Advancing across the frozen, forested swamps astride the Belyi-Dukhovshchina road in a driving snowstorm, Povetkin's 6th Stalin Volunteer Rifle Corps, supported by tank detachments from Solomatin's 1st Mechanized Corps, easily overcame the forward defenses of the XXXXI Panzer Corps' 246th Infantry and 2nd *Luftwaffe* Field Divisions and lunged eastward into the complex of villages scattered along the Vishenka River in the Germans' tactical rear

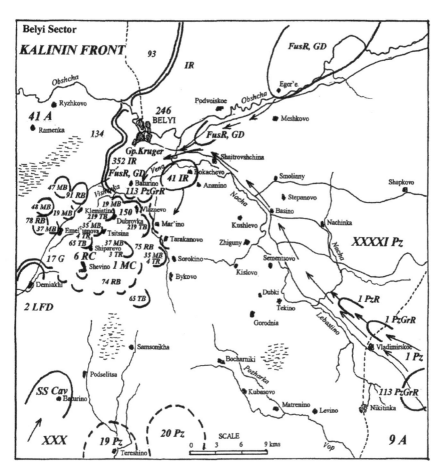

Map 14. The Belyi sector, the situation late on 26 November 1942

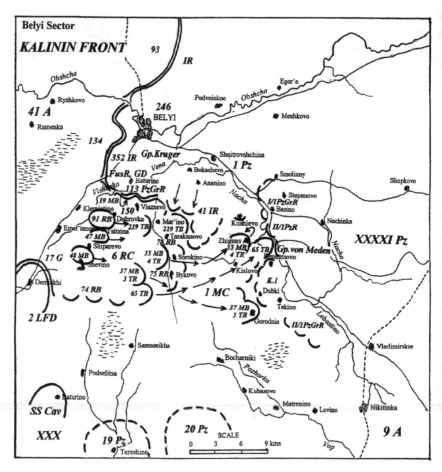

Map 15. The Belyi sector, the situation late on 27 November 1942

area.[44] Tarasov, heartened by the first day's successes, ordered Solomatin to commit his mechanized corps' main forces into action at dawn on 26 November. Marching in brigade column, with its 65th and 219th Tank Brigades in the lead, the mechanized corps' 15,200 men and 224 tanks recorded spectacular initial progress.[45] Moving painstakingly through the heavy and virtually roadless forests, by nightfall on 27 November, Solomatin's corps had torn a 20-kilometer-wide and nearly 30-kilometer-deep hole in the Germans' defenses, with his lead brigades reaching the Belyi-Vladimirskoe road astride the Germans' most vital communications routes into the town of Belyi (see Map 15).[46]

In spite of the dramatic forward progress of Solomatin's mechanized corps, the 41st Army's offensive experienced some potentially serious problems early on because the army commander deviated from the *front's* operational plan. Although his *front* commander, Purkaev, ordered Tarasov to avoid attacking the town of Belyi frontally for fear of a prolonged and costly struggle for the fortified town, the army commander was inexorably drawn to the enticing target since Belyi seemed ripe for the taking.[47] Drawn like a magnet to the town, Tarasov first committed Colonel N. O. Gruz's 150th Rifle Division against the city's southern defenses and, soon after, reinforced Gruz's division with additional brigades from Solomatin's mechanized and Povetkin's rifle corps.[48] Despite these reinforcements, strong German defenses on the southern outskirts of Belyi prevented Tarasov's forces from capturing the town.

Credit for the defense of Belyi belongs to Colonel General Joseph Harpe, the commander of the Ninth Army's XXXXI Panzer Corps. Harpe, after deciding to hold on to the town at all costs, first ordered his corps' 246th Infantry Division to establish and man a hedgehog defense south of the city and then asked for and received reinforcements in the form of *kampfgruppen* dispatched from the *Grossdeutschland* Panzer Grenadier and 1st Panzer Divisions, whose forces were situated in reserve positions northeast and southwest of Belyi. Thereafter, Harpe relied on a combination of fate and luck to save the situation around the vital town.[49] Racing forward along the frozen, snow-covered road, *Kampfgruppe* von Wietersheim from the 1st Panzer Division reached Belyi late on the morning of 26 November. *Kampfgruppe* Kassnitz from the *Grossdeutschland* Division arrived in the vicinity of the town several hours later.[50] Together, the two groups conducted a successful but prolonged and bloody struggle to hold on to the town.

Meanwhile, the bulk of Solomatin's 1st Mechanized Corps, which was now fighting unsupported and in relative isolation, continued its struggle along the critical Belyi-Vladimirskoe road against multiple battalion and company-size *kampfgruppen* the 1st Panzer Division deployed to defend its main supply route to Belyi.[51] An increasingly frustrated Solomatin tried to consolidate his positions along the critical supply artery and, at the same time, repeatedly and urgently requested Tarasov to reinforce his flagging attack with the two additional mechanized brigades in the army's reserve.[52] On 28 November, however, Tarasov denied Solomatin's request and, instead, committed these brigades along the Belyi axis on his army's flanks (see Map 16). One of these brigades, Colonel I. F. Dremov's 47th Mechanized Brigade, attacked due northward east of Belyi in an attempt to cut the Belyi-Vladimirskoe road and envelop the town from the east. Although Dremov's

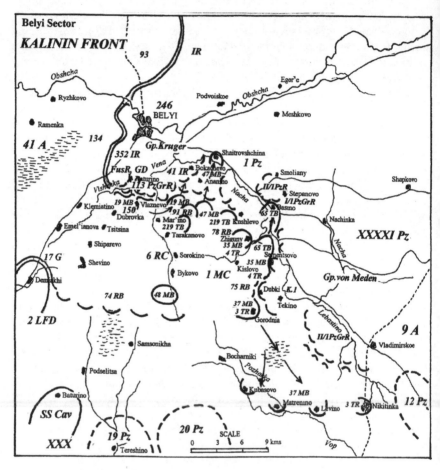

Map 16. The Belyi sector, the situation late on 28 November 1942

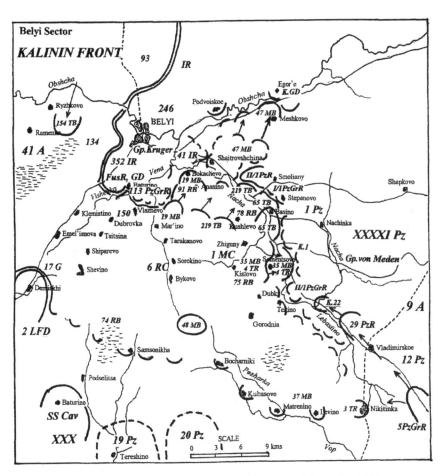

Map 17. The Belyi sector, the situation late on 30 November 1942

brigade did indeed manage to cut the critical road, it too ended up in an exposed and unsupported position northeast of the city.[53]

Solomatin's frustration mounted on 29 November when, after his overextended brigades had fought bitterly but in vain for a full day along a 30-kilometer-sector of the road, his forward brigades reported the arrival of fresh German panzer reserves in the region. By then Solomatin knew what his army commander, Tarasov, did not – that the momentum of the 41st Army's offensive was ebbing, and its prospects for success were vanishing. Solomatin, preparing for the inevitable, ordered his brigades over to the defense to await the anticipated German counterattacks.

Solomatin was indeed correct. The fresh German forces his reconnaissance units identified were the forward elements of the panzer force with which Harpe hoped to defeat the Soviet offensive. Harpe, only days before, had ordered the 1st Panzer Division to form a protective cordon around the town of Belyi with its forward *kampfgruppen*, and, with the remainder of its force, to erect a thin but durable defensive line stretching along the entire length of the Belyi-Vladimirskoe road. Harpe had also requested the Ninth Army and Army Group Center to send him all of its available panzer reserves. Harpe's superiors at army and army group, General Alfred Model and Field Marshal Guenther von Kluge, responded promptly by ordering their 12th, 20th, and 19th Panzer Divisions to march as quickly as possible to the sound of the guns. This regrouping, however, was no easy task because the regrouping panzer divisions had to conduct long road marches over difficult routes in the worst of winter conditions (see Map 17). Until they arrived, the fate of the XXXXI Panzer Corps and entire Ninth Army hung in the balance.

Other unpleasant factors only compounded the difficult situation the XXXXI Panzer Corps faced. For example, at this time Model's Ninth Army was preoccupied with other important concerns. Although his forces seemed to have stabilized the situation along the Vazuza River by containing the Western Front's assaults, other Red Army forces had breached his army's defenses along the Luchesa River north of Belyi and were conducting strong assaults on his defenses along the Molodoi Tud River at the northern extremity of the Rzhev salient. In addition, from Army Group Center's perspective, the deteriorating situation in Army Group B's sector in the Stalingrad region attracted its attention, as well as that of the OKH (Army High Command). These complicating factors only underscored the importance of Harpe's panzer corps conducting a successful defense in the Belyi region.[54]

Model had every reason to be concerned about the viability of his army's defenses elsewhere around the Rzhev salient. First and foremost, in addition to the assaults by the Western Front's 20th and 31st Armies along the Vazuza Riverfront and by the Kalinin Front's 41st Army south of Belyi, the army commander also had to contend with other dangerous large-scale attacks by armies subordinate to the Kalinin Front, including an offensive by its 22nd Army in the Luchesa River valley region and a smaller-scale assault by its 39th Army in the Molodoi Tud region, north of the key German communications center at Olenino at the northern extremity of the Rzhev salient. The offensive by Iushkevich's 22nd Army struck the left wing of his army's XXIII Army Corps, whose forces were responsible for defending the front astride the Luchesa River valley north of Belyi. Like

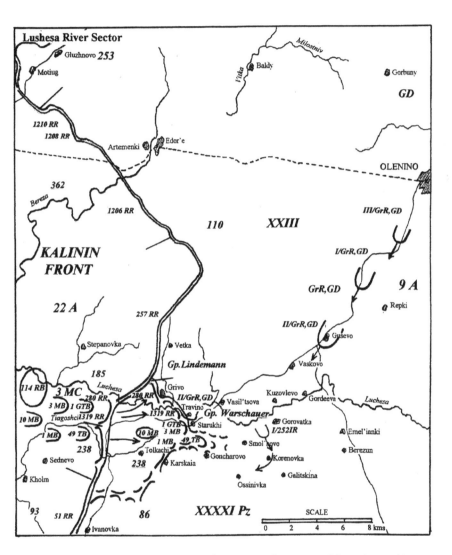

Map 18. The Luchesa River sector, the situation from 25-27 November 1942

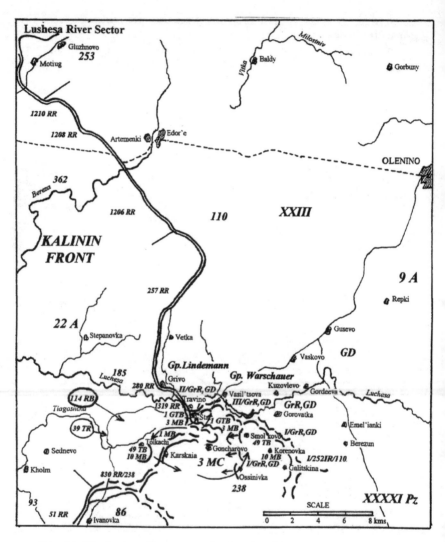

Map 19. The Luchesa River sector, the situation from 28-30 November 1942

Tarasov's 41st Army, Iushkevich's 22nd Army had also begun its offensive at dawn on 25 November. Attacking eastward up the Luchesa River valley, Iushkevich spearheaded his army's attack with Colonel I. V. Karpov's 238th Rifle Division, two regiments of Colonel M. F. Andriushchenko's 185th Rifle Division, and the 1st Guards and 49th Tank Brigades from Major General M. E. Katukov's 3rd Mechanized Corps (see Map 18). After routing a regiment of the German 86th Infantry Division in its initial assault, the 22nd Army's forces tore a gaping hole in the Ninth Army's defenses at the boundary between the XXXXI Panzer Corps' 86th Infantry Division and the XXIII Army Corps' 110th Infantry Division and threatened to advance further eastward to sever the Olenino-Belyi road, the main German communications and supply route running along the western face of the Rzhev salient. Iushkevich, elated by his army's initial success, then committed all four brigades of Katukov's mechanized corps to an eastward advance along the Luchesa valley.

The XXIII Army Corps, responding to this new threat, committed the *Grossdeutschland* Division's Grenadier Regiment into combat to block the advance by Katukov's armor.[55] During the ensuing three days, intense fighting raged for possession of the village of Starukhi, as Iushkevich's shock group drove inexorably eastward toward the vital Olenino-Belyi road, which lay just 10 kilometers beyond. Although the XXIII Army Corps had insufficient forces with which to close the yawning gap in its defenses torn by Iushkevich's exploiting forces, the extremely rough and roadless terrain the heavily-wooded region, deteriorating weather, together with the Germans' skillful defense and the arrival of fresh German reserves, exacted a heavy toll on the attacking forces, ultimately forcing the 22nd Army to halt its advance short of its objectives. By 30 November Iushkevich's army had carved an 8-kilometer-wide and almost 15-kilometer-deep salient in the German defenses; but, try as they did several times thereafter, his forces could not overcome the German resistance and reach the key Olenino-Belyi road (see Map 19).[56]

While the 22nd Army's forces were advancing eastward up the Luchesa River valley on the XXIII Army Corps' left wing, General Zygin's 39th Army exacerbated Model's problems by unleashing a series of attacks with more limited objectives on the XXIII Army Corps' right wing along the Molodoi Tud River (see Map 20).[57] Since the 39th Army was conducting only secondary attacks in support of the offensives at Belyi and the Luchesa River valley, although its forces achieved some spectacular successes during the first few days of its attack, Zygin's army proved to be too weak to exploit these fleeting opportunities.[58] Skillful reaction by German operational reserves, including the 14th Motorized Division and several battalions from the *Grossdeutschland* Division's Grenadier Regiment, prevented the 39th Army from exploiting its initial gains, and after 30 November the struggle along and south of the Molodoi Tud River degenerated into a costly slugfest during which Purkaev reinforced Zygin's army with forces from the neighboring 30th Army, and the former conducted successive assaults resulting in only limited gains (see Maps 21 and 22). Although these attacks forced the XXIII Army Corps' defending 206th Infantry and 14th Motorized Divisions to conduct several minor tactical withdrawals during this fighting, the Germans managed to maintained a

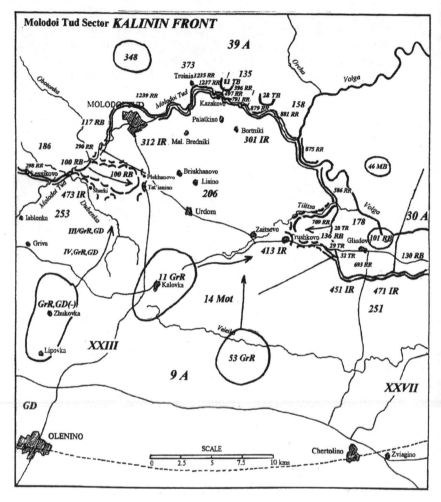

Map 20. The Molodoi Tud sector, the situation late on 25 November 1942

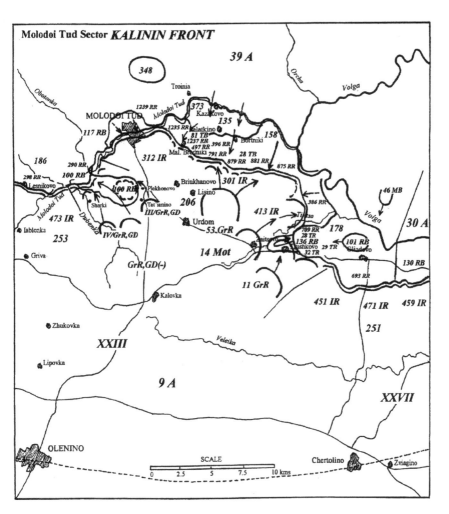

Map 21. The Molodoi Tud sector, the situation late on 27 November 1942

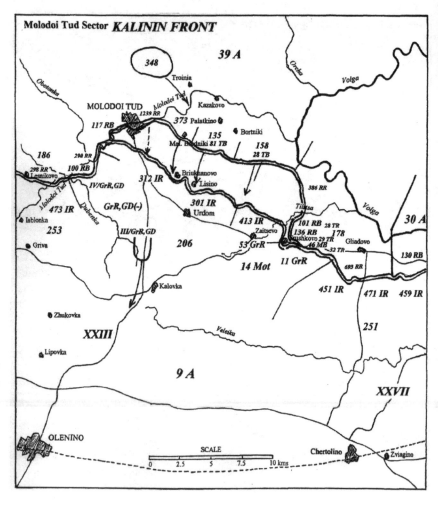

Map 22. The Molodoi Tud sector, the situation late on 29 November 1942

continuous coherent defense line south of the Molodoi Tud River and denied Zygin's forces access to their objective, the Olenino-Rzhev road and rail junction.

Thrust, Counterthrust, and Defeat
(30 November–15 December)

Resumption of the Offensive

Zhukov, Konev and Purkaev had mixed reactions to the results of the first five days of heavy fighting around the periphery of the Rzhev salient. On the negative side of the ledger, Zhukov and Konev were frustrated by the failure of the Western Front's main attack to achieve its objectives along the Sychevka axis and, in particular, by the 31st Army's dismal performance. Despite these disappointments, the *front's* 20th Army had captured a sizeable bridgehead on the Vazuza River's western bank, and Kriukov's cavalry-mechanized group still occupied positions, precarious as they were, astride the Rzhev-Sychevka road in the XXXIX Panzer Corps' rear. On the positive side of the ledger, Zhukov and Purkaev were elated by the Kalinin Front's successful advance along the Belyi and Luchesa River axes, where its 41st and 22nd Armies had successfully penetrated the Ninth Army's defenses and torn huge gaps through Model's defenses along the western face of the salient. Furthermore, Konev's Western Front had yet to commit its 29th Army's forces into the struggle and still possessed strong reserves, including the fresh 5th Tank Corps.

Zhukov, assessing these positive and negative factors, decided to press on with Operation Mars. First, he ordered Purkaev's Kalinin Front to accelerate the advance by its 41st and 22nd Armies along the Belyi and Luchesa River axes and reinforce the assaults by its 39th Army along the Molodoi Tud River. Second, he directed Konev's Western Front to reinforce its 20th Army with forces transferred from its 31st and 29th Armies and then resume its offensive to rescue Kriukov's cavalry-mechanized group isolated west of the Rzhev-Sychevka road. Once its main forces were across the road, Kiriukhin's 20th Army, supported by the mobile group, was to continue its advance toward the west and northwest and link up with the forces of Tarasov's 41st Army and Iushkevich's 22nd Army attacking from the west to encircle and destroy the Ninth Army's forces in the northern half of the Rzhev salient. Although this new plan reflected Zhukov's usual optimism, audacity, and determination, the *Stavka* coordinator did not realize that Model's Ninth Army was already preparing to strike back at his forces in the sectors where they had achieved their greatest successes.

Despite Zhukov's optimism, misfortune plagued his plan from the very start. First, Arman's 6th Tank Corps and the three cavalry divisions of Kriukov's 2nd Guards Cavalry Corps isolated west of the Rzhev-Sychevka road ran short of fuel, ammunition, and other critical supplies, leaving them no choice but to attempt a breakout to the east to rejoin the 20th Army in its bridgehead. Arman's force launched their desperate escape on the night of 29–30 November in conjunction with fierce relief attacks by the 20th Army's main forces in the Vazuza bridgehead (see Map 23). Although the ensuing intense and often chaotic fighting cost Arman's tank corps nearly all of its remaining tanks, most of the corps' personnel reached the safety of the bridgehead.[59] Far more fragile than the accompanying

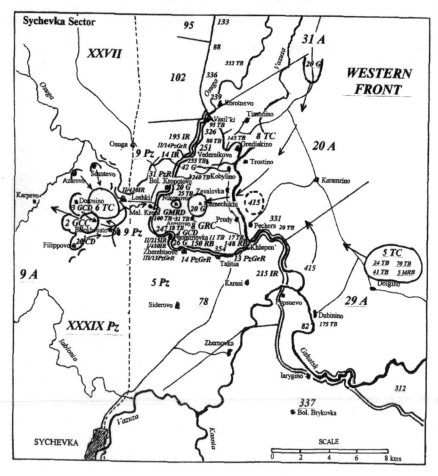

Map 23. The Sychevka sector, the situation from 29 November–1 December 1942

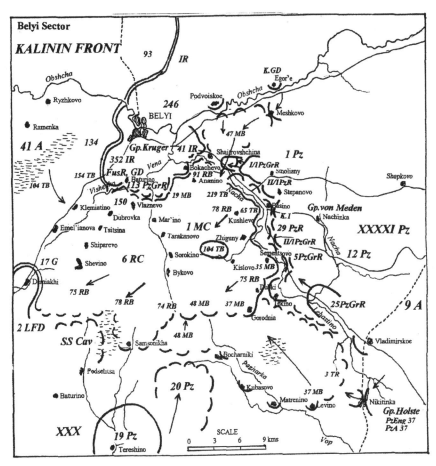

Map 24. The Belyi sector, the situation from 1–6 December 1942

tank units, Kriukov's cavalrymen fared worse. While many of them made it back to the bridgehead, either individually or in small groups, Colonel Kursakov's 20th Tadzhik Cavalry Division was not able to run the gauntlet of fire. Instead, Konev ordered it to drive deeper into the Germans' rear area and reach Soviet lines elsewhere around the salient. Thereafter, the cavalrymen from Tadzhikistan fought alongside Soviet partisans within the salient for weeks before their remnants finally reached the Soviet front lines in the Luchesa valley during early January.[60] Zhukov was bitterly disappointed. The 20th Army had lost over 30,000 men and 200 tanks in 5 days of vicious combat. Losses in 31st Army were just as severe, and little had been gained by the effort. Even more disconcerting, the 41st Army's seemingly certain victory in the Belyi sector along the western face of the Rzhev salient was about to degenerate into a catastrophic defeat.

The German Counterstroke

In fact, General Solomatin, the commander of the 41st Army's 1st Mechanized Corps, whose forces had already advanced deep into the Germans' rear area south of Belyi while spearheading the offensive by Tarasov's army, began realizing his worse fears were indeed materializing by the end of November. Not only did the Germans hold firm to their fortress in Belyi, but they were also beginning to orchestrate a potentially lethal counterstroke. The situation facing Solomatin's mechanized corps began deteriorating on 1 December, only days after his corps had begun shortening its lines and gone over to the defense (see Map 24). Thereafter, from 2–6 December, the 1st Panzer Division and newly arrived 12th Panzer Division of Harpe's XXXXI Panzer Corps regained control over most of the vital Belyi-Vladimirskoe road, cut off and destroyed Dremov's isolated 47th Mechanized Brigade northeast of the town of Belyi, and began applying pressure to Solomatin's defenses southeast of the city.[61] More devastating still, the freshly regrouped German 19th and 20th Panzer Divisions, both operating under the control of the Ninth Army's XXX Army Corps, began assembling opposite the southern flank of the 41st Army's penetration south of Belyi. The regrouping and assembly of this corps' panzer divisions was no easy task, since all German movements were severely hindered by terrible weather conditions, abysmal roads, and strong resistance offered by bands of Soviet partisans.[62]

Despite these formidable obstacles, the XXX Army Corps' two panzer divisions were prepared to strike back at the southern flank of Tarasov's 41st Army by late on 6 December. Attacking at dawn the next day, in conjunction with concentric assaults launched by the XXXXI Panzer Corps' 1st Panzer Division from assembly areas east and southeast of Belyi and by the *Grossdeutschland* Division's Fusilier Regiment from positions south of Belyi, in three days of intense fighting, the combined German force slashed through the 41st Army's flanks and into its rear area, encircling the bulk of Tarasov's army in a pocket southeast of Belyi (see Map 25). In this fashion, the dramatic advance of the 41st Army suddenly degenerated into an utter rout, leaving Tarasov's army in an inglorious trap. Solomatin, who now commanded both his own mechanized corps and Povetkin's 6th Rifle Corps, did everything in his power to organize an immediate breakout to the west.

Map 25. The Belyi sector, the situation from 7–10 December 1942

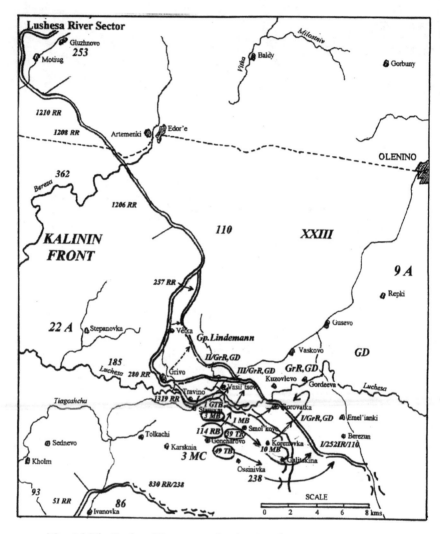

Map 26. The Luchesa River sector, the situation from 1–3 December 1942

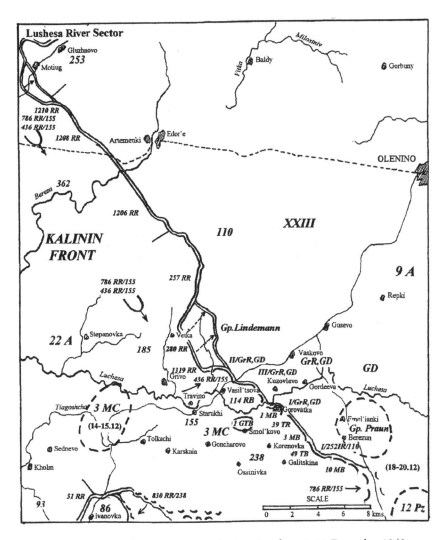

Map 27. The Luchesa River sector, the situation from 3–11 December 1942

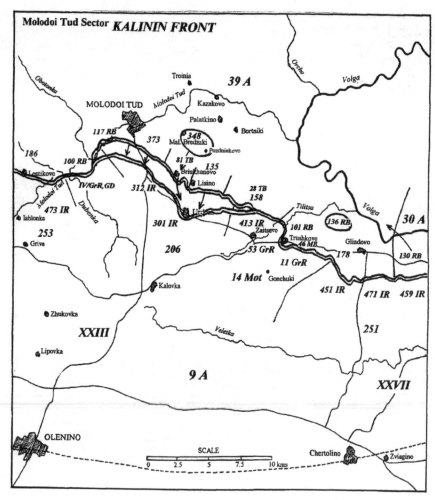

Map 28. The Molodoi Tud sector, the situation from 30 November–5 December 1942

When these initial escape attempts failed, Solomatin thereafter organized his two corps for an all-round defense of the pocket and awaited help that never arrived.[63]

Nor was the Kalinin Front's situation in the Luchesa River valley any more promising. Despite Iushkevich's strenuous efforts, his 22nd Army simply lacked the strength necessary to expand its penetration and reach and cut the Olenino-Belyi road. On the other hand, the XXIII Army Corps had insufficient forces with which to liquidate the 22nd Army's penetration. Therefore, although fighting in the valley ebbed and flowed for days on end, neither side could gain advantage (see Maps 26 and 27). Ultimately, this stalemate endured until events elsewhere around the Rzhev salient settled the fate of Zhukov's general offensive. Likewise, along the northern face of the Rzhev salient, Zygin's 39th Army registered only minor gains south of the Molodoi Tud River against stout German resistance. Ironically, however, the apparent sideshow in the north would ultimately represent Zhukov's last hope for victory (see Map 28).

Zhukov, unwilling to admit defeat, responded in characteristic fashion to the depressing news from the Belyi and Luchesa River valley sectors. First, he fired Kiriukhin, the 20th Army's commander, and replaced him with a proven "fighter," Lieutenant General M.S. Khozin, who had fought alongside Zhukov during the successful defense of Leningrad in September 1941. He then ordered Khozin to reinforce the 20th Army's main shock group on the Vazuza bridgehead "massively" and to prepare a fresh offensive from the bridgehead.[64] Second, while heavy fighting continued in the Belyi region, he ordered Khozin's 20th Army, supported on the left by Major General E. P. Zhuravlev's 29th Army, to resume its offensive on 11 December, in close concert with a renewed advance by Zygin's 39th Army against the Germans' defenses at Olenino. Finally, to support the 39th Army's assaults, Zhukov also began transferring a steady stream of divisions from the 30th Army in the Rzhev sector to reinforce Zygin's army.

Two documents illustrate Zhukov's resolve to salvage victory out of apparent defeat. The first, a directive Zhukov issued on 4 December, relieved Kiriukhin from command of the 20th Army, replaced him with Khozin, and reinforced the 20th Army:

> Instructions of the Supreme High Commander to the *Stavka* Representative [Zhukov] Concerning the Strengthening of the 20th Army
>
> The *Stavka* approves your proposals for improving the 20th Army's operations.
>
> Kiriukhin is relieved from his post as 20th Army commander. Lieutenant General Khozin is temporarily appointed to direct the 20th Army's operations. You can postpone the operation against Gzhatsk [ed., Jupiter or Neptune]. Take the required number of rifle divisions and the 5th Tank Corps from the grouping of force designated to conduct the Gzhatsk operation and transfer them to reinforce the 20th Army. One hundred and fifty tanks are being sent for Stepanov's [Konev's codename] use.
>
> Vasil'ev [Stalin's codename][65]

Then, at 2215 hours on 8 December, the *Stavka* issued yet another directive that fully sanctioned the continuation of Operation Mars:

Stavka VGK Directive No. 170700 to the Western and Kalinin Front
  Commanders Concerning the Missions to Destroy the
  Enemy's Rzhev-Sychevka-Olenino-Belyi Grouping

The *Stavka* of the Supreme High Command orders:

The combined forces of the Kalinin and Western Front will destroy
the enemy's Rzhev-Sychevka-Olenino-Belyi grouping and dig in firmly
along the Iarygino, Sychevka, Andreevskoe, Lenino, Novoe Azhevo,
Dentialevo, and Svity front by 1 January 1943.

While conducting this operation, the Western Front will be guided
by the following:

a) Penetrate the enemy's defenses in the Bol'shoe Kropotovo and Iarygino
sector on 10–11 December and capture Sychevka no later than 15
December. Commit no fewer than two rifle divisions into combat in the
Andreevskoe region to organize an encirclement of the enemy together
with the Kalinin Front's 41st Army.

b) After penetrating the enemy's defense and the main grouping reaches
the line of the railroad, wheel *front's* mobile group and no fewer than four
rifle divisions toward the north for an attack against the rear of the
enemy's Rzhev-Chertolino grouping.

c) The 30th Army will penetrate the defense in the sector from Koshkino
to the road junction northeast of Burgovo and reach the railroad in the
vicinity of Chertolino no later than 15 December. When [it] reaches the
railroad line, [it] will establish close combat cooperation with the *front*
mobile group and attack toward Rzhev by an advance along the railroad,
with the mission of capturing Rzhev on 23 December.

While fulfilling its missions, the Kalinin Front will be guided by the
following:

a) Continue to develop the 39th and 22nd Armies' attacks in the general
direction of Olenino, with the mission to destroy the enemy's Olenino
grouping and reach the Olenino region no later than 16 December.

Part of the 22nd Army's forces will conduct a secondary attack
toward Egor'e to assist the 41st Army in the destruction of the enemy's
Belyi grouping.

b) The 41st Army will destroy the enemy grouping that has penetrated
into the Tsytsyno region and restore its lost positions in the Okolitsy
region by 10 December.

Part of its forces will reach the Mol'nia, Vladimirskoe, and Lenino
regions, with the mission of enclosing the encircled enemy grouping from
the south no later than 20 December in cooperation with the Western
Front's forces.

Capture Belyi no later than 20 December.

Subsequently, after regrouping the forces of the Kalinin and Western
Fronts, I mean to destroy the enemy's Gzhatsk, Viaz'ma, and
Kholm-Zhirkovskaia grouping and reach our old defensive line by the
end of January 1943.

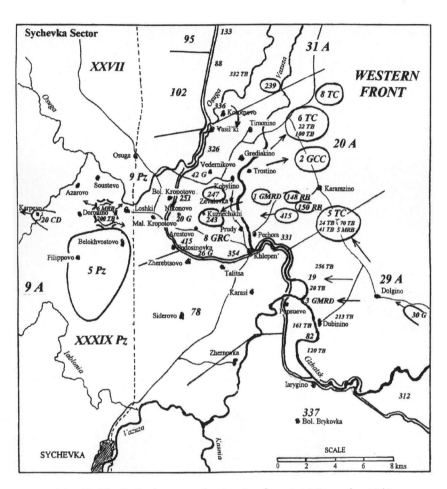

Map 29. The Sychevka sector, the situation from 2–10 December 1942

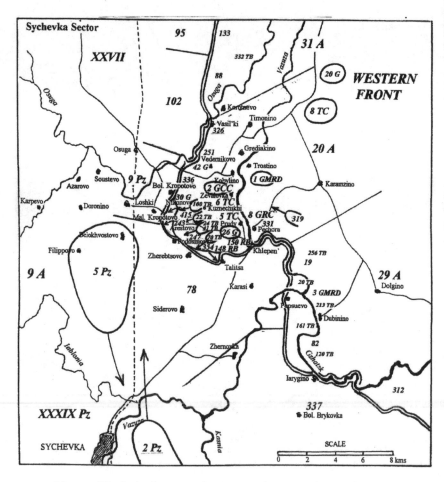

Map 30. The Sychevka sector, the situation from 11–14 December 1942

When our forces occupy Viaz'ma and reach last year's defensive positions west of the Rzhev-Viaz'ma [line], the operation will be considered to have been completed and the forces can go into winter quarters.

Confirm receipt and report fulfillment.

Pass this order to all commanders down to regiment.

The *Stavka* of the Supreme High Command

I. Stalin G. Zhukov[66]

Defeat

The curtain rose on the last act of the continuing drama of Operation Mars at mid-morning on 11 December in the valley of the Vazuza River (see Maps 29 and 30). After Soviet artillery pounded the Germans' defenses for over an hour, at precisely 1010 hours, the massed riflemen of the 20th and 29th Armies went over to the attack across the entire breadth of their armies' front. Defying a deadly curtain of German artillery, mortar, and machine gun fire, Konev and Khozin then ordered the 20th Army's 5th and 6th Tank Corps into the battle in support of the advancing infantry. Attacking with abandon across a 4-kilometer-wide sector into the teeth of reinforced German antitank defenses, the desperate assault cost the two tank corps well over 200 of their tanks in two days of incessant, deadly combat.[67] Despite the frightful carnage in the attack sectors of the two armies, Zhukov and Konev urged their forces on. The assaults continued for three more days before the offensive exhausted itself on 15 December. By this time it was clear to all, generals and soldiers alike, that defeat was at hand. And if the carnage along the Vazuza River failed to confirm this fact, the grisly fate experienced by Solomatin's forces isolated southeast of Belyi certainly did.

Solomatin's forces held their ground south of Belyi for as long as humanly possible. Lacking any logistical support within his pocket and any concrete assistance from without, his task was simply hopeless. Left with no other choice, on the night of 15–16 December, Solomatin ordered his forces to break out to the west (see Map 31). Drawing in his perimeter defense, the corps commander ordered his forces to destroy their remaining tanks and heavy weapons and thrust westward as infantry through a flaming gauntlet of heavy German fire. Although Solomatin's decision ultimately saved his life and the lives of many of the soldiers in his two corps, the human cost was still appalling. While the 1st Panzer Division reported it destroyed over 102 Soviet armored vehicles during the battle, in his after-action-report, Solomatin admitted that his 1st Mechanized Corps lost over 8,000 of its 12,000 soldiers either killed or wounded, and most of its over 200 tanks either destroyed or abandoned.[68] The casualty toll in the remainder of the 41st Army was equally grim.

Even the twin defeats along the Vazuza River and at Belyi did not totally destroy Zhukov's resolve. Although the Germans' stout and skillful resistance and counterstrokes thwarted his assaults against the Rzhev salient's eastern and western flanks, Zhukov ordered the 39th Army to continue its attack against the northern face of the salient until mid-December (see Map 32). Despite Zhukov's stubborn determination, however, Operation Mars was a shambles by 15 December. Though it took until mid-December for Zhukov to appreciate that the operation had failed, Stalin understood this reality long before and abandoned hope for any

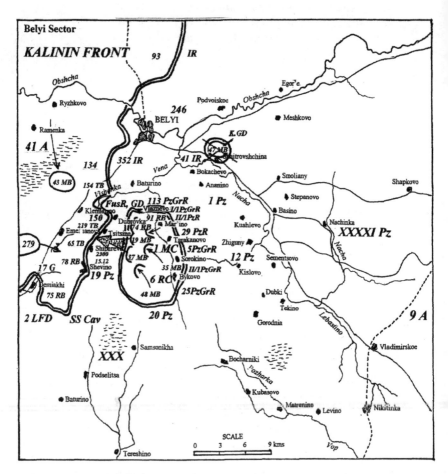

Map 31. The Belyi sector, the situation from 11–16 December 1942

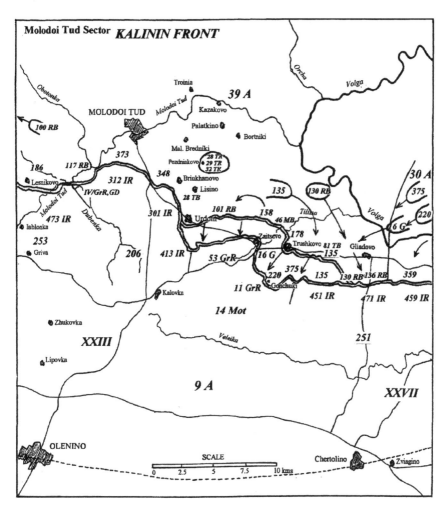

Map 32. The Molodoi Tud sector, the situation from 7–23 December 1942

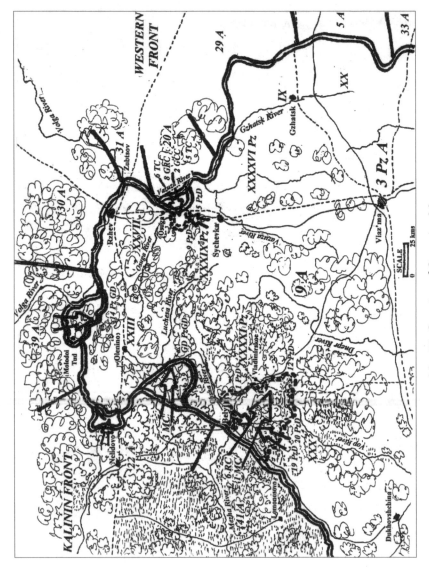

Map 33. Overview of Operation Mars

follow-on operation. Underscoring this grim reality, by early December Stalin was already dispatching his *Stavka's* reserves southward to reinforce Vasilevsky's successful Operation Uranus in the Stalingrad region.

Conclusions

Conducting Operation Mars in characteristic fashion, Zhukov's assaults were massive in scale and unsparing in manpower and material (see Map 33). Discounting the rough terrain and harsh weather conditions so prevalent in the fall, Stalin's "Hammer" sought to achieve victory by applying unrelenting pressure against the Germans' entire front and by conducting simple maneuver with his powerful mechanized and tank corps. Neither technique succeeded. The Germans defeated Zhukov's offensive by skillfully employing multiple small *kampfgruppen* in tactical defenses taking maximum advantage of the terrain to bottle up Zhukov's attacking mobile corps before they were able to reach their operational depths. During these battles these German *kampfgruppen* wore down the attacking Soviet infantry formations and separated them from the advancing mobile forces, denying the tank and cavalry forces necessary infantry and artillery support. Avoiding panic and holding only where necessary, the Ninth Army's corps then carefully assembled mobile reserves to conduct the successful counterattacks and counterstrokes necessary to produce victory. Nevertheless, despite the Ninth Army's ultimate victory, Operation Mars came enticingly close to succeeding. Although the intense fighting produced catastrophic casualties in the ranks of the Red Army's forces conducting the operation, it also seriously weakened the defending Germans. As a result, within months after achieving victory in Operation Mars, largely because his army could ill afford the costs of another such victory, Model requested and received permission for his Ninth Army to abandon the bloody Rzhev salient.

Archival sources concerning the Red Army's combat losses in Operation Mars remain contradictory. Although the German Ninth Army's records estimate that the Red Army incurred about 100,000 soldiers killed in the operation and as many as 200,000 more wounded or captured, recently released Russian casualty figures indicate that its attacking forces suffered 70,373 soldiers killed, captured, or missing-in-action and another 145,301 wounded or ill.[69] Whichever figures are correct, the Red Army's personnel losses were substantial, a fact documented by the 20th Army's tally of its own strength and losses in the operation (see Figures 1 and 2).

Figure 1. The 20th Army's Combat Losses during the Period from 25 November–18 December 1942

Formation	Killed	Wounded	Missing-in-Action	Total
251 RD	765	1,911	328	3,004
326 RD	1,248	3,156	81	4,485
42 GRD	1,118	2,858	175	4,151

336 RD	749	2,297	—	2,946
247 RD	1,143	5,301	—	6,444
1 GMRD	423	1,641	—	2,064
20 GRD	515	2,913	—	3,425
415 RD	692	1,865	—	2,557
30 GRD	652	1,768	170	2,590
354 RD	524	2,223	183	2,929
243 RD	748	1,954	4	2,706
8 GRC	2,311	7,434	360	10,105
331 RD	597	1,445	106	2,148
379 RD	182	527	—	709
2 GCC	1,222	2,858	49	4,129
2 Bn, ATR	8	22	3	33
52 Bn, ATR	22	28	—	50
Others	1,010	2,892	138	4,040
TOTAL	13,920	41,999	1,596	58,524

84883 Source: "Opisanie boevykh deistvii na rubezhe r. Vazuza za 25 noiabria–18 dekabria 1942 goda" [An account of combat operations along the Vazuza River line from 25 November–18 December 1942], Polevoe upravlenie 20 Armii [The 20th Army's field headquarters], *TsAMO RF* [Central Archives of the Russian Federation's Ministry of Defense], F. 373, Op. 6631, D. 65, Ll. 41–42 [sic] – [note that the numbers do not add up to the indicated totals].

For comparison's sake, Figure 2 shows the 20th Army's strength on 25 November and 11 December.

Figure 2. The 20th Army's Combat Strength on 25 November and 11 December 1942 (The Beginning of Each Phase of Operation Mars)

Category	25 November 1942	11 December
Personnel (Overall)	114,176	112,411
Personnel (Combat)	95,557	80,322*
Horses	10,976	9,774
Rifles	66,103	62,786
Heavy machine guns	455	410

AA machine guns	182	76
Light machine guns	1,902	1,927
PPD and PPSh	9,692	7,045
Mortars	1,473	1,159
Field guns	614	866
Guards mortars	334	345
Antitank guns and AA guns	365	74 (AA guns)
Antitank rifles	1,942	1,586
Vehicles	6,104	4,254
Tanks	334	91

*The 20th Army received 8,296 personnel replacements between 25 November and 18 December 1942.

Source: "Opisanie boevykh deistvii na rubezhe r. Vazuza za 25 noiabria–18 dekabria 1942 goda" [An account of combat operations along the Vazuza River line from 25 November–18 December 1942], Polevoe upravlenie 20 Armii [The 20th Army's field headquarters], *TsAMO RF* [Central Archives of the Russian Federation's Ministry of Defense], F. 373, Op. 6631, D. 65, Ll. 11, 17, 42

The Western and Kalinin Fronts' tank losses, which the Germans correctly estimated at about 1,700 armored vehicles, were equally staggering, since they exceeded the total number of tanks the Red Army employed in Operation Uranus.[70] The manner in which Zhukov conducted Operation Mars and the carnage the failed operation produced have few parallels in the later war years. In its most grisly form, the operation most closely resembles the 1st Belorussian Front's infamous frontal assault against the Germans' defenses on Seelow Heights during the battle for Berlin April 1945, an operation also conducted by Zhukov. Unlike the case in 1942, however, the victorious conclusion of the Berlin operation required no alteration of the historical record to preserve the pride of the Soviet Union or its Red Army or to protect the reputations of famous Red Army generals.

The legacy of Operation Mars was silence. Stalin and Soviet historiography dictated that Vasilevsky's feat at Stalingrad remained unblemished by Zhukov's failure at Rzhev. Indeed, Stalin recognized Zhukov's greatest quality — that he fought — and, at this stage of the war, Stalin needed fighters. Therefore, with help from the censors' pens, Zhukov's reputation remained unblemished and intact; furthermore, as Stalin's deputy Supreme Commander, he shared the plaudits for the victory at Stalingrad with Vasilevsky. In time, Zhukov would gain a measure of revenge for his defeat in operation Mars by achieving victories over his old nemesis, German Army Group Center, on the battlefield of Kursk during the summer of 1943 and, once again, in the vast expanse of Belorussia during the summer of 1944. Ironically, however, it would be Vasilevsky who, as key *Stavka* planner, would be instrumental in the final defeat of German Army Group Center in East Prussia during January and February 1945. Such is the fickleness of history.

Chapter 3

The Northwestern Fronts' Demiansk Offensive (26 November 1942–6 January 1942)

Introduction

In was no surprise that the *Stavka* added the German-occupied Demiansk salient to its list of vital strategic objectives in the fall of 1942. The German Sixteenth Army's II Army Corps, which Red Army forces had isolated and encircled in the salient during the winter campaign of 1941–42, remained a focal point of the *Stavka's* strategic attentions throughout all of 1942. This was particularly the case after May 1942, when, during Operation Seydlitz, the Army Group North's Sixteenth Army had carved a narrow corridor through the village of Ramushevo, linking up the beleaguered corps' defensive perimeter around Demiansk with the front lines of its parent army south of the city of Staraia Russa. The Soviets became even more preoccupied with the salient and its pesky corridor after the Sixteenth Army conducted a local offensive to widen the corridor between 27 September and 9 October 1942 (see Map 34).

The *Stavka* had good reason to include the Demiansk salient as one of its strategic objectives when it began planning the offensive operations it wished its Red Army to conduct during its winter campaign of 1942–43. First, since the salient jutted eastward from Army Group North's front lines south of Lake Il'men into the strategically located Valdai Hills north of Lake Ostashkov, it placed the German forces occupying the eastern tip of the salient only 50 kilometers west of the major highway that served as the Red Army's main supply line to the Novgorod region and just under 100 kilometers west of the Moscow-Leningrad railroad, the main supply route between the two cities and the most important route along which the Red Army could dispatch troop reinforcements, weapons, and other key supplies to its Leningrad and Volkhov Fronts.

Second, after failing to defeat Army Group North and raise its siege and blockade of Leningrad on several occasions during 1942, the *Stavka* hoped to use the Demiansk region as a launching pad for a more successful offensive during the forthcoming winter campaign. Previously, the Red Army had attempted to rescue Leningrad's besieged population and the forces of the Leningrad Front which defended it either by attacking through the Siniavino and Shlissel'burg regions immediately east of Leningrad or by attacking across the Volkhov River, farther to the southeast. However, all of these relief attempts had failed, often with catastrophically heavy losses. Furthermore, by late summer 1942, the Germans had erected a formidable array of elaborate fortifications and strong defensive lines protecting

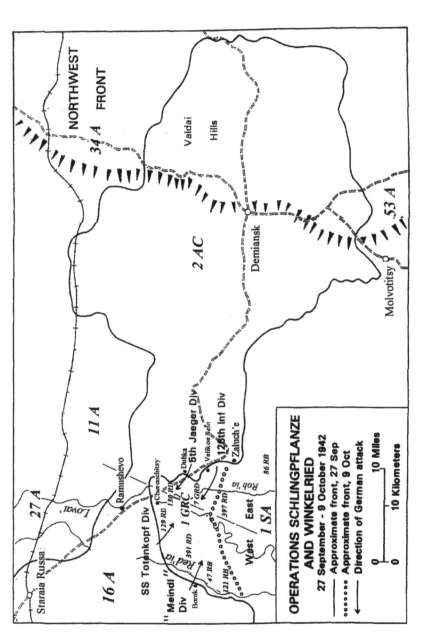

Map 34. German operations around the Demiansk salient, 27 September–9 October 1942

the eastern and southeastern approaches to the city, which promised to make any future Red Army offensives through these regions prohibitively costly, if not utterly impossible. Therefore, in the early fall, the *Stavka* began developing plans to raise the siege of Leningrad by conducting a much larger offensive operation designed to envelop, encircle, and destroy most of Army Group North's forces operating in the Leningrad region.

Planning

In outline form, the *Stavka's* new plan called for the armies of Colonel General P. A. Kurochkin's Northwestern Front to attack and penetrate the defenses of Army Group North's Sixteenth Army in the Staraia Russa region, just south of Lake Il'men' and 200 kilometers south of Leningrad, advance northeastward through the cities of Dno, Luga, and Pskov into the German army group's deep rear, and capture objectives on the eastern shores of either Lake Pskov or the Gulf of Finland. By conducting a successful penetration operation against the Sixteenth Army's right wing and then exploiting this success to either of its deep objectives, Kurochkin's forces could outflank and rout the Sixteenth Army and, by cutting off its withdrawal routes from the Leningrad region, place Army Group North's Eighteenth Army in an untenable situation. In short, if the Northwestern Front's offensive succeeded, its force would either encircle the bulk of both German armies south of Leningrad or force them to conduct a hasty withdrawal back to new defensive lines protecting the approaches to the Baltic region.

As sound as the *Stavka's* plan appeared to be on paper, however, it contained one potentially fatal flaw; the German-occupied salient around Demiansk denied the Northwestern Front's armies access to the assembly areas and jumping-off positions from which they could launch their new offensive. Therefore, the *front* could not launch the larger offensive to raise the siege of Leningrad unless and until its armies were able to liquidate German forces in the Demiansk salient and its associated Ramushevo corridor. Thus, when it planned Operation Mars, the *Stavka* also included in its plans yet another assault on the German defenses around Demiansk.

Existing German and Soviet accounts of the Red Army's offensive against Demiansk during November and December 1942 are sketchy at best. For example, in his book *Stalingrad to Berlin*, the most thorough account of the war from the German perspective, Earl Ziemke scarcely mentions the offensive, writing only, "On the Army Group North right flank, the Demiansk pocket had been under continuous attack since the end of November 1942. By mid-January the fighting in the pocket had drained off the last army group reserves."[71] Most Soviet (Russian) accounts of the war also avoid mentioning the offensive. Thus, the book, *Na severo-zapadnom fronte* [On the Northwestern Front], an account of the Northwestern Front's operations during the war, also only briefly mentions the *front's* November offensive through the eyes of its 202nd Rifle Division:

> In November 1942 the [11th Army's 202nd Rifle] division destroyed the enemy in his strongpoint and liberated the village of Pustynia Polavskogo near Novgorod. The village was located on heights jutting out into our defenses ... On 22 November the village was taken after a decisive attack

supported by artillery and volleys of guards-mortars – "*katiushas*." ....The Fascist garrison was completely destroyed in the battle for Pustynia village. Trophies [captured equipment] included about 200 heavy and light machine guns, 5 guns, and many other weapons ....

At the end of December, the Northwestern Front went over to the offensive against the enemy's Demiansk grouping. Our division operated in the Safronkovo region. A fierce struggle raged for one of the heights on the flank of the enemy's penetration into our defenses.[72]

The only exception to this general dearth of information concerning the Northwestern Front's offensive in November and December is the official history of the *front's* 1st Shock Army, which contains several pages on this army's role in the offensive, but virtually nothing about the operations of its neighboring armies. Fortunately, however, by exploiting the few existing sources, German records, and newly-released Soviet archival documents, we can now reconstruct a fairly accurate account of the *front's* offensive, at least in general form, if not in detail.

Although the Russians have yet to release the *Stavka* directive requiring Kurochkin's *front* to conduct its offensive against the Demiansk salient, it apparently did so on or about 16 October 1942. In terms of the directive's timing, the *Stavka* apparently dispatched it to the Northwestern Front several weeks after it issued its initial directives to the Kalinin and Western Fronts ordering them to conduct Operation Mars and the associated offensive in the Velikie Luki region. By this time the *Stavka* had decided to postpone Mars until November but added the Northwestern Front's assault on the Demiansk salient to its broad array of offensive operations associated with Mars. Ultimately, the *Stavka* ordered the Northwestern Front to begin its offensive several days before the Kalinin and Western Fronts began Operation Mars in an attempt to confound the German defenders and draw German reserves away from the Rzhev region.

After consulting with Kurochkin, Marshal of the Soviet Union S. K. Timoshenko, whom the *Stavka* had dispatched to the Demiansk region in July to serve as its representative and to supervise the Northwestern Front's operations in the region, sent his proposed plan for the assault on the Demiansk salient to Stalin at 1329 hours on 18 October:

> I am reporting my views regarding the conduct of the Northwestern Front's forthcoming operations.
>
> 1. The enemy has managed to achieve success with an offensive in the 1st Shock Army's sector during the first ten days of October. After reaching the Viazki, Khodyni, and Zaluch'e front, he widened the corridor to the Demiansk bridgehead and, at the same time, created favorable conditions for its offensive use. In these circumstances we must anticipate the possibility of [the following] future active operations:
>
> a) Against the 27th Army to reach the western bank of the Lovat River and widen the corridor further;
>
> b) Against the 11th Army to reach the 27th Army's rear area; and
>
> c) From the southern sector of the Demiansk grouping toward Molvotitsy to sever the 1st Shock Army's communications.

The main enemy grouping of up to eight infantry divisions (the 8th Jäger, 122nd, 123rd, 290th, SS, and 329th Infantry, 126th Motorized, and 5th Infantry Divisions) continues to remain the Aleksandrovka and Dedno sector, covering the Demiansk grouping's communications through the corridor and protecting its supply by road.

Enemy combat aircraft, operating groups of from 3 to 20 planes, are continuing to operate against the combat formations of our forces and the rear areas of our armies and *front*, at the same time creating a tense air situation in the *front's* sector.

2. The immediate aim of the *front's* operation is to split the enemy's Staraia Russa and Demiansk groupings apart and complete the encirclement of the latter, with the mission of subsequently destroying it

The general concept of the operation [is] to destroy the enemy in the Simanovo, Tsemena, and Dedno regions by an attack with the 11th Army's left wing to the south and southeast and by the 1st Shock Army's right wing to the north and northeast and, after reaching the Pola and Polomet' Rivers, completely encircle the enemy's Demiansk grouping and, at the same time, create favorable conditions for its final defeat and destruction.

On the remaining front, tie down enemy forces and weapons along separate axes with active and decisive actions by assault groups and prevent them from approaching the Simanovo, Tsemana, and Dedno regions.

The armies' missions:

The 11th Army's primary mission is to destroy the enemy in the sector between the Pola and Polomet' Rivers by an attack from the Strelitsy, Gorby, Viazovka, and Dedno (inclusive) line with the forces on the army's left wing and, after reaching the Rosino, Maslino, Kost'kovo, and Solov'evo front on the northern and western banks of these rivers, complete the encirclement of the enemy's Demiansk grouping in close coordination with forces on the 1st Shock Army's right wing, which will be attacking from the south. The army will conduct its main attack from the Gorby, Viazovka, and Nory regions with three rifle brigades, two rifle divisions, and one tank brigade (the 151st, 126th, and 127th Rifle Brigades, the 170th and 384th Rifle Divisions, and the 60th Tank Brigade), supported by all attached army reinforcements, to penetrate the enemy's defense along the Sorokino and Viazovka front, reach the Pola River in the Rosino and Kost'kovo sector, and, after severing the Demiansk grouping's main ground communications, split the enemy's Demiansk grouping away from the Staraia Russa grouping in cooperation with the forces of the 1st Shock Army.

Subsequently, after regrouping part of the forces conducting its main attack into the Rosino region, the army will liquidate the Tuganovskii defensive region by attacks from the north, east, and southeast.

Conduct a secondary attack through Dedno with the 133rd Rifle Brigade to reach the Polomet' River in the Bol'shoe Shumilovo and

Solov'evo sector (inclusive), where you will go over to a firm defense to prevent the enemy from reaching the western bank of the Polomet' River.

Before beginning the general offensive, to protect the shock grouping from the northeast and east, conduct a local operation to liquidate the center of resistance in Pustynia and reach the Vesiki, Pochinok, and Liubimka River front, where you will organize a firm defense.

In the remaining sectors of its front, the army will reliably tie down the enemy's forces and weapons by an active defense to prevent them from regrouping into the region between the Pola and Polomet' Rivers.

The 1st Shock Army will destroy the enemy in the forests between the Pakhinskii Mokh Swamp and the Starovskaia Rob'ia River by conducting its main attack along the Khakhileia axis on its right flank, with one rifle division (the 129th) and two rifle brigades (the 45th and 86th) and all army reinforcements, and, after severing the main communications of the enemy's Demiansk grouping in the Tsemena and Korpovo sector, split the Demiansk grouping away from the Staraia Russa grouping in cooperation with the forces on the 11th Army's left wing, which will be attacking from the north. Along the remainder of its front, the army will reliably defend the positions it occupies and tie down enemy forces and weapons with active operations by separate detachments in the center toward the road junction (3 kilometers west of Dubkov) and Kulakovo to prevent them from reaching the eastern bank of the Sutokskaia and Sredniaia Rob'ia Rivers.

The 27th Army will capture the unnamed swamp (2 kilometers west of Sychevo) and the Mikhalkino and Borisovo regions by short but powerful attacks with individual detachments from the vicinity of the northeastern bank of the unnamed swamp (2 kilometers west of Sychevo) to Mikhalkino and from the forested region (1 kilometer north of Borisovo) to Dmitrovo, and, at the same time, disrupt active enemy intentions to free up the Ramushevo highway completely. In the remaining sectors of its front, the army will reliably defend the positions it occupies and, at all costs, prevent an enemy penetration from the Staraia Russa region along the highway to Parfino.

The 34th Army will attack southwestward from the front between Volodikha (inclusive) and forest grove (1 kilometer southeast of Belyi Bor) with separate detachments to destroy the enemy in the Belyi Bor region and the forest west of that point, reach the Luzhenka River, and sever the Luzhno-Lychkovo highway in sector from Marker 55.4 to Iamnik and, at the same time, disrupt the normal supply of combat materiel to the enemy's Lychkovo grouping and prevent him from maneuvering his forces along the Luzhno-Lychkovo and Luzhno-Iamnik-Bardovka roads.

In the remaining sectors of its front, the army will tie down enemy forces and weapons with an active defense and prevent them from reaching the Demiansk region and launching an attack northwestward through Kost'kovo.

The 53rd Army will attack from the Bol'shoe Vragovo and Kopylovo front toward Pen'kovo with separate detachments to reach the rear of the enemy's Bel' grouping, cut his main communications in the sector from Pen'kovo to road marker 10.0 (2 kilometers southwest of Pen'kovo), and, at the same time, disrupt the enemy's active intent to conduct operations toward Molvotitsy. In the remaining sectors of its front, the army will reliably defend the positions it occupies and, under no circumstances, permit penetrations: a) by the enemy's Vatolino grouping toward Roven', Mosty, and Mashugin Gor; and b) by the Bel'-Budkovo grouping to Molvotitsy.

3. The missions of the *front* air forces:

a) Before the overall operation begins.

1) The chief mission is to protect the grouping and the concentration of the 11th Army's and 1st Shock Armies' shock groups from enemy reconnaissance and combat aviation, while paying special attention to protecting the 11th Army's shock group in the Pola and Beglovo village sector south of the railroad.

2) Neutralize and exhaust the enemy with bomber attacks at night against the region between the Pola and Polomet' Rivers.

3) Conduct continuous reconnaissance and observation over the enemy both in vicinity of the Demiansk grouping and west of the Pola River to the Dno meridian.

4) Prevent flights by enemy transport aircraft along the Staraia Russa-Demiansk route.

b) After the overall operation begins:

1) Neutralize the enemy's main artillery grouping in the Malye Rogy, Uchny, and Upolozy regions.

2) Destroy the enemy's crossings sites over the Pola River at Kolomna and Kost'kovo.

3) Prevent enemy counterattacks from the Sorokopenno region through Kolomna to the northeast and from the Demiansk region through Kost'kovo toward Viazovka and Savkino.

4) Prevent enemy reserves from the Staraia Rusa region from approaching the eastern bank of the Lovat' River.

5) Continue protecting the 11th Army's and 1st Shock Army's shock groups and fight against enemy transport aircraft.

4. The forces will be prepared for action by the end of 22 October 1942.

Timoshenko, Bogatkin, Pronin, Zlobin[73]

The next day the *Stavka* issued a directive of its own approving Timoshenko's and Kurochkin's proposed attack plan with only minor modifications:

1. Organize an attack from the Prismorzh'e and Bolota Suchan front in the general direction of Novosel'e with separate detachments, after coordinating with the operations of Romanovsky's [1st Shock Army] forces against Kulakovo.

2. In the Molvotitsy region, limit yourself to strong reconnaissance raids and do not conduct an attack. The principal mission along that axis is to defend stubbornly to attract [enemy] reserves to Molvotitsy.

3. Initiate small unit operations in the Glukhoe and Demidovo regions so that the enemy will not be able to operate from those regions against Romanovsky's flank.

Zhukov, Vasilevsky[74]

As was the case with Operation Mars, constant bad weather and a late frost delayed the Northwestern Front's preparations for its offensive, particularly the regrouping of its forces. As a result, the *Stavka* had no choice but to postpone the start date of the operation several times. Finally, however, in early November the *Stavka* and Timoshenko agreed upon an attack date of 28 November. Over a week before, on 17 November the *Stavka* had reshuffled the Northwestern Front's senior command cadre to place its most dynamic senior officers in key command positions. Its Directive No. 994280, dated 17 November, relieved Kurochkin from command of the *front*, assigning him instead to command the 11th Army, and appointed Marshal Timoshenko as his temporary replacement. The directive also replaced Lieutenant General V. Z. Romanovsky, the commander of the 1st Shock Army, with Lieutenant General V. I. Morozov, the former commander of the 11th Army, and assigned Romanovsky to the control of Peoples' Commissariat of Defense (NKO).[75] Although the Northwestern Front did not unleash its main offensive until 28 November, as indicated by the excerpt cited above concerning the 202nd Rifle Division's actions, the armies designated to launch secondary attacks conducted extensive reconnaissances-in-force across their fronts between 22 and 27 November to deceive the Germans regarding the *front's* actual main attack axes.

Aside from the *Stavka* directives cited above, the 1st Shock Army's history is the only detailed account of the ensuing offensive. Presumably, Morozov's shock army bore the brunt of the action, since the assaults by Kurochkin's 11th Army, as well as those launched by the other supporting armies, faltered from the very start.

As far as it goes, the 1st Shock Army's account of the fighting closely reflects the existing *Stavka* records of the offensive:

In November 1942 Marshal of the Soviet Union S. K. Timoshenko became the commander of the Northwestern Front. The *Stavka* assigned him the mission to destroy the enemy's Demiansk grouping in as short a period as possible …

In principal, the overall concept of the new offensive operation remained as before, "to encircle completely the enemy's Demiansk grouping with an attack by the 11th Army's left wing to the south and southeast and by the 1st Shock Army's right wing to the northeast and north, and, at the same time, to create favorable conditions for its final destruction."

Unlike previous operations, however, considering the reprimands from the *Stavka* for stereotyped operations by the *front's* forces, the commander selected a new offensive axis – at the eastern entrance of the Ramushevo corridor. In accordance with the army's directive, while its main forces continued to hold firmly to the positions they occupied in a sector of roughly 100 kilometers in the [army's] center and on its left wing, part of its forces were to "destroy the enemy's garrisons in the corridor between the Korpovka, Pola, and Starovskaia Rob'ia Rivers with surprise attacks by assault battalions operating across a broad front. [Thereafter], while protecting themselves against attacks from the east and organizing defenses along the Ankuta River facing to the west, [they] were to reach the Tsemena and Loznitsy sector along the Pola River, where they were to go over to a reliable defense." Major General G. I. Kulik, the [new] *Stavka* representative, arrived in the 1st Shock Army to coordinate its actions with the other forces of the *front*.[76]

As of 1 November 1942, the 1st Shock Army consisted of five rifle divisions (the 7th Gds., 129th, 130th, 391st, and 397th), five rifle brigades (the 44th, 45th, 47th, 86th, and 121st), one ski brigade (the 43rd), one separate tank battalion (the 103rd), and about eight supporting artillery regiments. The next day Timoshenko reinforced Morozov's shock army with the 23rd Guards Rifle Division (with 9,651 men) and the 167th Tank Regiment (with 24 T–34 tanks). Stronger than its counterpart shock group to the south, Kurochkin's 11th Army was made up of ten rifle divisions (the 22nd, 28th, and 43rd Gds., 55th, 170th, 200th, 202nd, 282nd, 370th, and 384th), five rifle brigades (the 126th, 127th, 133rd, 144th, and 151st), one tank brigade (the 60th), three tank battalions (the 161st, 411th, and 482nd), and 26 artillery regiments. Far smaller than the two armies launching the *front's* main effort, the armies conducting its supporting attack consisted of three-four rifle divisions, one-three rifle brigades, and a single tank brigade or battalion each.[77]

Morozov's offensive plan called for the 23rd Guards and 129th Rifle Divisions and 86th Rifle Brigade, supported by the 167th Tank Regiment, the 70th Guards-mortar [*Katiusha*] Regiment, and the bulk of his army's artillery, to conduct the army's main attack in the Rechki and Sarai sector (3 kilometers west of Tsemena), while the remainder of his forces conducted an "active" defense along the rest of the army's front. Although the exact composition of the 11th Army's main shock group remains obscure, it likely consisted of at least four rifle divisions, including the 202nd Rifle Division, which began its attack on Pustynia on the night of 23–24 November, several days before the shock group commenced its assault, the 133rd Rifle Division, and at least one supporting tank brigade.

Opposite the Northwestern Front's armies, Army Group North's Sixteenth Army defended the eastern and central portions of the Demiansk salient, with its II Army Corps' 122nd, 30th, 329th, 32nd, 12th, and 123rd Infantry Divisions deployed from left to right around the salient's elongated perimeter. At the base (western end) of the salient, the army's *Kampfgruppe* Höhne protected the narrow Ramushevo corridor, with its 126th Infantry Division and part of the II Army Corps' 123rd Infantry Division deployed along the corridor's southern face and its

8th Jäger and 290th and 81st Infantry Divisions defending along its northern face. Once deployed for the attack, the 1st Shock Army's shock group faced roughly three German infantry regiments, supported by 15–20 tanks; the 11th Army's shock group opposed a German force roughly twice as large. Thus the correlation of forces favored the Red Army's attacking forces by a ratio of over three to one in infantry and five to one in tanks, although the rough and roadless terrain and often stormy weather largely negated the Soviets' numerical superiority.

As the 1st Shock and 11th Armies prepared their forces for the offensive, a prolonged thaw began during mid-November, which severely hindered their efforts. The force regrouping in both armies was especially difficult as the seemingly endless columns of Soviet trucks and carts carrying the troops forward frequently bogged down in the muddy, deeply rutted roads. As a result, neither Morozov nor Kurochkin was able to regroup and concentrate all of his forces by the designated attack date. In the 1st Shock Army, for example, the divisions and brigades already concentrated at the front had only one-two combat loads of artillery shells, 0.9 combat loads of rifle ammunition, and only two-four days worth of combat rations, far less than what was required to conduct, much less sustain, a major offensive.

The Offensive

Regardless of these vexing problems, Timoshenko, with the *Stavka* constantly urging him on, had no choice but to order the offensive to proceed as planned (see Map 35). Therefore, on the night of 23–24 November, the 11th Army's 202nd Rifle Division, leading the assault by its army's shock group, attacked the German 122nd Infantry Division's strongpoint at Pustynia on the northern face of the Ramushevo corridor. Simultaneously, the 1st Shock Army's 86th Rifle Brigade, advancing in the vanguard of the 1st Shock Army's main shock group, struck the corridor's defenses from the south. Striking hard at the boundary between the defending 126th and 123rd Infantry Divisions, the 86th Brigade's mission was to penetrate the German defenses, exploit northward, and link up with the 202nd Rifle Division's forces advancing southward west of Pustynia. This preliminary assault, however, was only partially successful. Although the 202nd Rifle Division captured Pustynia after three days of heavy fighting, it was unable to advance any further to the south, and the 86th Rifle Brigade's attack stalled short of its initial objective in a welter of deep mud and intense German fire. Undeterred by this failure, on 27 November Timoshenko ordered the two armies to commit the main forces of their two shock groups into action in an attempt to break the stalemate. Accordingly, the main forces of Kurochkin's shock group moved forward into their jumping-off positions west of Pustynia, on the northeastern face of the corridor, and the 23rd Guards and 129th Rifle Divisions of Morozov's shock group did the same on the corridor's southeastern face. Protected by aircraft from the 674th Aviation Regiment, which flew 36 sorties over their heads, the 23rd Guards and 129th Rifle Divisions' assault groups conducted a complex passage of line through the 86th Rifle Brigade's forward positions and occupied their jumping-off positions overnight on 27–28 November.

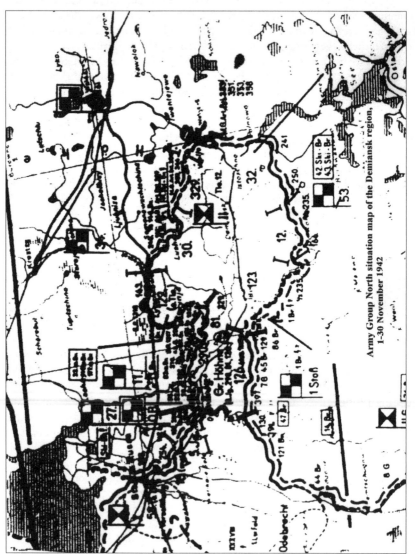

Map 35. Army Group North's situation in the Demiansk region, 1–30 November 1942

Although no detailed description of the 11th Army's assault exists, evidently it faltered almost immediately after it began. The 1st Shock Army's shock group, however, achieved some limited successes, but apparently with heavy losses.[78] The assault groups from the 23rd Guards and 129th Rifle Divisions' first echelon rifle regiments, supported by tanks from the 167th Tank Regiment and the 410th and 103rd Tank Battalions, launched their attack against the German forward defensive positions at 1115 hours on 28 November, after the army's artillery had pounded the German defenses for 45 minutes. Supported by tanks operating in small groups because of the rough terrain, the riflemen, machine gunners, and sappers constituting the carefully-tailored shock groups advanced 2 to 2.5 kilometers deep through the German's forward security outposts and across extensive networks of wooden obstacles and minefields, all the while subjected to intense German fire, and reached the forward edge of the German defense at 2000 hours, well after dark. Here the advancing forces ran onto a veritable wall of exploding metal fragments from German barrier fires, reportedly, "4–5 artillery and mortar battalions firing more than 4,500 rounds."[79] After seizing only pitifully small footholds in the German forward defenses, the heavy German artillery and mortar fire, punctuated by numerous German counterattacks in company and battalion strength, drove the advancing Red Army troops back to their starting positions. The 1st Shock Army history simply noted, "One ought to mention that the attacking units suffered heavy losses both from destructive machine gun fire and from numerous enemy 'cuckoos' [*kukushek* – presumably the '*Nebelwerfer*' multi-barreled engineer mortars]."[80]

Although the 1st Shock Army's attacking forces suffered heavy losses in their initial assault, Morozov ordered them to resume the offensive several times over the next few days, but to no avail. The other attacking armies also recorded only minimal gains against heavy resistance with ever-increasing losses. The only significant accomplishment was the capture of the German strongpoint at Pustynia by the 11th Army's 202nd Rifle Division. Though the *Stavka* realized Timoshenko's offensive had indeed failed, as was the case in Operation Mars, it insisted his armies continue their futile attacks. Thus, at 2235 hours on 8 December, it sent yet another directive to the Northwestern Front:

> The *Stavka* of the Supreme High Command orders:
>   Penetrate the orifice of the enemy's Demiansk grouping [the Ramushevo corridor] from the north in the Maloe Stepanovo and Viazovka sector and from the south in the Marker 63.5 and Bol'shoe Kniazevo sector with the combined forces of the 11th and 1st Shock Armies. Firmly dig in and erect a defense facing toward the west along a line extending from Maloe Stepanovo through Bol'shoe Zasovo and the western edge of the forest east of Kokorino to Matasovo and facing eastward along a line extending from Viazovka through Savkino and Tsemena to Marker 63.5 by 30 December.
>   When this has been accomplished, we will consider the first stage of the offensive to have been completed.
>   The *front's* subsequent mission is to regroup its forces and weapons and, when additional reserves from the *Stavka's* reserves approach, be prepared to liquidate the enemy's Demiansk grouping by 10 January.

Complete the liquidation of the Demiansk grouping by 20–25 February, after which your forces will go into winter quarters.

Pass this order down to regimental commanders in the 11th and 1st Shock Armies.

Acknowledge receipt and report fulfillment.

The *Stavka* of the Supreme High Command

I. Stalin, G. Zhukov[81]

Despite the *Stavka's* numerous threats and entreaties, all of Timoshenko's subsequent attempts to revive the offensive during November and early December ended in failure (see Map 36). As a result, on 11 December Timoshenko halted the *front's* offensive operations, albeit temporarily, to provide his formations an opportunity to rest, refit, and regroup their exhausted forces. During the ensuing ten days, the *front* commander dispatched fresh reinforcements to the 11th Army and 1st Shock Army, the 12th Guards Rifle Corps' headquarters, the 55th Rifle Division, the 20th and 87th Rifle Brigades, and four tank regiments to the former and the 14th Rifle Corps' headquarters, the 53rd Guards Rifle Division, the 177th Tank Brigade, the 1st Guards-mortar Division, and the 55th Engineer-Sapper Brigade to the latter.[82]

After this brief respite to rest and reinforce their forces, Timoshenko ordered the Kurochkin's and Morozov's two armies to resume their assaults on 23 December, roughly a week after Zhukov's Operation Mars collapsed in bloody defeat. Despite being significantly reinforced, when they resumed their attacks, the two armies' forces once again encountered heavy German resistance, in particular, devastating German artillery and mortar blocking fires which smashed their assault groups and compelled them to withdraw. When they launched renewed assaults four days later, the 1st Shock Army's history recorded the ensuing carnage:

Anticipating the [the 1st Shock Army's] attack, the enemy conducted a strong artillery counter-preparation on the morning of 27 December, with 9–10 battalions firing more than 14,000 shells. The army artillery was in no condition to conduct an appropriate counter-battery struggle. As a result, the army's shock group suffered critical losses, its communications and command and control were destroyed, and its crossing sites over the Korpovka River were destroyed.[83]

Despite yet another failure, on the evening of 27 December, Timoshenko submitted a new operational plan to the *Stavka* for what he termed "the second stage of the offensive," which apparently required the 11th Army and 1st Shock Army to renew their assaults in even narrower sector of attack. The *Stavka* responded to Timoshenko's proposal at 0400 hours the next morning by issuing two new directives of its own, the first approving the *front* commander's revised plan and the second urging him on:

[The first directive]

The *Stavka* of the Supreme High Command approves the plan you submitted for the second stage of the operation to destroy the enemy's Demiansk grouping.

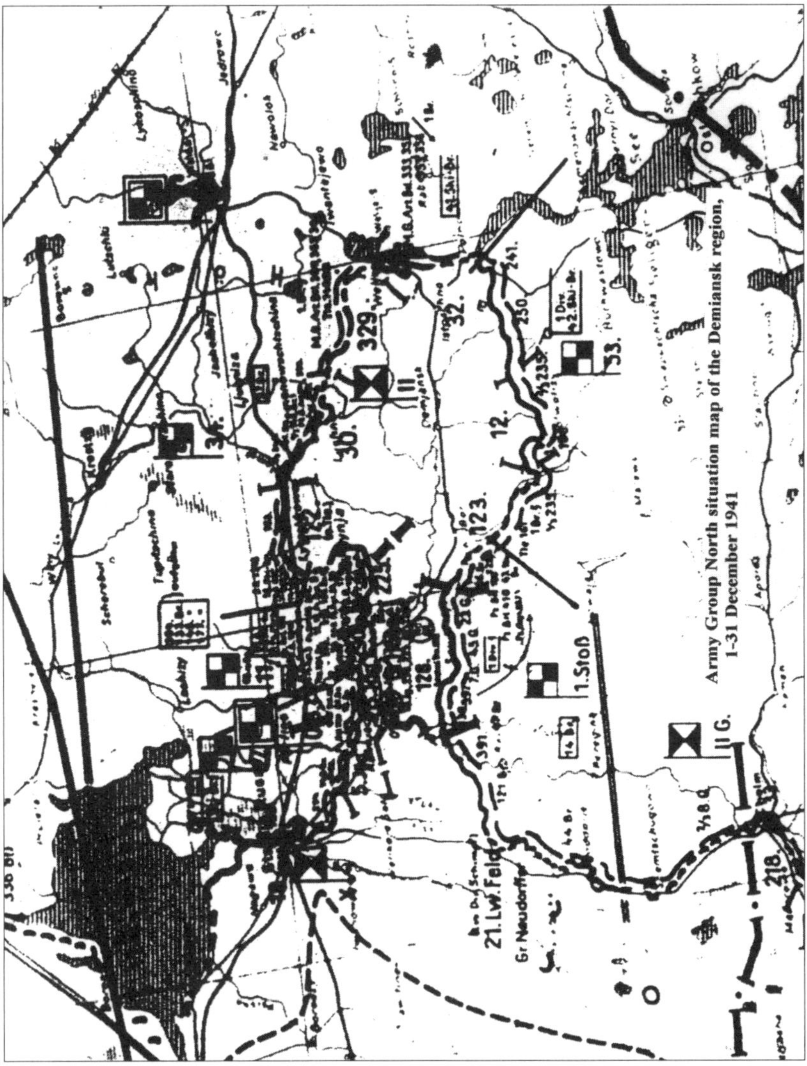

Map 36. Army Group North's situation in the Demiansk region, 1–31 December 1942

To conduct the operation, the *Stavka* of the Supreme High Command orders that 6 rifle divisions, 3 tank penetration regiments, 4 line tank regiments, 4 122-mm howitzer regiments, 1 122-mm gun regiment, and 14 M–30 multiple rocket launcher battalions be placed at the disposal of the Northwestern Front's commander.

Be prepared to conduct the offensive no later than 8 January 1943.

The *Stavka* of the Supreme High Command

I. Stalin[84]

[The second directive]

To liquidate the enemy's Demiansk grouping as rapidly as possible, the *Stavka* of the Supreme High Command orders you to complete an operation to penetrate the enemy's fortified positions in the Ramushevo corridor with the 11th Army and 1st Shock Army and link up the forces of both armies along the Pola River no later than 3 January 1943.

The *Stavka* of the Supreme High Command

I. Stalin[85]

Although the 11th Army's role and performance in the operation remain unknown, during the second stage of the Demiansk offensive, the 1st Shock Army conducted its attack with the 129th and 397th Rifle Divisions and the 177th Tank Brigades concentrated in far narrower sectors than before. Once again, the army's history recorded the offensive's dismal results:

Summarizing the second stage of the operation, the forces of the 129th and 397th Rifle Divisions and 177th Tank Brigade succeeded in wedging 2–3 kilometers into the enemy's defenses in a narrow sector. However, from 3 to 6 January, groups of enemy forces succeeded in cutting off some of these forces by conducting counterattacks at night against the flanks of the penetrating units. During the first half of January, the army devoted its efforts to rescuing the 2nd Battalion of the 129th Rifle Division's 518th Rifle Regiment, together with an attached battalion from the 43rd Ski Brigade, the 397th Rifle Division's 447th and 448th Rifle Regiments, and the forces of the 177th Tank Brigade, which were encircled in the small woods 1.5 kilometers southwest of Tsemena. The encircled group, which was commanded by Lieutenant Colonel P. G. Saenko, the commander of the 448th Rifle Regiment, fought selflessly for 18 days, while experiencing critical shortages of ammunition and food. Senior Lieutenant Golovin, a deputy battalion commander in the 397th Rifle Division's 447th Regiment, became one of the heroes of this epic. After the death of his battalion commander, he assumed command. On 2–3 January alone, his battalion repelled 16 enemy attacks, and Golovin himself is reported to have killed 37 Germans, for which he later received the Order of Lenin. On the night of 20 January, Major P. I. Iakovenko, Saeno's assistant, who had taken command of the group after his commander perished, led 140 soldiers, 122 of which were either wounded or sick, out of the encirclement.

The 11th Army's forces also achieved no significant success. The enemy managed to hold on to his occupied positions and liquidated the small penetrations our forces made in his defenses. The operations at Tsemena cost the army great losses.[86]

Conclusions

The multiple offensives Timoshenko's Northwestern Front conducted in the Demiansk region during November and December 1942 were as futile and unsuccessful as those it conducted in previous months and years. From the perspective of the *front's* exhausted troops, the only saving grace was that this defeat was the last they would suffer in this region. Although the *Stavka* would order the Northwestern Front to mount yet another offensive in mid-February 1943, this time the Germans would beat them to the punch by abandoning the Demiansk salient and withdrawing to new defensive positions east of Staraia Russa.

In their intent, course, and outcome, the Red Army's offensives at Demiansk during November and December 1942 closely resembled the army's experiences in conducting Operation Mars; that is, despite its repeated failures to break through the German defenses, the *Stavka* insisted the Northwestern Front continue the offensive without regard to the immense cost in human lives. Although neither the Soviet nor the Russian government has released official casualty figures for the operation, within the context of the losses it suffered during its previous offensives in 1942, the Northwestern Front's armies likely suffered between 15,000 and 30,000 casualties in the November and December operations, most of them in its 11th Army and 1st Shock Army.

PART 2

SOVIET OFFENSIVE OPERATIONS ALONG THE SOUTHWESTERN AXIS (FEBRUARY–MARCH 1943)

Chapter 4

The Southwestern Front's Voroshilovgrad (Donbas) Offensive (Operation Gallop [*Skachok*]) (29 January–18 February 1943)

Introduction

While Soviet forces were destroying the German Sixth Army, which they had encircled in the Stalingrad region in November 1942, in mid-January 1943, the *Stavka* ordered the Red Army to commence a new series of offensives operations, referred to collectively as the Voronezh-Khar'kov strategic offensive, which ultimately encompassed the entire southern wing of the Soviet-German front. In reality only an expansion of the series of counteroffensives the Red Army began conducting on 19 November 1942, this strategic offensive consisted of eight separate operations conducted simultaneously or consecutively by the Red Army's Briansk, Voronezh, Southwestern, and Southern Fronts between mid-January and early March 1943. During these operations Soviet forces advanced roughly 350 kilometers westward from the Voronezh and Rostov regions along the Don River to a front extending from the Kursk region southward to the Sea of Azov. The offensive finally ended when General Erich von Manstein's Army Group South conducted twin successful counterstrokes, the first, in the Donbas region in mid-February and, the second, in the Khar'kov and Belgorod regions in early March.

The Red Army's Southwestern and Southern Fronts played an instrumental role in these operations, first by clearing Germans from the "great bend" in the Don River and the region east of Rostov during the Millerovo and Rostov operations in January, and then by advancing deep into the Donbas region in February (see Maps 37 and 38). During this Donbas operation, the two *fronts* sought to destroy all German forces in the region and liberate all of the German-occupied territory east of the Dnepr River.

As recently as 20 years after the war's end, the Soviet government forbade Soviet historians from writing detailed accounts about the Red Army's military operations in the Donbas during early 1943, primarily because they failed. The government finally relented and permitted its historians to discuss these operations during the historical "thaw" [*ottepel'*] which occurred during the early 1960s when Nikita Khrushchev was Communist Party First Secretary and, later, during the period of "*glasnost*," which occurred during the late 1980s when Mikhail Gorbachev was Party First Secretary. Yet, despite the loosening of the historical fetters, these historians were permitted to investigate and expose only the South-

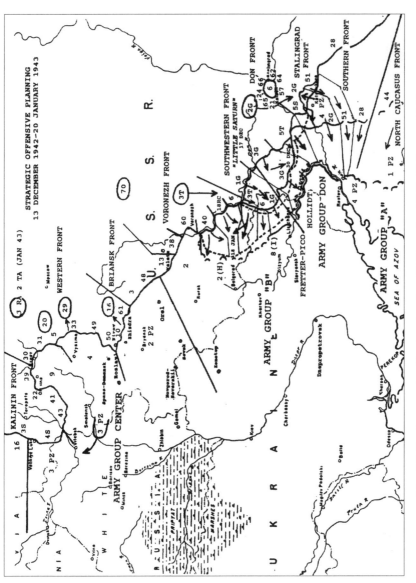

Map 37. *Stavka* strategic offensive planning, 13 December 1942–20 January 1943

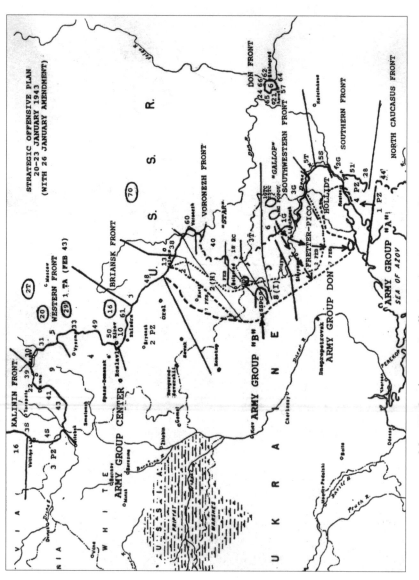

Map 38. *Stavka* strategic offensive planning, 20–26 January 1943

western Front's participation in the operations and von Manstein's famous counterstrokes which ensued.

During these two brief periods of historical candor, Soviet historians published two major studies about the Red Army's operations in the Donbas region. The first of these works, a 1963 article written by V. Morozov, provocatively entitled, "Why Was the Offensive in the Donbas during the Spring of 1943 not Completed?" [*Pochemu ne zavershilos' nastuplenie v Donbasse vesnoi 1943 goda?*], addressed the *Stavka's* strategic planning during the late winter of 1942–1943 and described the course and conduct of the Donbas operation for the first time, but included no *Stavka* or *front* documents related to the operations.[87] This account focused on the Southwestern Front's involvement in the offensive, incorrectly implying that no other major forces took part. The second work, a more detailed assessment of the Donbas operation written in 1973 by A. G. Ershov and entitled *Osvobozhdenie Donbassa* [The Liberation of the Donbas], provided considerably greater details about the Southwestern Front's role in the offensive and mentioned a raid conducted by the 8th Cavalry Corps southwest of Voroshilovgrad, supposedly in support of the Southwestern Front's offensive. However, Ershov provided no further details about other forces involved in the offensive. Based on these two accounts and extensive German archival materials, this author published a more comprehensive study of the Donbas operation in 1991. Entitled *From the Don to the Dnepr: Soviet Offensive Operations, December 1942-August 1943*, although it focused its attention primarily on only the Southwestern Front's operations, this book provided far more operational detail than previous accounts.[88]

In the wake of the Soviet Union's collapse in 1991, the new government of the Russian Federation declassified and released significant amounts of new archival materials, including many wartime *Stavka* and *front* directives, orders, and reports hitherto unavailable, which proved the Red Army's offensive into the Donbas region during February 1943 was far more extensive and ambitious than previously assumed. Specifically, in addition to the Southwestern Front, Mobile Group Popov, and several other mobile corps, the Southern Front, with several more mobile corps, also took part in the offensive. This article corrects the historical record by providing a brief review of the Southwestern Front's operations in the Donbas region, an expanded survey of the Southern Front's participation in the offensive, and newly released archival documents related to the offensive as a whole. As these new documents indicate, by mid-February 1943, Vatutin's modest initial offensive in fact grew into a full-fledged offensive by two Red Army *fronts* aimed at liquidating all German forces operating east of the Dnepr River.

Planning

The scope and scale of the Donbas operation, code-named operation Gallop ["*Skachok*"], itself underwent a considerable transformation from the moment Army General N. F. Vatutin, the commander of the Southwestern Front, first proposed its conduct to the *Stavka*. Originally, Vatutin's operational concept envisioned only an advance by the Southwestern Front into the Donbas region. However, as the Southwestern Front's forces advanced westward toward

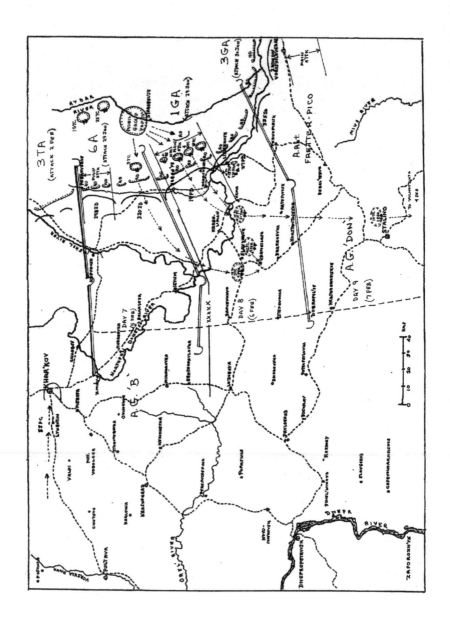

Starobel'sk on the Aidar River, the Northern Donets River, and the city of Voroshilovgrad against weakening German resistance, at 0730 hours on 20 January, Vatutin presented the *Stavka* with his initial proposal for an offensive to liberate the entire Donbas region (see Map 39):

> I firmly expect to reach the Pokrovskoe, Tarasovka, Starobel'sk, Aidar River, and Northern Donets River front and capture the Kamensk, Likhaia, Zverevo, and Krasnyi Sulin regions by 22 January 1943.
>
> The forces on the right [the Voronezh Front's 3rd Tank Army] have captured the Valuiki and Urazovo regions.
>
> As a result I am making the following corrections in the South-western Front's plan for subsequent operations:
>
> 1. I will conduct the next attack from the Tarasovka (30 kilometers north-east of Svatovo) and Starobel'sk front in the general direction of the Kramatorsk-Artemovsk front and beyond to Stalino, Volnovakha, and Mariupol' with a strong and mobile group consisting of the 3rd, 10th, and 18th Tank Corps, three rifle divisions, three antitank [tank destroyer] artillery regiments, three guards-mortar regiments, and three antiaircraft artillery regiments, reinforced by the three ski brigades that are due to arrive by railroad, to cut off the entire Donbas region, encircle and destroy enemy forces in this territory, and seize back all equipment, reserves, and other riches in this territory without permitting the enemy to withdraw anything.
>
> A smaller part of the forces will be directed toward Starobel'sk, Debal'tsevo, and Makeevka. My deputy, Lieutenant General Popov, will lead the group and personnel from the *front's* headquarters, and 4th Guards Tank Corps' headquarters, reinforced with radio communications equipment, will serve as its staff.
>
> The tank corps will be concentrated in the Tarasovka and Starobel'sk regions by 24 January 1943. By this time the corps will be replenished with three refills of fuel and three combat loads of ammunition.
>
> The arrival of the three rifle divisions and the ski brigades is lagging. However, I intend to transport two new rifle divisions to Starobel'sk Station by 25 January 1943 by using auto-transport.
>
> The operation will begin on approximately 26–27 January 1943.
>
> The [*front's* forces] will reach the Mariupol' region within the next seven days according to the following plan:
>
> a) To the Northern Donets on the first day;
>
> b) To the Kramatorskaia, Konstantinovka, Nikitovka, and Debal'tsevo regions on the third day;
>
> c) To the Kurakovka, Stalino, and Makeevka regions on the fourth day;
>
> d) To the Volnovakha region on the fifth day; and
>
> e) To Mariupol' on the seventh day.
>
> The *front's* main forces will support the mobile group's operations.

The operations by the *front's* remaining forces will coincide with the plan indicated above.

2. The next most importance role will fall to the 3rd Guards Army, which will attack from the region southwest of Kamensk toward Stalino, and its mobile group, consisting of the 23rd and 2nd Tank Corps, the 2nd Guards Tank Corps, and the 1st Mechanized Corps, will reach the Debal'tsevo, Makeevka, and Stalino front on the third or fourth day of the operation, where it will link up with Popov's mobile group to encircle and destroy all enemy forces in the Donbas.

3. The 5th Tank Army will attack from the region west of Krasnyi Sulin toward Volnovakha and, with part of its forces, toward Taganrog.

4. The 6th Army will attack toward Kupiansk and, with part of its forces, toward Izium.

5. The Voroshilovgrad region will be encircled by the two divisions on the 1st Guards Army's left wing and by two divisions on the 3rd Guards Army's right wing.

6. As a result of the operation, the armies' rifle divisions must reach:

a) The 6th Army – the Dvurechnaia and Savintsy front on the seventh day of the operation;

b) The 1st Guards Army – the Savintsy, Barvenkovo, and Devshino (inclusive) front on the eighth day of the operation;

c) The 3rd Guards Army – the Devshino, Krasnoarmeiskoe, and Kurakovka front on the ninth day of the operation; and

d) The 5th Tank Army – the Kurakovka and Volnovakha front on the ninth day of the operation.

Therefore, the operation must be completed by 5 February 1943. This will make it possible to conduct yet another operation before the end of the winter period and to reach a more favorable line, namely, from Akhtyrka through Poltava, Perevolochnaia, Dnepropetrovsk, and Zaporozh'e to Melitopol' and, if the situation is favorable, also seize the Kakhovka, Kherson, Perekop, and Genichesk regions and cut off the Crimea.

However, this operation must be closely aligned with the operations of neighboring *fronts*, in particular, the Voronezh Front.

The 1st and 4th Guards and 25th Tank Corps, all without weapons and equipment, will remain my reserve.

All the while, I will fully outfit the 1st Guards Tank Corps at the expense of scattered arriving tanks. There are insufficient tanks for the 4th Guards and 25th Tank Corps.

I request [you]:

1. Approve the plan set forth above (the preparatory work is underway).

2. Provide tanks to fully equip the two tank corps.

3. Additionally, provide three regiments and one battalion of M–13 multiple rocket launchers.

4. Designate boundary lines with neighboring *fronts* to great depth.

5. It would be beneficial if we received one fresh cavalry corps.

6. Appoint Major General Shlemin to replace Comrade Popov as commander of the 5th Tank Army.

Fedorov [Vatutin]
Fomin [Lieutenant General A. S. Zheltov][89]

In its original form, Vatutin's plan required his mobile groups to conduct a double envelopment of all German forces defending the Voroshilovgrad region of the Donbas, with the 1st Guards Army and Mobile Group Popov attacking from the north and the 3rd Guards and 5th Tank Armies attacking from the south. At this stage Vatutin did not expect the Southern Front, whose forces were still engaged in heavy fighting east of Rostov, to be able to support his offensive. Therefore, he ordered the 3rd Guard Army's mobile group, which consisted of the 23rd and 2nd Tank Corps and the 2nd Guards Tank and 1st Mechanized Corps, to penetrate the German defenses south of Voroshilovgrad and then advance westward through Debal'tsevo and Makeevka to link up with Mobile Group Popov in the Stalino region.

Stalin approved Vatutin's plan at 2315 hours on 20 January:

The *Stavka* of the Supreme High Command approves your plan for subsequent operations. The boundary line on your right, with the Voronezh Front, is through Aleksandrovka, Pokrovskoe, Kupiansk, Shevchenkovo, Zmiev, and Poltava (all inclusive for the Southwestern Front). The boundary line between the Southwestern and Southern Fronts is from Proletarka Station to Golodaevka (all inclusive for the Southwestern Front).

The *Stavka* of the Supreme High Command
Vasil'ev [Stalin][90]

Vatutin assigned specific missions to the forces on his *front's* right wing on 23 January:

1. Having been defeated along the Valuiki and Starobel'sk axes, the enemy is attempting to resist our forces resolutely along the line from Bol'shoi Sukhodol, Kamensk, and the mouth of the Northern Donets [River] to the mouth of the Don River and, apparently, is hurriedly withdrawing his forces from the Northern Caucasus to the Rostov region. It is possible that enemy reserves will appear from the direction of Khar'kov and Dnepropetrovsk. A large enemy headquarters, which is in communication with radios located in France, has been detected in Dnepropetrovsk.

2. Delivering its main attacks with its right wing from the Pokrovskoe and Starobel'sk front toward Stalino and Mariupol' and with its left wing from the region west of Kamensk toward Roven'ki and Stalino, and,

depending on the situation, with part of its forces toward Taganrog, the Southwestern Front's armies will cut off, encircle, and destroy the entire enemy grouping located on the territory of the Donbas and in the Rostov region and prevent them from withdrawing to the west and evacuating any sort of material with them. The armies will reach the Stalino and Volnovakha regions with their mobile formations on the 5th–6th day, and the Mospanovo, Balakleia, Petrovskaia, Barvenkovo, Krasnoarmeiskoe, and Mariupol' regions with their rifle formations on the 7th–9th day.

The forces will be prepared for the offensive by 27 January 1943. The time of the artillery preparation will be provided later.

The boundary line on the right, with the Voronezh Front, will extend through Aleksandrovka, Pokrovskoe, Kupiansk, Shevchenko, Zmiev, and Poltava (all points inclusive for the Southwestern Front) and, on the left, with the Southern Front, through Proletarka and Golodaevka (Kuibyshev) (all points inclusive for the Southwestern Front).

I order:

a) The 3rd Guards Army, in its present configuration (without the 229th Separate Rifle Brigade) and while continuing active operations to tie the enemy down along the Gundorovskoe, Kamensk, and Kalitvenskaia front, will firmly defend the northern bank of the Northern Donets River and the bridgeheads it captured on the southern bank, including Malaia Kamenka and the northwestern part of Kamensk.

Before the operation begins, widen the bridgehead along the western bank of the Northern Donets River on your right wing and concentrate a shock group consisting of five rifle divisions, three tank corps, one mechanized corps, and one motorized rifle brigade with the greater part of your reinforcements, in the Kruzhilovka, Davydo-Nikol'skii, Uliashin, and Verkhnii Grachinskii regions along that axis, with the mission to conduct the *front's* main attack from the Makarov Iar and Bol'shoi Sukhodol front toward Roven'ki and Stalino beyond and, together with other *front* units, encircle and destroy the enemy on the territory of the Donbas and capture that territory. Envelop the Voroshilovgrad region from the south and west with part of your forces and, together with the 1st Guards Army's forces, encircle and destroy the enemy's Voroshilovgrad grouping.

Deliver an attack with part of your forces southeastward from the Likhaia and Krasnyi Sulin front and, in cooperation with the 5th Tank Army, encircle and destroy the enemy grouping in the Kamensk, Likhaia, and Krasnyi Sulin regions.

To do so, penetrate the enemy's defensive front in the Mokryi Iar and Bol'shoi Sukhodol sector, commit the mobile group into the penetration, and, by exploiting your success in the direction of Roven'ki and Stalino, reach the Debal'tsevo, Makeevka, and Stalino front by the end of the first day of the operation. At that line, link up with Lieutenant General Popov's mobile group, which will be attacking from the north, bearing in mind that part of the mobile group's forces will subsequently be re-subordinated by special order to Lieutenant General Popov, and the remaining forces will prepare either to destroy the enemy's encircled grouping or for an attack toward the south or southeast.

Attacking decisively from behind the mobile group, the rifle divisions will reach the Annovka, Krasnoarmeiskoe, and Elizavetovka front no later than the 9th day of the operation, in readiness for subsequent operations. The attached map shows the operational plan with the indicated operational axes of the formations and the lines to be attained on each day.

The boundary line on the left will extend through Kostino-Bystrianskii, Kalitvenskaia (incl.), Verkhnii Sazonov, Likhaia Station, Roven'ki, Ilovaiskaia Station, and Elizavetovka.

b) The 5th Tank Army, in its present configuration and with the 229th Separate Rifle Brigade, will relieve the 3rd Guards Army's units in the Kalitvenskaia and Ust'-Belokalitvenskaia sector by the morning of 24 January 1943. Continue to widen the bridgeheads on the western bank of the Northern Donets River and, simultaneously, concentrate a shock group on your right wing by the end of 26 January 1943, with the mission to destroy the opposing enemy in cooperation with the 3rd Guards Army by conducting a main attack from the Kalitvenskaia and Muravlev front toward Repnoe and Krasnyi Sulin and a secondary attack from the Kamenev region toward Krasnyi Sulin and encircling and destroying the enemy in the Kamensk, Likhaia, and Krasnyi Sulin regions. Capture the Platov, Sokolov, and Krasnyi Sulin regions on the 3rd day of the operation and, subsequently, by exploiting the attack toward Krasnyi Sulin, Kuibyshevo, and Volnovakha, capture the Dmitrievka, Kuibyshevo, and D'iakovo regions on the 5th day of the operation and reach the Elizavetovka, Petrovskaia, and Ianisal' region on the 9th day of the operation, in readiness for further operations. Upon capture of the Kuibyshevo region, be prepared to attack with part of your force toward Taganrog.

The plan of operations by day is in accordance with the attached map.

Maintain communications with the Southern Front during the offensive to protect the boundary on your left.

c) In accordance with a special plan, the 17th Air Army will destroy enemy aircraft at airfields in the Voroshilovgrad, Stalino, and Shakhty regions with part of the *front's* air forces before the beginning of the operation.

After the operation begins, protect the 3rd Guards Army's shock group and mobile formations and assist them in destroying the enemy on the field of battle and in reserve.

d) The army commanders will submit their operational plans, drawn on a map and in handwriting, to me by messenger by 1200 hours on 26 January 1943.

The mobile formations will have three refills [of fuel] and three combat loads [of ammunition] by the beginning of the operation.

e) Attachment: a map with the operational plan.

Vatutin, Zheltov, Ivanov[91]

Lieutenant General V. I. Kuznetsov, the commander of the 1st Guards Army, submitted his army's plan for operations north and west of Voroshilovgrad to Vatutin on 26 January:

1. The enemy, after being defeated in the region between the Derkul and Aidar Rivers and along the Starobel'sk axis, is trying to offer stubborn resistance along the Svatovo and Kremennaia line and further along the right bank of the Northern Donets River. We cannot exclude the possibility of enemy reserves appearing from the direction of Khar'kov and Dnepropetrovsk.

2. The mission of the army is to conduct a main attack from the Starobel'sk region, penetrate the enemy's front, protect the commitment of the *front* mobile group's forces into the penetration, and, by attacking decisively farther to the west and enveloping the enemy from the north, encircle and destroy him and reach the Petrovskaia, Barvenkovo, and Annovka front by the end of the eighth day of the operation while conducting deep reconnaissance.

On the right the 6th Army is penetrating the enemy's front in the Pokrovskoe and Tarasovka sector and will, while exploiting its attack to the west, reach the Mospannovo, Balakleia, and Pokrovskoe front by the end of the seventh day of the operation. The boundary line with it will extend through Novo-Markovska (incl.), Gaidunovka, Kaban'e, the mouth of the Oskol River, and along the Northern Donets River (incl.) to Petrovskaia.

On the left the 3rd Guards Army is enveloping the Voroshilovgrad region from the south and southwest with two rifle divisions and attacking along the Debal'tsevo and Stalino front with its remaining forces and will reach the Annovka and Elizavetovka front no later than the ninth day of the operation. The boundary line with it will extend through Makeevka, Nikol'skaia (incl.), Kruzhilovka (incl.), Parizhskaia Kommuna, Annovka, and Petropavlovka.

3. Decision. Conduct a main attack with the 4th Guards Rifle Corps from the Kalmykovka, Nizhniaia Pokrovka, Shevchenko, Novo-Astrakhan', and Petrenkovo line in the general direction of Lisichansk, Artemovsk, Slaviansk, and Barvenkovo, while securing the operation on the right by an attack by one rifle division toward Drobyshevo and Bol'shaia Andreevka.

The 6th Guards Rifle Corps will attack from the Nizhnee, Krymskaia, Slavianoserbsk, and Zheltoe line in the general direction of Sergo and Artemovsk. Capture Voroshilovgrad with one rifle division in coordination with the 3rd Guards Army.

4. Specific missions of the corps: a) The 4th Guards Rifle Corps, with the 212th and 213th Howitzer Artillery Regiments, 47th Gun Artillery Regiment, 456th Antitank Artillery Regiment, 411th and 426th Guards-Mortar Battalions, 633rd Antiaircraft Artillery Regiment, 127th

Tank Regiment, and a battery of the 139th Separate Antiaircraft Artillery Battalion, after deploying its main forces along the Shevchenko, Novo-Astrakhan, and Petrenkovo line, will attack toward Artemovsk, Slaviansk, and Barvenkovo. The 35th Cavalry Division will protect the army's operation from the right by an attack toward Drobyshevo.

Reach the Kaban'e, Kremennaia, Lisichansk, and Nizhnee (incl.) line by the end of the first day. Reach the Shandrotolovo, Krasnyi Liman, Petrovskoe (incl.), and Artemovsk line by the end of the third day and the Bogorodichnoe, Slaviansk, and Kramatorskaia line by the end of the sixth day.

Subsequently, the 78th and 195th Rifle Divisions will capture Barvenkovo by concentric attacks and dig in along the Petrovskoe, Iasnaia Poliana, Barvenkovo (incl.), and Andreevka line with three divisions on the eighth day of the operation. Upon reaching the Bogorodichnoe, Slaviansk, and Kramatorskaia line, allocate one rifle division to the army reserve, which will be concentrated in the Khristishche and Maiaki region. Upon arriving at the final line, conduct reconnaissance toward Oleiniki and Lozovaia.

The boundary line to the left will extent through Novo-Aidar (incl.), Bobrovo (incl.), Novo-Nikolaevka (incl.), Artemovsk (incl.), and Andreevka.

b) The 6th Guards Rifle Corps, with the 230th Howitzer Artillery Regiment, will destroy enemy forces resisting in the Irmino and Sergo region with concentric attacks by the 244th Rifle and 44th Mountain Rifle Divisions from the Nizhnee, Krymskaia, Slavianoserbsk, and Zheltoe front and reach the Rudnoi Zolotoi, Irmino, and Voroshilovsk front by the end of the first day, and, simultaneously, the 58th Guards Rifle Division, cooperating with the 44th Mountain Rifle Division and the 3rd Guards Army, will capture Voroshilovgrad, after which it will revert to the corps' reserve.

The corps will capture Artemovsk by the end of the third day and reach the Krasnotorka, Druzhkovka, and Konstantinovka line by the end of the sixth day, and the 244th Rifle Division and 44th Mountain Rifle Division will dig in along the Andreevka (incl.) and Krasnoarmeiskii Rudnik line by the end of the eighth day, while conducting reconnaissance toward Iur'evka and Boguslav. Dispatch the 58th Guards Rifle Division to the army's reserve in the Kramatorskaia region.

5. Command and Control.

a. Command posts:

Army headquarters — Belovodsk. Axis of movement: Belovodsk, Novo-Aidar, Lisichansk, Slaviansk. Displacement: Novo-Aidar — on the second day of the operation; Lisichansk — on the fifth day of the operation, and Slaviansk — on the eighth day of the operation.

4th Guards Rifle Corps – headquarters, southwestern outskirts of Starobel'sk. Axis of movement: Starobel'sk, Novo-Astrakhan', Proletarsk, Rai-Aleksandrovka, Bylbasovka, Prelestnoe.

6th Guards Rifle Corps – headquarters, Petrovka. Axis of movement: Trekhizbenka, Irmino, Artemovsk, Druzhkovka, Novo-Aleksandrovka.

b. Army Report Collection Points [*punkty sbora donosenii* – PSD]: Alekseevka, Borovskoe, Rai-Aleksandrovka.

c. Communications with the corps — wire, radio, and liaison officers. In addition, each corps headquarters will have two aircraft. Flights – two times per day (in the morning and evening).
Attachment: one operational planning map.

Kuznetsov, Rybinsky, Paniukhov[92]

While Vatutin was issuing orders to his subordinate armies, on 26 January the *Stavka* enjoined Colonel General A. I. Eremenko, the commander of the Southern Front, to speed up his *front's* advance toward Rostov so it would be in position to support Vatutin's offensive into the Donbas region:

Enemy resistance is being overcome as a result of the successful operations of our forces in the Voronezh, right wing of the Southwestern, Don, and North Caucasus Fronts. The enemy defense is being penetrated on a broad front. The absence of deep reserves is forcing the enemy to commit approaching formations [into combat] piecemeal and from the march. Many empty spots and sectors have been formed that are being protected by separate small detachments. The Southwestern Front's right wing is hanging over the Donbas, and the seizure of Bataisk will lead to the isolation of the enemy's Trans-Caucasus grouping [Army Group "A"]. Favorable conditions have set in for the encirclement and piecemeal destruction of the enemy's Donbas, Trans-Caucasus, and Black Sea groupings.

In these circumstances, the Southern Front's center and the left wing along the Bataisk axis are marking time, the unwarranted delay by Group Rotmistrov along the vital approaches to Bataisk, the surrender to the enemy of the bridgehead on the southern bank of the Don River without any real resistance, and the indecisiveness displayed by the commander of the 2nd Guards Army, Malinovsky, are providing the enemy with an opportunity to withdraw his forces through the Bataisk gate.

You have organized the command and control of your forces poorly. As a rule, the *front's* headquarters does not know the situation, and Malinovsky and his staff are trying to avoid commanding and controlling combat along the most critical axis to Bataisk.

The attacks by the 51st and 28th Armies' units are developing very slowly and in uncoordinated fashion and are [they are] out of communications with the 2nd Guards Army.

The *Stavka* of the Supreme High Command orders:

1. Decisively improve command and control of the *front's* forces.

2. Accelerate the tempos of the 51st and 28th Armies' offensives and reach the Ol'ginskaia and Bataisk line by 28 January 1943.

3. Move the 2nd Guards Army's auxiliary command post forward to the forces immediately.

4. Transfer direct control over the 2nd and 5th Guards Mechanized and 3rd Guards Tank Corps to Comrade Malinovsky.

5. Confirm receipt and report fulfillment.

I. Stalin, G. Zhukov[93]

The Advance Across the Northern Donets River (30 January–14 February)

The Thrust to Slaviansk and Krasnoarmeiskoe

Vatutin, within hours after his *front* resumed its offensive, dispatched another situation report to the *Stavka* at 2400 hours on 30 January:

1. The forces of the Southwestern Front, after firing an artillery raid, went over to the offensive along the entire front at 0850 hours on 30 January 1943. The *front's* forces, overcoming stubborn resistance by an enemy in centers of resistance along the movement routes of the forces and in populated points across the entire front, inflicted heavy losses on the enemy, pressed him back in all sectors, and penetrated the front on the axis of the main attack, advancing 15 kilometers on the main axis. The enemy, having brought forward two new assault battalions, counterattacked in some sectors with infantry and tanks. Especially fierce enemy attacks occurred in the 3rd Guards Army's sector.

2. The 6th Army continued its offensive during the day, advancing on its right flank and in its center. On the army's left wing, the enemy halted the offensive in the Nizhniaia Dubanka and Svatovo regions by fire and counterattacks with infantry, tanks, and self-propelled guns.

The army's forces captured [populated points] and reached the Korzhovka, Man'kovka, Osinovka, Lipovka 2, Lipovka 1, Sarikovka, Apanovka, Iasinovka, Tarasovka, and Varvarovka regions and, enveloping Verkniaia Dubanka from the north and south, reached Lebedevka, Aleksandrovka, and Novo-Aleksandrovka, penetrated into Verkhniaia Dubanka, cleared the enemy from the southern outskirts of Novo-Krasnoe, penetrated into the northern and eastern outskirts of Nizhniaia Dubanka, captured Preobrazhennoe and Goncharovka, and advanced forward.

Small groups of enemy aircraft operated against the 6th Army's combat formation throughout the day.

The roads, particularly on the army's right flank, are snow-covered and difficult for all wheeled transport to use.

3. Lieutenant General Popov's group has launched its offensive in cooperation with the 6th Army and 1st Guards Army.

The 3rd Tank Corps, overcoming a roadless region, attacked with two columns, and, by the end of the first day, the first column captured Verkhniaia Dubanka, and the smaller part of the force was fighting for Nizhniaia Dubanka.

The 57th Guards Rifle Division penetrated into the southeastern outskirts of Svatovo, while tying the enemy down along the Melovatka and Novo-Nikol'skoe line.

The 52nd Guards Rifle Division, after driving off up to a regiment of enemy infantry and 20 tanks, captured Novo-Aleksandrovka, Kaban'e, and Belosvitovka.

The 10th Tank Corps assisted the 35th Guards Rifle Division's attack with part of its forces and, following the infantry, advanced into the Novo-Krasnianka region, but did not enter the penetration.

The 18th Tank Corps fought with [enemy] infantry and tanks during the day and, after repelling several counterattacks and defeating the enemy, captured the villages of Smolianinova, Aleksandrovka, Purdovka, Zamulovka, Voevodovka, and Metelkin, and by evening part of the force was fighting for the bridge over the Northern Donets River at Proletarsk, while continuing its advance toward the Northern Donets River.

The 38th Guards Rifle Division captured Krymskaia, destroying up to a battalion of enemy infantry.

4. The 1st Guards Army, cooperating with Lieutenant General Popov's group of forces, continued to attack during the day with its right wing, while blockading Novo-Astrakhan', and, on its left wing, carried out a regrouping of forces and conducted an attack with part of its forces.

The 4th Guards Rifle Corps blockaded Novo-Astrakhan with part of the 41st Guards Rifle Division's forces, and its remaining forces, continuing their attacks, captured Bunchuzhnaia, Peschanoe, and Zhitlovka.

The 6th Guards Rifle Corps' forces, carrying out a regrouping, captured the large towns of Krymskaia, Slavianoserbsk, and Zheltoe on the right bank of the Northern Donets River, repelling all attempts by the enemy to restore the situation in that sector.

5. The forces on the 3rd Guards Army's right wing and in its center attacked during the day and, on its left wing, tied the enemy's resisting forces down with active operations. The 59th Guards Rifle Division, after penetrating the forward edge of the enemy's defense in the sector from Kruzhilovka to the unnamed lake (4 kilometer west of Nizhnii Grachinskii), repelled several counterattacks by 1–2 companies of enemy infantry and 8–13 tanks, reached the line through the eastern outskirts of Makarov Iar, 0.5 kilometers east of Khoroshilov, and Hill 162.0, and, continuing its attack, enveloped enemy strongpoints from the north and south.

The 14th Rifle Corps reached the line through Hill 153.0 (2 kilometers northeast of Ivanovka) and Hill 160.0 and was fighting to capture Ivanovka by the end of the day.

The 266th Rifle Division fought an unsuccessful battle for possession of Bol'shoi Sukhodol after encountering and repelling a counterattack by up to a regiment of enemy infantry from the direction of Malyi Sukhodol and Belen'kii Farm.

The 2nd Guards Tank Corps forced the Northern Donets River east of Kruzhilovka, reached the region 0.5 kilometers east of Il'evka by day's end, repelled a counterattack by 63 enemy tanks, and will continue to fulfill its assigned mission on the night of 31 January.

The 1st [Guards] Mechanized Corps entered the penetration at 1430 hours, captured Petrovka, and fought for Shirokii and Voroshilovsk by the end of the day.

The 2nd Tank Corps reached the northern outskirts of Ivanovka and will continue to fulfill its assigned mission during the night.

The 23rd Tank Corps was situated in the second echelon during the day and will be concentrated in the Davydo-Nikol'skoe region by morning, with the mission to sever the railroad line in the Krasnodonskaia-Verkhnii Duvannyi sector by the morning of 31 January.

Comrade Monakhov's group (the 60th Guards and 203rd Rifle Divisions) tied the enemy down in the Nizhnii Vishnevetskii and Kalitvenskaia sector by active operations. Its attack was unsuccessful, and, during the day, the enemy repulsed Group Monakhov's attack with repeated counterattacks by up to battalion and 10–18 tanks supported by 4–6 bombers. These counterattacks held up the entire army's offensive, and, while bringing reserves forward to the 3rd Army's right wing, the enemy tried to halt the offensive by our forces.

According to incomplete information, the enemy has suffered significant losses. Three 105mm, 3 75mm, and 2 small caliber guns, 30 carts, 5 automobiles, and 2 warehouses with ammunition were captured. No fewer than 1,500 enemy soldiers and officers, 28 tanks, 22 guns, 32 machine guns, 4 mortars, and 15 automobiles were destroyed. Four enemy aircraft were shot down. Our losses included 7 tanks.

6. The 5th Tank Army went over to the attack at 0850 hours on 30 January 1943. The army's forces, after advancing up to 2 kilometers in some sectors, reached the right bank of the Northern Donets River at a number of points, overcame stubborn resistance, and repelled a number of enemy infantry and tank counterattacks. Ten enemy tanks and armored vehicles were destroyed or burned, and up to 500 enemy soldiers and officers were destroyed.

The army's aircraft destroyed 60 automobiles, 6 tanks, 9 cargo trucks, and up to 400 soldiers and officers during the day of fighting. Three enemy aircraft were shot down in air combat.

7. A supplementary report will be sent concerning the 17th Air Army's operations.

8 The *front's* forces are continuing to fulfill their assigned missions.

Vatutin, Zheltov, Ivanov[94]

The armies of Vatutin's Southwestern Front recorded spectacular progress during early February, particularly on the *front's* left wing. Lieutenant General F. M. Kharitonov's 6th Army drove German forces back toward the Northern

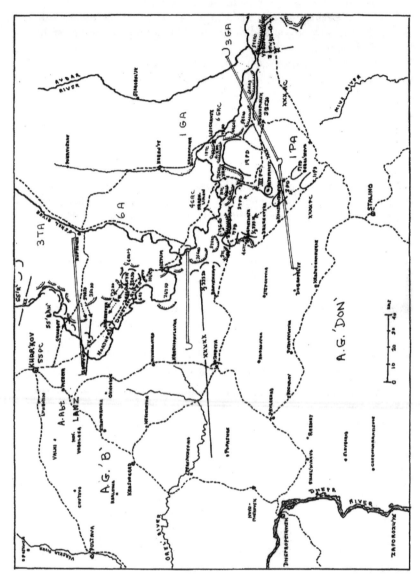

Map 40. The Donbas operation, the situation on 5 February 1943

Donets River south of Khar'kov, encircled the 320th and 290th Infantry Divisions, and seized bridgeheads across the river by 5 February (see Map 40). However, the two German divisions managed to extricate themselves from the trap and escape across the river. On the 1st Guards Army's right wing, the 4th Guards Rifle Corps and Mobile Group Popov also forced their way across the Northern Donets River and lunged southward into the Donbas region. Once south of the river, however, they became bogged down in heavy fighting for possession of the towns of Slaviansk, Kramatorskaia [Kramatorsk], and Artemovsk.

Manstein, whose Army Group "B" was about to be renamed Army Group South, struggled strenuously to contain and defeat Vatutin's offensive. Ultimately, the army group commander decided to withdraw his First Panzer Army, which was increasingly isolated in the Caucasus region, back to safety through the Rostov "gate," which the Fourth Panzer Army was barely holding open. In the meantime, Manstein ordered Army Detachment Hollidt to defend the sector from Voroshilovgrad along the bend in the Northern Donets River north of Rostov. Manstein's most pressing problem was to parry Vatutin's advance north and south of Voroshilovgrad. To do so, he quickly regrouped elements of the First Panzer Army's III Panzer Corps to contain Vatutin's attempt to envelop Voroshilovgrad. The III Panzer Corps was to anchor its defenses around Slaviansk and Artemovsk, while other forces stoutly resisted the Soviet forces driving on Voroshilovgrad from the east.

While Manstein regrouped his forces to defend the Donbas region, since the *Stavka* was disturbed over the slow progress of the right flank of Kuznetsov's 1st Guards Army and Lieutenant General D. D. Leliushenko's 3rd Guards Army in the Voroshilovgrad region, on 6 February Vatutin issued two orders that applied the whip to Kuznetsov's and Leliushenko's forces:

[The first order — to the 3rd and 1st Guards Armies]
I order:
While decisively fulfilling your assigned missions along the main axes, encircle and destroy the enemy's Voroshilovgrad grouping and capture Voroshilovgrad city and the adjacent region by the end of 7 February. To do so:

1. The 3rd Guards Army will capture Voroshilovgrad with part of its forces by enveloping Voroshilovgrad from the south and southwest and subsequently operate according to the plan.

2. The 1st Guards Army will assist the 3rd Guards Army in capturing Voroshilovgrad by enveloping the city of Voroshilovgrad from the northwest and west with the 58th Guards Rifle Division and will clear the enemy from the entire region north and northwest of Voroshilovgrad.

3. Report fulfillment by 2000 hours 7 February 1943 and by radio signal immediately after Voroshilovgrad falls.

Vatutin, Zheltov, Ivanov[95]

[The second order — to the 1st Guards Army]

1. Gagen's [4th Guards Rifle Corps] and Kulagin's [35th Rifle Division] actions merit all kinds of praise. Please thank them in my name. I attach

special importance to the capture of the Barvenkovo region, which they must hold on to very firmly.

2. In these circumstances I order:

The 1st Guards Army's forces will continue a swift offensive. In cooperation with Group Popov, capture Slaviansk, Konstantinovka, and Artemovsk on 7 February 1943.

Secure the Kamyshevakha and Kaganovichi Farm regions with part of your forces and cooperate with the 3rd Guards Army in the capture of Voroshilovgrad city. Capture the Lozovaia and Krasnoarmeiskoe regions by a decisive attack and reach the Orel'ka (25 kilometers west of Lozovaia), Slavianka, and Novo-Troitskoe (10 kilometers southwest of Krasnoarmeiskoe) front no later than 9 February 1943, while reliably protecting yourself against attacks from the Lozovaia and Krasnoarmeiskoe regions. Capture Debal'tsevo with part of the forces of [Major General I. P.] Alferov's [6th Guards Rifle Corps]. Eliminate the overextension of your corps' and divisions' combat formations as soon as possible by energetically bringing forward units lagging behind the forward edge. Prevent the artillery and multiple rocket launchers, ammunition, and fuel from lagging behind.

3. On the right, Kharitonov's [6th Army] forces will reach the Taranovka, Efremovka, and Orel'ka line simultaneously with your forces. The boundary line with [the 6th Army] will extend through Petrovka as before and further to Orel'ka (inclusive for the 1st Guards Army).

Group Popov, after capturing Konstantinovka and Artemovsk, will capture Krasnoarmeiskoe by the end of 8 February and, subsequently, will operate in accordance with the plan. You know the 3rd Guards Army's mission. The boundary line with [the 3rd Guards Army] will extend through Parizhskaia Kommuna as before and further to Debal'tsevo and Novo-Troitskoe (10 kilometers southwest of Krasnoarmeiskoe). Both points are inclusive for the 1st Guards Army.

4. Send your plans for fulfilling these missions and copies of your orders to me by 2200 hours 7 February 1943.

Vatutin, Zheltov, Ivanov[96]

Two days later, at a time when his forces were still well short of their initial objectives but while Vatutin was still optimistic about his prospects for success, at 2310 hours on 9 February, he once again reported to the *Stavka* about his *front's* forward progress (see Map 41):

I am reporting:

1. According to the information at hand, the enemy has begun withdrawing westward and northwestward from the Rostov and Shakhty regions. Sensing a mortal threat from Group Popov, the enemy is now concentrating his main efforts against Group Popov and the center of Kuznetsov's army, on the one hand, and, on the other, is offering stubborn resistance to Leliushenko's army. Units of the enemy's 6th, 7th, 11th, 19th, 27th, and 3rd Panzer Divisions have been identified along the

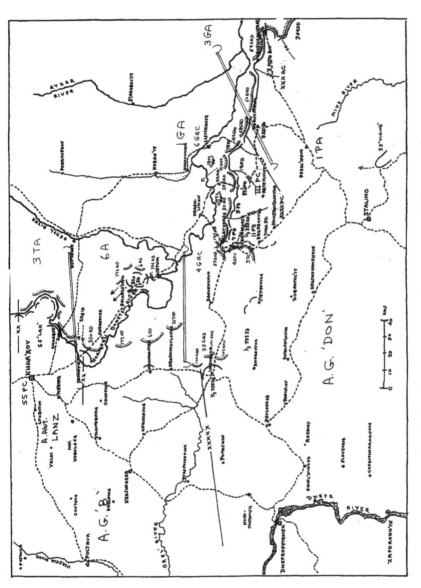

Map 41. The Donbas operation, the situation on 9 February 1943

Konstantinovka, Artemovsk, and Kaganovichi Farm front. Apparently, the enemy is bringing up to two infantry divisions forward to the Konstantinovka and Barvenkovo regions.

In addition, units of the enemy's 23rd Panzer Division and the 335th and 302nd Infantry Divisions, [the latter] recently-arrived from France, have been identified operating against Leliushenko's army in the Krasnodon region. The enemy has concentrated the main efforts of his aircraft against Group Popov.

2. In these circumstances I decided to envelop and cut off the enemy's routes west of Stalino and, at the same time, to continue my right wing's advance to the west and southwest and, simultaneously, during the same time frame, to prepare a strong mobile group for a deeper attack from the Krasnopavlovka and Lozovaia regions toward Pavlograd, Sinel'nikovo, Zaporozh'e, and Melitopol' to cut the enemy off from the crossings over the Dnepr River and prevent him from withdrawing to the west. Simultaneously, I must try to reach the Poltava, Kremenchug, and Dnepropetrovsk regions on my right wing and capture bridgeheads on the western bank of the Dnepr River along the Kremenchug, Krivoi Rog, and Kakhovka front.

On the left wing, when the mobile group reaches the Melitopol' region, I intend to reinforce it quickly, swiftly reach the lower course of the Dnepr River, and seize bridgeheads in the Crimea south of Perekop and Chongar.

To do so:

A. Group Popov, together with the 1st Guards Army, will capture Krasnoarmeiskoe, Konstantinovka, and Artemovsk and clear the enemy out of Slaviansk by the end of 11 February 1943. Subsequently, I will envelop the Stalino region from the west with the forces of Group Popov, after regrouping them closer to Krasnoarmeiskoe, and seize Volnovakha with part of its force. Simultaneously, I will attack through Gorlovka and Makeevka toward Stalino with the left wing of Kuznetsov's army and toward Stalino from the east with part of Leliushenko's army. Subsequently, the forces of Group Popov will seize Mariupol'.

Group Popov has already been reinforced with one tank brigade (the 9th) and one ski brigade, on 10 February yet another tank brigade (the 13th) will arrive, and two more ski brigades and, possibly, 152 reinforcing tanks will succeed in arriving by 12 February 1943.

Five rifle divisions, with reinforcing weapons from Kuznetsov's army, will operate with Group Popov during the fighting described above.

b. Kharitonov's 6th Army, which is already fighting along the Khar'kov-Lozovaia railroad line, will reach the Orel River line and capture Lozovaia by 1 February 1943 and, subsequently, will attack in the general direction of Krasnograd and reach the Poltava, Kremenchug, and Dnepropetrovsk regions. The 6th Army will be reinforced with no fewer than two divisions from those divisions approaching the railroad line and one RVGK [*Stavka* reserve] artillery division.

c. The 1st Guards Army, together with Group Popov, will capture the Slaviansk, Konstantinovka, and Artemovsk regions by 11 February 1943 and advance part of its forces to the Lozovaia and Krasnoarmeiskoe front (inclusive). Subsequently, the smaller part of the force, together with Group Popov and the 3rd Guards Army, will capture the Stalino region. The rest of the [army's] forces will swiftly reach the Dnepropetrovsk, Zaporozh'e, and Vasil'evka front and capture bridgeheads on the western bank of the Dnepr River.

d. Leliushenko's 3rd Guards Army will capture the Voroshilovgrad city region by the morning of 10 February 1943 and swiftly attack further toward Chistiakovo and Volnovakha and capture Stalino region with part of its forces. Subsequently, depending on the situation, it will advance toward the west.

e. The 5th Tank Army (consisting of five very small rifle divisions) will pursue the enemy toward Kamensk and Kuibyshevo and will later revert to the *front's* reserve.

f. A mobile group newly formed by me, consisting of the 1st Guards and 25th Tank and 1st Guards Cavalry Corps, four antitank artillery regiments, one antiaircraft artillery division, and the 1st Guards Army's 4th Guards Rifle Corps, must play the most important role by displaying the greatest mobility and great ardor while on the march. I have entrusted Lieutenant General Kharitonov with command of this group, and his deputy, Major General Firsov, will temporarily serve as the 6th Army's commander.

This group will be concentrated in the Krasnopavlovka and Lozovaia regions at approximately day's end on 16 February 1943, with the mission of attacking toward Pavlograd, Sinel'nikovo, Zaporozh'e, and Melitopol'.

This group will begin its attack on 17 February 1943 and reach the Melitopol' region at about day's end on 22 February 1943.

g. The seven approaching rifle divisions will advance by forced march from behind the *front's* right wing, and the two lead divisions will be included in the 6th Army.

3. No fewer than three tank corps and one cavalry corps (the 8th) will be allocated to the *front* reserve during the operation for routine replenishment.

I request you:

1. Approve the proposed operational plan.

2. Besides the reinforcements you have already assigned to the *front* (one RGK artillery division, one PVO division, a fighter-aviation corps, and

bombers), provide the *front* with three M–13 multiple rocket launcher regiments.

3. Issue enough tanks to fill out three tank corps.

Fedorov [Vatutin], Fomin [Zheltov], Ivanov[97]

The *Stavka*, however, was not yet prepared to approve fully the bold measures Vatutin proposed. Although Kharitonov's 6th Army had registered significant progress in its westward advance toward the Northern Donets River, the First Panzer Army's III Panzer Corps still held firmly to Slaviansk, Kramatorsk, and Artemovsk and, most important, Voroshilovgrad. While Vatutin focused his attention on a rapid advance westward toward Poltava, Kremenchug, and the Dnepr River, the *Stavka* was more concerned with seizing Voroshilovgrad, the Donbas region, and Mariupol' on the northern coast of the Sea of Azov. Therefore, after reviewing Vatutin's proposal, at 0405 hours on 11 February the *Stavka* directed Vatutin to scale back his intended objectives:

> Instead of the operational plan you suggested, it would be better to adopt another plan — with limited objectives, but better suited to the existing conditions. You should consider that Khar'kov has still not been taken by our forces. It is apparent that when Khar'kov is taken, we can broaden the plan.
>
> I propose you neither break up the 6th Army nor create Group Firsov but instead maintain the 6th Army in its present form, after reinforcing with several rifle divisions and one or two tank formations and the cavalry corps being sent to you.
>
> Assign the 6th Army the mission to occupy Sinel'nikovo reliably and then Zaporozh'e to prevent the enemy's forces from withdrawing to the western bank of the Dnepr through Dnepropetrovsk and Zaporozh'e.
>
> Do not assign the 6th Army any other missions, such as advancing on Kremenchug. Regarding the missions of Group Popov and the 1st Guards Army, they can remain accordance with your plan.
>
> The *front's* general mission in the immediate future is to prevent the enemy from withdrawing to Dnepropetrovsk and Zaporozh'e and to undertake all measures with the *front's* entire force to squeeze the enemy Donets group into the Crimea, to block the passages through Perekop and Sivash, and, thus, to isolate the enemy Donets group from its remaining forces in the Ukraine. Begin the operation as soon as possible.
>
> Send an information copy of your decision to the General Staff.
>
> Vasil'ev [Stalin], Bokov[98]

Three days later, after the forward elements of Kharitonov's 6th Army were well on their way to Zaporozh'e, the lead elements of Group Popov finally reached the Krasnoarmeiskoe region, and the 3rd Guards Army's 18th Rifle Corps began its assault on Voroshilovgrad, at 0200 hours on 14 February, Vatutin once again approached the *Stavka* with another proposal to expand his offensive:

> The enemy on the *front's* right wing, having concentrated up to one infantry division, presumably units of the 333rd and 298th Infantry Divisions, and 25–30 tanks in the Efremovka and Taranovka regions, is

holding on to the positions he occupies and is trying to conduct strong reconnaissance toward Novo-Beretskii Farm and Alekseevka.

Enemy attempts to counterattack toward Zanki Station were repulsed with heavy losses to his forces.

During the day the remnants of the 320th Infantry Division (400–500 soldiers) encircled in Liman tried several times to penetrate toward Zmiev. All of the enemy's attempts to escape from encirclement were repulsed. The fighting will go on until the enemy is completely destroyed.

As a result of fighting in the Balakleia region, the route from Ol'khovatka to Balakleia, Verbovka, and Andreevka is strewn with enemy bodies and destroyed equipment, horses, and supplies.

While holding on to his previous positions in the center, the enemy strove to dislodge our units from Krasnoarmeiskoe, Kramatorskaia, and Slaviansk by repeated fierce counterattacks with infantry and tanks. All counterattacks have been repelled.

Resisting stubbornly, the enemy facing the 3rd Guards Army's front is continuing to hold on to Voroshilovgrad, Semeikino, Samsonov, Vodianoi, and Malyi Sukhodol and is trying to halt the attacks by the 3rd Guards Army's forces by fires and counterattacks.

On the *front's* left wing, the [enemy's] main forces are continuing to withdraw toward the west, protected by rear guards units.

2. The 6th Army, while holding on to its previous positions, was preparing to resume its offensive on 13 February 1943 and was continuing to destroy the remnants of the smashed 320th Infantry Division in the Liman region with part of its forces.

After clearing the entire region from Savintsy to Liman of enemy, by day's end on 13 February 1943 [the army] was continuing to liquidate an encircled enemy grouping numbering up to 600 men with tanks and field artillery with part of its forces, and, in the Liman region, was holding on to its previous positions with its main forces, while repelling attacks by enemy reconnaissance groups.

3. On 13 February 1943, Comrade Popov's Group of Forces was fighting fierce battles with enemy tanks and infantry, while repelling numerous attacks. The group's units occupied [the following] positions at day's end:

— The 57th Rifle Division is continuing to fight on the northern and northwestern outskirts of Slaviansk, pushing the enemy towards the center of the town;

— The 3rd Tank Corps, repelling repeated attacks by enemy infantry and tanks from Krasnogorka, Veselyi, and Petrovka, continues to hold on to Kramatorskaia;

— The 10th Tank Corps was fighting in the vicinity of Hill 198 (5 kilometers north of Bylbasovka) throughout the day with enemy infantry and 30 tanks, which were trying to attack northward and westward to threaten the communications of Comrade Popov's Group of Forces;

— The 4th Guards Tank Corps, with the 9th Tank Brigade, while firmly holding on to Krasnoarmeiskoe, during the day repelled several fierce counterattacks by enemy tanks and infantry toward Grishino, Zverevo No.2, and Novo-Ekonomicheskoe. A group of tanks and three self-propelled [guns] penetrated from Novo-Ekonomicheskoe to the northern outskirts of Krasnoarmeiskoe. Fighting is underway to destroy the penetrating enemy group. An enemy force of more than a battalion captured Novo-Pavlovskaia and Chunishino Station by enveloping Chunishino Station from the east. The corps' units destroyed up to 2,000 enemy soldiers and officers during its seizure of Krasnoarmeiskoe. Ten trains with material, 20 guns, a train with 20 tanks, and several warehouses were seized. Antiaircraft artillery shot down six enemy aircraft on 11 and 12 February 1943. The corps destroyed up to 1,200 Germans and 300 Italians, took 200 prisoners, and seized 600 automobiles during combat on 12 February 1943. The positions of the remaining units of Comrade Popov's Group of Forces are unchanged.

4. On its right wing, the 1st Guards Army captured Orel'ka and Iur'evka by night operations on 13 February 1943 and, while holding on to Lozovaia and Barvenkovo, dug in along the positions it occupied.

In its center, while repelling repeated counterattacks by enemy infantry and tanks, [the army] is continuing fierce fighting for Slaviansk. The forces of the 41st Guards Rifle Division abandoned Bylbasovka on the night of 13 February and withdrew to the northern outskirts under pressure from repeated enemy counterattacks.

On its left wing, after resuming their attack toward Artemovsk, the army's forces encountered stubborn enemy resistance and, after repelling several counterattacks by infantry and tanks, captured the strongly fortified strong point at Berestovaia. In the process, it destroyed up to a battalion of enemy infantry. The army's units destroyed 650 enemy soldiers and officers and knocked out 8 tanks during the day.

5. During 13 February 1943, the 3rd Guards Army, while protecting its left wing along the Vodianoi (incl.), Malyi Sukhodol (incl.), and Popovka (incl.) line and further along the left bank of the Northern Donets River to Nizhnii Vishnevetskii, continued fierce offensive fighting with enemy motorcycles and tanks in the Krasnyi Iar, Chkalova State Farm, the eastern and southeastern outskirts of Voroshilovgrad, and the Debal'tsevo regions on its right wing.

During this fighting the army occupied the towns of Popovka, Andrianopol', Sofievka, Gorodishche, and Chernukhino and was fighting for possession of Krasnyi Iar, Chkalova State Farm, Voroshilovgrad, and west of Rozalinovka, west of Petrovka, and west of Znamenka [sic] at 1700 hours.

The 8th Cavalry Corps, while continuing to accomplish its mission, captured Andrianopol', Sofievka, Gorodishche, and Chernukhino and was fighting on the eastern outskirts of Debal'tsevo at 1300 hours.

The 2nd Guards Tank Corps, after completing its march to the Krivorozh'e and Brianskii regions, was fighting in the Uspenka and Kutserbovka regions at day's end.

The 14th Rifle Corps, while continuing to advance behind the 8th Cavalry Corps, approached Lutugino and Uspenka with the lead element of its 14th Guards Rifle Division at 1400 hours. The 61st Guards Rifle Division was at Grafirovka at 1000 hours.

The 50th Guards Rifle Division, after capturing Pervozvanovkaia, Suvorovskii, Orekhovskii, and Mikhailo-Lazarevskii, was continuing its advance toward Makedonovka.

The 1st Guards Mechanized Corps, while advancing on Parizhskaia Kommuna during the first half of the day, passed through Georgievskoe and was fighting with the enemy in the Uspenka region.

As a result of the day's fighting, the 203rd Rifle Division captured Gundorovskaia, Bol'shaia Kaminskaia, and Makar'ev.

According to far from complete information, during the day the army's forces destroyed more than 450 soldiers and officers, 5 tanks, 4 guns, and 20 enemy aircraft at the Voroshilovgrad airfield.

6. The 5th Tank Army, while destroying enemy rear guards along its entire front, captured the towns of Kamensk, Malaia Kamenka, Kosonogov, Podskel'nyi, Popovka Station, Severo-Donetskaia, Fedortsov, Verkhne-Goveinyi, Lavrov Station, Likhaia Station, Likhaia (northern and southern), Rudniko, Chicherina State Farm, Komissarovskii, Tatsin, Zamchalovo Station, Iasnyi, Zverevo, Mal. Zverevo, Russko-Prokhorovskii, and Vladimirskaia, after advancing from 12 to 30 kilometers during the day.

Reaching the Malaia Kamenka, Likhaia, and Zverevo line, the army completely cleared the Stalingrad-Likhaia railroad and the Millerovo-Rostov railroad in the Kamensk-Zverevo sector.

7. The 17th Air Army assisted the *front's* offensive by bombing and assault operations, bombed the Gorlovka airfield, the railroad junction at Debal'tsevo, and railroad trains carrying forces to Chunishino station (south of Krasnoarmeiskoe), conducted reconnaissance, and protected our forces. Incomplete data indicates it conducted 121 sorties, 27 of them at night. It destroyed or damaged 18 aircraft, 1 tank, 20 automobiles with cargo, 9 carts, and 3 railroad cars and dispersed or destroyed piecemeal up to a company of infantry. [Aircraft] detected a direct hit on the Debal'tsevo depot and a strong explosion in Gorlovka. Four air battles were conducted in which 4 enemy aircraft were shot down and 2 were destroyed. One FV–189 was destroyed in air combat on 12 February 1943.

Vatutin, Zheltov, Ivanov[99]

The forces of Vatutin's Southwestern Front captured Voroshilovgrad on 14 February, the same day as the Southern Front's forces captured Rostov. By this time, Vatutin's plan seemed to be developing beyond his wildest hopes (see Map 42). The 1st Guards Army's 4th Guards Rifle Corps and Popov's Mobile Group

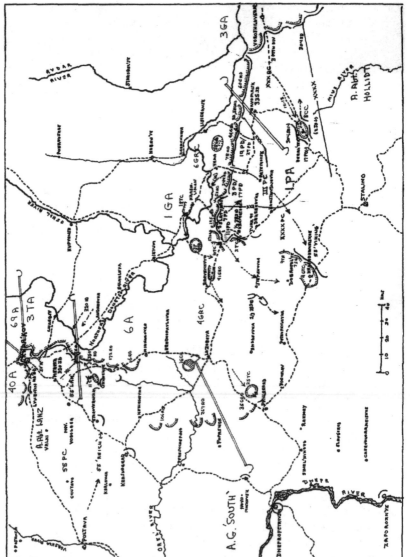

Map 42. The Donbas operation, the situation on 15 February 1943

were besieging Slaviansk and Kramatorsk, west of Voroshilovgrad, and Major General P. P. Poluboiarov's 4th Guards Tank Corps made a dash for and captured Krasnoarmeiskoe, which was astride the vital railroad line in the III Panzer Corps' rear, on 11 February. To the east, Leliushenko's 3rd Guards Army broke out of its bridgehead across the Northern Donets River south of Voroshilovgrad after 5 February and reached the eastern outskirts of the city on the 12th.

The Thrust to Debal'tsevo

At this point, Vatutin decided to employ an even large *front* mobile group to advance even deeper to the west in the 3rd Guards Army's sector, while Leliushenko's army was capturing Voroshilovgrad. The new mobile group consisted of Major General M. D. Borisov's 8th Cavalry Corps, which was already fighting in the southern suburbs of Voroshilovgrad on 12 February and was to spearhead the mobile group's advance on the city, and Major General V. M. Badanov's 2nd Guards Tank Corps, Major General I. N. Russianov's 1st Guards Mechanized Corps, and Major General F. E. Sheverdin's 14th Rifle Corps. As this mobile group advanced westward, Major General M. I. Zaporozhchenko's 18th Rifle Corps was to capture Voroshilovgrad city by attacking from the north, east, and southeast, supported the tanks from Major General A. F. Popov's 2nd Tank Corps. While Leliushenko's infantry fought for possession of Voroshilovgrad, Badanov's tank corps and Russianov's mechanized corps, spearheaded by Borisov's cavalry corps, were to advance rapidly westward and link up with Popov's mobile group at Stalino, thereby encircling all German forces between Artemovsk and Voroshilovgrad.

However, Leliushenko's 3rd Guards Army and its subordinate mobile group failed to accomplish the tasks Vatutin assigned to them. Borisov's 8th Cavalry Corps, which consisted of the 21st, 35th, and 112th Cavalry Divisions, the 148th Mortar Regiment, and the 263rd Cavalry Artillery and 8th Separate Antitank Battalions, succeeded in penetrating the Germans' defenses south of Voroshilovgrad in cooperation with the 18th Rifle Corps' 279th Rifle Division on the night of 7–8 February. Advancing rapidly to the southwest, it passed through the village of Rozalinovka, on the main road south of Voroshilovgrad, on the night of 9–10 February, where it wheeled to the southwest, heading thorough the open country along and south of the Debal'tsevo-Voroshilovgrad railroad line (see Map 43). Continuing its rapid advance, Borisov's cavalry captured the villages of Sofievka, Adrianopol', Gorodishche, and Chernukhino, and its lead elements reached the eastern outskirts of Debal'tsevo at nightfall on 13 February.[100]

Despite Borisov's spectacular advance, his supporting infantry and the mobile group's other tank and mechanized corps lagged far behind. By the time Borisov's cavalrymen reached Debal'tsevo, the 14th and 50th Guards Rifle Divisions, which were in the vanguard of the supporting 14th Guards Rifle Corps, were still trudging across the Voroshilovgrad-Kuibyshevo road over 60 kilometers to the rear. The 2nd Guards Tank and 1st Guards Mechanized Corps were still fighting to reach Uspenka, west of the road and more than 50 kilometers away from Borisov's cavalrymen, and, farther to the east, the remainder of the 3rd Guards and 5th Tank Armies were making barely perceptible progress in their advance south of the Northern Donets River.

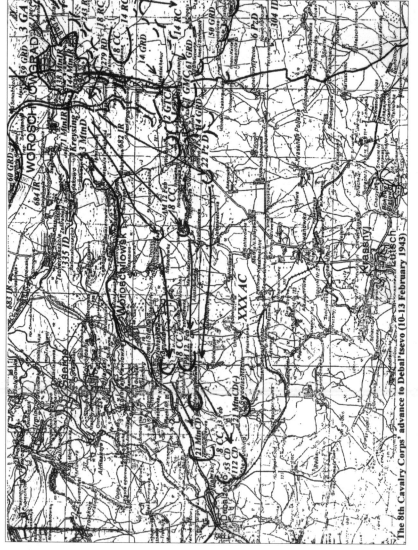

Map 43. The 8th Cavalry Corps' advance to Debal'tsevo, 10–13 February 1943

Determined to fulfill Borisov's mission, his cavalrymen attacked the Germans' defenses at Debal'tsevo on 14 February, but, although his forces briefly captured the town, German reinforcements forced them to withdraw to the town's eastern suburbs. Once it received Borisov's report, on the spot, the *Stavka* awarded his corps and its subordinate divisions with honorific "guards" status. With a stroke of the pen, the 8th Cavalry Corps became the 7th Guards Cavalry Corps and its 21st, 35th, and 112th Cavalry Divisions, the 14th, 15th, and 16th Guards Cavalry Divisions, respectively.

Although the Germans reacted swiftly to Borisov's deep thrust and recaptured most of the town and its surrounding extensive network of supply depots, they did so too late to undo the initial damage done to the town's installations. The raid on Debal'tsevo also contributed to the Germans' decision to abandon Voroshilovgrad and fall back to a new defense line further to the west. Just how far west this would have to be depended on whether German forces could recapture Debal'tsevo and isolate and destroy the marauding cavalry before reinforcements arrived. From Manstein's perspective, the far more serious issue was whether or not his army group's forces would be able to halt Vatutin's twin offensives toward Krasnoarmeiskoe and Debal'tsevo before the Southwestern Front's forces reached the Stalino region.

Manstein's Reaction

As the fighting raged on in the Debal'tsevo region and along the railroad line back to Voroshilovgrad, on 14 February Manstein began regrouping his forces to contain and eliminate the threat, a process only complicated by the necessity of arranging similar countermeasures in the Krasnoarmeiskoe region. The fact that Borisov's cavalry had struck the German defenses at the boundary between his First Panzer Army and Army Detachment Hollidt made the task of coordination that much more difficult. Initially, the First Panzer Army sent a *kampfgruppe* made up of elements of the 17th Panzer Division and the 335th Bicycle Battalion to Gorlovka, west of Debal'tsevo, with orders to sever the raiding cavalry's lines of communications. Together with local German reserves, this *kampfgruppe* managed to contain any further Soviet advance westward from Debal'tsevo on 15 February, but only barely. By day's end, German forces confined Borisov's cavalry into "a defensive perimeter encompassing Debal'tsevo, Chernukhino, and Gorodishche."[101]

Manstein, who was in the midst of reorganizing his forces to conduct a more extensive counterstroke against Vatutin's main shock group in the Krasnoarmeiskoe region, castled the headquarters of Colonel General Hermann Hoth's Fourth Panzer Army westward from the Rostov region to Zaporozh'e on the Dnepr River, recreated Hoth's army to fill the gap between his army group's left flank, where *Armeeabteilung* [Army detachment] Kempf was defending the Khar'kov region, and his center and right flank, where Colonel General Eberhard von Mackensen's First Panzer Army was defending the sector from Slaviansk eastward to Voroshilovgrad and *Armeeabteilung* Hollidt, the sector from Voroshilovgrad southward along the Mius River to the Sea of Azov. As a result of this regrouping, Manstein left the Fourth Panzer Army's XXXXVIII Panzer Corps behind in the eastern Donbas, assigned it to the First Panzer Army, and ordered it

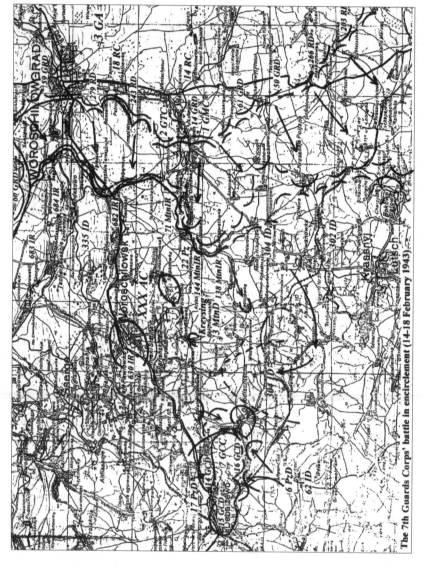

Map 44. The 7th Guards Cavalry Corps' battle in encirclement, 14-18 February 1943

to liquidate the Soviet cavalry threatening the Debal'tsevo region. At this time Lieutenant General of Panzer Troops Otto von Knobelsdorff's XXXXVIII Panzer Corps consisted of the 304th and 62nd Infantry and the 17th and 6th Panzer Divisions (the latter transferred from the First Panzer Army).

Since the 304th Infantry Division was defending a sector of the front southeast of Voroshilovgrad that was still intact, Knobelsdorff relied primarily on his 6th and 17th Panzer and 62nd Infantry Divisions to clear Borisov's cavalry from the Debal'tsevo region (see Map 44). His plan called for Major General Walter von Hünersdorff's 6th Panzer Division to attack Borisov's cavalry from the east and southeast and Lieutenant General Fidolin von Senger und Etterlin's 17th Panzer Division, supported by the 62nd and part of the 304th Infantry Divisions, to attack Borisov's cavalry from the Gorlovka region in the west. Along the previous front lines south of Voroshilovgrad, the 335th Infantry and 3rd Mountain Divisions, together with the remainder of the 304th Infantry Division, were to contain the follow-on Soviet mobile forces and restore the front lines somewhere east of Debal'tsevo. Knobelsdorff's *kampfgruppen* were to begin their counterattacks at dawn on 17 February.

The Battles for Krasnoarmeiskoe and Debal'tseco (15–23 February)

Altered Plans

As Manstein was formulating his plans to halt the menacing Soviet advance, Vatutin's appeals to the *Stavka* to permit the Southern Front to join his offensive were finally bearing fruit. After the Southern Front's forces captured Rostov on 14 February, the *Stavka* appointed Colonel General R. Ia. Malinovsky, then commander of the 2nd Guards Army, to command the *front* in place of Eremenko and ordered Malinovsky to accelerate his advance to reach and cross the Mius River as soon as possible. As a result, while Vatutin's mobile groups, specifically, Mobile Group Popov, the 3rd Guards Army's mobile group (the 8th Cavalry and the 2nd Guards Tank and 1st Guards Mechanized Corps), and the 1st Guards Army's mobile group (the 1st Guards Tank and 25th Tank Corps), were advancing into the Donbas from the north, Malinovsky's mobile groups were supposed to cross the Mius and invade the Donbas from the east. Therefore, the operations by Malinovsky's mobile groups, described in a separate section below, were an integral part of the *Stavka's* overall strategic plan for recapturing the Donbas region.

Emboldened by the two days of dizzying successes, at 1800 hours on 16 February, Vatutin whipped Leliushenko's 3rd Guards Army to accelerate its offensive, in particular, its lagging armored and mechanized forces:

> 1. The enemy is continuing his withdrawal in front of the 5th Tank Army and further south, trying to hold on to his previously-prepared positions along the Slaviansk, Artemovsk, Debal'tsevo, and Mius River line and tie down the forces of Group Popov and the 1st Guards Army as much as possible.

2. The forces of your army, with the exception of Zaporozhchenko's [18th Rifle Corps] and Borisov [7th Guards Cavalry Corps], are operating in incomprehensibly passive fashion, marking time in front of the enemy's separate rearguard detachments, and not fulfilling and even ignoring our orders, especially Badanov and Russianov [of the 2nd Guards Tank and 1st Guards Mechanized Corps], who are not only conducting themselves criminally and passively but are also whining and citing every objective reason to justify their inaction. And you, unfortunately, are listening to all of this quietly instead of using your strong will to compel the commanders of your formations to fulfill your orders and to supervise the fulfillment of these orders. As a result, you are permitting the enemy to complete his planned withdrawal and are not undertaking real measures to rescue the 8th Cavalry Corps, which has accomplished much but which may perish without your rapid support.

I order:

While continuing to operate within the spirit of the plan you submitted to me, you and your staff will personally organize the combat operations of the 2nd Guards Tank Corps, the 1st Guards Mechanized Corps, and the 14th Guards Rifle Corps in the Lutugino and Orekhovo regions. Encircle and destroy the enemy in the Uspenka and Ivanovka regions and, impetuously exploiting the 8th Cavalry Corps' success, quickly link up with it no later than 18 February 1943, capture the Debal'tsevo and Chistiakovo regions, and, subsequently, continue the offensive in the direction of Stalino.

Demand that your formation commanders attack energetically and cease marking time in place and conducting so-called "battles by fire." Warn Badanov, Russianov, and Sheverdin [of the 14th Guards Rifle Corps] in the strongest terms of severe punishment, including relief from their commands and being brought to trial, if they do not attack immediately. Demand your forces exert every effort to defeat the enemy and completely accomplish their missions.

Report all measures you have taken and copies of all orders you have given. Our forces occupied Khar'kov today.

Vatutin, Zheltov, Ivanov[102]

After scolding Leliushenko, but still brimming with optimism, at 1125 hours on 17 February, Vatutin submitted yet another plan to the *Stavka*, this time proposing his forces advance all the way to the Dnepr River:

In fulfillment of your [order] no. 30044 dated 11 February 1943, I have assigned the *front's* forces the following missions:

1. The 6th Army:

a. Attack toward the west with the forces of the 15th Rifle Corps (the 350th, 172nd, and 6th Rifle Divisions), the 267th Rifle Division, and the 106th Rifle Brigade and, since Khar'kov has been taken by our forces, capture the Krasnograd, Poltava, and Kremenchug regions and reach the Poltava and Kremenchug front with the forces indicated above by 23

February 1943 and conduct observation along the northern bank of the Dnepr River with part of your forces.

b. Capture Pavlograd by day's end on 18 February, Sinel'nikovo by day's end on 19 February, and Zaporozh'e by day's end on 20 February 1943 with the forces of the 1st Guards Tank Corps, 25th Tank Corps, 4th Guards Rifle Corps, three multiple rocket launcher battalions, three anti-tank artillery regiments, two howitzer artillery regiments, one gun artillery regiment, and six antiaircraft artillery regiments.

Further, while holding on to Pavlograd, Sinel'nikovo, and Zaporozh'e, seize Bol'shoi Tolmak and the railroad station at Fedorovka with part of your force and prevent the enemy from withdrawing across the Dnepr through Dnepropetrovsk, Zaporozh'e, and Nikopol' at all costs. Seize bridgeheads on the western bank of the Dnepr River in the Zaporozh'e region and to the north with part of your forces. If the circumstances are favorable, also seize Melitopol'.

This group of the 6th Army's forces will be supported by almost all of the *front's* aircraft and will be reinforced by yet another rifle division during the battle.

2. Group Popov:

Assemble the group's main forces in the Krasnoarmeiskoe, Krasnoarmeiskii Rudnik, and Bodropol'e regions.

Prevent an enemy penetration or withdrawal toward the west along the Slaviansk and Stalino front at all costs. Encircle and destroy the enemy's main forces (up to seven panzer divisions and several infantry divisions) in the Konstantinovka, Stalino, and Artemovsk regions, in cooperation with the units of the 3rd Guards and 1st Guards Armies. Seize Volnovakha with part of your force no later than 19 February 1943.

In the event the enemy begins to withdraw his main forces south of Stalino, prevent their withdrawal beyond the Dnepr through Zaporozh'e at all costs by conducting flanking attacks from the north and press the enemy toward the sea by means of a parallel pursuit, while cutting off his withdrawal routes to Zaporozh'e.

Group Popov has already received two separate tank brigades and three ski brigades.

3. The 1st Guards Army, less the 4th Guards Rifle Corps, consisting of a total of six rifle divisions (the 57th, 195th, 52nd, and 78th Rifle and the 44th and 58th Guards Rifle Divisions), with reinforcements:

a. Tie down the enemy along the Slaviansk and Krymskaia front with the forces of four rifle divisions and capture Slaviansk by the end of 18 February 1943.

b. Immediately move the remaining two rifle divisions by forced march toward Barvenkovo, Lozovaia, Gubinikha, and Petrikovka, 30 kilometers northwest of Dnepropetrovsk.

Reach the Petrikovka region by 25 February 1943. Subsequently, the 1st Guards Army's remaining divisions will move forward behind these two rifle divisions as soon as they are freed up from the Slaviansk and Krymskaia front.

The entire 1st Guards Army will be concentrated in the Shul'govka, Kolkhozovka, Chaplinka, and Petrikovka regions on about 1 March 1943. While doing so, the 1st Guards Army will be reinforced at the expense of the 3rd Guard Army and additional newly-arrived divisions so as to consist of up to 12 rifle divisions, reinforced by one RGK [*Stavka* reserve] artillery division and eight mortar regiments (formed on the basis of the 300 mortars already provided to you).

The army will be reinforced by the 1st Guards Cavalry Corps, which will be assembled by roughly 1 March, and, perhaps, by one tank corps.

After its concentration, the army must force the Dnepr River in cooperation with the *front's* other forces to fulfill the mission of securing bridgeheads on the Dnepr River's western bank, as I will explain below.

We cannot exclude the possibility that, as the armies are moving westward from Slaviansk, they will have to turn to the south to conduct flank attacks against the enemy if he succeeds in penetrating the Slaviansk and Konstantinovka front.

4. The 3rd Guards Army, attacking toward Debal'tsevo and Stalino in cooperation with the forces of Lieutenant General Popov's and the 1st Guards Army's groups, will encircle and destroy the enemy in the Donbas region.

Reach the Debal'tsevo and Chistiakovo front by day's end on 18 February 1943, capture the Stalino region by day's end on 22 February 1943, and, subsequently, swiftly develop your attack toward Zaporozh'e, while denying the enemy the opportunity to break contact and complete a planned withdrawal. When you reach the Debal'tsevo and Chistiakovo line, allocate two tank corps without equipment from the 3rd Guards Army to the *front's* reserve.

5. The 5th Tank Army, consisting of five rifle divisions and one tank corps, will swiftly continue its attack toward Roven'ki and Donetsko-Amvrosievka and reach the Ilovaisk, Kuteinikovo, and Tsybulianovka front by 20 February.

Subsequently, attack impetuously along the Orekhov and Bol'shoi Tokmak front and, if the boundary line with the Southern Front is moved to the north, then the 5th Tank Army will be gradually withdrawn into the *front's* reserve for replenishment and castling to the main axis.

6. The *front's* air forces will primarily assist the 6th Army and Group Popov.

Regarding the seizure of bridgeheads on the western bank of the Dnepr River, I am providing you with the following [guidance]: this mission is exceptionally important and must be fulfilled now, quickly and at any price, in order to disrupt the enemy's intentions and plans to organize a [new] front and defenses along the western bank of the Dnepr River.

Now the enemy still does not have sufficient forces to occupy positions along the Dnepr River; however, engineer forces and the local population are preparing entrenchments and, according to our information, he is transferring his forces by aircraft from the North Caucasus to the Zaporozh'e region, and he is bringing forces by rail to the Zaporozh'e region from the Crimea.

As they conduct operation to secure these bridgeheads, our forces must reach the Kremenchug, Krivoi Rog, and Kherson front and, if the conditions are favorable, the Kirovograd and Nikolaev front.

In any event, an air base must be seized in the Kirovograd region. I have entrusted fulfillment of this mission to the 1st Guards Army, as constituted above, which will concentrate in the Shul'govka, Petrikovka, and Chaplinka regions, with the mission of forcing the Dnepr River in the Verkhne-Dneprovsk and Dneprodzerzhinsk sector, after which it will exploit its success toward Krivoi Rog and to Dnepropetrovsk and Zaporozh'e with part of its forces.

I will conduct another strong attack with the mobile formations and the 4th Guards Rifle Corps and, if they manage to move forward, with Leliushenko's forces from the Zaporozh'e and Nikopol' sector toward Krivoi Rog and with part of his force toward Dnepropetrovsk.

The 1st Guards Cavalry Corps will be employed along the 1st Guards Army's axis.

The 6th Army will be reinforced with three divisions, which must force the Dnepr River in the Mishen'ka region, 40 kilometers southeast of Kremenchug, for operations toward Krivoi Rog.

Special attention will be paid to engineer, aviation, and artillery support.

I am reporting to you about my plan to seize the bridgehead because this will require a considerable amount of preparatory work. In particular, considerable time will be spent concentrating the forces, and it is necessary to do so now so in order to complete all of the preparations by 1 March 1943 and begin the work during the first few days [of March].

By this time the floods [*rasputitsa*] may already be beginning; however, the engineer services and forces must be prepared to cope with forcing the river during the flood period, since we cannot give the enemy time.

Air assault formations could play a great role in the operation to seize the bridgehead. Unfortunately, the seven rifle divisions and the 1st Guards Cavalry Corps, which are arriving by railroad, are late.

I request [you]:

1. Approve the plan described above for Kharitonov's operations and the proposal for the conduct of an operation to seize the bridgehead.

2. If possible, provide air assault formations to the Southwestern Front.

3. Accelerate the movement of trains with newly arriving formations for the Southwestern Front.

Map 45. The *Stavka's* concept for the Donbas operation, February 1943

4. Hasten the dispatch of tanks to the Southwestern Front to replenish the tank army.

Fedorov [Vatutin], Fomin [Zheltov], Ivanov[103]

Encouraged by Vatutin's report, Stalin immediately approved his plan (see Map 45):

I approve your operational plan, which the *Stavka* received today. While doing so, I request you take into account my remarks about the missions of the 6th Army, which I expressed in a telephone conversation with you on the matters concerning operation "Gallop" [*Skachok*].[104]

Vasil'ev [Stalin], Bokov[105]

The Advance Falters

As Vatutin's forces resumed their offensive, his chief of staff, Ivanov, dispatched another progress report to the *Stavka* at 2400 hours on 18 February:

1. The enemy on the right wing of the *front* is continuing to withdraw slowly toward the west, protected by rear guards. In the central sector of the *front*, the enemy, in his previous configuration and grouping, is continuing to resist our attacking forces stubbornly, particularly, along the Belogorovka, Kamyshevakha, Orekhovo, Krasnogorovka, Petroven'ki, Khoroshee, Cherkasskoe, and Sukhodol' line and in the Debal'tsevo region. On the left wing, he is continuing to withdraw toward the west, fighting rear guard actions.

2. The 6th Army continued to develop its attacks toward the southwest on 18 February 1943. The army's units captured Riabukhino, Semenovka, Sharlaevka, Pisarevka, Andreevka (Kokhanovka), Dmitrovka (Skotovaia), and Znamenka by 1000 hours on 18 February 1943 and were continuing to fight for possession of Okhochae, Lozovaia (7 kilometers west of Efremovka), and Par-Shchliakhovaia, with [its] forward detachments at Marker 201 (southwest of Riabukhino), in Andreevka (Kokhanovka), and on the western outskirts of Orlovshchina. The positions of the army's units at day's end are not yet confirmed.

No new information has been received about the 106th Rifle Brigade's and 267th Rifle Division's positions.

3. Comrade Popov's Group of Forces continued to fight intense battles with enemy motorized infantry and tanks throughout the day on 18 February 1943 while holding firmly to Kramatorskaia, Krasnoarmeiskii Rudnik, and Krasnoarmeiskoe.

The 10th Tank Corps captured Verevka with one brigade, and another brigade was fighting for Krivorozh'e (west of Krasnoarmeiskii Rudnik). The positions of the remaining units are unchanged.

The 18th Tank Corps captured Mikhailovka and Lavrovka and cleared the enemy from the Cherkasskoe-Oktiabr'skii road.

The 57th Guards Rifle Division, after capturing Andreevka, linked up with the 3rd Tank Corps' forward detachments and advanced into the Kramatorskaia region.

The positions of the remaining units are essentially unchanged.

4. The 1st Guards Army, having repulsed several small enemy counterattacks, on 18 February 1943 fortified the positions it occupied and conducted reconnaissance and, on its left wing, conducted a regrouping and relieved units for replenishment and future missions.

The 4th Guards Rifle Corps (the 35th and 41st Guards and 244th Rifle Divisions) was transferred to the 6th Army.

5. The 3rd Guards Army, overcoming stubborn enemy resistance, continued to develop its offensive toward the southwest on 18 February 1943, encircling and destroying the remnants of the enemy's Voroshilovgrad grouping.

During this fighting the units on the army's left wing occupied up to 25 towns and villages and, having advanced up to 10 kilometers during the day, were fighting along the Krinichnyi, Petroven'ki, Cherkasskoe, Sukhodol, Sabovka, Veselaia Tarasovka (all points inclusive), Sbornaia Station, Kalinin State Farm, Ushakovka, Vodino, Uspenka, Kruglik, Krasnaia Poliana, Kolpakovo, Shchetovo Station, and Fominovka line by day's end on 18 February 1943.

The 7th Guards [former 8th] Cavalry Corps is continuing to fight fierce battles on the eastern outskirts of Debal'tsevo. A detachment (12 tanks and 120 men) sent out to link up with the 7th Guards Cavalry Corps was fighting in the Fedorovka region (northwest of Ivanovka) on the night of 18 February 1943.

6. The 5th Tank Army continued to develop its offensive on 18 February 1943, pressing the enemy back toward the Mius River. The army's units reached the Verkhnii Nagol'chik, Nizhnii Nagol'chik, D'iakovo, Novaia Nadezhda, and Zhelobok line by day's end and are continuing their offensive toward Dmitrievka and Kuibyshevo. The army advanced from 10 to 15 kilometers during the day and occupied 15 populated points. Three enemy tanks were destroyed in the battle for D'iakovo.

7. The 17th Air Army bombed the railroad center and enemy forces in the Artemovsk and Kaganovichi State Farm regions during night operations.

34 aircraft sorties were conducted, and 6 hits were noted against stationary targets and 2 direct hits on the main railroad line. The army's units did not carry out combat operations on 18 February 1943 because of the unfavorable weather conditions.

Fedorov and Fomin are located with the 3rd Guards Army.

Ivanov[106]

It was clear to Vatutin by the evening of 18 February that the 7th Guards Cavalry Corps would have to fight for its very survival. Reports from Borisov's headquarters indicated that German forces began attacking his beleaguered cavalrymen from three different directions on 17 February. Although his 15th and 16th

Guards Cavalry Divisions clung grimly to the village of Chernukhino, 5 miles east of Debal'tsevo, and the eastern outskirts of Debal'tsevo against intensifying enemy attacks, his 14th Guards Cavalry Division, whose forces were now separated into two parts, held on to part of the village of Gorodishche, 6 miles east of Chernukhino, and sagging perimeter defenses along the railroad line 8 miles northeast of Debal'tsevo.

On 17 February a *kampfgruppe* from Senger und Etterlin's 17th Panzer Division, with 40 tanks, recaptured Baronskii Station, Demchenko State Farm, and the village of Sofievka from the 14th Guards Cavalry Division by the evening, and a smaller *kampfgruppe* from Hünersdorff's 6th Panzer Division captured Gorodishche and then moved north to link up with the 17th Panzer's *kampfgruppe* the following day. With his cavalry corps now virtually surrounded, Borisov had no choice but to form a hedgehog defense around the village of Chernukhino and wait for promised relief, while his supply of fuel and ammunition steadily dwindled. In the meantime, the forces of the 3rd Guards and 5th Tank Armies probed German defenses to the east, but the former made only limited progress in the Krasnaia Poliana sector and the latter equally slow progress in the Nizhnii Nagol'chik region to the south.

The stubborn German resistance and diminishing offensive gains on his *front's* left wing prompted Vatutin to renew his emphasis on Mobile Group Popov's operations. As a result, at 1145 hours on 19 February, the *front* commander ordered Popov "to encircle and destroy the enemy in the Krasnoarmeiskoe region and fully restore the situation. Prevent the enemy from withdrawing to the west at all costs. Report fulfillment every two hours. Our forces have occupied Sinel'nikovo."[107] However, the day before Vatutin sent this message, Manstein's forces had already begun attacking Popov's forces, which by now were semi-isolated in the Krasnoarmeiskoe region. By late on 19 February, the intensity of these assaults indicates they were far too strong to be merely local counterattacks (see Map 46). Therefore, at 1110 hours on 20 February, Vatutin dispatched the first of many increasingly frantic orders to General Popov, evidencing the *front* commander's increasing concern: "Immediately radio me about the situation in the Krasnoarmeiskoe region and all of the measures you have taken. I confirm, restore the situation, destroy the enemy, and prevent him from withdrawing toward the west. Subsequently, carry out your mission in accordance with my orders. Accelerate the advance by Bakharov [18th Tank Corps commander] and your other commanders."[108] At the same time he radioed Kharitonov's 6th Army:

> Popov temporarily abandoned the Krasnoarmeiskoe region and is withdrawing toward north, thus opening the enemy's withdrawal routes to Dnepropetrovsk. Popov has been sharply censured for this action, and he has been ordered once again to take up positions in the Krasnoarmeiskoe region on the enemy's routes of withdrawal by the morning of 21 February 1943. However, I cannot exclude the possibility that part of the enemy's forces will slip through along the route toward Dnepropetrovsk.
>
> Take measures to destroy this enemy and in no circumstances allow him to withdraw beyond the Dnepr River. To this end, conduct deep reconnaissance to the east, sever all possible enemy routes of withdrawal, and destroy him with fire and skillful and decisive attacks by our shock

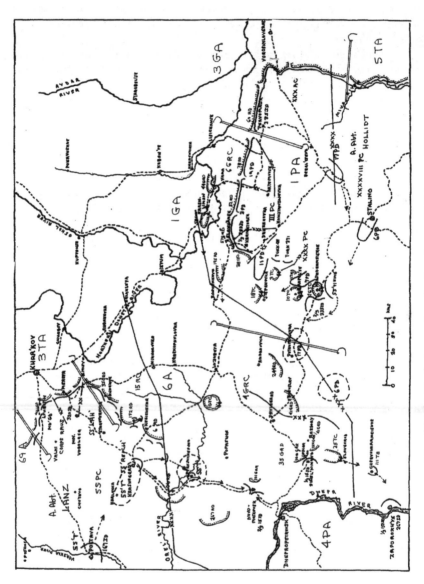

Map 46. The Donbas operation, the situation on 20 February 1943

groups. Move all of your remaining forces, especially Kukushkin [1st Guards Tank Corps], forward energetically.

Vatutin, Zheltov, Ivanov[109]

Despite the disconcerting news from the front, as indicated by the Southwestern Front's daily intelligence summary for 20 February, the *Stavka's* and the Southwestern Front's intelligence organs remained supremely confident victory was just around the corner:

> The enemy operating in front of the Southwestern Front fought sustained defensive battles during the period from 10 to 20 February 1943, trying to hold on to control of the territory of the Donets Basin.
>
> On the *front's* right wing (the Krasnograd axis), lacking sufficient forces with which to resist the offensive by our forces, the enemy withdrew westward and southwestward through 19 February 1943.
>
> Simultaneously, since 17 February [he] began concentrating new tank formations (the SS Panzer Divisions "*Grossdeutschland*," "Adolph Hitler," and "*Reich*" and the 17th Panzer Division) for the purpose of attacking to liquidate the penetration and free up his communications for the withdrawal of forces from the territory of the Donbas across the Dnepr. In the central sector of the front — Slaviansk and Voroshilovgrad, the enemy waged fierce defensive fighting all ten days, striving to prevent our forces from reaching the rear of his fortified line along the Mius River. On the left wing, beginning on 11 February, he withdrew the forces of his Shakhtinsk grouping to the 1941–42 defensive positions along the western bank of the Mius River without offering serious resistance.
>
> The enemy in the Krasnoarmeiskoe and Debal'tsevo regions tried to their utmost to destroy our mobile forces and free up their communications so they could withdraw their forces. As a result of the ten days of fighting on the *front's* wings, the enemy was forced to abandon a large amount of territory with a great number of large population points. In the fighting the German 320th Infantry Division, 617th and 619th Training Regiments, and 298th Infantry Division were almost completely routed. The 335th Infantry Division, the 302nd Infantry Division, and a whole range of separate specialized and march units suffered a serious defeat.

I. Enemy Actions

A. The Krasnograd axis. The enemy on the right wing of the axis, after being driven back to the Liman, Nizhne-Rus, Bishki, Verkhnie Bishki, Alekseevka, Mironovskoe (16 kilometers southwest of Alekseevka), Ligovka, Orel'ka, and Lozovaia line by 10 February, is stubbornly resisting the offensive by our forces with units of the 298th Infantry Division, the 1st SS Regiment of SS Division "Adolph Hitler," the 193rd and 393rd Assault Gun Battalions, and various specialized and rear service subunits.

The forces of the 320th Infantry Division, reinforced by subunits of the 617th and 619th Training Regiments, were fighting in encirclement in the Balakleia, Borshchevoe, and Verbovka regions.

The 320th Infantry Division was completely crushed as a result of the fighting from 11 through 14 February, losing up to 4,000 soldiers and officers killed. The division's remnants, numbering up to 2,500 men, fought their way to the Zmiev region by February 15, but were dislodged from this region on 16 February 1943.

Along the Alekseevka axis, units of the 298th Infantry Division, the 193rd and 393rd Assault Gun Battalions, and the SS "Adolph Hitler" Division's 1st SS Regiment held up the advance by our forces until 16 February but were also forced to withdraw toward the northwest and were fighting along a line from west of Riabukhino and Okhochae through Staroverovka, Tsiglerovka, and Kegichevka by day's end on 19 February. Along the Pereshchepino, Novo-Moskovsk, and Pavlograd axis, the enemy, lacking close operational reserves to oppose the offensive of our forces, offered weak resistance with separate police and gendarme detachments and, up to 18 February, hurriedly withdrew toward the southwest and was thrown back to the Buzovka (25 kilometers northwest of Pereshchepino), Magdalinovka, Novo-Moskovsk, and Razdory (13 kilometers east of Sinel'nikovo) line. Simultaneously, in order to liquidate the threat of the Red Army's forces encircling his Donbas grouping, the enemy began to concentrate large tank forces along the flanks of the penetration during the second half of the ten-day period, with the further objective of a concentric attack to liquidate it. To this end he withdrew all of his SS panzer divisions ("Adolph Hitler," "*Grossdeutschland*," and "*Reich*") from the Khar'kov axis and transferred them to the Krasnograd, Pereshchepino, and Novo-Moskovsk regions. The 17th Panzer Division, transferred from the Southern Front, was concentrated in the Vasil'kova region.

B. The Krasnoarmeiskoe axis. The enemy has directed his main efforts along the Krasnoarmeiskoe axis during the last 10 days at liquidating the groups of our forces that have penetrated into the Krasnoarmeiskoe region and to defending the Slaviansk region. In the Krasnoarmeiskoe region, since 14 February the enemy has been trying to capture the town and clear the main Avdeevka-Sinel'nikovo railroad line with bitter attacks by units of the SS Division "*Wiking*," the 333rd Infantry Division, and a whole series of other units and subunits so that he can transport his forces from the Donbas to the west. As a result of sustained fighting, the enemy succeeded in driving our units from the town and extended combat operations into the Dobropol'e, Krasnoarmeiskii Rudnik, and Stepanovka regions by 20 February.

In the Slaviansk region, the enemy engaged in stubborn defensive fighting until 17 February, holding up the advance by our forces with an unyielding defense in previously prepared positions and by relying on urban fortifications designed for prolonged defense. Attacks by our forces drove the enemy units defending Slaviansk away from the town's lines on 17 February and threw them back to the Belen'koe, Nikonorovka, and Orekhovatka line, where they halted the further advance of our *front's* forces on 20 February. The enemy held on to the positions he occupied in the Nikiforovka, Nikolaevka, Berestovaia, Gorskoe, and Zhelobok sector with fire and local counterattacks during the entire ten-day period, while protecting the withdrawal of the forces of his Shakhtinsk grouping.

C. The Ordzhonikidze axis. From 10 through 13 February, the enemy conducted sustained defensive fighting in the Voroshilovgrad region and to the south with the units of the 335th Infantry Division, subunits of the 620th Infantry Training Regiment and 144th Mountain Infantry Regiment, and several march [replacement] and specialized battalions, while striving to throw our attacking units back with repeated counterattacks.

At a cost of heavy losses, by 13 February the enemy succeeded in pressing our units back from positions at Davydovka State Farm to a line through the populated points of Rozalinovka and Petrovka and Voroshilovo State Farm. Subunits of the 144th Mountain Infantry Regiment, units of the 6th Panzer Division, and subunits of the 321st March [Replacement] Battalion were defeated in the Lysyi, Novo-Svetlovka, Beloskelevatyi, Orlovka, and Popovka regions, and their remnants were thrown back toward the west and southwest on 12 and 13 February.

Along the Samsonov, Popovka, and Gundorovaia line, units of the 6th Panzer Division, remnants of the 304th Infantry Division, units of the 302nd Infantry Division, and specialized march battalions held up the advance of our forces until 13 February.

After fierce fighting, the enemy was driven back from Voroshilovgrad and a number of populated points north and south of Voroshilovgrad during the second half of 14 February. By day's end [the enemy] was fighting along the Zheltoe, Zemlianoi, *Metallist* [Metal Workers] State Farm, Davydovka State Farm, and Hill 220.5 (4 kilometers north of Uspenka) line.

The enemy units defending the Krasnoe, Semeikino, Samsonov, Vodianoi, Malyi Sukhodol, and Belen'kii line were thrown back toward the south and southwest by the end of 14 February and were fighting along the Orekhovka (12 kilometers northwest of Semeikino), Rosa Luxemburg State Farm, Krasnyi Iar, Novaia Aleksandrovka, Shevyrevka, Verkhnee Sorokino (incl.), and Verkhniaia Gerasimovka line.

From 15 through 20 February, the enemy continued to withdraw slowly to the west along the entire front of this axis, retarding the advance of our forces with fires and numerous counterattacks. As a result of the fighting, the enemy was driven back to a line from Zhelobok (incl.) through Khoroshee, Cherkasskoe, Sukhodol, Beloe, and Kamyshevakha, west of Illiriia and Elizavetovka, and through Shterovka (incl.) to Bokovo-Platovo by 20 February, where he halted the further advance by our units.

In the Komissarovka region northeast of Debal'tsevo and Chernukhino, the enemy conducted active combat operations from 14 through 20 February to destroy the mobile group of our forces which had penetrated into this region.

D. The Chistiakovskoe axis. Along the Chistiakovskoe axis, the enemy withdrew the units of his 306th and 294th Infantry and 22nd Panzer Divisions and subunits of several specialized and march battalions westward beyond the Mius River from 11 through 20 February without offering serious resistance, while destroying railroad installations, blowing up warehouses, and carrying off with him all males capable of work during the withdrawal.

The enemy halted the advance by our forces by 20 February in previously prepared defensive positions along the Bokovo-Antratsit, Esaulovka, and Glubokaia Balka line and further along the western bank of the Mius River to Skelianskii.

II. The Grouping of the Enemy in Front of the Southwestern Front on 20 February 1943

All types of reconnaissance and force combat activities have established that a total of up to 17 enemy divisions, 6 separate regiments, and 15–18 separate battalions, whose overall combat strength has been determined to be [as follows], are operating in front of the *front* on 20 February 1943:

1. Soldiers and officers	135,000–136,000
2. Machine guns	4,570
3. Antitank guns	620
4. Field guns	660–700
5. Mortars	1,210
6. Tanks	460

Of these, [the following] are identified:

1. Infantry divisions (German) – 7 (the 294th, 298th, 302nd, 304th, 306th, 320th, 333rd, and 335th Infantry Divisions).

2. Panzer divisions – 8 (the 3rd, 6th, 7th, 11th, 19th, and 27th Panzer Divisions, and SS Panzer Division "*Wiking*")

3. Separate regiments –the SS "Adolf Hitler" Division's 1st Motorized Regiment, the 620th Infantry Training Regiment, the 162nd Infantry Division's 314th Infantry Regiment (requires confirmation), the 3rd Mountain Infantry Division's 144th Mountain Infantry Regiment, the 901st Panzer Training Regiment, and an unidentified regiment.

4. Separate battalions – the 1st, 2nd, 313th, 314th, 427th, 8th, and 100th March Battalions, operating as independent entities, the 200th Reserve Assault Battalion, the 193rd and 393rd Assault Gun Battalions, the "Eisenach," "Gol'dringer," and 27th Latvian Battalions, and 3–4 police and gendarme battalions.

The Grouping of the Enemy's Formations and Units

A. The Krasnograd axis. The following enemy units are operating along the Riabukhino (west of Taranovka), Krasnograd, Pereshchepino, Novo-Moskovsk, and Sinel'nikovo front: the remnants of the 320th and 298th Infantry Divisions, the SS Division "Adolph Hitler's" 1st Regiment, the 193rd and 393rd Assault Gun Battalions, up to an infantry division (identity unknown), and up to two mixed police battalions. By 20 February the main mass of all of the enumerated forces was grouped along a line from west of Riabukhino and Okhochae through Melikhovka, Paras'koveia, Vlasovka, and Tsiglerovka (the remnants of the 320th Infantry Division, units of the 298th Infantry Division, the remnants of the destroyed 1st Regiment of the SS Division "Adolf Hitler," and the remnants of the 193rd and 393rd Assault Battalions) and in the Novo-Moskovsk region (the unnamed infantry division, up to a battalion of gendarmes, and separate rear service units that do not represent any sort of serious force). By 20 February the enemy did not have any sort of forces capable of organized resistance to the advance of our forces in the sector from west of Krasnograd through Buzovka (25 kilometers northwest of Pereshchepino), Magdalinovka, and Korneevka (northwest of Novo-Moskovsk).

Lacking operational reserves, on 18 February the enemy began assembling all kinds of mixed units, hastily formed from rear service and specialized units, along the Krasnograd axis.

B. The Krasnoarmeiskoe axis. On 20 February the enemy concentrated units of the 3rd, 7th, 11th, 19th, and 27th Panzer Divisions, the SS Panzer Division "*Wiking*," the 333rd Infantry Division, the 162nd Infantry Division's 314th Infantry Regiment, the "Hamburg" Special-Designation Battalion, the 1st and 2nd Special Designation Battalions, the 232nd Assault Gun Battalion, 2–3 police and gendarme battalions, and various rear service and specialized subunits of the 9th, 50th, and 96th Infantry Divisions (requires confirmation) in the Krasnoarmeiskoe region and along the Sergeevka (northwest of Kramatorsk), Krasnogorovka (south of Kramatorsk), Malinovka, Bondarnoe, Nikolaevka (15 kilometers northeast of Artemovsk), Belogorovka, and Gorskoe line. On 18 February the enemy unloaded units newly arrived in that region at Mezhevaia and Udachnaia Stations (both west of Krasnoarmeiskoe). Up to a regiment of infantry with 30 antitank guns were unloaded at these stations on 18 February.

The enemy forces along the Krasnoarmeiskoe axis are grouped as follows. Up to 12 battalions, 20 artillery batteries, and 50 tanks from the SS Division "*Wiking*," the 333rd Infantry Division, the 162nd Infantry Division's 314th Infantry Regiment, rear service and specialized subunits of the 9th, 50th, and 96th Infantry Divisions, and up to a regiment (unnamed), which unloaded on 18 February at Mezhevaia and Udachnaia Stations, are operating in the Krasnoarmeiskoe and Dobropol'e region. Of the entire enemy grouping in the Krasnoarmeiskoe region – up to 5 battalions with 15–20 tanks are operating along the Roksha and Shidlovka line, attacking toward

Krasnoarmeiskoe from the north. Up to 4 battalions with 10–12 tanks are attacking toward the northeastern outskirts of the town, up to 3 battalions are attacking from the south, and up to 3 battalions from the west.

According to unverified data, the presence of the 620th Grenadier Training Regiment, which arrived from the region west of Voroshilovgrad, has been noted in the Krasnoarmeiskoe region.

On 20 February the remnants of defeated units of the 7th Panzer Division (the 25th Panzer Regiment), the 1st and 2nd Special Designation Battalions, and up to two police and gendarme battalions were continuing to withdraw from the Slaviansk region. Part of the forces from the Slaviansk grouping withdrew southwestward toward Shabel'kovka and Sergeevka and the main mass toward Artemovsk. The exact location of the enemy forces withdrawing from Slaviansk has not been determined by 20 February.

Units of the 3rd and 11th Panzer Divisions are operating in the Kramatorsk, Malinovka, Bondarnoe, and Nikolaevka sectors.

Units of the German 27th and 19th Panzer Divisions, an unnamed special designation battalion, and the 27th Latvian Battalion are defending along the Nikolaevka, Belogorovka, Kamyshevakha, Gorskoe, and Zhelobok front.

C. The Ordzhonikidze axis. Units of the 335th and 302nd Infantry Divisions, the remnants of the 304th Infantry Division, the 22nd and 6th Panzer Divisions, the 3rd Mountain Infantry Division's 144th Mountain Infantry Regiment, the 620th Infantry Training Regiment, a mixed battalion of the 62nd Infantry Division, and the "Eisenach," "Gol'dringer," and 5th, 313th, 314th, 321st, and 417th March Battalions have been detected operating along the Zhelobok (8 kilometers southeast of Nizhnee), Khoroshee, Cherkasskoe, Sukhodol, Rodakovo, Beloe, Ivanovka, Orlovka, Kolpakovo Station, Kolpakovo, and Bokovo-Platovo front (incl.).

By 20 February the enemy's units were occupying the following positions: the 335th Infantry Division's 683rd and 684th Infantry Regiments, specialized subunits of the 335th Infantry Division, a mixed battalion of the 62nd Infantry Division's remnants, the "Gol'dringer" Battalion, and, presumably, units of the German 7th Panzer Division along the Zhelobok, Khoroshee, and Sukhodol line (incl.), and the 144th Mountain Infantry Regiment, the 335th Infantry Division's 682nd Infantry Regiment, and the 313th and 314th March Battalions in the Sukhodol (incl.), Rodakovo, Beloe, and Sdornaia (incl.) sector.

Subunits of an infantry training regiment were withdrawing toward Kalinin State Farm.

The "Eisenach" and 5th March Battalions and subunits from the 22nd Panzer Division were operating in the sector west of Illiriia and Elizavetovka. The remnants from the 304th Infantry Division and units of the 302nd Infantry and 6th Panzer Divisions were detected operating along the Azarovka, Novobulakhovka, Orlovka, Kolpakovo Station,

Kolpakovo, and Bokovo-Platovo line by captured prisoners and documents taken from the dead.

Because of the withdrawal and the associated shortening of the front, enemy units operating along the Ordzhonikidze axis were so intermingled that prisoners from two to three different units and even formations were seized at various points.

D. The Chistiakovskoe axis. Units of two divisions (the 306th and 294th Infantry Divisions), reinforced by separate tank subunits and, presumably, the 6th and 22nd Panzer Divisions, with infantry subunits from rear service organs and specialized units, were operating along the Bokovo-Antratsit and Kuibyshev front.

The enemy occupied [the following positions] by day's end on 19 February: units of the 306th Infantry Division in the Bokovo-Antratsit, Esaulovka, Zhelobok, and Glubokaia Balka sector; and also operations by subunits from the 302nd Infantry Division in the Bokovo-Antratsit region were noted from documents and dead.

Units of the German 294th Infantry Division are occupying defenses along the Dmitrievka, Kuibyshevskie, and Kuibyshevo line on the western bank of the Mius River (confirmed by prisoners from all three infantry regiments).

III. The Enemy's Reserves

The enemy in front of the Southwestern Front possessed no operational reserves whatsoever by 20 February. The enemy began concentrating forces along the Krasnograd axis by withdrawing units from divisions on other fronts (the SS Division "*Wiking*" and 17th Panzer Division from the Southern Front and the SS Panzer Divisions "*Grossdeutschland*," "Adolph Hitler," and "*Reich*" from the Voronezh Front).

It is possible a part of the enemy forces from his Caucasus grouping, which is withdrawing across the Taman' Peninsula to the Crimea, and also new divisions transferred from Karelia (the 163rd and 169th Infantry Divisions) and Norway (the 196th and 197th Infantry Divisions) will reach the Southwestern Front.

According to agent reports, the enemy is preparing to withdraw his forces from the Iukhnov, Viaz'ma, Rzhev, and Nelidovo regions (in the Western Front), which will provide the enemy with the opportunity to free up as many as 20 divisions by shortening his front lines, of which 5–6 divisions can be transferred for operations against the Southwestern Front.

IV. The Political-Morale State of the Enemy's Forces

The Red Army's attacks have seriously undermined the morale of the German Army's soldiers and officers. Faith in German victory in this war is wavering not only among the soldiers but also among the mass of officers, and there is an increasing sense of doom. Conversations among the soldiers about a separate peace are growing to massive proportions. The soldiers are saying Germany rather than Russia must make concessions for peace (from the testimony of prisoners in the 385th Infantry Division's 537th Infantry Regiment, the 298th Infantry Division's 526th Infantry Regiment, the 385th Infantry Division's 539th Infantry Regiment, an officer from the VIII Army Corps, and others).

Because of its heavy losses, the German command is being forced to accept a large contingent of soldiers from non-German nationalities (Poles, Czechs, and others), a fact which is leading to national dissension within the German Army.

As a result of the almost general levy [conscription] of adult males in the 17 to 55 year age range into the army, many former members of the Left Democratic Party have joined the army, which has also led to cracks in the state of the forces' morale.

Recently, the quantity of soldiers and non-commissioned officers voluntarily deserting to the Red Army's side has increased significantly.

As a result, the commander of Army Group "B" has issued special order No. 499.

Despite of all of these facts, however, discipline in the German Army is still sufficiently firm. Instances of non-fulfillment of orders and desertion remain isolated.

The contradictions between soldiers and officers are still not showing signs of deep cracks. The soldiers behave stoically. During this period we did not observe instances when groups deserted to the Red Army. The main reason German Army soldiers are not surrendering is the excessive intimidation of the soldiers by their officers with the "horrors" of becoming prisoners of the Red Army.

Conclusions:

1. The enemy in front of the Southwestern Front is making every effort to prevent the advance by our forces along the Krasnograd and Krasnoarmeiskoe axes, while concentrating large tank forces at the expense of panzer divisions transferred from the Voronezh and Southern Fronts.

2. In the near future, we should expect active enemy offensive operations to liquidate the penetration along the Krasnograd axis and to protect the withdrawal routes of the forces of the Donbas grouping.

3. All available information indicates that the enemy will abandon the territory in the Donbas and withdraw his forces across the Dnepr River.

Ivanov, Rogov [chief of Intelligence][110]

Although some of Ivanov's and Rogov's judgments indeed proved correct, most were also irrelevant, since they totally misjudged Manstein's intentions. Within hours after they went into action, the forces conducting Manstein's planned counterstrokes tore into and through the forces on the Southwestern Front's right wing and in its center, dampening Vatutin's optimism and shattering his confidence and offensive ardor. On his *front's* right wing, the SS Panzer Corps' Panzer Divisions "*Reich*" and "*Totenkopf*" [Death's Head] shattered his defenses in the Krasnograd sector, just as the regrouped divisions of the XXXXVIII and XXXX Panzer Corps routed the forces in his *front's* center in the sector from Pavlograd eastward to Krasnoarmeiskoe). With his *front* facing imminent collapse, at 1025 hours on 20 February, a still calm Vatutin attempted to improve cooperation between his *front* and Malinovsky's Southern Front, perhaps in the hope of rekindling his offensive:

1. The *Stavka* of the Supreme High Command has established the following boundary line between the Southwestern and Southern Fronts, effective 2400 hours 22 February 1943 — to Kuibyshevo, as before, and further from Kuibyshevo through Amvrosievka, Blagodatnoe, Ilovaisk, Makeevka, Spartak, Tsukurikha, Ivanov, Pokrovskoe, and Sofievka to Velikii Lug. All points are inclusive for the Southern Front.

2. Consequently, I am establishing the following boundary lines between the armies effective 2400 hours 20 February 1943:

a. Between the 6th and 1st Guards Armies – as before.

b. Between the 1st and 3rd Guards Armies – as before and further through Kamyshevakha, Artemovsk, and Konstantinovka to Dobropol'e. All points except Artemovsk are inclusive for the 1st Guards Army.

c. Between the 3rd Guards and 5th Tank Armies — to Lozovaia State Farm, as before, and further from Novopavlovka through Ordzhonikidze, Gorlovka, and Krasnoarmeiskoe to Poputnyi. All points except for Poputnyi are inclusive for the 3rd Guards Army.

3. To liquidate the enemy in the Donbas completely and as rapidly as possible, I order:

a. The 6th Army commander will fulfill his previous mission energetically without considering his boundary line.

b. Lieutenant General Popov, fulfilling his previous mission energetically, will prevent the enemy from penetrating from the Kramatorskaia and Stalino front toward Dnepropetrovsk and Zaporozh'e at all costs.
    Prevent the enemy from reaching the left flank and rear of Kharitonov's [6th Army] shock group.

c. The commander of the 1st Guards Army, while fulfilling your previous mission and the operational plan you submitted, will capture Konstantinovka no later than 21 February 1943.

d. The commander of the 3rd Guards Army will capture the Debal'tsevo region by concentric attacks no later than 21 February 1943. Subsequently, attack toward Nikitovka and Krasnoarmeiskoe and from Nikitovka toward Artemovsk and from Nikitovka toward Konstantinovka with part of your forces.

e. The commander of the 5th Tank Army will continue a swift pursuit of the enemy and reach the Ordzhonikidze (incl.) and Makeevka line no later than the morning of 22 February 1943. Subsequently, attack toward

Semidovka and toward Krasnoarmeiskoe with part of your force. Ensure close operational coordination with the right wing.

4. Report copies of all orders given to me immediately.

Vatutin, Zheltov, Ivanov[111]

Later in the day, however, an increasingly alarmed Vatutin began issuing new orders and messages reflecting his growing concern over deteriorating situation and the fate of his forces and his plan. Dispatched at 1850 hours, the first of these urgent messages asked General Popov, whose forces were still under heavy German assault in the Krasnoarmeiskoe region, to clarify his situation, "Immediately report about the situation. Are you holding on to Krasnoarmeiskoe? What are the positions of your forces? What enemy do you face? What is the air situation?"[112]

Several hours later, at 0300 hours on 21 February, Vatutin tried to provide the *Stavka* with a clearer picture of what was actually transpiring:

1. The enemy on the *front's* right wing, while enveloping from the Khar'kov axis toward Dnepropetrovsk with the forces of his SS Division "Adolph Hitler," is pushing our forces back toward the Pereshchepino and Gubinikha line.

The enemy is continuing to offer strong resistance to the advance by our forces by reinforcing his grouping in the Novo-Moskovsk and Sinel'nikovo regions.

After reinforcing his grouping in the Krasnoarmeiskoe region and launching a counteroffensive, the enemy captured Krasnoarmeiskoe and Dobropol'e on 20 February 1943.

As previously configured, the enemy is continuing to resist our attacking forces stubbornly in the remaining sectors of the *front*.

Beginning on the morning of 20 February 1943, air reconnaissance has detected the movement of dense columns of vehicles and tanks from the Stalino region through Pokrovskoe to Zaporozh'e and from the Nikitovka region to Krasnoarmeiskoe.

2. The forces of the *front* fought intense offensive battles with enemy motorized infantry and tanks on 20 February 1943 and, repelling repeated counterattacks, were continuing to fight to capture Sinel'nikovo, Krasnoarmeiskoe, and the Mius River line. Especially heavy fighting took place along the *front's* right wing, where the enemy succeeded in pressing our units back and captured Krasnograd.

The enemy is continuing to hold on to Novo-Moskovsk and has fought a prolonged battle for the town.

In the center, our units abandoned Krasnoarmeiskoe under the pressure of a superior enemy force.

In the remaining sectors of the *front*, encountering heavy resistance, our forces occupied seven populated points.

3. The 6th Army continued to conduct intense offensive fighting with enemy infantry and tanks on 20 February 1943, while repelling repeated counterattacks by his motor-mechanized units and, on the left wing,

engaged in bitter fighting for possession of Novo-Moskovsk and Sinel'nikovo.

The army's units were fighting along the [following] lines by day's end:

The 350th Rifle Division – Riabukhino and eastern outskirts of Melikhovka.

The 172nd Rifle Division, after being pushed back by the enemy, was fighting for Shliakhovaia and Rossokhovatoe by day's end.

The 6th Rifle Division, withdrawing to the Lipianka, Dal'niaia, Rogoven'ka, and Vol'nyi line, continued exchanging fire with the enemy, while repelling repeated counterattacks.

The 106th Rifle Brigade's position has not been verified.

The 267th Rifle Division was fighting in Kulebovka and Novo-Moskovsk by the morning of 20 February 1943; at 0900 hours 20 February 1943, the enemy pushed the division's units back, and two of the division's regiments concentrated in Spasskoe at day's end.

The 4th Guards Rifle Corps continued to fight stubbornly on the northern outskirts of Novo-Moskovsk with part of its forces and fought to capture Sinel'nikovo with its main forces.

The 244th Rifle Division is on the march to the Prishtopovka region.

According to incomplete information, the army's units destroyed more than 2,500 enemy soldiers and officers, destroyed 27 tanks, 8 armored vehicles, 1 armored train, 2 self-propelled guns, 23 guns, 37 mortars, 63 machine guns, and 130 vehicles during the day of fighting.

It captured 95 platforms [railroad] and wagons with coal, 2 damaged locomotives, 1 tank, and other equipment.

4. Comrade Popov's Group of Forces, while continuing fierce fighting with enemy infantry and tanks in the Krasnoarmeiskoe region, moved its units to the Krivorozh'e and Krasnoarmeiskoe line on 20 February 1943.

After reinforcing his grouping in the Krasnoarmeiskoe region, the enemy launched a counterattack and captured Krasnoarmeiskoe and Dobropol'e by day's end on 20 February.

Two enemy aircraft were shot down by rifle fire in the Dobropol'e region.

The 4th Guards Tank Corps, the 10th and 18th Tank Corps, the 9th and 11th Tank Brigades, and the 7th Ski Brigade repelled repeated attacks by enemy infantry and tanks while holding on to Aleksandrovka and Krasnoarmeiskii Rudnik.

The 10th Tank Corps captured Krivorozh'e with one tank brigade at 1300 hours.

The 3rd Tank Corps is fighting in the Novo-Aleksandrovka region after repelling two counterattacks by up to 15 tanks on the southern outskirts of Sergeevka.

The 38th Guards Rifle Division completed its march to Krasnoarmeiskii Rudnik and reached Sergeevka during the second half of the day with its main forces, while holding on to Kramatorskaia with one regiment.

The 5th Ski Brigade fought in the Novo-Troitskoe region and with part of its forces in Stepanovka at day's end.

5. The 1st Guards Army was defending along the Kramatorskaia, Aleksandrovka, and Krymskaia front with three divisions on 20 February 1943.

The 6th Guards Rifle Corps completed its march and reached [the following positions] by the end of the day:

The 44th Guards Rifle Division – Bogorodichnoe and the 58th Guards Rifle Division — the approaches to Slaviansk.

6. The 3rd Guards Army continued prolonged fighting with enemy motorized infantry and tanks and occupied six populated points on 20 February 1943.

The 61st and 60th Guards Rifle Divisions, the 279th Rifle Division, and the 229th Rifle Brigade conducted a regrouping during the night and the first half of the day. They went over to the attack from the Kripaki and Smelyi front toward Krivorozh'e beginning at 1600 hours on 20 February 1943.

The 18th Rifle Corps (the 54th Guards Division, the 243rd Rifle Division, and the 59th Guards Rifle Division), in cooperation with the 1st Guards Mechanized Corps, fought along their previous line, after advancing 3 kilometers west of Illiriia.

The 14th Rifle Corps (the 259th Rifle Division, the 50th Guards Rifle Division, and the 346th Rifle Division) conducted prolonged offensive fighting and, after destroying up to two companies of enemy infantry, advanced and captured Khartsizskaia, Karakash Shakhtaia, and Piatikhatka.

The 7th Guards Cavalry Corps penetrated the encirclement ring on the night on 20 February and reached the Striukovo and Rassypnaia region, where it smashed the enemy's rear area.

7. The 5th Tank Army, resuming its offensive on the morning of 20 February 1943, forced the Mius River in several sectors during the day but was unable to exploit its success.

All of its attempts to attack were repelled by enemy fire from pillboxes, which had (barbed) wire and other obstacles in front of them.

8. The 17th Air Army destroyed enemy forces in the Krasnoarmeiskoe region and columns of automobiles along the Andreevka, Gavrilovka, and Pokrovskoe road on 20 February 1943, while assisting the *front's* forces with bombing and assault operations. It bombed the airfield at Stalino and Gorlovka and the railroad stations at Debal'tsevo, Makeevka, Dnepropetrovsk, Vishnevetskii, and Illarionovskii. According to far from complete data, it carried out 135 aircraft sorties. It destroyed or damaged 6 aircraft at the Stalino airfield, 10 [railroad] wagons, and 45 automobiles and suppressed the fire of 7 artillery batteries. It scattered and destroyed piecemeal up to a company of enemy infantry. Ten air battles occurred, during which it shot down 6 enemy aircraft.

Vatutin, Zheltov, Ivanov[113]

Shortly before he notified the *Stavka* about the deteriorating situation, at 0220 hours Vatutin sent a blistering rebuke to Popov, with information copies going to the General Staff and 6th Army:

> You have committed a stupid and unforgivable mistake by withdrawing your main forces away from the Krasnoarmeiskoe region and even the Dobropol'e region contrary to my categorical order, and, by so doing, you have opened the road for the enemy to withdraw to Dnepropetrovsk and have exposed the flanks and rear of the shock group of Kharitonov's [6th Army]. Don't you understand that this sharply contradicts the mission I entrusted to you and has now created a situation in which the enemy will hasten to withdraw his forces from the Donbas across the Dnepr with all of the means at his disposal?
>
> In this situation your proposal concerning the withdrawal of your forces to the Stepanovka region and then the conduct of an attack from that region clearly deviates from fulfilling your combat mission since your attack will be too late. I categorically forbid you to withdraw your forces to the north and order you to launch a swift attack along the shortest route from the Dobropol'e region to Grishino and the southwest. Your mission is to occupy positions astride the enemy's withdrawal routes once again and to capture the Grishino and Udachna-Sergeevka region and, if conditions are favorable, Krasnoarmeiskoe as well, by the morning of 21 February 1943. Encircle and destroy the enemy's rear guard units in the Novo-Aleksandrovka region. Prevent the enemy from withdrawing to Dnepropetrovsk and sever his withdrawal routes to Zaporozh'e with part of your forces at all costs.
>
> After capturing the regions indicated above, you can abandon them only as a last resort, but you are subsequently obligated to withdraw westward to link up with Kharitonov, all the while blocking the enemy's withdrawal routes to Dnepropetrovsk and Zaporozh'e. You are permitted to withdraw no farther westward than the Volch'ia River line.
>
> Vatutin, Zheltov, Ivanov[114]

After Popov passed these new instructions to his subordinate corps, Major General of Tank Forces P. P. Poluboiarov, the commander of Mobile Group Popov's strongest tank corps, the 4th Guards Tank Corps, which was almost entirely encircled in the Krasnoarmeiskoe region, reported back directly to Vatutin on 22 February:

> Profiting by the visit by Colonel Guliaev [Colonel V. G. Guliaev, the tank corps' military commissar] to the *front's* headquarters, I am sending you this short official report regarding the actions and condition of the 4th Guards Tank Corps. He will report to you personally about the nature and details of the corps' almost superhuman efforts in holding off the enemy's colossal onslaught as it ripped into the enemy's entire Donets grouping.

The corps itself, with all of its equipment, both combat and supporting, as well as its personnel, has been put out of action almost completely.

Beginning with me and finishing with the last soldier, the guards corps has fulfilled the *front's* mission to the very end, with honor and simple soldierly determination. After capturing Krasnoarmeiskoe, the corps has held on to it for 10 days with its forces alone. Although the enemy suffered colossal losses during this period, my corps was also reduced to a state requiring general and complete overhaul [capital repair] as a result of this fighting.

Since I have been out of direct communications with you, up to this time, I have no final evaluation of the corps' operations.

I am basically troubled over the issue of whether the cost we have had to pay to hold on to this main nerve center in the Donbas was too high. Although they have forced me to withdraw to Barvenkovo at the present time, I will still continue to consider myself in forward positions and will operate in the group's and *front's* interests. Yesterday and last evening I formed a single tank brigade, using all of the corps' remaining soldiers and equipment to form it. I expect to create a full-blooded 13th Guards Tank Brigade by day's end today. I am having difficulty only with fuel. I have reported to Comrade Popov about this formation.

To make a decision about the future fate of the guards corps, I request you dispatch Comrade Chernobaia to me, who will give me your decision on the spot or permit me to report to you personally.

Poluboiarov[115]

The Debaltsevo Encirclement

While Vatutin was attempting to deal with the catastrophes looming over his *front's* right wing and center, Borisov's isolated and increasingly desperate 7th Guards Cavalry Corps was suffering its death agonies on his *front's* left wing. After failing to receive any assistance whatsoever from the 3rd Guards Army's mobile corps to its rear, Borisov's cavalrymen attempted to escape to the east before dawn on 19 February (see Map 47). The night before, after his reconnaissance units detected German forces concentrating at Chernukhino Station for an all out assault on their shrinking perimeter, Borisov radioed Leliushenko:

The [encirclement] ring is tightening. There is no ammunition, and I have received none. Today, enemy aviation conducted heavy bombing. None of our units are approaching. I request you take immediate measures, in particular, aviation operations; otherwise a catastrophe is possible."[116]

According to Major General I. T. Chalenko, the commander of the cavalry corps' 15th Guards Cavalry Division, who survived the harrowing operation, Leliushenko promised to supply Borisov's corps by air and ordered Borisov to hold on to his position "at all costs" and, if the situation deteriorated further, to begin partisan operations. When he determined a final German assault was imminent, Borisov decided to remove his forces from the Chernukhino region before the

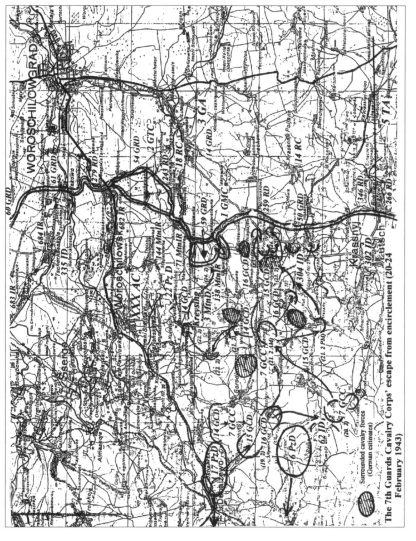

Map 47. The 7th Guards Cavalry Corps' escape from encirclement, 20–24 February 1943

encirclement ring snapped shut around them. To conduct the escape attempt, Borisov ordered Guards Major G. A. Chernikov, the chief of the 16th Guards Cavalry Division's Operations Section, to conduct a feint westward from Debal'tsevo, while Borisov himself led the corps' main body southeastward through Fashchevka Station, 10 kilometers southeast of Chernukhino, and then southward to the Striukovo region, 11 kilometers south of Fashchevka, with the 15th Guards Cavalry Division bringing up the rear. The 17th Panzer Division engaged Borisov's rear guards at dawn with heavy artillery fire but was unable to intercept his corps' main body once it headed to the south. However, when the main body of Borisov's retreating force reached Striukovo, elements of the 6th Panzer and 62nd Infantry Divisions, which counterattacked northward from Rassonoe, 5 kilometers south of Striukovo, blocked his forces, once again threatening them with encirclement.

Trapped once again, Borisov then ordered his corps to withdraw northeastward to Illiriia in the hope of linking up with the 1st Guards Mechanized Corps, which was supposed to be marching to Borisov's rescue. Marching northeastward overnight, with the 15th Guards Cavalry Division in its vanguard, the cavalry corps' main body passed through Popovka and Artema, 18–19 kilometers east of Chernukhino, heading toward Illiriia, on the railroad line south of Voroshilovgrad. After Borisov's forces captured Artema early on the morning of 21 February, the 3rd Guards Army radioed the cavalry corps commander that help was being sent to his corps by way of Krasnyi Kut, 10 kilometers northwest of Krasnyi Luch'. Convinced that smaller forces could better dodge the ever-increasing number of German pursuers, Borisov decided to split up his forces and make his final escape along three divergent routes.

Borisov's breakout plan called for Major General N. P. Iakunin's 14th Guards Cavalry Division to attack northward through Utkino, Fedorovka, and Illiriia to reach Uspenka, Major General M. M. Shaimuratov's 16th Guards Cavalry Division to advance northeastward through Ivanovka and Petrovo-Krasnosel'e, and Chalenko's 15th Guards Cavalry Division to strike eastward toward Krasnyi Kut, with all three divisions ultimately linking up with various elements of the 3rd Guards Army's relief forces along or west of the Voroshilovgrad-Krasnyi-Luch' road. After beginning its breakout on 21 February, by evening the 15th Guards Cavalry Division's column neared Krasnyi Kut, a 5 kilometer long and 1 kilometer wide village extending along a *balka* [ravine] formed by a tributary of the Mius River. After a short but intense fight, Iakunin's cavalrymen destroyed the defending German garrison, reportedly the headquarters of the German 62nd Infantry Division, and captured the division's commander.

The next day the 3rd Guards Army commander, Leliushenko, radioed new orders to Borisov's now dispersed corps, directing it "to link up with [3rd Guards] army's units in the direction of Shirokii Farm and then deliver a blow against the enemy from the rear, while operating to meet the 14th Guards Rifle Corps attacking from the east."[117] Borisov tried to comply, but, after marching about 8 kilometers eastward through a snow-covered roadless region, the corps encountered elements of the 302nd Infantry Division blocking its path at the village of Fromandirovka, 16 kilometers north of Krasnyi Luch' (see Map 48). While the cavalrymen of Chalenko's 15th Guards Cavalry Division fought fiercely with the

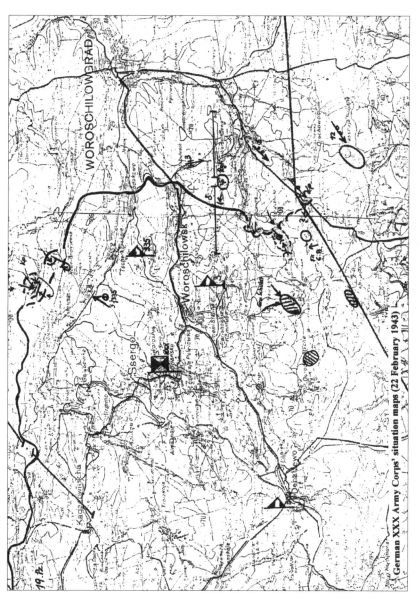

Map 48. German XXX Army Corps' situation, 22 February 1943

German force at Fromandirovka all day on 23 February, the remainder of Borisov's forces engaged the small German garrisons at Iulino 1 and Iulino–2 State Farms, 2–3 kilometers south of Fromandirovka, all the while pounded unmercifully by German artillery firing from Zhuravlevka, a fire base of the 302nd Infantry Division about 6 kilometers to the south. The corps suffered heavy casualties during these engagements, including Borisov, who was wounded and captured along with many other soldiers and officers in his corps.

Before he was wounded, Borisov ordered Shaimuratov's 16th Guards Cavalry Division to bypass Iulino 1 from the south, penetrate the Germans' defenses along the Voroshilovgrad-Krasnyi Luch' road, and advance eastward through Shirokii to Malonikolaevka, 23 kilometers northeast of Krasnyi Luch. However, heavy German artillery fire halted Shaimuratov's cavalrymen as they tried to cross the road. To the rear, supported by intense artillery fire, infantrymen from the 302nd Infantry Division inflicted heavy casualties on Borisov's corps headquarters and several battalions from Shaimuratov's 16th Guards Cavalry Division at Petrovskii State Farm. After several hours of intense fighting, the attacking Germans destroyed or dispersed the 7th Guards Cavalry Corps' headquarters and the remnants of its 16th Guards Cavalry Division, killing Major General I. S. Dubko and Colonels I. D. Saburov and A. A. Karpushenko, the corps' deputy commander, chief of staff, and political officer, as well as Shaimuratov, the famous Bashkir commander.[118]

During the heavy fighting on 23 February, German blocking forces attacked Chalenko's 15th Guards Cavalry Division as it was approaching Iulino 2. After suffering heavy losses in an intense firefight, the remnants of Chalenko's division escaped through the Zapadnaia [Western] *Balka* to the northeastern outskirts of Ivanovka, where they joined the remnants of the 16th Guards Cavalry Division and the corps' headquarters. After assuming command of the combined group, which now numbered about 6,000 of its original 10,000 men, Chalenko reconnoitered and decided to make one last attempt to break out of encirclement and reach the safety of the 3rd Guards Army's lines, now less than 2 kilometers distant.

Chalenko made his first attempt to break out late in the afternoon on 23 February, with a force on foot led by Guards Major S. A. Strizhak, the 15th Cavalry Division's chief of staff, and a group on horseback under his personal command. However, this attack failed, and Strizhak died in the fighting. Chalenko then reorganized his force into three mixed regiments: the first consisting of the 15th Guards Cavalry Division's survivors led by Captain S. S. Oleiniko; the second with the 16th Guards Cavalry Division's remnants commanded by Colonel G. E. Fonderantsev; and the third made up of the corps staff and specialized subunits led by Major F. P. Muzypia, and ordered all three regiments to break out toward the east after nightfall. After running a gauntlet of artillery, machine gun, and small arms fire overnight on 23–24 February, during which they once again suffered heavy losses, the remnants of the three regiments finally reached the 3rd Guards Army's lines near Malonikolaevka. For several days thereafter, the scattered remnants of Borisov's once proud cavalry corps infiltrated back to Soviet lines individually and in small groups.

Meanwhile, after becoming separated from its parent corps on 21 February, Iakunin's 14th Guards Cavalry Division headed northeastward from the region west of Krasnyi Kut, crossing the railroad 19 kilometers east of Chernukhino, and reached Utkino. After dodging pursuing German forces for two days north of the railroad, Iakunin's force zigzagged northward through Lenin State Farm and Andrianopol' and then northeastward to Seleznevka, where the Germans detected its whereabouts and surrounded it once again. Finally, on the night of 22–23 February, Iakunin's cavalrymen broke out eastward through Illiriia *balka* and reached the 3rd Guards Army's lines at Elizavetovka, although also after suffering heavy losses.

Borisov's 7th Guards Cavalry Corps lost well over half of its 15,000 men, most of its horses, and virtually all of its heavy weapons and equipment during the so-called Debal'tsevo "raid." The corps' combat reports assert that Borisov's cavalrymen killed, wounded, or captured 12,000 German soldiers, destroyed 28 tanks, 70 motorcycles, 50 guns, 35 mortars, 54 machine guns, 2 armored trains, 1 fuel train, 20 locomotives, 5 trains loaded with weapons and equipment, and 30 warehouses, and caused other significant damage in the Germans' rear area.[119] However, as daring and dramatic as Borisov's operation was, it had only minimal impact on Manstein's counterstrokes or the Red Army's overall success elsewhere in the Donbas region.

Despite the Debal'tsevo raid and the loss of Voroshilovgrad, Army Group South's First Panzer Army and *Armeeabteilung* Hollidt were able to reestablish stable defensive lines west of Voroshilovgrad and southward along the Mius River, block Leliushenko's mobile group before it could reinforce Borisov's cavalry corps, and cut off, encircle, and virtually destroy over half of the 7th Guards Cavalry Corps before it could make its escape. Nor did the raid by Borisov's cavalry corps materially contribute to the success of Mobile Group Popov since, at the same time, the XXXX Panzer Corps' 7th and 11th Panzer Divisions, deployed on the First Panzer Army's left wing, were able to contain and defeat Group Popov's operations in the Krasnoarmeiskoe region. By 20 February the First Panzer Army had the situation at Debal'tsevo so well in hand it was able to regroup its 6th and 17th Panzer Divisions westward to join the assault against Group Popov and the Southwestern Front's right wing just as Vatutin was dispatching yet another mobile group toward the Dnepr River at Zaporozh'e.

Vatutin's Plan

Although Soviet and Russian historians have routinely called the operations by Borisov's cavalry corps the "Debal'tsevo raid," the term "raid" clearly did not reflect Vatutin's original intent. On the contrary, Vatutin regarded the 8th Cavalry Corps as the vanguard of a much larger and far more formidable armored group whose mission was to reach and capture Stalino, link up with Mobile Group Popov, advancing on Stalino from the north, and together advance southward toward Mariupol' to encircle and destroy all of *Armeeabteilung* Hollidt. In an even broader context, Vatutin's ambitious maneuver plan required another mobile group (the 1st Guards and 25th Tank Corps), which was operating on his *front's* right wing, to advance to Zaporozh'e on the Dnepr River and several mobile groups under the Southern Front's control to advance across the Mius River into the Donbas region from the east (see below). However, Mobile Group Popov's defeat at Krasnoarmeiskoe at the hands of the First Panzer Army's 7th and 11th Panzer Divisions, SS Panzer Division "*Wiking*," and 333rd Infantry Division and the defeat of Borisov's cavalry corps at Debal'tsevo by the same army's 6th and

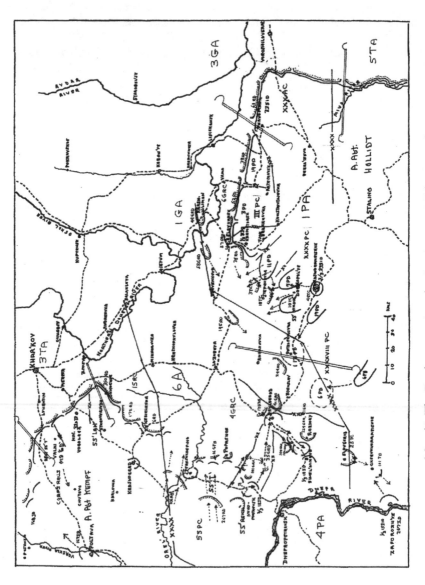

Map 49. The Donbas operation, the situation on 22 February 1943

17th Panzer and 62nd and 302nd Infantry Divisions thwarted Vatutin's ambitious plan and began transforming what had begun as a spectacular success into what would end as a catastrophic failure (see Map 49).

Vatutin began displaying his increasing frustration over the rapidly deteriorating situation across his entire front in a report he submitted to the *Stavka* at 0500 hours on 23 February:

1. The enemy, in spite of [conducting] fierce counterattacks toward Krasnograd, Lozovaia, Novo-Moskovsk, and Pavlograd on the *front's* right wing with the forces of three infantry divisions and 300 tanks during the day, failed to advance successfully. The enemy is constantly bringing fresh forces forward to Dnepropetrovsk from the southwest to reinforce this grouping and is then dispatching them from Dnepropetrovsk toward Novo-Moskovsk and Sinel'nikovo. Simultaneously, the enemy is continuing to withdraw his Donbas grouping. On 22 February the largest columns were moving along the Gorlovka, Stalino, and Pokrovskoe; the Artemovsk and Konstantinovka; and the Krasnoarmeiskoe, Andreevka, and Pokrovskoe axes.

A large concentration of tanks and vehicles has been detected in Gavrilovka.

The enemy in the central sector of the *front's* sector and on its left wing is continuing to protect the withdrawal of his main forces with a stubborn defense, while striving to hold back the offensive by our forces.

Up to 300 aircraft are concentrated at the airfield in Dnepropetrovsk, up to 200 at Poltava, up to 70 in Debal'tsevo, and up to 80 at Stalino. Up to 20 railroad trains are at Volnovakha Station.

2. The forces on the *front's* right wing engaged in heavy fighting with enemy motorized infantry and tanks on 22 February 1943, while repelling repeated counterattacks. Especially intense fighting took place in the Novo-Moskovsk, Pavlograd, Sinel'nikovo, and Krasnoarmeiskii Rudnik regions, where the enemy was striving to free up his communications with Dnepropetrovsk at all costs.

In the central sector of the *front*, our units occupied several populated points along separate axes, while overcoming stubborn enemy resistance.

On the left wing, our forces carried out local regroupings in their existing positions, while preparing to resume the offensive on the morning of 23 February 1943.

3. The 6th Army conducted offensive fighting against enemy motorized infantry and tanks on 22 February 1943. Encountering heavy resistance and repelling several enemy counterattacks during the day, it had no success and was continuing to fight along the [following] lines:

The 15th Rifle Corps – Riabukhino, Melikhovka, Leninskii Zavod [Factory], the southern outskirts of Kegichevka, Krasnoarmeiskoe, and Grigor'evka.

The 106th Rifle Brigade – Shevskoe, Vodianoi, and Magdalinovka.

The 267th Rifle Division – fought its way into the Vol'noe and Svobodnoe regions.

The 4th Guards Rifle Corps continued fierce fighting for Novo-Moskovsk and Sinel'nikovo and also street battles in Pavlograd.

The 1st Guards Tank Corps fought for Pavlograd during the second half of the day and for Marienfel'd and Burakovka with part of its force, while protecting Sinel'nikovo from the northwest.

The 25th Tank Corps, advancing toward Zaporozh'e, seized Slavgorod on 21 February, during which it destroyed a railroad train and seized prisoners. On 22 February it was fighting [as follows]: advancing toward Razdol'e and Zelenyi and operating toward Pavlovskii with one tank brigade, with its forward units in the Platonovskii region; toward Mikhailovo-Lukashevo with another tank brigade, whose forward detachment cut the road in the Udachnyi region; and in the Rudo-Nikolaevka and Mikhailovskii regions with its third tank brigade.

In this fashion, the 25th Tank Corps cut off the enemy's withdrawal routes to Zaporozh'e.

4. Comrade Popov's Group of Forces conducted prolonged fighting with withdrawing enemy units all day on 22 February, while repelling repeated tank counterattacks along the Aleksandrovka and Krasnoarmeiskii Rudnik line. The units of the group units were fighting at [the following locations] at day's end:

The 3rd Tank Corps and 5th Ski Brigade are in the Slavianka region. The results of the fighting have not been received.

The 10th and 18th Tank Corps, repelling repeated attacks by enemy tanks, held on to Aleksandrovka and Krasnoarmeiskii Rudnik with a reliable all-round defense all day and fought a column of enemy, which was penetrating from Novo-Troitskoe toward the west, with part of their forces.

The 38th Guards Rifle Division went over to the defense with two regiments, protecting the axis to Stepanovka, and the 10th Ski Brigade is in the Bezzabotovka region.

The units of Comrade Popov's Group destroyed 30 tanks and 100 vehicles during the day.

5. The 1st Guards Army. The 6th Guards Rifle Corps completed a march to its new concentration areas on 22 February 1943, and the units of the corps reached [the following locations] by day's end:

The 44th Guards Rifle Division moved forward into Bogodarovo along the Aleksandrovka and Verkhniaia Samara march-route.

The 58th Guards Rifle Division reached the Nadezhdino region with its lead column and continued moving toward Lozovaia.

The 195th Rifle Division approached Dubovo with its lead column, with the mission of being in the Iakobinka region by day's end.

Comrade Semenov's Group [of Forces], overcoming enemy resistance and repelling repeated counterattacks, continued to conduct intense offensive fighting and captured Pervomar'evka and Belogorovka by day's end on 22 February 1943.

6. The 3rd Guards Army, resuming its offensive on the morning of 22 February, repulsed several enemy counterattacks during the day, while recording an insignificant advance in individual sectors.

The 7th Guards Cavalry Corps, operating against the enemy's rear area, captured and held the Liman State Farm, Timiriazevka, Krasnyi Kut, Mines Nos. 10 and 21, Sofievka, Aleksandrovka, and Davydovka regions.

The 1st Mechanized Corps was fighting 1 kilometer northwest and east of Shterovka. Essentially, there were no changes in the positions of the army's other units.

The units of the army destroyed more than 700 enemy soldiers and officers, 3 tanks, 6 automobiles during the day of fighting, and fire from infantry weapons shot down 1 enemy aircraft. Three guns, 3 mortars, 8 heavy machine guns, 2 motorcycles, and 2 portable radios were captured. One hundred enemy soldiers and officers were taken prisoner.

7. The 5th Tank Army, holding onto its previous positions, carried out a partial regrouping of its forces on 22 February and brought ammunition and fuel forward on 22 February 1943, while preparing to continue its offensive beginning on the morning of 23 February 1943.

The army's units captured enemy mobile equipment, including 16 locomotives, 35 platforms, and 662 wagons [railroad] during the period from 12 through 20 February 1943.

8. The 17th Air Army, cooperating with the forces of the 1st Guards Army, the 6th Army, and Comrade Popov's Group, destroyed enemy forces in the Gavrilovka, Andreevka, Gradovka, Konstantinovka, Novo-Ekonomicheskoe, Veseloi Gory, and Novotroitskoe regions by bombing and assault operations, bombed Artemovsk, Nikitovka, the airfield at Stalino, and the railroad center at Volnovakha, and conducted reconnaissance on 22 February, while protecting its forces.

According to incomplete information, it conducted 317 aircraft sorties (111 at night), and destroyed or damaged 17 aircraft (at the Zaporozh'e and Stalino airfields), 4 tanks, 175 automobiles, 15 carts, 1 fuel tank, 1 bus, 2 antiaircraft guns, and 2 antiaircraft gun mounts. Eight strong explosions were observed at Volnovakha Station. We destroyed 30 wagons and dispersed and destroyed up to a company of enemy infantry piecemeal. We conducted nine air battles, during which six enemy planes were shot down and one was damaged.

Vatutin, Zheltov, Ivanov[120]

Defeat

Manstein's Counterstroke

As these and other reports indicated, the forces operating on the right wing and in the center of Vatutin's Southwestern Front were unwittingly falling victim to an ambitious plan hatched by Manstein. In fact, Manstein was already orchestrating a classic double envelopment maneuver against Vatutin's overextended mobile groups aimed at nothing less than cutting off and destroying all of his forces exploiting deeply between the Krasnograd region in the west eastward through the Pavlograd region to the Krasnoarmeiskoe region. Manstein's plan required the SS Panzer Corps' "*Das Reich*" ("DR") and "*Totenkopf* [Deaths Head]" ("T") Panzer Divisions, the former regrouped from the Khar'kov region and the latter from the West, to assault eastward from the Krasnograd and Dnepropetrovsk regions and link up with the XXXXVIII Panzer Corps' 6th and 17th Panzer Divisions and the XXXX Panzer Corps's SS "*Wiking*," and 7th and 11th Panzer Divisions, which were attacking northwestward from positions north and south of Krasnoarmeiskoe. The twin pincers of Manstein's three panzer corps threatened to encircle and destroy all of Mobile Group Popov, the 25th Tank and 1st Guards Tank Corps, half of Kuznetsov's 1st Guards Army, and all of Kharitonov's 6th Army, most of whose forces were still advancing with utter abandon toward the Dnepr River.

Finally appreciating the deadly threat Manstein's pincers posed to his overextended forces, at 0410 hours on 24 February, Vatutin ordered Popov's Mobile Group, which had been, in essence, already defeated, to disband and dispatch its remnants to reinforce the 1st Guards Army's defenses (see Map 50):

> The situation no longer warrants the further independent existence of Group Popov.
>
> I order Comrade Popov's Group to disband and to transfer all of its personnel, excluding the group's headquarters, with its materiel reserves, to the 1st Guards Army by 0800 hours on 25 February 1943. Lieutenant General Popov will turn over his group by the designated time, and the commander of the 1st Guards Army will accept the group after establishing reliable communications with the group's formations and units beforehand.
>
> Until the completion of the handover and acceptance of the group, Lieutenant General Popov will remain responsible for the defense of sectors occupied by the group.
>
> After the handover of the group, Lieutenant General Popov will be at my disposal as my deputy.
>
> I am establishing the following boundary line between the 6th Army and the 1st Guards Army, effective 1800 hours on 24 February 1943: to Lozovaia, as before, and further to Ternovka, inclusive for the 6th Army.
>
> The mission of the [1st Guards] army – will be in accordance with specially given orders.
>
> For information's sake, I am reporting that the 6th Army's forces are being withdrawn from the Zaporozh'e and Sinel'nikovo regions to the Pavlograd region.
>
> Vatutin, Zheltov, Ivanov[121]

Despite this order, Vatutin soon realized Popov's Mobile Group could not disband because it was decisively engaged. Therefore, at 1350 hours on 24 February, he assigned Popov's now bedraggled forces the new mission of defending the Barvenkovo region at all costs:

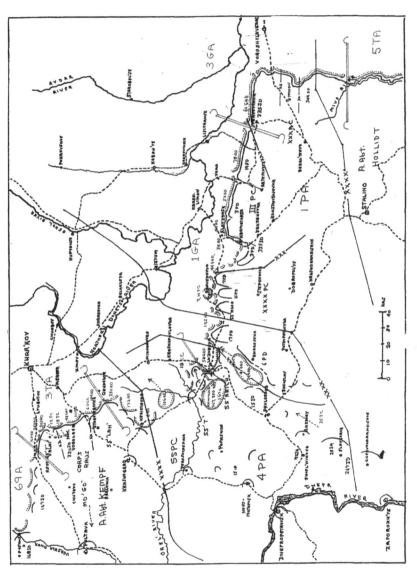

Map 50. The Donbas operation, the situation on 25 February 1943

Hold on to the Barvenkovo region at all costs and contain the enemy along the approaches to Barvenkovo. Defeat him and prevent him from reaching the rear of our forces and [illegible, but probably "the communications"] of the 6th Guards Rifle Corps and, to do so, bring the 11th Tank Brigade and 3rd Tank Corps forward immediately. Once again – assemble your group for the defense of the Barvenkovo axis, for which I am completely entrusting you personally the responsibility. Coordinate your actions with the 6th Guards Rifle Corps. The 52nd Rifle Division is located in the Cherkasskaia and Privol'e regions.

I am permitting you to employ it after coordinating your actions with Kuznetsov [the 1st Guards Army].

Vatutin, Zheltov, Ivanov[122]

Vatutin described his increasingly precarious situation to the *Stavka* at 0400 hours on 25 February, this time relating the full extent of the damage to his *front* and the 7th Guards Cavalry Corps' defeat, although without revealing the degree of damage suffered by Borisov's cavalry corps:

1. The enemy resumed his offensive against the right wing and central sector of the *front* on the morning of 24 February 1943 by attacking along the Pavlograd and Lozovaia axes and, especially, along the Krasnoarmeiskoe and Barvenkovo axes, while simultaneously forming a grouping of more than 100 tanks and up to 2–3 motorized infantry regiments in the Rossokhovatoe and Kegichevka regions and in the Konstantinovka and Artemovsk regions, where large enemy columns were moving forward all day.

An enemy force of more than 100 tanks penetrated the 4th Guards Rifle Corps' front at 1630 hours on 24 February, captured Iur'evka and Zhemchuzhnaia, and advanced toward Lozovaia.

Attacking in the Dobropol'e and Aleksandrovka sector in the central sector of the *front*, an enemy force of up to three infantry regiments with 60–70 tanks pushed our units back, and a small group reached the southern outskirts of Barvenkovo.

On the left wing, as before, the enemy, relying on prepared defensive positions, offered stubborn resistance while trying to halt the offensive of our forces.

2. The forces on the right wing and in the central sector of the Southwestern Front continued heavy fighting with enemy tanks and motorized infantry in the Novo-Moskovsk, Pavlograd, and Sinel'nikovo regions on 24 February. Particularly fierce fighting took place along the Krasnoarmeiskoe and Barvenkovo axis, where, at great cost, the enemy pushed Popov's units back and reached Barvenkovo with his forward units.

In the remaining sectors of the *front*, after resuming the offensive on the morning of 24 February 1943 and encountering strong enemy resistance, [our forces] essentially achieved no results.

3. The 6th Army continued to exchange fire with the enemy and repelled enemy attempts to conduct combat reconnaissance with groups of tanks and motorized infantry on its right wing and conducted intense holding actions and withdrew its units north of Pavlograd on its left wing on 24 February 1943.

The army's units occupied the [following] positions at day's end on 24 February:

The 15th Rifle Corps is defending the front from Riabukhino through Okhochae, the eastern outskirts of Melikhovka, Nizhniaia Orel', Pisarevka, and Andreevka (Kokhanovka) to Bezzabotovka.

The 106th Rifle Brigade is continuing to fight in encirclement in the Malaia Kozyrshchina, Pereshchepino Station, and Aleksandrovka regions.

The 267th Rifle Division, with the 16th Tank Brigade, is continuing to fight fiercely in the vicinity of the forested region south of Ivano-Mikhailovka and Andreevka.

The 4th Guards Rifle Corps, with 1st Tank [Guards] Corps, is fighting fierce holding actions with enemy motorized infantry and tanks north of Viazovska and Verbki.

The 41st Guards Rifle Division is fighting in the Aleksandrovka and Levadki regions, in readiness to withdraw northward on the night of 25 February.

The 25th Tank Corps is fighting in the Platonova region (15 kilometers east of Zaporozh'e) and will withdraw to its designated defensive region on the night of 25 February.

4. Comrade Popov's Group of Forces continued intense fighting with enemy motorized infantry and tanks attacking toward Krasnoarmeiskii Rudnik and Barvenkovo on 24 February 1943.

As a result of the intense fighting, the units of Group Popov abandoned Stepanovka and withdrew to Barvenkovo on the night of 24 February 1943. After repelling several counterattacks by enemy infantry and tanks during the day, it was fighting in the Barvenkovo region.

The positions of its units will be defined more precisely by day's end. According to incomplete information, 5 enemy tanks were destroyed while repelling these infantry and tank attacks. One enemy aircraft was shot down by fires from the ground forces.

5. The 1st Guards Army, while continuing to fulfill its assigned mission and holding on to Lozovaia on 24 February 1943, fought a prolonged battle with attacking enemy forces on its right wing all day. In its center and on its left wing, it dug in along its previous positions. The units of the army were fighting in [the following] positions by day's end:

The 6th Guards Rifle Corps – [in] Parkhomenko, Nizhnii Ukrainskii, Dobropol'e, Sofievka, Blagodat', and Razdol'e, while repelling attacks by up to 2–3 infantry regiments, supported by 60–70 tanks.

The 52nd Rifle Division is being concentrated in Barvenkovo.

Comrade Semenov's Group of Forces is continuing to fight in its previous positions. Up to an infantry division and 50–60 tanks are operating in front of Semenov's Group of Forces.

6. The 3rd Guards Army, while conducting a partial regrouping of forces to its right wing, continued intense offensive fighting on 24 February 1943 and, after repelling several enemy counterattacks, occupied [the following] positions by day's end:

The 18th Rifle Corps, on the [army's] left wing, after capturing Kamyshevakha, Hill 167.1 (0.5 kilometers northwest of Kamyshevakha), Hill 224.5 (1.5 kilometers southwest of Kamyshevakha), and Hill 227.4 (2.5 kilometers east of Bashtevicha), continued to fight for Shinshinovka and Annovka.

The 1st Guards Mechanized Corps, after capturing Hill 287.4 (1 kilometer northeast of Nikitovka), attacked toward Fedorovka (northern and southern) and Shterovka (northern).

The 14th Rifle Corps, overcoming stubborn resistance and repelling repeated enemy counterattacks, is continuing to attack toward Fromandirovka and Iulino from the Red'kino *Balka* (2.5 kilometers east of Shterovka) and Velikii Dolzhik *Balka* (1 kilometer east of Ivanovka) line.

The 7th Guards Cavalry Corps, attacking northeastward from the Vladimirovka, Davydovka, and Aleksandrovka region, reached the Red'kino *Balka*, Petrovskoe State Farm, Shirokii, and Orlova line, where it linked up with units of the 14th Rifle and 1st Guards Mechanized Corps. It has the mission of concentrating in the Orekhovo and Shelkovyi Protok regions. During the fighting from 11 through 24 February, the units of the 7th Guards Cavalry Corps destroyed the headquarters of the 62nd Infantry Division and inflicted considerable losses on the 62nd and 304th Infantry Divisions. Up to 4,000 soldiers and officers were destroyed, the 22nd Panzer Division's Tank School, 25 tanks, 20 trains with various weaponry and equipment, 8 locomotives, and 30 warehouses were completely destroyed, and the railroad right of way and a number of stations were blown up in several places. A train with prisoners-of-war was also seized.

The positions of the army's remaining units are essentially unchanged.

During the day of fighting on 24 February, more than 2,150 enemy soldiers and officers, 2 tanks, 11 machine guns, and 31 guns were destroyed. Three guns, 9 machine guns, 94 rifles, 550 shells, and 20,000 bullets were captured. Ten prisoners were captured.

7. The 5th Tank Army resumed its offensive on the morning of 24 February 1943, but, having met with strong enemy resistance, its offensive was unsuccessful, and it continued to fight in its previous positions at day's end.

8. The 17th Air Army, while assisting the *front's* forces, destroyed enemy forces and equipment in Sakhnovshchina, Stepanovka, Mar'evka,

Annovka, Novotroitskoe, and Novo-Aleksandrovka with bombing and assault operations,. It bombed the airfields at Stalino and Andreevka and enemy forces in Artemovsk and Nikitovka, and it conducted reconnaissance and protected its forces.

According to incomplete data, [the air army] conducted 328 aircraft sorties, 120 of these at night. Up to 30 enemy aircraft, 10 tanks, and 100 automobiles were destroyed or damaged, 2 fuel warehouses were blown up, the fires of 2 field artillery batteries and 1 antiaircraft artillery battery were suppressed, and 2 strong explosions were noted in Artemovsk. Up to two companies of enemy infantry were dispersed and destroyed in piecemeal fashion. Three air battles were conducted, during which 2 enemy aircraft were shot down.

Vatutin, Zheltov, Ivanov[123]

Later in the day, with more than just a touch of ruthlessness, at 1140 hours Vatutin issued Mobile Group Popov new orders spelling out in even greater detail how he intended its commander withdraw his already defeated (and, in many instances, still encircled) forces to new defensive positions south of the Northern Donets River. Always the fighter, Vatutin was still trying to figure out a way to revive his faltering offensive by forming new shock groups:

Given the existing situation, I have decided to withdraw Kharitonov's [6th Army's] units and organize an active defense along the Riabukhino, Okhochae, and Orel'ka River line to Orel'ka and to Kondrashovka and Starye Bliznetsy beyond to prevent the enemy from penetrating into the Lozovaia region and from Kegichevka toward Alekseevskoe. Destroy the enemy attacking from Barvenkovo and capture the Barvenkovo region. To do so:

A. The 1st Guards Army's 6th Guards Rifle Corps, after leaving one rifle division in the Lozovaia region, will break contact with the enemy and reach the Barvenkovo region by forced march by the morning of 25 February with its remaining divisions.

Together with your group, the 52nd Rifle Division will attack and defeat the enemy and capture the Barvenkovo region. Construct a defensive front along the line of the Bliznetsy and Barvenkovo railroad stations

B. Your group will gather into a fist and destroy the enemy in the Barvenkovo region, in cooperation with the 6th Guards Rifle Corps.

C. All of the *front's* aviation will work for the destruction of the enemy in the Barvenkovo region and along the approaches from the southeast.

Since Kuznetsov [1st Guards Army] has not established communications with your formations and has not taken over your group, I entrust you with organizing all details of the battle to destroy the enemy in the Barvenkovo region and demand you prevent the enemy from reaching this region from the north and northwest at all costs.

Bring the 3rd Tank Corps and the 4th Guards Tank Corps' 13th Tank Brigade forward. Understand that today the enemy is bringing columns forward from Debal'tsevo to Artemovsk, from Gorlovka to

Konstantinovka, and from Krasnoarmeiskii Rudnik to Kramatorskaia. Therefore, you should expect the enemy to reinforce his attack along the Barvenkovo axis on 25 February 1943. I demand that you and Kuznetsov be personally responsible for preventing the enemy from taking a step further.

Vatutin, Zheltov, Ivanov[124]

Vatutin dispatched even more detailed instructions to Mobile Group Popov and to the 6th Army and the 1st Guards Army at 1905 hours on 25 February:

I am informing you that the units on the Voronezh Front's left wing are starting to fulfill the mission of attacking into the enemy's flank toward Krasnograd and Kegichevka.

As a result of this attack, the forward units of the cavalry [the 1st Guards Cavalry Corps] will reach the Lozovaia and Efremovka front by the end of 24 February 1943, from which they attack toward Shliakhovaia and Kegichevka.

Two rifle divisions are moving southward from Merefa.

The 156th Rifle Division is fighting for Novaia Vodolaga, and the 12th Tank Corps is fighting for Fedorovka, 10 kilometers east of Valki.

I order:

The commanders of the armies and Lieutenant General Popov will display maximum persistence while fulfilling their assigned missions and, everywhere conditions permit, will undertake active operations, while encircling and destroying the scattered enemy units.

The commander of the 6th Army will immediately order the commander of the 350th Rifle Division, together with the Voronezh Front's cavalry [6th Guards Cavalry Corps], to go over to the offensive and attack into the enemy's flanks in the direction of Shliakhovaia and further to the south.

The units escaping from encirclement will operate skillfully and decisively against the enemy's rear area and headquarters and destroy his separate garrisons.

This regards the cavalry division, in particular.

I confirm the mission of Lieutenant General Popov and Lieutenant General Kuznetsov – to destroy the enemy along the Barvenkovo axis.

Vatutin, Zheltov, Ivanov[125]

At 0700 hours on 26 February, Vatutin contacted Kharitonov, the commander of the beleaguered 6th Army, by radio-teletype in a conversation underscoring the increasing desperateness of the situation:

Kharitonov speaking.

Fedorov [Vatutin] speaking.

Fedorov: Hello, Comrade Kharitonov. Our communications with you are no good at all. You and I have to take measures to improve it. Now report on your situation, how you are fulfilling my orders, where is Sokolov [the 6th Guards Cavalry Corps] located, and where and what enemy you are facing?

Kharitonov: I am reporting: all attempts to determine Sokolov's precise whereabouts have been unsuccessful. We know his units were fighting in the Shliakhovaia region and somewhere to the west. Despite inadequate supplies, [Major General A. G.] Griaznov [the 15th Rifle Corps] was conducting active operations together with Sokolov and, holding his positions firmly, did not lag behind Sokolov. [Colonel A. M.] Mel'nikov [the 115th Tank Brigade] is assisting Griaznov. The sector between Griaznov and Gagen [the 4th Guards Rifle Corps] is the most dangerous for me, and cavalrymen on foot and separate groups made up of the remnants of [Major General A.V.] Kukushkin [the 1st Guards Tank Corps] and [Major General P. P.] Pavlov [the 25th Tank Corps] are operating in this region. I am preparing a position for Moshliak [unknown unit], and he should show up soon.

The enemy is massing toward this sector from the north. We have not determined his strength. The enemy is continuing to operate actively in Gagen's sector. No fewer than 100 tanks and up to a division of infantry are in action. Derebin [unknown unit] is fighting to hold this point and has requested assistance by available fire support. The promised antitank regiments have not yet arrived.

My neighbors to the left, on his right wing, are obviously in a bad way. I hear a fire fight nearby.

Tanks and motorized infantry are seeping through Gagen's left wing.

Fedorov: What do you know about Pavlov [the 25th Tank Corps] and [Colonel V. A.] Gerasimov [the 267th Rifle Division] and the others like them? Have they pushed down [southward] from [Colonel L. M.] Goriakin [the 6th Rifle Division]? Reply.

Kharitonov: I have no information about Gerasimov or Pavlov. Krasovsky's [17th Air Army] equipment, which is serving me, has poor connections with Zlatotsvetov [unknown unit]. They have not reported what they are doing and how and where they are regarding their assigned missions. In the morning, I must once again search for and determine Pavlov's march-route. There must be enemy opposite Gagen. I have assigned him missions but doubt he can accomplish them. Goriakin [the 6th Rifle Division] is in contact with the enemy and is partially fulfilling his mission to the south. Over.

Fedorov: What positions has the enemy in front of Gagen reached? Perhaps it would be useful to visit Gagen and [Major General A. P.] Gritsenko [the 350th Rifle Division] or [Colonel N. S.] Timofeev [the 172nd Rifle Division] and Mel'nikov [the 115th Tank Brigade]? Is your 212th Tank Regiment operational? What is your opinion? Answer.

Kharitonov: I am answering. Gritsenko is fully working in Sokolov's group. They are fighting. Timofeev has just enough to hold his position somewhat and cannot be withdrawn. I already reported to you about Goriakin; he cannot be castled [moved left]. Mel'nikov has the mission to work with Goriakin, initially to the southwest and then with Gagen to the northeast. All of this requires time and knowledge of the enemy's impending actions. The 212th Tank Regiment has still not arrived ... its equipment is approaching. I am clarifying the exact place, and think I will send it to Gagen. Its approach is required for a good turning point. Over.

Fedorov: You did not tell me which points the enemy has reached in front of Gagen. Reply.

Kharitonov: I report. Dmitrievka (the southern outskirts of the larger point). And on the neighboring side, Bratoliubovka. Over.

Fedorov: Comrade Kharitonov. First of all, you must defeat the enemy facing Gagen and hold on to your own lines. Therefore, assist Gagen [the 4th Guards Rifle Corps] more decisively by castling [forces] from Griaznov [the 15th Rifle Corps].

Sokolov must help, but if you have a crisis in Gagen's sector; then bear in mind Sokolov's operations themselves can be compromised. Understand this and take appropriate measures. Fight with everything at hand to bring out Pavlov, Gerasimov, and the others. Do not lose communications with them, [it is better] to find out about them rather than help them. We will undertake measures. Your neighbor to the left has received a strict order not to withdraw a step. However, if the enemy penetrates into the junction with him, destroy him. Recently, order no. 227 ["Not a Step Back"] has been violated with impunity in some sectors, in particular, in Popov's. Demand stubborn and sharp increased steadfastness. I forbid the abandonment of occupied positions without my approval. Fulfill order no. 227 exactly. Organize your blocking service [to prevent desertion or unauthorized withdrawals] carefully. Acquaint all personnel with order no. 227. Reinforcements will arrive. That is all. Do you have any questions?

Kharitonov: I have no questions, and the orders are clear. I will act. I will fight to the end. Over.

Fedorov: I just received news about Sokolov. His forces were along the Kazach'ii Maidon, Shliakhovaia, and Par-Shliakhovaia line at day's end on 25 February. Understand this and make an appropriate effort to help Gagen. That is all. I wish you success. Goodbye.

Kharitonov: Gritsenko will occupy that line. That is all from me. Goodbye.

Vatutin, Zheltov, Ivanov[126]

As Manstein's forces accelerated their counterstroke, steadily increasing the pressure brought to bear against the right wing and center of Vatutin's Southwestern Front, on 27 February the beleaguered *front* commander tried once again to shore up his sagging defenses. This time he did so by freeing up forces from less active sectors, in particular, from the sectors of the 1st and 3rd Guards and 5th Tank Armies on his *front's* left wing, and by hastily transferring them to the most threatened sectors on the *front's* right wing and center:

According to available information, the enemy is strengthening his forces in the Artemovsk, Gorlovka, and Debal'tsevo regions with the intent of attacking toward the north. I have decided to strengthen the sector of the front from Slaviansk to Krymskaia immediately.

I order:

1. The commander of the 3rd Guards Army will bring up an additional three rifle divisions, one howitzer artillery regiment, two antitank regiments, one gun artillery regiment, and two battalions of antitank rifles to the Slaviansk and Krymskaia sectors no later than 4 March 1943 to strengthen the defense in that sector and to create a deep defense, paying special attention to the Artemovsk, Kaganovich Coal Pits, and Lisichansk axis.

Hold firmly to the designated lines and prevent any sort of enemy movement toward the north.

Immediately transfer the 57th Guards Rifle Division and its sector to the 1st Guards Army.

I am establishing the following boundary line between the 1st Guards and 3rd Guards Armies effective 2400 hours on 27 February 1943: to Krasnyi Liman, as before, and further to Veselyi (2 kilometers southeast of Kramatorskaia), inclusive for the 1st Guards Army. Give the 5th Tank Army the Kolpakovo and Mine No. 33 sector of the front by 0800 hours on 1 March 1943 once the units of the 5th Tank Army have relieved your forces.

I am establishing the following boundary line between the 3rd Guards Army and the 5th Tank Army effective 0800 hours on 1 March 1943: to Verkhnie Krasnianka, as before, and further to Rebrikovo (incl.), Kolpakovo (incl.), Krasnyi Kut, and Ordzhonikidze. Immediately go over to a tough defense along the Rodakovo and Meterovka front after allocating up to two rifle divisions and a tank regiment to your second echelon.

Implement timely measures to fill out the divisions and replenish them with ammunition and fuel up to required norms. Conduct continuous force reconnaissance day and night along the army's entire front.

2. The commander of the 5th Tank Army will take over the Kolpakovo and Mine No. 33 sector from the 3rd Guards Army by 0300 hours on 1 March 1943, after the units of the 3rd Guards Army relieve you there.

The army will immediately go over to a tough defense along its existing lines, after allocating no less than one rifle division to its second echelon. Implement timely measures to fill out the divisions and replenish them with ammunition and fuel up to required norms.

3. The commander of the 1st Guards Army will immediately accept the 57th Guards Rifle Division and its sector. Report copies of all orders given.

Vatutin, Zheltov, Ivanov[127]

The End

However, nothing Vatutin could do halted the violent attacks by Manstein's three panzer corps. In addition to the SS, XXXXVIII, and XXXX Panzer Corps, which had already caved in Vatutin's defenses from Krasnograd eastward to Barvenkovo, the First Panzer Army's III Panzer Corps joined the counterstroke at day's end on 27 February by assaulting northward from the Slaviansk region. Vatutin dutifully announced the bad news in a report he dispatched to the *Stavka* at 0200 hours on 28 February:

1. The enemy, in his previous configuration and grouping, continued constant attacks against our forces on the *front's* right wing all day on 27 February 1943, displaying the greatest toward Lozovaia and Barvenkovo. Our units succeeded in pressing the enemy back along several axes of the 1st Guards Army. Attempts by the enemy to capture Barvenkovo were unsuccessful, and, as before, our forces held on to Barvenkovo.

The enemy is continuing to hold onto his previous positions in front of the 3rd Guards Army and the 5th Tank Army, while offering stubborn resistance to the offensive of our forces.

Operations by the units of the SS Panzer Division "*Totenkopf*" have been detected in the Orel'ka region by documents taken off the dead.

2. The forces of the Southwestern Front continued intense fighting with enemy motorized infantry and tanks on 27 February 1943, particularly along the Lozovaia and Barvenkovo axes, and part of its forces fought in encirclement and to escape from encirclement and link up with their own forces.

The 6th Army, while attacking toward the southwest with part of its forces, captured Logvinaia and Kotliarovka.

Our units east of Barvenkovo, after repelling several enemy counterattacks, once again captured Nikopol' and Cherkasskoe.

Our units in the remaining sectors of the *front* had no offensive success and continued to fight along previous lines.

3. The 6th Army, while holding on to Riabukhino (northern) and Paraskoveia on its right wing, developed its offensive toward the southwest on 27 February 1943, captured Logvinaia and Kotliarovka, and, while repelling enemy counterattacks from Berezovka and Vlasovka toward Efremovka, fought for possession of Vlasovka and Shliakhovaia,

In the center and on the left wing, while repelling attacks by enemy infantry and tanks, the units of the army held on [to the following] positions: The 172nd Rifle Division — Dmitrovka and Sharlaevka; the 6th Rifle Division — Pisarevka and Bessarabovka; and the 106th Rifle Brigade fought for Sakhnovshchina and Ligovka.

The 244th Rifle Division fought encircled in the Iur'evka region with part of its force and, together with the 267th Rifle Division, is holding on to Nizhnee Razdory and Shirokov with its main forces.

The 112th Tank Regiment and the 115th Tank Brigade are being concentrated in the Krasnopavlovka region in readiness to repel enemy tank attacks.

The 35th and 41st Guards Rifle Divisions are holding on to positions between Krasnopavlovka and Grushevakha.

The 58th Guards Rifle Division, repelling fierce enemy infantry and tank attacks, is holding on to Lozovaia.

4. The 1st Guards Army continued fighting heavy holding actions against enemy tanks and motorized infantry in the Kamyshevakha, Barvenkovo, and Slaviansk regions all day on 27 February 1943, while repelling repeated counterattacks.

The units of the army occupied [the following] positions at day's end:

The 195th Rifle Division continued to fight encircled in the Mar'inopol'e, Valer'ianovka, Novo-Morokino, and Chervonogo Shpil regions at 1600 hours.

The 44th Guards Rifle Division, repelling enemy attacks, continued holding on to the Grushevakha (incl.) and Velikaia Kamyshevakha line.

The 52nd Rifle Division, after repelling all enemy tank and infantry attacks against Barvenkovo, continued to hold Barvenkovo firmly at day's end and Nadezhdovka and Nikopol', with one regiment facing toward the east,.

The 57th Guards Rifle Division was concentrated in the Slaviansk region and fought along the line through Krasnoarmeisk, Bylbasovka, the western and southern outskirts of Slaviansk and Mandrichino, and the southeastern outskirts of Slaviansk during the day.

The 78th Rifle Division — in its previous positions, repelled an attack by up to a battalion of infantry from Karbonit toward Gorskoe on its left wing.

The 19th Rifle Corps: the 60th Guards Rifle Division withdrew from the Malaia Kamyshevakha and Sukhaia Kamenka line to the Dmitrievka, Brazhevka, Suligovka, and Dolgen'kaia regions to organize a defense along this line.

The 229th Separate Rifle Brigade – along the Malaia Eremovka, Iarovaia, and Maiaki line.

Up to 700 enemy soldiers and officers were destroyed and 18 tanks destroyed and burned in the Dubovo region and east of the state farm on 24 February. Twenty-five enemy tanks were destroyed in the Nikopol' region on 26 and 27 February.

5. The 3rd Guards Army, fulfilling its assigned missions, continued prolonged fighting with enemy infantry and tanks during the day on 27 February 1943, repelling repeated attacks. It continued fighting in its previous positions to day's end, while replenishing its ammunition and personnel and preparing to fulfill new missions.

The positions of the army's units are essentially unchanged.

6. The 5th Tank Army, after resuming the offensive along its entire front beginning on the morning of 27 February 1943, encountered organized enemy fire resistance and, after repelling repeated counterattacks, made insignificant gains in separate axes during the day.

7. The 17th Air Army destroyed enemy personnel and equipment with bombing and assault operations in the Barvenkovo, Lozovaia, Sergeevka,

and Konstantinovka regions. It protected its own forces and conducted reconnaissance. 141 aircraft sorties were conducted.

According to incomplete data, 10 tanks, 92 automobiles, 5 carts, and 1 tanker truck were destroyed or damaged, 5 field guns and 2 antiaircraft gun mounts were suppressed, and up to 250 enemy soldiers and officers were scattered and destroyed piecemeal. It conducted four air battles during which it shot down one Me–109 aircraft.

Vatutin, Zheltov, Ivanov[128]

As Manstein's attacking forces continued demolishing his *front's* defenses, in the process encircling large chunks of his forces, Vatutin had no choice but to turn to the *Stavka* for assistance. The *front* commander did so by asking Stalin to order the Voronezh Front, whose forces were advancing adjacent to Vatutin's right wing and had recently captured Khar'kov, to send forces to assist him. In response, at 0430 hours on 28 February, the *Stavka* ordered Colonel General F. I. Golikov, the commander of the Voronezh Front, to transfer Lieutenant General P. S. Rybalko's 3rd Tank Army, Major General S. V. Sokolov's 6th Guards Cavalry Corps, and their supporting rifle divisions to Vatutin's control:

The *Stavka* of the Supreme High Command orders:

1. Transfer the Voronezh Front's 3rd Tank Army, including Group Sokolov [the 6th Guards Cavalry Corps], to the Southwestern Front, effective at 2200 hours on 28 February.

2. The commander of the Southwestern Front will employ the 3rd Tank Army and Group Sokolov to conduct a flank attack against the attacking enemy forces.

3. Before forces arrive from the *Stavka's* Reserve, the commander of the Voronezh Front will transfer several divisions from other sectors of the *front* and send them to strengthen the *front's* left wing.

4. Report fulfillment.

I. Stalin[129]

The *Stavka's* intent in issuing this directive was to wheel the 3rd Tank Army and 6th Guards Cavalry Corps, which were conducting exploitation operations southwestward from the Khar'kov region toward Poltava, ninety degrees to the left and then employ the massed tanks and cavalry for an attack southward against the SS Panzer Corps' left wing and flank. However, regrouping Rybalko's tank army was no mean task. The tank army's 12th and 15th Tank Corps and supporting rifle divisions had been engaged in near constant fighting from more than a month, and, as a result, its forces were woefully under-strength and suffering from short- ages of tanks, fuel, and ammunition. Nevertheless, the *Stavka's* directive was clear, and Rybalko had no choice but launch his tank army into the teeth of the SS Panzer Corps regardless of cost.

Rybalko's force, which consisted of the 12th and 15th Tank Corps, with a total of fewer than 80 operational tanks, supported by the 111th, 184th, and 219th Rifle Divisions, approached the Kegichevka region from the north on 1 March. By this time, the SS Panzer Corps' SS Panzer Divisions *"Leibstandarte Adolf Hitler"* (*"LAH"*), *"T,"* and *"Reich"* were approaching the Kegichevka region from three directions; the "*LAH*" Division eastward from the Krasnograd region and the "*T*" and "*Reich*" Divisions northward in tandem from the Lozovaia region. By this time, the remnants of the 6th Army's 172nd and 6th Rifle Divisions defended the Kegichevka region (see Map 51). Therefore, as it advanced southward into the Kegichevka region, Rybalko's 3rd Tank Army encountered the SS Panzer Corps' three converging panzer divisions, in what soon became a "death ride" with utterly predictable results for Rybalko's threadbare tank army.

As Rybalko's forces were completing their ill-fated march toward Kegichevka, Vatutin apprised the *Stavka* of the situation at 0300 hours on 1 March, but without even mentioning Rybalko's tank army:

1. The enemy on the *front's* right wing, in his previous configuration and grouping, continued constant attacks against our forces all day of 28 February 1943, while displaying the greatest activity along the Barvenkovo and Izium axis.

The enemy launched his heaviest attacks in the 1st Guards Army's sector, where an enemy force of more than 300 enemy tanks and motorized infantry penetrated our forces' defensive front and captured Petrovskoe and the Novo-Ivanovka, Novo-Dmitrovka, and Khrestishche by day's end on 28 February 1943 and continued to develop his offensive toward Chervonyi, Shakhter, Malaia Kamyshevakha, and Dolgen'kaia, while delivering his main attack toward Izium. His forward detachments reached the southern bank of the Northern Donets River.

The enemy in front of the 3rd Guards Army's front, while firmly holding the positions he occupied, attacked the right wing of the 78th Rifle Division with a force of more than an infantry regiment and 40–50 tanks during the first half of the day, delivering his attack toward Nikolaevka and Rai-Aleksandrovka.

The enemy penetrated into these populated points by day's end and cut the Nikolaevka, Rai-Aleksandrovka, Beskrovnyi, and Kalenniki road.

On the left wing, while offering stubborn resistance, he is occupying his previous defensive positions.

2. The forces of the Southwestern Front fought intense defensive battles with attacking enemy tanks and motorized infantry units all day on 28 February 1943, particularly in the sector of the 1st Guards Army, where the enemy penetrated the defenses of the 6th Guards Rifle Corps with a large tank force with motorized infantry and reached the rear area of our units.

A part of the 1st Guards Army's forces are fighting in encirclement or half encircled. In the sector of the 3rd Guards Army, remaining in their previous positions, part of its forces repelled attacks by enemy tank and motorized infantry penetrating into Nikolaevka and Rai-Aleksandrovka.

No offensive operations were conducted on the *front's* left wing.

3. The 6th Army continued to fight with attacking enemy tanks and motorized infantry and organized a defense along the Petrovskoe, Kuibyshevo, Aseevka, Gusarovka, and Chepel' line and farther along the eastern bank of the Northern Donets River on 28 February 1943.

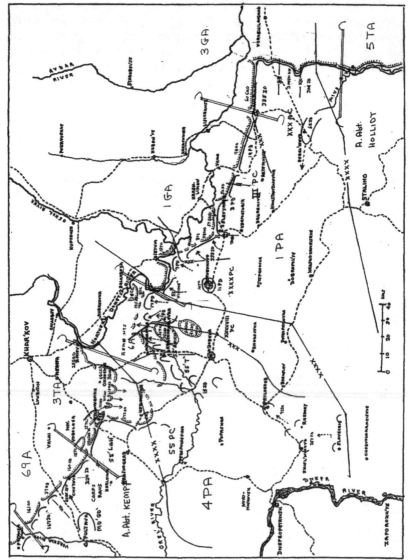

Map 51. The Donbas operation, the situation on 28 February 1943

The army's units occupied [the following] positions by day's end: the 350th Rifle Division advanced from the Vlasovka, Kotliarovka, and Lozovaia (northern) line to the Shliakhovaia and Par-Shliakhovaia line; the 172nd Rifle Division – along the Dmitrievka and Nizhnii Orel'ka line; the 6th Rifle Division – at Pavlovka and Bessarabovka; the 106th Rifle Brigade, attacking eastward from Sakhnovshchina, captured Ligovka; the 267th Rifle Division fought along the Elizavetovka 2, Elizavetovka 1, and Chernokamenka line and, while withdrawing toward Lozovaia, was attacked by enemy tanks and forced to withdraw to Mikhailovka on 27 February 1943.

The 58th Guards Rifle Division continued street fighting in Lozovaia. It has the mission to destroy the railroad center and withdraw to Mikhailovka on the night of 1 March 1943.

The 1st Guards Tank Corps and 2nd Guards Cavalry Regiment, as a result of the fighting for Krasnopavlovka, withdrew toward Krasnyi Kut, Razdol'e, and Petrovskoe.

The 244th Rifle Division [should read the 263rd Rifle Division] (without one regiment) and the 2nd Mixed Cavalry Division continued their escape from encirclement in small subunits and groups toward Krasnopavlovka and Mikhailovka.

The 25th Tank Corps withdrew from encirclement, and its advanced elements are approaching Krishtopovka.

4. The 1st Guards Army continued conducting intense holding actions with enemy tanks and motorized infantry on 28 February 1943, which were especially severe in the Slaviansk region along the Barvenkovo and Izium axis.

The units of the army occupied [the following] positions at day's end:

The 195th Rifle Division continues to fight in encirclement in the Mar'inopol'e', Valer'ianovka, Novo-Morokino, and Chervonyi Shpil' regions, with the mission to reach the Velikaia Kamyshevakha and Dmitrovka line;

The 18th Tank Corps conducted offensive operations toward Bobrov and Novo-Ivanovka axis, while protecting the Pashkovo region;

The 44th Guards Rifle Division is defending Velikaia Kamyshevakha;

The 244th Rifle Division: fought in the Dmitrovka, Novo-Kamyshevakha, and Vernopol'e region with one rifle regiment: and one rifle regiment, with a battalion from the 11th Tank Brigade, withdrew from Bazaleevka to Brazhevka and Malaia Kamyshevakha;

The 52nd Rifle Division, while repelling constant enemy tank attacks, held on to Barvenkovo;

The 57th Guards Rifle Division is fighting half encircled, while holding on to Slaviansk; and

The 19th Rifle Corps prepared a second defensive line in the Dmitrievka and Maiaki sector during the day.

The positions of the remaining units are being verified.

5. The 3rd Guards Army, remaining in its occupied positions, carried out a regrouping and repelled attacks by enemy tank and motorized infantry penetrating toward Nikolaevka and Rai-Aleksandrovka with part of its forces on 28 February 1943.

The enemy began simultaneous attacks on Nikolaevka and Rai-Aleksandrovka with a force of more than an infantry regiment supported by 40–50 tanks at 1000 hours on 28 February and, as a result of a day-long battle, cut the Nikolaevka – Rai-Aleksandrovka and the Beskrovnyi – Kalenniki roads.

The units of the 78th Rifle Division, occupying all-round defenses in Nikolaevka and Rai-Aleksandrovka, continue fierce street fighting with enemy infantry and tanks.

The army's units are continuing to hold firmly to the positions they occupy in the remaining sector of the front.

6. The 5th Tank Army, while holding on to its previous positions, replenished its reserves and exchanged fire with the enemy on 28 February 1943. The positions of the army's units remain unchanged.

Vatutin, Zheltov, Ivanov[130]

While the forces of Rybalko's 3rd Tank Army were preparing to go into action in the Kegichevka region, employing a curious mixture of threats and exhortations, at 0945 hours on 1 March, Kharitonov enjoined the commanders in his 6th Army to contain the German advance in cooperation with Rybalko's armor:

1. The enemy is continuing to develop his offensive along the Balakleia and Alekseevka axes with tank units and motorized infantry, and his forward units, consisting of small tank groups (3–5 tanks), with small groups of submachine gunners, are brazenly bursting through to the Northern Donets River.

2. Our units, completely encircled by the enemy, are fighting heroically in Lozovaia, in the Pavlograd region, and in the region northeast of Zaporozh'e.

The units of the 15th Rifle Corps successfully repelled all enemy attempts to attack southwest from Kegichevka.

The 267th Rifle Division, 106th Rifle Brigade, 16th Tank Brigade, and the 3rd, 8th, and 19th Cavalry Regiments fought their way out of encirclement and are continuing to fight.

The units of the 4th Guards Rifle Corps, having falling victim to heavy attacks by the enemy's tank groups, suffered losses and, thanks to the very poor organization of the withdrawal from the fighting by their command cadre and staff, cannot delver the required rebuff to the penetrating enemy forces. The commanders and staffs of the rifle corps inadequately prepared obstacles in their rear and poorly fulfilled NKO order no. 227, and, as a result, a great number of commanders and soldiers forgot their obligation to their Homeland, deserted the field of battle, and ended up in the army's deep rear area. Many commanders and their staffs displayed extreme confusion and, sometimes, clear cowardice in these recent battles.

The army's mission – while exerting maximum energy, initiative, will, and decisiveness, prevent the enemy [from advancing] further than the Dmitrovka, Alekseevskoe, Aseevka, Gusarovka, and Chepel' line and, especially beyond the Northern Donets River, with whatever forces and weapons are necessary. All units located south and southwest of the Northern Donets River have received the mission to hold firmly to this designated line.

I order:

1. The commanders of rifle corps, rifle divisions, and rifle brigades and the commanders of all artillery and mortar units to undertake immediately the most decisive measures to organize their forces and fulfill their assigned missions. No one has the right of withdrawing his subunit across the Northern Donets River. The headquarters of the divisions and regiments, in the last resort, must be located on the southern bank of the Northern Donets River, while grouping all of their forces and weapons around themselves and repelling any enemy attacks on them. Those who have abandoned the Northern Donets River and crossed to its northern bank must return immediately and occupy firm defensive positions on its southern bank.

2. The commander of the 15th Rifle Corps will force the river with the forces of the 172nd and 6th Rifle Divisions and organize a defense along the Dmitrovka, Alekseevskoe, and Petropavlovskoe line. Immediately set about organizing intermediate defenses along the Efremovka, Oktiabr'skii, Kamenka, and Kiseli line and in Bereka and Verkhne-Byshkin. Bear in mind that the forward edge of the main defensive belt, which the newly arriving units must reach, must be along the Taranovka, Bereka, Verkhne-Byshkin, and Geevka line.

3. The commander of the 4th Guards Rifle Corps, after absorbing the remnants of the 41st Guards Rifle Division, the 16th Tank Brigade, and Levin's 1249th Antitank Regiment, as well as the remaining artillery of all attached units, will firmly defend the Kuibyshevo and Aseevka line with the forces of the 267th and 35th Guards Rifle Divisions, and, simultaneously, prepare intermediate positions through Melovoi Iar, Novo-Nikolaevka, Sokolovka, Zhebelinka, Piatigorsk State Farm, and Melovaia. Employ the local population to prepare the positions.

4. The commander of the 1st Guards Cavalry Corps, while exploiting detachments from withdrawing units in his defense, will continue to hold firmly to the Aseevka, Gusarovka, and Chepel' line with the forces of the 5th Cavalry Division and the 21st Separate Rifle Brigade, reinforced by one gun from Levin and the weapons of the 1st Guards Cavalry Corps, and, simultaneously, will prepare strong positions for approaching units along the northern bank of the Northern Donets River from Melovaia to Krasnyi Gusarovka, while paying special attention to defending firmly the crossing in the Krinichnyi and Zadonetskii regions.

5. The defense of all units must be resolute to the end, carefully organized for antitank fighting, and protected by obstacles (engineer and natural).

6. The chiefs of staff of the units and formations are personally responsible for maintaining reliable and uninterrupted communications with all of their units and subunits by all means at their disposal.

7. Once again disseminate NKO order no. 227 widely, strictly warn all command cadre in advance about their responsibility to the country and its people for fulfilling their assigned missions, and give short shrift to panic and desertion mercilessly and immediately.

8. Ensure this order is fulfilled with all measures of your Special Department [*Osobyi otdel'* – OO for counterintelligence], procurator, and tribunal.

9. Report receipt and fulfillment immediately.

Kharitonov, Klokov, Fomin[131]

Nor was there anything the hapless Vatutin could do to escape the inevitable as the panzer corps of Army Group South's Fourth and First Panzer Armies bore down the overextended, collapsing, and often isolated forces in his *front's* center and on its shattered left wing. Continuing their assaults northward from the Lozovaia and Barvenkovo regions, the 6th and 17th Panzer Divisions of the Fourth Panzer Army's XXXXVIII Panzer Corps, flanked on the east by the SS "*Wiking*" and 7th and 11th Panzer Divisions of the First Panzer Army's XXXX Panzer Corps, shattered the remnants of Kharitonov's 6th Army, the 4th Guards Rifle Corps, and Mobile Group Popov on the left wing of Kuznetsov's 1st Guards Army and reached the southern bank of the Northern Donets River between Andreevka and Izium by day's end on 3 March. Simultaneously, operating in Army Group South's center, the 3rd and 19th Panzer Divisions of the First Panzer Army's III Panzer Corps pressed the 1st Guards Army's 6th Guards Rifle Corps northward from the Slaviansk region to the Northern Donets River in the sector from Izium eastward toward Voroshilovgrad. South of Voroshilovgrad, on Army Group South's right wing, the First Panzer Army's XXX Army Corps and the forces of *Armeeabteilung* Hollidt kept the 3rd Guards and 5th Tank Armies of Vatutin's Southwestern Front and the armies of Malinovsky's Southern Front at bay along the Mius River front southward to the Sea of Azov.

Meanwhile, on the left wing of Manstein's army group, the Fourth Panzer Army's SS, soon supported by the XXXXVIII Panzer Corps, completely demolished Rybalko's counterattacking 3rd Tank Army and its supporting rifle divisions in the Kegichevka and Okhochae regions from 3 through 5 March, in the process turning the rescuers into new victims. After encircling and largely destroying Rybalko's 12th and 15th Tank Corps and his four supporting rifle divisions in converging assaults, sending their survivors reeling back northward toward Khar'kov, the SS Panzer Corps' "LAH," ""T," and "Reich" Panzer Divisions advanced to roughly 32 kilometers from the southern outskirts of Khar'kov (see Map 52). Before Golikov's Voronezh Front could patch together a new defensive line south and west of Khar'kov, Manstein's SS and XXXXVIII Panzer Corps, now joined on the left by *Armeeabteilung* Kempf's Corps Raus and the Second Army to the west, struck violently at Golikov's defenses west and south of Khar'kov. Catching the *Stavka* and Golikov by surprise, Manstein quickly transformed his victorious counterstroke in the Donbas into an equally spectacular counterstroke toward Khar'kov, this time with Golikov's Voronezh Front as its intended victim.

Despite this looming developing disaster, on 8 March an ever optimistic Vatutin sent another proposal to Stalin, this time requesting the *Stavka's* permission to launch an even more ambitious offensive:

I am reporting for you for consideration:

1. The immediate aim: to encircle and destroy the enemy armed forces situated in the Donbas and east of the Poltava, Kremenchug, and Dnepr River line in the Ukraine and to capture these regions.

2. Enemy forces: in front of the Southwestern Front — 9 panzer divisions, 12 infantry divisions, and up to 12 separate regiments; in front of the Southern Front — 2 panzer divisions, 1 motorized division, and 5–6 infantry divisions; and in front of the Voronezh Front's left wing — 5 panzer divisions and 2 infantry divisions in. In all, a total of 16 panzer divisions, 1 motorized division, and 20 infantry divisions. To sum up — 37 divisions.

3. I will accomplish the encirclement and destruction of the enemy in the following fashion:

A. The Southwestern Front will attack from the Novoberetskii (12 kilometers south of Taranovka) and Chepel' front toward Lozovaia, Sinel'nikovo, and Melitopol' with two armies (no fewer than twelve reinforced rifle divisions) in a dense combat formation.

Two tank armies will develop their attack to clear the entire eastern bank of the Dnepr River.

Two [other] armies (no fewer than twelve reinforced rifle divisions) will attack from the Izium and Saiaki front in the general direction of Barvenkovo, Krasnoarmeiskoe, and Mariupol' with their fronts turned toward the east. No less than one tank army, one separate tank corps, and one cavalry corps will develop their attack.

The 3rd Guards Army will conduct a supporting attack from the Voroshilovgrad axis.

The *front's* reserve: up to five rifle divisions, one tank corps, and one cavalry corps.

B. Neighbors: The Voronezh Front must attack toward Krasnograd and Dnepropetrovsk and toward Poltava and Kremenchug with its left wing.

The Southern Front must attack toward Volnovakha to envelop Stalino from the south.

I will present a more detailed plan later.

Fedorov [Vatutin][132]

If it responded at all, the *Stavka's* reaction to Vatutin's utterly unrealistic proposal remains unknown.

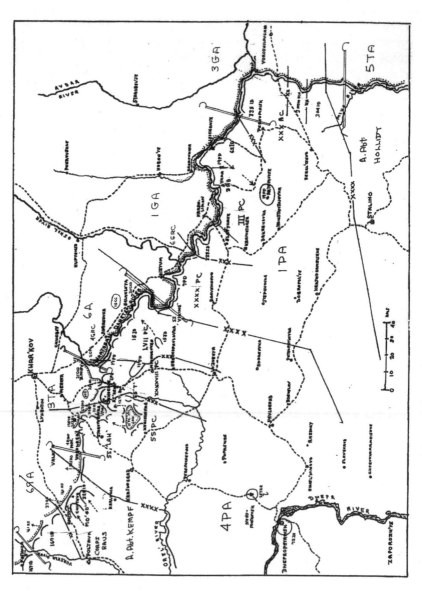

Map 52. The Donbas operation, the situation on 5 March 1943

Conclusions

The failure of the Southwestern Front's offensive into the Donbas region, which was readily apparent to German commanders as early as 20 February but acknowledged by their Soviet counterparts days later, also marked the end of the *Stavka's* ambitious Voronezh-Khar'kov strategic offensive operation. Despite its spectacular initial successes, ultimately the offensive proved immensely costly to Vatutin's forces. Although the Russians have yet to release a comprehensive unit-by-unit listing of the casualties the Red Army suffered during the operation, fragmentary archival records indicate that the Southwestern Front (less the 6th Army) initially committed 265,180 men in the offensive and, including reinforcements received during the operation, lost 101,733 soldiers, including 38,049 killed, missing, or captured and 63,684 wounded or sick during the period from 1 January through 22 February 1943.[133]

In addition, during the period from 13 January through 3 March 1943, the Southwestern Front's 6th Army lost 20,423 soldiers, including 8,268 killed, captured, or missing and 12,155 wounded or sick out of the 60,200 soldiers it initially committed to combat. Thereafter, the 6th Army lost 28,225 more soldiers, including 15,412 killed, captured, or missing and 12,813 wounded or sick during its retreat to the Northern Donets River.[134] Although grim in their own right, these figures do not include the losses suffered by the Southwestern Front's other armies during the offensive and defensive fighting between 23 February and 8 March, which probably exceeded the 100,000 losses it suffered during the offensive stage of its operations.

An after-action-report Vatutin dispatched to the *Stavka* on 15 March 1943, which contained specific requests for personnel reinforcements and additional weapons, confirms that his *front's* personnel losses likely exceeded 200,000 men:

> The forces of the Southwestern Front, conducting constant offensive operations, advanced about 1,000 kilometers during the period from 16 November 1942 through 15 March 1943.
>
> Before the beginning of the combat operations, the forces were under-strength, at about 70–80 percent of their authorized strength, and they suffered considerable losses in personnel and weapons in the fighting they conducted, particularly, the most recent.
>
> On 10 March 1943 the shortages in the combat units constituted: personnel — 256,000 men, horses — 35,000 head, guns of all calibers — 1,041, mortars of all calibers — 1,628 mortars, tanks — 1,013, and cargo trucks — 5,900.
>
> There are considerable shortages in communications equipment and in engineer and chemical weapons.
>
> To replenish the forces with personnel, during the period from 1 November 1942 through 10 March 1943, [the following] were received: as march replacements detailed by the GLAVUPROFORM [Main Directorate for the Formation and Manning of the Red Army] — 36,500 men; mobilized from territory liberated by the *front* — 39,191 men; liberated from Fascist captivity — 38,000 Red Army soldiers;

released from *front* and army hospitals — 80,439 men; and at the expense of replacing young men in the *front's* and armies' rear services by the mobilization of women — 6,470 men. All told, during this period [the following] were received: detailed by the Directorate of Red Army Reserve Units — 365,000 men, and from local and *front* resources — 163,691 men.

During the month of March, I assigned the mission: to bring 8 rifle divisions up to a strength of 7,500–8,000 men each at the expense of local resources and at the expense of those arriving at the direction of the Center [the NKO], to fill out the 1st Antitank Brigade, the 2nd Tank Corps, and the 1st Guards Mechanized Corps (their motorized rifle brigades), and to form 14 antitank rifle battalions and 1 automatic weapons battalion. I have rehabilitated four antitank artillery regiments and four antiaircraft artillery regiments.

I request you assign [the following] to fill out the rifle divisions, fifteen regiments, and a number of units of other types of forces with personnel and horses, artillery, and other types of weapons:

1. Personnel

Command personnel: combined-arms — 5,000 and artillery — 1,000; and non-commissioned officers, rank and file soldiers, and those suited to the construction service — 7,000.

2. Artillery weapons

Guns: 122-mm – 58, 76-mm field – 45, 76-mm divisional — 235, 45-mm – 550, 37-mm antiaircraft guns — 148, 76-mm antiaircraft guns – 5, large stereoscopes (BST) — 547, survey compasses — 1,094, and binoculars — 11,941.

Mortars: 82-mm – 780, 120-mm – 52, and 50-mm — 790.

Rifles and carbines — 108,250, revolvers and pistols — 27,870, and 12.7-mm DShK large-caliber machine guns – 322.

Antitank rifle — 4,380, heavy machine guns — 2,738, sub-machine guns — 7,400, and PPD and PPSh [sub-machine guns] — 18,300.

3. Tanks: T–34 – 614, T–70 — 400. Armored transporters – 72, armored cars — 106.

4. Engineer weapons

Small shovels — 64,300, sapper shovels — 32,000, military axes — 19,000, carpentry axes — 18,200, normal crow bars — 4,500, traverse saws — 3,300, sets of N2P [pontoon] parks — 2, vehicles for N2P parks – 416, heavy and light pickaxes — 9,400, sheers for cutting barbed wire — 8,500, mine detectors — 750, antitank mines — 1,000,000, antipersonnel mines — 90,000, explosives (MUV) — 65,000, detonator capsules — 35,000, and demolition vehicles — 100.

5. Chemical weapons

Gas masks — 156,000, protective wraps — 43,000, protective stockings — 331,000, chemical reconnaissance satchels — 750, and inflammable bottles [Molotov cocktails] — 200,000.

6. Communications equipment

High-power radios — 30, medium-power radios — 54, low-power radios — 702, RUK — 26, radio receivers — 104, wave meters – 40, charging units — 81, BODO apparatuses — 5, ST–35 apparatuses — 146, Morse apparatuses — 12, ShK–20 apparatuses — 11, telegraph satchels — 88, R–60 switchboards — 4, KOF switchboards — 315, numerators — 22, UNA-I telephones — 166, UNA-F telephones — 1,619, UNA-FI telephones — 1,013, telephone packs No. 257 — 816, telephone packs No. 259 — 2,770, ASP No. 271 sets — 43, NKN–22 storage batteries — 6,262, NKN–45 storage batteries — 2,166, line laying instrument sets No. 278-A — 64, line laying instrument sets No. 278-B – 53, line laying instrument packs No. 275 — 166, six-line instruments sets No. 283 — 62, field line sets No. 285 — 178, ASK–33 — 153, cable telephones — 2,934, telegraph coils — 1,355, telephone cables — 3,350, telephone coils — 11,808, standardized instrument sets — 141, [*politnish. peredn.*] lines — 745, two-peg telephone — 1,109, two-peg cable — 164, two-peg [*gestovikh*] — 47, two-peg telegraph — 62, and two-peg chain-stitch — 16.

7. Trucks – 3,650

8. Horses for the cavalry corps – 8,500 and for artillery units – 5,000

Vatutin, Zheltov, Ivanov[135]

Chapter 5

The Southern Front's Mariupol' (Donbas) Offensive (16–22 February 1943)

Introduction

When Vatutin's Southwestern Front began its offensive into the Donbas region on 29 January, tentatively at least, the *Stavka's* offensive plan required the Southern Front, then under Eremenko's command, to play an active role in the operation. At the time, Eremenko's *front* consisted of five field [combined-arms] armies, one air army, one cavalry-mechanized group, and eight mobile corps. These included Lieutenant General V. D. Tsvetaev's 5th Shock, Lieutenant General Ia G. Kreizer's 2nd Guards, Major General N. I. Trufanov's 51st, Lieutenant General V. F. Gerasimov's 28th, and Major General V. A. Khomenko's 44th Armies, Major General of Aviation T. T. Khriukhin's 8th Air Army, and Lieutenant General N. Ia. Kirichenko's Cavalry-Mechanized Group (CMG).

Eremenko retained direct control over Kirichenko's CMG, which consisted of his own 4th Guards Cavalry Corps and Major General A. G. Selivanov's 5th Guards Cavalry Corps, and two of his *front's* five mobile corps, but assigned the other three mobile corps to support his *front's* armies. Specifically, Major General K. Z. Sviridov's 2nd Guards Mechanized Corps, Major General S. I. Bogdanov's 5th Guards Mechanized Corps, and Lieutenant General P. A. Rotmistrov's 3rd Guards Tank Corps remained under the *front* commander's direct control, while Eremenko assigned Major General T. I. Tanaschishin's 4th Guards Mechanized Corps, Major General A. P. Sharogin's 3rd Guards Mechanized Corps, and Major General N. S. Oslikovsky's 3rd Guards Cavalry Corps to support the 2nd Guards, 51st, and 5th Shock Armies, respectively.

Although formidable on paper, the forces of Eremenko's *front* were severely under-strength in both men and material because they had been fighting incessantly since early January, driving the Fourth Panzer Army's forces westward south of the Don River from the Aksai River toward Rostov. In early February the forces on the Southern Front's left wing (the 44th, 28th, and 51st Armies and the Cavalry-Mechanized Group) were advancing westward along the southern bank of the Don River toward Rostov, engaging the forces of Army Group South's Fourth Panzer Army and those on *Armeeabteilung* Hollidt's right wing. In the *front's* center, the 2nd Guards Army was advancing westward toward the Don River south of Razdorskaia against the forces in *Armeeabteilung* Hollidt's center, and, on the *front's* right wing, the 5th Shock Army, flanked on the right by the 5th Tank Army, was advancing against the forces on *Armeeabteilung* Hollidt's left wing, which were protecting the Northern Donets River line south of

Kamensk-Shakhtinskii and the approaches to Shakhty in the bend of the Northern Donets River. When Eremenko fell ill on 2 February, the *Stavka* appointed Malinovsky to command the Southern Front.

Although the forces of Vatutin's Southwestern Front successfully penetrated the German defenses along the Northern Donets River and began advancing into the northern Donbas region during the first week of February, those of Malinovsky's Southern Front remained bogged down opposite the German defenses along the Don and Northern Donets Rivers. To speed up his offensive, late on 8 February, Malinovsky ordered his *front's* forces to "destroy the enemy's Rostov-Novocherkassk grouping by the end of 9 February and to [capture Rostov and] reach the Bol'shekrepinskaia, Gorskaia Porada, Blagodat', and Sambek front with its left wing by day's end 10 February."[136] However, because Malinovsky's offensive once again faltered in the face of skillful German resistance, his forces were not able to capture the city of Rostov until 14 February (see Map 53). By this time Vatutin's forces were across the Northern Donets River, and Malinovsky's forces had not yet reached positions from which they could support Vatutin's advance. However, the fall of Rostov on 14 February and the ensuing withdrawal by Army Group South's Fourth Panzer Army and *Armeeabteilung* Hollidt to defenses along the Mius River opened the way for Malinovsky's forces to participate more actively in operations to liberate the Donbas region.

Planning

Responding to a fresh directive from the *Stavka,* which ordered his Southern Front to pursue the withdrawing German forces to the Mius River more vigorously, Malinovsky assigned new missions to the armies of his *front* armies at 2340 hours on 14 February (see Map 54):

1. The enemy, fighting rear guard actions, is withdrawing to the Mius River.

2. The forces of the Southern Front, pursuing the withdrawing enemy, will disorganize his withdrawal, destroy his units piecemeal, and reach the Mius River by day's end on 17 February and the Donets-Amvrosievka, Anastasievka, and Fedorovka line with its mobile units by 16 February, and cut off the enemy's routes of withdrawal toward the northwest and west.

3. The 5th Shock Army, pursuing the enemy toward Agrafenovka and Uspenskaia, will reach the Vlasovo-Bytovka, Balabanov, and Novo-Dmitrievskii line by day's end on 15 February and the Zhelobok and Novo-Spasovka line by day's end on 16 February, and capture Uspenskaia by day's end on 17 February.

The 3rd Guards Cavalry Corps will capture Kuibyshevo by the morning of 16 February and prevent the enemy from withdrawing toward the northwest.

The 4th Guards Mechanized Corps will reach the Donetsko-Amvrosievka and Mokryi Elanchik regions by the morning of

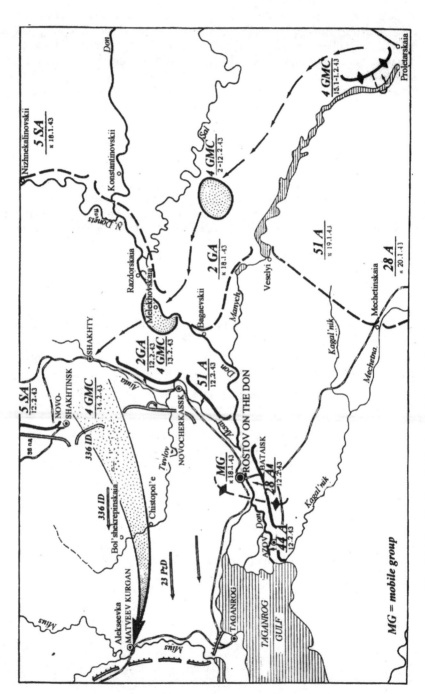

Map 53. The 4th Guards Mechanized Corps' advance to the Mius River, 12–16 February 1943

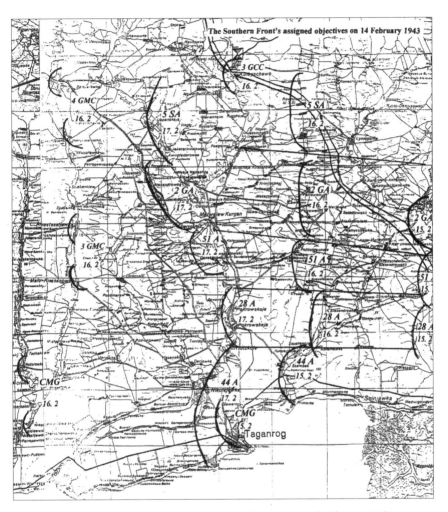

Map 54. The Southern Front's assigned objectives on 14 February 1943

16 February, cut the railroad and main road, and prevent the enemy from withdrawing toward the northwest and west.

The CP [command post] of the army – Sidoro-Kadamovskaia and Verilo-Krepinskaia.

The boundary to the left: [through] Rodionovo-Nesvetaiskoe – as previously and farther — Iasinovskii (Mar'evka).

4. The 2nd Guards Army, destroying the enemy withdrawing toward Bol'shekrepinskaia and Matveev Kurgan, will reach the lines: by day's end on 15 February — Bol'shekrepinskaia and Karshino-Ivanovskii; by day's end on 16 February — Novoveselyi and Vidnyi; and by day's end on 17 February — Pervomaiskii and Doroganov.

The 3rd Guards Mechanized Corps will reach the Anastasievka and Malo-Kirsanovka region by the morning of 16 February and prevent the enemy from withdrawing toward the northwest and west.

CP – Grushevskaia and Bol'shekrepinskaia.

The boundary line to the left: [through] Novocherkassk, Nesvetai, and Matveev Kurgan.

5. The 51st Army, pursuing the enemy toward Kirpichevo-Aleksandrovskii and Riazhenaia, will reach the lines: by day's end on 15 February — Russko-Leont'evskii, Kalmykov, and Aleksandrovka; by day's end on 16 February — Politotdel'skoe and Buzinov; and by day's end on 17 February — Stepanovksii and Riazhenaia.

CP – Aksaiskaia, Bol'shie Saly, and Sovet.

The boundary line on the left: [though] Bol'shie Saly, Aleksandrovka, and Riasnyi.

6. The 28th Army, developing its offensive toward Pokrovskoe, will reach the lines: by day's end on 15 February — Aleksandrovka and Hill 106; and by day's end on 16 February — Blagodat' and Abramovka; and capture Pokrovskoe by day's end on 17 February.

CP — Bataisk and Sultan-Saly.

The boundary line on the left: through Bataisk (incl.), Krym (incl.), Vodianoi (incl.), and Troitskoe.

7. The 44th Army — will crush enemy resistance and reach the lines: by day's end on 15 February — Kurlatskoe, Sambek, and Varenovka; and by day's end on 17 February — Troitskoe, Nikolaevka, Grecheskie Roty, and Novo-Bessergeevka.

CP – Podazov'e and Sambek.

8. The Cavalry-Mechanized Group of Kirichenko, developing its attack toward Taganrog, will capture Taganrog by day's end on 15 February, reach the Fedorovka and Mar'evka regions by the morning of 16 February, and seize the crossings over the Miusskii Liman [River] and prevent the enemy from withdrawing toward the west.[137]

9. The 8th Air Army will protect the 4th Guards Mechanized Corps and CMG Kirichenko and, in cooperation with them, destroy the enemy's withdrawing units.

10. Report on all orders received and given.

Malinovsky, Khrushchev, Varennikov[138]

The Southern Front's 28th Army and CMG captured Rostov at 0800 hours on 14 February. But before Malinovsky could organize a proper coordinated pursuit, Manstein ordered his army group to regroup its forces and withdraw them behind the Mius River, out of harm's way, as quickly as possible.[139] First, he ordered Hoth's Fourth Panzer Army, which had just protected the withdrawal of Mackensen's First Panzer Army from the northern Caucasus region to the Donbas region through the "Rostov gate," to conduct an orderly fighting withdrawal from the Rostov region to prepared defenses along the Mius River and, subsequently, prevent Soviet forces from penetrating westward across the river. Second, once Hoth moved his Fourth Panzer Army's forces to safety west of the Mius River, Manstein ordered him to turn his defenses along the river to *Armeeabteilung* Hollidt, whose forces then became responsible for defending the entire Mius River line. Finally, after passing control of the Mius River front to Hollidt's army detachment, Hoth was to regroup the headquarters of his Fourth Panzer Army westward to the Dnepropetrovsk region in the western Donbas, where it was to take control of new forces and mount a powerful counterstroke against the western flank of the Southwestern Front's armies attacking into the Donbas region from the north.

As it conducted its tricky withdrawal back to the Mius River line, Hoth's panzer army consisted of the LVII Panzer Corps's 23rd Panzer, 16th Infantry (Motorized), 15th *Luftwaffe* Field, and 111th Infantry Divisions, the XXIX Army Corps' Divisional Groups 79 and 177 (the former 79th and 177th Infantry Divisions), the headquarters of the Romanian II Army Corps, the 454th and 444th Security Divisions, and two separate regiments.

When Malinovsky realized that Hoth's skillful withdrawal was effectively thwarting his *front's* general advance, at 1530 hours on 15 February, he ordered Kirichenko's CMG and Khomenko's 44th Army to mount a hasty dash forward to reach and cross the Mius River and capture Taganrog by the evening of the same day:

> To forestall the enemy from going over to the defense in previously prepared positions along the Mius River, I order the *front's* forces to pursue the withdrawing enemy energetically day and night with their full efforts.
>
> Avoiding combat with separate centers of resistance, reach the western bank of the Mius River with your mobile units as quickly as possible and destroy the withdrawing enemy from the rear, denying him the opportunity to conduct an organized transition to the defense along the Mius River.
>
> In they failed to do so on 15 February, Kirichenko's Cavalry-Mechanized Group and the 44th Army will fulfill the mission of seizing Taganrog on the night of 15–16 February by a dash through Rostov.
>
> Malinovsky, Khrushchev, Varennikov[140]

When Kirichenko's cavalrymen encountered strong German resistance along the Sambek River west of Rostov, at 0525 hours on 16 February, Malinovsky directed his forces to accelerate their advance (see Map 55):

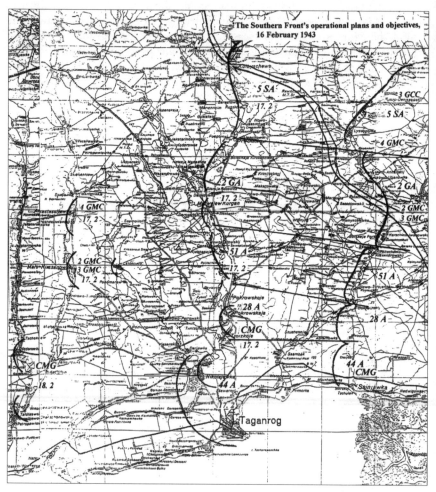

Map 55. The Southern Front's operational plans and objectives, 16 February 1943

1. The Southwestern Front is directing its efforts at capturing Donetsko-Amvrosievka with its left wing.

2. With the objective of cutting off the enemy and pressing him toward the sea, I order:

The commander of the 5th Shock Army to direct the 4th Guards Mechanized Corps to capture Matveev Kurgan and then Anastasievka, which it will reach by the morning of 17 February.

The commander of the 2nd Guards Army to send the 2nd and 3rd Guards Mechanized Corps through Riazhenaia to Latonovo and Malo-Kirsanovka, which they will seize by the morning of 17 February.

The commander of the CMG – Kirichenko, enveloping the enemy's centers of resistance from the north, has the main missions to reach the Pokrovskoe and Nikolaevka regions, cut off the enemy's withdrawal from Taganrog by the morning of 17 February, and reach the Fedorovka and Mar'evka regions by the morning of 18 February.

The commander of the 44th Army will smash enemy resistance and, enveloping it from the north, capture Taganrog by day's end on 17 February.

3. Confirm receipt and report all orders given.

Malinovsky, Khrushchev, Varennikov[141]

The Offensive

To the Mius River

After pausing briefly to regroup its forces, Tanaschishin's 4th Guards Mechanized Corps had accelerated its advance late on 15 February and, attacking westward with the 2nd Guards Army's 33rd Guards Rifle Division following close behind, captured the town of Matveev Kurgan and a small bridgehead on the Mius River's western bank on the evening of 16 February. Shortly after the 4th Guards Mechanized seized the key town and nearby bridgehead, Malinovsky ordered Tanaschishin "to force the Mius River from the march, penetrate the enemy's defenses, capture Marfinka [Marfinskaia], Anastasievka, and Malo-Kirsanovka [30 kilometers deep], and subsequently exploit success southwestward 40 kilometers and reach the Grintal', Tel'manovo, and Rosenfel'd line."[142] After completing these missions, Tanaschishin's corps was to wheel southward and advance toward Mariupol' in the Germans' deep rear to outflank *Armeeabteilung* Hollidt's defenses along the Mius River.

Pausing shortly to catch its breath on 16 February, on the 17th Tanaschishin's corps lunged westward audaciously and captured the villages of Anastasievka and Marfinskaia on the Mokryi Elanchik River 30 kilometers behind *Armeeabteilung* Hollidt's forward defenses along the Mius River (see Map 56). However, as Malinovsky noted in a report he dispatched to the *Stavka* at midnight on 18 February, the rest of his *front's* armies failed to keep pace with Tanaschishin's bold thrust to and across the river:

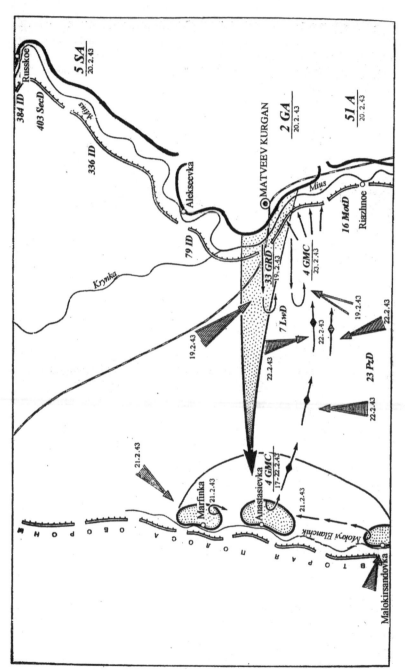

Map 56. The 4th Guards Mechanized Corps' penetration of the main enemy defensive belt on the Mius River and its combat in encirclement, 17–23 February 1943

1. The forces of the *front* were continuing to arrive along the Mius River on the right wing on 18 February and, along the remainder of the front, conducted offensive fighting against enemy forces which went over to the defense along the Mius River. As a result more than 20 populated points were occupied during the day, including Iasinovskii (Mar'evka), Bol'shaia Kirsanovka, and Staraia Rotovka.

2. Along the entire front of the offensive by our forces, the enemy occupied last year's defense lines along the western bank of the Mius River and Sambek River and offered stubborn resistance throughout the entire day.

3. The 5th Shock Army, continuing to push the enemy's rear guards units back, was fighting [in the following locations] at day's end: the 3rd Guards Cavalry Corps – for possession of Kuibyshevo; the 315th Rifle Division – the eastern outskirts of Berestovo and Russkoe; and the 40th Guards Rifle Division — after crushing enemy resistance, captured Petropol'e and Iasinovskii (Mar'evka) and, wedging into the enemy's defenses, was continuing to widen the bridgehead it seized with its right wing.

The 2nd Guards Army fought along the Alekseevka and Matveev Kurgan line with the forces of its 300th, 44th, 387th, and 33rd Rifle Divisions.

The 33rd [Guards] Rifle Division, exploiting the success of the 4th Guards Mechanized Corps, was moving forward southwest of Matveev Kurgan.

The 4th Guards Mechanized Corps forced the Mius River, penetrated the enemy's defense, fought for Stepanovskii, and approached Marfinskaia with part of its forces (its arrival in Marfinskaia is being verified).

The 3rd Guards Mechanized Corps was continuing to fight for possession of Riazhenaia.

The 51st Army reached the eastern bank of the Mius River in the Kolesnikov and Riazhenoe Station sector with its 87th and 126th Rifle Divisions and, together with the units of the 3rd Guards Mechanized Corps, is fighting to reach the western bank of the Mius River.

The 2nd Guards Mechanized Corps captured Riazhenoe Station and is fighting for Riasnyi.

The 28th Army, together with the 2nd Guards Mechanized Corps, is fighting to capture Riasnyi with units of the 156th Rifle Brigade, the 248th Rifle Division is fighting 2 kilometers south of Sedovskii, and the 159th Rifle Brigade is at Kopani.

The 52nd and 152nd Rifle Brigades are fighting to capture height marker 108, and the 34th Guards Rifle Division is 4 kilometers west of height marker 77.

The 44th Army, having encountered stubborn enemy resistance along the Sambek River, is fighting to capture Sambek, Varenovka, and Primorskaia.

CMG Kirichenko is concentrating in the Matveev Kurgan and Riazhenaia region for an attack toward Mar'evka and Fedorovka.

4. The *front's* force will continue their offensive to destroy the opposing enemy and reach the Mokryi Elanchik River on 19 February (in accordance with Order No. 0019)[143]

Malinovsky, Khrushchev, Varennikov[144]

Even before he was able to concentrate the bulk of his *front's* main forces along the Mius River line, Malinovsky decided to exploit the 4th Guards Mechanized Corps' bold preemptive advance toward the west by organizing a series of follow-on assaults, first with his other mobile corps and later with his *front's* main forces, once they reached the river line. After directing Tanaschishin's mechanized corps to expand its foothold along the Mokryi Elanchik River, the *front* commander ordered Kreizer's 2nd Guards Army to reinforce Tanaschishin's forces as quickly as possible with rifle divisions from its main forces as they reached and crossed the Mius River. He then ordered his *front's* other mobile corps, the 3rd Guards Cavalry Corps, the 2nd and 3rd Guards Mechanized Corps, and the two corps of Kirichenko's Cavalry-Mechanized Group to launch similar deep strikes westward across the river in support of Tanaschishin's corps as soon as they were capable of doing so. In the grander scheme of things, by exploiting Tanaschishin's successes west of the Mius with similar deep operations by all of his *front's* mobile corps, Malinovsky hoped his *front's* mobile corps could ultimately link up with those of the Southwestern Front (Mobile Group Popov's four tank corps and the 3rd Guard Army's 8th Cavalry, 2nd Guards Tank, and 1st Guards Mechanized Corps) somewhere in the Stalino region. If they did so successfully, it would be possible to encircle and destroy most of Army Group South's forces in the eastern Donbas region.

Although Malinovsky's reports to the *Stavka* do not describe the operations by Tanaschishin's corps west of the Mius River in any detail, the 4th Guards Mechanized Corps' official history provides a fairly accurate account of the corps' operations. Since Tanaschishin's corps had been engaged in heavy fighting for weeks on end, by mid-February it was severely under-strength in tanks and other weapons and equipment, and its rear services were lagging far behind. Tanaschishin himself reported on about 17 February, "There is no fuel. We have a total of 15–20 kilometers [to traverse], and we have only 50 percent of our equipment. Twenty tanks are operational, and the rest lack fuel. My men have not slept for four nights. I request three days of rest to put the corps in order."[145]

Pressured unrelentingly by Stalin and his *Stavka*, Malinovsky simply refused to grant Tanaschishin's forces any respite. Led by the forces of Lieutenant Colonel V. I. Zhdanov's 15th Guards Mechanized Brigade, which defeated a small German force at the villages of Greko-Ul'ianovka and Mar'evka, 20 kilometers east of Matveev Kurgan, on 15 February, the 4th Guards Mechanized Corps' main body approached the Mius River during the evening of the same day. After the corps' 13th Guards Mechanized Brigade forced the Mius River and captured the village of Alekseevka, 8 kilometers north of Matveev Kurgan, late in the evening, the remainder of Tanaschishin's corps attacked and captured Matveev Kurgan overnight on 15–16 February. When a German counterattack forced the 13th Guards Mech-

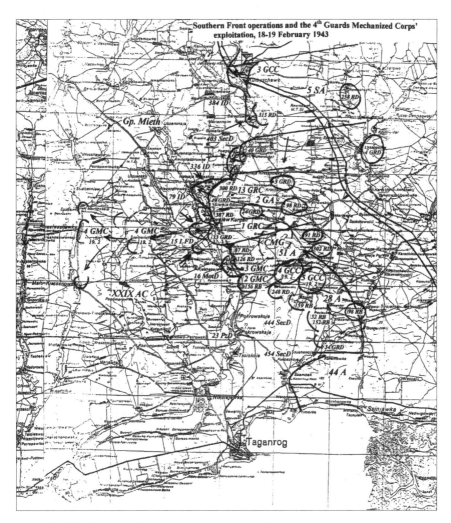

Map 57. The Southern Front's operations and the 4th Mechanized Corps' exploitation, 18–19 February 1943

anized Brigade to withdraw back to the river's eastern bank during the night, Tanaschishin spent all day on 16 February regrouping his forces for a concerted assault to breech the Mius River line once and for all. By this time the lead elements of Kreizer's 2nd Guards Army were still 25–30 kilometers to Tanaschishin's rear.

To the Mokryi Elanchik River

Attacking at 1000 hours on 17 February after a 15-minute artillery preparation, Tanaschishin's forces pierced the Germans' defenses along the Mius River at the boundary between *Armeeabteilung* Hollidt's 79th Infantry and 7th *Luftwaffe* Field Divisions and began a to exploit rapidly toward the west at 1900 hours (see Map 57). Responding to this new threat, Hollidt hastily erected a new defensive line along the Mokryi Elanchik River, 25 kilometers to the west, manning it with rear service forces and "scratch" ad hoc units formed from whatever combat troops he could assemble. He then ordered these small groups to defend this line at all costs and, whenever and wherever possible, conduct counterattacks against the flanks of the exploiting Russian force to cut its lines of communication and prevent its reinforcement. Conducting its exploitation with all three of his mechanized brigades deployed abreast, Tanaschishin's mechanized corps captured the town of Anastasievka on the Mokryi Elanchik River at nightfall on 17 February, where it reportedly dispersed the headquarters of the German XXIX Army Corps, and, soon after, also seized the towns of Marfinka and Malo-Kirsanovka, on the Mokryi Elanchik River 5 and 8 kilometers north and south of Anastasievka, respectively.

As Tanaschishin's forces advanced westward toward the Mokryi Elanchik River, the 88th and 91st Guards Rifle Regiments of Major General A. I. Utvenko's 33rd Guards Rifle Division (from the 2nd Guards Army) also assaulted across the Mius River to support Tanaschishin's thrust and protect his flanks. Reacting quickly, the 79th Infantry and 7th *Luftwaffe* Field Divisions immediately attacked the flanks of Utvenko's advancing division at the villages of Doroganov and Stepanovo, 5–6 kilometers west of the Mius River, with hastily assembled battalion- and company- size *kampfgruppen*. Since Utvenko's division lacked air support, these counterattacks overwhelmed his two forward rifle regiments, encircling them west of the Mius River, and drove the remainder of his division back to a small bridgehead on the river's western bank west of Matveev Kurgan, by doing so severing all communications between Tanaschishin's mechanized corps and the supporting 2nd Guards Army. Simultaneously, the Germans also began bombing Tanaschishin's lines of communications to cut off his support, particularly, his reserve supplies, which the 2nd Guards Army's 33rd Guards Rifle Division was transporting forward.

After reevaluating his situation, late on 18 February, Tanaschishin ordered his three mechanized brigades to erect and man all-round defenses in their present positions and wait for assistance from the 2nd Guards Army's rifle divisions, which he hoped were advancing to assist his forces. In the meantime, the corps commander exploited captured German equipment, fuel, and supplies to sustain his force and formed armed partisan detachments from the local populace to help his brigades defend Marfinka and Malo-Kirsanovka.

As Tanaschishin's mechanized brigades dug themselves in around the villages they occupied along the Mokryi Elanchik River, the main body of Kreizer's 2nd

Guards Army finally reached the Mius River on 18 and 19 February. During these two days, the 300th Rifle and 49th Guards Rifle Divisions of Major General P. G. Chanchibadze's 13th Guards Rifle Corps forced their way across the Mius River, captured Alekseevka, and fought for Aleksandrovka, while the same corps' 3rd Guards Rifle Division captured Bol'shaia Kirsanovka, 8 kilometers further to the north. At the same time, the 387th Rifle Division of Major General I. I. Missan's 1st Guards Rifle Corps captured Shaposhnikov Farm, on the river's western bank 4 kilometers north of Matveev Kurgan, and Utvenko's 33rd Guards Rifle Division, two of whose regiments were still fighting encircled west of Matveev Kurgan, prepared to break through to the west to rescue its two beleaguered regiments and Tanaschishin's now isolated mechanized corps. Utvenko, however, required considerable assistance before he could do so.

While the 2nd Guards Army was concentrating its forces along the Mius River near Matveev Kurgan, preparing to support Tanaschishin's mechanized corps to the west, *Armeeabteilung* Hollidt struggled to assemble sufficient forces to prevent Malinovsky from inserting even more forces into its rear area west of the Mius River. Ultimately, these forces included elements of the 79th, 336th, and 384th Infantry, the 403rd Security, and the 16th Panzer Grenadier and 23rd Panzer Divisions. Hollidt then ordered the bulk of these forces to dig in along the Mius River's western bank, while the 23rd Panzer Division, with minimal infantry support, prepared plans to deal with Tanaschishin's corps. From the 2nd Guards Army's perspective:

> The enemy command understood the important significance of the defensive line along the Mius River, which protected the southern Donbas region. The Hitlerites well understood that, if they failed to hold the "Mius Front" position, they would have to withdraw from the entire steppe region right up to the Dnepr River. All of this forced the enemy to fight stubbornly for that position.
>
> The 2nd Guards Army, which approached the Mius River on 18 February, was severely weakened from prolonged battles. It was experiencing severe shortages in ammunition and fuel. The roads were deteriorating from the advancing thaw. Even though the advancing army's front shrank from 120 to 18 kilometers, the army was not able to exploit the 4th Guards Mechanized Corps' success. By the time it reached the Mius River, the enemy had managed not only to seal the breech made by the mechanized corps but also to consolidate significantly his units' combat formations.
>
> The army made numerous attempts to penetrate the enemy's defenses along the Mius River during the last ten days of February and the first ten days of March, but all of them failed. Two regiments of the 33rd Guards Rifle Division and the 4th Guards Mechanized Corps distinguished themselves during this fighting by their special actions while operating encircled and while breaking out from the [encirclement].[146]

As Malinovsky pondered how best to rescue his forces encircled west of the Mius River and, if possible, re-ignite his flagging offensive, he sent another situation report to the *Stavka* at 2400 hours on 19 February:

1. On 19 February the forces of the *front* fought fiercely to reach the Mius River's western bank and captured Kuibyshevo, Russkoe, Demidovka, and Shaposhnikov.

2. The enemy, having been reinforced, is offering stubborn resistance with four infantry divisions (the 306th, 336th, 294th, and 79th), two separate infantry regiments (the 177th and 179th), three air force divisions (the 7th, 8th, and 15th), two security divisions (the 444th and 454th), one panzer division (the 23rd), and one motorized division (the 16th). The enemy launched a series of counterattacks with tanks and infantry supported by aircraft during the second half of the day and pushed our forces, which had occupied Berestovo, Petropol'e, Podgornyi, and Kucherovo, back. His aircraft bombed the combat formations of the 4th Guards Mechanized Corps and 2nd Guards Army.

3. The 5th Shock Army, after capturing Kuibyshevo, was continuing its offensive and fighting 2 kilometers west and southwest of Kuibyshevo with units of its 3rd Guards Cavalry Corps. The enemy's counterattacks on Kuibyshevo were repelled.

The 315th Rifle Division, after capturing Berestovo and Russkoe, was counterattacked and was fighting along the eastern outskirts of Berestovo.

The 40th Rifle Division, after being counterattacked by the enemy, withdrew to Iasinovskii (Mar'evka) and is fighting on the eastern bank of the Mius River.

The 2nd Guards Army fought with mixed success. Alekseevka changed hands twice. The 300th and 49th Rifle Divisions, after driving the enemy away, were continuing to fight for Aleksandrovka at day's end.

The 387th Rifle Division, repelling enemy counterattacks, is holding on to Demidovka and Shaposhnikov.

The 33rd [Guards] Rifle Division advanced forward slowly and is fighting 3 kilometers east of Verkhne-Shaposhnikov and for possession of Doroganov.

Volleys of multiple rocket launchers and infantry fire halted a counterattack in the Stepanovskii region conducted by 20 tanks and motorized infantry mounted on 15 armored personnel carriers.

The 4th Guards Mechanized Corps is fighting heavily in the southeastern part of Anastasievka. All of the attempts by the 2nd Guards Army's units to break through to it have not been crowned with success.

Enemy aircraft bombed the units of the corps and burned some of the fuel transporters being sent to the 4th Guards Mechanized Corps.

The units of the 3rd and 2nd [Guards] Mechanized Corps fought in the Riazhenaia region with mixed success. Pressed by the enemy, they were fighting in the eastern part of Riazhenaia during the second half of the day.

The 51st Army, after encountering stubborn resistance and flanking artillery and mortar fire, was unable to advance.

The 28th Army captured Riazhenoe Station and Riasnyi with units of the 156th Rifle Brigade but were pushed back north of Riazhenoe Station by enemy counterattacks.

Encountering strong resistance from enemy fire, no success was achieved in the remaining sectors of the army.

The 44th Army fought intensely for possession of Sambek and Varenkovka during the day, but had no success.

Kirichenko's Cavalry-Mechanized Group concentrated in [the following] regions: the 4th Guards Cavalry Corps — in the Turchaninov, Bogdanov, and Sedovskii regions; the 5th Guards Cavalry Corps — in the Ivanovka, Poliev, and Buzonov region; and the tank group — in the Turchaninov region.

4. According to our calculations, [the following] trophies were seized during the occupation of Bataisk: railroad cars — 3,984, of these, with cargo — 2,018, and empty — 1,955; automobiles (inoperable) — 411; tanks — 49; guns — 20; ammunition – 106 railroad cars, bread — 39 railroad cars; motorcycles — 1 railroad car, bicycles — 1 railroad car; rails — 34 railroad cars; cable — 14 railroad cars; sleepers – 45 railroad cars; motors — 4 railroad cars; medical supplies — 4 railroad cars; furniture — 18 railroad cars; electrical equipment — 7 railroad cars; tinned [canned] goods — 16 railroad cars; carbide — 2 railroad cars; iron casks — 47 railroad cars; durable goods — 1,052 railroad cars; petrol engines — 19 railroad cars; coal tenders — 14; and locomotives — 48.

We identified 195 damaged and partially burned enemy aircraft, mainly "Henkel–111," "Ju–83," and "Me–110" models, at the Rostov, Novocherkassk, and Shakhty airfields, 15 of which can be restored.

5. The forces of the *front* will continue the destruction of the opposing enemy on 20 February and will reach the Anastasievka and Malo-Kirsanovka regions with the units of the 3rd and 2nd Guards Mechanized Corps and also Kirichenko's Cavalry-Mechanized Group and link up with the units of the 4th Guards Mechanized Corps.

Malinovsky, Khrushchev, Varennikov[147]

Malinovsky himself traveled to Matveev Kurgan on 20 February to assist the 2nd Guards Army as it prepared its forces to breach the Mius River line and rescue Tanaschishin's beleaguered mechanized corps. Under Malinovsky's direct supervision, Kreizer's guards army commenced its assaults at dawn the next morning:

The army commander transferred the 24th Guards Rifle Division from his reserve to assist the encircled units and the mechanized corps. It was supposed to link up with the units of the 33rd Guards Rifle Division by attacking from the Matveev Kurgan region, in cooperation with the 387th Rifle Division, and then toward Anastasievka to assist the 4th Guards Mechanized Corps. The attack began in the morning

Simultaneously, the 33rd Guards Rifle Division's 84th Guards Rifle Regiment and the 4th Guards Mechanized Corps' 12th Guards Mechanized Brigade launched active operations to advance to the encircled regiments [from the east and west]. They reached the heights by day's end but ended up north of its [the 33rd Guards Division's] units, where they occupied a defense.[148]

Still encircled and lacking communications with their parent division, the 88th and 91st Guards Rifle Regiments of Utvenko's 33rd Guards Rifle Division continued to repel heavy German attacks throughout the day and overnight on 20–21 February. Thereafter, operating individually or in small groups, the survivors of the two regiments managed to break out eastward through the German lines, finally reaching the safety of the Mius River.

As the 2nd Guards Army's forces fought to rescue Tanaschishin's and Utvenko's encircled forces, on 21 February Lieutenant General A. N. Bogoliubov, the deputy chief of the Red Army General Staff's Operations Directorate discussed the operation's progress with Malinovsky's chief of staff, Varennikov:

General Varennikov is at the phone.

Lieutenant General Bogoliubov is at the phone.

Bogoliubov: I am conducting this conversation at Comrade Stalin's personal order. Where is Malinovsky?

Varennikov: Comrade Malinovsky is with the forces along the Matveev Kurgan axis.

Bogoliubov: Good. First question, report on the situation in your *front*: what is the situation in Tanaschishin's corps, what help are you providing him, and is he in an encirclement? I await your report.

Varennikov: I am reporting. Tanaschishin's corps is continuing to hold on to the Marfinskaia and Anastasievka [regions] and, while widening his sector, is fighting for possession of Malo-Kirsanovka and toward Vasil'evka with separate groups.

  The combat operations by the 5th Shock, 2nd Guards, and 51st Armies have had no success up to 1200 hours on 21 February. The enemy, relying on his old defensive lines along the Mius River, is offering stubborn resistance. The units were occupying the following positions at 1200 hours:

a) The 5th Shock Army. The 3rd Guards Cavalry Corps is in the Kuibyshevo region and the grove to the west; the 315th Rifle Division – Russkoe; and the 40th Guards Rifle Division — Iasinovskii. The [enemy] 336th Infantry Division, 384th Infantry Division (newly formed), and 403rd Air Force Division are defending forward of its front. According to prisoner reports, these units received up to four battalions of march replacements during the last few days. The 258th Rifle Division is at Kartashovo, in the army's second echelon, and the 4th Guards Rifle Division is moving from Novo-Poltavka to Iasinovskii.

b) The 2nd Guards Army. The 300th Rifle Division is fighting on the southeastern outskirts of Novaia Nadezhda, Alekseevka, and Aleksandrovka (I repeat, on the southeastern outskirts of those points), the 49th [Guards] Rifle Division — in the southern outskirts of Aleksandrovka and the eastern slopes of height marker 115.2 (I will provide you the coordinates on a 1:100,000 map); the 387th Rifle Division – occupies Demidovka and Shaposhnikovo and is fighting for height marker 114,9; the 33rd [Guards] Rifle Division is fighting for Doroganov; the 24th [Guards] Rifle Division — on the eastern slopes of height marker 105.7; the 3rd [Guards] Rifle Division — behind the 49th [Guards] Rifle Division; and the 98th Rifle Division — Poltavskii. The 7th Air Force Division and units from the 79th Infantry Division and the 16th Motorized Division are in front of the 2nd Guards Army's front.

c) The 51st Army. The 3rd Guards Mechanized Corps — 2 kilometers northeast of Stepanovskii; the 87th Rifle Division — on the western bank [of the Mius River], in the southeastern outskirts of Riazhenaia; the 126th Rifle Division — on the western bank [of the Mius River], in the southeastern outskirts of Riazhenaia; and Group Kirichenko — in the Matveev Kurgan, Kolesnikov, Bednovskii, and Novo-Rotovka regions. Units of the 16th Motorized Division and 23rd Infantry Division are defending in front of the 51st Army's front.

There are no changes on the 28th and 44th Armies' fronts. They are conducting an active defense.

Today I received two radiograms from Tanaschishin. He reports that he himself is not bad, but there is little ammunition. Tomorrow night we will organize an ammunition drop by aircraft. None of the units operating along the front have as yet fought their way through to him. Beginning in the second half of the day, the 5th Shock, 2nd Guards, and 51st [Armies] were putting themselves into order, bringing ammunition forward, and preparing for operations to penetrate the enemy's defense toward Tanaschishin this evening. Malinovsky and Khrushchev are working on this matter. The weather is exceptionally wet, the roads are bloody [messy], and supply is exceptionally difficult. That is all.

Bogoliubov: Tell me clearly whether or not Tanaschishin's corps is in encirclement? What is Tanaschishin reporting about the enemy? Why has he not attacked Doroganov with part of his forces?

Varennikov: Tanaschishin's corps is cut off from the front line but, according to reports, is not being subjected to special enemy ground actions, and he has prisoners who are saying that they must soon withdraw toward Stalino. He has orders to attack toward Verkhne-Shirokii with part of his forces, but he is reporting in radiogram that he will temporarily refrain from fulfilling this mission because of the shortage of ammunition.

Bogoliubov: Your report provides nothing new. Apparently, you yourself poorly understand the situation. I believe that the assessment of the enemy which you gave me is exaggerated. We have accurate information that, yesterday, the enemy was withdrawing from the Donbas in dense columns. Thus, yesterday, on 20 February, our aircraft observed an enemy column (of infantry, artillery, and vehicles) with its head at Pokrovskoe and its tail in Stalino, that is, a length of up to 150 kilometers. Tanaschishin's prisoners speak truthfully. The enemy is defending in front of you with weak forces. The forces of the Southern Front, having decisive superiority in personnel and weapons and having large mobile formations, have marked time along the line of the Mius River for four days without any results. Comrade Vasil'ev [Stalin] believes this marking time is taking place because:

1. The forces are operating sluggishly and indecisively, command and control is exercised poorly, and cooperation between the types of forces and the armies is not being organized.

2. The movement of the armies straight forward has led to an even distribution of forces along the front. This is no way to conduct an operation.

3. The mobile formations are lagging behind the infantry and, besides Tanaschishin's corps, are not participating in the fighting.

4. The success of Tanaschishin's corps is not being exploited. The corps is being left by itself in the Anastasievka region and is not receiving support from the *front*.

5. You are underestimating the fact that every day of fighting without results is allowing the enemy to withdraw his personnel and equipment from the Donbas. The enemy has imposed his will on you with his weak forces and is compelling you to drag yourself along behind him. This situation is intolerable.

Comrade Vasil'ev ordered you to transmit the following to Malinovsky:

1. Immediately take measures to provide real help to Tanaschishin and exploit the success of this corps to the utmost.

2. Create a strong shock group on the right wing of the *front* and, continuously overwhelming the enemy, deny him the opportunity to withdraw from the Donbas and destroy and capture him.

3. Comrade Vasil'ev ordered me to convey to Malinovsky that, if he does not improve the command and control of his forces, if there is no turning point in the situation, and if, as before, the forces continue to mark time, he will relieve him from his post as the *front* commander.

Report our conversation to Comrades Malinovsky and Khrushchev.

Just now, by telephone Comrade Vasil'ev demanded you point out exactly where Malinovsky is at this very moment so he can talk to him by VCh apparatus [enciphered radio].

Varennikov: Comrade Bogoliubov, the demand of Comrade Vasil'ev is perfectly clear, and I will now try to pass it to Malinovsky. He was located at ....

Bogoliubov: Not where he was located but where he is located?

Varennikov: When I came to the phone he was located in Sovet, but an hour and a half have already passed. I have communications with Sovet by BODO [type of radio], and I am now going there to pass on the contents of Vasil'ev's demand and your conversation with me. When he left, Malinovsky told me if VCh transmissions cannot reach the military council today, then he will return here, where I am located.

Bogoliubov: Is all of this clear to you, and do you have any questions at all of me? Our conversation is only for you and the *front's* Military Council, and everyone must understand this.

Varennikov: Everything is clear. Everything is perfectly understandable. Comrade Bogoliubov, I request that you clarify exactly where the left flank of our neighbor to the right is located. My information is that the line is through Dmitrievka and to the south along the Mius River. Is he [Vatutin] not advancing forward?

Bogoliubov: Fedorov's forces are operating extraordinarily successfully. His right wing is located beyond Pavlograd, and the delay on his left wing is occurring because of insufficiently active operations by your *front.* Shlemin's army [5th Tank] was located along the Nagol'chik, Dmitrievka, and Kuibyshevo line by the morning of 21 February.[149]

The Breakout and Retreat

These and other conversations between Stalin, the *Stavka,* and the two subordinate *front* commanders did nothing to alter the stark reality that Tanaschishin's corps was indeed isolated and would perish if it remained where it was without receiving significant assistance. This assistance was not forthcoming. Therefore, at 1230 hours on 22 February, Malinovsky subordinated Tanaschishin's mechanized corps to the 2nd Guards Army and ordered it to break out of encirclement toward the east to reach the safety of the Southern Front's positions along the Mius River (see Map 58).

1. The enemy, protecting his general withdrawal, is stubbornly defending prepared positions along the Mius River from Riasnyi and further to the south along the Sambek River.

2. The Southwestern Front is attacking on the right, and the boundary with it is through Kuibyshevo — as before, and further through Amvrosievka (Blagodatnoe), Ilovaisk, Makeevka, Spartak, and Tsukurikha Station.

3. The Southern Front, while actively defending with its left wing, will concentrate its main efforts in its center and on its right flank and, while attacking in the general direction of Zakadychnoe Station, Mokryi Elanchik, and Kuteinikovo, will try to cut off the enemy's grouping in the central Donbas, in cooperation with the Southwestern Front.

4. The 5th Shock Army, conducting its main attack with its left wing, will attack decisively beginning on the morning of 23 February 1943 to pene-

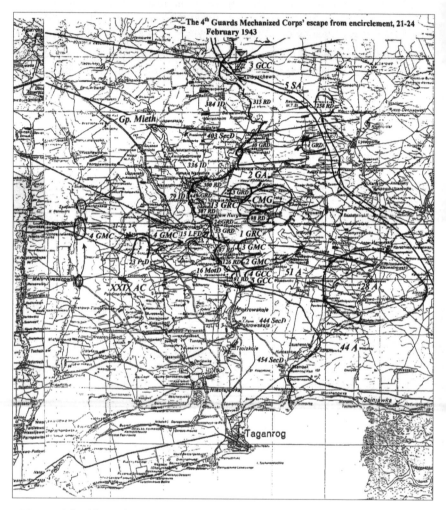

Map 58. The 4th Mechanized Corps' escape from encirclement, 21–24 February 1943

trate the enemy's defense and capture the Semenovskii and Uspenskaia line by day's end. Subsequently attack toward Donetsko-Amvrosievka.

The boundary on the left: (incl.) Rodionovo-Nesvetaiskoe, Iasinovskii (Mar'evka), Uspenskaia, and Donetsko-Amvrosievka.

The army's CP — Lysogorka and subsequently — Pisarevskii.

5. The 2nd Guards Army, conducting its main attack toward Zakadychnoe Station and Novo-Nikolaevka, will attack decisively beginning on the morning of 23 February and, in coordination with the 4th Guards Mechanized Corps' attack against the rear of the enemy's defense, will penetrate his defense and capture the Sukhaia Krynka and Verkhne-Shirokii line by day's end.

Subsequently attack toward Mokryi Elanchik and Tsybulianovka.

The boundary on the left: Nesvetai (incl.), Sovet (incl.), Politotdel'skoe, Matveev Kurgan, Verkhne-Shirokii, and Novoivanovka.

The army's CP – Petrovskii and subsequently Staro-Rotovka.

6. The 51st Army will combine all of the army's tanks into a single group under the command of Major General Sviridov, the commander of the 2nd Guards Mechanized Corps, and, after directly subordinating the 4th and 5th Guards Cavalry Corps to him, attack decisively beginning on the morning of 23 February 1943 and penetrate the enemy's defense, after combining its tank group with the 4th Guards Cavalry Corps. Capture the State Farm No. 15, Samoilov, and Sharon line by day's end. Subsequently attack toward Anastasievka and Pokrovo-Kireevka.

The left boundary — as before.

The army's CP —Politotdel'skoe.

7. The 44th Army will relieve the units of the 28th Army by the morning of 24 February and, having taken over its sector, go over to an active defense along the Riasnyi, Kurgan [burial mound] 83, Kopani, and Sambek River line. At the first indication of an enemy withdrawal, go over to a decisive offensive and reach the Sharon, Nikolaevka, and Petrushina line.

The army's CP — Vodianoi.

8. The 28th Army — After transferring its sector to the 44th Army, will concentrate the army in the Novo-Sergenevka, Blagodat', Golovinskii, and Aleksandrovka (east) regions by the morning of 24 February and take every measure to replenish its formations quickly with men and material. Plan to exploit the offensive of the 2nd Guards and 51st Armies in the general direction of Anastasievka and Karakubstroi upon receipt of a special order.

The army's CP — Aleksandrovka (western).

9. The commander of the 8th Air Army will concentrate all of his efforts on protecting the forces of the 2nd Guards and 51st Armies. Direct your assault efforts in the interests of the 2nd Guards and 51st Armies, to which you must send representatives, beginning on the morning of 23 February.

10. The commander of the *front's* artillery and the chief of the GMCh [guards-mortar units] groups will ensure the forward movement of artillery and guards-mortars into the 2nd Guards and 51st Armies' sectors so as to provide maximum fire and volleys at first light on 23 February.

11. I will take notice of indecisive actions and the absence of energy in the fulfillment of assigned missions on the part of commanders in the 2nd Guards and 51st Armies and, especially, on the part of the acting commander of the 3rd Guards Mechanized Corps, Major General Sharogin, and the commander of the 4th Guards Cavalry Corps, Lieutenant General Kirichenko.

I categorically demand the most decisive and energetic actions from the forces and their commanders in order to penetrate the defenses of the enemy's covering units and crush his withdrawing units.

12. The artillery and mortar raid will begin at 0740 hours on 23 February 1943 and the attack at 0800 hours.

Report decisions made and orders given by 2200 hours on 22 February 1943.

My forward CP – Sovet, and main — Koisug.

Malinovsky, Khrushchev, Kotelkov[150]

As for the breakout of Tanaschishin's 4th Guards Mechanized Corps from its encirclement along the Mokryi Elanchik River, the 2nd Guards Army's history provides the most graphic description:

The mechanized corps' strength was weakened considerably after three days of combat in the Anastasievka region. After repelling a particularly heavy enemy attack by three motorized rifle battalions and 40 tanks from the enemy's 16th Motorized Division, which lasted for more than seven hours, the corps had a total of only seven operational tanks by day's end on 21 February. After deploying them to the head of his column, Major General T. I. Tanaschishin penetrated the enemy's screen and withdrew the corps from Anastasievka on the night of 21–22 February. After bypassing the enemy's tank covering forces along their route, the column encountered the enemy around Samoilov State Farm. General T. I. Tanaschishin then sent the tanks around the farm to the south, while firing on the enemy to attract his attention from the south. Thanks to the commander's resourcefulness, the corps' main force bypassed the enemy and linked up with their units.

When the column approached Stepanovskii State Farm, German tanks blocked the corps' path to the east. Lacking a bypass route and anticipating an enemy attack from the east and west, the corps turned to the north. Soon after, the column was struck by massive artillery fire. The soldiers organized an all-round defense and repelled the enemy attacks until nightfall on 22 February. After holding their position all night, the corps reached the eastern bank of the Mius River in the Matveev Kurgan region on the morning of 23 February.[151]

Largely substantiating the account in the 2nd Guards Army's history, the history of the 4th Guards Mechanized Corps added that the soldiers of Tanaschishin's mechanized corps broke out of encirclement mounted on 80 vehicles, as well as on foot. It correctly asserts that the enemy forces opposing the corps' breakout included the 23rd Panzer Division and elements of the 5th [should read 15th] *Luftwaffe* Field, 79th Infantry, and 16th Motorized Divisions, as well as elements of various German security units.

Although Tanaschishin and at least half of his corps' personnel succeeded in escaping from the encirclement intact by 23 February, the corps had no choice but to abandon most of its weapons and heavy equipment before and during its retreat. Thereafter, it required considerable time to rest and refit the corps before it again became combat capable. In fact, by this time most of the Southern Front's mobile corps, as well as its rifle formations, were in a similar dilapidated and weakened state. Nonetheless, the *Stavka* granted Malinovsky's forces no respite. Just as the directives the *Stavka* issued to Malinovsky's forces in mid-February demanded they join Vatutin's offensive into the Donbas so that it would succeed, the directives it issued to Malinovsky's *front* in late February enjoined his forces to continue their attacks so that Vatutin's forces would survive.

Therefore, when Manstein's counterstroke threatened to collapse Vatutin's defenses in the western Donbas and encircle and destroy his *front's* forces south of the Northern Donets River, Stalin ordered Malinovsky to organize even stronger attacks along the Mius River. Reluctantly, at 0215 hours on 25 February, Malinovsky issued new attack orders to his exhausted forces:

1. The enemy, in his previous grouping, is offering stubborn resistance along his old defensive line along the Mius River and further through Riasnyi, height marker 108, Sambek, and Varenovka.

2. On the right — the Southwestern Front, the boundary with it — as before.

3. The Southern Front is continuing to fulfill the mission of penetrating the enemy's defense with the immediate mission of reaching the Semenovskii, Uspenskaia, Samoilov, and Sharon line, while concentrating its main efforts in the general direction of Mokryi Elanchik and Mospino.

4. The 5th Shock Army, with the 3rd Guards Cavalry Corps, 5th Destroyer Brigade, 274th and 331st Howitzer Artillery Regiments, 1162nd Gun Artillery Regiment, 507th and 764th Antitank Artillery Regiments, and 21st Guards-mortar Regiment, will move its artillery forward, refill its units with ammunition, and attack and penetrate the enemy's defense along the Skelianskii and Metropol'e front on the morning of 27 February 1943 and, enveloping and destroying the enemy's centers of resistance, will capture the Semenovskii and Uspenskaia line by the morning of 28 February. Subsequently conduct an attack toward Ilovaisk.

The boundary on the left: Dar'evka, Lysogorka, Iasinovskii, Uspenskaia, and Donetsko-Amvrosievka.

CP – Lysogorka, subsequently, Pisarevskii.

5. The 2nd Guards Army, with the 1095th Corps Artillery Regiment, 648th, 1100th, and 1101st Gun Artillery Regiments, 435th and 1250th Antitank Regiments, 488th Mortar Regiment, 2nd, 19th, 23rd, 48th, and 88th Guards-mortar Regiments, and 408th, 409th, and 334th Separate Guards-mortar Battalions, will move its artillery forward and replenish its units with ammunition by the end of 26 February, attack and complete the penetration of the enemy's defense in the Aleksandrovka and Doroganov sector beginning on the morning of 27 February, and capture the Sukhaia Krynka and Novo-Nikolaevka line by the morning of 28 February. Subsequently, conduct an attack toward Mokryi Elanchik and Kuteinikovo.

The boundary on the left: Voloshino, Nizhne-Tuzlovskii, Novo-Andrianovka, Matveev Kurgan, and Novo-Ivanovka.

CP — Petrovskii, subsequently, Staro-Rotovka.

6. The 51st Army, with the 3rd and 2nd Guards Mechanized Corps, 4th and 5th Guards Cavalry Corps, 85th Howitzer Artillery Regiment, 491st, 492nd, 665th, and 1246th Antitank Regiments, 125th and 486th Mortar Regiments, and 4th, 80th, 90th, and 51st Guards-mortar Regiments, will move its artillery forward and replenish its units with ammunition by the end of 26 February, attack and penetrate the enemy's defensive front in the Stepanovksii and Riazhenaia sector beginning on the morning of 27 February, and, enveloping and destroying the enemy's main centers of resistance, capture the Verkhne-Shirokii, Samoilov, and Zharkov line by the morning of 28 February. Subsequently, conduct an attack toward Anastasievka, Ul'ianovka, and Isaeva *Balka*.

The boundary on the left: Bol'shie Saly, Novoselovka, Riazhenaia, and Malo-Kirsanovka.

CP — Politotdel'skoe.

7. The 44th Army will actively defend the Riazhenaia, Kopani, and Primorka line.

CP — Vodianoi.

8. The 28th Army will replenish its formations and bring its ammunition up to one combat load by day's end on 2 March 1943.

9. The 4th Guards Mechanized Corps will concentrate in the Kriukovo and Grekovo-Ul'ianovka regions by day's end on 25 February, move its tanks and motorized infantry forward, replenish its ammunition, and be prepared to fulfill combat missions by 1 March 1943.

10. The 8th Air Army — will protect the forces of the 2nd Guards and 51st Armies and direct its assault efforts in the interests of these armies, to which it must send its representatives, beginning on the morning of 27 February.

11. The hour of the general attack on 27 February will be provided later.

Malinovsky, Khrushchev, Varennikov[152]

Malinovsky dispatched his new attack plan to the *Stavka* for approval at 2330 hours on 27 February:

1. The forces of the Southern Front remained in their previous positions during the day, exchanged fire with the enemy, and completed their regrouping.

The enemy strengthened his air activity considerably on 27 February 1943, especially during the second half of the day, bombed the combat formations of the forces in the center of the *front* continuously with groups of from 4 to 15 aircraft, and subjected populated points situated a distance of 20 kilometers from the front to repeated attacks. He subjected Bol'shaia Kirsanovka, Riazhenaia, Matveev Kurgan, and Politotdel'skoe and the road in the Matveev Kurgan, Politotdel'skoe, and Sovet sector to particularly heavy bombing.

Enemy aircraft conducted 200 aircraft sorties. Sixteen aircraft were shot down by antiaircraft fire and in air combat, including 10 "He–111s," and 6 "Ju–88s."

Our aircraft bombed the enemy along the forward edge, suppressed immediate reserves and artillery positions, and bombed Zakadychnoe Station and the railroad in the Uspenskaia and Donetsko-Amvrosievka sector during the night. Our aircraft reconnoitered, protected our forces, and fought eight air battles during the day. There were no losses.

The 5th Shock, 2nd Guards, and 51st Armies, continuing to hold on to their positions, exchanged fire with the enemy and completed their regrouping.

The enemy, not launching attacks by ground units, conducted fires against the combat formations of the 5th Shock Army all day long and heavier fire raids against the units of the 2nd Guards and 51st Armies and enemy aircraft also operated vigorously against the forces of these armies.

The left wing units of the 44th Army were also subjected to intense artillery and mortar fire during the day and pressure by aircraft against its right wing.

2. On 27 February [the following] enemy [forces] were destroyed or neutralized:
— artillery batteries 3;
— mortar batteries 3;
— machine guns 8;
— vehicles 12;
— up to two companies of infantry; and
— the railroad line at Zakadychnoe Station demolished.

3. Decision: Penetrate the enemy's defensive belt beginning at 1200 hours on 28 February 1943 with an attack by the 5th Shock Army toward Uspenskaia and by the 2nd Guards and 51st Armies in the general direction along the railroad to Sukhaia Krynka Station and Anastasievka and, after destroying him, reach the Uspenskaia, Sukhaia Krynka, Verkhne-Shirokii, Samoilov, and Zharkov front with the armies by the morning of 29 February.

The 44th Army will assist the offensive by the 51st Army with its right wing and will conduct an active defense along the remainder of its front.

The 28th Army, remaining in its previous region, will replenish its forces in readiness to exploit subsequently the success of the 2nd Guards and 51st Armies.

Malinovsky, Khrushchev, Kotelkov[153]

As the forces of Army Group South completed collapsing the Southwestern Front's defenses in the northern Donbas region and Manstein began planning a subsequent counterstroke to expel the forces of Kuznetsov's Voronezh Front from the Khar'kov region, as indicated by a report Malinovsky dispatched to the *Stavka* on 3 March, although exhausted, the Southern Front's forces continued pounding *Armeeabteilung* Hollidt's defenses along the "Mius River Wall," but to no avail:

1. The enemy, offering stubborn resistance, is continuing to defend along the western bank of the Mius River.

2. The Southern Front is continuing offensive operations to seize bridge-heads on the western bank of the Mius River.

3. The 5th Shock Army, after fortifying itself in the positions it seized on the western bank of the Mius River, will capture the heights with the burial mounds, 2–2.5 kilometers northeast of Gustafel'd Collective Farm, by successive attacks.

The boundary — as before.

4. The 2nd Guards Army, while firmly defending along the Bol'shaia Kirsanovka and Alekseevka line, will completely capture Hill 115.2, the hill with two burial mounds, Hills, 105.9 and 111.9, and the southern slope of Hill 111.9 up to the railroad at Doroganov by a series of local operations. It will firmly dig in along the positions it has seized as a bridgehead for subsequent offensive operations.

Include the 5th Guards Mechanized Corps in the army and withdraw it into reserve in the Mar'evka, Shelkovnikov, Sokolovskii, and Chebatarov regions for rest and refitting.

The Boundary line on the left: up to Matveev Kurgan — as before, and further to Doroganov and Novoivanovka.

5. The 51st Army, while firmly holding on to the eastern and south-eastern slopes of Hill 105.7, will continue offensive operations and capture the Stepanovka, Hill 115.2, and Panchenko (incl.) line before 6 March; subsequently, after digging in along this line, be prepared to continue the offensive.

Withdraw the 2nd [Guards] Mechanized Corps to the Mar'evka, Shelkovnikov, Sokolovskii, and Chebatarev region by the end of 5 March and transfer it to the control of the commander of the 2nd Guards Army.

6. Conduct combat operations continuously with all of the armies, while preventing the enemy from strengthening his defense and erecting new defensive works.

Increase the supply of ammunition, fuel, and foodstuffs so as to fill the reserves up to the levels required by the norms by 10 March 1943.

7. Confirm receipt of orders and report all decisions made.

Malinovsky, Gurov, Varennikov[154]

It is not surprising that Malinovsky's report, which contained the last attack order he issued to his forces before the winter campaign formally ended, spoke only of actions designed to consolidate his forces' defenses around the bridgeheads they had already seized on the Mius River's western bank and nothing more. Thus, his report clearly indicated that his *front* had indeed "shot its bolt" and was no longer capable of conducting major offensive operations of any sort. Nothing Stalin, Zhukov, or Malinovsky could do altered the sad reality that the Red Army's Donbas offensive had ended in complete and utter defeat.

Conclusions

The Russians have yet to release a definitive count of the number of casualties the Southern Front suffered while it was conducting offensive and defensive operations from 14 through 24 February 1943. However, recently released statistics indicate that, when the *front* began its participation in the Red Army's North Caucasus strategic offensive operation on 1 January 1943, its strength was 393,800 soldiers. Of this number, including the roughly 10,000 personnel replacements it received during this period, by 4 February 1943, the Southern Front had suffered 101,717 casualties, including 54,364 killed, captured, or missing and 47,364 wounded or sick.[155] Subsequently, during the Rostov offensive operation, which took place from 5 through 18 February, the Southern Front began the offensive with 259,440 soldiers and lost another 28,231 soldiers, including 9,809 killed, captured, or missing and 18,422 wounded or sick, by the time the operation ended.[156] According to other sources, thereafter, the Southern Front lost 6,766 soldiers, including 2,254 killed and missing and 4,512 wounded or sick, during the period from 20 February through 1 March 1943, and another 2,672 men between 1 and 10 March 1943.[157]

Therefore, including the roughly 30,000 personnel replacements it received while these operations were under way, the Southern Front's personnel strength at any given time ranged between 240,000 to 250,000 soldiers assigned to its five field armies, one air army, and supporting *front* units. Stripping out the air army, its nine mobile corps (four mechanized, one tank, and four cavalry), and its supporting artillery and logistical support units, the strength of the *front's* 22 rifle divisions and 7 rifle brigades could not have exceeded a total of much over 150,000 soldiers or, at best, roughly 5,000 soldiers per division and brigade. In fact, many of the *front's* divisions and brigades were far weaker. These estimated strength figures graphically explain why the Malinovsky's Southern Front, which faced a German force with an estimated strength of just over 100,000 men, could not prevail.

It is no coincidence that the Southwestern and Southern Fronts' mobile corps, which shared the common task of spearheading their *fronts'* offensives into the Donbas, destroying Manstein's Army Group Don (South), and reaching the Dnepr River and the Sea of Azov, all perished at roughly the same time and in the same harrowing circumstances. As impressive as these mobile corps were on paper, excluding the 1st Guards and 25th Tank Corps, which were near full strength when they entered combat, like their parent armies, the four tank corps of Mobile Group Popov, as well as the 1st and 7th Guards Cavalry and 4th Guards Mechanized Corps, were only pale reflections of their former selves. Although all were near full strength when they began their operations in January 1943, by mid-February the rigors of time, distance, deteriorating weather, and skillful German resistance had taken a terrible toll on their combat strength. By mid-February only a combination of excessive optimism on the part of Soviet commanders, increasingly unrealistic and often brutal *Stavka* orders, and sheer grit propelled them forward.

In the final analysis, Vatutin's and Malinovsky's mobile groups suffered defeat at the hands of hastily assembled and regrouped, equally exhausted, but better led German forces. The Germans prevailed in the Donbas region, first and foremost, because of Manstein's determination in the face of a recalcitrant Hitler and the operational skills he displayed in orchestrating an imaginative series of counter-strokes designed to exploit the superior tactical skills of numerous threadbare German divisions, regiments, and even battalions. As a result, Manstein's forces achieved victories of operational and, ultimately, strategic significance against an overconfident and numerically superior foe.

Blinded by excessive optimism, Stalin, the *Stavka*, and the commanders of the Red Army's Southwestern and Southern Fronts marched their forces into a trap in the Donbas region. As a result, both *fronts* suffered embarrassing defeats that doomed the *Stavka's* entire winter offensive to failure. As bitter as the defeat in the Donbas was, however, neither Stalin nor the *Stavka* would appreciate its full effects until mid-March 1943, when their equally ambitious strategic offensives along the northwestern and western (central) axes of the Soviet-German front would also falter. To a great extent, Manstein's victories in the Donbas and, later, in the Khar'kov region were the reasons why the *Stavka's* far grander winter offensive failed. Finally, judged within a strategic context, in terms of its scale, scope, and potential significance, it is now clear that the Southwestern and Southern Fronts' February offensive into the Donbas region was a far more ambitious and important undertaking then previously believed.

PART 3

SOVIET OFFENSIVE OPERATIONS ALONG THE WESTERN (CENTRAL) AXIS (FEBRUARY–MARCH 1943)

Chapter 6

The Briansk Front's Orel Offensive and the Voronezh Front's (60th and 38th Armies') L'gov and Sumy Offensives (26 January–12 February 1943)

Introduction

Military historians have correctly credited Field Marshal Eric von Manstein with staving off disaster on Germany's Eastern Front during the winter of 1942–43. As Soviet forces attempted to exploit their unprecedented victory in Operation Uranus at Stalingrad, Manstein overcame the twin obstacles of an obstinate Hitler, who refused to consider resort to a maneuver defense, and a Red Army, which, inspired by its victory at Stalingrad, was poised to exploit that victory, to inflict a stunning setback on the advancing Soviet host and to restore stability to the southern wing of the *Wehrmacht's* Eastern Front. Manstein did so in February and March 1943 by unleashing two powerful counterstrokes that halted the Red Army's advance, defeated its forces in the Donbas and Khar'kov regions, and drove them back to a new defensive line protecting the southern approaches to Kursk.

History has fairly assessed that Manstein's feat was indeed remarkable and probably thwarted ambitious Soviet plans for total victory in southern Russia. There is, however, increasing evidence that, while justifiable, this praise heaped on Manstein fell far short of the credit he actually deserved. It now appears that Manstein's victories in the Donets Basin (Donbas) and Khar'kov regions during late February and early March 1943 were far more significant than historians have previously supposed, since Soviet strategic aims during the winter of 1942–43 far exceeded simple defeat of German forces in southern Russia. Instead, by launching these offensives, the *Stavka* sought to collapse German defenses across virtually the entire expanse of the Soviet-German front.

Existing assessments of Soviet strategic intentions during the winter of 1942–43 and the contributions Manstein made to restoration of German fortunes in the East are well documented in a multitude of sound histories.[158] The Soviets, historians have maintained, placed great hope, first, in the success of their Stalingrad counteroffensive and, second, in their exploitation of that signal victory. Therefore, subsequent Soviet offensive actions from December 1942 to February 1943 were a logical outgrowth of the Stalingrad victory. The ensuing Winter Campaign then developed in three distinct stages. First, during late November and early December 1942, the *Stavka* tightened its encirclement ring around Stalingrad and sought frantically to parry German attempts to relieve their beleaguered Stalingrad forces. By astutely shifting its strategic and operational reserves (in particular, the 2nd Guards Army) and by capitalizing on luck and Field Marshall Friedrich Paulus' timidity is refusing to ignore the Führer's stand fast order and break out of Stalingrad with his Sixth Army, the German relief attempts failed.

The Soviets then began a series of offensives, known collectively as the Winter Offensive, designed to clear German and Axis satellite forces from the southern bank of the Don River and the southwestern approaches to Stalingrad. From 17 December 1942 through late January 1943, Soviet forces engaged and severely mauled, in succession, Italian Eighth, Hungarian Second, and German Second Armies. Although they failed to seize Rostov and block the egress of German Army Group "A" from the Caucasus region, they did ravage German and allied forces along the Don River from Veshenskaia to Voronezh, and, in so doing, they created a gaping hole in German defenses in southern Russia.

Finally, in late January, the *Stavka* exploited this gap by hurling the Voronezh and Southwestern Fronts' forces westward into the Donbas and Khar'kov regions in an attempt to collapse the remaining weakened German defenses, reach the Dnepr River and Sea of Azov, and destroy the remainder of German Army Group Don.[159] During the final planning stages of the Khar'kov and Donbas operations, the Soviets added the city of Kursk to their formidable list of strategic objectives.

In February 1943 increasingly threadbare Soviet forces, operating at the extremities of overextended logistical umbilicals, advanced with abandon into a trap set by Manstein. By skillfully regrouping his forces (in particular, First and Fourth Panzer Armies), employing the newly arrived SS Panzer Corps, and obtaining Hitler's reluctant permission to resort to a maneuver defense, Manstein orchestrated the brilliant Donbas and Khar'kov counterstrokes. The former, which commenced on 20 February 1943, smashed the overextended Southwestern Front and drove its remnants back to the Northern Donets River. Then, on 6 March, Manstein's SS and XXXXVIII Panzer Corps struck the equally vulnerable armies of the Voronezh Front south of Khar'kov. The furious counterstrokes collapsed that *front*, drove its armies northward in disorder, and captured Belgorod, forcing the *Stavka* to abandon its ambitious Winter Offensive and to erect hasty defenses along the Northern Donets River and along what would become the southern face of the famous Kursk "bulge."

While historians disagree over whether Manstein could have done more, they all agree that this sequence of events set the stage, geographically and strategically, for the ensuing famous Battle of Kursk.

Already, some aspects of this conventional interpretation of the Soviet Winter Campaign and Offensive require fundamental reassessment. We now know that German relief efforts at Stalingrad were futile, since Paulus' force had limited capabilities for breaking out, and Soviet strategic deployments (principally of the 2nd Guards Army) rendered breakout and linkup exceedingly unlikely. We also know that, as a follow-on to its Operation Uranus, in early December 1942, the *Stavka* was already formulating plans for so-called Operation Saturn, which required its forces in southern Russia to smash large elements of Army Group "B", capture Rostov, and isolate and destroy Army Group "A" before it could escape from the Caucasus region. However, Soviet miscalculation of German strength at Stalingrad forced an alteration to this plan. We also now know that Soviet overconfidence and outright ineptitude, in particular regarding the interpretation of intelligence information, and not just Soviet force weakness conditioned Manstein's victories in February and March. Finally, we know that newly-appointed Marshal Zhukov, exultant over the success of the Soviet offensives, added Kursk to the list of Soviet objectives in early February.

Virtually all historians have concluded that Soviet strategic planning throughout winter 1943 focused their attention on the southwestern axis [direction], specifically the strategic line extending from the Don River north of Stalingrad through Millerovo and Kotel'nikovskii and through Khar'kov and Stalino to the Dnepr River and Sea of Azov. The clear goal of this offensive, they believed, was the destruction of German Army Groups "A", Don, and the southern wing of Army Group "B."

What has been overlooked in this interpretation was a second Soviet strategic line extending from Voronezh through Kastornoe, Livny, Kursk, and Orel to Briansk, and beyond toward Smolensk. Soviet military historians have written much about the Ostrogozhsk-Rossosh' and Voronezh-Kastornoe operations of January 1943 but somewhat less about the February operation to secure Kursk. There the Soviet general accounts tend to end abruptly as they shift their focus to the seemingly more important fighting taking place in the Khar'kov and Donbas regions to the south. To learn more about subsequent operations along this strategic axis (Kursk, Orel, Briansk, and Smolensk), one must consult more detailed Soviet memoirs and unit histories, which contain only fragmentary information about these operations.

Examination of these sources, along with extensive German archival materials, now reveals that the Soviet Winter Offensive had far more ambitious goals, which, if achieved, would have added German Army Group Center to the list of planned victims of the Soviet strategic offensive. In short, the *Stavka* formulated and attempted to implement strategic plans which, if realized, would have rent the German Eastern Front in two and placed in jeopardy the entire German defense along its Eastern Front. The fact that the planned Soviet offensive did not succeed increases the significance of Manstein's successful counterstrokes and, in fact, elevates them to the importance of a full counteroffensive.

Strategic Planning

Stavka strategic planning from spring 1942 through February 1943 was remarkably consistent in terms of Soviet strategic aims. Convinced of the vital importance of defending Moscow, during spring 1942 the *Stavka* concentrated its most powerful forces along the Western (Moscow) axis, where it hoped to blunt an anticipated German offensive and then conduct a decisive counteroffensive to drive German forces back to the Smolensk region. Although he accepted defense along the Western axis, an impatient Stalin also sought to distract German attention from Moscow and weaken their expected advance on the Soviet capital by conducting smaller-scale preemptive offensives in the Khar'kov region and the Crimea in May 1942. However, both of these operations failed at a cost to the Red Army of almost a half million casualties. Exploiting these failures, Hitler then unleashed his forces in Operation Blau, his planned summer offensive toward Stalingrad and the Caucasus region. Attacking on 28 June 1942, the armies on Army Group South's northern wing smashed the Briansk and Southwestern Fronts' forward defenses east of Kursk and Khar'kov and began a rapid exploitation toward the Don River at Voronezh. Just over a week later, the armies on Army Group South's southern wing joined the offensive, routing the Southern Front's armies and driving deep into the eastern Donbas region. Although this German onslaught across southern Russia surprised the *Stavka*, it did not lessen Stalin's belief in the decisive importance of the Western axis. Therefore, although the *Stavka* took measures to halt and defeat Army Group South's (now reorganized into Army Groups "A" and "B") offensive, it also continued its planning for future offensive actions along the Western axis.

Faced with a major German strategic offensive across southern Russia, the Soviets sought to destroy German Army Groups "B" and "A" by conducting counterstrokes against the nose and flanks of its advancing forces. As they did so, the *Stavka* also raised new armies in its strategic reserves and deployed them forward into defenses along the Don River and on the western approaches to the Stalingrad region. During the second week of July 1942, as German forces were advancing toward the Don River at Voronezh, the *Stavka* attempted to launch the first of many counterstrokes designed to halt the German juggernaut. However, the first counterstroke, which was conducted by the Briansk Front's newly-formed 5th Tank Army west of Voronezh, ended in total defeat. Undeterred by this failure, in late July and early August, the *Stavka* struck once again, this time with a poorly coordinated series of counterstrokes conducted by the Briansk Front, with the reinforced remnants of its 5th Tank Army west of Voronezh, the Voronezh Front at Voronezh proper, and the newly-formed Stalingrad Front's 1st and 4th Tank Armies in the "Great Bend" of the Don River west of Stalingrad.[160] However, despite slowing the *Wehrmacht's* advance and inflicting heavier than expected losses on some German forces, these counterstrokes also failed. Thereafter, throughout the remainder of August, the *Stavka* settled for a series of lesser counterattacks designed to halt the German advance and stabilize the front on the immediate approaches to Stalingrad.

In the meantime, along the Western axis, during late July and August, the forces of the Kalinin and Western Fronts, operating under Marshal Zhukov's direct supervision, conducted a large-scale counterstroke against the defenses of the Army Group Center's Ninth Army in the Rzhev salient, and, during the same period, the forces on the left wing of Zhukov's Western Front conducted a series of counterstrokes against Army Group Center's Second Panzer Army in the Zhizdra and Bolkhov regions north and northeast of Orel. Throughout these fierce defensive battles, the *Stavka* never abandoned its hopes for renewed large-scale offensive operations both along the Western axis and in the south.

By late September 1942, German offensive momentum in southern Russia had ebbed. Army Group "A's" forces were spread deeply into the Caucasus region, and those of Army Group "B" deployed along an immensely broad front extending from south of Stalingrad, northward through the city proper, and then northwestward along the Don River to the Livny region, west of Voronezh. Since the bulk of Army Group "B's" once powerful but now steadily weakening Sixth Army and Fourth Panzer Armies were locked in costly street fighting for Stalingrad and the city's factory district, by this time the army group had no choice but to reinforce the German forces defending its short right wing south of Stalingrad and its far longer left wing along the Don River northwest of the city, first, with the Hungarian Second and Romanian Fourth Armies and, later, with the Italian Eighth and Romanian Third Army.

At this juncture, Stalin directed the *Stavka* to formulate plans to conduct two mutually-supporting strategic offensives, the first code-named Operation Mars, aimed at enveloping and destroying Army Group Center's Ninth Army in the Rzhev salient, and, the second, code-named Operation Uranus, designed to encircle and destroy Army Group "B's" Sixth Army in the Stalingrad region. If they succeeded, the *Stavka* planned to exploit these operations by conducting two follow-on efforts, the first, likely code-named Operation Neptune or Jupiter, to destroy the bulk of Army Group Center and reach the Smolensk region and, the second, called Operation Saturn, to damage or destroy Army Groups "B" and "A" and capture the Rostov region."[161] Initially, Stalin intended to launch Operations Mars on 28 October 1942 and Operation Uranus either shortly before or shortly after Mars. However, the uncertain situation in the Stalingrad region and difficulties encountered while regrouping and concentrating the required assault forces, primarily due to deteriorating weather conditions, forced the *Stavka* to postpone both operations until mid- and late-November.

The Soviets launched their Stalingrad counteroffensive, which, by design, was to be the first stage in an even broader Winter Campaign, on 19 November. Although Operation Mars, which Zhukov's forces unleashed six days later, ultimately faltered (see Chapter 2) within days, Soviet optimism soared as their mobile forces, conducting a successful double envelopment operation, linked up near Kalach-on-the-Don, encircling an Axis force far greater than anticipated.[162] While devising methods to digest the large encircled force, the *Stavka's* appetite for even greater victory prompted drafting of Plan Saturn, an ambitious undertaking designed to seize Rostov and, in doing so, place Army Group "A," then overextended in the Caucasus, in jeopardy. Although intense combat on the approaches to Stalingrad, prompted by German attempts to relieve the beleaguered garrison, caused truncation of Operation Saturn into Little Saturn with correspondingly less ambitious objectives, the pattern was set for future Soviet offensive planning. Meanwhile, after Operation Mars sputtered to an end at the end of November, the *Stavka* began dispatching forces from its strategic reserves southward in an expanding torrent to reinforce success in the Stalingrad region. This set the stage for a wholesale expansion of the Red Army's Winter Offensive.

Planning for Operation Little Saturn was completed on 13 December, and the conduct of the operation itself (16–29 December) coincided with the launch and repulse of German attempts to relieve Stalingrad from the southwest. Soviet success in Little Saturn and the Kotel'nikovskii operation (24–30 December) destroyed Italian Eighth Army, drew German XXXXVIII Panzer Corps away from its efforts to penetrate toward Stalingrad from the west, defeated an attempt by the Fourth Panzer Army's LVII Panzer Corps to relieve the Stalingrad garrison from the southwest, and, far more important, threatened the safe withdrawal of Army Group "A" from the Caucasus.

Building on these successes, in January 1943 the *Stavka* prepared plans to continue the process begun by Little Saturn. The targets for the new series of offensives were Hungarian and German forces defending northward along the Don River and the remnants of German and Rumanian forces now clinging desperately to the land bridge east of Rostov, through which Army Group "A" would have to pass to reach the safety of German lines. The first of the new offensives, the

Ostrogozhsk-Rossosh' operation, conducted by the Voronezh Front from 13–27 January, severely damaged the Hungarian Second Army and paved the way for a follow-on operation with the cooperating Briansk Front against the German Second Army defending the Don River line north and south of Voronezh (the Voronezh-Kastornoe operation, 24 January–5 February 1943). By 5 February Soviet forces had routed the Second Army and were approaching Kursk and Belgorod.[163] At the same time, the armies of the Southwestern and Southern Fronts exerted unrelentingly pressure against German forces defending Rostov.

Even before the beginning of the Voronezh-Kastornoe operation, from 20–23 January, the *Stavka* developed plans to expand the strategic offensive. While Soviet forces continued their attacks along the Voronezh and Rostov axes, the Voronezh and Southwestern Fronts were tasked with conducting Operations Star and Gallop. Launched from the march, the twin operations were designed to collapse weakened Army Group Don and propel Soviet forces to Khar'kov and into the Donbas region. Planned seizure of Mariupol' on the Sea of Azov by exploiting Soviet armored columns (Mobile Group Popov) would cut off the withdrawal of Army Group "A" from the Rostov area and permit further Soviet exploitation to the Dnepr River

Preparations for Operations Star and Gallop established a new planning pattern for the winter campaign. Specifically, the *Stavka* formulated new operational plans while current operations were being prepared or were underway. True to this pattern and due to immediate and spectacular success of Soviet forces around Voronezh, on 26 January the *Stavka* added Kursk to the list of objectives to be secured in Operation Star.

Launched on 29 January and 2 February, respectively, Operations Gallop and Star developed spectacularly. By 6 February Soviet forces threatened Kursk, Belgorod, Khar'kov, Slaviansk, and Voroshilovgrad (see Map 59). Although German First and Fourth Panzer Armies had escaped to Rostov, it too was threatened.[164] With gaping holes in German defenses north and south of Kursk and between Khar'kov and Slaviansk, it seemed to the *Stavka* that the German position around Kursk and Khar'kov and in the Donbas was untenable. Not only was the destruction or forced withdrawal of Army Group Don likely, but it also seemed that German defenses throughout southern Russia were in jeopardy. If this was so, then German Army Group Center's southern flank also seemed vulnerable. Because Zhukov's forces had inflicted serious damage on this army group months before in Operation Mars, the *Stavka* was optimistic that it could expand the winter offensive to encompass this army group as well.

At this juncture, therefore, the *Stavka* revived strategic hopes which had been dashed by the Germans in the winter of 1941–42. Assured of victory in the south, it began thinking of ways to expand that victory to embrace the old Soviet nemesis, Army Group Center.

The first stage in this expansion process occurred in late January 1943, when, as Stalin's Deputy Supreme Commander, Marshal Zhukov, convinced the Generalissimo to add Kursk to the Red Army's list of objectives to be seized in the winter offensive. Zhukov assigned this task to the Briansk and Voronezh Fronts, whose forces were recording spectacular advances during the initial stages of the Voronezh-Kastornoe operation. At 2200 hours on 26 January, Zhukov issued new

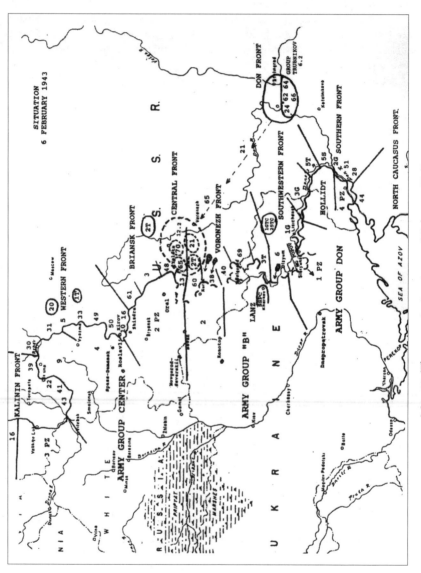

Map 59. The strategic situation on 6 February 1943

orders requiring the forces of the Voronezh and Briansk Fronts to capture the Arkhangel'sk and Kursk regions:

> In connection with the [enemy] withdrawal from the Voronezh region and the successful advance by our forces towards Kastornoe, the *Stavka* of the Supreme High Command orders:
>
> 1. Establish [the following] boundary line between the Briansk and Voronezh Fronts, effective beginning at 2000 hours 27 January 1943: Dobroe, Vodop'ianovo, Dolgorukovo, Aleshki, Volovo, Koz'modem'iansk, Gemiachka, Isakovo, Kosorzha, Zolotukhino, Fatezh, Dmitriev-L'govskii. All points, with the exception of Dobroe, are inclusive for the Briansk Front.
>
> 2. Smash the enemy in the Studenoe, Kolpny, Maloarkhangel'sk, and Droskov region with the units of the Briansk Front's left wing by an attack through their rear and, attacking toward Kolpny and Maloarkhangel'sk, reach the Pokrovskoe, Maloarkhangel'sk, and upper Smorodnoe front.
>
> 3. Attack in the general direction of Kastornoe and Kursk with the units on the Voronezh Front's right wing to destroy the resisting enemy, capture the Kursk region, and reach the Sergeevskoe, Drenevo, and Anokhino line.
>
> 4. Confirm receipt and report fulfillment.
>
> *Stavka* of the Supreme High Command
> Zhukov[165]

Thus, Zhukov's order directed the Briansk and Voronezh Fronts to pursue new objectives even before the two *fronts* accomplished those assigned to them in the Voronezh-Kastornoe operation. Nevertheless, by the time the two *fronts* completed this operation on 2 February, they had demolished the defenses of German Second and Hungarian Second Armies, encircled the bulk of both Axis armies in the Kastornoe region, and forced the encircled forces to commence a harrowing retreat westward toward Kursk and Belgorod. The Briansk Front's Military Council (commander, commissar, and chief of staff) described their forces' progress in daily situation reports it issued on 2, 3, and 5 February.

[2 February]

1. The forces of the *front*, developing the penetration, were advancing westward and northwestward successfully on 2 February 1943.

The left wing divisions of the 48th Army (the 143rd and 137th Rifle Divisions), having cleared the eastern bank of the Zelenka and Foshnia Rivers in the Manino, Tatarinovo, and Beketovo sector of enemy, are prepared to attack northwestward beginning on the morning of 3 February.

The forces of the 13th Army fought their way [to the following locations] by 1600–1700 hours on 2 February:

The 74th Rifle Division on the Panikovets and Skorodomka line and operating toward Kolpna from the northeast;

The 148th Rifle Division – Temenskoe and Krasnyi Ugolok and — Pokrovka — with its forward units;

The 81st Rifle Division – on the western bank of the Kobylin River and captured Berezovka 2. Nikolaevka, and Aleksandrovka;

The 211th Rifle Division captured Lugovskii, Kazanka 2, Zales'e, and Mozhaevka after throwing a mobile detachment forward to cut the Orel-Kursk railroad in the region north of Zolotukhino;

The 280th Rifle Division captured Kosorzha;

The 132nd Rifle Division, attacking toward Shchigry, captured Lavrovka and Nikitskoe during the second half of the day. The division smashed up to a battalion of infantry and destroyed 11 tanks;

The 15th Rifle Division reached the Nikol'skoe, Isakovo, and Ostriki region and was continuing to move into the Kosorzha region; and

The 8th Rifle Division – in the Lipovets, Uspenskoe, and Kunach region.

The forces of the 13th Army captured up to 500 German soldiers and officers.

A large number of trophies have been seized. I will report about the trophies later.

The positions of the remaining forces of the *front* are changed.

2. The *front's* aviation conducted 64 aircraft sorties on 2 February, while striking the enemy's forces and rear area.

Eight enemy aircraft have been shot down in air battles.

3. The enemy, while resisting along the lines of the 48th and 13th Armies with his previous units, is withdrawing toward the west and southwest. He bombed the combat formations of our attacking units.

On the attack axes of the 280th and 132nd Rifle Divisions, [the enemy] employed a group of 10–15 tanks and on the approaches to Shchigry — motorized infantry in undetermined strength.

According to a report by a prisoner seized in the Somovo 1 region (the sector of the 3rd Army), the enemy relieved units of the 4th Panzer Division with units of the 34th Infantry Division from 29 to 31 January and dispatched the former to the southwest.

Radio reconnaissance noted a radio station of the 18th Panzer Division operating in the Verkhniaia Sosna region on 1 and 2 February.

According to information from an agent, the 1st Panzer Division is being transferred from the Briansk region to Orel.

Thus, the enemy is concentrating up to three panzer divisions to liquidate the offensive operations by the *front's* left wing.

4. I have decided:

a) To commit additionally the 48th Army's 73rd Rifle Division to develop the success of the 48th Army's 143rd and 137th Rifle Divisions to the northwest and to attack toward Verkhniaia Sosna.

b) To continue the uninterrupted offensive by the 13th Army, with the objective to capture Zolotukhino with mobile detachments by the morning of 3 February and cut the Orel-Kursk railroad line with two to three divisions by the end of the day.

c) To transfer the 8th Rifle Division to the commander of the 13th Army for operations toward Viazovik, Sychevka, and Maloarkhangel'sk.

Lieutenant General Reiter, Commander of the
Briansk Front
Major General of Tank Forces Susaikov, Member
of the Briansk Front's Military Council
Major General Sandalov, Chief of Staff of the
Briansk Front[166]

[2200 hours 3 February]

1. The forces on the left wing of the *front* were continuing the offensive and defending the positions they occupied along the remainder of the front.

The enemy offered fire resistance and conducted counterattacks in separate sectors.

2. The 3rd Army was continuing to defend the sectors it occupied, exchanging fire and reconnoitering by observation.

The enemy did not conduct active operations.

A deserter — a Russian from among captured Red Army soldiers — came over to our side in the Nizhnaia Zaroshcha region, who, during his initial interrogation, said that he belonged to the 34th Infantry Division. According to his testimony, the division arrived in Dumchino on 18 January by rail and reached Mtsensk on foot where it occupied the defenses of a battalion in which [Russian] prisoners were located.

Enemy aircraft dropped three bombs in the Vudugovishche region. There were no casualties or damage.

The positions of the army's units were unchanged.

3. The 48th Army was defending the positions it occupied and was attacking with the two divisions on its left wing.

The 143rd Rifle Division, having captured Ul'ianovka and Ivanovka by 1400 hours, was fighting along the Dobroe, Nachalo, and Novofedorovka line.

The 137th Rifle Division, having captured Rozhdestvenskoe, Pavlovka, Sychevka, and Panikovets 2, was fighting along the Novofedorovka and Pavlovka line.

The remaining units of the army are defending their existing positions.

4. The 13th Army was continuing its offensive, overcoming fire resistance and repelling enemy counterattacks.

Enemy aviation bombed and assaulted the combat formations of our army's units with small groups of aircraft.

The units of the army were occupying [the following positions] at 1700 hours:

The 74th Rifle Division, after repelling repeated counterattacks by up to a battalion of enemy infantry from the Panikovets and Ostrov region during the day, captured Panikovets 1, Gustyi Tychinok, Paperetskoe, and Krivets.

Subunits of the 45th Infantry Division were identified operating in the sector of the division. A foodstuffs warehouse was seized in Panikovets.

The 148th Rifle Division, continuing its attack along the Sosna River, captured Temenskoe and Kartashevka and was continuing to fight in the Pokrovka region.

The 81st Rifle Division, overcoming enemy fire resistance and under attack by [enemy] aircraft, continued its attack and captured Alisovo, Krasnyi, and Zarei and will attack toward Chibisovka.

The enemy, protecting himself with strong detachments, withdrew toward the west.

The 211th Rifle Division was continuing to develop the success it achieved and, in fighting, captured the western bank of the Polevaia Snova River in the Goriainovo and Bukreevka sector. It will protect itself [against attack] from the north with part of its forces along the Oklinskii line.

The 280th Rifle Division, with the 79th Tank Brigade, while continuing its attack, reached the Kosogor and Kondrinka line and was fighting for these villages, while protecting itself [against attack] from the south with part of its forces along the Timskaia line.

The 15th Rifle Division concentrated in the Mokhovoe, Dlinnoe, and Rozhdestvenskoe regions with its main forces, with two battalions along the Vrazhnoe and Stakanovo line.

The 132nd Rifle Division is fighting for Nikitskoe with the units on its right wing, while repelling counterattacks by enemy infantry and four tanks, and was continuing to attack toward Dubrovka with the units on its left wing, after blockading up to 900 enemy infantry troops in the Petrovka, Ivanovka, Pozhidaevka, and Krasnaia Poliana regions.

The 8th Rifle Division — on the march to the Miliaevo, Vazhovo, and Vezovik regions beginning at 1500 hours.

The positions of the remaining units of the army are unchanged.

5. The positions of the units of the *front's* reserves are unchanged.

6. The 15th Air Army destroyed enemy forces in the Rakitino, Morozovo, Nikol'skoe, and Maloarkhangel'sk regions during the day, bombed columns of enemy motor-mechanized forces in Viazovoe, and protected our forces [advancing] along the road from Viazovoe.

As a result of the operations, up to 50 automobiles with troops and cargo and 60 carts were destroyed, three warehouses with ammunition were blown up, and two batteries of field artillery, three mortar batteries, and up to 400 enemy infantrymen were destroyed. Five air battles were conducted, as a result of which five enemy aircraft were shot down.

7. On the right, on the 61st Army's front, there was no essential change in the situation.

On the left, the 38th Army, destroying small groups of enemy infantry, was continuing its advance toward the west.

8. Wire communications are working with infrequent interruptions.

9. Weather. Variable cloudiness at 0–10 percent. The wind is from the south at 3–7 meters/second. The temperature is 10–15 degrees.

Major General Sandalov, Chief of Staff of
Briansk Front
Major General Antonov, Chief of the
Operations Department[167]

[2400 hours 5 February]

1. The forces of the Briansk Front were continuing their offensive operations toward the west and northwest on 5 February 1943.

The 48th Army, having encountering stubborn enemy fire resistance and having cleared a number of populated points of enemy, captured the Krasnyi Pakhar', Nepochataia, Nikol'skoe 2, Shalimovo 1 and 2, and Kishevka line with its left wing (the 73rd, 143rd, and 137th Rifle Divisions) by day's end and are fighting for Enino 1 and Kriukovo.

Its 6th Guards Rifle Division, with the onset of darkness – in movement from the Trusy, Berezovyi, and Pokrovka line to the left wing of the army.

The 13th Army captured the Belozerovka, Lukovets, and Legostaevo 2 line with its right wing (the 74th and 148th Rifle Divisions) by day's end.

The 81st Rifle Division – on the Ponyri 2 and Krasnyi Oktiabr' line and Stanovoe — with one regiment.

The 211th Rifle Division – on the Nizhnee Smorodnoe and Derlovo line.

The forward detachments of the 81st and 211th Rifle Divisions — Teploe, Khmelevoe, Veselaia Plota, and Telegino. Mobile detachments are being dispatched to cut the Orel-Kursk highway and capture Fatezh.

The 280th Rifle Division — in movement to from Zolotukhino to Kursk beginning on the morning of 5 February. It crossed the Tuskar' River at 1200 hours.

The 15th Rifle Division — in the Tishino, Zolotukhino, and Matveevka region.

The 132nd Rifle Division, in the Shchigry region, is being temporarily subordinated to the commander of the 60th Army for operations against Kursk.

The 307th Rifle Division — in the Kolpny region.

The 19th Tank Corps, the *front's* reserve — in movement from the Pen'shino region to the Kolpny region.

The forces of the 13th Army destroyed up to 1,000 enemy soldiers and officers on 4 February 1943.

During the capture of Shchigry by the 132nd Rifle Division, up to a battalion of enemy were destroyed. It has prisoners.

Based on incomplete data, 2 tanks, 5 guns, 26 automobiles, 12 motorcycles, and 8 warehouses were seized on 4 February.

The trophies taken in Shchigry are being counted.

During the capture of Kshen' Station by the units of the 132nd Rifle Division, a grain elevator was taken, and General Bensch [Lieutenant General Alfred Bäntsch, killed on 31 January], the commander of the 82nd Infantry Division, was killed.

2. The air forces of the *front* destroyed the enemy defensive system, forces, and rear area by bombing and ground attack operations.

81 aircraft sorties were conducted.

Three tanks, 100 vehicles with troops and cargo, 60 carts, 6 field batteries, 5 antiaircraft guns, 2 warehouses with ammunition, and up to 500 enemy soldiers and officers were destroyed.

Four batteries and 10 machine gun nests were suppressed.

Five enemy aircraft were shot down in air battles.

3. The enemy is offering stubborn resistance to the 48th Army's forces with units of the 45th Infantry Division. [The enemy] is carrying out a withdrawal toward the west in the remaining sectors. No new enemy units have been identified. The enemy bombed the combat formations of our units with small groups [of aircraft].

4. I have decided: To continue to fulfill my plan to destroy the enemy's Maloarkhangel'sk grouping beginning on the morning of 6 February by attacking in the Droskovo, Voronovo, and Kishevka sector with four divisions of the 48th Army with the mission of reaching the Lipovets River; to continue the attack toward the northwest and capture the Alekseevka and Kurakino Station line with four divisions of the 13th Army; cut the Orel-Kursk highway and seize Fatezh with forward detachments of the 13th Army's central group of forces; and continue operations toward Kursk with the 280th Rifle Division of the 13th Army.

Reiter, Susaikov, Sandalov[168]

Since the forces of the Briansk and Voronezh Fronts were making such spectacular progress in their advance toward Kursk, Belgorod, and Khar'kov, on 6 February the *Stavka* decided to capitalize on their success by shifting the axis of their advance northwestward toward Orel. This projected path promised to propel their forces around the right flank and into rear of the Second Panzer Army, commanded by Colonel General Rudolf Schmidt, whose forces were anchoring Army Group Center's right wing. Simultaneously, the *Stavka* began sketching out in outline form an even more ambitious plan for a large-scale offensive against German forces in the central sector of the Soviet-German front, which, if successful, could propel Soviet forces forward to the Dnepr River (see Map 60). The day before, the *Stavka* had already ordered creation of a new Central Front formed around the nucleus of the former Don Front and had begun ordering selective formations from the Don Front to deploy northward and assemble in the

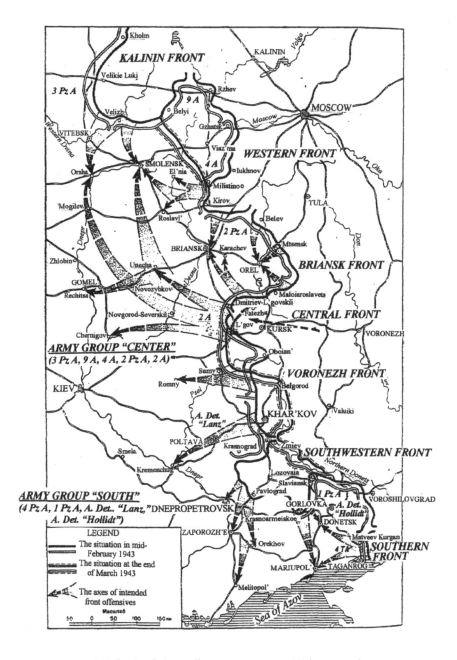

Map 60. The *Stavka's* overall strategic concept, 6 February 1943

Briansk Front's rear area, where they would join other forces from its strategic reserves to form an important new shock grouping.

As it assembled this new shock grouping, at 0140 hours on 6 February, the *Stavka* ordered Colonel General M. A. Reiter, the commander of the Briansk Front, to add the city of Orel, a vital hub in the German command and control, communications, and logistics system, to his list of priority objectives:

> To achieve the most rapid encirclement and destruction of the enemy's Orel-Briansk grouping, the *Stavka* of the Supreme High Command orders:
>
> 1. With the arrival of the 48th and 13th Armies along the Droskovo, Maloarkhangel'sk, and Fatezh line, the 48th Army will attack toward Orel, while enveloping it from the southwest.
>
> Prepare an offensive by the 61st Army from the Belev region in the general direction through Bolkhov to Orel to link up with this attack.
>
> The 61st Army will be subordinate to you beginning on the morning of 8 February 1943.
>
> With the arrival of 48th Army in the Zmievka region, go over to the attack with the 3rd Army, launching an attack in the general direction of Orel.
>
> 2. Simultaneously with the offensive by the 48th, 3rd, and 61st Armies on Orel, continue the offensive toward Karachev and Briansk by the 13th Army with the mission of forming a second encirclement ring around the enemy and seizing the cities of Briansk and Karachev.
>
> Bear in mind, the 16th Army of the Western Front will attack from the Bryn' and Zavod regions in the general direction through Zhizdra to link up with the 13th Army's attack.
>
> 3. Complete the encirclement and destruction of the enemy's Orel grouping with the forces of the 48th, 3rd, and 61st Armies by 15–17 February 1943.
>
> The 13th Army, in cooperation with the 16th Army of the Western Front, will seize Briansk by 23–25 February 1943.
>
> 4. Bear in mind, the forces of Colonel General Rokossovsky are deploying on your left – approximately along the Fatezh and L'gov line –and will attack in the general direction of Sevsk and Unecha Station.
>
> 5. The boundary line with the Western Front, effective beginning on the morning of 8 February 1943, will be: Kozel'sk, Khvostovichi, and Zhurinichi. All points are inclusive for the Western Front. The boundary line with Rokossovsky's forces will be provided later.
>
> 6. Report your decision in code via BODO [enciphered teletype] by 2400 hours 6 February 1943.
>
> The Stavka of the Supreme High Command
I. Stalin   G. Zhukov[169]

The Advance

The 60th Army's Sizure of Kursk

While the *Stavka* was forming Colonel General K. K. Rokossovsky's new Central Front and regrouping its forces to the Elets region, the 48th and 13th Armies of Reiter's Briansk Front continued their drive toward Orel from the southeast, in close coordination with the two armies thrusting westward on the Voronezh Front's right wing, Lieutenant General I. D. Cherniakhovsky's 60th Army, which was advancing toward Kursk, and, on the 60th Army's left, Lieutenant General M. E. Chibisov's 38th Army, which was attacking toward Sumy. Although subordinate to the Voronezh Front, since the 60th Army was on the *front's* right wing, its forces were to protect the left flank of the Briansk Front's 13th Army as the latter attacked toward Orel. However, since the 60th Army's advance was delayed as it helped liquidate and pursue German forces encircled in and west of Kastornoe, the army was not able to resume its advance toward Kursk until 4 February. As described in an extract from a Voronezh Front report dated 2400 hours on 8 February 1943, the 60th Army finally captured Kursk late in the day:

1. The *front* continued the offensive toward the west and southwest, fought for possession of the cities of Kursk and Belgorod, and repelled enemy counterattacks in separate sectors with its main forces on 8 February and was continuing to destroy the enemy grouping encircled in the Sennoe, Chepelki, and Verkhne Apochki and Pokrovka, Krutye Verkhi, and Mochagi regions with part of its forces.

The city of Kursk was taken by our forces at 1500 hours on 8 February 1943.

The 60th Army. The forces of the army fought intensely for possession of Kursk on 8 February 1943. The enemy offered stubborn resistance with the remnants of the 82nd Infantry Division, the 340th Infantry Division, and the 4th Panzer Division, which approached from the Orel region, while counterattacking our units from the vicinity of Kursk with a force of up to a regiment of infantry.

The forces of the army captured Kursk at 1500 hours on 8 February 1943.

The units of the army, after cutting the Kursk-Oboian' highway, captured a series of populated points, including Medvenskoe, Znamenka, and Kochegurovka.

A battalion of the 104th Rifle Brigade was thrown into the Ploskoe region, with its front facing toward the east, to prevent the enemy, who was penetrating through the combat formations of the 38th Army's units, from escaping from the encirclement. The enemy's penetrating groups were approaching Afanas'evka.

The 38th Army. The units of the army engaged in intense fighting with the enemy group encircled in the Sennoe, Chepelki, and Verkhne Apochki and the Pokrovskoe, Krutye Verkhi and Mochagi regions during the day ….

Filippov [General Kuznetsov]
Fedotov
Petrov[170]

Map 61. The 13th and 48th Armies' operations, the situation from 6–8 February 1943

The Briansk Front's Advance

As the *Stavka* struggled to accelerate the Central Front's regrouping and forward deployment, the Briansk Front's 48th and 13th Armies, commanded by Major General G. A. Zhaliuzin and Major General N. P. Pukhov, respectively, continued their rapid advance toward the west and swept into the Fatezh region, splitting the German Second Panzer and Second Armies apart (see Map 61). The Briansk Front's daily report issued at 2400 hours on 9 February recorded its progress:

1. As a result of the offensive, the forces of the 48th and 13th Armies, overcoming stubborn enemy resistance, captured [the following] lines on 9 February: the southeastern slopes of Hill 238.9 at Salomatovka, the southeastern part of Salomatovka (the 73rd Rifle Division), Hill 236.4 northeast of Orlovka (the 143rd Rifle Division), the southwestern outskirts of Smirnye (the 137th Rifle Division), Hill 242.9 and the eastern outskirts of Topki 2 (the 6th Guards Rifle Division), Novoselki (the 8th Rifle Division), Hill 238.8, Alekseevka, and Hill 228.4 (the 74th Rifle Division), Dobroe Nachalo and Malaia Plotka (the 148th Rifle Division), Iudinka and Petrovka (the 15th Rifle Division), and Ponyri, Ponyri 1, and Shirokoe Boloto (the 81st Rifle Division). The 129th Tank Brigade is fighting with units of the enemy's 20th Panzer Division in the vicinity of Maloarkhangel'sk Station.

The 211th Rifle Division was concentrating in the Molotochi, Khmelevoe, and Teploe region.

The 280th and 132nd Rifle Divisions – in movement from Kursk to the Fatezh region.

Active combat operations are not being conducted in the remaining sectors of the *front*.

The forces of the 48th and 13th Armies liberated 19 populated points, including Ponyri Station, during the day.

More than two battalions were destroyed, and 30 enemy soldiers and officers were taken captive.

Trophies seized: 105-mm guns — 3, antiaircraft guns — 4, large caliber machine guns — 2, RP's — 4, rifles — 60, rifle rounds — 50,000, motorcycles — 2, vehicles — 1, carts with cargo — 6, horses — 88, and warehouses with ammunition and foodstuffs — 2.

In addition, 18,000 aerial bombs, a warehouse with ammunition, and a considerable amount of other equipment were seized at Ponyri Station. The count of trophies is continuing.

2. *Frontal* aviation conducted no combat operations because of poor meteorological conditions, and reconnaissance flights were limited to the Orel and Sevsk axes.

3. The enemy offered exceptionally stubborn resistance in all of the offensive sector of the 48th and 13th Armies' forces with counterattacks by infantry, groups of tanks with submachine gunners, and organized artillery fire from artillery, mortars, and infantry weapons.

According to information from prisoners, the enemy's units have received orders to die rather than fail to stop our offensive.

The 130th and 133rd Infantry Regiments of the 45th Infantry Division, units of the 18th Panzer Division (in the Ponyri region), the 1st, 9th, 10th, and 11th Jager Battalions (the latter in the Protasovo region), and motorcycle (ski) battalions of the 20th Panzer Division (in the region of Maloarkhangel'sk Station) have been identified and confirmed by captured prisoners and their reports.

4. I have decided:

1) To continue fulfilling the plan for the destruction of the enemy's Maloarkhangel'sk grouping on 10 February;

2) To bring the 211th Rifle Division forward from the Molotochi and Khmelevoe region toward Trosna and Kromy beginning on the morning of 10 February;

3) To concentrate the 19th Tank Corps and the 1st and 2nd Ski Brigades in the Tsurikovo and Man'shino region by the morning of 10 February; and

4) To commit the 132nd and 280th Rifle Divisions at the boundary of the 13th Army.

Reiter, Susaikov, Sandalov[171]

As the Briansk Front's 48th and 13th Armies pressed their attacks in the Maloarkhangel'sk and Fatezh regions, the assault by the Lieutenant General P. A. Belov's 61st Army north of Bolkhov aborted almost immediately after it commenced. Attacking a dawn on 12 February, the army's 12th Guards, 342nd, and 356th Rifle Divisions, supported by the 68th Tank Brigade, struck the defenses of the Second Panzer Army's 112th Infantry Division in the Ulanova and Merkulavskii sector, just west of the Bolkhov-Belev road. Within hours, the assault faltered in the face of withering German fire. Belov explained just why his assaults failed in two reports entitled "Reports Nos. 4 and 5 by the Commander of the 61st Army to the Commander of the Briansk Front Concerning the Reasons for the Unsuccessful Attack," which he sent to General Reiter, his *front* commander, on 12 February:

[1400 hours]

The attack obviously misfired. We have not managed to exploit the insignificant successes of the 12th Guards Rifle Division.

The enemy is conducting heavy fire from mortars and machine guns and is stubbornly defending in strong points.

Strong and gusty head winds are hindering the tank fire. There are many targets, but our artillery's activity has fallen off sharply because of insufficient ammunition.

I am organizing a second attack using assault groups saturated with accompanying direct fire guns.

I also intend to fight the battle all night. I have been forced to resort to the latter in light of the absence of ammunition and the inactivity of our supply organs.

I am suffering losses from enemy fire.

Belov

[Notation by the recipient] "Ammunition has been sent. Continue the attack at first light. Reiter."[172]

[1700 hours]

The second attack has had no success. The fighting revealed the presence of really strongly fortified enemy positions. Reliable means of suppression are required in order to penetrate such a [defensive] belt, but the artillery is not strong (one heavy artillery regiment), and, at the most decisive moment (the attack), aviation refused to support because of the weather. I am determining my losses.

I have come to the conclusion about the uselessness of wasting people in hopeless attacks without the support of reliable weapons.

I request your approval to withdraw the forces from their jumping-off positions.

The ammunition of various types that you promised me two days ago did not arrive and will not arrive earlier than the morning of 13 February. And days will be required to move it from the railroad line to the units.

Strong winds are constantly covering the just-cleared roads with snow and are blinding the eyes of the riflemen, machine gunners, and the artillerymen who are firing over open sights.

If you do not approve my proposal, then I will attack during the night, using the 0.2 combat loads of artillery shells designated for repelling the day's counterattacks.

Belov[173]

General Reiter summarized the results of the day's actions in a report he submitted to the *Stavka* at 2400 hours on 12 February (see Map 62):

1. The forces of the Briansk Front were continuing offensive fighting along the previous axes and in the sector of the 61st Army on 12 February.

As a result of the day's fighting, the forces of the 61st Army penetrated into the first trench line of the enemy's defense in the Ulanova and Merkulovskii sector. The fighting is continuing.

The 48th Army's 6th Guards Rifle Division captured Novaia Slobodka and an unnamed populated point (1 kilometer north of Novaia Sloboda). The remaining units of the army were fighting in their previous positions.

The 13th Army's 15th and 81st Rifle Divisions, with the 118th and 129th Tank Brigades, captured the line through Hill 249.9 (6 kilometers northeast of Ponyri), Hill 251.9, Hill 253.6, Sorevnovanie, Hill 245.2, and Rzhavets, and the 132nd Rifle Division, having encountered resistance by units of the 258th Infantry Division and police detachments,

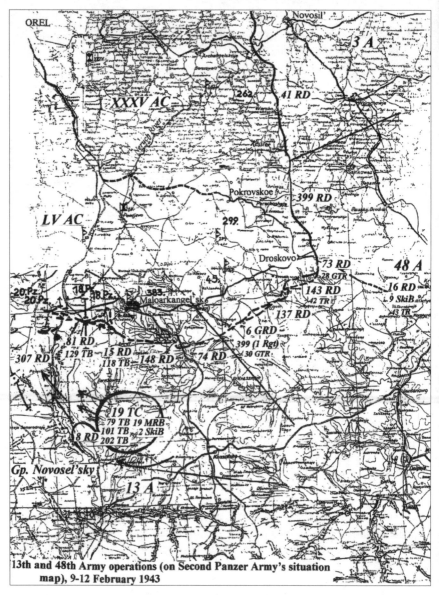

Map 62. The 13th and 48th Armies' operations, the situation from 9–12 February 1943

was fighting in the General'shino (Novoselovka), Belyi Kolodez', and Zaslonka region at 1600 hours.

159 prisoners were seized by the divisions.

The 307th Rifle Division, after marching from the Tsurikovo and Man'shino region, was committed to combat toward Berezovyi Log, Aleksandrovka, and Arkhangel'skoe from behind the 81st Rifle Division's left wing during the second half of the day. The remaining units were fighting along previous lines.

Group Novosel'sky's 211th Rifle Division captured Chermoshnoe and was continuing to attack toward the north. The remaining formations of the group, with the onset of darkness, were continuing to move forward northwestward toward Chermoshnoe.

The 280th Rifle Division [is moving forward] from the Novaia Golovinka and Verknii Liubazh region; the 19th Tank Corps from the Brekhovo and Sotnikovo region, and the ski brigades [the 1st and 2nd] — from the Goriainovo and Koronino region.

During the day of fighting, 190 prisoners, 3 tanks, 2 guns, and other trophies were seized by the *front's* forces. One enemy aircraft was shot down by infantry fire.

The artillery destroyed one troop train.

During the course of repelling numerous enemy counterattacks, about 1,000 soldiers and officers were destroyed, and 10 tanks were blown up by units of the 81st Rifle Division.

2. *Frontal* aviation did not conduct combat operations because of the poor meteorological conditions.

3. The enemy is continuing the transport of fresh units to the Maloarkhangel'sk Station region to protect Maloarkhangel'sk, Kromy, and Dmitriev-L'govskii.

In the Maloarkhangel'sk region, the enemy conducted constant counterattacks during the day with forces of up to 2 battalions and 30 tanks each. These forces were thrown into counterattacks immediately after unloading from the railroad cars and vehicles. He defended with increasing persistence in the remaining sectors.

Enemy units that were operating [in the region] before and, in addition, the 52nd Motorized Regiment of the 18th Panzer Division, the 112th Motorized Regiment of the 20th Panzer Division, the 258th Infantry Division, and the 502nd Sapper Battalion have been confirmed by prisoners. Prisoners from the 258th Infantry Division indicated the division was transferred by auto-transport from the Gzhatsk region to Dmitriev-L'govskii with the mission to halt the Red Army's offensive.

Small groups of enemy aircraft bombed the combat formations of the 48th and 13th Armies, Group Novosel'sky, and the town of Fatezh.

4. I will continue to fulfill my mission according to the plan on 13 February 1943.

Reiter, Susaikov, Sandalov[174]

As indicated by Reiter's report, by 12 February it was becoming increasingly difficult for the Briansk Front's armies to sustain their offensive momentum. Underscoring this problem, the assaults by Belov's 61st Army's along the Bolkhov axis toward Orel had stalled, and both Zhaliuzin's 48th Army and Pukhov's 13th Army were encountering ever-increasing resistance along the southeastern approaches to Orel. Days before, the German OKH (Army High Command), realizing the 48th and 13th Armies' advance had torn a huge gap between its Second Panzer and Second Armies – a gap that threatened the viability of its strategic defenses in the East — had begun shifting forces from other sectors of the front to block the Soviet advance and repair the breech. Compounding Reiter's problems, the attrition resulting from weeks of near-constant fighting was literally wearing his forces out, and they were experiencing shortages of critical ammunition, fuel, and rations. Reiter acknowledged as much in an order he dispatched to his subordinate commands on 12 February.

> During the course of the fighting, large-scale shortages and interruptions in the supply of foodstuffs, ammunition, and fuel have been evident in individual attacking units. It has been determined that the interruptions in the supply of units are occurring because the commanders and political workers and, especially, the supply apparatuses of the units are displaying insufficient concern for this matter. As a result, the division exchange points [DOP] in some of the formations are lagging 60–70 kilometers behind their forward units (the 74th, 148th, and other rifle divisions).
>
> I order:
>
> 1. Immediately undertake measures to move the DOP's nearer to the forward units and constantly position them at distances envisioned by RKKA orders and regulations.
>
> 2. Demand that the supply organs of the units be more agile in the supply of their units with all that is required. Do not [merely] establish the fact that foodstuffs, ammunition, and fuel are lacking, but [instead] implement all possible measures so as to satisfy the units with all necessities and, by doing so, insure successful offensive fighting.
>
> 3. I am taking notice and demanding that the matter of supplying foodstuffs, ammunition, and fuel will remain at the center of attention of all commanders and political workers.
>
> Reiter, Susaikov, Sandalov[175]

At 1800 hours the following day, Reiter complained to the *Stavka* about the increasing German resistance, implying his forces required reinforcement:

> From interrogations of prisoners seized in the Maloarkhangel'sk Station region, in the Chermoshnoe region along the Kursk-Kromy road, and along the approaches to Dmitriev-L'govskii it has been determined that the enemy has concentrated the 18th and 20th Panzer Divisions, the 45th and 258th Infantry Divisions, the 10th and 11th Jager Battalions, and other separate units in these region with the mission — to attack into the flank of the Briansk Front's shock group, destroy it, and capture Kursk.
>
> Reiter, Susaikov, Sandalov[176]

Conclusions

In light of the strengthening German resistance, by mid-February it was apparent to Stalin and his *Stavka* that the fate of the Briansk Front's offensive, as well as their ambitious plan to expand the Winter Offensive to encompass the entire central sector of the Soviet-German front, hinged on the ability of Rokossovsky to regroup the armies of his Central Front into the region northeast of Kursk and commit them into the gap formed by the Briansk and Voronezh Front's exploiting armies as soon as possible. Therefore, as the Briansk Front's armies were advancing toward Orel during the second week of February, with the *Stavka's* assistance, Rokossovsky struggled to commit his forces into battle at the most decisive time and place. Initially, the *Stavka* decided the decisive time was 15 February, and the decisive place was the so-called Fatezh corridor, the gap separating the forces of the defending German Second Panzer and Second Armies.

Chapter 7

The Central, Briansk, and Western Fronts' Orel, Briansk, and Smolensk Offensive (15 February–6 March 1943)

Strategic Planning and Regrouping

Strategic Plans

Central to Soviet strategic planning in early February 1943 was the fact that the German Stalingrad garrison had surrendered on 2 February. This released the six field armies and one air army of Rokossovsky's Don Front (the 21st, 24th, 62nd, 64th, 65th, and 66th Armies and the 16th Air Army) to the *Stavka's* control for it to employ elsewhere across the front.[177] Obviously these armies required refitting after their almost two months of fighting in the Stalingrad region. Some refitting had been accomplished before the German surrender, and, therefore, forces were shifted among the six armies. In addition, other strategic reserves were available for assignment to Rokossovsky's new Central Front. These included Lieutenant General A. G. Rodin's 2nd Tank Army, which was formed during January and early February 1943 on the base of the Briansk Front's 3rd Reserve Army and then assigned to the Briansk Front's reserve, and Lieutenant General G. F. Tarasov's 70th Army, which was created between October 1942 and early February 1943 and was composed of NKVD border guards and internal security forces from the Far Eastern, Central Asian, and Trans-Baikal Military Districts. These new forces would play a key role in the formulation of new *Stavka* plans.

The overall concept for this, the culminating stage of the Winter Offensive, envisioned conduct of a three-phase strategic offensive, which would ultimately involve the participation of four Red Army *fronts*. First, beginning on 12 February, as the Central Front assembled its armies in the Fatezh region, the combined forces of the Western and Briansk Fronts were to encircle and destroy German forces in the Orel salient (see Map 63). Then, between 17 and 25 February, the two *fronts*, joined by the Central Front.were to clear the Briansk region of German forces and secure bridgeheads across the Desna River. During this phase, the Central Front was to employ its tank army and cavalry-rifle group to capture crossings over the Desna River near the towns of Novgorod-Severskii and Trubchevsk (see Map 64). During the final phase of the operation, between 25 February and mid-March, the Kalinin and Western Fronts would join combat to seize Smolensk and, in concert with their sister *fronts*, encircle and destroy German Army Group Center in the Rzhev-Viaz'ma salient (see Map 65). The Kalinin Front's forces were to attack

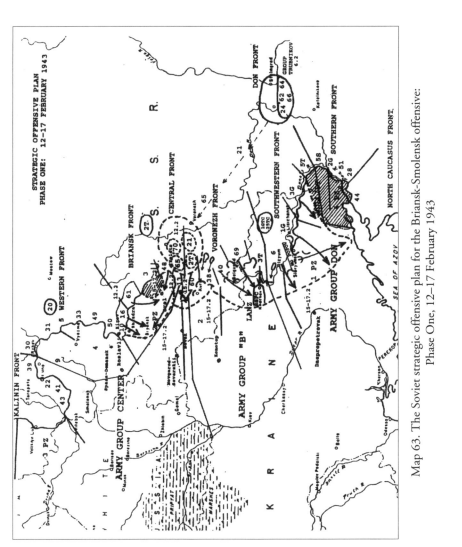

Map 63. The Soviet strategic offensive plan for the Briansk-Smolensk offensive: Phase One, 12–17 February 1943

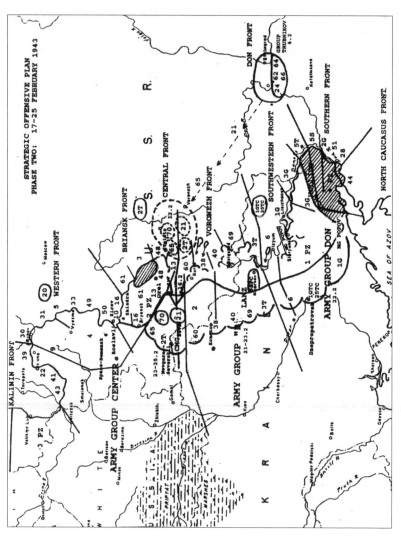

Map 64. The Soviet strategic offensive plan for the Briansk-Smolensk offensive: Phase Two, 17–25 February 1943

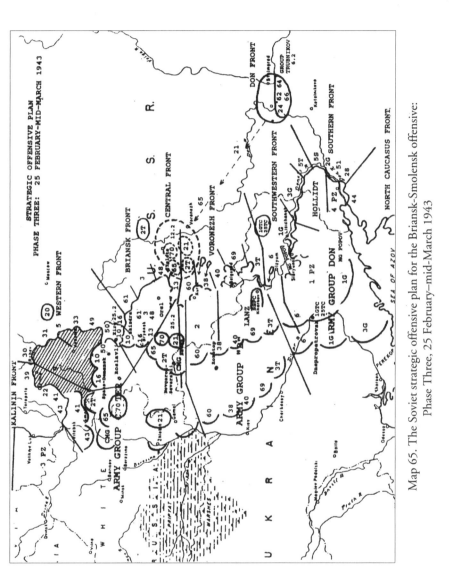

Map 65. The Soviet strategic offensive plan for the Briansk-Smolensk offensive: Phase Three, 25 February–mid-March 1943

southward through Vitebsk to link up with Central Front's forces near Orsha on the Dnepr River. The Western Front's forces were to advance along two axes; first, westward from the Kirov region across the base of the Rzhev-Viaz'ma salient to attack Smolensk from the southeast and, second, southward from the Kirov region to envelop German forces defending Orel from the north. The entire offensive was timed to coincide with anticipated successful operations by the Voronezh and Southwestern Fronts so that by mid-March the strategic offensive would have propelled Soviet forces to the line of the Dnepr River from Vitebsk southward through Dnepropetrovsk to the Sea of Azov.

Obviously, Rokossovsky's new Central Front would play the key role in determining how successful this expanded offensive would be. Marshal A. M. Vasilevsky, then deputy chief of the General Staff, recalled:

> While discussing the situation in the south and reckoning that the complete defeat of the Paulus' [German Sixth Army] grouping was merely a matter of days, the Supreme High Command was planning the further use of Don Front's forces, which were being released from Stalingrad. At the end of January and beginning of February, after numerous conversations between the Supreme Commander and leading figures at the Center and in the *fronts*, yet another decision had matured: besides the operations in the south, to carry out a series of large-scale offensive operations linked with a single strategic design and plan, with the aim of defeating the main forces of German Army Group Center. The idea was to use primarily the Briansk Front and left wing of the Western Front to defeat the German 2nd Panzer Army in the Orel area and then, bringing up forces of the former Don Front and renaming it the Central Front, attacking Smolensk through Briansk and launching an offensive so as to emerge into the rear of the enemy's Rzhev-Viaz'ma grouping, in conjunction with forces of the Kalinin and Western Fronts. A concrete plan of action was drawn up, and, in the early part of February, the *Stavka* issued directives to the *fronts* involved.[178]

The *Stavka* began issuing preliminary orders for the assembly of Rokossovsky's new *front* on 2 February, immediately after General Paulus surrendered his Sixth Army in Stalingrad. At 1410 hours the same day, it transferred the Don Front's 21st and 64th Armies to it own control and ordered them to concentrate as soon as possible in the Elets and Livny regions, in the Briansk Front's rear area.[179] At 0220 hours the next day, it directed the Don Front's headquarters and many units and installations subordinate directly to the *front* to move northward into the same regions and allocated 30 railroad trains to transport the regrouping forces.[180] Early on 4 February, however, the *Stavka* amended this directive by ordering the 65th Army to move to Elets and the 64th Army to remain the Stalingrad region.[181] Over the next few days, it sent similar movement directives to many other formations, including the 12th Antitank Artillery and the 4th Artillery Divisions. Then, at 1750 hours on 5 February, Zhukov appointed Lieutenant General K. P. Trubnikov, the deputy commander of the Don Front, to command all of the *front's* forces remaining in the Stalingrad region, including the 62nd, 64th, and 66th Armies, and assigned him the task of preparing these armies for future commitment to combat wherever required.[182]

Meanwhile, the *Stavka* also began assembling other forces designated to take part in Rokossovsky's new offensive. In addition to Rodin's 2nd Tank Army, which was already situated in the Briansk Front's rear area, the most important of these formations was General Tarasov's Separate NKVD [Peoples Commissariat of Internal Affairs] Army, whose subordinate formations were scattered throughout the central and eastern reaches of the Soviet Union. At 1800 hours on 5 February, Zhukov issued two directives: the first ordering this army to begin concentrating in the Briansk Front's deep rear and the second assigning it, with a new numerical designation, to the Red Army:

[To the commander of the Separate Army]

[Copies to the deputy People's Commissar of Internal Affairs [A. N. Apollonov] and the chief of the General Staff's Operations Directorate]

The *Stavka* of the Supreme High Command orders:

1. Relocate the Separate Army of Major General Tarasov to a new region. Carry out the relocation by railroad in the following order:

a) The field headquarters of the army, with reinforcing units and rear service units and installations – load in [the vicinity] of Sverdlovsk, Iset', Rezh, and Kunara Stations beginning at 1200 hours on 6 February 1943. Tempo – 3.

b) The Stalingrad Division – load at Cheliabinsk Station beginning at 1200 hours on 6 February 1943. Tempo – 3.

c) The Siberian Division – load at Krasnoufimsk Station beginning at 1800 hours on 8 February 1943. Tempo – 3.

d) The Far Eastern Division – load at Vereshchagino Station beginning at 1800 hours on 9 February 1943. Tempo – 3.

e) The Ural Division – load at Revda Station beginning at 1800 hours on 9 February 1943. Tempo – 2.

f) The Trans-Baikal Division – load at Shchadrinsk Station beginning at 1800 hours on 9 February 1943. Tempo – 3.

g) The Central Asian Division – load in [the vicinity] of Zlatoust, Satka, and Tundush Stations beginning at 1800 hours on 11 February 1943. Tempo – 3.

2. Dispatch the army's headquarters and formations complete, with all of their personnel, weapons, transport, and equipment.

3. Only the commanders of the formations should know about the transportation plan, which will be given to them in person and to each separately.

4. Carefully camouflage all equipment following on open rail cars.
   Explain everything to the personnel, and strictly forbid whomever it may be to speak about where his unit is going.

5. Provide the departing [forces] with: ammunition — 1 combat load, fuel — 2 refills, rations during the movement — 10 days, and, in addition, 10 days of disembarkation reserves.

Maintain reserves of foodstuffs, ammunition, and fuel in each train to insure its independence. Under no circumstances permit the reserves of an entire formation to be transported on one train.

6. Report to the General Staff at 1800 hours daily about the movement of each of the army's formations.

Deputy Supreme High Commander
Zhukov[183]

[To the deputy People's Commissar of Internal Affairs and the chief of the Main Directorate for the Formation and Manning of Forces]

The *Stavka* of the Supreme High Command orders:

1. Name the Separate Army formed by the People's Commissariat of Internal Affairs of the USSR, consisting of six rifle divisions, with separate reinforcing and support units, the 70th Army and include it in the Red Army on 1 February.

2. Give the formations of the 70th Army the following designations:
The 102nd Far Eastern Rifle Division,
The 106th Trans-Baikal Rifle Division,
The 140th Siberian Rifle Division,
The 162nd Central Asian Rifle Division,
The 175th Ural Rifle Division,
The 181st Stalingrad Rifle Division

3. Determine the numbering and table of organization and composition [TO&E] of the units of the 70th Army in accordance with the instructions of the Chief of the Red Army *Glavupraform* [Main Directorate for the Formation and Manning of the Red Army].

By direction of the Supreme High Command
G. Zhukov[184]

After mobilizing the NKO's vast organizational structure to form and move the 70th Army and the other forces designated to participate in Rokossovsky's offensive, on 5 February the *Stavka* issued a formal directive establishing the new Central Front by the 15th:

The *Stavka* of the Supreme High Command orders:

1. Form a Central Front by 15 February 1943.

2. Rename the field headquarters of the Don Front the field headquarters of the Central Front. Station the headquarters of the *front* in the Ol'shanets region (10 kilometers east of Elets).

3. Appoint:
As commander of the Central Front — Colonel General K. K. Rokossovsky;

As the Member of the *front's* Military Council {commissar] — Major General K. F. Telegin; and

As the *front's* chief of staff — Lieutenant General M. S. Malinin.

4. The composition of the Central Front will include: the field headquarters of the 21st, 65th, and 70th Armies; the 16th Air Army; the 2nd Tank Army; the 2nd Guards Cavalry Corps; the 37th, 51st, 52nd, and 67th Guards Rifle Divisions; the 23rd, 69th, 112th, 149th, 193rd, 194th, 246th, 325th, 354th, and 375th Rifle Divisions; the six divisions of the 70th Army; the 10th Antiaircraft Artillery Division; the 502nd, 1180th, and 1188th Antitank Artillery Regiments; the 114th, 136th, and 143rd RGK [*Stavka* reserve] Mortar Regiments; the 56th and 92nd Guards-mortar Regiments; the 12th Antiaircraft Artillery Battalion; the 4th RGK Artillery Division; and six line tank regiments.

5. Guarantee concentration of the units and formations included in the Central Front to the Chief of the General Staff by 12 February 1943; the 112th, 37th Guards, 51st Guards, 67th Guards and 193rd and 23rd Rifle Divisions and the 4th Artillery Division — by 17 February 1943; and the six rifle divisions of the 70th Army — by 23 February 1943.

6. The operational tasks of the *front* will be spelled out in a separate directive.

7. Leave your deputy, Lieutenant General K. P. Trubnikov, with a group of commanders, in the Stalingrad region, to which you will assign the tasks of directing combat training and putting the remaining forces in order and responsibility for their timely dispatch to new points in accordance with directives of the *Stavka* and the General Staff. Practical orders governing the work of Trubnikov will be issued separately.

8. Confirm receipt. Report fulfillment.

The *Stavka* of the Supreme High Command
I. Stalin, G. Zhukov[185]

Operational Missions

Specific *Stavka* directives issued on 6 February assigned missions to participating *fronts*.[186] Colonel General I. S. Konev's Western Front was to transfer its left-wing 61st Army to the Briansk Front control. By 12 February the Western Front's 16th Army, reinforced by the 9th Tank Corps, was to join the Briansk Front's 61st Army in an offensive through Zhizdra to Briansk to link up with the Briansk Front's 13th and 48th Armies and encircle the German Orel grouping. By 25 February Konev's *front* was to prepare an additional offensive by its 50th and 10th Armies, reinforced by two tank corps, toward Roslavl' and El'nia in concert with the Briansk and Central Fronts' expanding offensive.

Colonel General Reiter's Briansk Front was to cooperate with the Western Front and encircle rapidly and eliminate the German Orel-Briansk grouping. Reiter's 13th and 48th Armies were to advance on 12 February to the Droskovo, Maloarkhangel'sk, and Fatezh line. Subsequently, the 13th Army was to facilitate commitment to combat of the Central Front's forces and advance on the Karachev-Briansk axis, while the 48th Army was to envelop Orel from the south. Meanwhile, the Briansk Front's 61st Army was to join the Western Front's 16th Army in an attack from the Belev region through Bolkhov to link up with the 48th Army at Orel. When the 61st Army had reached Zmievka, Reiter's 3rd Army was to join the offensive on Orel. The first phase of the operation was to culminate on 15–17 February with the destruction of the German Orel grouping. The second phase would climax from 23–25 February when the 13th Army linked up with the Western Front's 16th Army to destroy German forces around Briansk. Both the Western and Briansk Fronts would then join the Central Front in the final drive to Smolensk and the Dnepr River.

Rokossovsky received detailed instructions from the *Stavka* at 0140 hours on 6 February:

> In order to further exploit the Briansk and Voronezh Fronts' success and reach the rear area of the enemy's Rzhev-Viaz'ma-Briansk grouping, the *Stavka* of the Supreme High Command orders:
>
> 1. By 12 February 1943, concentrate:
>
> a) The 2nd Tank Army — in the Dolgoe region;
>
> b) The 2nd Guards Cavalry Corps, with three ski brigades and two tank regiments in the Cheremisinovo region; and
>
> c) The 65th Army — in the region north of Dolgoe and south of Livny.
>
> Bring the 2nd Tank Army, 65th Army, and 2nd [Guards] Cavalry Corps from their concentration regions up to the Kursk and Fatezh deployment line by the end of 14 February 1943. Concentrate the remaining units of the 21st and 70th Armies in the Volovo, Dolgorukovo, and Livny regions as they arrive and send them after the advancing forces of the *front's* first echelon.
>
> 2. The 2nd Tank Army, 65th Army, and 16th Air Army will launch an offensive in the general direction of Sevsk and Unecha Station beginning on the morning of 15 February 1943, with the immediate mission of cutting the Briansk-Gomel' railroad line.
>
> Deploy Kriukov's cavalry-rifle group on the left wing and send it through Novgorod-Severskii, Staryi Bykhov, and Mogilev, where it is to cross to the Western bank of the Dnepr and, after securing the crossings, reach the Orsha region.
>
> Bear in mind, the Briansk Front's 13th Army will be advancing toward Briansk on your right and the Western Front's 16th Army will launch an offensive through Zhizdra toward Briansk.
>
> 3. When the *front's* armies reach the Briansk and Gomel' line, conduct your main attack through Klimovichi and Khislovichi to Smolensk, with the missions of seizing the Smolensk region and cutting off the withdrawal routes of the enemy's Viaz'ma-Rzhev grouping. After your main force reaches the Unecha Station region, seize Gomel' and the western

bank of the Dnepr River in the Rechitsa and Zhlobin sector with a force of two rifle divisions.

Simultaneously with your forces launching the offensive against Smolensk from the Briansk-Gomel' line, the Western Front will conduct an offensive to Roslavl' and, further, to Smolensk, and the Kalinin Front will advance to Vitebsk and Orsha, and part of its forces to Smolensk, to link up with your main attack.

4. The boundary line of the *front* will be provided later. Bear in mind that, on the *front's* left, the 60th Army of the Voronezh Front will be attacking in the general direction of L'gov, Glukhov, and Chernigov.

The *Stavka* of the Supreme High Command

I. Stalin

G. Zhukov[187]

To plan such an operation was one thing. To carry it out was an altogether different matter, even if the Germans permitted continued Soviet offensive progress in the south. Only six days remained for concentration of Rokossovsky's shock force in the Livny area, and 11 days before the offensive itself was supposed to commence. Although the 2nd Tank Army and 2nd Guards Cavalry Corps were already concentrated in the Livny region, the 70th Army's forces, after their long rail journey from the Stalingrad region, had to traverse another 200 kilometers of rain-soaked roads from the Elets region, and the 65th and 21st Armies had to complete arduous rail and road movement from Stalingrad. Heavy Spring snows hampered movement, the *rasputitsa* [spring rainy season] was due any day, and roads from Livny and Elets to the front were already in poor condition.

Rokossovsky, objecting to the stringent time requirements imposed by the *Stavka*, nevertheless moved with his staff to Elets, leaving his deputy, Lieutenant General K. P. Trubnikov, in Stalingrad to facilitate further troop movements north. There he coordinated with the Briansk Front commander, General Reiter, and established his own *front* command post. He later described the tremendous chore confronting his staff as its strove to meet the *Stavka's* ambitious offensive timetable:

> From the outset we encountered tremendous difficulties. There was only one single-track railroad functioning – the only one that had been restored by then. Naturally, it could not handle such traffic. Our transportation plans were bursting at the seams. Traffic schedules collapsed, there were not enough troop trains, and, in those that were available, the trucks were, as often as not, unsuited for carrying personnel or horses.[188]

Since Rokossovsky's deployment problems were insurmountable, the *Stavka* was left with no choice but to delay the start of the Central Front's offensive from 15 to 25 February. Accordingly, on 15 February Rokossovsky too altered his *front's* operational plan:

> I. The missions of the *front* in accordance with the stages of the operation.
> The first stage – overcome enemy resistance along the Nikol'skoe, Vysokoe, Karmanovo, General'shino, Mashkina, Belitsa, and Ol'shanka

line and reach the Briansk-Konotop railroad line in the Sviatoe Station and Mikhailovskii Farm Station sector.

Subsequently, conducting the main attack toward Sevsk and Unecha Station, cut the Briansk-Gomel' railroad line in the Rassukha Station-Klintsy Station-Novozybkov Station sector.

Kriukov's Cavalry-Rifle Group, attacking through Novgorod-Severskii and Semenovka on the left wing of the *front's* shock group, will capture the Novozybkov region.

The second stage of the operation – with the arrival of the *front's* forces along the Briansk-Gomel' railroad line, conduct a main attack through Klimovichi and Khislovichi with the mission to capture the Smolensk region and cut of the withdrawal routes of the enemy Viaz'ma-Rzhev grouping to the west and southwest.

Kriukov's Cavalry-Rifle Group, while continuing its offensive through Bykhov Station toward Mogilev on the left wing of the *front's* shock group, will cross to the right bank of the Dnepr River and, while protecting the crossings, will reach the Orsha region with its main forces.

With the arrival of the main forces of the *front's* first combat echelon at the Sviatoe, Trubchevsk, and Novgorod-Severskii line, move two rifle divisions from the *front's* second combat echelon forward toward Semenovka and Gomel', with the mission to capture the Gomel' region and the western bank of the Dnepr River in the Zhlobin and Rechitsa sector.

II. The tempo of the operation and the time required for its conduct.

Considering the deep snow cover and the absence of roads conducive to movement of auto-transport and artillery, the tempo of the operation will accord with the success of the road building: on the first day of the operation — 10 kilometers [per day] and, subsequently, 15 kilometers per day.

The forces of the *front* will have to overcome a distance of 250 kilometers during the first stage of the operation, and during the second stage of the operation — up to 250 kilometers.

Pauses necessary for putting the units into order, organizing command and control, bringing up artillery and rear services, replenishing reserves, possible local regroupings of combat formations, and committing the forces of the *front's* second combat echelon into combat will be inescapable during the operation.

One should reckon on three days in each stage of the operation as the minimum amount of time for pauses.

Based on these calculations, 36 days will be required to overcome a distance of 500 kilometer and 6 days — on pauses, for a minimum total of 42 days for the operation.

III. The *front's* boundary lines:

a) To the right – Lebedian', Verkhov'e, Ponyri Station, Radogoshch, Sviatoe, Pochep, and Roslavl'.

b) To the left – (incl.) Voronezh, Kursk, Kalinovka, Marchikhina Buda, Novgorod-Severskii, and Rechitsa.

IV. The grouping of forces and missions according to the stages of the operation.

The 65th ARMY consisting of:

— The 194th, 354th, 69th, 193rd, 246th, and 149th Rifle Divisions, the 37th Guards Rifle Division, and the 42nd Rifle Brigade;

— The 255th, 84th, 240th, 40th, and 30th Separate Tank Regiments; and

— The 321st Separate Engineer Battalion and the 163rd and 168th Motorized Engineer Battalions.

The 1st Stage of the Operation

Hold on to Ponyri 1, Stepnoe, Podsoborovka, Berezovka, and Sergeevka line with two rifle divisions, and conduct an attack beginning on the morning of 24 February 1943 by three rifle divisions, with one tank regiment each, with the mission of smashing enemy resistance in the Radogoshch and Radubichi sector, and, exploiting success toward Vysokoe and Androsov, reach the Makarovo, Androsovo, and Khlynino line by day's end on 24 February 1943.

Have two rifle divisions, one rifle brigade, and two tank regiments in the second combat echelon of the army.

Subsequently, while protecting your right wing against counterattacks by the enemy from the north and northeast, conduct the main attack toward Razvet'e, Asmon', Uparoi, Arkino, Altukhovo, Liubozhichi, Pliuskovo, and Kotovka, with the mission to cut the Briansk-Konotop railroad line in the Sviatoe Station-Kokarevka Station sector – by 3 March 1943 and the Briansk-Gomel' railroad line in the Pochep Station-Zhudilovo Station sector — by 10 March 1943.

The 2nd Stage of the Operation

Attack in the general direction of Roslavl' – in accordance with a supplementary plan.

The boundary line to the left: Sedmikovka, Vozy Station, Liubosh (incl.), Kuban', Kokarevka (incl.), and Rassukha Station.

The 2nd TANK ARMY consisting of:

— The 11th Tank Corps (the 53rd, 59th, and 160th Tank Brigades and the 12th Motorized Rifle Brigade);

— The 16th Tank Corps (the 107th, 109th, and 164th Tank Brigades and the 15th Motorized Rifle Brigade);

— The 11th Separate Guards Tank Brigade;

— The 51st Separate Motorcycle Battalion;

— The 112th and 60th Rifle Divisions and the 115th Rifle Brigade;

— The 563rd and 567th Tank Destroyer [Antitank] Artillery Regiments;

— The 37th Guards-Mortar Regiment;

— The 167th and 170th Engineer Battalions and the 169th and 171st Motorized Engineer Battalions;

— The 14th and 17th Battalions of Armored Transporters; and
— The 10th Antiaircraft Artillery Battalion.

The 1st Stage of the Operation
Pass over to the offensive beginning on the morning of 24 February 1943, with the mission of crushing enemy resistance in the Kopenki, Zorino, Mikhailovka, Karmanovo, General'shino, and Obukhovka sector and, while exploiting success toward General'shino and Dmitriev-L'govskii, capture the Mikhailovka, Rotmanovo, Stezha, and Novoe Pershino line by day's end on 24 February 1943. Subsequently, while exploiting the attack toward Sevsk, Pogar, and Unecha Station, cut the Briansk-Konotop railroad line in the Kholmechi Station-Suzemka Station sector — by 2 March 1943 and the Briansk-Gomel' railroad line in the Rassukha Station-Klintsy Station sector — by 10 March 1943.

The 2nd Stage
Attack in the general direction of Klimovichi, Khislovichi, and Smolensk — in accordance with a supplementary plan.
The boundary line to the left: Verkhniaia Ol'khovataia, Budanovka, Shemiakino, Sevsk, Starodub, and Klintsy.
The CAVALRY-RIFLE GROUP consisting of:
— The 2nd Guards Cavalry Corps (the 3rd and 4th Guards and 7th Cavalry Divisions);
— The 28th, 29th, and 30th Separate Ski Rifle Brigades;
— The 251st and 250th Separate Tank Regiments; and
— The 172nd and 173rd Motorized Engineer Battalions.

[The 1st Stage of the Operation]
Pass over to the offensive beginning on the morning of 24 February 1943, with the mission of smashing enemy resistance in the Bulgakova, Mashkina, Belitsa, Savenki, Turas'ka, and Pankeevo sector and, while exploiting success, capture the Aleshenka, Arsen'evka, Chernichina, and Tolkachevka line by the end of 24 February 1943. Subsequently, attack toward Fateevka, Charnatskoe, Kostobobr, and Novozybkov, with the mission to cut the Briansk-Konotop railroad line in the Zernovo Station-Mikhailovskii Farm Station sector — by 3 March 1943 and the Briansk-Gomel' railroad line in the Unecha (incl.)-Novozybkov Station sector — by 12 March 1943.

The 2nd Stage of the Operation
Continuing the offensive through Bykhov Station toward Mogilev, capture Mogilev on 28 March 1943, cross over to the western bank of the Dnepr River, and, while protecting the crossing, capture the Orsha region with the main forces by 5 April 1943.
The 70th ARMY consisting of:
— The 140th, 102nd, 175th, 162nd, 181st, and 106th Rifle Divisions.
The forces of the army will concentrate in the Fatezh, Kursk, Besedino, and Zolotukhino regions by day's end on 23 February 1943.

Attack in the *front's* second echelon after the 2nd Tank Army and Kriukov's Cavalry-Rifle Group in the general direction of Dmitriev-L'govskii, Sevsk, Seredina-Buda, Chernatskoe, and Zhuravki beginning on the morning of 24 February 1943.

With the arrival of the main forces of the first combat echelon along the Sviatoe, Trubchevsk, and Novgorod-Severskii line, bring two rifle divisions from the army forward in the general direction of Semenovka and Gomel', with the mission to capture the Gomel' region by 20 March 1943 and the western bank of the Dnepr River in the Zhlobin and Rechitsa sector by 27 March 1943.

The remaining forces of the army will continue the offensive in readiness to develop the attack in the general direction of Karachev, Mstislavl', Monastyrshchina, and Smolensk.

The 21st ARMY consisting of:

— The 51st, 52nd, and 67th Guards and 23rd, 325th and 375th Rifle Divisions

As the rifle divisions arrive along the railroad line, the forces of the army will concentrate in the Kobzeva, Drovosechnoe, Gorodetskoe, and Pokrovka regions.

Without waiting for the full concentration of the army's forces, as the rifle divisions reach their concentration regions, attack in the second echelon of the *front* after the 65th Army in the general direction of Berezovets, Ol'khovatka, Radogoshch, Kurbakino, Troianov, and Aptukhovo, with the mission of establishing a covering force or counterattacking to protect the right wing of the *front* against counterattack by the enemy from the north and northeast.

Subsequently continue the offensive in readiness to repel counterattacks by the enemy from Briansk and exploit success toward Pochep and Roslavl'.

V. The 16th AIR ARMY consisting of [no numbers provided] aircraft, including;

    a) Bombers —
    b) Assault aircraft —
    c) Fighters —
    d) Night bombers —

1. Assist the forces of the 2nd Tank Army in capturing the Svapa River line with assault aviation operations against the combat formations of infantry in the Mikhailovka, Ratmanovo, Morynevy, and Dmitriev-L'govskii regions on the western bank of the Svapa River.

2. Prevent counterattacks by the enemy against the right wing of the first combat echelon of the *front* from the north and northeast and against the left wing from the south and southwest with assault and bomber aviation operations.

3. Conduct continuous reconnaissance and observation of enemy movements and regroupings on the flanks of and in the offensive sector of the *front*.

4. Protect the shock group of the *front* in the Staryi Buzets, Zlobino, Zaslonka, Volkovo, and Verkniaia Zhdanova regions from 0800 hours through 1700 hours on the first day of the operation.

5. Subsequently, aviation will fulfill missions in accordance with a special plan.

VI. The organization of command and control in the operation

a) With the transition of the *front's* forces to the offensive, carry out command and control from the *front's* main command post — in Fatezh.

b) With the arrival of the first combat echelon along the Radogoshch, Komarichi, and Sevsk line, the main command post will be relocated to Dmitriev-L'govskii, from which it will command and control the *front's* forces.

c) With the arrival of the forces along the Briansk-Konotop railroad line, the command post will be relocated to Sevsk, and, with the arrival along the Krasnaia Sloboda, Pochar, and Kostobobr line, the command post will be relocated to Trubchevsk.

d) The subsequent axis of movement — Unecha, Klimovichi, and Mstislavl'.

VII. Material-technical support of the operation

1. The entire period of the operation – from 24 February 1943 through 7 April 1943 requires:

a) Food and forage – 42 daily rations.

b) Ammunition – 4 combat loads, based on the calculation of 0.5 combat loads on the first two days of the operation and 0.1 combat loads on each subsequent day.

c) Fuel and lubricants:
　　— On combat vehicles – 12 refills based on the calculation of a 60 kilometer range of one refill of a warmed up vehicle at a stop.
　　— On auxiliary and specialized wheeled vehicles – 8 refills based on a calculation of a range of 80 kilometers of one refill of a warmed up vehicle at a stop.

2. Of this amount, it is necessary to have [the following] by the beginning of the operation:

a) Food and forage – 10 daily rations.

b) Ammunition – 2 combat loads.

c) Fuel and lubricants – 3 refills for tracked vehicles and 2 refills for wheeled.

3. Repair, evacuation, and restoration of damaged and broken down vehicles — by means available to the force units and formations, reinforced by the army equipment attached to them.

Attachments:
 1) 1: 500,000 map, with the decision.
 2) 1: 200,000 map, with the decision.
Colonel General Rokossovsky, Commander of the
Central Front
Major General Telegin, Member of the Military
Council of the Central Front
Lieutenant General Malinin, Chief of Staff of the
Central Front[189]

The *Stavka*, after studying Rokossovsky's proposals, issued a new directive on 17 February adjusting the boundaries of his *front* to match the objectives contained in his new operational plan:

The *Stavka* of the Supreme High Command orders:
 Establish the following boundary lines between the Briansk, Central, and Voronezh Fronts effective at 1200 hours on 19 February 1943:

a) Between the Briansk and Central Fronts: Lebedian', Verkhov'e (incl.), Droskovo, Ponyri Station, and Dmitriev-L'govskii – all for the Central Front.

b) Between the Central and Voronezh Fronts: (incl.) Voronezh, Kursk, Kalinovka, Novgorod-Severskii, Dobrianka, and Rechitsa – all for the Central Front.

The *Stavka* of the Supreme High Command
I. Stalin[190]

Because the *Stavka* decided to delay the commitment of Rokossovsky's Central Front, it also directed the Kalinin and Western Fronts to postpone their general offensives until late February or early March.

The Briansk Front's Orel Offensive (12–21 February 1943)

In the meantime, the 48th and 13th Armies on the Briansk Front's left wing continued their offensive according to the original plan based on the assumption that, if successful, these operations would improve the situation for the Central Front when it finally launched its offensive. Operating in tandem with the Voronezh Front's 60th Army on its left, the forces of Pukhov's 13th Army drove the forces of Schmidt's Second Panzer Army westward toward Maloarkhangel'sk and turned the right flank of Schmidt's panzer army, seizing Fatezh on 8 February and reaching the eastern outskirts of Maloarkhangel'sk on the 13th. Pukhov then formed a special operational group on his army's left wing to exploit this success. Consisting of the 211th and 280th Rifle Divisions, three ski brigades, and the 19th Tank Corps, all under the command of Lieutenant General Novosel'sky, this group was to thrust northward from Ponyri and Fatezh toward Trosna to threaten the Second Panzer Army's open right flank (see Map 66). However, increasingly stubborn German resistance soon markedly slowed the forward progress of all of Pukhov's shock groups.

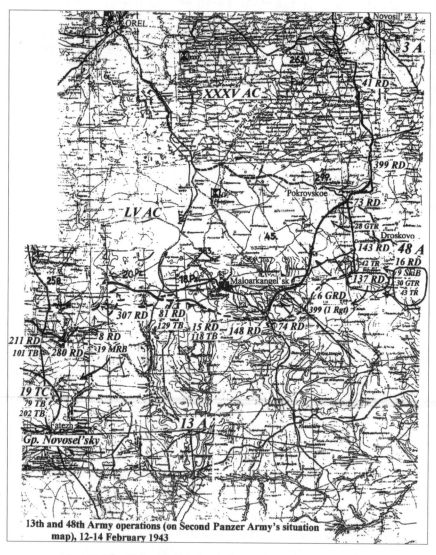

13th and 48th Army operations (on Second Panzer Army's situation
map), 12-14 February 1943

Map 66. The 13th and 48th Armies' operations, the situation from
12–14 February 1943

Concerned over the flagging momentum of his offensive, General Reiter, the commander of the Briansk Front, directed his chief of staff, General Sandalov, to urge Novosel'sky forward. Sandalov did so in a caustic message he sent to the group commander at 2030 hours on 16 February, "The commander is pointing out that you are still continuing to mark time in place because you are attacking populated points frontally. Bypass the centers of resistance and fulfill your assigned mission."[191]

Despite Reiter's entreaties, as indicated by its report to the *Stavka* at 1000 hours the next day, the Briansk Front's forces continued to encounter resolute and stiffening German resistance:

> 1. The forces on the left wing of the *front*, while continuing their offensive, were engaged in stubborn fighting with the enemy who are launching constant counterattacks. The fiercest fighting was under way in the Maloarkhangel'sk and Trosna sector.
>
> The enemy, trying to hold back the advance of the units of the *front*, is throwing fresh forces forward.
>
> Operations of the 23rd Airborne Regiment are being detected in the Verkhniaia Sergeevka region and the 119th Motorized Regiment of the 25th Motorized Division's and a signal battalion of the 293rd Infantry Division — in the Tureiki region (25 kilometers west of Maloarkhangel'sk Station).
>
> The 727th Infantry Regiment (the 707th Infantry Division), in full complement, is in the Dmitriev-L'govskii region.
>
> 2. On the front of the 61st Army, fighting was continuing throughout the night to destroy the enemy in the Ozhigovo region, and, along the remainder of the front, active operations are not occurring, and the units are defending their previous positions.
>
> The enemy is continuing to hold on to the trenches he seized in the Ozhigovo region and is conducting heavy artillery and mortar fire against the combat formations of the units along the remainder of the front.
>
> The 105th Rifle Brigade is continuing to fight with the enemy who is holding on to the first trench line in the Ozhigovo region.
>
> The positions of the remaining units of the army — are unchanged.
>
> The losses of the 105th Rifle Brigade for the period from 11 through 15 February 1943 – killed – 36, wounded – 58 men.
>
> The losses of the 108th Rifle Brigade from 11 through 15 February 1943 killed — 6, wounded – 16 men.
>
> 3. On the front of the 3rd Army, enemy reconnaissance raids took place during the night and the usual exchanges of fires were noted.
>
> The 283rd Rifle Division is defending the Gorodishche Farm (incl.) and Troitskoe line with one regiment and is concentrating in the forests north and northeast of Lunino with its remaining forces.
>
> 4. The 269th Rifle Division is defending its previous positions with two regiments and will commit its third regiment into the Viazhi, Zadushnoe, and Zaversh'e region.

The positions of the remaining units of the army are unchanged.

5. The 13th Army continued its offensive toward the north during the night with its left wing units, with the mission of enveloping the Maloarkhangel'sk grouping from the west. It was occupying its previous lines with its right wing units and, while putting its units into order, was preparing an offensive beginning on the morning of 17 February 1943.

The 74th Rifle Division put its units in order overnight in its previous positions and prepared for an offensive along its previous axis in the morning.

The 148th Rifle Division, as a result of repeated counterattacks by the enemy from the Orlianka and Leski regions, withdrew to the Hill 221.9 (2 kilometers west of Kuznechik 2), Bakhmatskie Vysoty, and Hill 234.1 (1 kilometer west of Uderava) line and was putting its forces in order along this line and preparing for an offensive beginning on the morning of 17 February 1943. The division was driving the enemy toward the north by 1000 hours and once again captured Dobroe Nachalo, Uderevo, and Peresukhaia.

Losses for 16 February 1943 – killed and wounded — 370 men.

The 15th Rifle Division is continuing to occupy its previous positions.

The 307th Rifle Division, with the 118th Tank Brigade, was continuing to fight for possession of Arkhangel'skoe and Sel'kovo, while enveloping these points from the west with part of its forces. Its ski battalion reached the vicinity of the stream 0.5 kilometers west of Sin'kovo.

Losses for 16 February 1943 – killed and wounded — 229 men.

The 81st Rifle Division, with the 129th Tank Brigade, was continuing to fight with subunits of the 258th Infantry Division in positions through the northern outskirts of Verkhnee Tagino, Hill 221.4 (1 kilometer west of Verkhnee Tagino), Krasnaia Zaria, and Hill 238.5 (0.5 kilometers northwest of Grinets).

The 132nd Rifle Division is continuing to fight for possession of Dmitriev-L'govskii.

The 8th Rifle Division reached the Podlesnaia, Ozerki, and Novyi Khutor line, with the mission of attacking toward the north.

6. The positions of the units of the *front's* reserve are unchanged.

7. The 15th Air Army did not conduct combat sorties because of the poor weather conditions.

8. To the right there were no changes on the front of the 16th Army. To the left the 60th Army was fighting in its previous positions, while repelling counterattacks by the enemy

9. Wire communications are absent with Group Mikhailov and are working with interruptions with the Red Army General Staff, the 48th Army, and Group Novosel'sky; along remaining axes – they are reliable.

10. Weather. Stratified rainy clouds 10 percent, ceiling of 100–200 meters. Drizzle and rain with snow. Visibility – 0.5–2 kilometers. Wind

from the south at 2–4 meters/second. Temperature – from –3 to +2 degrees.

Lieutenant General Sandalov, Chief of Staff of the
Briansk Front
Colonel Sidel'nikov, Deputy Chief of Staff of the
Briansk Front[192]

When the progress of Group Novosel'sky around the left flank of Schmidt's Second Panzer Army continued to remain painfully slow, at 1720 hours on 18 February, Sandalov reminded the group's commander of his duty:

1) According to Tkachenko's report, your tank brigades have been provided with three refills of fuel, however they have not made use of it.

2) Your headquarters is reporting the situation in distorted fashion and 12–18 hours late. According to your reports, the enemy has been withdrawing for several days, and you are pursuing, but, in fact, you are not moving. Clearly, Gritsenko [Novosel'sky's chief of staff] cannot cope with his work and is displaying a lack of discipline when called upon to report. Inform me of your views about replacing Gritsenko.

3) The boss [Reiter] demands a concrete report on the reasons you are marking time.

Sandalov[193]

Novosel'sky responded to Sandalov's critical remarks with two blunt situation reports of his own. The first, which he dispatched at 1125 hours on 20 February, complained bitterly about his group's lack of air support: "Enemy aviation is systematically bombing the forces and headquarters, inflicting casualties and disrupting communications. Not one of our aircraft can be seen, regardless of numerous requests. I request you give instructions to Piatykhin [Major General of Aviation I. G. Piatykhin, the commander of the 15th Air Army]."[194] The second, sent by Novosel'sky on 21 February, summarized his group's many problems in even greater detail:

I have repeatedly reported on the reasons for the inaction of the 19th Tank Corps as a whole. There are no roads. Now we cannot even move by road. The small tanks cannot operate.
The 101st Tank Brigade and 19th Motorized Rifle Brigade are being employed along one axis, and Vasil'ev [Major General of Tank Forces I. D. Vasil'ev, the commander of the 19th Tank Corps] is moving to the degree that the roads are prepared.
The results of four days of work have been destroyed by the snowstorm.
If you think that the 16 kilometer-advance by the 280th and 211th Rifle Divisions, with a maximum of 800 rifles against a full-blooded division plus two separate battalions [enemy], and the 50-kilometer advance by the ski battalions along absolutely roadless areas in combat is marking time in place, then I am in a quandary.
I understand the mission, and I am doing all that I can. I hope I will do it.

[Note: The following notation was on the enciphered telegram. "Immediately order Novosel'sky to mobilize 5,000 men from the local population to clear the roads. Reiter, 21 February."][195]

The heavy fighting in the 13th Army's sector from Trosna eastward to Maloarkhangel'sk and in the 48th Army's sector east of Maloarkhangel'sk was producing very little real progress. As a result, growing frustration began taking its toll on Red Army generals and soldiers alike. A 21 February memorandum sent by the military commissar of the 13th Army to the Briansk Front regarding the award of honorific "guards" status to the army's 307th Rifle Division illustrated this frustration:

In connection with the proposed award of a guards banner to the 307th Rifle Division, which is operating in the 13th Army, I consider it my duty to report to you that, in my opinion, the state of affairs in the division and the course of its combat operations at present do not provide a sufficient basis for the award of that high status, since, from 13 through 21 February of this year, the division has not fulfilled even one of its assigned missions.

What then prevents the award of a guards' banner to the 307th Rifle Division?

1. The required organization, precision, and vigilance is absent in the division's headquarters, units, and subunits. Work and the fulfillment of missions is going on without a deep approach, without analysis of the state of affairs, and often haphazardly. For example, not all of the soldiers have bayonets, helmets, gas masks, and spades, and the headquarters of the division and the commanders of its units do not know how many of these inadequately equipped soldiers there are and are not trying to equip them fully.

Wartime procedures are not being observed in populated points occupied by the headquarters of the division's regiments and rear services, security is not being organized, the local inhabitants walk about at any time of night, and matters in the event of a surprise attack by the enemy (his tank raids, diversionary groups, and aviation) have not been worked out by the headquarters. Instances have already been noted of spies penetrating [the units] in the guise of local inhabitants.

2. The division inadequately displays concern about the skillful fulfillment of combat missions during its operations, and, as a result, the division's units are suffering excessive personnel losses. [These deficiencies include:]

Imprecise assignment of missions to units, subunits, and soldiers;

The absence of proper training for offensive actions;

Disdain for reconnaissance of the terrain and observation posts;

Poor reconnaissance of enemy firing points and his forces and inadequate instruction of command cadre on the use of the main tenets of the new infantry combat regulations; and

Poor cooperation between units and subunits.

The characteristics of enemy operations are being inadequately studied and learned in the sector of the division. The operational experiences of the units and subunits of the division are not being generalized, and deficiencies — mistakes in the actions of the units — are not being prevented (either in the operational documents of the headquarters of the division or in the personal instruction of the unit commanders by the commander of the division).

The supervisory workers of the division do not properly think about how to fulfill missions better, more rapidly, and with fewer losses, and they do not learn from the opinions and experience of their subordinates. The division commander, Comrade [Colonel G. S.] Laz'ko, displays considerable conceit, [excessive] self-confidence, and unnecessary arrogance; he keeps distant from his units and the command cadre, he "always" leads from his office, and, when assigning missions, he does not listen to the opinions of his service chiefs.

To a great degree, the losses the division [experienced] in personnel, combat equipment, and horses while it was completing its march into the Ponyri region resulted from thoughtlessness and carelessness (72 men, 103 horses, and other equipment were lost). The artillery lagged behind the rifle units also as a result of carelessness and lack of coordination.

The division's personnel losses during the recent battles could have been significantly fewer with more careful training and skillful actions by the division commander and his staff (according to incomplete data, the division lost 1,174 men killed and wounded from 13 through 21 February).

3. Military discipline is not at the required level. There have been instances of drunkenness and dissipation among the command cadre, low standards among the personnel, and the presence of instances of false information about the fulfillment of combat missions by units and subunits.

4. The division's rear services function exceptionally poorly. The soldiers in a number of subunits have not received bread or sugar in several days, to say nothing about other foodstuffs and other articles.

They have not changed their underclothing for a long time, many are lice-ridden, and recently 16 instances of typhus were registered. The division commander displays complete indifference to all of these outrages and deficiencies.

The 307th Rifle Division has not yet achieved that level worthy of the award of the guards' banner. The question of awarding the guards' banner can be resolved only after these and other enumerated shortcoming have been eliminated, after the division has fulfilled its assigned combat missions, and after careful inspection of its condition.

Major General Popov, probationary Deputy Commander
for Political Affairs of the Rifle Division and Chief of the 13th Army's
Political Department[196]

Despite the Briansk Front's trials and tribulations, the forces on its left wing managed to achieve some minor tactical successes along the Fatezh and Sevsk axis, where the forces of Rokossovsky's Central Front were to be committed into action. For example, the 13th Army's 132nd Rifle Division, advancing on the extreme left flank of Pukhov's army, reached the eastern outskirts of Dmitriev-L'govskii, a key road junction midway between Fatezh and Sevsk, on 23 February. This advance turned the right flank of Schmidt's Second Panzer Army and separated it from Colonel General Walter Weiss' Second Army, operating to the south. At the same time, the forces of the 48th Army, now commanded by Lieutenant General P. L. Romanenko who had replaced General Khaliuzin only days before, continued their slow but steady advance against German defenses at the eastern tip of the Orel salient, by 22 February reaching positions extending southwestward from the Novosil' region, 70 kilometers east of Orel, to the northern outskirts of Maloarkhangel'sk, 70 kilometers southeast of Orel.

During this advance, Romanenko's forces briefly pierced German defenses northeast of Maloarkhangel'sk and drove northwestward over 20 kilometers before hastily organized German counterattacks halted their thrust. Curiously enough, despite releasing vast quantities of archival materials related to the 13th and 48th Armies' operations, the Russians have remained largely silent about the heavy fighting in the region northeast of Maloarkhangel'sk, whose negative results aborted the Briansk Front's opportunity to capture Orel on its own. Despite the absence of Soviet archival materials, we can now reconstruct the course of the heavy fighting in this region by exploiting German records and older open-source Soviet military literature. This material indicates that, after capturing Droskovo, 40 kilometers east-northeast of Maloarkhangel'sk, in heavy fighting between 8 and 12 February, over the next three days the 48th Army concentrated a sizeable shock group consisting of the 6th Guards Rifle Division and 9th Ski Brigade, supported by three separate tank regiments and, later, the 399th Rifle Division, and committed it into combat in the Pokrovskoe sector, midway between Novosil' and Maloarkhangel'sk. This group, whose commander remains unknown, was to penetrate the Second Panzer Army's defenses at the boundary between its XXXV and LV Army Corps, advance northwestward to seize a bridgehead across the Neruch River, 50 kilometers southeast of Orel, and then wheel westward to sever the vital German rail and road communications routes between Orel and Maloarkhangel'sk.

Attacking the German defenses at the boundary between the XXXV Army Corps' 299th Infantry Division and the LV Army Corps' 45th Infantry Division on 14 February, the 48th Army's shock group advanced almost 30 kilometers in four days of heavy fighting, reaching the bank of the Neruch River at day's end on 17 February (see Map 67). The 9th Ski Brigade, leading the shock group's thrust, forced its way across the Neruch River on the evening of 18 February only to be halted just short of the Orel-Maloarkhangel'sk railroad line by dug-in units of the 45th Infantry Division. Following in the ski brigade's wake, the 6th Guards Rifle Division and two accompanying tank regiments encircled several German battalions in small hamlets east of the river. General Schmidt, the commander of the Second Panzer Army, barely averted disaster in this sector by dispatching his army's 216th Infantry Division from Orel to reinforce the 45th Infantry Division's de-

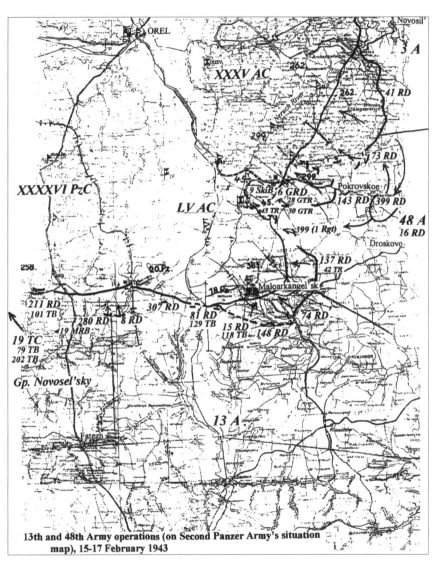

13th and 48th Army operations (on Second Panzer Army's situation map), 15-17 February 1943

Map 67. The 13th and 48th Armies' operations, the situation from
15–17 February 1943

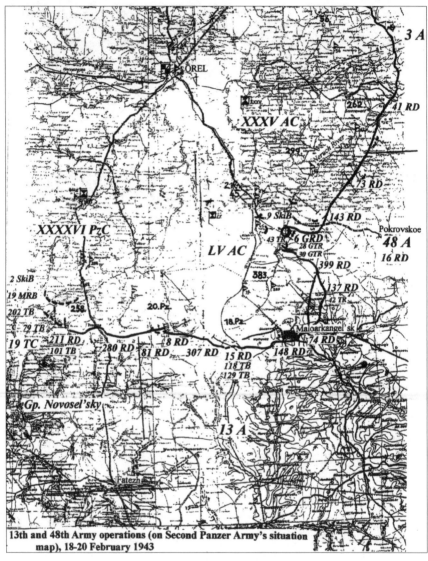

Map 68. The 13th and 48th Armies' operations, the situation from
18–20 February 1943

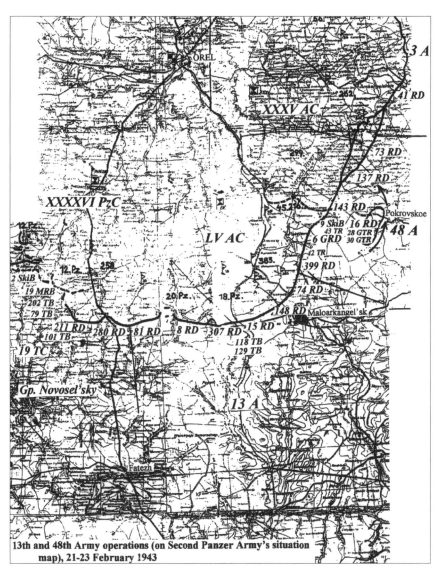

13th and 48th Army operations (on Second Panzer Army's situation map), 21-23 February 1943

Map 69. The 13th and 48th Armies' operations, the situation from
21–23 February 1943

fenses. In three days of intense fighting, the two German infantry divisions smashed the Russian ski brigade, relieved their encircled comrades, and restored a contiguous front east of the Neruch River (see Maps 68 and 69). The failure of the 48th Army's thrust to the Neruch River thwarted the *Stavka's* hopes that Reiter's forces could seize Orel by means of an offensive from the southeast.

The Voronezh Front's (60th Army's) L'gov-Ryl'sk Offensive (12–20 February 1943)

Meanwhile, on the Voronezh Front's left wing, Cherniakhovsky's 60th Army drove the 4th Panzer Division of Weiss' Second Army from Kursk on 8 February. Together, the 60th and 13th Armies opened a 60-kilometer breach between the German Second Panzer and Second Armies — a breach Rokossovsky's Central Front was expected to exploit.[197]

The Voronezh Front informed the *Stavka* of the 60th Army's encouraging progress along the L'gov axis at 2400 hours on 16 February:

1. The forces of the *front*, having concentrated their main efforts on capturing the city of Khar'kov, were simultaneously continuing their offensive fighting for possession of Oboian', Graivoron, and Bogodukhov.

As a result of five days of intense combat, our forces captured Khar'kov during the first half of the day after defeating crack enemy SS units by attacks from the west, east, and southeast.

The 60th Army. The forces of the army were putting their units in order on the night of 16 February and preparing to continue their offensive; and, during the day, they resumed their attack toward L'gov.

The enemy offered stubborn resistance to the offensive by our units.

The units of the army, while repelling counterattacks by subunits of enemy infantry, were continuing to fight along previous lines up to 1600 hours on 16 February.

The 38th Army. The forces of the army were continuing to advance toward the southwest, while destroying scattered small groups of enemy infantry with their forward units.

The main forces of the army were approaching the Kotovo, Bobryshevo, and Belenikhino line by the end of 15 February.

More up to date information has not been received about the positions of the units ....

3. On 17 February 1943, the forces of the *front* will continue the offensive on the left wing and, on the right wing, will reach their army axes within the limits of new boundary lines: the 60th Army – will attack toward L'gov; the 38th Army – will arrive for an attack toward Sumy; the 69th Army – toward Akhtyrka; and the 3rd Tank Army – toward Poltava.

Filippov, Fedorov, Petrov[198]

As Rokossovsky's Central Front was completing preparations for its offensive, the Voronezh Front had ordered Cherniakhovsky's 60th Army to capture L'gov by 15 February and Ryl'sk by 17 February to erect a protective barrier along the southern flank of Rokossovsky's intended penetration:

> 1. The mission of the 60th Army. Destroy the opposing enemy and, after capturing the cities of L'gov, Ryl'sk, and Korenevo, reach the Arbuzova Station, Studenok, Ryl'sk, and Snagost' line by day's end on 17 February 1943. Have the following grouping of the army along the given line: on the right wing – Arbuzova, Griady — the 248th Separate Rifle Brigade, with the mission of protecting the right flank of the army; in the center – Studenok, Ryl'sk (incl.), and Korenevo — a shock group consisting of the 322nd, 121st, and 141st Rifle Divisions, the 129th Rifle Brigade, and the 150th Tank Brigade, with the mission to be ready to attack toward Glukhov or Putivl'; and, on the left wing — in the Korenevo and Snagost' region — the 104th Separate Rifle Brigade with the 8th Destroyer Brigade, with the mission of protecting the left flank of the army. Keep the 14th Destroyer Brigade in reserve in the Suchkino region, having in mind to employ it to consolidate success along the central axis. Use the 129th Rifle Brigade, which is approaching late, to relieve the 141st Rifle Division on the given line, and withdraw the latter into reserve in the Ivanovskoe region.

> 2. The concept of the operation. Conduct the main attack in the center in the general direction of L'gov-Ryl'sk, while avoiding any sort of complex regrouping and by using the existing army grouping as the jumping-off position for the new operation.

> 3. The stages of the operation:
> The 1st Stage (13–15 February 1943) – The capture of L'gov and Sherekino. The entire army will reach the St. Sokovninka, Konyshevka, Prilepy, Shirkovo, Kudintsevo, Sergeevka, Sherekino, Liubomirovka, Vyshnie Dereven'ki, Kromskie Byki, Anastas'evka, Khitrovka, Pogrebki, and Viktorovka front by the end of 15 February 1943.
> The 2nd Stage (16–17 February 1943) – The capture of Ryl'sk and Korenevo. The army, having captured Ryl'sk, will reach the line: Arbuzovo, Studenok, Ryl'sk, Korenevo, and Snagost' line by the end of 17 February 1943.
> Major General Krylov, the Chief of Staff of the 60th Army[199]

Cherniakhovsky's army, without pausing to regroup or reorganize its forces, lunged westward from Kursk on 17 February in an attempt to seize L'gov from the march before the Germans could send forces to defend it. Weiss, the commander of the German Second Army, responded by hastily dispatching two regiments from its already severely weakened 88th Infantry Division to defend the town and, if possible, restore communications with Schmidt's Second Panzer Army. Although the German division failed to reestablish contact with Schmidt's panzer army, it did halt Cherniakhovsky's advance on the eastern approaches to L'gov on 20 February. Frustrated over his failure to seize the town by a coup de main,

Cherniakhovsky ordered his army's 248th Student Rifle Brigade to envelop L'gov from the north and west to ensure that the gap between the two German armies remained open.

The Central Front Altered Plan
(18–24 February 1943)

While Pukhov's 13th Army and Cherniakhovsky's 60th Army were fighting to widen the breach between the Second Panzer and Second Armies from Dmitriev-L'govskii southward to L'gov, on 19 February Rokossovsky finalized plans for his Central Front's delayed offensive to exploit this breach and dispatched them to the *Stavka* for approval:

> In fulfillment of the instructions given by you regarding corrections to the *front's* offensive operational plan No. 0020 that I presented to you on 15 February 1943, I am reporting:
>
> First. With the arrival of the forces of the *front's* first combat echelon along the Dmitriev-L'govskii, Verkhniaia Kuban', and Fateevka (30 kilometers southwest of Dmitriev-L'govskii) line, I will concentrate three rifle divisions from the 70th Army in the Trofimovka (12 kilometers southeast of Dmitrovsk-Orlovskii), Rechitsa (18 kilometers southeast from Dmitrovsk-Orlovskii), and Ploskoe region. All three divisions, reinforced by tanks and artillery, will launch an offensive from that region in the general direction of Karachev on 27 February 1943 (the fourth day of the operation), with the mission to cut the Orel-Briansk railroad line and highway in the sector east of Karachev. The three remaining rifle divisions of the 70th Army will attack in the second echelon toward Karachev as they arrive and concentrate in the Dmitrovsk-Orlovskii region.
>
> With the arrival of the first combat echelon in the Karachev region, the forces of the 70th Army will be assigned the mission to exploit success in the general direction of Briansk, Roslavl', and Smolensk.
>
> Second. With the arrival of the forces of the *front's* first combat echelon along the Sviatoe, Trubchevsk, and Novgorod-Severskii line, I will move the two rifle divisions from the 2nd Tank Army forward toward Semenovka and Gomel', with the mission to capture the Gomel' region by 20 March 1943 and the western bank of the Dnepr River in the Zhlobin – Rechitsa sector by 27 March 1943. The divisions will be reinforced by tanks at the expense of the 2nd Tank Army and by artillery at the disposal of the *front*.
>
> It is necessary to have a corps headquarters to control the fighting of these two divisions.
>
> The *front* does not have the forces and equipment necessary to form a corps headquarters.
>
> I consider it possible to entrust the commander and staff of one of these rifle divisions with the responsibility of corps command by strengthening his command cadre and communications equipment.

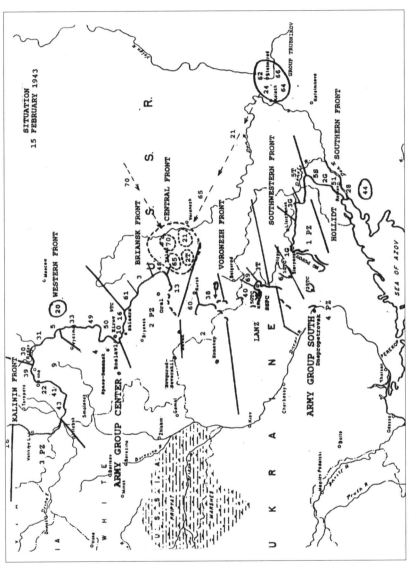

Map 70. The strategic situation on 15 February 1943

I myself will affect direct control of the combat activities of these two divisions united under the command of a single division commander through my VPU [auxiliary command post], at first from the Novgorod-Severskii region, subsequently from Semenovka, and then from Gomel'.

Rokossovsky, Telegin, Malinin[200]

As the Central Front's 65th Army, 2nd Tank Army, and Cavalry-Rifle Group struggled to regroup their forces forward into the Fatezh region in the face of terrible weather and terrain conditions, at 1830 hours on 19 February, Rokossovsky issued final instructions regarding precisely how they were to occupy their final jumping-off positions for the offensive (see Map 70):

[To the 2nd Tank Army]

1. The 132nd Rifle Division (Briansk Front) is fighting with units of the enemy 258th and 707th Infantry Divisions along the Ostapovo, Polozovka, Morshnevka, Dmitriev-L'govskii, and Arbuzovo line.

2. To the right, the 65th Army will reach the Chistye Bugry, Gremiach'e, Mokhovoe, Makarovo, and Khlynino line by the morning of 22 February.

The boundary line to the right: Sedmikovka (incl.), Vozy Station (incl.), Verkhnii Liubazh (incl.), Verkniaia Kuban', and Kokorevka (incl.).

To the left the Cavalry-Rifle Group of Kriukov will reach the Staraia Belitsa, Verkhniaia Sokovninka, and Konyshevka line by the morning of 22 February.

The boundary line to the left: Verkhnee Ol'khovatoe, Budanovka, Shemiakino, Arbuzovo Station, Sevsk, and Gorozhanka.

3. Occupy a jumping-off position along the Mikhailovka, Rotmanovo, Staryi Gorod, and Sukhoi Rovets line with the forces of the 2nd Tank Army by the morning of 21 February 1943 for an offensive in the general direction of Dmitriev-L'govskii, Sevsk, and Trubchevsk.

4. Be prepared to attack – beginning on the morning of 22 February 1943.

Confirm receipt.

Rokossovsky, Telegin, Malinin[201]

[To the 65th Army]

1. The enemy offering resistance to the units of the Briansk Front along the Kritovo (2 kilometers northeast of Zmievka), Berezovka, Petrovka, Matiukhina, Maloarkhangel'sk, Maloarkhangel'sk Station, Nizhnee Tagino, Malakhova, Svoboda, Ploskoe, Ostapovo, Polozovka, and Dmitriev-L'govskii line.

2. To the right, the units of the 13th Army (Briansk Front) are fighting along the Perovskii, Lishkovo, Moliushino, Verkhnee Tagino, Shepelevo, Volkovskaia Sloboda, and Mikhailovka line.

The boundary line to the right: Lebedian', Verkhovoe, Droskovo (incl.), Ponyri Station, and Dmitrovsk-Orlovskii.

To the left, the 2nd Tank Army will reach the Mikhailovka, Rotmanovo, and Gorod Station line by the morning of 21 February 1943. The boundary line to the left: Sedmikovka, Vozy Station, Verkhnii Liubazh, Verkhniaia Kuban' (incl.), and Kokorevka.

3. Occupy jumping-off position along the Chistye Bugry, Gremiach'e, Mokhovoe, Makarovo, and Khlynino line with the forces of the 65th Army by the morning of 22 February 1943 for an offensive in the general direction of Razvet'e, Asmon', Komarichi, Lokot', and Altukhovo.

4. Be prepared to attack – beginning on the morning of 23 February 1943.
Confirm receipt.

Rokossovsky, Telegin, Malinin[202]

[To the Cavalry-Rifle Group]

1. The remnants of the [enemy] 340th, 37th, and 88th Infantry Divisions and units of the 4th Panzer Division are offering resistance to the units of the 13th Army (Briansk Front) and 60th Army (Voronezh Front) along the Arbuzovo, Naumovka, Tolkachevka, Poliachkovo, and Lukashevka line.

To the right, the 2nd Tank Army will reach the Mikhailovka, Rotmanovka [sic], Staryi Gorod, and Sukhoi Rovets line by the morning of 21 February 1943.

The boundary line to the right: Verkhnee Ol'khovatoe (incl.), Budanovka, Shemiakino (incl.), Arbuzovo Station (incl.), Sevsk (incl.), and Gorozhanka.

To the left, the units of the 60th Army (Voronezh Front) are fighting along the Prilepy, Ol'shanka, and Rossolovo line.

The boundary line to the left, effective 1200 hours 19 February 1943: Voronezh (incl.), Kursk, Kalinovka, and Novgorod-Severskii.

3. Occupy jumping-off positions along the Staraia Belitsa, Verkhniaia Sokovninka, and Prilepy line with the forces of the Cavalry-Rifle Group by the morning of 19 February 1943 for an offensive in the general direction of Selino, Zhuravka, and Novgorod-Severskii.

4. Be prepared to attack – beginning on the morning of 23 February 1943.

Rokossovsky, Telegin, Malinin[203]

Lieutenant General P. I. Batov, the commander of the 65th Army, moved his headquarters to Elets on 18 February to supervise his army's forward deployment, and by 24 February his divisions began reaching their assigned concentration areas north of Fatezh. Their attack on 25 February would thus, of necessity, be literally from the march. Similarly, Rodin's 2nd Tank Army had the daunting task of moving his tank army (with 408 tanks) 200–220 kilometers from the region north of Livny to jumping-off positions near Fatezh. Despite the appalling road conditions, he did so within seven days, but at a cost of 96 tanks left behind in his assembly areas and 130 tanks broken down or mired along the treacherously muddy march route.[204] Rodin would commit 182 of his tanks into combat on 25 February, but the remaining armor would catch up later. Similarly, Major General V. V. Kriukov's 2nd Guards Cavalry Corps completed its concentration west of Fatezh by 24 February in somewhat better condition.[205]

With Rokossovsky's regrouping and concentration nearing completion, at 2345 hours on 23 February, the *Stavka* dispatched new instructions to the Briansk Front through General Vasilevsky, its representative designated to coordinate the offensive, to ensure that Reiter's plan and objectives accorded with those of Rokossovsky's Central Front:

> In a change to directive No. 30041 of 6 February 1943, the *Stavka* of the Supreme High Command orders:
>
> 1. Assign the Briansk Front the main and immediate missions of destroying the enemy Orel-Kromy grouping and seizing the city of Orel.
>
> 2. Free the Briansk Front from fulfilling the mission of seizing Karachev and Briansk.
>
> The Stavka of the Supreme High Command
Vasil'ev [Stalin]
Transmitted by telephone by Comrade Stalin
Bokov[206]

Despite the strenuous efforts by the *Stavka* and Rokossovsky to ensure timely regrouping and concentration of the Central Front's forces into their assembly areas and jumping-off positions for the offensive, persistent poor weather and deteriorating road conditions once again hindered the planned regrouping. Reluctantly, the *Stavka* was left with no choice but to postpone the start of the offensive for two more days, this time to the morning of 25 February. A situation report prepared by Rokossovsky's chief of operations early on 24 February explained why this delay was necessary:

> The 65th ARMY – Transportation by railroad has, on the whole, been completed.
>
> The march by the main forces of four rifle divisions (the 69th, 149th, and 354th Rifle and 37th Guards) from the Ponyri and Leninskii line to jumping-off positions at Dubrova, Mokhovoe, and Androsovo by day's end on 23 February is continuing. The distance of the march is 60 kilometers. The divisions can be concentrated in their jumping-off positions by the end of 25 February. The 1st Artillery Division and 84th Separate Tank Regiment are expected to arrive by this time.
>
> The army will begin active operations by reinforced forward detachments (one rifle regiment per each rifle division) on the morning of 26 February and will go over to the offensive with the main forces of the first combat echelon beginning on the morning of 27 February.
>
> [The following] will be committed in the second combat echelon:

The 193rd Rifle Division, which passed through Ponyri on the evening of 23 February and must be concentrated in the Frolovka, Studenok, and Pavlovo region by the end of 26 February;

The 246th Rifle Division – was concentrated in the Nikol'skoe and Man'shino (12 kilometers northeast of Zolotukhino) region at the end of 23 February and is continuing its march to the Belyi Kolodez' (incl.), Radogoshch, and Chermoshnoe region;

The 42nd Rifle Brigade – will arrive in the Vysokoe, Pokrovskii, and Igino regions; and

The 112th Rifle Division (transferred to the army to replace the 194th Rifle Division) – passed through Kolpny on 23 February.

The 255th, 240th, 40th, and 30th Separate Tank Regiments (the 30th Tank Regiment has still not unloaded) and the 210th, 226th, and 218th Mortar Regiments – on the march after unloading.

The headquarters of the army – Ol'khovatka and will relocate to Iasenok by day's end on 26 February.

The condition of the forces: the 37th Guards Rifle Division – 10,000 men; the 69th Rifle Division – 7,600 men; the 193rd Rifle Division – 9,000 men; the 149th Rifle Division – 6,800 men; and the 354th Rifle Division – 7,500 men, and the situation of the remaining divisions is being determined.

The howitzers of all artillery units have lagged behind – and there are no tractors.

The 2nd TANK ARMY – reached its jumping-off position along the Svapa River with its motorized rifle units [traveling] on foot by day's end on 23 February and will conduct reconnaissance beginning on the morning of 24 February.

The 194th Rifle Division – will conduct reconnaissance by fire along the Pervomaiskii and Polozovka (15 kilometers northeast of Dmitriev-L'govskii) line on the morning of 23 February.

The 60th Rifle Division – began concentrating in the Romanovka, Belyi Kolodez', and Dmitrievskaia Koloniia (12 kilometers southeast of Dmitriev-L'govskii) region by the morning of 24 February.

The artillery of these units is still on the march.

The tank formations are located in [the following] regions:

The 16th Tank Corps – Bugry, Milenino, and Soleevka;

The 11th Tank Corps – Shmarnoe, Kasilovo, and Kochetki;

The 11th Separate Guards Tank Brigade – Bychek and Trubitsyn (Sorokovye Dvory); and

The 29th Guards Tank Regiment – Koneva, where it is moving up the equipment it left behind and transporting fuel.

The tank formations will reach their jumping-off position by day's end on 26 February and will begin operations on the morning of 27 February.

Condition:

The 11th Tank Corps – operational KV's – 11, T–34's – 1, T–60s and T–70s – 41, and MK–2 and MK–3 – 49, for a total of 102 tanks;

The 16th Tank Corps – operational T–34's – 33, and T–70s and T–60s – 14, for a total of 47 [tanks];

The 11th Guards Tank Brigade – operational T–34's – 25 and T–70s – 15, for a total of 40 [tanks]; and

The 29th Guards Tank Regiment – operational KV's — 15.

[The following] can arrive and will be rehabilitated by the beginning of the advance:

The 11th Tank Corps – 33 tanks; and

The 16th Tank Corps – 23 tanks.

Eighty-five tanks for the army, which are beginning to arrive at Livny Station on 24 February, are going by railroad to fill out the tank formations.

The heavy material losses in the 16th Tank Corps are explained by the poor command and control on the part of the commander of the corps, Major General Maslov, and his chief of staff— Colonel Pupko.[207]

[The tank formations] had up to one refill of fuel at the end of 23 February, and, in addition, fuel cisterns [barrels] being sent to the army by the Directorate of the Rear are still following.

The army has containers necessary for one refill of fuel, but transport is complicating things. There is insufficient grease. They have captured lubricants in Kursk, which is now being tested for possible use.

Reinforcing units – the 1188th Antitank Artillery Regiment and the 143rd Mortar Regiment – on the march from the Elets region – have passed through Livny. The 567th and 563rd Antitank Artillery Regiments are on the march from Livny. Fifty percent of their tractors ("Willys" jeeps) are inoperable.

The 10th Antiaircraft Artillery Division – is completing its concentration in the region east of Fatezh.

The CAVALRY-RIFLE GROUP of Kriukov has concentrated its cavalry divisions [as follows] by the morning of 24 February:

The 4th Guards Cavalry Division – Kotlevo and Iur'evka (7 kilometers east of Komysheva); and

The 3rd Guards Cavalry Division – in the Shirkova region (30 kilometers northwest of Kursk).

The artillery of these divisions has lagged behind and will be brought forward by 25 February.

The ski brigades were on the march at the end of 23 February [at]:

The 30th Ski Brigade – Zhernovets (16 kilometers northeast of Kursk); and

The 28th and 29th Ski Brigades – in the Ukolovo region.

The 251st and 259th Separate Tank Regiments — are located in Livny without fuel.

The group will begin active operations with its forward units on the morning of 26 February and will go over to the offensive with its main forces beginning on the morning of 27 February.

Condition:

There is little fuel in the group and, therefore, transport had been hindered.

The main reserves of ammunition are situated in Efremov.

There are no wild oats. Sufficient hay is concentrated in the region.

Horse transport is in a poor state in the ski brigades, and transport can be provided with difficulty. The horses are worn out.

The 21st ARMY – is continuing to unload from railroad trains.

They have completed unloading [the following] by the end of 23 February:

The 51st and 67th Guards Rifle Divisions, the 325th and 375th Rifle Divisions, and the 52nd Guards Rifle Division still have not competed their unloading.

The units that have unloaded were on the march [as follows] by the end of 23 February:

The 51st Guards Rifle Division – from the Uspenskoe region.

The 325th Rifle Division – from the Navesnoe region.

The 375th Rifle Division – continues to remain the Kalinino region (15 kilometers east of Livny).

The remaining units will approach Livny on the march as they are unloaded.

The 70th ARMY – on the whole has completed its unloading and is continuing its concentration.

The divisions, following two march routes, were located [as follows] by the end of 23 February:

The 162nd, 175th, and 106th Rifle Divisions – the head [of the column] was approaching Kolpny and their rear was passing through Livny.

The 102nd, 140th, and 181st Rifle Divisions – were approaching Kosorzha with their head and Volovo with their rear.

Some subunits of these divisions were still following from the unloading station at Dolgorukovo.

The composition of the divisions – roughly 9,000–11,000 personnel in each.

There are no tractors for the guns; therefore, their weaponry, in particular the howitzers, are located at the unloading stations.

Shortages of horses amount to 75 percent; as a result, transport [supply] is very difficult.

GUARDS-MORTAR UNITS: The 37th Guards-Mortar Regiment – following in the 2nd Tank Army, passed though Zolotukhino on the morning of 24 February, and the 86th Guards-Mortar Regiment as well.

The 94th Guards-Mortar Regiment – following in the 65th Army — on the march in the Ol'khovatka region.

The 92nd Guards-Mortar Regiment unloaded and concentrated in Elets by day's end on 22 February but was without fuel. After receiving fuel on 23 February, it is completing its march to the Vodianoe region.

ARTILLERY: The 1st Guards Artillery Division – following in the 65th Army, was approaching Kosorzhe by the end of 23 February;

The 210th, 226th, and 218th Mortar Regiments – after unloading, are following in the 65th Army on the march from the Elets region.

The 114th and 136th Mortar Regiments – after unloading, are following in the 65th Army, and their positions are being verified;

The 12th Antiaircraft Division – is traveling on its own from Moscow following in the 65th Army. It passed through Elets on 22 February.

The 502nd Antitank Artillery Regiment – is following in the 2nd Guards Cavalry Corps and is on the march in the Livny region;

The 1188th Antitank Artillery Regiment and 143rd Mortar Regiment – after unloading, is following in the 70th Army, and their position on the march is being verified;

The 10th Antiaircraft Artillery Division – sent to the 2nd Tank Army and completing its concentration in the Ol'khovatka region.

The 398th, 504th, and 1428th Antitank Artillery Regiments – after unloading, are on the march following in the *front* reserve.

Deputy Chief of the Central Front's
Operations Department
Colonel Kramar[208]

The strongest and most critical force in the Central Front's main shock group were the two tank corps and single tank brigade in General Rodin's 2nd Tank Army, which Rokossovsky designated to spearhead and exploit his *front's* offensive. Rodin put the finishing touches of his army's operational plan in accordance with Rokossovsky's instructions on 24 February, just as his forces were closing into their assembly areas in the region west of Fatezh:

I. Explanation of the missions

The 2nd Tank Army [with its rifle and motorized rifle formations], in cooperation with the Central Front's 65th Army and the Cavalry Group of Kriukov, will penetrate the enemy's defense in the Mikhailovka, Morshneva, Dmitriev-L'govskii, and Arbuzovo sector on 23 February 1943 and destroy the opposing units of the 707th Infantry Division and the 5th Regiment of the Kaminski Brigade.

Exploit success into the operational depth by committing the tank corps in the general direction of Trubchevsk and Unecha.

The immediate mission of the army is to cut the Briansk-Konotop railroad line, and its final aim — reach the northwestern bank of the Desna River and capture Trubchevsk.

Subsequently, the army must be prepared for operations along the Pochep and Unecha axes.

The army, as a part of the *front*, will fulfill one of the principal missions, presenting itself as a powerful battering ram separating the northern and the southern groupings of the enemy operating in front of the Briansk and Central Fronts. When fulfilling the immediate mission during the first two days, it is necessary to destroy the enemy forces in his tactical defense zone with two rifle divisions and the first echelon's motorized infantry in cooperation with the partisan brigades and to protect the operations of the tank corps from the southwestern direction.

When fulfilling the subsequent missions, the army will protect its main grouping against likely counterattacks [by the enemy] from Briansk, Pochep, Pogar, and Gremiach'e.

The overall depth of the operation — 120 kilometers. The line for fulfilling the immediate mission – arrival at the northwestern bank of the Desna River — 35 kilometers. The operational tempo for the tank formations and the motorized infantry on the third day — 40–45 kilometers and for the infantry — 25–30 kilometers after destruction of the enemy in the tactical zone.

II. Decision

a) The concept of the operation: The army will penetrate the enemy defense with two rifle divisions, the motorized infantry of the tank corps, and the 132nd Rifle Division (Briansk Front) with part of its forces and, in cooperation with the 65th Army and the Cavalry Group of Kriukov, will destroy his forces in the tactical zone and commit its tank corps into the operational depth with the objective of separating the enemy's Briansk and southern groupings, while capturing the railroad line in the Kokorevka-Suzemka sector.

The immediate mission of the army – to reach the Kokorevka and Suzemka front; subsequently — arrival at the northwestern bank of the Desna River and the capture of Trubchevsk.

b) Deployment of the Army: Carry out the regrouping of the army and combat deployment one day before the penetration. Accomplish the supply of the army's forces only at night.

The combat formation in the jumping-off position will be formed in three echelons.

In the first echelon — two rifle divisions, the motorized infantry, two regiments of the 132nd Rifle Division, and all of the artillery of the rifle divisions and motorized rifle brigades.

The second echelon — two tank corps and one tank regiment.

The third echelon – one tank brigade and one rifle brigade.

III. Stages of the operation

Conduct the operation in three stages:

The preparatory stage – two days. All work in the preparatory stage will be completed in the concentration region. The jumping-off region will only be the place for additional commanders' reconnaissance [*rekognostsirovka*], preliminary reconnaissance, and preliminary refueling of tanks for the first echelon.

The first stage –for the tank formations 3–4 days and for the infantry 5–6 days.

The second stage – presumably on the Pochep and Unecha axes, for the tank formations 2–3 days and for the infantry 3–4 days.

The missions by stages of the operation for the formations and units – according to combat instructions and orders.

IV. Supporting the operation
Reconnaissance:
In the preparatory stage – Determine the system of fires of the enemy along the forward edge. Determine the dispositions of the artillery of the enemy along the forward edge and in the depths. Determine the concentration regions of close reserves. Monitor the unloading areas for operational reserves, especially in the Konotop and Bakhmach regions.

In the first stage – Determine the system of defensive works in the tactical defense zone. Pay special attention to the establishment of anti-tank works and regions. Determine the possibility of the regrouping of the Hungarian VIII Army Corps and the approach of operational reserves from the Konotop and Bakhmach region, as well as the grouping and routes of withdrawing enemy. Clarify the system of defensive works along the Desna River.

V. Material support of the operation
The Army must have during the operation:
— Ammunition – 3 combat loads;
— Fuel and lubricants [GSM] for combat machines [tanks] – 5–6 refills;
— Fuel and lubricants [GSM] for transport vehicles – 8 refills; and
— Foodstuffs – 10 daily rations.
Rifle divisions must have two combat loads.
For successful fulfillment of the operation, it is necessary to reinforce the army [with]:
— two tank destroyer [antitank] regiments – 76-mm;
— two light artillery regiments;
— two howitzer artillery regiments; and
— two aviation divisions (mixed aviation divisions).

Lieutenant General of Tank Forces Rodin, Commander of
the 2nd Tank Army
Major General of Tank Forces Latyshev, Member of the
2nd Tank Army's Military Council
Major General of Tank Forces Onuprienko, Chief of Staff
of the 2nd Tank Army[209]

After these last minute delays to permit adequate concentration of his forces, Rokossovsky commenced his offensive on the morning of 25 February. Since Major General G. F. Tarasov's 70th Army and Lieutenant General I. M. Chistiakov's 21st Army were still on the move, they were to join the attack as soon as they arrived in the region, even before their full concentration.

The Expansion of the Briansk, Western, and Central Offensives (22 February–6 March 1943)

The Western and Briansk Fronts Zhizdra and Bolkhov Offensives (22–27 February)

As the 13th and 48th Armies of Reiter's Briansk Front continued pounding the defenses on the German Second Panzer Army's weakened right wing south of Orel, on 22 February shock groups from the Western Front's 16th Army and the Briansk Front's 61st and 3rd Armies joined the *Stavka's* ambitious offensive by striking the panzer army's defenses along the northern and northeastern face of the Orel salient. Striking simultaneously, Lieutenant General I. Kh. Bagramian's 16th Army attacked the defenses of Corps Group Scheele's 208th and 211th Infantry Divisions north of Zhizdra, Belov's 61st Army attacked the defenses on the left wing of the LIII Army Corps' 112th Infantry Division north of Bolkhov, and Lieutenant General P. P. Korzun's 3rd Army assaulted the defenses on the right wing of the LIII Army Corps' 112th Infantry Division at the nose of the Orel salient north of Mtsensk. Together, all three attacks formed a coordinated effort to collapse the Second Panzer Army's defenses north and northeast of Orel and capture the salient in concert with converging attacks by the shock groups of the Briansk Front's 13th and 48th Armies from the south.

Bagramian's 16th Army conducted the strongest and most promising of these simultaneous offensives with a shock group consisting of six rifle divisions (the 18th, 11th, and 31st Guards and the 97th, 326th, and 324th Rifle Divisions), supported by three tank brigades. The shock group's mission was to penetrate German defenses at the boundary between Corps Group Scheele's 208th and 211th Infantry Divisions and capture Zhizdra, which was situated 20 kilometers to the south (see Map 71). Subsequently, after reinforcing his shock group with two rifle divisions (the 247th and 64th) and two more tank brigades, Bagramian planned to commit his army's mobile group, Major General of Tank Forces A. A. Shamshin's 9th Tank Corps, to an exploitation southward toward the Orel-Briansk highway, where it was to cut the highway west of Orel and link up with the forces of the Briansk Front's 48th and 13th Armies, which were attacking northeastward and northward from the regions east and west of Maloarkhangel'sk. Specifically, the 16th Army's 9th Tank Corps was to link up with the 48th Army's shock group advancing northwestward from the Neruch River toward the southeastern approaches to Orel and with the 13th Army's Group Novosel'sky and 19th Tank Corps which were advancing northward through Kromy toward the Orel-Briansk road west of Orel.

Bagramian's shock group commenced its assault early on 22 February after pounding Group Scheele's defenses with an intense artillery preparation. Despite the formidable strength of the attacking force, rainy weather, mud-clogged roads, and a stubborn and skillful defense by the two German infantry divisions kept Bagramian's forward progress to a minimum (see Map 72). After suffering significant losses in manpower and material, the 16th Army's shock group managed to advance only 7 kilometers by 25 February, reaching the northern bank of the Iasenka River (see Map 73). Because the fighting was so intense and the 16th

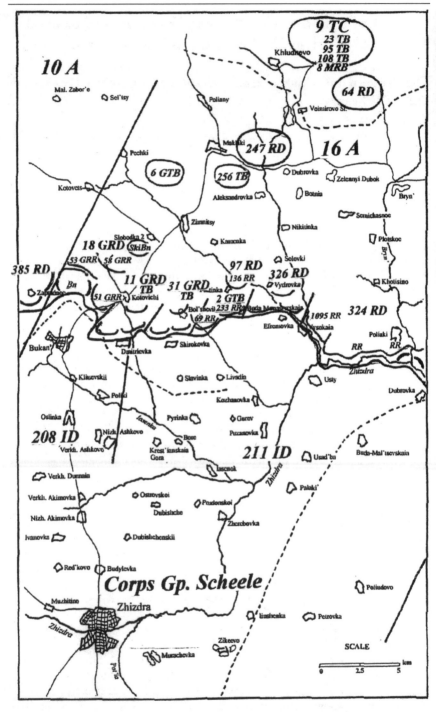

Map 71. The 16th Army's (Western Front) operations, the situation on
21 February 1943

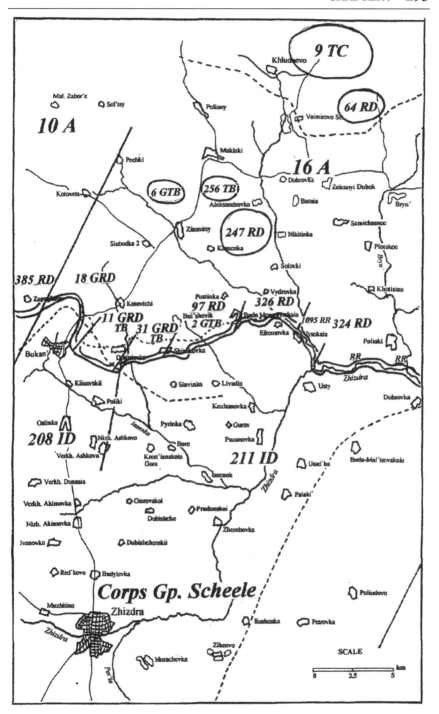

Map 72. The 16th Army's operations, the situation on 23 February 1943

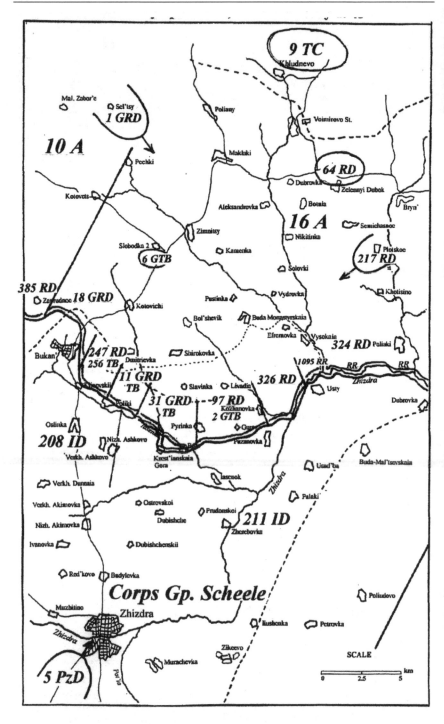

Map 73. The 16th Army's operations, 25-26 February 1943

Army's shock group made such limited progress, Colonel General I. S. Konev, the commander of the Western Front, denied Bagramian's request to commit Shamshin's 9th Tank Corps into combat to complete the penetration. Later Bagramian complained bitterly about this decision, criticizing both Konev and his successor, Colonel General V. D. Sokolovsky, for their failure to support his offensive adequately.[210] Nonetheless, Bagramian had no choice but to continue his costly, futile assaults in support of Rokossovsky's offensive. By 27 February, the newly arrived German 5th Panzer Division had contained Bagramian's forces along the Iasenka River line. Bagramian then regrouped his forces to renew the assaults with increased ferocity in early March.

On the same day that Bagramian's 16th Army was striking the defenses of Schmidt's Second Panzer Army north of Orel, the shock groups of General Belov's 61st and General Korzun's 3rd Armies began their supporting attacks in the sectors north and east of Bolkhov. Belov's plan required the 12th Guards Rifle Division, supported by the 68th Tank Brigade, to attack and penetrate the 112th Infantry Division's defenses in the Vygonovskie and Merkulovskii sector, 18 kilometers north of Bolkhov. If this assault succeeded, Belov's shock group, now reinforced by the 342nd and 356th Rifle Divisions, was to exploit southward toward Bolkhov in concert with the attack by the shock group of Korzun's 3rd Army toward Bolkhov from the east. However, the 112th Infantry Division's forces (about one regiment) repulsed the 12th Guards Rifle Division's assault with relative ease, inflicting heavy losses on the guardsmen. Acknowledging failure in this sector, General Reiter, the Briansk Front commander, ordered Belov to transfer the 342nd, 356th Rifle and 12th Guards Rifle Divisions to the control of the 3rd Army and, once they regrouped southward, to use them to reinforce the bridgehead Korzun's army seized on the western bank of the Oka River.

Meanwhile, Korzun's 3rd Army planned to conduct its attack in the Butyrki and Krasnyi sector along the eastern bank of the Oka River, 20 kilometers east of Bolkhov and 25–30 kilometers north of Mtsensk. His shock group, which consisted of the 5th and 283rd Rifle Divisions, the 116th Naval Infantry Brigade, and the 155th Tank and 116th Motorized Rifle Brigades of Colonel A. K. Pogosov's 20th Tank Corps, was to penetrate the defenses on the right wing of the LIII Army Corps' 112th Infantry Division, exploit westward to capture Bolkhov in cooperation with the 61st Army's shock group attacking from the north, and then wheel southward to support the 16th Army's advance on Orel (see Map 74). Korzun planned to use his two rifle divisions and single tank brigade to penetrate the defenses of the single German regiment on the 112th Infantry Division's right wing and conduct his exploitation to Bolkhov with the tank corps' 116th Motorized Rifle Brigade, the 116th Naval Infantry Brigade, and, if necessary, reinforcements transferred from adjacent sectors.

Korzun's shock group began its assault at dawn on 22 February and, in three days of heavy fighting, seized a 5-kilometer-wide and 4 kilometer-deep bridgehead on the western bank of the Oka River anchored on the villages of Chegodaeva and Gorodishche (see Map 75). However, the defending regiment of the 112th Infantry Division, supported by forces from the 34th Infantry Division on its right, managed to contain Korzun's attack by shifting their artillery fires and skillfully maneuvering company- and battalion-size tactical reserves. After containing

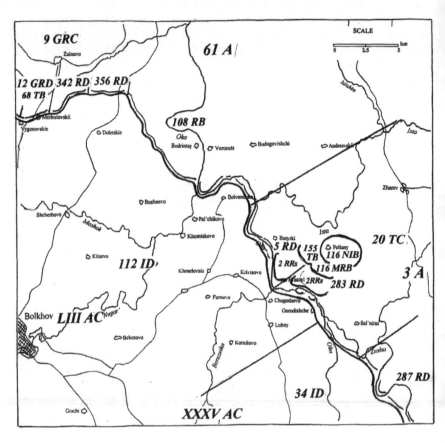

Map 74. The 61st and 3rd Armies' (Briansk Front) operations, the situation on 21 February 1943

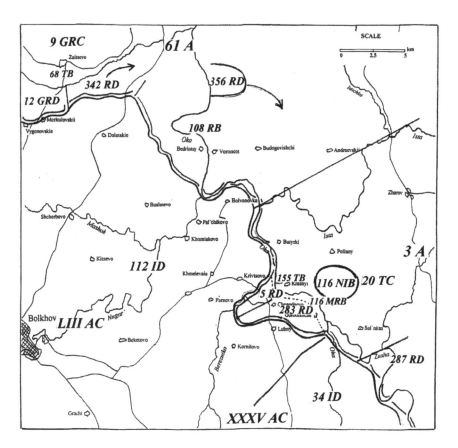

Map 75. The 61st and 3rd Armies' operations, the situation on 23 February 1943

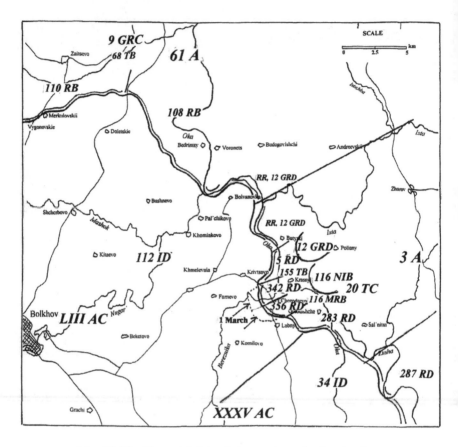

Map 76. The 61st and 3rd Armies' operations, the situation from
27 February–1 March 1943

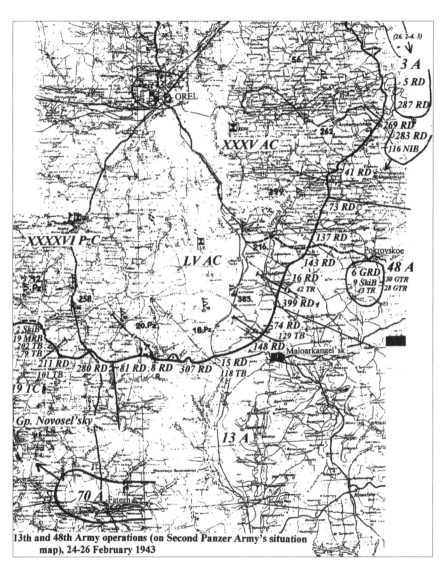

Map 77. The 13th and 48th Armies' operations, the situation from
24–26 February 1943

the shock group's advance by late on 26 February, the two German infantry divisions conducted numerous counterattacks between 27 February and 1 March that steadily shrank Korzun's bridgehead. During this fighting, Reiter reinforced the 3rd Army's shock group with the 356th and 342nd Rifle and 12th Guards Rifle Divisions, in succession, from Belov's 61st Army so that it could retain its foothold on the Oka River's western bank.

Once the Germans contained his shock group's attack, Korzun began searching for a more vulnerable sector in the German defenses further to the south where he could resume his attacks (see Map 76).[211] After detecting what he thought was a suitable weak spot on 26 February in the sector along the Neruch River 40 kilometers southeast of Orel, adjacent to the 48th Army's right boundary, between 26 February and 3 March, Korzun regrouped his army's 5th, 283rd, and 287th Rifle Divisions and 116th Naval Infantry Brigade southward into this sector, where he hoped they could resume operation together with the 48th Army's forces (see Map 77). However, events elsewhere ultimately frustrated these hopes. As for his army's foothold on the western bank of the Oka River, repeated counterattacks by German forces compelled Korzun to order his forces to abandon the bridgehead by 12 March.

The Western Front's Gzhatsk and Viaz'ma Offensives (22–27 February)

In addition to these major attacks by the Western Front's 16th Army and the Briansk Front's 61st, and 3rd Armies, the *Stavka* also ordered Konev's Western Front to conduct other attacks of a more limited nature to tie down German forces along the Moscow axis and prevent the OKH from shifting forces from this region southward to reinforce the defenses of Schmidt's Second Panzer Army opposite Rokossovsky's Central Front. In response, Konev ordered his *front's* 5th and 33rd Armies to conduct local assaults in their respective sectors beginning on 22 February. The 5th Army, commanded by Colonel General Ia. T. Cherevichenko, employed its 29th Guards Rifle Division and 153rd Rifle and 153rd Tank Brigades in an assault against a narrow sector defended by the Fourth Army's 35th Infantry Division (the XI Army Corps) east of Gzhatsk.[212] Simultaneously, the 33rd Army, commanded by Lieutenant General V. N. Gordov, conducted its attack against the defenses of Fourth Army northeast of Temkino, east of Viaz'ma, with several divisions, probably including its 7th Guards Rifle Corps' 5th Guards Rifle Division and 112th Rifle Brigade and elements of its 160th Rifle Division. Both attacks failed within a matter of hours.

Realistically, the *Stavka* understood that these attacks, conducted against strong and battle-tested German defenses, could achieve little more than simply to distract the Germans from the more important events taking place to the south. Although Army Group Center's defenses around the Rzhev-Viaz'ma salient held firm throughout February, the die was already cast for its defenders. The Red Army's persistent assaults against the salient, which had begun in July and August 1942, reached a climax in November and December 1942 and continued on a lesser scale throughout February 1943, inflicted heavy casualties on Army Group Center's Ninth Army and significantly weakened the salient's defenses. Coupled with the new threat to the forces of Schmidt's Second Panzer Army in the Orel salient, which provided ample reasons for the Germans to consider shortening their front in the East, the OKH concluded that further defense of the salient would be futile. Therefore, after obtaining Hitler's approval on 6 February, beginning on 1 March, Army Group Center began Operation *Büffel* [Buffalo], a phased withdrawal of its forces from the salient that took 23 days to complete. The *Stavka's* apparent awareness of German plans prompted it to maintain unrelenting pressure on the salient's defenses throughout February, first with the 5th and 33rd Armies' assaults and later with lesser efforts. Despite these assaults, Army Group Center began withdrawing the Ninth Army from the salient about one week later. Although this withdrawal lessened the threat to Moscow immeasurably, it also meant Rokossovsky would soon have to contend with a large number of new German divisions transferred from the north.

The Western Front's failure to collapse Army Group Center's defenses around the Rzhev-Viaz'ma salient in November and December 1942 and, once again, in February 1943 prompted the *Stavka* to effect several changes in the command cadre of the Western Front and at least one of its armies. Therefore, on 27 February the *Stavka* issued two new orders, the first two relieving Konev from his duties as commander of the Western Front and, the second, Cherevichenko as commander of the 5th Army:

1. Relieve Colonel General I. S. Konev from his duties as commander of the forces of the Western Front for not coping with his task of directing the *front* and place him at the disposal of the *Stavka* of the Supreme High Command.

2. Appoint Colonel General V. D. Sokolovsky as commander of the forces of the Western Front, releasing him from his duties as the chief of staff of the *front*.

3. Complete the receipt and handing over of *front* business by 0200 hours on 28 February, after which Comrade Sokolovsky will assume command of the forces of the *front*.

4. Appoint Lieutenant General A. P. Pokrovsky as the chief of staff of the Western Front, releasing him from his duties as chief of the operations department of that *front*.

The *Stavka* of the Supreme High Command
I. Stalin[213]

1. Relieve Colonel General Ia. T. Cherevichenko from his duties as commander of the forces of the 5th Army for not being able to cope with fulfilling his combat missions and place him at the disposal of the *Stavka* of the Supreme High Command.

2. Appoint Lieutenant General V. S. Polenov as the commander of the forces of the 5th Army, releasing him from command of the forces of the 31st Army.

3. Appoint Major General V. A. Gluzdovsky as commander of the forces of the 31st Army, releasing him from his duties as chief of staff of that army.

The Stavka of the Supreme High Command
I. Stalin[214]

At 2130 hours the same day, the *Stavka* issued yet another order, this time a directive "lighting a fire" under Bagramian, the commander of the *front's* 16th Army, and directing the new commander of the Western Front, Colonel General V. D. Sokolovsky, to provide Bagramian with reinforcements necessary to reinvigorate his army's offensive in support of Rokossovsky's offensive, which was just getting under way:

With the goal of further development of the success of the penetration of the enemy's defense by the forces of the 16th Army, the *Stavka* of the Supreme High Command orders:

1. Reinforce the shock group of the 16th Army at the expense of the *front's* reserves and bring [its strength] up to eleven rifle divisions, three rifle brigades, five tank brigades, one tank corps, and one separate ski regiment.

2. Continue to conduct the main attack in the general direction of Diad'kovo and Briansk, while enveloping Briansk from the west.

Bear in mind that units of the forces of the Central Front will attack from the south from the Dmitrovsk-Orlovskii region toward Karachev.

3. Conduct a flank attack from the Bukan' region toward Krutaia and Ignatovka with a force of two-three rifle divisions, with the mission of destroying the enemy in front of the 10th Army's front.

Subsequently, commit the forces of the 10th and 50th Armies in flank attacks from behind the right wing of the 16th Army, while rolling up the combat formation of the enemy.

Simultaneously, with the objective of rolling up the combat formation of the enemy in the Dubrovka and Rechitsa regions, conduct an attack toward Dubrovka and Buda with a force of no fewer than two rifle divisions.

4. Begin fulfilling this directive out immediately while continuing the offensive of the 16th Army against Zhizdra with all of its strength.

The Stavka of the Supreme High Command
Vasil'ev [Stalin][215]

At 1700 hours on the 28th, the *Stavka* reiterated its intent by notifying the Western Front it was dispatching it four additional rifle divisions and directing Sokolovsky to use them to reinforce Bagramian's 16th Army:

The *Stavka* of the Supreme High Commander orders:

1. Reassign four rifle divisions (the 173rd, 260th, 273rd, and 298th) to the Sukhinichi region at the disposal of the commander of the Western Front.

2. Carry out the transfer by railroad. The time and order of dispatch – will be in accordance with the instructions of the Chief of the General Staff.

3. Fill out all of the rifle divisions with personnel, horses, weapons, and other types of equipment in their new stationing regions according to the instructions of the chiefs of the main NKO directorates, bringing the strength of each rifle division, including guards, up to 8,000 men.

4. Report fulfillment.

The *Stavka* of the Supreme High Command
I. Stalin[216]

However, none of these four rifle divisions reached Bagramian's army. Instead, General Sokolovsky, the Western Front commander, reinforced Bagramian's army with the 17th, 49th, and 108th Rifle Divisions and the 125th and 128th Rifle Brigades between 28 February and 3 March.

The Changing Strategic Situation in Mid-February

At the time Rokossovsky's Central Front commenced its offensive, there were already ominous signs that the overall Soviet strategic offensive was encountering unanticipated difficulties. Contrary to the *Stavka's* expectations, the frenetic and poorly coordinated offensives by the Southwestern and Southern Fronts faltered by mid-February. Thwarted in attempts to reduce German defenses at Slaviansk and Voroshilovgrad, despite being well under-strength, the bulk of the Southwestern Front's mobile formations raced haphazardly into the deep German rear. The lead elements of Mobile Group Popov's four tank corps reached the Krasnoarmeiskaia region, south of Slaviansk, on 15 February, and the *front's* 25th Tank Corps approached the outskirts of Zaporozh'e on the Dnepr River on 20 February.[217]

After a skillful regrouping of his forces designed to bring the full force of the First and Fourth Panzer Armies and the newly arrived SS Panzer Corps to bear on the Southwestern Front's advancing forces, Manstein, commander of German Army Group South (as Don was renamed on 14 February), struck back at overextended Soviet forces. Attacking on 20 February, Manstein's XXXX Panzer Corps smashed Mobile Group Popov's forces in the Krasnoarmeiskaia region and pursued its remnants back through Barvenkovo to the Northern Donets River.[218] A few days later, the SS Panzer and XXXXVIII Panzer Corps, attacking along converging axes, inflicted a similar crushing defeat on the Southwestern Front's overextended forces near Pavlograd and Lozovaia, completely destroying the 25th Tank Corps and pushing the *front's* forces back to the Northern Donets River. Simultaneously, in the central and southern Donbas region, the forces of the First Panzer Army and *Armeeabteilung* Hollidt isolated and demolished two more Red Army mobile corps (8th Cavalry and 4th Guards Mechanized) that had penetrated into the Debal'tsevo and Anastasievka regions.

At first the *Stavka* discounted the seriousness of the situation and remained optimistic that the German counterstrokes would either expire or become irrelevant in light of Rokossovsky's anticipated successes further north. The *Stavka* stubbornly refused to alter its plans, trusting that the Voronezh Front, whose forces

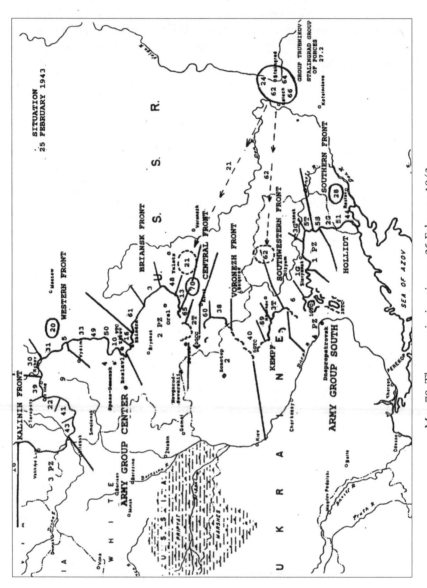

Map 78. The strategic situation on 25 February 1943

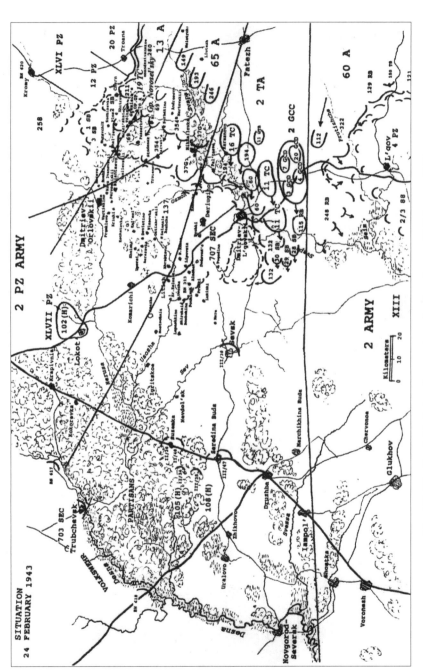

Map 79. The Sevsk-Trubchevsk operation, the situation on 24 February 1943

were still advancing successfully south and west of Khar'kov, could cope with the temporary setback in the Donbas. In essence, a deadly race was about to begin between Rokossovsky's forces attacking toward Briansk and Manstein's armored spearheads now approaching Khar'kov from the south. At stake were *Stavka* strategic expectations and the ultimate fate of its winter campaign.

The Central Front's Sevsk-Truschevsk Offensive and the Briansk Front's Orel Offensive (25 February–6 March)

The two armies spearheading Rokossovsky's Central Front finally struck into the gap between German Second Panzer and Second Armies on the morning of 25 February, two days after General Pukhov had reported his 13th Army's seizure of Maloarkhangel'sk (see Maps 78 and 79).[219] While the 13th Army's 132nd Rifle Division and Group Novosel'sky provided protection for his right flank against any attack by the Second Panzer Army from the north, the lead rifle divisions of Batov's 65th Army advanced in regimental column against light enemy resistance towards Komarichi and Dmitriev-Orlovskii. On the army's extreme right wing, the regiments of Colonel I. A. Kuzovkov's 69th Rifle Division', deployed across a broad front, maintained only loose contact with General Novosel'sky's operational group from the 13th Army, whose mission now was to facilitate the 65th Army's advance. To the south, in the 65th Army's center and on its left wing, the 354th and 37th Guards Rifle Divisions advanced in similar fashion against equally fragmented opposition by elements of the German 137th Infantry Division.[220]

At this juncture, the defending Germans sought only to monitor and slow Soviet forward progress until reinforcements arrived to establish a more solid defense. However, because Batov's rifle forces were advancing in dispersed attack formations across a broad front, they generated only weak offensive momentum and, unless and until Rokossovsky could commit his armor into action, Batov's forces could do little more than slowly press the defending Germans back. Complicating the situation for Batov was the fact that his units also had to operate in the adjacent sector of the 70th Army, whose boundaries had been designated but whose troops had not yet arrived. Within two days an operational group from General Tarasov's 70th Army reached the Gremiach'e area and began directing the Army's divisions into their respective offensive sectors.[221] On 25 February, however, these divisions were still struggling forward along the mud-clogged roads forward from Livny.

General Rodin's 2nd Tank Army attacked westward from concentration areas west of Fatezh through a screen erected by the 13th Army's 132nd Rifle Division, which had driven German forces from the 707th Security Division back to the outskirts of Dmitriev-L'govskii. There, the Germans also attempted to maintain positions covering the critical road junction until reinforcements could establish firmer defenses, since the town sat astride the vital roads leading westward to Sevsk and northward to Briansk. The tank army's two rifle divisions (the 194th and 60th) fought their way through the swamps along the Svapa River and pushed toward Dmitriev-L'govskii and Deriugino, 10 kilometers to the north, against spirited resistance, while Rodin's two tank corps (the 11th and 16th) followed.[222] Given the stiffening German resistance at Dmitriev-L'govskii, Major General of

Tank Forces I. G. Lazarov, the commander of the 11th Tank Corps, swung his armor columns southward to bypass the town, crossed the Svapa River, and began a headlong drive toward Sevsk, more than 50 kilometers to the west, to envelop the Second Panzer Army's right wing. Meanwhile, Colonel Grigor'ev's 16th Tank Corps remained along the Svapa River to support the two rifle divisions in their struggle for Dmitriev-L'govskii. General Kriukov's Cavalry-Rifle Group, with its three ski brigades in the lead and the army's 115th Rifle Brigade attached, exploited the 11th Tank Corp's enveloping maneuver by following Lazarov's tank corps into the breech.

The tenacious German defense of Dmitriev-L'govskii forced Rodin to split his tank army, with more than half of its forces left to engage in close combat for the town and the remainder to detour around the German flank. Hence, almost immediately, Grigor'ev's 16th Tank Corps and both the 60th and 194th Rifle Divisions became involved in what would become a heavy and complex five-day struggle to overcome the Germans' Dmitriev-L'govskii and Deriugino defense line. Meanwhile, Lazarov's 11th Tank Corps and Kriukov's Cavalry-Rifle Group skirted south of the German defenses and moved toward Sevsk along deteriorating roads, but against lighter German resistance.

While Rokossovsky's forces were achieving some initial successes despite the bad weather and atrocious road conditions, General Reiter's Briansk Front forces recorded a signal victory on 23 February, when the forces of the 148th and 74th Rifle Divisions of General Pukhov's 13th Army finally captured Maloarkhangel'sk. This success, however, was only fleeting since German forces driven from the town withdrew to an even stronger defense line situated along the Neruch River, 10 kilometers to the north. The Briansk Front kept the *Stavka* informed of its progress, as indicated by the report it dispatched at 2400 hours on 25 February:

> First. The forces of the *front* continued offensive fighting on 25 February 1943, with the shock groups of the 61st and 3rd Armies, and also in the sectors of the 48th and 13th Armies and Group Novoscl'sky – the assistant commander of the Briansk Front's forces. The following will be included in the group of forces: the 19th Tank Corps, the 6th Guards Rifle Division, and the 137th Rifle Division.[223] Having encountered stubborn fire resistance and counterattacks by enemy infantry in strengths of up to one to two battalions, with 10–20 tanks, they successfully repelled them.
>
> The most intense fighting developed in the Saburovo and Krivtsovo sector along the approaches to the Neruch River. In this sector, the units of the 74th and 148th Rifle Divisions twice repelled counterattacks by the enemy in strengths of up to two battalions with 20 tanks and destroyed up to a battalion of infantry and knocked out 7 tanks.
>
> The forces of the *front* were continuing to fight along previous lines at the end of the day.
>
> Second. The aviation of the *front* conducted no combat operations during the day.
>
> Third. The enemy is offering stubborn resistance to the offensive by our units and is continuing to throw fresh forces forward from other axes.

Prisoners reportedly belonging to the 216th Infantry Division, which has been transferred from the Rzhev region, have been captured in the Fetishchevo and Khoroshevskii regions.

Fourth. I have decided:

a) To cease the offensive operations of the shock groups of the 61st and 3rd Armies and go over to the defense in the Ozhigovo (incl.), Mtsensk, and Maloe Kritsyno sector with the forces of the 61st Army;

b) To castle [move laterally] the 3rd Army to the south, with its main grouping on its left wing; and

c) To continue to fulfill the previously assigned mission with the 48th and 13th Armies and Group Novosel'sky.

Reiter, Susaikov, Sandalov[224]

In accordance with Reiter's instructions, the 61st and 3rd Armies immediately halted their attacks east of Bolkhov, and the 3rd Army began regrouping its forces southward to form a new shock group along the Neruch River near Krasnogor'e, 45 kilometers northeast of Maloarkhangel'sk, adjacent to the 48th Army's right wing. On 2400 hours 26 February, Reiter dispatched two more reports to the *Stavka*, the first providing details of the day's action and the second recounting the Briansk Front's successes during the previous month (see Maps 80 and 81):

[The first report]

First. On 26 February 1943, the forces of the *front* fought stubborn battles with counterattacking units of enemy infantry in strengths of up to one-two battalions supported by small groups of tanks in separate sectors; the 61st and 3rd Armies carried out a regrouping of forces for the fulfillment of new missions, and part of the forces of the 61st Army, having fortified their newly achieved lines, repelled attacks by the enemy in the Gos'kovo, Zheleznitsa, and Fetishchevo regions.

The 41st Rifle Division (48th Army) captured Khitrovo and Dorogoe as a result of a surprise attack.

The forces of the 13th Army fought intense battles in the Trosna (eastern) and Arkhangel'skoe regions.

The 132nd Rifle Division turned its sector over to units of the 194th Rifle Division (65th Army) and concentrated in the Sukhachevo, Bugry, and Banino region, from which, when darkness falls, it will join Novosel'sky's Group in the Radogoshch' region.

The remaining units of the *front* were fighting in their previous positions.

More than 200 Germans were destroyed, and three tanks were knocked out by the units of the 13th Army on 26 February and [the following] were seized as trophies on 25 February: mortars – 2, machine guns – 3, rifles – 20, shells – 2000, rounds — up to 400,000, and hand grenades – 300.

Second. The aviation of the *front* aviation conducted no operations during the day because of poor weather conditions.

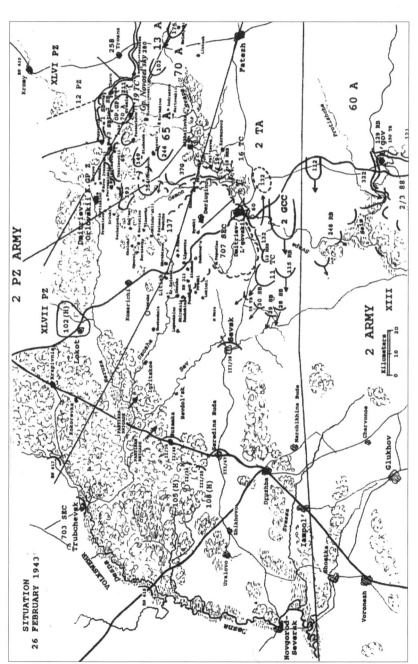

Map 80. The Sevsk-Trubchevsk operation, the situation on 26 February 1943

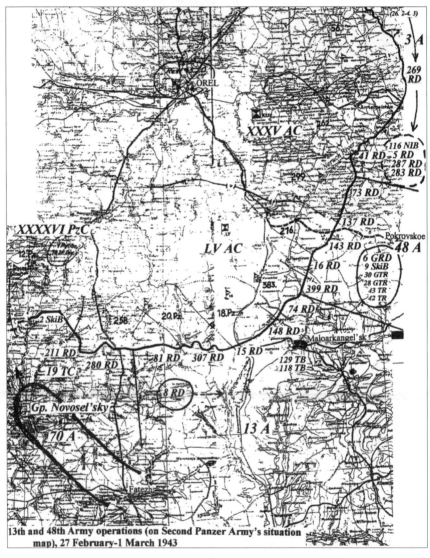

13th and 48th Army operations (on Second Panzer Army's situation map), 27 February–1 March 1943

Map 81. The 13th and 48th Armies' operations, the situation from
27 February–1 March 1943

Third. The enemy offered stubborn resistance to the offensive of our units in all sectors by fire and counterattacks. On the right wing of the 61st Army, the enemy attacked Gos'kovo with a force of about two battalions from the 25th Motorized Division and penetrated into its northeastern outskirts, where the fighting is continuing.

The enemy attacked Fetishchevo and captured it with a force of more than a battalion from the 216th Infantry Division's 348th Infantry Regiment; attempts by the enemy to advance from Fetishchevo toward Chegodaeva were repulsed.

Up to a battalion of infantry with four tanks conducted a counterattack from Aleksandrovka 2 and Glazunov and occupied Trosna (eastern) at 0730 hours.

All enemy counterattacks were repelled in the remaining sectors of the *front*.

No new enemy units were identified during the day.

Fourth. I have decided:

a) To fulfill the missions according to the projected regrouping plan with the 61st and 3rd Armies; and

b) To conduct a regrouping with seven reinforced rifle divisions (three — from the 48th Army and four — from the 13th Army) into the Sandrovka, Krasnaia Sloboda, and Glazunovka sector [along the Neruch River 10–12 kilometers north and northwest of Maloarkhangel'sk], concentrate all of the artillery, tank, and mortar units of the 48th and 13th Armies in this sector, carry out a penetration, and attack toward Kromy.

Reiter, Susaikov, Sandalov[225]

[The second report]

Fulfilling your order [of 25 January 1943], the forces of the Briansk Front went over to the offensive on 26 January 1943 and, penetrating the defenses of the enemy along a front of 160 kilometers, reached to a depth of 220 kilometers.

As a result of the offensive operations by the forces of the Briansk Front, [the following] have been smashed, partially destroyed, or captured during the period from 26 January through 26 February: the 82nd, 383rd, and 45th Infantry Divisions, the 377th Artillery Regiment (the 377th Infantry Division), the 44th, 320th, 654th, and 630th Security Battalions, the 742nd Sapper Battalion, the 273rd Antiaircraft Artillery Battalion, the 524th Army Transport Battalion, and a battalion of the 63rd High Command Artillery Regiment. The 299th, 258th, and 216th Infantry Divisions, the 18th and 20th Panzer Divisions, the 12th Panzer Division, the 9th, 10th, and 11th Jäger Battalions, the 350th Infantry Regiment (the 221st Infantry Division), the 727th Infantry Regiment (the 107th Infantry Division), and a special designation battalion of the Second Panzer Army have suffered heavy losses. In addition, the remnants of the German 340th, 68th, 75th, and 377th Infantry Divisions and the Hungarian 23rd Infantry Division were destroyed in the Kastornoe region.

The enemy, striving to halt the offensive actions of our units and to prevent our forces from reaching the rear of the Orel grouping, committed fresh units transferred from other fronts and from the depths into the fighting. During the period from 26 January through 25 February, the enemy transferred to the left wing of the front: the 4th Panzer Division from the Mtsensk region, replacing it with units of the 34th Infantry Division [from the Western Front]; the 18th Panzer Division from the Zhizdra region; the 20th Panzer Division from the Viaz'ma region; the 12th Panzer Division from the Nevel' region; the 258th Infantry Division from the Gzhatsk region; the 727th Infantry Regiment (707th Infantry Division) from the Zhukovka region; the 1st Jager Battalion from Belgium; the 9th, 10th, and 11th Jager Battalions from the Belyi region; the 742nd Sapper Battalion from the Western Front; the 1st Parachute-Destroyer Regiment from France; a student battalion of the Second Panzer Army from Orel; and the 216th Infantry Division from the Rzhev region. Further transfers of forces into the Briansk and Ordzhonikidzegrad regions and, further to the south, into the Lokot' and Dmitrovsk-Orlovskii regions from the Western Front and from the depths have been noted, as well as the arrival of the headquarters of the 29th Motorized Division, the 75th Infantry Division, and the SS Panzer Division "Deaths Head" in the Navlia region.

The enemy has suffered losses: 46,431 soldiers and officers destroyed and 6,783 captured. Destroyed: tanks – 37, aircraft — 7, armored transporters — 14, guns — 94 guns, mortars – 70, machine guns — 677, vehicles – 103, artillery depots – 8, and one armored train blown up.

As a result of the offensive — 12,300 square kilometers of territory was seized by our forces. 1,472 populated points, including the cities of Kastorne, Shchigry, Fatezh, and Maloarkhangel'sk, the regional centers of Droskovo, Pokrovskoe, Volovo, Vyshne-Dolgoe, Kolpny, Zolotukhino, and Ponyri have been liberated from the Fascist invaders. Captured trophies: guns – 722, mortars — 281, rifles — 7,201, machine guns – 932, automatic weapons — 336, tanks — 121, vehicles — 7,844, tractors – 59, armored transporters – 4, motorcycles — 544, bicycles — 1,697, armored trains — 1, rifle rounds — 16,542,000, shells and mines — 4,068,150, radio sets — 130, telephone apparatuses — 92, horses — 2,169, carts — 1,500, hand grenades — 9,450, antitank and antipersonnel mines — 12,150, railroad trains with foodstuffs – 2, railroad cars with cargo—920, and warehouses with ammunition, supplies, and goods — more than 300.

Reiter, Susaikov, Sandalov[226]

Reiter once again reported on his *front's* slow progress at 2400 hours on 27 February:

First. The 48th Army conducted local operations on its right wing with part of its forces on the morning of 17 February 1943, but, encountering heavy enemy fire and counterattacks in strengths of up to a battalion, had no success.

Active offensive operations were not conducted in the remaining sectors of the *front*, and the forces of the 3rd, 48th, and 13th Armies and Group Novosel'sky were putting themselves in order and regrouping to fulfill new missions.

Up to 270 soldiers and officers were destroyed, 4 tanks were knocked out, and prisoners from the 25th Motorized Regiment and the 12th Panzer Division were taken by the units of Group Novosel'sky during fighting in the Grankino region on 26 February.

Second. The aviation of the *front* did not conduct operations during the day.

Third. The enemy launched counterattacks in strengths of up to battalion with the aim of resisting local operations by our forces in separate sectors of the front and conducted artillery, mortar, and rifle-machine gun fire in the remaining sectors of the front.

According to information from agents, increased movements of troops by auto-transport from Briansk to Orel, involving the movement of up to 300 automobiles daily, has been detected. New enemy units have not been identified during the day.

Fourth. I have decided: to continue preparing the forces for the fulfillment of the projected plan.

Reiter, Susaikov, Sandalov[227]

General Reiter's revised offensive concept envisioned his armies conducting fresh and even larger-scale offensive operation beginning in early March against German forces defending along the Neruch River southeast of Orel. Therefore, in late February he ordered General Korzun's 3rd Army to accelerate the regrouping of his forces southward into its new offensive sector along the Neruch River adjacent to the 48th Army's right wing. To deceive the Germans regarding the 3rd Army's planned assault, on 28 February the Briansk Front ordered Belov's 61st Army to posture its forces as if intending to attack in the sector where they had done so on 22 February, specifically, in the Zaitsevo and Bobriki sector, 20–22 kilometers north of Bolkhov:

The *front* commander orders:

1. Beginning on 1 March 1943, set about implementing measures designed to create an impression on the part of the enemy concerning preparations for a repeat attack in the Bobrovka and Zaitsevo sectors.

To that end:

a) Prepare passages through the enemy's and our barbed wire obstacles and minefields;

b) Imitate reinforcement work by clearing the roads and moving forces along them;

c) Represent the approach of vehicles and tanks to the front and their concentration in designated regions by lighting fires and the sounds of motors; and

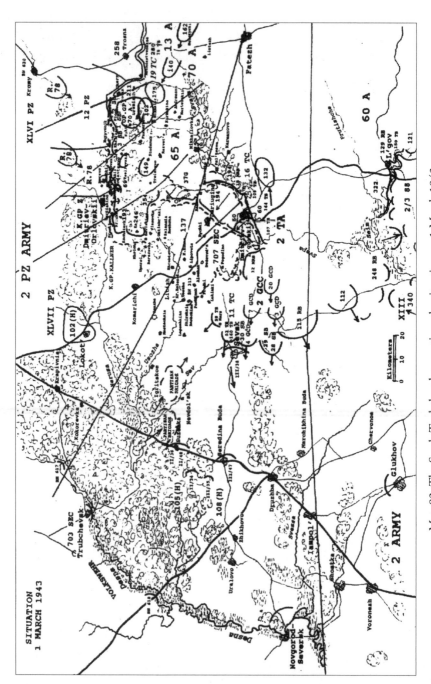

Map 82. The Sevsk-Trubchevsk operation, the situation on 1 March 1943

d) Imitate the work of groups of command cadre by increasing command-ers' reconnaissances [*rekognostsirovka*] and a series of other measures.

2. Plan the work for the designated period and report fulfillment by enci-phered message by 1800 hours 1 March 1943.

Sidel'nikov[228]

By 1 March the armies of Rokossovsky's Central Front had achieved consider-able success, even though the attacks by the Briansk Front's 13th and 48th Armies north and northeast of Maloarkhangel'sk had faltered (see Map 82). On his *front's* right wing, Batov's 65th Army had carved a deep salient extending toward Komarichi and Trosna, which threatened both the left flank of the German forces clinging to Dmitriev-L'govskii and the right flank of German forces defending Kromy. Although Batov's thrust forced the 707th Security Division to abandon Dmitriev-L'govskii late on 2 March, his forces were unable to exploit the penetra-tion since the Germans reinforced their sagging defenses with the newly-arrived 78th Assault Infantry Division. Unknown to Batov, the 78th Division had just arrived from German Ninth Army, which was just then beginning to withdraw its forces from the Rzhev-Viaz'ma salient. This was the first of several fresh German divisions soon flowing southward to help thwart the Central Front's offensive. However, Batov still exuded an air of optimism because he could now count on support from Tarasov's 70th Army, whose lead divisions were beginning to assemble in the Gremiach'e region and preparing to enter combat in their hitherto vacant sector. On Rokossovsky's left, Lazarov's 11th Tank Corps and Kriukov's Cavalry-Rifle Group seized Sevsk from its Hungarian defenders and prepared for a precipitous exploitation westward against dwindling resistance.[229]

Just before the Central Front's forces captured Sevsk, on 1 March the head-quarters of the Partisan Movement in the Briansk Front prepared a plan containing instructions for mutual cooperation between Rokossovsky's advancing forces and the sizeable partisan detachments and bands operating along his projected axis of his advance. Among other things, this plan called for active participation of partisan forces in combat during the offensive:

General missions

1. Cut the railroad line and main highway in the Briansk-Karachev sector and prevent the movement of enemy trains, vehicular columns, and supplies along these routes.

2. Cut the railroad line and main highway in the Zhukovka-Briansk sector and prevent the movement of enemy trains, vehicular columns, and supplies along these routes.

3. Cut the railroad line in the Briansk-Unecha sector and prevent the movement of enemy trains along this route.

4. Blow up the railroad bridge across the Desna River in the vicinity of Vygonichi Station.

5. Prepare positions along the right and left banks of the Desna River in the Uruch'e-Vitemlia sector for the approach of attacking units of the Red Army.

Specific missions

1. Scorning death, the Kravtsov Brigade, in its full complement of 600 men, and the "Death to the German Occupiers" Brigade, with 1,000 men, under the overall command of Comrade Duka, the commander of the Kravtsov Brigade, will enter the Belye Berega region along the Briansk-Karachev railroad line and, by all possible methods and means, prevent the movement of enemy trains along the railroad line and the movement of automobiles and transport along the Briansk-Karachev road.

Reconnaissance missions

1. Determine the strength, composition, weapons, and fortifications system of the enemy in the vicinity of the cities of Briansk and Karachev.

2. The Shchors Brigade, with its full complement of 800 men, and the Voroshilov Detachment No. 1, with 525 men, under the overall command of Comrade Romashin, the commander of the Shchors Brigade, will blow up the railroad bridge across the Desna River in the vicinity of Vygonichi.

After fulfillment of the mission of blowing up the bridge, the Shchors Brigade and the Voroshilov Detachment No. 1 will take under its control the dirt road in the Briansk-Uty sector, preventing the movement along it of enemy vehicles and transport, and prepare positions along the right bank of the Desna River in the Uruch'e-Riabchevsk sector.

3. The Chapaev Brigade will leave forces to protect its base and, with its remaining forces of up to 800 men, together with the Voroshilov Detachment No. 2, under the overall command of the Chapaev Brigade commander, reach the Romassukhskie Forest, with the mission to cut the railroad line in the Pochep-Krasnoe sector and prevent the movement of enemy trains along this route.

Prevent the movement of enemy vehicular columns and cargo along the Pochep-Krasnyi Rog-Vygonichi, Krasnyi Rog-Svetlovo, and Zhiriatino-Krasnoe roads.

The primary reconnaissance mission: monitor the garrisons in Unecha, Pogar, and Pochep and the enemy movements in that region.

4. The "Death to the German Occupiers" Brigade will secure control over the road in the Uty-Trubchevsk sector and provide security for its own base with its remaining forces and, together with the Shchors Brigade, prepare positions along the right bank of the Desna River in the Uruch'e-Riabchevsk sector for the approach of attacking units of the Red Army.

5. The Stalin Brigade, with its full complement of 1,000 men, will reach the western bank of the Desna River in the Riabchevsk-Radutino sector and hold on to it until the approach of the units of the Red Army.

Prevent the movement of enemy forces from moving along the Pochep-Trubchevsk main highway.

6. The Frunze Brigade, with 500 men, and the "All Power to the Soviets" Brigade, with 1,000 men, under the overall command of Comrade Baliasov, the commander of the "All Power to the Soviets" Brigade, will reach the western bank of the Desna River in the Selets-Vitemlia sector and hold on to it until the approach of the units of the Red Army. Prevent the movement of enemy forces along the Pogar-Gremiach'e and Gremiach'e-Trubchevsk roads. Provide security for the airfield, prevent the enemy from entering the forests from the east and south, and hold on to the main Suzemka-Trubchevsk highway with the remaining forces of both brigades.

7. The "For the Fatherland" Brigade, remaining in its previous region, will provide security for the airfield from the northeast, prevent the movement of the enemy along the Altukhovo-Dol'sk main road, and maintain control over the Lokot'-Sevsk dirt road.

8. 1/ The northern group of partisan detachments, consisting of: the Zhukovka Nos. 1 and 3 and the Briansk, Dubrovskii, Sterzhskii, Loibokhinskii, Ivatskii, Diat'kovskii Nos. 1 and 2, and Kletnianskii Regional Brigades, under the overall command Major Shurukhin, will cut the railroad line and road in the Zhukovka-Sel'tso sector and prevent the movement of enemy trains, automobile columns, and transport along the indicated roads.

2/ The Ordzhonikidzegrad and Bytoshevsk Partisan Detachments, under the overall command of Comrade Ryzhkov, will reach the Belye Berega region along the Briansk-Karachev railroad and, together with the Kravtsov Brigade, will cut the railroad in the Briansk-Karachev sector and prevent the movement of enemy trains, vehicular columns, and transport along the Briansk-Karachev railroad line and road.

3/ The Liudinovskii and Diat'kovskii Partisan Detachments Nos. 3 and 4 will remain Major Zhurukhin's reserve.

Senior Major of the State Security Services Matveev,
Chief of Staff of the Partisan Movement in the headquarters of the
Briansk Front[230]

As Rokossovsky's forces subsequently thrust westward through Sevsk, these partisan forces carried out their missions and, ultimately, found themselves defending a sizable portion of the Central Front's front-line positions, albeit in virtually impenetrable swampy and forested regions.

Despite progress on his left and right wings, the situation in Rokossovsky's central sector was less encouraging. There, although German forces finally abandoned Dmitriev-L'govskii late on 1 March, they began a fighting withdrawal to newly prepared defenses covering Deriugino and the main road to Briansk. Despite committing the 16th Tank Corps to combat, Soviet forward progress remained agonizingly slow. Moreover, the heavy fighting diverted Rodin's forces from their original attack axis (Sevsk-Trubchevsk) and sent them instead toward Komarichi and Lokat', points to which German reserves were gravitating.

During the ensuing five days, Rokossovsky's force made only grudging gains on the right and in the center and spectacular, but misleading, progress on the left. Batov's 65th Army was now joined on the right by an increasing flow of 70th Army divisions, which took over an expanded front sector and struggled with the 65th Army's formations to penetrate the German 78th Infantry and 12th Panzer Divisions' defenses covering the southern approaches to Orel. Rokossovsky hounded his two army commanders to intensify their attacks. Tarasov's 70th Army pounded German defenses west of Trosna unmercifully, but at high cost, and, although Batov's forces pushed the German defenders back to positions south of the Usozha River and took some villages on the approaches to Komarichi, progress was slow, and it was becoming apparent to all involved that continued advance was unlikely without significant Soviet reinforcements.

Nor was the situation much better to the east in the region north of Maloarkhangel'sk, where the Briansk Front's 13th, 48th, 3rd, and 61st Armies were attempting to reinvigorate their offensive, but with little success. The situation report the Briansk Front submitted to the *Stavka* at 2400 hours on 6 March summed up Reiter's frustration:

> First. The shock groups of the 48th and 13th Armies went over to the offensive along the Krest'ianka, Maiskaia Zorka, and Soglasnyi front at 0830 hours on 6 March 1943 after a 30-minute artillery preparation, encountering stubborn fire resistance in all sectors and counterattacks by enemy infantry in strengths of up to two companies with tanks.
>
> Advancing forward slowly, they are fighting [in the following regions] at day's end: the 48th Army, having captured the grove 2 kilometers northwest of Verkhniaia Gnilusha with its left wing, is fighting for possession of Nikitovka and Panskaia with its right wing; and the 13th Army, after capturing Trosna, is fighting for Neskuchnaia, Saburov, Krivtsovo, and Glazunov.
>
> As a result of the fighting, up to a battalion of enemy infantry have been destroyed, 5 tanks have been knocked out, and [the following] have been captured by the units of the 13th Army: guns — 18, machine guns — 28, rifles — 25, mortars – 1, and shells — 500. Prisoners have been taken from the 532nd Infantry Regiment of the 383rd Infantry Division, the 101st and 52nd Heavy Howitzer Regiments, the 88th Reserve Battalion, and 18th Motorcycle Battalion of the 18th Panzer Division.
>
> The 61st Army fought stubborn battles during the day with units of the 12th Guards Rifle Division against enemy forces attacking in the Sivkovo and Gorodishche sector. Active offensive operations were not conducted in the remaining sectors of the *front*.
>
> Second. The aviation of the *front* destroyed enemy forces on the battlefield during the day. 42 aircraft sorties have been conducted, of which 21 combat aircraft returned without having fulfilled their missions because of bad weather.
>
> Third. The enemy in the offensive sectors of the 48th and 13th Armies offered stubborn fire resistance with units of the 383rd Infantry and 18th Panzer Divisions and subunits of the 10th and 11th Jager

Battalions, while going over to counterattack with infantry in strengths of up to two companies with tanks in several sectors.

On the front of the 61st Army, the enemy launched attacks on Sivkovo, Chegodaevo, Kukuevka, and Gorodishche in a strength of more than a regiment of infantry at 0730 hours, after a 1.5-hour artillery preparation by eight artillery batteries and six mortar batteries. Throwing in small groups of fresh infantry, the enemy captured Sivkovo after intense fighting and penetrated into Chegodaevo and Gorodishche. The battle was continuing in these points at the end of the day.

Aviation of the enemy bombed and assaulted the combat formations of the attacking units of the 48th and 13th Army units with groups of 10–12 aircraft.

Fourth. I have decided: to continue the offensive by shock groups of the 48th and 13th Armies [and] to begin the offensive by the shock groups of the 3rd Army on the morning of 7 March 1943.

Reiter, Susaikov, Sandalov[231]

Conclusions

Despite Reiter's best efforts, the Briansk Front's offensive was a shambles by day's end on 6 March. Not only were the shock groups of the 48th and 13th Armies at a dead standstill, but the 3rd Army had also lost its bridgehead on the western bank of the Oka River east of Bolkhov. Nor was their much hope that the 3rd Army's attack across the Neruch River on the 48th Army's right wing would achieve anything appreciable without support from other sectors of the front. The fact was that nearly three months of near constant combat had sapped the strength and will of those Soviet soldiers who had survived the long march westward from the Don River.

To the south and west, however, Rokossovsky's forces still seemed to be faring far better, in particular, the forces of Rodin's 2nd Tank Army. After its forward elements captured Sevsk on 1 March, Lazarov's 11th Tank Corps rolled steadily westward, seizing the key road junctions at Seredina Buda and Suzemka, 30 kilometers west and 35 kilometers northwest of Sevsk, respectively, on 4 March (see Map 83). The corps' 59th Tank Brigade then cooperated with partisan units in operations northeastward toward Igritskoe on the Usozha River, 25 kilometers north of Sevsk, as it attempted to locate and turn the open right flank of Schmidt's Second Panzer Army. Meanwhile, the remaining brigades of Lazarov's corps fanned out toward the west and south in support of Kriukov's Cavalry-Rifle Group as it advanced westward toward its objective, Novgorod-Severskii, a key city on eastern bank of the Desna River which sat astride vital German communications routes linking the Second Panzer and Second Armies. Kriukov's cavalrymen reached the eastern outskirts of Novgorod-Severskii and the bank of the Desna River, 160 kilometers into the German rear, by 7 March. His success, however, was deceptive, since his forces were spread thinly across a front of over 100 kilometers. This thin screen of cavalrymen and rifle troops could contend with the remnants of Hungarian light divisions. It could not, however, successfully deal with a new and refreshed German panzer division.[232] This was, in fact, was what it was about to be asked to do.

The most logical ultimate source of reinforcements for Rokossovsky's faltering offensive was Lieutenant General I. M. Chistiakov's 21st Army, which had been en route to the Livny area from Stalingrad since early February.[233] The lead elements of Chistiakov's army reached concentration areas around Fatezh on 5 March. Not wishing to repeat the mistake he made in the piecemeal commitment of the 70th Army, Rokossovsky gave the new army several days to assemble before going into combat in support of Batov and Tarasov. The reinvigoration of Rokossovsky's offensive, however, now faced new time imperatives imposed by events taking place well outside of his area of operations. And these imperatives required that he renew his attack and achieve success before Chistiakov's army was fully ready.

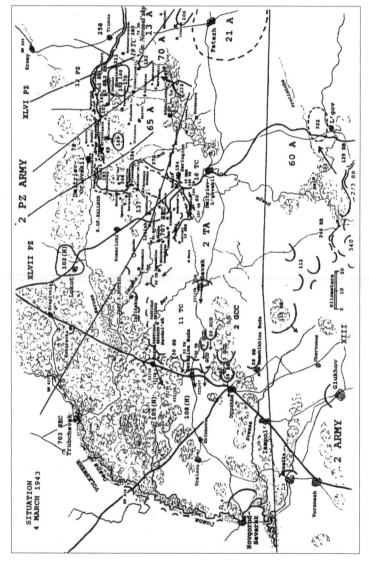

Map 83. The Sevsk-Trubchevsk operation, the situation on 4 March 1943

Chapter 8

The Kalinin, Western, Briansk, and Central Fronts' Orel, Briansk, and Smolensk Offensive (7–21 March 1943)

The *Stavka's* Revised Plan

The most serious of the many new factors affecting the fate of the *Stavka's* offensive along the Orel, Briansk, and Smolensk axis were the successful counterstrokes by Manstein's forces in the south. In the wake of Army Group South's victory over the Soviet Southwestern and Southern Fronts in the Donbas region during the last ten days of February, in heavy fighting between 1 and 5 March, the Fourth Panzer Army of Manstein's army group had encircled and utterly destroyed the Voronezh Front's 3rd Tank Army south of Khar'kov. Now two of his panzer corps (the SS Panzer Corps and XXXXVIII) threatened the *front's* defenses protecting the key city. The *Stavka*, beginning to appreciate the gravity of the situation during the last few days of February, immediately reoriented the flow of its strategic reserves to restore the situation, including the 24th, 62nd, 64th, and 66th Armies, most of which it had already planned to employ as reinforcements for Rokossovsky's Central Front (see Map 84). The allocation of these and other armies from its strategic reserves was of immense importance not only for the fate of Rokossovsky's offensive but also for the ultimate outcome of Manstein's counterstroke, particularly if Manstein decided to continue it through the remainder of March and into April.

The *Stavka* began reassigning its reserve armies at 1700 hours on 28 February, when it dispatched directives to the commanders of the 66th, 24th, 64th, and 66th Armies and the Kalinin, Southwestern, and Voronezh Fronts, as well as Lieutenant General V. V. Kosiagin, its representative controlling the armies in its strategic reserve:

> [To the representative of the *Stavka* and the commanders of the forces of the Kalinin Front and the 66th Army]
>
> The *Stavka* of the Supreme High Command orders:
>
> 1. Re-station the 66th Army, consisting of six rifle divisions (the 13th Gds., 66th Gds., 116th, 226th, 299th, and 343rd) and the 815th Separate Artillery Reconnaissance Battalion, to the Toropets region at the disposal of the commander of the Kalinin Front.
>
> 2. Carry out the re-stationing by railroad. The time and order of dispatch – in accordance with the instructions of the Chief of the General Staff.

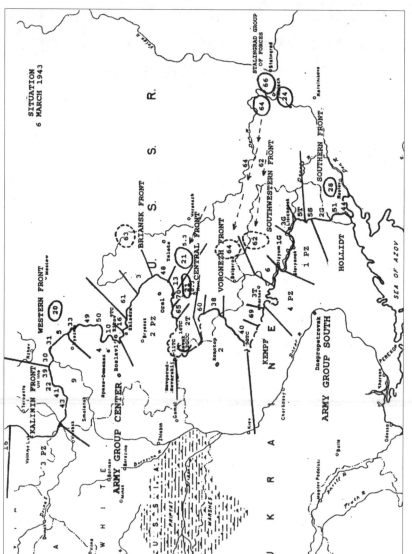

Map 84. The strategic situation on 6 March 1943

3. Fill out all rifle divisions in the new stationing region with personnel, horses, weapons, and equipment based on orders of the chiefs of the main directorates of the NKO [Peoples' Commissariat of Defense], bringing the strength of each rifle division, including guards, up to 8,000 men.

Report fulfillment.

The *Stavka* of the Supreme High Command
I. Stalin[234]

[To the representative of the *Stavka* and the commander of the 24th Army]

The *Stavka* of the Supreme High Command orders:

1. Re-station six rifle divisions (the 68th and 69th Gds., 84th, 214th, 233rd, and 252nd) to the Valuiki region in the composition of 24th Army in the reserve of the *Stavka* of the Supreme High Command.

2. Carry out the re-stationing of the rifle divisions by railroad. Carry out the re-stationing of the headquarters of the 24th Army from the Voronezh region in march order. The order and time of dispatch – in accordance with the instructions of the Chief of the General Staff.

3. The chiefs of the main directorates of the NKO will fill out the divisions in the Valuiki region with personnel, horses, weapons, and other types of missing equipment, bringing the strength of each rifle division up to eight thousand men

4. Report fulfillment.

The *Stavka* of the Supreme High Command
I. Stalin[235]

[To the representative of the *Stavka* and the commanders of the forces of the Southwestern Front and the 62nd Army]

The *Stavka* of the Supreme High Command orders:

1. Re-station the 62nd Army, consisting of six rifle divisions (the 27th Gds., 39th Gds., 24th, 45th, 99th, and 284th), the 99th and 671st Gun Artillery Regiments, the 184th, 565th, and 386th Tank Destroyer (Anti-tank) Artillery Regiments, the 8th Guards Separate Artillery Reconnaissance Battalion, and the 5th and 9th Guards Tank Regiments to the Kupiansk region in the reserve of the Southwestern Front.

2. Carry out the re-stationing by railroad. The time and order of dispatch — in accordance with the instructions of the Chief of the General Staff.

3. Fill out all rifle divisions in the new stationing region with personnel, horses, weapons, and equipment based on orders of the chiefs of the NKO's main directorates, bringing the strength of each division, including guards, up to 8,000 men.

Report fulfillment.

The *Stavka* of the Supreme High Command
I. Stalin[236]

[To the representative of the *Stavka* and the commanders of the forces of the Voronezh Front and 64th Army]

The *Stavka* of the Supreme High Command orders:

1. Re-station the 64th Army, consisting of six rifle divisions (the 15th Gds., 36th Gds., 29th, 38th, 204th, and 422nd), the 156th and 1111th Gun Artillery Regiments, the 186th, 493rd, 496th, and 500th Tank Destroyer (Antitank) Artillery Regiments, the 838th Separate Artillery Reconnaissance Battalion, the 27th Guards Tank Brigade, and the 224th and 245th Tank Regiments (the latter two from Gor'ki), to the Valuiki region at the disposition of the commander of the Voronezh Front.

2. Carry out the re-stationing by railroad. The beginning of the dispatch will be on 1 March of this year. Complete the transfer of the army to the new stationing region by 15 March of this year.

3. Carry out the filling out of all rifle divisions with personnel, horses, weapons, and equipment in the new stationing region based on orders of the chiefs of the NKO's main directorates, bringing the strength of each rifle division, including guards, up to 8,000 men.
Report fulfillment.

The *Stavka* of the Supreme High Command
I. Stalin[237]

When the situation in the Khar'kov region continued to deteriorate, at 2300 hours on 1 March, the *Stavka* issued a fifth directive ordering the NKO to transfer the 66th Army from the Kalinin Front to the Southwestern Front, with instructions for it to assemble in the Starobel'sk region:

[To the representative of the *Stavka*]
In a change to *Stavka* directive No. 46059, the *Stavka* of the Supreme High Command orders:

1. Send the 66th Army, consisting of the 13th Gds., 66th Gds., 116th, 226th, 229th, and 343rd Rifle Divisions and the 815th Separate Artillery Reconnaissance Battalion, to the Southwestern Front reserve in the Starobel'sk region.

2. Carry out the re-stationing of the army by railroad. Begin loading the formations of the army on 12 March. Complete the transfer by 24 March.

3. Carry out the filling out of the divisions of the 66th Army with missing personnel, horses, weapons, and equipment in the Starobel'sk region based on the instructions of the chiefs of the main directorates of the NKO, bringing the strength of each division up to 8,000 men
Report fulfillment.

The *Stavka* of the Supreme High Command
I. Stalin[238]

This directive was the first of many that, considered collectively, ultimately deprived Rokossovsky of the reinforcements he needed to conduct his offensive successfully. Even at this juncture, however, the *Stavka* demurred and refused to halt Rokossovsky's offensive.[239] Instead, at 2130 hours on 7 March, it changed Rokossovsky's mission. Now, rather than striking deep at Briansk and beyond, the *Stavka* ordered Rokossovsky to regroup his forces northward toward Orel and cooperate with the Briansk and Western Fronts in a shallower envelopment of German positions defending the Orel salient (see Map 85):

> The advance by the forces of the Central Front is being held up because the Briansk Front has not been able to defeat the enemy's Orel group of forces, and the forces of the enemy on the right wing of the Central Front are threatening the forces of the Central Front with attacks against their flank and rear.
>
> The *Stavka* thinks that an advance by the forces of the Central Front toward Roslavl' is not possible without prior liquidation of the enemy's Dmitrovsk-Orlovskii group of forces.
>
> The *Stavka* of the Supreme High Command orders:
>
> 1. Temporarily slow down the advance of the forces of the Central Front toward Unecha and Pochep, while organizing reconnaissance toward the northwest and west with reinforced detachments.
>
> 2. Turn the forces of General Batov's, Tarasov's, and Chistiakov's armies from the west toward the north and northeast, with the missions to destroy the enemy's Dmitrovsk-Orlovskii group of forces and cut the railroad line between Briansk and Orel somewhere east of Karachev with the combined forces of these armies and, by doing so, help the Briansk Front liquidate the enemy's Orel group of forces.
>
> 3. After fulfillment of this mission, continue a decisive offensive toward Roslavl' with the forces of the Central Front, together with the units of the Briansk Front, with new resolve.
>
> 4. Begin fulfilling this mission immediately.
>
> The Stavka of the Supreme High Command
I. Stalin[240]

Specifically, Rokossovsky was ordered to consolidate his forces along the Usozha River and drive northward through Lokot' toward Orel, with the 2nd Tank, 65th, and 70th Armies deployed from left to right. Chistiakov's 21st Army was to join the attack as soon as his army was fully concentrated and fit to do so. Bagramian's 16th Army of the Western Front, which had already been locked in over two weeks of fruitless combat on the Zhizdra axis, was reinforced and ordered to renew its strikes, simultaneous to those by Rokossovsky. Completing this ambitious mosaic of offensive operations, in between Bagramian's and Rokossovsky's shock groups, the Briansk Front's 3rd, 13th, and 48th Armies were to conduct supporting attacks along the entire eastern perimeter of the Orel salient, and, to protect Rokossovsky's long left wing and exposed left flank, Kriukov's Cavalry-Rifle Group was to continue its advance westward toward Novgorod-Severskii on the Desna River. To the south, Cherniakhovsky's 60th Army of the Voronezh Front was to capture Ryl'sk and continue its attack westward toward Glukhov.

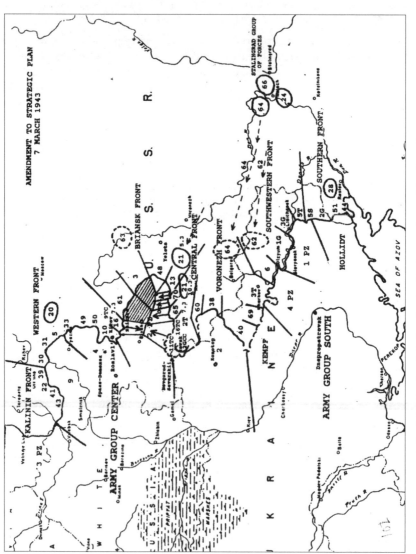

Map 85. The *Stavka*'s plan for the Orel operation, 7 March 1943

The Kalinin and Western Fronts' Rzhev-Viaz'ma Offensive (Pursuit) (6 March–1 April 1943)

However, even before the *Stavka* decided to reorient the axes of its offensive to destroy German Army Group Center's forces defending the Orel salient, the German OKH confounded Stalin's plans by implementing Operation Büffel, the evacuation of Army Group Center's Ninth and Fourth Armies from the Rzhev-Viaz'ma salient. After receiving Hitler's permission to do so in early February, between 1 and 31 March, Army Group Center initiated a deliberate time-phased withdrawal of its Ninth and Fourth Armies from their defenses around the salient back to a new and shorter defense line it had constructed between Velizh and Kirov. Although this delicate and tricky retrograde operation offered the *Stavka* an opportunity to strike the Ninth and Fourth Armies while they were most vulnerable, it also posed a less obvious threat to its offensive plans by permitting the Germans to regroup many of the divisions from its withdrawn Ninth Army southward to assist in the Second Panzer Army's defense at Orel. The *Stavka's* solution to this dilemma was to order the armies of its Kalinin and Western Fronts to attack across the entire periphery of the Rzhev-Viaz'ma salient as the Germans were attempting to withdraw.

Although few German or Soviet histories describe the fighting around the Rzhev-Viaz'ma salient in detail, depending on their perspective, those few that mention it either minimize or overstate the ferocity of the ensuing struggle. On the one hand, German-based accounts routinely treat Operation Büffel as a carefully planned and relatively peaceful withdrawal:

> Although the Army Group Center zone was quiet in the early winter of 1942–43 except for partisan activity, its front, in the long run, clearly was untenable …. On 26 January Kluge recommended to Hitler a large-scale withdrawal that would shorten the front and eliminate the danger of the Fourth and Ninth Armies' being encircled. As was to be expected, Hitler resisted bitterly, but finally, on 6 February, he yielded to Zeitzler's and Kluge's arguments.
>
> During the rest of the month the army group readied itself for the withdrawal, which was given the code name BUEFFEL ….
>
> On 1 March Ninth Army began withdrawing back its front north and west of Rzhev. In twenty-three days Operation BUEFFEL was completed. The units that originally stood furthest east had covered a distance of 90 miles. The length of the front in the BUEFFEL area was reduced from 320 to 110 miles.[241]

On the other hand, Soviet accounts, which term the Kalinin and Western Fronts' actions against the salient as the so-called "Rzhev-Viaz'ma offensive," describe the operation as a victorious penetration and pursuit operation that expelled German forces from the salient in relatively intense fighting. Documentary evidence now indicates that the Soviets did indeed attempt to disrupt the Germans' orderly withdrawal but failed to do so despite often heavy fighting. Specifically, it is now clear that Soviet intelligence organs detected the Germans' preparations to withdraw their forces from the salient, and, in response, the *Stavka* ordered the Kalinin and Western Fronts' armies around the salient to attack and disrupt the German withdrawal both before it commenced and while it was underway.

As early as 25 February, for example, the 369th and 220th Rifle Divisions of the Western Front's 30th Army struck the defenses of the German Ninth Army's 251st and 87th Infantry Divisions along the Volga River west of Rzhev and managed to seize a bridgehead on the river's southern bank. This action prompted a German account to speculate:

> Had the Russians expected something? The Russians repeatedly attacked the main combat line. The troops defended, and the enemy suffered losses. In the 87th Infantry Division area of operations alone, on 25 February the enemy achieved a penetration across the Volga into the forward-most positions, where they established themselves and could not be driven back. On 17 February the 251st Division realized that the enemy had already allocated his divisions for immediate pursuit of the Germans with tanks and was particularly vigilant. On 18 February the Russians announced over their loudspeakers, "The Ninth Army has packed up and is preparing to withdraw." Thus, the Russians did suspect something.[242]

The Western Front conducted similar operations in the sectors of its 5th and 33rd Armies during the second half of February. On 22 February, for example, the 5th Army's 29th Guards and 352nd Rifle Divisions assaulted the defenses of the Fourth Army's 35th Infantry Division east of Gzhatsk, tearing a small breech in the division's defenses. The 5th Army then committed, first, its 153rd Tank Brigade and a ski battalion from the 49th Rifle Brigade and, later, a full ski brigade, into the breech. After days of heavy fighting, the exploiting Soviet forces reached the vicinity of the German division headquarters at Leskovo on 26 February before counterattacking German forces encircled and largely destroyed the marauding Soviet force.[243] Thereafter, the Kalinin and Western Fronts ceased their offensive operations against the salient's defenses until early March. However, the *Stavka*, obviously concerned about the potential impact of the evacuation on its critical offensive in the Orel region, issued new attack orders to the Kalinin and Western Fronts at 1715 hours on 2 March:

> The enemy in front of the left wing of the Kalinin Front and the right wing of the Western Front has begun withdrawing his forces toward the south and southwest. The pursuit of the withdrawing enemy is being conducted sluggishly and indecisively.
>
> The *Stavka* of the Supreme High Command orders:
>
> 1. Immediately undertake measures to pursue the withdrawing forces of the enemy energetically.
>
> 2. Create mobile pursuit detachments from various types of forces under the command of brave and enterprising commanders and dispatch them into the enemy's rear.

3. The overall pursuit of the enemy must be guided by the offensive plan of our forces rather than by the march-routes of his withdrawal.

4. The *Stavka* obliges you to present an offensive plan for the forces on the left wing of the Kalinin Front and the right wing of the Western Front with regard to the withdrawal of the enemy no later than 2300 hours on 2 March 1943.

The *Stavka* of the Supreme High Command
I. Stalin[244]

Just as the *Stavka* demanded, the Kalinin and Western Front's armies began their pursuit operations on 2 March and intensified their pursuit of withdrawing German forces in virtually every sector on 4 March (see Map 86). Nor was the ensuing fighting bloodless. Since the Germans carefully prepared their withdrawal, most of the bloodletting occurred on the Soviet side:

> We must point out how carefully and logically the withdrawal plan was thought out. It went like clockwork. During the withdrawal, the enemy was tentative and later followed cautiously. At times, on 2 March, the rear guards had to repulse enemy scouts and even attacks by up to 200 men. Where earlier there had been nine groups, there were now only three. However, by constantly changing their positions, they gave the impression of greater strength and, by their accurate fire, beat the Russians back. At 1800 hours on 2 March, the rear guards evacuated the main combat line as ordered and, therefore, also the city of Rzhev.
> A Ninth Army report stated:
> 'On the evening of 2 March 1943, the last German rear guard troops left Rzhev under no enemy pressure. Therefore, in the interests of the entire operation and without enemy pressure, the army has given up an area that it fought hard for and successfully defended for over a year while dashing to pieces massive attacks by enemy formations and which the enemy still lacks the necessary strength to re-conquer. Thus, the Rzhev fighters leave their front sector undefeated, [a sector] which embodies the full test of being a soldier, and which, in the future, will inspire them to full combat readiness.'[245]

The same account then qualified the assertion that the withdrawal remained peaceful:

> On 5 March the troops reached the Sychevka-Belyi defensive line, which was held until 7 March. Fierce combat operations were conducted here, but the Russians did not achieve any success. For the first time, the enemy employed a seven-meter long motorized sled, armored in the front, with two mounted machine guns in the front and a propeller on the back. They attacked the companies obliquely. After being baffled for a short time by this new combat equipment, our antitank gunners destroyed one motorized sled after another, while the machine gun crews successfully engaged their crews and the unarmored side of the sleds. Seven [of these] lay in front of one regiment, and another eight were destroyed in front of another. The Russians attacked eight times without success. However,

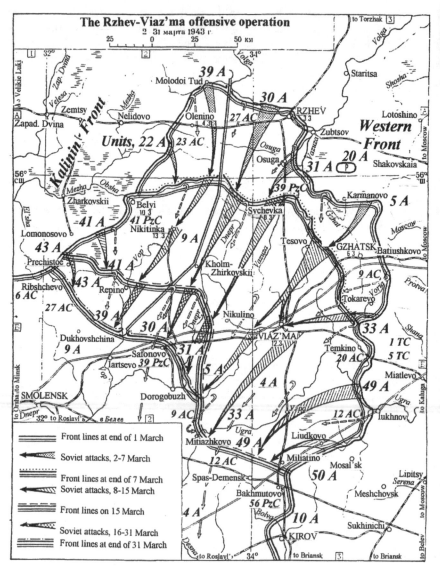

Map 86. The Rzhev-Viaz'ma offensive [pursuit] operation, 9–31 March 1943

local crises did emerge because the combat conditions in the largely primeval-like forest west of Sychevka, in which the Russian formations were attacking, were especially difficult. Also, the partisans were making themselves noticeable as they cut our telephone lines and shot up individual vehicles and advanced parties.[246]

Particularly sharp fighting took place during the latter stages of the German withdrawal:

> During the day, the enemy attacked with tanks after heavy mortar fire, and, later, the artillery would also support them. The troops defended themselves. Occasionally, the Russians would penetrate .... During the withdrawal on the evening of 13 March, the Russians pursued closely. They had no success and none again on 14 March when they attacked ten times. Bit by bit the divisions were withdrawn, some to occupy the "Bueffel" positions and some relinquished to other armies. During the final days, due to heavy losses, the enemy only pursued the Germans troops cautiously, who conducted the withdrawal in full order and with surprisingly small losses. The "Bueffel" positions were ready to be occupied and defended because, for the better part of seven weeks, over 100 kilometers of it was reconnoitered and constructed by 29,000 engineers, construction troops, and other support elements, and it was secured by wire obstacles and minefields and reinforced by shelters. The troops were able to face the enemy attacks with confidence. Timidly, the Russians advanced. They were, as the expression goes, "confronted by a veritable fortress." .... During the withdrawal, the enemy lost more than 42,000 dead and wounded. These casualties equaled the strength of almost six rifle divisions.[247]

Soviet and German archival materials now permit reconstruction of this forgotten, or at least understated, operation. Russian archival sources now indicate that the Western Front's 5th Army, commanded by Lieutenant General V. S. Polenov, began its pursuit on 4 March, with special reconnaissance detachments formed by all of its forces conducting probes along the army's entire front. Thereafter, the 5th Army formed a special mobile group consisting of the 153rd Tank Brigade, a ski battalion, and the 7th and 40th Aerosleigh Battalions [as referred to by Grossman's account], which, together with the army's 153rd Rifle Brigade, captured the abandoned city of Gzhatsk early on 6 March, while the remainder of the army advanced toward Viaz'ma.[248] The combined forces of the Western Front's 5th and 33rd Armies captured the Viaz'ma region on the evening of 12 March, with the 5th Army's 144th Rifle and 3rd Guards Motorized Rifle Divisions and the 33rd Army's 110th Rifle Division leading the advance into the city proper. The next day General Sokolovsky, the commander of the Western Front, committed two tank corps (the 1st and 5th) to lead his pursuit, and each of the corps employed their brigades along separate axes in support of the exploiting riflemen.

As indicated by the official history of the 5th Army, however, most Soviet accounts fall deafeningly silent about the heavy fighting that took place after 23 March, probably because these operations failed to achieve their objectives. Its account asserts, "While pursuing the enemy, the 5th Army reached the Bykovo,

Polibino, Teplianka, and Gorodok line by 23 March. Offensive action was halted along this line because of the spring *rasputitsa* [thaw]. Both sides went over to the defense,"[249] A notable exception to this rule is a far more detailed and candid account contained in the official history of the Western Front's 31st Army, commanded by Major General V. A. Gluzdovsky, which, after pursuing German forces from the Rzhev region and enduring several sharp engagements, most notably near Sychevka, encountered intense enemy resistance and appalling weather and terrain obstacles during the final stages of its operations:

> While developing the successes achieved, the 88th and 42nd Guards Rifle Divisions captured the regional center of Izdeshkovo on 18 March and, together with the 118th and 30th Guards Rifle Divisions, reached the eastern bank of the Dnepr River. The entire army forced the river on 20 March and advanced 20–25 kilometers toward the southwest.
>
> The roads had become completely impassible because of the spring *rasputitsa* [rainy season], even for horse transport. The impassible mud bogged down the artillery tractors and trucks. Extraordinary problems surfaced in supplying ammunition and provisions and evacuating the wounded. The situation required the organization of supply by aircraft and parachute drops. However, the heavy transport aircraft suffered heavy losses from antiaircraft fire and enemy aircraft and were unable to supply the forces with all that was necessary to continue the offensive. To this end, the commanders were forced to undertake extreme measures. Daily, each regiment dispatched a company or a battery to the Dnepr River, to which cargo was brought forward, also with difficulty, from the army and *front* supply bases. The soldiers traversed the 25–30 kilometers along field tracks and the sides of the roads. They returned to their units carrying as much as they could on their shoulders ....
>
> The situation in the army's sector of the front was also complicated by the fact that, during their withdrawal, the Hitlerites blew up and burned all of the towns and villages along the Viaz'ma River lines and turned the terrain west of the Dnepr into a "desert" zone. [They] blew up all bridges and culverts along the Moscow-Minsk highway and also road embankments along the edges of swampy terrain. The railroad was completely destroyed.
>
> Nevertheless, the forces continued to carry out their combat missions. On 22 March reconnaissance determined that the enemy 6th and 337th Infantry Divisions had occupied defenses along previously prepared lines along the western banks of the Vopets and Dnepr Rivers, northeast of Iartsevo, and further to the south along the Os'ma River. Here, he occupied a well-developed network of trenches and full-profile communications trenches, with a large quantity of pillboxes and fortifications protected by dense barbed wire and mine fields. After regrouping, the units of the 133rd, 82nd, and 42nd Guards Rifle Divisions attempted to launch an attack. Overcoming the barbed wire, the divisions' forward battalions penetrated the first trench line, commenced a fierce firefight, but could advance no further.[250]

Curiously enough, the 31st Army also employed several aerosleigh battalions (the 6th and 20th, plus the 37th and 38th from the disbanded 20th Army) in its pursuit operations.

The history of the Western Front's 50th Army also provides a brief description of its role in the offensive. The army, which was commanded by Lieutenant General I. V. Boldin, attacked on the left wing of the Western Front's shock force and then pivoted northward toward Miliatino to confront the German Fourth Army's XII Army Corps, manning strong defenses north of Spas-Demensk. Laconically, the army's history provides a skeletal description of the fighting in late March:

> The 50th Army's formations reached the enemy's main defensive belt on 17 March, where they encountered stiff resistance. Attempts to penetrate [the German defenses] failed in spite of the commitment of the second echelon 139th Rifle Division into combat and the subsequent reinforcement of the army with the 277th Rifle Division and artillery units. The army's forces went over to the defense along a line northeast and east of Spas-Demensk on 1 April.[251]

In reality, the *Stavka* did indeed order the Western Front to conduct a concerted effort to smash the German forces even after they had completed their withdrawal successfully, despite the obvious strength of the new German defensive line. Urged on by directives from the *Stavka*, the Western Front mounted twin assaults beginning on 18 March, the first by its 31st and 5th Armies in the Dorogobuzh sector and the second by the 49th and 50th Armies opposite the strong German defenses at Spas-Demensk. In the first instance, the 31st Army's 133rd, 82nd, and 42nd Guards Rifle Divisions, supported by tank brigades, assaulted German defenses east and northeast of Dorogobuzh but failed to do more than dent the German defenses (see Maps 87 and 88). Meanwhile, to the south, combined shock groups from the Western Front's 33rd, 49th and 50th Armies, with a total of about eight rifle divisions and seven separate tank brigades, mounted an even larger scale attack at Spas-Demensk. In addition, Sokolovsky committed the entire 5th Tank Corps in support of the 33rd Army and the full 1st Tank Corps in support of the 49th Army. However, hindered by appalling terrain conditions and heavy German fortifications, these assaults too collapsed in complete exhaustion by 1 April, after the attacking Soviet forces suffered heavy losses (see Maps 89 and 90).

The pursuit and penetration operations the Kalinin and Western Fronts conducted against German forces evacuating the Rzhev-Viaz'ma salient in March failed to inflict any serious damage on the German Ninth and Fourth Armies. However, the fighting was far heavier and certainly more complex and costly than previous accounts have claimed. Although not yet available, German losses could not have amounted to more then a few thousand soldiers killed or wounded. On the other hand, by official Soviet calculation, the Kalinin and Western Fronts suffered 138,577 casualties in the operation, including 38,862 killed, captured, or missing and 138,577 wounded or sick.[252] This toll in dead alone exceeded the entire combat strength of the 31st Army, which fielded 31,000 officers and men at the beginning of the operation.[253]

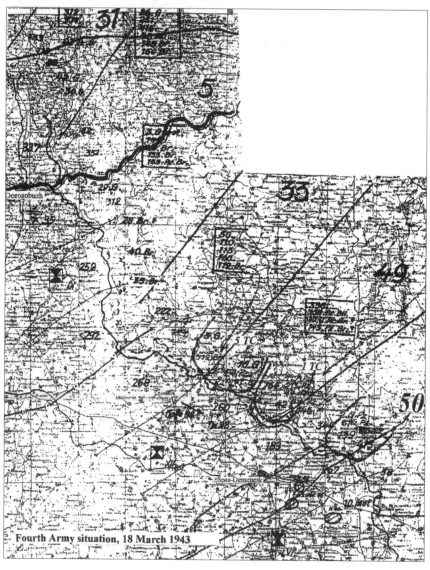

Map 87. The Fourth Army's situation on 18 March 1943 (the Dorogobuzh and Spas-Demensk operations)

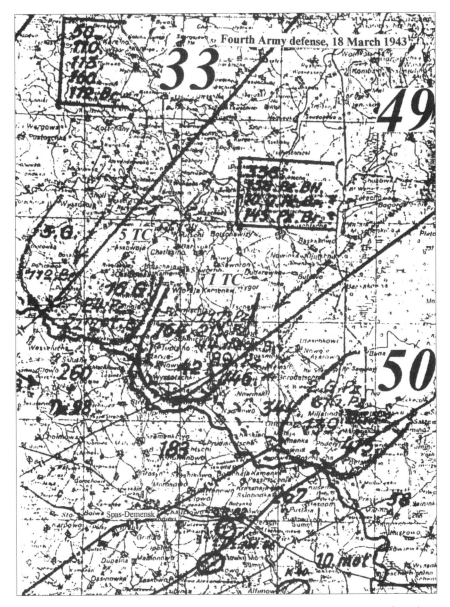

Map 88. The Fourth Army's defense (the Spas-Demensk operation), 18 March 1943

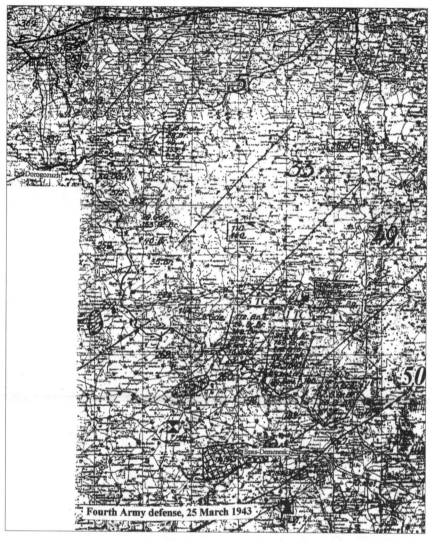

Map 89. The Fourth Army's defense, 25 March 1943 (the Dorogobuzh and Spas-Demensk operations)

Map 90. The Fourth Army's situation on 25 March 1943 (the Dorogobuzh and Spas-Demensk operations)

More important still, Army Group Center, by successfully withdrawing all of the forces of its Ninth Army and about half of those of its Fourth Army from the Rzhev salient without major losses, was able to shorten its front lines and dispatch many of the Ninth Army's divisions southward in time to reinforce Schmidt's beleaguered Second Panzer Army in its struggle with Rokossovsky's Central Front. For example, to Rokossovsky's increasing frustration, by mid-March Army Group Center reinforced the Second Panzer Army's defenses south of Orel with the Ninth Army's 72nd and 102nd Infantry Divisions, and more divisions followed by month's end.

The Central, Briansk, and Western Fronts' Orel Offensive (7–10 March 1943)

Revised Plans

Just as the Germans were beginning their withdrawal from Rzhev, Rokossovsky set about fulfilling the *Stavka's* new directive. The *front* commander ordered Rodin to reassemble his tank army south of the Usozha River and, in cooperation with Batov's 65th Army, deliver a concentrated blow along the Lokot' and Orel axis. Tarasov's 70th Army was to cooperate with Pukhov's 13th and Romanenko's 48th Armies of the Briansk Front in smashing German defenses from west of Trosna to north of Maloarkhangel'sk. Rodin, in turn, ordered Lazarev's 11th Tank Corps and the 115th Rifle Brigade to turn over their offensive sectors west of Sevsk to Kriukov's Cavalry-Rifle Group, march northeastward, and assemble on the 2nd Tank Army's left flank along the southern bank of the Usozha River opposite the Second Panzer Army's exposed right flank. This left Kriukov's fragile cavalry forces deployed in an operational sector of over 150 kilometers at a time when Weiss, the commander of the German Second Army to the south, was assembling forces to launch a concerted counterattack.

In addition to requiring Rokossovsky's forces to assault toward Orel from the south, the *Stavka* also ordered the forces of the Briansk and Western Fronts to renew their attacks toward Orel from the east and north, respectively. Bagramian's 16th Army, now significantly reinforced, was to penetrate through Zhizdra toward Orel, and Korzun's 3rd Army was to attack northwestward across the Neruch River toward Orel in concert with renewed assaults by the 13th and 48th Armies against German defenses due north of Maloarkhangel'sk.

Rokossovsky, pursuant to the *Stavka's* 7 March directive, ordered his forces to reorient their attacks toward Orel in three orders he dispatched between 1300 and 1830 hours on 8 March, all of which anticipated the early arrival of Chistiakov's fresh 21st Army:

[To the commander of the 21st Army, 1300 hours]

1. Units of the enemy 258th Infantry and 12th Panzer Divisions are offering organized resistance to the offensive of our forces along the Voronets, Trosna, Chernod'e, Krasnikovo, Grankino, Muravchik, and Rashnovskii Station line.

2. On the right and on the front, the forces of the 13th Army are fighting along the line through Verkhnee Tagino, the southern outskirts of Trosna, Lomovets, and Zhiriakino.

On the left the forces of the 70th Army are attacking from the Kucheriavka and Trofimenko line in the general direction of Volobuevo, Apal'kovo, Dashkovo, and Orel.

The boundary line on the left: Chern', Kutafino (incl.), Mar'inskii, and Antsifrovo.

3. The 21st Army, consisting of the 51st, 52nd, and 71st Guards Rifle Divisions and the 375th Rifle Division, will go over to the offensive from the Trosna and Chern' line beginning on the morning of 10 March 1943, pass through the combat formation of the 13th Army's Group Novosel'sky, and, while delivering its attack in the general direction of Kromy and Orel, maintaining close contact with the forces of the 13th Army, and protecting its right wing against counterattacks from the east, will capture [the following] lines successively:

10 March 1943 – Krivtsovo, Karavaevo, Progress, Hill 251, and Sergeevskii;

11 March 1943 – Bol'shaia Kolchevka, Kromskii Most, Malaia Dragunskaia, and Mar'inskii;

12 March 1943 – Shorokhovo, Ul'ianovka, and Volobuevka; and

13 March 1943 – Lavrovo, Malaia Fominka, and Rzhavets.

Subsequently, in cooperation with the forces of the 70th Army, capture the Orel region by an attack with part of the forces from the south and with the main forces from the southwest.

Leave the 67th Guards Rifle Division in my reserve in its previous position — Miroliubovo.

Have no less than one rifle division in second echelon and commit it before [reaching] Kromy on the army right wing and, subsequently — behind the center along the highway on the western bank of the Oka River.

Deploy the army CP in the Chermoshnoe region by day's end on 9 March 1943 and, subsequently, relocate it successively to the Chernod'e and Zakromskii Khutor [Farm] regions.

4. Submit your decision and order for the offensive by 1800 hours on 9 March 1943. Report on your forces' readiness to attack by 2100 hours on 9 March 1943.

5. Confirm receipt.

Rokossovsky, Telegin, Malinin[254]

[To the commander of the 70th Army, 1300 hours]

1. Units of the enemy's 258th Infantry, 12th Panzer, and 78th Infantry Divisions are offering organized resistance to the offensive of our forces along the Trosna, Chernod'e, Krasnikovo, Grankino, Muravchik, Strashnovskii, and Promklevo line.

2. On the right, the units of the 13th Army are fighting along the line through Verkhnee Tagino, the southern outskirts of Trosna, Lomovets, and Zhiriakino line, and the forces of the 21st Army, after passing through the combat formation of the 13th Army, will go over to the offensive from the Trosna and Chern' line beginning on the morning of 10 March 1943 and will develop the attack toward Kromy and Orel.

The boundary line on the right: Chern' (incl.), Kutafino (incl.), Mar'inskii (incl.), and Antsiferovo.

On the left, the forces of the 65th Army will attack with the mission to capture the Dmitrovsk-Orlovskii region and, subsequently, will exploit success toward Abrateevo, Zhukharevo, Shakhovtsy, Gorodishche, and Miud State Farm.

The boundary line on the left: Trofimovka (incl.), Gnezdilovo, Verkhniaia Boevka, and Naryshkino.

3. The 70th Army with attached reinforcing units will continue its offensive on the morning of 9 March 1943 in the general direction of Volobuevo, Apal'kovo, and Naryshkino and, while protecting its left flank against counterattacks by the enemy from the west and northwest, will capture [the following] lines successively:

10 March 1943 – Kutafino, Krasnaia Roshcha, and Egino;

11 March 1943 – Novyi Khutor [Farm], Verkhniaia Fedotovka, and Verkhniaia Boevka;

12 March 1943 – Pikalovka, Ostanina, and Novaia Zhizn'; and

13 March 1943 – the southern bank of the Orlik River in the Nadezhda, Opraksino, and Volodarskii sector.

Subsequently, capture the Orel region by attacks from the west and northwest in cooperation with the forces of the 21st Army.

Have three rifle divisions in the second combat echelon before the arrival of the first combat echelon at the Zhiriatino and Koshelevo line; subsequently — two rifle divisions, and shift them to follow the army's left wing.

After the penetration of the enemy's main defensive belt, demand a swift offensive from the forces and throw forward strong mobile detachments made up of tank, rifle, and sapper units — on tanks, on vehicles, on aero sleighs, and on skis, with the mission to cut the Orel-Karachev road and railroad line, seize the line of the Orlik River in the Dashkovka-Naryshkino sector, and hold it until the approach of the main forces of the army.

Have the CP in the Opeki region before the arrival of the forces of the army to the Kutafino and Kirovo line.

Relocate the CP to Krupyshino with the arrival of the forces of the army along the Verkhniaia Fedotovka and Verkniaia Boevka line; subsequently — Apal'kovo and Bogdanovka.

4. Confirm receipt.

Rokossovsky, Telegin, Malinin[255]

[To the commanders of the 65th Army and 2nd Tank Army, 1830 hours]

1. Units of the enemy's 12th Panzer and 78th Infantry Divisions, the 1st SS Cavalry Group, the 45th, 137th, and 707th Infantry Divisions, and the Kaminsky White Guards Brigade are offering stubborn resistance to the offensive by our forces along the Uspenskii, Strashnovskii, Promklevo, Hill 235, Kuznetsovka, northern part of Litizh, northern part of Usozha, Ugreevichi, Mostechnia, and Igritskoe line.

2. On the right, the forces of the 70th Army are attacking in the general direction of Krupyshino, Apal'kovo, Sebiakino, and Orel.

The boundary line on the right: Trofimovka, Gnezdilovo (incl.). Verkhniaia Boevka (incl.), and Naryshkino.

On the left, Major General Kriukov's Cavalry-Rifle Group is fighting along the Stegailovka, Dubrovka, Shatryshchi, Iampol', and Marchikhina Buda line, and the 112th and 325th Rifle Divisions — are defending the Lemeshovka, Strekalovka, and Skovorodnevo line.

3. The forces of the 65th and 2nd Tank Armies will continue the offensive swiftly, with the immediate missions — to destroy the enemy in the Dmitrovsk-Orlovskii, Lokot', Igritskoe, Ugreevichi, and Kuznetsovka region, and subsequently attack toward the northeast and north.

4. The 65th Army, with attached reinforcing units, will continue its attack swiftly and, while delivering its main attack from the left wing toward Khlebtovo, Uporoi, and Domakha, will capture the Dmitrovsk-Orlovskii region and subsequently, exploit the blow in the general direction of Abrateevo, Shakhovtsy, Gorodishche, and Miud State Farm, with the mission of cutting the Orel-Karachev railroad line and main highway and capturing the line of the Orlik River in the sector from the mouth of the Orlik River to Bol'shie Riabinki.

The boundary line on the left: up to Verkhniaia Kuban' as before and farther – Khlebtovo, Kavelino, Zhuravka, Borodino, Shablykino, and Krasnye Riabinki.

The CP, before the capture of the Dmitrovsk-Orlovskii region – Razvet'e. Subsequently, shift the CP to the Dmitrovsk-Orlovskii, Zhikharevo, and Shakhovtsov region, successively.

5. The 2nd Tank Army, with attached reinforcing units, will continue its offensive swiftly with two strong groups toward:

a) The 16th Tank Corps, 11th Guards Tank Brigade, and 194th Rifle Division – Komarichi, Radogoshch, and Gremuchee; and

b) The 11th Tank Corps, 60th Rifle Division, and 115th Rifle Brigade – Bobrik, Lokot', and Brasovo, with the mission to destroy the enemy in the Chernevo, Radogoshch, Lokot', Igritskoe, Ugreevichi, and Usozha Station region, in cooperation with the units of the 65th Army, and reach the Nizhnee Gorodishche, Stolbovo, and Brasovo line with its main forces. Subsequently, develop the blow toward Verebsk, Somovo, and Karachev with all of the forces of the army except the 194th and 60th Rifle Divisions and the 115th Rifle Brigade, with the mission to cut the Orel-Briansk highway and railroad line and capture the Karachev region.

With the arrival of the forces of the army along the Gremuchee, Nikolaevskoe, and Brasovo line, withdraw into my reserve and concentrate in [the following] regions:

The 194th Rifle Division – Gremuchee, Stolbovo, and Radogoshch;

The 115th Rifle Brigade – Brasovo and Lokot'; and

The 60th Rifle Division – Arkino, Luboshevo, Solov'evskii, and Komarichi.

With the arrival of the army's forces along the Liuboshch, Komarichi, and Bykovo line – relocate the army's CP from Dmitriev-L'govskii to the Latizha region and subsequently relocate the CP to the Radogoshch, Verebsk, and Somovo regions successively.

7. The commanders of the 65th Army and 2nd Tank Army will demand decisive actions and a swift offensive from their forces.

With the arrival of the forces of the armies along the Dmitrovsk-Orlovskii, Nizhnee Gorodishche, and Brasovo line, throw forward strong mobile forward detachments made up of tank, rifle, motorized rifle, and sapper units on tanks, on vehicles, on aero-sleighs, and on skis, with the missions to cut the Orel-Briansk highway and railroad line and seize and hold [the following] until the approach of the main forces:

a) For the 65th Army – the Naryshkino, Bednoty Station, Shakhovo, and Bezdrevo line (incl.); and

b) For the 2nd Tank Army – the Khotynets, Maiaki, Verbnin, Iakhontovo, Krasnaia Poliana, Kozlovskii, Trykovka, and Riasniki line.

8. Confirm receipt.

Rokossovsky, Telegin, Malinin[256]

The Central Front's Attack

Rokossovsky's forces began their new offensive on 7 March with heavy attacks in the 65th Army's sector against German forces at Berezovka, east of Komarichi. However, the offensive developed in piecemeal fashion due to the time delay in assembling the 2nd Tank Army's 11th Tank Corps, which was still deploying northward to its designated jumping-off positions. Despite the 11th Tank Corps' absence, Grigor'ev's 16th Tank Corps and the 2nd Tank Army's organic 60th and 194th Rifle Divisions, cooperating with the 65th Army on their right flank, drove German forces back to the Usozha River and, in desperate fighting, gained small footholds on the river's northern bank (see Map 91). On 10 March the 11th Tank Corps finally joined the fray and drove across the Usozha River toward Aposha, 10 kilometers southwest of Komarichi. By this time, the twin assaults by the 2nd Tank and 65th Armies were threatening to envelop and encircle all of the German forces defending south of Komarichi (see Map 92). These efforts, however, were in vain, for Schmidt's Second Panzer Army now shifted fresh reserves (the 45th and 72nd Infantry Divisions) into the path of Rokossovsky's forces.

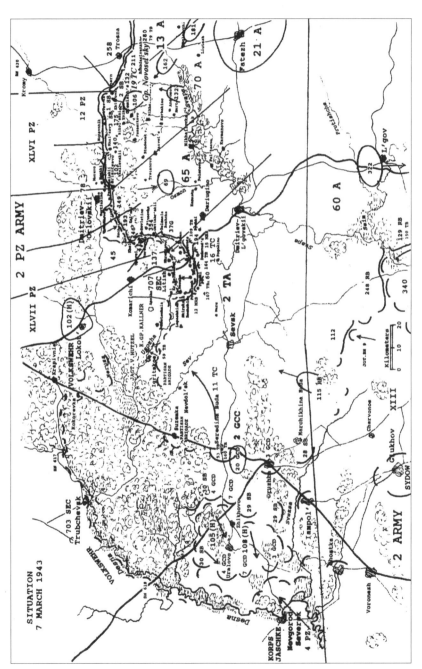

Map 91. The Orel operation, the situation on 7 March 1943

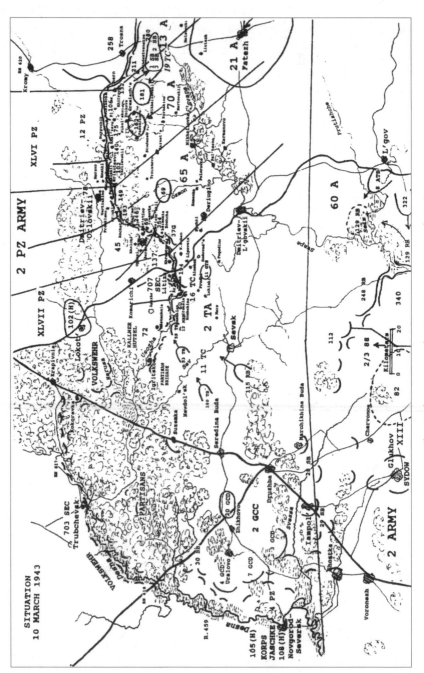

Map 92. The Orel operation, the situation on 10 March 1943

The Briansk Front's Attack

Meanwhile, farther to the east, the newly-arriving divisions of Tarasov's 70th Army and the armies of Reiter's Briansk Front exhausted themselves conducting fruitless frontal attacks against the German prepared defenses east of Bolkhov and east and west of Trosna. Reiter planned to launch his assault northwestward and westward across the Neruch River along the 55-kilometer-wide front from the village of Vasil'evskii, 15 kilometers northwest of Maloarkhangel'sk, northeastward along the river to the village of Krasnoe Pole, 25 kilometers southwest of Novosil'. Three shock groups from the 13th and 48th Armies were to attack in the southern half of the sector, and a single shock group from the 3rd Army was to assault in the north. Deployed from left to right in the 23-kilometer-wide sector from Vasil'evskii to Sandrovka, 20 kilometers north of Maloarkhangel'sk, the 13th and 48th Armies' main shock groups were to penetrate the defenses of the Second Panzer Army's LV Army Corps (the 18th Panzer and 383rd Infantry Divisions), cross the Neruch River, and advance northwestward to sever German rail and road communications routes south of Orel, and then march on Orel in tandem with Rokossovsky's 70th and 21st Armies, advancing from the south.

The shock group of Pukhov's 13th Army, which was to attack northward astride the Maloarkhangel'sk-Orel road, consisted of four rifle divisions (the 15th, 8th, 148th, and 74th), supported by tank brigades (the 118th and 129th). The main shock group of Romanenko's 48th Army, which was to conduct its assault in the Krasnaia Slobodka-Sandrovka sector north of Maloarkhangel'sk, consisted of three rifle divisions (the 399th, 6th Guards, and 16th), a ski brigade (the 9th), and two tank regiments (the 42nd and 43rd), supported by over half of the *front's* available artillery (see Map 93). Yet another shock group from the 48th Army, consisting of the 143rd and 137th Rifle Divisions, supported by the 28th and 30th Guards Tank Regiments, was to conduct a supporting attack further north by attacking westward along the Pokrovskoe-Orel road against the LV Army Corps' 216th Infantry Division.

In addition, Reiter ordered General Korzun's 3rd Army to form a shock group to conduct an assault across the Neruch River near Krasnoe Pole, 10 kilometers south of Arkhangel'skoe on the main railroad line running into Orel from the east. This shock group consisted of four rifle divisions (the 41st, 283rd, 287th, and 5th), one tank brigade (the 155th), and one naval infantry brigade (the 116th), most regrouped into this region from the army's previous attack sector north of Mtsensk. This group was to advance northwestward to cut the railroad line into Orel, engage the German XXXV Army Corps' 262nd and 299th Infantry Divisions to prevent them from reinforcing their neighbors to the south, and protect the right flank of the 13th and 48th Army's shock groups. Despite their imposing size and strength on paper, by this time all four of Reiter's shock groups suffered from the same problems – because they had been fighting constantly for more than a month, all were severely under-strength, with divisions counting as few as 3,000–4,500 men each.

Reiter's four shock groups began their assaults at dawn on 6 March. In two days of intense fighting, during which all four shock groups suffered heavy casualties, three of the shock groups failed to even dent the German defenses. The fourth shock group, the 3rd Army's force conducting the supporting attack in the Krasnoe

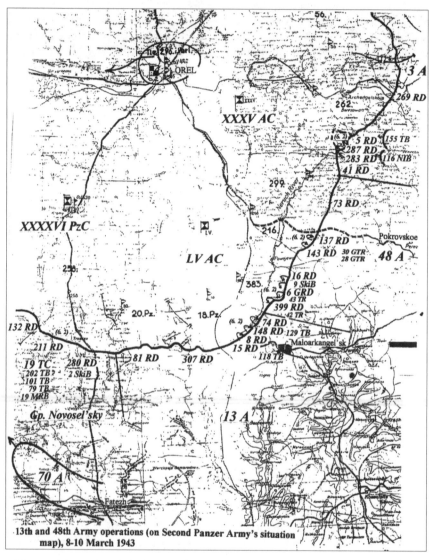

13th and 48th Army operations (on Second Panzer Army's situation map), 8-10 March 1943

Map 93. The 13th and 48th Armies' operations, the situation from 8–10 March 1943

Pole sector, recorded the *front's* only success by seizing a shallow bridgehead on the western bank of the Neruch River near Krasnoe Pole. As before, however, the defending German corps and divisions, their defenses anchored on well-prepared defensive positions covered by interlocking artillery fire, skillfully employed their tactical reserves to snuff out and contained the fierce but futile Soviet assaults. The daily report the Briansk Front dispatched to the *Stavka* at 2400 hours on 8 March reflected the *front's* lack of progress and the frustration of its commander:

> First. The shock group of the 3rd Army's forces was continuing offensive fighting along its previous axis on 8 February 1943. Stubborn fighting is raging for full possession of Vskhody and Vasil'evka and for possession of the villages of Krasnoe Pole, Kokurinka, and Dorogovskii at day's end. Four counterattacks by the enemy in strengths of up to a battalion each have been repelled.
>
> The 48th Army, in the sector of its shock group, had been fighting since 1600 hours to destroy the enemy on the eastern bank of the Neruch River, while replenishing its ammunition, fuel, and foodstuffs. As a result of the prolonged fighting, the 6th Guards Rifle Division penetrated into Panskaia and is fighting street battles. The remaining units of the army's shock group are fighting along previous lines.
>
> The forces of the 13th Army repelled counterattacks by the enemy along the Neruch River, dug into the positions they seized, and replenished their ammunition, fuel, and other types of material support on 8 February 1943, with the aim of preparing for a further offensive. The 132nd Rifle Division fought to regain the position it lost on 7 March 1943. Up to 100 enemy soldiers and officers were destroyed during the day.
>
> Second. The aviation of the *front* destroyed forces of the enemy directly on the battlefield, supported the operations of the shock groups of the 3rd and 48th Armies, bombed the railroad stations and forces of the enemy on the roads, and opposed enemy aircraft during the day.
>
> A total of 250 aircraft sorties were carried out. Up to a battalion of enemy infantry, field guns — 24, antiaircraft guns — 10, mortar batteries — 7, machine gun nests — 19, automobiles with forces and cargo — 20, carts with cargo — 30, pillboxes — 1, and dug-outs – 3, were destroyed, warehouses with ammunition – 4 were blown up, and 55 buildings – were destroyed.
>
> Seven enemy aircraft were shot down in 15 air battles, including 5 Fw–190s and 2 Me–109's.
>
> Third. The enemy is continuing to offer stubborn resistance to the offensive by our forces. The movement of columns toward the sectors of attack of the 48th and 3rd Armies at the expense of tactical reserves and the transfer of forces from Orel to Kromy and to the Zmievka and Glazunovka regions has been ascertained.
>
> The aviation of the enemy displayed great activity during the day. Up to 30 or more aircraft appeared simultaneously over the 3rd Army's field of battle and, in other sectors, from 10–12 aircraft. Overall the enemy carried out up to 200 aircraft sorties.

Fourth. I have decided: to rest and refit my forces, provide ammunition and foodstuffs, and improve the state of the *front* and army roads. [I] will continue offensive operations by the shock groups of the 3rd and 13th Armies and Group Novosel'sky.

Reiter, Susaikov, Sidel'nikov[257]

As evidenced by two reports Reiter's Briansk Front dispatched to Moscow on 10 March, there were many reasons why the assaults by his armies' shock groups faltered other than their relative numerical weakness and the utter exhaustion of their troops. The first of these reports, submitted to G. M. Malenkov, a member of the State Defense Committee, complained bitterly about his *front's* supply difficulties:

Two *fronts* [the Briansk and Central] are based on the one-way dead-end Elets-Verkhov'e railroad line, with a load capacity of nine steam trains. The roads operate poorly. Four trains have been allocated to the Briansk Front in this sector, which meet half of the daily requirements of the *front*. In fact, on average, one train per day serves the *front*.

The *front* planned to receive 212 wagons [railroad cars] with ammunition, 6,477 tons of fuel, and 746 wagons with food and forage during the period from 23 February through 5 March. We received 155 wagons of ammunition, 4,882 tons of fuel, and 233 wagons with food and forage. Of this quantity, 61 wagons of ammunition, 2,255 tons of fuel, and 85 wagons with food and forage have been brought forward to the final unloading station. The absence of food and grain resources, which, on the whole, have been exhausted in this region, has aggravated the difficult situation in the forces with obtaining food and forage. As of the situation on 6 March, the armies have been provided with the following foodstuffs and forage: the 13th Army – 2 days of rations; the 48th Army – 5 days of rations; and the 3rd Army – 10 days of rations (which must be brought up by auto-transport).

Provisioning of the *front* requires moving 7 transporters with ammunition, 4 with weapons, 11 with fuel and lubricants, and 40 with food and forage of the amounts already en route up to the *front's* distribution stations by 15–20 March. In addition, we must move forward 2,000 tons of automobile gasoline, 250 tons of *legroin* [unknown word], 250 tons of kerosene, 130 tons of grease, and 50 tons of diesel grease. It is essential that the NKPS [People's Commissariat of Communications Routes] immediately put the Elets-Verkhov'e railroad sector in working order and strengthen supervisory control and the technical operations of this sector.

The burden on dirt road transport has increased considerably because of the existing situation. The auto-transport we have on hand is insufficient.

I request that you allocate three automobile battalions to the *front* in order to organize uninterrupted supply of the forces.

Reiter, Susaikov[258]

The second report, to the commander of the Red Army's Armored and Mechanized Forces, contained similar complaints about the state of the *front's* armored forces:

> KV [tanks] – A total of 23 were lost, of which 12 were burned and 4 knocked out by artillery fire, 1 was burned by aircraft, 4 fell into ravines and burned, and 2 were missing in action. Ten were abandoned to the enemy.
>
> T–34s – A total of 29 were lost, of which 20 were burned, and 7 knocked out by artillery fire, 7 were destroyed by aircraft, and 1 sank. Five were abandoned to the enemy.
>
> MK–2s [British Matilda tanks] – A total of nine were lost, all missing in action.
>
> MESs – A total of 27 were lost, of which 22 were burned by artillery fire, and 5 were missing in action.
>
> T–70s – A total of 10 were lost, of which 9 were burned by artillery fire, and 1 from aircraft. Seven were abandoned to the enemy.
>
> T–60s – A total of 9 were lost, of which 3 were burned, and 1 was knocked out by artillery fire, 1 was burned, and 1 was knocked out by aircraft, and 3 exploded in minefields. Nine were abandoned to the enemy.
>
> We lost a total of 107 tanks.
>
> Sukhorukhin[259]

A report Reiter dispatched to the *Stavka* at 2400 hours on 11 March summed up the *front's* progress or lack thereof:

> First. The forces of the 3rd Army were continuing sustained offensive fighting along the previous axis while encountering heavy fire resistance. The forces of the army repelled three counterattacks by the enemy in strengths of one-two battalions each. The units are fighting along previous lines at day's end. Up to a battalion of enemy infantry was destroyed.
>
> The 48th and 13th Armies replenished their ammunition, fuel, and food and forage during the day. They conducted reconnaissance in individual sectors and repelled actions by small groups of enemy scouts. The 74th Rifle Division repulsed an enemy reconnaissance group up to two companies strong east of Pokhval'naia, destroying up to 120 German soldiers and officers.
>
> The units of Group Novosel'sky are continuing to be replaced by units of the 21st Army and are returning in the positions they previously occupied.
>
> Second. The aviation of the *front* destroyed enemy forces on the field of battle in front of the 3rd Army's front and operated against enemy aircraft during the day. A total of 65 aircraft sorties have been conducted.
>
> Destroyed: automobiles with troops — 15, carts — 4, field artillery batteries – 1, and up to 250 soldiers and officers. Four dug-outs were destroyed, and five antiaircraft artillery positions were suppressed by fire.

Third. The enemy in the sector of the 3rd Army is striving to clear the western bank of the Neruch River of our forces with counterattacks and strong artillery fire. He counterattacked our units three times during the day with a force of one-two battalions, protected by strong artillery and mortar fire and aviation, and pushed them back somewhat in separate sectors west of Krasnoe and Sergeevskoe. [The enemy], limiting himself to reconnaissance and fire activities, did not conduct active operations in the remaining sectors of the *front*.

Reiter, Susaikov, Sandalov[260]

The Western Front's Attack

As the armies of Reiter's Briansk Front expended their remaining strength conducting fruitless assaults east and south of Orel, the Western Front's 16th Army, now reinforced by fresh forces dispatched by the *Stavka*, also resumed its offensive towards Zhizdra and Orel from the north. Bagramian's army, attacking at dawn on 4 March, spearheaded its assault with a powerful shock group formed around a nucleus of the newly-formed 8th Guard Rifle Corps' 11th and 31st Guards and 217th Rifle Divisions and 125th and 128th Rifle Brigades, supported by three tank brigades (see Map 94). The 8th Guards Rifle Corps' shock group attacked southward from a 6-kilometer-wide bridgehead on the southern bank of the Iasenka River, 11 kilometers north of Zhizdra, while forces of two rifle divisions each conducted supporting attacks on its left and right flanks. Despite creating overwhelming force superiorities in his penetration sector, in four days of intense fighting, Bagramian's shock group registered only minimal gains of 3–4 kilometers at a heavy toll in casualties. The Second Panzer Army's Corps Group Scheele conducted its successful defense south of the Iasenka River with its 208th Infantry, 5th Panzer, and the left wing regiment of its 211th Infantry Divisions, reinforced by late on 5 March by the fresh 9th Panzer Division, which Scheele deployed forward from Zhizdra to reinforce his forward defenses.

After regrouping his forces and reinforcing his shock group, Bagramian renewed his assaults on 7 March; however, his forces managed to advance only a kilometer more before being halted by determined counterattacks by German tanks and infantry. After three more days of heavy fighting, his forces' staggering losses left Bagramian with no choice but halt the assaults on 10 March (see Map 95). Nine days later, Corps Group Scheele orchestrated yet another the counterattack with its 5th and 9th Panzer Divisions, this time driving Bagramian's worn out shock group back to its initial positions of 4 March (see Map 96). In retrospect, the 16th Army's offensive turned into a massive exercise in futility.

The German Counterstroke (11–21 March)

The Altered Strategic Situation

While the Western, Briansk, and Central Fronts continued their seesaw struggle to collapse the defenses of Schmidt's Second Panzer Army around the Orel salient, once again, events elsewhere disrupted the *Stavka's* and Rokossovsky's grandiose

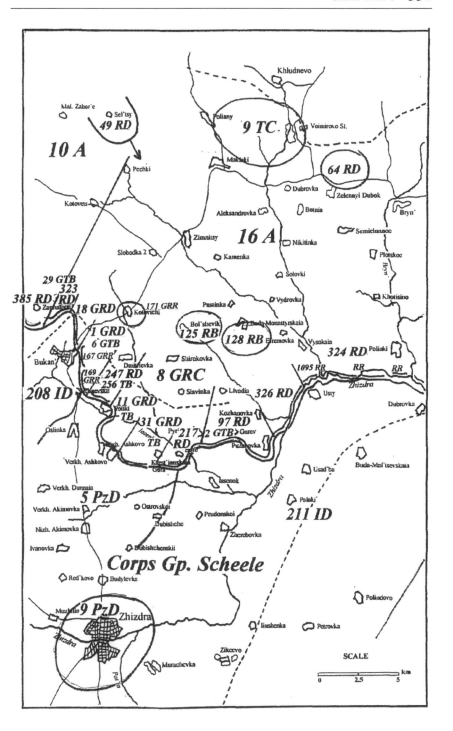

Map 94. The 16th Army's (Western Front) operations, the situation on 2 March 1943

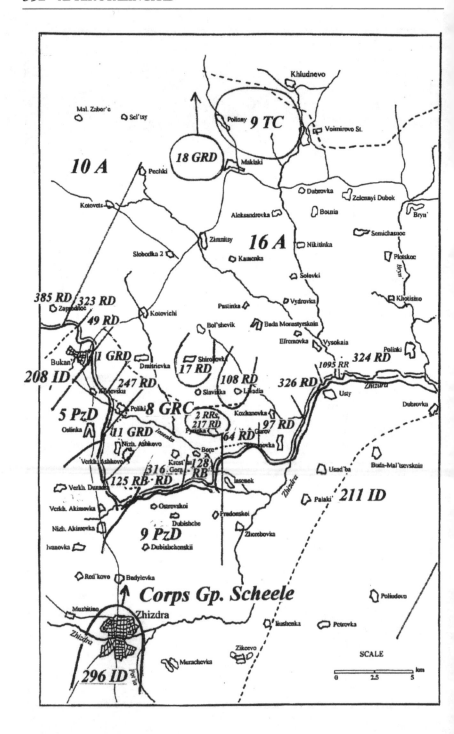

Map 95. The 16th Army's (Western Front) operations, the situation on 10 March 1943

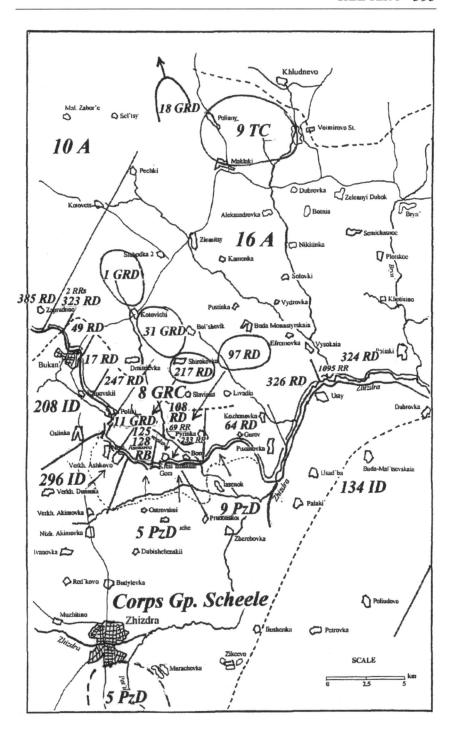

Map 96. The 16th Army's (Western Front) operations, the situation on 19 March 1943

plans. By the first week of March, the forces of Rokossovsky's Central Front, together with the Voronezh Front's 60th and 38th Armies on their left, had torn an immense breach nearly 100-kilometers wide and 140-kilometers deep in the German strategic defenses between the forces of Schmidt's Second Panzer Army defending the Orel salient and those of Weiss' Second Army, which was attempting to cover the broad sector extending from the Ryl'sk region, 100 kilometers southwest of Kursk, westward through Glukhov to the Desna River at Novgorod-Severskii, 200 kilometers west of Kursk.

By 7 March, however, Weiss's Second Army had completed regrouping some of the forces from the Belopol'e and Sumy regions in its center and on its right wing northward to his army's long left wing in the sector from Ryl'sk westward to the Desna River at Novgorod-Severskii. Weiss deemed these forces sufficient to begin conducting operations to close the yawning gap between his forces and those of Schmidt's Second Panzer Army. As a first step in this process, the forces of his army's 340th Infantry Division had already contained the advance by General Cherniakhovsky's 60th Army along the eastern approaches to Ryl'sk. With this threat addressed, Weiss then ordered the 82nd and 88th Infantry Divisions to concentrate along the southern flank of the forces of Kriukov's Cavalry-Rifle Group from Ryl'sk westward to the Glukhov region and attack northward to defeat Kriukov's group.

More importantly, at the same time, Weiss regrouped Lieutenant General Erich Schneider's 4th Panzer Division into the Novgorod-Severskii region, with orders to cross the Desna River and strike the nose of Rokossovsky's exploiting forces as they approached the river. Although still fatigued from the prolonged de-laying action it had conducted westward from Kursk, which it completed only days before, Schneider's panzer division attacked from the small German bridgehead on the eastern bank of the Desna River at Novgorod-Severskii on 11 March, striking the overextended cavalry divisions and ski brigades of Kriukov's Cavalry-Rifle Group (see Map 97). The Soviet light infantry and cavalry could not withstand the blow of even a weakened German panzer division and began withdrawing eastward.

The *Stavka's* Revised Plan

As Kriukov's diminished force recoiled steadily eastward, Rodin's, Batov's, and Tarasov's weakened armies hammered in vain at German defenses covering Komarichi, Dmitrovsk-Orlovskii, and Kromy, and the Briansk Front's exhausted 13th, 48th and 3rd Armies expended their remaining strength in fruitless assaults south and east of Trosna. In the midst of this looming crisis, the *Stavka* issued two new directives on 11 March. The first directives, issued at 0130 hours and addressed to G. M. Malenkov, member of the State Defense Committee, A. I. Antonov, the representative of the *Stavka*, and the commanders of the Western, Briansk, and Central Fronts, ordered Reiter's Briansk Front disbanded, assigned its 61st Army to the Western Front, and its 3rd, 48th, and 13th Armies to the Central Front. This expanded the size of Rokossovsky's *front* to six armies (the 3rd, 48th, 13th, 70th, and 21st Armies and 2nd Tank Army) and assigned him responsibility for controlling all Soviet forces along the eastern and southern faces of the German Orel salient so that he could better coordinate operations against the city of Orel.

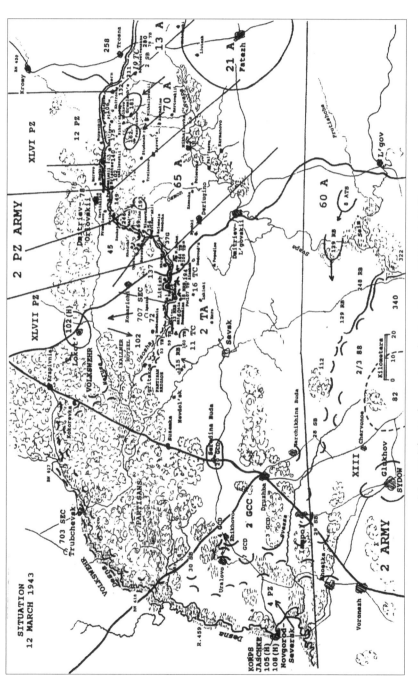

Map 97. The Orel operation, the situation on 12 March 1943

The *Stavka* of the Supreme High Command orders:

1. Disband the Briansk Front, effective on 12 March 1943.

2. Transfer the forces of the Briansk Front, effective at 2400 hours on 12 March 1943:

a) To the Western Front — the 61st Army, with all reinforcing units and rear service units; and

b) To the Central Front — the 3rd, 48th, and 13th Armies, the 28th Rifle Corps, the 19th Cavalry Corps, and all of the units reinforcing the *front*.

3. Withdraw the headquarters of the Briansk Front, with its communications, rear service, and road service units, to the *Stavka's* reserve in the Voronezh region.

4. Establish the [following] boundary line between the Western and Central Fronts: Plavsk, Medvezhka, Verkhniaia Zaroshcha, Dumchino Station, and Stal'noi Kon' Station, effective at 2400 hours on 12 March 1943. All points are [inclusive] for the Central Front.

5. Member of the GKO [State Defense Committee], Comrade Malenkov, and representative of the *Stavka*, Lieutenant General Antonov, will determine the composition of the rear service and road units and communications units of the Briansk Front, which it is necessary to leave in the composition of the Central Front.

Confirm receipt and report fulfillment.

The *Stavka* of the Supreme High Command

I. Stalin[261]

The second directive, issued five minutes later to the commander of the Briansk Front, formed a new Reserve Front, assigned the headquarters of the former Briansk Front, three new armies, and a separate tank corps to the new *front*, appointed Reiter as its commander, and ordered the *front's* forces to deploy into positions in the Central and Voronezh Front's deep rear to prevent German forces from advancing eastward to the Don River:

The *Stavka* of the Supreme High Command orders:

1. Form a Reserve Front effective at 2400 hours on 13 March 1943.

2. The Reserve Front will include:

a) The 2nd Reserve Army, consisting of the 129th, 235th, 250th, 348th, 380th, and 397th Rifle Divisions, re-stationed in the Elets, Lipetsk, and Lebedian' regions;

b) The 24th Army, consisting of the 68th and 69th Guards Rifle Divisions and the 84th, 214th, 233rd, and 252nd Rifle Divisions, which have arrived in the Ramon', Voronezh, and Davydovka regions;

c) The 66th Army, consisting of the 13th and 66th Guards Rifle Divisions and the 226th, 299th, and 343rd Rifle Divisions, which have arrived in the Ostrogozhsk and Alekseevka regions; and

d) The 4th Guards Tank Corps – in Kastornoe, the 10th Tank Corps – in Staryi Oskol, and the 3rd Tank Corps — in Alekseevka.

3. Rename the headquarters of the Briansk Front as the headquarters of the Reserve Front.

4. Appoint Colonel General Reiter as commander of the forces of the Reserve Front and Lieutenant General Sandalov — as chief of staff of the Reserve Front.

> The *Stavka* of the Supreme High Command
> I. Stalin[262]

Later on the same day, Rokossovsky issued an order of his own acknowledging the organizational changes in his Central Front mandated by the *Stavka*:

In fulfillment of Order No. 300702 of the Supreme High Commander, Marshal of the Soviet Union Comrade I. V. Stalin, dated 11 March 1943, I order:

1. Include in the composition of the Central Front, effective at 2400 hours on 12 March 1943:
   The 3rd, 48th, and 13th Armies;
   The 28th Rifle Corps;
   The 19th Tank Corps;
   The 19th Cavalry Corps; and
   All reinforcing units of the Briansk Front.

2. My deputy for the Rear [Rear Services], Lieutenant General Comrade Sovetnikov, and the chiefs of all of the supply directorates and departments will take account of all types of supplies in the transferred formations and units.

> Rokossovsky, Telegin, Malinin[263]

Despite the wholesale expansion in the size of his Central Front, the situation facing Rokossovsky's forces remained critical. The 2nd Tank Army's daily combat report for 12 March vividly described the dilemmas facing Rodin's tank army and Rokossovsky's expanded Central Front:

The army, having begun the operation on 23 February 1943, half-prepared, has been fighting continuously for 15 days up to the present. During this period the army penetrated the enemy's defensive belt along the Osmanka, Svapa, and Kharaseia Rivers. It smashed the 707th Infantry Division and one regiment of the Hungarian 108th Infantry Division and thoroughly wore out the 137th Infantry Division. Up to 6,000 enemy soldiers and officers have been destroyed, up to 1,500 soldiers and officers had been captured, and 220 populated points have been liberated, including the regional centers of Dmitriev, Sevsk, Seredina Buda, and Suzemka.

Considering that the operation was begun almost from the march, with limited quantities of ammunition and fuel and also in roadless conditions, and that the offensive has been conducted for four days by rifle divisions and motorized infantry with limited quantities of artillery and without tanks, it had led to excessive losses in infantry and motorized infantry.

As a result of the over-extension of the rear up to 200 kilometers, the absence of roads, and the extremely limited quantities of fuel and ammunition, especially in the rifle formations, less than 50 percent of the combat vehicles [tanks] and a similar amount of the artillery have been committed to combat.

The situation with regard to fuel and ammunition as well has not improved to this day, and the infantry and part of the tanks are continuing to fight, but whole units and formation remain the rear without fuel — the 10th Antiaircraft Artillery Division, the 1188th Antitank Artillery Regiment, the 37th Guards-Mortar Regiment, and up to 50 percent of the artillery and tanks.

The arrival of the army along the Suzemka and Seredina Buda line with its left wing and the turn by its main forces toward Komarichi and Lokot' has created a clear threat of destruction to the enemy's Orel-Briansk grouping.

The successful advance of the army to the west and then its turning movement toward the northwest and north has forced the enemy to transfer frantically up to three infantry divisions (the 72nd, 45th, and SS) and up to 100 aircraft into the Komarichi, Igritskoe, and Lokot' regions and occupy defenses along the Usozha River with the forces of the 72nd and 45th Infantry Divisions and a second defensive belt along the Nerussa River with the SS Division.

As a result, the forces of the army have encountered strong enemy resistance along the Nerussa River, supported by up to 75–100 aircraft sorties per day by bomber aircraft conducted in groups of from 3 to 15 aircraft, and up to 50 aircraft bombed the Litizh' region on 11 March 1943.

The enemy is counterattacking daily in strengths of from a company to a battalion, supported by 7–10 tanks, along the Litizh' and Ugreevichi axes.

The constant attacks and daily bombing of the combat formations of our forces have had their effect on the attacking forces.

As a result of the losses suffered and the lagging behind of combat support units due to the absence of fuel in the rear, the operational situation of the army and the correlation of forces to date is as follows:

The enemy:

With the objective of preventing the further advance of our forces toward the north and encircling the Orel-Kromy grouping, the enemy, after withdrawing the remnants of his 137th and 707th Infantry Divisions to the line of the Usozha River and having thrown new infantry and tank units forward, is offering stubborn resistance in the positions he occupies by fire and local counterattacks with infantry and tanks, with aviation support. The strongest fortified points in the enemy defense on the forward edge are Mal'tsevskii, Kozinka, Dobreichik, Ugreevichi, and

Mostechnia and in the depths of the defense – Komarichi, Lokot', Barsovo, and Krasnyi Kolodez'.

The enemy has in the first line of defense the remnants of the 707th Infantry Division (the 727th and 747th Infantry Regiments), the 133rd Infantry Regiment of the 45th Infantry Division, 124th and 105th Infantry Regiments of the 72nd Infantry Division, and 313th Security Battalion of the of the 532nd Rear Service Corps – overall, up to five infantry regiments, reinforced by artillery and tanks, and one security battalion — for a total of 16 battalions, are defending in the first line.

The enemy has two infantry regiments – a regiment of the 45th Infantry Division and a regiment of the 72nd Infantry Division — as divisional reserves.

The operational reserves of the enemy – the SS Division in the Nerusskikh Dvorikov region, the 102nd Infantry Division (Hungarian) in the Lokot' region, and the 7th Panzer Division situated in the Komarichi and Nerusskikh Dvorikov regions.

Artillery of the enemy:

Antitank — 167 guns; regimental – 46 guns; divisional — 120 guns; heavy — 35 guns; and mortars — 306.

Tanks: One tank [panzer] division with 70–80 tanks.

Aviation: up to 100 aircraft.

Our forces:

The 2nd Tank Army, which is operating on the outflanking wing of the Central Front, in cooperation with the 65th Army and the partisans, is destroying the opposing units of the enemy and will reach the Briansk-Orel railroad line and road, completing the operational encirclement of the enemy's Orel-Kromy grouping.

The army is fulfilling the main mission as part of the Central Front.

The army has at its disposal by day's end on 11 March 1943:

Infantry – the 194th and 60th Rifle Divisions, the 115th Rifle Brigade, the 12th and 15th Motorized Rifle Brigades, and the motorized rifle battalions of the tank brigades – in all, 35 battalions (which have suffered up to 40 percent losses as a result of 15 days of offensive combat operations).

Artillery – antitank — 135 guns, with 58 more guns approaching; regimental — 19 guns, with 4 more guns approaching; divisional — 42 guns, with 53 more guns approaching; no heavy artillery; mortars — 379 mortars; and multiple rocket launchers — 14, with 29 more launchers approaching. (The approaching artillery remains an average of 90 kilometers from the region of combat operations.)

Tanks — the 16th and 11th Tank Corps and the 11th Guards Tank Brigade – in all, 100 tanks operational, with 21 on the march from the jumping-off regions, and 41 are situated in the previous concentration regions without fuel.

Support:

— In ammunition – the 16th and 11th Tank Corps and 11th Guards Tank Brigade with one combat load each, the 194th Rifle Division – 0.1 combat load, the 60th Rifle Division – 0.5 combat load, and the 115th Rifle Brigade – 0.1 combat load; and

— In fuel – the 11th Guards Tank Brigade –0.3 refills, the 16th Tank Corps – 0.1 refills; and the 11th Tank Corps – 0.5 refills.

The distance of the supply stations, the poor state of the roads, the insufficient support by army auto-transport, and the absence of fuel and lubricants in the *front* and army bases and also ammunition in the front base at Fatezh deny us the capability of bringing necessary material means forward to support the operation.

For the normal course of fulfilling combat missions, it is necessary to have 3 refills of fuel for tanks, 5–6 refills for wheeled vehicles, and no less than 2 combat loads of ammunition for all of the formations of the army.

Conclusions:

1. The Second Panzer Army of the enemy, reinforced by the 72nd and 137th Infantry Divisions and 75–100 aircraft from the Western Front [western Europe], is firmly holding on to defensive lines along the Usozha River on the left wing and a series of populated points north of the Usozha River on the right wing, while launching local counterattacks supported by tanks and aircraft.

The enemy has as his objective to throw our units on the right wing back to the southern bank of the Usozha River and, subsequently, in cooperation with the Dmitrovsk-Orlovskii grouping, to go over to a general offensive toward the southeast.

2. The army, suffering great losses in infantry and motorized infantry, and also as a consequence of the shortages of fuel and ammunition and the stretching out of artillery and tanks in the deep rear, and having encountered new enemy divisions in the second defensive line, will not be in a state to fulfill its assigned mission with its existing forces and combat material until it brings all of its serviceable tanks and artillery forward and replenishes its motorized rifle and rifle formations with personnel.

3. The fulfillment of present missions notwithstanding, the absence of army reserves places the army in an extremely difficult position.

4. The absence of the army's artillery regiments denies us the capability of suppressing the main centers of resistance and artillery of the enemy. Based on the above, the military council of the army requests:

a) Do not begin the operation before provision of the army with fuel and ammunition;

b) Replenish the motorized rifle and rifle formations with personnel;

c) Reinforce the army with one rifle division as a reserve;

d) Cover the main grouping of the army with aircraft in the preparatory period and support the offensive of the army with bomber and fighter aviation; and

e) Reinforce the army with artillery of the RGK [reserve of the *Stavka*].

The main mission of the forces of the army during the period of preparation of the operation is to hold on to the positions it occupied, chiefly on the northern bank of the Usozha River.

Lieutenant General of Tank Forces Rodin,
commander of the 2nd Tank Army
Major General of Tank Forces Latyshev, member
of the military council of the 2nd Tank Army[264]

Rodin's report, which by this time applied as well to the condition of the Central Front's other armies, made it abundantly clear that his forces operating along the Orel axis had literally "shot their bolt." Faced with this grim reality, Rokossovsky's principal challenge was to protect his forces in the deep wedge they had carved between the German Second Panzer and Second Armies by preventing the Germans from counterattacking from the north and south and encircling and destroying his exposed forces.

The German Counterstroke (12–17 March)

Cherniakhovsky, the commander of the 60th Army, whose forces were operating in the Ryl'sk region well south of the left flank of Rokossovsky's *front*, was acutely aware of the threat posed to his right flank by the possible collapse of Kriukov's Cavalry-Rifle Group, which, if it occurred, would uncover his right flank and Rokossovsky's left. Therefore, on 12 March Cherniakhovsky shifted some of his forces, including the 129th Rifle Brigade and 8th Antitank Artillery Brigade, to his army's right wing to protect the southern flank of the gap by extending his army's front to the west. As prudent as this measure was, however, it weakened the 60th Army's pressure against the Second Army's defenses at Ryl'sk, permitting Weiss to regroup the army's 82nd and 88th Infantry Divisions westward into concentration areas from which they could strike the southern flank of Kriukov's Cavalry-Rifle Group.

Weiss' Second Army unleashed its counterattack early on 14 March, with its 82nd and 88th Infantry Divisions thrusting northeastward across a broad front east of Glukhov (see Map 98). These assaults collapsed the thin defensive screen manned by the 28th and 29th Ski Brigades and 112th Rifle Division on the southern wing of Kriukov's group and, coupled with the continuing attacks by Schneider's 4th Panzer Division against the main forces Kriukov's 2nd Guards Cavalry Corps east of Novgorod-Severskii, placed Kriukov's entire force in an untenable position. Kriukov was left with no choice other than to begin an agonizing but increasingly hasty retreat eastward and appeal to Rokossovsky for help.

As Rokossovsky heard Kriukov's calls for assistance, there was little he could do. Again events beyond his control had tied his hands. His assaults had recorded only limited progress south of Orel, the attack by Bagramian's 16th Army north of Orel had failed miserably, Reiter's supporting attacks had faltered, and Manstein's Army Group South had renewed its offensive, this time against the Voronezh Front's equally overextended and exhausted armies defending south of Khar'kov. To the apparent surprise of the *Stavka*, on 6 March Manstein's SS Panzer Corps and Corps Raus (which included the powerful *Grossdeutschland* Panzer Grenadier

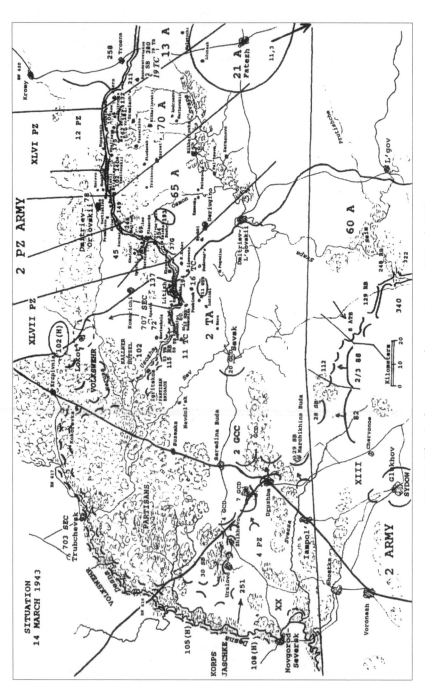

Map 98. The Orel operation, the situation on 14 March 1943

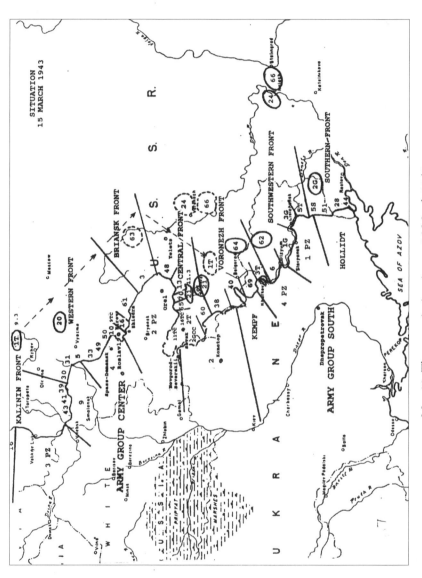

Map 99. The strategic situation on 15 March 1943

Division) struck directly at Soviet forces defending Khar'kov, took the city by storm on 15 March, and on 17 March struck northward in concert with the Second Army against Soviet positions around Belgorod (see Map 99).

Manstein's renewed assaults tore apart the Voronezh Front's 3rd Tank and 69th Armies and threatened the latter and the *front's* 40th Army with encirclement between Belgorod and Sumy. Any subsequent successful German advance would clearly threaten the southern flank and rear of Rokossovsky's Central Front. If the experiences of the Southwestern and Voronezh Fronts were an accurate indicator of German capabilities, the Central Front was indeed in jeopardy. For the first time in weeks, the *Stavka* now fully appreciated the deteriorating situation. The crisis was, indeed, real.

Reorganization of Soviet Defenses (11–19 March)

Spurred to action, the *Stavka* began implementing a series of measures it hoped could compensate for the offensive failures in the Western, Briansk, and Central Fronts' sectors and the embarrassing defeats suffered by the Voronezh and Southwestern Fronts. Although few in the *Stavka* harbored any illusions that the general offensive could continue, all agreed that damage had to be limited, and the Red Army had to preserve as many of the precious gains it had made during the winter offensive as possible. Therefore, it began reorganizing its forces frenetically in an attempt to find the right combination of forces necessary to contain the German advance and retain its gains. At the same time, it struggled to reconstitute its strategic reserves, including Reiter's Reserve Front, and it continued deploying its "Stalingrad" armies (the former Don Front's 24th, 62nd, 64th, and 66th) to the most critical points to back up its forward *fronts*.

Soon after the *Stavka* reassigned the bulk of the Briansk Front's armies to Rokossovsky's control, it dealt a mortal blow to Rokossovsky's expectations by transferring Chistiakov's 21st Army from his Central Front to the Voronezh Front's control. Although now fully assembled in the Fatezh region and prepared to join Rokossovsky's offensive, at 0200 hours of 11 March, the *Stavka* issued a directive requiring Chistiakov to move his army by rail to the region north of Belgorod. There, together with the 1st Tank Army, which the *Stavka* had already begun regrouping southward from the Northwestern Front's sector, it was to deal with the threat posed by Manstein's counterattacking panzers:

> [To the commander of the forces of the Central Front, the representative of the *Stavka* [A. M. Vasilevsky], and the commander of the forces of the Voronezh Front]
> The arrival of the enemy's southern group in the Kazach'e Lopan' region north of Khar'kov is creating a difficult situation for the Voronezh Front and poses a threat of the destruction of the Central Front's entire rear. The enemy has the intention to reach the vicinity of Belgorod, penetrate to Kursk, and link up with the German Orel group of forces to reach the Central Front's rear area.
> The *Stavka* has decided to move the tank army [the 1st] of Katukov toward the enemy who are advancing to the north with the mission,

together with the 21st Army, to smash the enemy's southern grouping and liquidate the threat created to the Central and Voronezh Fronts.

The *Stavka* orders:

1. Immediately move the 21st Army to the vicinity of Kursk so that it will reach [the region] south of Kursk no later than 13 March, intercept the main road, and begin an accelerated movement to the vicinity of Oboian'.

2. Provide Katukov's cooperating tank army with all possible assistance regarding its unloading and its movement forward as rapidly as possible side by side with the 21st Army.

The *Stavka* is informing you that both the 21st Army and the Katukov's tank army will be transferred to the subordination of the commander of the Voronezh Front on 13 March.

The *Stavka* of the Supreme High Command

I. Stalin[265]

At 0330 hours the same day, the *Stavka* ordered the 9th Tank Corps, which remained uncommitted in the sector of the Western Front's 16th Army, also to deploy southward to the region north of Kursk under the Central Front's control to support the 21st Army and the 1st Tank Army when they reached the Kursk and Oboian' regions.[266]

As Chistiakov began moving his 21st Army southward through Kursk to the Oboian' region, Rokossovsky's last hopes for inflicting defeat on the German Orel grouping disappeared. Furthermore, in addition to reflecting its increased desperation, the *Stavka's* decision to transfer Katukov's 1st Tank Army southward from the Staraia Russa region to Kursk to back up the Voronezh Front effectively ended its hopes for conducting a major offensive operation along the Northwestern axis and in the Leningrad region (see Chapter 5).[267] During this period, the *Stavka* completed deploying the Reserve Front's 24th and 66th Armies forward from the Stalingrad region into their new concentration areas in the Voronezh Front's deep rear area. It judged, correctly as it turned out, that the Voronezh Front's forces, joined soon by the 21st Army and 1st Tank Army, and backed up by the Reserve Front's 24th and 66th Armies, together with the Southwestern Front's forces, backed up by the 62nd and 64th Armies newly arrived from Stalingrad, would be sufficient to bring Manstein's juggernaut to a halt. As it turned out, the weather and sheer exhaustion did so shortly after German forces seized Belgorod, creating what would soon become the southern face of the Kursk Bulge.

The forces of Rokossovsky's Central Front attempted to continue their offensive operations south and southeast of Orel through 21 March, although on a far more limited basis than before. As he did so, the Central Front commander also regrouped a part of his forces westward to assist Kriukov in extricating his beleaguered cavalry and rifle forces from their precarious positions around Seredina Buda and Druzhba, halfway between Sevsk and the Desna River, back to new defensive positions around Sevsk proper (see Maps 100–103).

In mid-March, after Manstein's forces seized Khar'kov and Belgorod and while the German Second Panzer and Second Armies were liquidating the penetration by the forces on the left wing of Rokossovsky's Central Front west of Kursk, the *Stavka* once again reorganized its forces operating along the Orel, Kursk, and

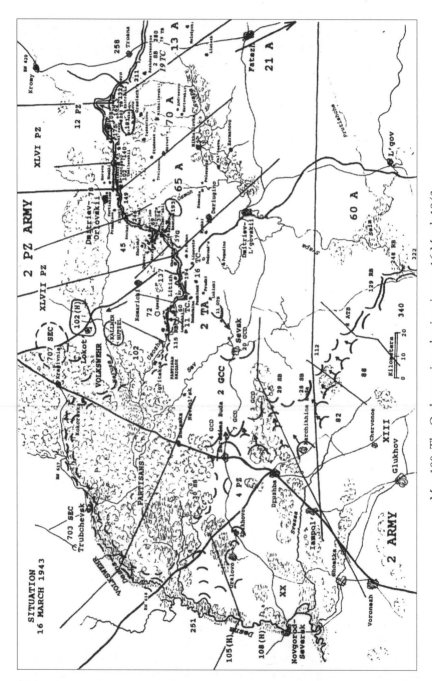

Map 100. The Orel operation, the situation on 16 March 1943

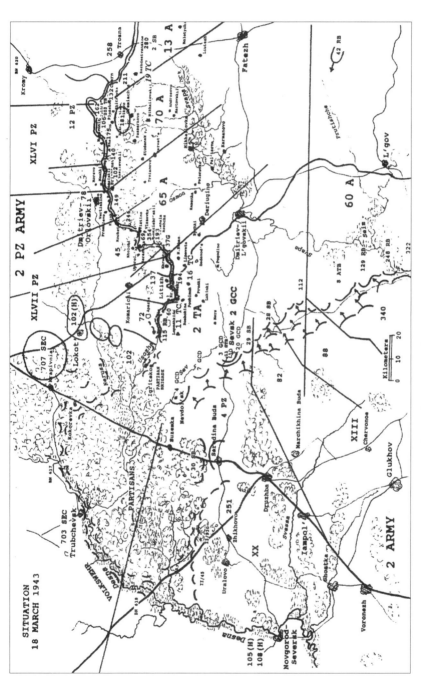

Map 101. The Orel operation, the situation on 18 March 1943

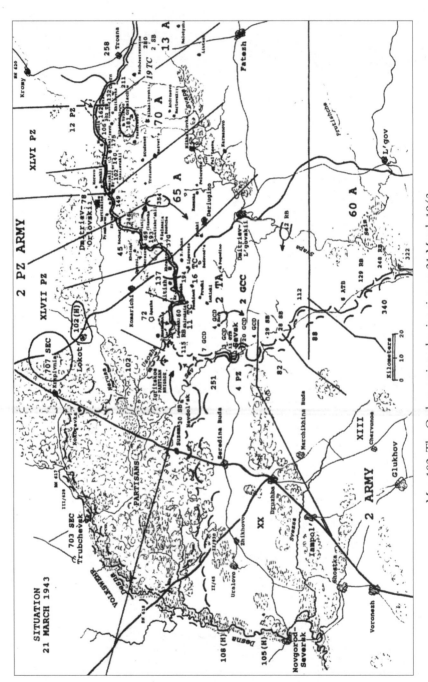

Map 102. The Orel operation, the situation on 21 March 1943

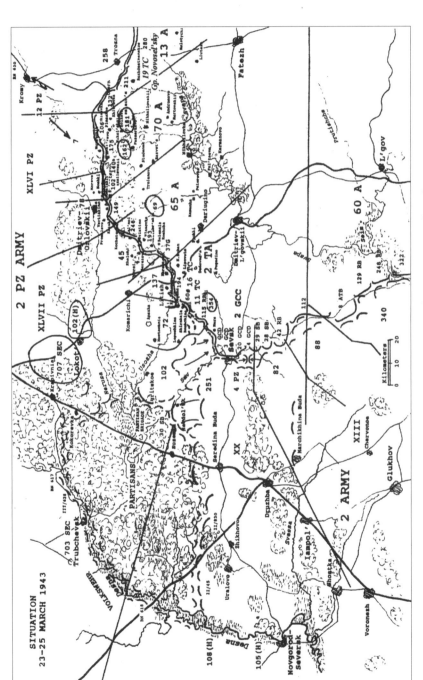

Map 103. The Orel operation, the situation from 23–25 March 1943

Voronezh axes. It did so to prevent German forces operating on both flanks of the emerging Kursk Bulge from capturing the vital communications center at Kursk and from inflicting further defeats on the forces of the Voronezh and Southwestern Fronts and continuing their advance eastward to the Don River near Voronezh.

Roughly a week after it abolished the Briansk Front, created the Reserve Front, and assigned most of the Briansk Front's forces to the Central Front, the *Stavka* began issuing a flurry of new directives designed to bolster its strategic defenses along the Orel, Kursk, and Voronezh axes. The first of these directives, dated at 0410 hours on 19 March, ordered the newly created 5th Guards Tank Army, commanded by Lieutenant General of Tank Forces P. A. Rotmistrov, to regroup from its home station in the Millerovo region to positions in the Voronezh Front's rear area:

> The *Stavka* of the Supreme High Command orders the 5th Guards Tank Army, consisting of the 29th Tank and 5th Guards Mechanized Corps and reinforcing units, with the army headquarters and all reserves of ammunition, fuel, and foodstuffs, to concentrate in the Pukhovo Station, Rybal'chino, Evdakovo Station, Khrestiki, and Kolomeitsevo region by 24 March 1943. To this end:
>
> 1. Immediately ship the unloaded trains of the army in Millerovo and all remaining units that have arrived in Millerovo by rail at a tempo of nine trains per day and disembark them in the Pukhovo Station and Evdakovo Station region day's end on 24 March.
>
> 2. Immediately turn around the army's trains located in the Liski and Millerovo sector and disembark them at Pukhovo Station and Evdakovo Station.
>
> 3. Unload all of the remaining trains of the army not passing through Liski at Pukhovo Station and Evdakovo Station.
>
> 4. Report daily to the General Staff about the course of loading and unloading.
>
> Confirm receipt. Report fulfillment.
>
> The *Stavka* of the Supreme High Command
> I. Stalin[268]

The second directive, issued at 1650 hours on 19 March, formed a new Kursk Front, commanded by General Reiter and consisting of the 60th and 38th Armies and the 15th Air Army:[269]

> [To General Reiter, the commander of the forces of the Briansk Front, and the commanders of the forces of the Central and Voronezh Fronts, with copies to G. K. Zhukov, G. M. Malenkov, and A. M. Vasilevsky]
>
> The *Stavka* of the Supreme High Command orders:
>
> 1. Form the Kursk Front by 2400 hours on 23 March 1943.
>
> 2. Include in the composition of the Kursk Front: the 60th and 38th Armies, with all reinforcing units, rear services, installations, and trans-

port, having removed them from the Voronezh Front. Have in mind the inclusion of one additional army in the *front* in the future.

3. Appoint Colonel General Comrade M. A. Reiter as the commander of the Kursk Front, Major General of Tank Forces Comrade I. Z. Susaikov — as the member of the military council of the *front*, and Lieutenant General Comrade L. M. Sandalov — as the chief of staff of the *front*.

4. Reorganize the headquarters of the Reserve Front into headquarters of the Kursk Front and station it in the Kursk region with it arrival by 21 March 1943.

5. Establish the [following] boundary lines:

a) On the right — between the Central and the Kursk Fronts: Voronezh, Kastorne, Kursk, and Novgorod-Severskii (Voronezh and Kursk — inclusive for the Kursk Front).

b) On the left – between the Kursk and Voronezh Fronts: Boromlia, Krasnopol'e, Peschanoe, and further along the Psel River to Kazatskaia and Staryi Oskol (all – [inclusive] for the Voronezh Front).

6. Carry out support for the Kursk Front with communications units, rear service installations, and transport at the expense of the Central and Voronezh Fronts.

Lieutenant General Comrade Peresypkin will determine the quantity of allocated communications units, and Colonel General Khrulev — the quantities of rear service and transport units.

7. Confirm receipt and report fulfillment.
The *Stavka* of the Supreme High Command
I. Stalin
Reported by telephone to Comrade Stalin and approved by him.
Bokov[270]

The Kursk Front, once formed, was to employ its 60th and 38th Armies, which had previously been operating on the Voronezh Front's right wing but had emerged relatively intact from the preceding operations, to defend the critical western extremity of the Kursk Bulge together with the Central Front's depleted Cavalry-Rifle Group. The *Stavka* also promised to reinforce Reiter's *front* with an additional army as soon as feasible, probably either the 63rd or the 66th Armies.

However, evidencing the complexity of the situation, if not its own indecision, the *Stavka* soon changed its mind and issued two new directives at 1200 hours on 24 March that countermanded its previous order. The first of these directives transformed the Kursk Front into a new Orel Front:

The *Stavka* of the Supreme High Command orders:

1. Instead of the Kursk Front, whose creation is no longer called for by the military situation and which is liquidated by this order, form the Orel Front, effective at 2400 hours on 27 March 1943.

2. Transfer to the composition of the Orel Front: from the Western Front — the 61st Army and from the Central Front — the 3rd Army. Transfer the armies with all reinforcing units, rear services installations, transport, and communications units.

Subsequently have in mind including one additional army in the *front*.

3. Appoint Colonel General M. A. Reiter as the commander of the forces of the Orel Front, Lieutenant General of Tank Forces I. Z. Susaikov and Major General of the Quartermaster Service S. I. Shabalin — as members of the military council, and Lieutenant General L. M. Sandalov — as the chief of staff.

4. Station the headquarters of the Orel Front headquarters in the Plavsk region.

5. Establish [the following] boundary lines:

a) Between the Orel and Western Fronts: Aleksin — Peremysl', Kozel'sk, Kliuksy, Belokamen', Zhukovo, Durnevo, Khvostovichi, and Zhurinichi – all points inclusive for the Western Front.

b) Between the Orel and Central Fronts: Kurkino, Efremov, Mikhailovskoe, Verkhov'e, Gorodishche, Nikol'skoe, and Stish' Station – all points except Nikol'skoe [inclusive] for the Orel Front.

6. Transfer all communications units, rear service installations, and transport designated for the Kursk Front, with their full complement, to the Orel Front.

7. Assign responsibility for defense of the meeting points [junction] between the Western and Orel Fronts to the commander of the forces of the Western Front and the defense of the meeting points between the Orel and Central Fronts – to the commander [of the forces] of the Orel Front.

8. Confirm receipt and report fulfillment.

The Stavka of the Supreme High Command
I. Stalin
Reported by telephone to Comrade Stalin and approved by him.
Bokov[271]

A second directive issued simultaneously with the first transferred the two armies on the left wing of the Orel Front to the Central and Voronezh Fronts and redrew the boundaries between the two latter *fronts*:

The *Stavka* of the Supreme High Command orders:

1. Transfer the 60th Army, with all of its reinforcing units and rear service and transport units to the Central Front, effective at 2400 hours on 25 March.

2. Transfer the 38th Army with all of its reinforcing units and rear service and transport units to the Voronezh Front, effective at 2400 hours 25 March.

3. Establish [the following] boundary line between the Central and Voronezh Fronts, effective at 2400 hours on 25 March 1943: Staryi Oskol, Dezhovka, Verkhnii Reutets, Soldatskoe, Lokinskaia Station, Korenevo Station, and Krolevets. All points except Staryi Oskol, inclusive for the Central Front.

Entrust responsibility for defense of the meeting points between the Central and Voronezh Fronts to the commander of the forces of the Central Front.

4. Confirm receipt and report fulfillment.

The *Stavka* of the Supreme High Command

I. Stalin

Reported by telephone to Comrade Stalin and approved by him.

Bokov[272]

By assigning the 38th Army to the Voronezh Front, this directive enabled the *front* to stabilize its defenses on a line extending from just north of Belgorod westward to the Sudzha region, forming the southern face of the Kursk Bulge.[273] Likewise, the assignment of the 60th Army to the Central Front made it possible for Rokossovsky to create firm defenses along the bulge's northern face, astride the dangerous Briansk-Kursk and Orel-Kursk axes. The newly formed Orel Front had the mission of protecting the eastern extremity of the German Orel salient with its 3rd and 61st Armies, with the 15th Army providing air support. However, for reasons that remain unknown, at 0300 hours on 28 March, the *Stavka* issued yet another directive, the last in this flurry of reorganizations, which renaming the Orel Front the Briansk Front:

The *Stavka* of the Supreme High Command orders:

1. Rename the Orel Front as the Briansk Front, effective at 2400 hours on 28 March 1943.

2. Confirm receipt.

The *Stavka* of the Supreme High Command

I. Stalin[274]

This process of reconfiguring and renaming the Red Army's operating *fronts*, although seemingly trivial, vividly underscored the *Stavka's* near frantic efforts to reorder the strategic offensive configuration of its forces into a force posture capable of conducting an effective strategic defense. If nothing else, it illustrated the scope of the battlefield setback suffered by the Red Army in February and March 1943.

Conclusions

The Red Army's ambitious Orel-Briansk-Smolensk offensive ended as it had begun, but with a whimper rather than in glory (see Map 104). Just as the *Stavka* began the offensive by committing its forces to combat in piecemeal fashion, adding layer after layer of new offensive operations to ongoing successful ones, the offensive petered out when regrouping and counterattacking German forces forced

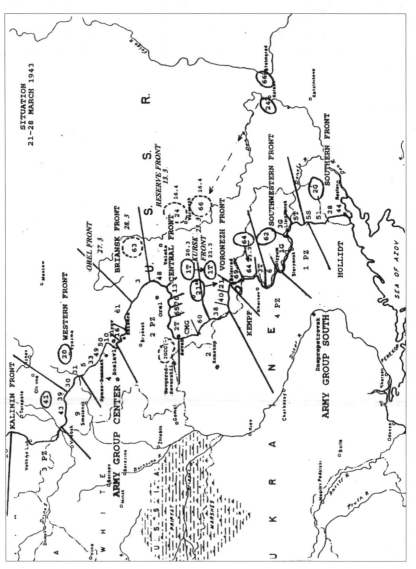

Map 104. The strategic situation, 21–28 March 1943

the Red Army's attacking *fronts* to detached force after force from the axes of their main attacks to deal with growing threats and crises on their flanks. Throughout this entire process, deteriorating weather conditions and over-stretched Soviet supply lines steadily eroded the strength and staying power of the Red Army's advancing forces. As a result, when the expanded winter offensive expired in mid-March, Rokossovsky's Central Front was left with only its initial objective in its hands, the city of Kursk and, with it, the associated infamous Kursk Bulge.

Soviet archival materials vividly underscore the problems the Red Army encountered during Rokossovsky's failed offensive. First and foremost, the *Stavka* and the operating *fronts* conducting the Orel-Briansk-Smolensk offensive required their soldiers, who were exhausted by months of near constant combat, to perform tasks far beyond their capabilities. The resulting high losses and immense human suffering were therefore predictable. The combat records of the 13th Army's 15th Rifle Division serve as a gruesome example. This rifle division participated in the Voronezh-Kastornoe operation in late January and February 1943, assisted in the seizure of Maloarkhangel'sk after mid-February, and then took part in the intense struggle northwest of this town for almost a month in late February and March. As a result, the division suffered 2,806 casualties from 13 January through 20 February 1943, including 683 dead, 1,581 wounded, and 542 missing, or about 25 percent its original combat strength. Thereafter, the division's agony continued unabated as it lost another 475 men, including 119 dead, 243 wounded, and 53 missing in the heavy fighting at and northwest of Maloarkhangel'sk between 21 and 28 February and 28 dead and 164 wounded on 17 March, three days before its parent army finally ordered it over to the defense on 20 March.[275] The 15th Rifle Division's personnel losses, which ultimately totaled over 50 percent of its original strength in mid-January, typified the losses suffered by most of the rifle divisions and brigades in the Briansk and Central Front's 3rd, 13th, 48th, 65th, and 70th Armies, as well as the Western Front's 16th Army and the Voronezh Front's 60th Army.

Understandably, since it played the most decisive role in the Orel-Briansk-Smolensk offensive, Rokossovsky's Central Front suffered the highest casualties, which numbered a total of 762,536 soldiers lost between 24 February and 31 December 1943. Subtracting the 428,546 soldiers the *front* lost during the Kursk, Orel, Chernigov-Pripiat', and Gomel'-Rechitsa operations during the period from early July through 31 December 1943 and the intervening periods between these operations, Rokossovsky's *front* suffered about 300,000 casualties, including roughly 90,000 dead, captured, and missing and 210,000 wounded during the period from mid-February through mid-March 1943.[276]

Rokossovsky was particularly upset by the losses suffered by Tarasov's 70th Army, which he considered unnecessary and excessive, especially those that resulted from the fruitless assaults by the army's divisions against the 18th Panzer Division's defenses west of Trosna between 8 and 17 March. According to Rokossovsky's reports, Tarasov's 70th Army lost 8,849 men and significant quantities of equipment during this period. In addition to these combat losses, as of 30 March it was short "7,802 rifles, 2,145 heavy machine guns, 326 submachine guns, 556 PPSh [sub-machine guns], 20 45-mm guns, 44 82-mm mortars, 93 50-mm mortars, and 240 antitank rifles."[277]

The armies operating within the *fronts'* conducting offensive operations in support of Rokossovsky's Central Front fared little better. For example, the Kalinin and Western Fronts suffered 138,577 casualties during their pursuit of German forces withdrawing from the Rzhev-Viaz'ma salient during the period from late February through 31 March 1943. This gruesome figure included 1,381 dead, 2,765 wounded, and 21 missing suffered by the 20th Army alone, as it attempted to penetrate the defenses of the Ninth Army's rear guards on 4 and 5 March.[278] Overall, Reiter's Briansk Front suffered 134, 903 casualties between 1 January and 12 March 1943, when the *Stavka* disbanded the *front*. This figure included 37,423 soldiers lost during the Voronezh-Kastornoe operation in late January and the first half of February and almost 100,000 men lost during operations in the second half of February and the first half of March. Thereafter, the casualties suffered by the *front's* former armies were included in the loss figures of the Western and Central Fronts.

Although the records of the Southwestern and Voronezh Fronts are still incomplete, fragmentary reports are indicative of the losses their divisions suffered while attempting to defend against the counterstroke by Manstein's forces in the Donbas and Khar'kov regions. For example, counting the replacements it received during the winter campaign, the *front's* 38th Guards Rifle Division, which began operations with roughly 10,000 men, suffered 12,285 casualties, including 1,997 dead, 9,740 wounded, and 548 missing, during the period from December 1942 through 1 March 1943.[279] Likewise, despite receiving 6,920 replacements during the same period, on 17 March 1943, the Voronezh Front's 350th Rife Division fielded only 2,557 men out of its authorized strength of 10,594 men. Despite the division's weakness, it remained in the field.[280] Finally, the Voronezh Front's 184th Rifle Division, which participated in the seizure of Khar'kov, fielded only 400 "bayonets" out its original strength of about 8,000 men by mid-March.[281]

Therefore, discounting the casualties suffered by the Voronezh Front's 60th Army in its L'gov and Ryl'sk operations, which have yet to be released, the Kalinin, Western, Briansk, and Central Fronts suffered combined losses of roughly one half million soldiers during the February-March offensive.

Considering the severity of these losses, the most intriguing question is how the Red Army's attacking *fronts* were able to sustain the offensive in so many sectors of the front. The fact that they were able to do so as long as they did underscores the effectiveness of the Red Army's personnel replacement system, which fed a steady stream of march companies and battalions into the forward area. This system was supplemented by relentless and often ruthless impressments of fresh levies from the newly liberated regions into the army's ranks. This process was exemplified by a report submitted by the Voronezh Front's 121st Rifle Division to its parent 60th Army in late March:

> The division took part in the battles for Voronezh, Kursk, and L'gov. The division suffered heavy losses in fighting for the Lukashevka and Soldatskoe line because of the unskillful leadership of the former commander of the division, Colonel [M. A.] Bushin, who was relieved from his duties. The division's strength was 7,025 men on 25 March 1943, of which 5,573 arrived as replacements at the expense of a mobili-

zation on the territory of Kursk region, which was liberated from the German invaders.[282]

At roughly the same time, the 60th Army's 248th Student [*Kursantnaia*] Rifle Brigade reported on its experiences with replacements:

[The brigade] joined the composition of the 60th Army on 30 January 1943. It took part in the battles for Kursk and L'gov .... The brigade operated particularly skillfully and energetically during the L'gov operation. Having been dispatched far forward to the Nizhne Chupakhino and Konoplianovka line (on the western bank of the Svapa River) on the army's flank, the brigade threatened the city of Ryl'sk from the north and, by doing so, essentially resolved the outcome of the operation for possession of L'gov. During this period, U–2 aircraft supplied the brigade with ammunition, and the division obtained its foodstuffs from local resources. The strength of the brigade on 25 March 1943 – is 2,389 men, of which 774 arrived as replacements by means of a mobilization conducted in the Kursk region, which has now been liberated from the Fascist invaders, and at the expense of the disbanded partisan detachment of Drozdov.[283]

Although the brigade had lost about half of its authorized combat strength, the report concluded, "The brigade is fully combat ready. Materials are being assembled for the awarding of a guards banner for [its] exemplary fulfillment of combat missions in the destruction of the German invaders, while displaying good organization and firm discipline."[284]

Despite the effective measures the advancing armies employed to obtain fresh levies for their ranks, some armies reported that their blocking detachments, which were formed either by the armies themselves or accompanying NKVD brigades to prevent soldiers or units from deserting, were not always fully effective. For example, an order the 13th Army sent to its blocking detachments on 16 March suggested measures to remedy the apparently persisting problem:

[To the commanders of the 1st, 2nd, and 3rd Army Blocking Detachments]

Replacements are arriving in the ranks of the Red Army from regions liberated from the forces of the enemy. With the objective of the struggle against possible instances of desertion and avoidance of military service, the commander of the army orders:

1. Strengthen the blocking duties of army blocking detachments;

2. Systematically conduct universal inspections of the entire male population in all population points;

3. Comb all forests and orchards thoroughly and examine all haystacks, uninhabited buildings, and especially dugouts situated along the lines of the old defenses; and

4. Strengthen the inspection of documents of those passing through the populated points and suspicious persons.

Report on all implemented measures by 25 March 1943.

Major General Petrushevsky, the chief of staff of the 13th Army[285]

However, the draconian measures the *fronts* and armies employed to obtain replacements for their divisions and brigades did not always improve discipline within the forces. For example, a 12 March report by the 60th Army's 121st Rifle Division, which it submitted when the army unsuccessfully attempting to capture Ryl'sk from the German Second Army, touched on disciplinary matters, providing a glimpse of pettiness that masked genuine morale problems within Cherniakhovsky's forces:

> The discipline of the [division's] personnel fell precipitously in the units of the division during the period of offensive combat operations. The soldiers and commanders ... no longer maintain their required military bearing ... [they] neither tuck in [their boots] nor salute their seniors in rank. Therefore, I am ordering:
>
> 1. Organize one hour of military training daily with all the personnel in all of the units of the division.
>
> 2. In the military training, first and foremost, work out [the troops'] external appearance (the correct wearing of headgear, the tucking in of greatcoats, waist belts, equipment, leg-wrappings, etc.) ... [286]

Given the inordinately prolonged duration of campaign, the high casualties, and the seemingly endless combat, it is understandable the morale of the officers and men alike began to flag. Among the many manifestations of this problem were the growing instances of drunkenness and self-mutilation among the troop and even the officers, as evidenced by a 31 March order Major General I. I. Ladygin, the commander of the 60th Army's 121st Rifle Division (General Bushin's successor), dispatched to his subordinate units and soldiers:

> Recently, a great many instances of behavior unacceptable to Red Army soldiers and commanders have been observed in the units of the division — drinking binges, which, to a great degree, have spread among the command personnel. Instead of ceasing this unnecessary phenomenon, in some instances the commanders of units and subunits are encouraging these persons and often themselves participating in the brawls, which lead to a loss of Red Army's soldiers state of mind and, in other instances, to the divulging of military secrets. Persons in an inebriated state are using weapons in all instances of drunkenness, and, as a result, unnecessary and completely unwarranted losses occur. On 27 March 1943, while in an inebriated state and without cause, the commander of an automatic weapons company in the 383rd Rifle Regiment, Senior Lieutenant Remizov, shot two Red Army soldiers in a burst of submachine gun fire.
>
> The commander of the 121st Rifle Division, Major General Ladygin
> The chief of staff of the 121st Rifle Division, Lieutenant Colonel Generalov [287]

Batov acknowledged a similar deterioration of discipline is his 65th Army in an order he issued on 25 March 1943:

The presence of unstable elements, carrying out various crimes motivated by cowardice, has appeared in the units of our army during the course of active combat operations. Among these crimes, self-mutilation [self-inflicted wounds] is found to have been especially widespread. During the first half of March 1943 alone, 22 men have been exposed and judged as self-mutilators in the 246th Rifle Division alone, of which the largest portion have appeared in the 908th Rifle Regiment. Self-mutilation is the most widespread in the 37th Guards, 246th, and 354th Rifle Divisions ....

> The commander of the 65th Army, Lieutenant General Batov
> The member of the Military Council, Colonel Luchko
> The chief of staff of the army, Major General Glebov[288]

Numerous archival documents contain extensive self-critiques by the forces conducting the offensive themselves and General Staff observers, as well as lessons-learned from combat experiences, which the General Staff later studied to improve the combat performance of its armies in the future. While these documents address virtually every facet of these operations, the most valuable focused on how to conduct combined-arms operations in the harsh conditions of the winter and spring *rasputitsa* [rainy season]. For example, during the early stages of the operation, the 13th Army's chief of staff and Operational Department directed the army's divisions to "cease employing infantrymen in attacks without artillery support."[289] On 3 February, The Briansk Front, before commencing its pursuit westward toward Orel and Kursk, issued the forces of its 13th and 48th Armies detailed instructions regarding infantry tactics:

> The experience of the initial fighting shows that a number of commanders of units and subunits are violating the Infantry Combat Regulations. Some parts of the commanders are situating themselves in the general lines and, sometimes, even in front of their subunits. As a result, units have suffered unnecessary losses of command cadre ... command and control is lost, and the tempo of the offensive is decreased .... Thus, in the 132nd Rifle Division, the division lost 167 mid-level command cadre alone during three days of combat operations. In addition, two deputy division commanders, the chief of staff of a regiment, a deputy regimental commander for political affairs, and a number of others were put out of action.
>
> I order:
>
> 1. All commanders of formations and units to lead strictly in accordance with the Infantry Combat Regulations. I will severely punish for deviating from the Regulations during offensive operations.
>
> Reiter, Susaikov, Sandalov[290]

Sometimes, however, these and similar orders seemed to be contradictory. For example, on 4 February Reiter and his colleagues criticized the 13th and 48th Armies for the reverse problem:

> The experience of the offensive fighting of the 13th Army and especially the 48th Army shows that the weak command and control of forces on

the battlefield depends chiefly on the fact that the commanders of divisions and even battalions are directing the battle from warm peasant houses in populated points with the help of telephones .... rather than from their command posts, from which they would be able to see the battle on the main axis.

I order:

1. The commanders of divisions, regiments, and battalions to direct the fighting exclusively from their command posts so that they can better see the field of battle on the main axis and respond to the situation in more timely fashion ...

Inform the commanders of divisions, regiments, and battalions of this directive without delay.

Reiter, Susaikov, Sandalov[291]

Still other combat reports, including a 1 February order by the Briansk Front, provided clear evidence that the attrition suffered by the forces was indeed undermining troop discipline during operation, in this case including numerous instances of looting:

It has been established that, when occupying populated points liberated from the enemy, the chiefs of the armies' rear services and the commanders of corps and divisions are not immediately appointing garrison commandants and are not establishing necessary military order. In light of such a situation, stations along the railroad line, public and state buildings and facilities, trophy property, and other material of value are not being protected at all, and property is being plundered.

I order:

1. When occupying a populated point immediately appoint a chief of garrison and commandant to set about fulfilling their responsibilities and establishing revolutionary order.[292]

Above and beyond the high attrition rate and associated disciplinary problems among the Red Army's forces, archival documents indicate that poor logistical support represented the most serious Achilles heel for advancing Soviet forces and one of the primary reasons why the offensive ultimately failed. Among the many documents identifying this problem was an order the Briansk Front order issued to its subordinate units on 6 February, which stated, "Demand that rear service units be more agile when supplying units with all necessities. Do not simply note the fact that foodstuffs, ammunition, and fuel are absent, but instead implement yourself all measures necessary to supply the units with all necessities and, by doing so, support the successful offensive battles."[293]

Another directive issued by the Briansk Front on 17 February criticized the poor cooperation between tank and infantry forces and, once again, also linked this recurring problem with persistent logistical difficulties:

The employment of the *front's* tank forces during the recent combat period shows that, in connection with the snowdrifts and the considerable gap between the tank units and the armies' forward supply bases, a considerable quantity of tanks are not taking part in the fighting because of insufficient fuel and ammunition. The combined-arms commanders with which the tanks are cooperating are not evidencing concerns about their support and are not providing them with assistance. By failing to do so they are violating NKO USSR's Order No. 325.

I order:

1. Place responsibility for combat support of the tanks on the combined-arms commanders with which the tank units are cooperating and on the commanders of the tank units.

2. Employ all types of transport, including the cart [horse] transport of the rifle divisions and regiments, for the support of tank units with POL and ammunition.[294]

Often, the wholesale congestion along the few snowbound roads prompted force commanders to take the easy way out by positioning their headquarters lumped together in the warmth and relative comfort of buildings and houses in towns and villages. As indicated by a 17 February Briansk Front report about the 48th Army's operations east of Maloarkhangel'sk, this indiscretion created lucrative targets for Germans gunners and aircraft and frequently produced costly casualties among command cadre and their staffs:

Subject: Concerning the inadmissibility of [having] a great number of headquarters of formations and units in a single populated point. On 11–12 February, the headquarters of the 137th Rifle Division, the headquarters of the 12th Artillery Division, and the headquarters of a guards-mortar regiment gathered in the village of Markino .... On 12 February enemy aircraft bombed the village of Markino .... We had intolerable losses in men and equipment.

I order:

1. Do not permit the placing of several headquarters in a single populated point. The commanders of formations and units will place their headquarters in the offensive sectors of their own formations/units;

2. When placing headquarters and forces in a populated point, carefully conceal them from the air; and

3. In all instances, the chiefs of staff will provide antiaircraft measures and organize the repulsion of enemy air raids with not only existing weaponry but also with infantry weapons (rifles, machine guns, antitank rifles, etc.).[295]

Another combat report prepared by the 13th Army on 2 March, a week after the army's second major assault north of Maloarkhangel'sk, catalogued some of the recurring command deficiencies in the conduct of tactical combat by the units of Pukhov's army:

The offensive fighting conducted by the units of the army revealed a number of existing deficiencies in the tactical operations of the forces:

1. The established requirement that battalion commanders be granted 2–3 hours of daylight to organize cooperation between tanks and artillery on the ground and within the battalions is being overlooked or forgotten .… The attack against the enemy was delivered without the concentration of forces and weaponry along the required axis at the requisite moment of combat .…

3. The requirement for continuous reconnaissance is being entirely forgotten.

4. The attack is being carried out in disorganized fashion, there is no swiftness and deception, and advances [rushes] are excessively long …

5. The commanders of the units are frequently forgetting to develop the success of their subunits in timely fashion, and they are not exploiting weak spots in the enemy's defense for decisive movement forward and the envelopment of his strong points.

6. Recently, separate instances have taken place of nothing less than unwarranted withdrawals by separate subunits and even units under attack by counterattacking enemy battalions and companies.

7. The enemy is very sensitive to night attacks and fears them; nevertheless, often the night attacks have no success. This can be explained by the absence of the element of surprise and weak discipline in a night attack (clamor and noise).

8. During fighting in populated points, assault groups are being employed insufficiently, and fire from indirect fire guns is seldom being applied in practice .…

9. Infantry weapons and antitank rifles are seldom used to combat low-flying aircraft, and, when they are, they are employed in disorganized fashion .… Infantry weapons can successfully conduct combat with enemy aircraft .…

12. The regulation requires the elimination of all possible intervals between the end of the artillery preparation and the beginning of the attack.

Indeed, these requirements are not being observed. Often the infantry is late in going over to the attack (such as the 148th Rifle Division), and the enemy regains his senses … and meets the attackers with organized fires.

> The commander of the 13th Army, Lieutenant General Pukhov
> The member of the Military Council, Major General Kozlov
> The chief of staff of the 13th Army, Major General Petrushevsky[296]

Despite Pukhov's protestation, these and other related problems persisted in his army until the very end of the offensive and continued contributing to unnecessarily high casualties, as evidenced by an order issued by the army on 21 March:

Combat operations have of late been limited to only night raids ["snatches"] by small groups of reconnaissance scouts; however, the losses of the forces in conditions of the lull along the front remain considerable. During the period from 1 through 20 March 1943, the army has lost 555 men, including 108 command personnel and 59 horses. The main reasons for this situation, which will be intolerable in the future, are the absence of required order in the forward edge of the defense, the failure to observe elementary *maskirovka* [camouflage] measures and the absence of a struggle against senseless losses in combat personnel.

> The chief of staff of the 13th Army, Major General Petrushevsky
> The chief of the 13th Army's Operational Department, Colonel Grechikhin,[297]

The records of the Central Front and its subordinate armies also cast considerable light on the employment of penal battalions and companies in combat, which was apparently both routine and extensive. For example, on 18 March the Central Front issued a directive lamenting the failure of the *front's* armies to employ penal subunits properly throughout the offensive:

> An investigation has established the following facts regarding treachery to the Homeland that took place in the 13th, 70th, 65th, and 48th Armies:
>
> ....
>
> 4. Weak discipline and unsatisfactory organizational work in the training and education of the rank-and-file personnel of penal companies and battalions and the flagrant violation of NKO USSR Order No. 227 regarding the employment of penal subunits. Especially intolerable was the fact of the desertion to the enemy side of 19 men from the 179th Penal Company of the 13th Army's 148th Rifle Division, who had been dispatched on reconnaissance by the commander of the division, Major General [A. A.] Mishchenko. The commander of the 148th Rifle Division grossly violated the NKO USSR's Order No. 227, which envisioned the employment of penal subunits for particularly difficult missions, with obligatory allocation of blocking detachments following after them, and this was not done in the 148th Rifle Division, the penal troops displayed cowardice, a portion of them fled from the field of battle, and 19 men surrendered to the enemy. The command personnel in that company did not train its personnel satisfactorily, and, evidently, the representatives of the special department [*osobyi otdel*] worked ineffectively, since the squad's timely preparations for treachery remained unknown to them.
>
> The Military Council of the *front* demands that: ...
>
> 4. Penal subunits be employed only in situations that permit blocking detachments to be deployed immediately behind them.
>
> Rokossovsky, Telegin[298]

Rokossovsky was even blunter in his criticism of the manner in which his *front's* armies conducted their operations, in particular, Tarasov's 70th Army, whose performance was dismal. He expressed his displeasure in a long decree his *front* issued on 4 April 1943, at the same time requesting the *Stavka* relieve General Tarasov of his command:

The unsuccessful offensive operations by the 70th Army for the seizure and retention of the Svetlyi Luch, Novaia Ialta, Rzhavchik, Muravchik, and Hill 260.2 regions and the heavy losses in personnel (8,849 men) and equipment suffered during them are explained by the unsatisfactory preparations for these operation on the part of the Military Council and, first and foremost, by the commander of the army, Major General Comrade Tarasov; the weak organizational role and unsatisfactory control on the part of the staff; and the perfunctory attitude of the commanders of the formation and units to the organization of combat.

The personnel demonstrated a high degree of courage and heroism, and, on the whole, they displayed fearlessness in the fulfillment of their combat missions, however, this could not compensate for the serious shortcomings in the organization of combat and command and control. Thus:

1. The necessary careful reconnaissance of enemy forces and weapons and the system of his defense was not conducted.

2. At the beginning of the combat operations of the army (8–12 March 1943), the Military Council did not take energetic measures to bring the artillery, mortars, and ammunition forward to the front lines and did not organize artillery support for the offensive of the army.

3. After the abandonment of the population points Novaia Ialta, Strelitsa, Svetlyi Luch, Rzhavchik, and Muravchik and Hill 260.2 by the units of the army, and the heavy losses suffered in the process, the appropriate conclusions were not reached, and, as a result, the local operations for the seizure of Hills 260 and 260.2 and the village of Muravchik, conducted from 18 through 28 March, once again repeated the series of mistakes, which entailed an unsuccessful outcome and new heavy losses:

a. The working out of missions with the commanders on the ground and the organization of cooperation with artillery and tanks was conducted superficially and without the direct participation by the commander of the army and his control. This led to the fact that the attacks of the infantry subunits were not supported in timely fashion by the reserves and by neighboring units, and the accompaniment of the infantry by the artillery and its support by direct fire was poorly organized, as a result of which the subunits that had advanced forward for the capture of Hill 260.2 and Muravchik came under strong fire and counterattacks by enemy infantry and perished heroically almost to a man and hundreds withdrew back, abandoning the seized positions.

b. The supervision of the fighting on 28 March 1943 in the 162nd Rifle Division was extremely unsatisfactory, and the chief of staff of the division, while remaining at his CP, was in fact eliminated from participation in the organization of the fighting and from control over the fulfillment of the order, and, as a result, both the information about the enemy and also about the situation of his own forces sent to the headquarters of the army from the CP of the commander of the division turned out to be implausible and disoriented.

4. The Military Council of the army and the commanders of the rifle divisions did not struggle to fulfill NKO USSR's Order No. 456 and permitted huge losses in command-political personnel and at the battalion and company level.

Thus, the former commander of the 278th Rifle Regiment of the 175th Rifle Division, Colonel Sedlovsky, ordered all of his command cadre to go directly to the forward lines (including the chief of staff of the regiment), as a result of which, all of the commanders of battalions and their deputies political affairs and the majority of the commanders of companies and platoons and all of their deputies for political affairs were put out of action in the course of a single battle. In light of such intolerable practices and the flagrant violation of NKO USSR's Order No. 306, in the 175th Rifle Division alone, 224 commanders and political workers were put out of action as killed or wounded during the final days of fighting.

5. The Military Councils and commanders of the formations did not take appropriate measures to collect weapons on the field of battle, carry their wounded to the PMP [medical assistance points], care for them during the march, and organize their careful registration, as a result of which, as of 30 March 1943, the army was missing (with combat losses): rifles — 7,802, heavy machine guns — 2,145, submachine guns — 326, PPSh [submachine gun] — 556, 45-mm guns — 20, 82-mm mortars — 44, 50-mm mortars — 93, and PTR [antitank rifles] — 240.

6. The Military Council did not ensure the fulfillment of the order of the Military Council of the *front* about the preparation of army and *front* roads for spring [*rasputitsa*] and their maintenance in a trafficable state. The army road in the Iasenok-Studenok-Bobrovo sector has proven to be unfit for auto-transport and the military roads out of trafficable condition since 29 March 1943, and the reserves of supplies and ammunition envisioned by decision of the Military Council of the Central Front in Order No. 0100 of 21 March 1943 have not been created.

All of this placed the forces in an extraordinarily serious situation with foodstuffs as a result of which exhaustion has appeared and even instances of death because of this (according to a report by the chief of the medical service of the 102nd Rifle Division, Military Doctor 2nd Rank Lebedev — 112 instances, in the 175th Rifle Division – 2, and others). All of this bears witness to the fact that the Military Council of the army (Comrades Tarasov, Savkov, and Vasin) have not displayed the required organizational skill and persistence in overcoming the range of difficulties confronting the army and have not managed to elicit high discipline and precision work from their command and control apparatus.

The Military Council decrees:

1. Ask the Peoples' Commissar of Defense of the USSR to relieve Comrade Tarasov from command of his army for being unsuited for command based on his inadequate practical experience.

2. Reprimand the members of the Military Council, Comrades Savkov and Vasin, for the inadequacy of their measures in the struggle for ensuring successful combat operations by the units of the army, for the unsatisfactory state of the army and force roads, and for tolerating the disruption in the supply of provisions and ammunition.

3. The Military Procurator of the Central Front, Major General of Juris-prudence Comrade Iachenin, will conduct an urgent investigation of the guilty parties [regarding]:

a. The withdrawal without orders cited above;

b. The disruption in the feeding of the soldiers and the toleration of death from exhaustion;

c. The disruption of measures for preparing the roads for the spring *rasputitsa* [rainy season]; and

d. The toleration of losses and the unwarranted combat losses of weapons – hand the judgment over to a Military Tribunal.

4. Demand the Military Council and the chief of staff of the army:

a. Carefully work out the lessons of the conducted fighting with all of their command personnel ....

10. The Military Council of the army will reach the necessary conclusions from the lessons of the 70th Army and will take energetic measures to prevent the repetition of these grossest deficiencies in leadership.

Rokossovsky, Ponomarenko, Stakhursky, Telegin[299]

Rokossovsky's harsh criticism of the commander of the 70th Army was entirely justifiable since Tarasov had long displayed his unfitness for command. Only months before, in November and December 1942 while commanding the Kalinin Front's 41st Army in Operation Mars, Tarasov's poor leadership and ineptitude in command had led to his army's embarrassing defeat in the Belyi region. This time, however, the *Stavka* recognized its mistake, heeded Rokossovsky's advice, and relieved Tarasov from command. Despite the relief, however, the damage was done.[300]

Careful examination of newly-released archival materials related to the Red Army's offensive along the Orel-Briansk-Smolensk axis in February and March vividly indicates that, as had been the case a year before, in the winter of 1942–43, the *Stavka's* offensive expectations exceeded the Red Army's capabilities. Inspired by its November victory at Stalingrad and emboldened by its seemingly endless series of subsequent successes, in February 1943 the *Stavka* broadened its initial strategic goal of destroying German forces in southern Russia to include the destruction of German forces in central Russia, in particular, its old nemesis, Army Group Center. This *Stavka* over-optimism was not unprecedented, for, during the earlier Moscow operation, it had also striven to accomplish too much. Although

Soviet planning in 1943 was more thorough, it still bore the mark of haste and impatience. Decisions were made too quickly, concentration of forces was slow and difficult, inadequate attention was paid to requisite fire support, and logistical support was inadequate at best. In short, the *Stavka* still had to master the art of the possible in terms of assessing realistic goals and both planning and conducting large-scale operations.[301]

It is now clear the offensive aims of the *Stavka's* 6 February strategic plan were excessive. Within the context of the times, however, the bold decision to expand the offensive was at least understandable. Success in the south was striking and seemingly limitless. Numerous and powerful new armies were available after the surrender of the German Stalingrad group, and these new armies could be employed in a variety of ways. It seemed prudent to employ them *en masse* to spur on an already successful offensive against reeling German forces subject to collapse at any moment rather to retain them for a summer offensive, when German fortunes might have improved. Unfortunately for the Soviets, since they did not (or could not) employ them *en masse*, in the end their impact was only limited.

Several other factors combined to limit the utility of the newly available "Stalingrad" armies. First, the German force encircled at Stalingrad held out until 2 February 1943, thus limiting critical time for deployment of the armies of Rokossovsky's *front* into their new operational sectors by the time specified in the *Stavka's* ambitious offensive timetable. Second, the deteriorating weather conditions in late winter and the *rasputitsa* of early spring combined with the dilapidated state of existing Russian road and railroads to render all movement difficult at best and impossible at worst. The agonizingly slow strategic redeployments that ensued forced the *Stavka* to delay the launch of offensive operations repeatedly, and, when the operations finally began, they developed in uncoordinated fashion and were conducted by only partially assembled forces. As a consequence, the ensuing offensive actions unfolded in only piecemeal fashion. Third, Hitler's decision to appoint Manstein to command Army Group Don (later South) and the Führer's belated decision to permit the latter to conduct a maneuver defense contributed materially to the subsequent Soviet defeat. Making matters even worse for the Soviets, the German decision to abandon the Rzhev-Viaz'ma salient upset the *Stavka's* offensive plans by releasing sufficient forces to tip the military balance in the Orel region in the Germans' favor.

Finally, and most important, the imaginative and impulsive counterstroke launched by Manstein mid-February and the skill with which German forces carried out the counterstroke spoiled the ambitious Soviet strategic venture. Had it not been launched at all or if it had experienced any sizeable delay, it is likely that the Soviet strategic offensive would have fared better, especially if the 21st Army had been able to join the Central Front's March thrust. It also remains unclear what impact the 62nd and 64th Armies, which were dispatched to the regions east of Belgorod and Khar'kov in early March, would have had on Rokossovsky's subsequent operations. Had all three armies (the 21st, 62nd, and 64th) become available to Rokossovsky, the German position would have been far more perilous. Finally, the 24th and 66th Armies, which deployed from Stalingrad to the Voronezh region in early April, were also waiting in the wings. Thus, it is safe to say that Manstein's counterstrokes, long credited with temporarily restoring German fortunes on the Eastern Front, had significantly greater implications than has hitherto been judged. In fact, measured by their achievements, which had strategic rather than operational impact, the counterstrokes amounted to nothing less than a successful counteroffensive.

The failure of its February offensive also had considerable impact on the strategy the *Stavka* adopted during the summer of 1943. For the first time in the war, in the summer it demonstrated prudence, patience, and restraint as it formulated a strategic offensive plan which incorporated a defensive initial phase and was followed by a series of counteroffensives with fairly realistic and, hence, achievable objectives. It is not coincidental that the ultimate Soviet strategic objective in summer 1943 was the Dnepr River line. The Soviets thoroughly rehearsed that scenario in the winter of 1943, and, by virtue of their experiences, in the summer they had a clearer understanding of the art of the possible.

The Red Army's unsuccessful strategic offensive operation in February and March also left a legacy of operational lessons for the *Stavka* and for its *front* and army commanders. Soviet counteroffensives planned for July and August 1943 focused on main German force groupings in the Belgorod-Khar'kov and Orel salients rather than on breaking out westward from the Kursk Bulge along the Sevsk axis. Some Soviet commanders argued for a repeat of the February plan and the conduct of extensive maneuver with deep thrusts westward and southwestward to encircle German forces north of Khar'kov and reach the Dnepr River. Stalin and the *Stavka*, however, insisted on striking German forces directly "on the nose" in the Orel and Belgorod regions. While justifying this plan on the basis of Soviet commanders' inexperience and their weakness in conducting sophisticated maneuver, at least part of their rationale for such an offensive was based on February operational experiences when German forces had used these positions to strike Rokossovsky on the flanks. The Soviets ultimately attacked along the Sevsk axis at the apex of the Kursk salient, however, only after the German flank threats had been eliminated.

Finally, the February offensive had an effect on German plans and fortunes in July 1943. First, Hitler's plan for Operation "Citadel" attempted to replicate the lethal effects of Manstein's February counteroffensive on an even grander scale by attacking the flanks of Soviet forces defending the Kursk Bulge, both northward along the Belgorod-Kursk and along the Orel-Kursk axes toward the south. Second but of more marginal importance, sizable Soviet forces were left behind German lines in the Briansk forests after the failed February offensive. These forces consisted of partisan brigades and elements of encircled 2nd Guards Cavalry Corps. Since the Germans were unable to clear the region by July, when the titanic Battle of Kursk began, elements of the 4th Panzer Division and other units were still tied up containing Soviet forces in the region and could not participate in the offensive. Moreover, these Soviet forces probably provided valuable intelligence information to the Soviets about the impending German offensive.

In the last analysis, the *Stavka's* offensive in February and March, which began with expectations of victory but ended in embarrassing defeat, was a bold gamble that failed. The price of this boldness was the loss of 500,000 Red Army soldiers. Although the *Stavka* managed to stabilize the front in March, it would take seven more months, the Battle of Kursk, and the price of about 3.5 million more casualties for the Red Army to reach the Dnepr River once and for all.

PART 4

SOVIET OFFENSIVE OPERATIONS ALONG THE NORTHWESTERN AXIS (FEBRUARY-MARCH 1943)

Chapter 9

The Leningrad, Volkhov, and Northwestern Fronts' Operation Polar Star (Demiansk) (15–28 February 1943)

Introduction

As the *Stavka* developed a strategy for the Red Army to pursue during its winter offensive of 1942–43, the northwestern axis had figured significantly in its calculations. During the preceding fall, for example, it had included the German salient at Demiansk in its list of key objectives when it planned and conducted Operation Mars. Although Mars failed, as did the assaults on Demiansk, the victories the Red Army achieved in the Stalingrad region during November and early December prompted the *Stavka* to revisit the idea of resuming offensive action in the north. Consequently, in mid-December it ordered the Red Army to plan offensives in two key sectors along the northwestern axis, first, at Leningrad, where the forces of German Army Group North's Eighteenth Army were still blockading the city, and, second, in the region east of Staraia Rusa (south of Lake Il'men'), where its forces had confined a portion of Army Group North's Sixteenth Army in the Demiansk salient. By conducting offensives in these regions, the *Stavka* hoped to break the German stranglehold on Leningrad, which had endured since September 1941, and eliminate the pesky salient, whose proximity to the strategically important region of the Valdai Hills still posed a threat to Soviet rail communications between Moscow and Leningrad.

The *Stavka* authorized its Leningrad and Volkhov Fronts to conduct a joint offensive aimed at raising the blockade of Leningrad on 2 December 1942.[302] During this offensive, which bore the code-name Operation Spark [*Iskra*], the two *fronts* were to attack, penetrate, and capture the eastern portion of the German cordon. Surrounding the city. Specifically, their target was the 13–16-kilometer-wide salient jutting northward from the Mga region through the town of Siniavino to the fortress of Shlissel'burg on the southern shore of Lake Ladoga that separated the city of Leningrad and its defenders from the main Soviet lines further to the east. Attacking from the west and east, respectively, the Leningrad and Volkhov Fronts were to capture Shlissel'burg and Siniavino and link up their forces to form a new and continuous front extending southeastward from the city. By doing so, the *Stavka* hoped to restore direct communications between its forces defending Leningrad and its main front to the east and form a base from which it could conduct future offensives to drive Army Group North's forces away from the region south of Leningrad.

Operation Spark, which took place from 12–20 January 1943, did indeed end the Leningrad blockade, but only barely and only in a technical sense. Although the two attacking *fronts* were able to restore ground communications with the city by carving a narrow corridor 8–10 kilometers wide through the German defense lines east of the city, those communications lines remained tenuous at best and subject to German artillery interdiction. In reality, since the operation ended in stalemate before they could widen the corridor, Operation Spark cracked rather than broke the German blockade.[303] As it reflected on the difficulties it experienced in the offensive and its many previous efforts to break the German stranglehold on Leningrad, in particular the heavy losses their forces suffered and the meager gains they achieved, the *Stavka* well understood the difficulties entailed in mounting an offensive solely in the immediate vicinity of Leningrad. These experiences vividly underscored how difficult it would be to overcome strong German defenses in such difficult terrain. Therefore, it was quite natural that the *Stavka* would consider an even more ambitious offensive option that avoided major attacks near Leningrad proper.

In mid-January 1943, the *Stavka* began seriously considering an even more ambitious offensive option aimed at defeating and destroying all German forces in the Leningrad region. Rather than resuming offensive operations around Leningrad proper, this time it began thinking about conducting a massive offensive operation from the Staraia Russa region south of Lake Il'men' through the Dno and Pskov region toward the southern shore of the Baltic Sea with the forces of its Northwestern Front. If successful, such an offensive could envelop Army Group North's forces in the Leningrad and Novgorod regions and either encircle and destroy them or force them to withdraw westward into the Baltic region. There were, however, two prerequisites the *Stavka* had to satisfy before it could accomplish this imposing task. First, to seize a launching pad for its new offensive in the Staraia Russa region and to amass supplies necessary to sustain such a large-scale offensive, it had to eliminate the German salient at Demiansk and take control of the vital railroad line extending from Moscow through the Valdai Hills to Staraia Russa. Second, it had to prevent the Germans from reinforcing their forces in the Leningrad and Demiansk regions by conducting successful strategic operations elsewhere along the Soviet-German front.

Initially, the *Stavka* sought to satisfy these prerequisites by ordering the Northwestern Front to resume its assaults on the Demiansk salient and its *fronts* operating in southern Russia to expand their offensives toward the west to tie down German operational reserves. However, as the Red Army achieved success after offensive success, first, along the southwestern axis in late January and then along the southwestern and the western axis in early February, the scale and ambitiousness of the *Stavka's* plans in the north soared. Consequently, throwing all caution to the winds, the *Stavka* devised an entirely new plan code-named Operation Polar Star in early February. Unprecedented in its scale and the ambitiousness of its objective, Polar Star envisioned the unprecedented employment of a special Army operational group, including a full tank army, in a strategic-scale offensive from the Staraia Russa region to the southern shore of the Baltic Sea aimed at nothing short of the envelopment and destruction of all German forces in the Leningrad region.

Although older Soviet histories of the war provide few details about this offensive, the official history of the war published in 1976 did describe the operation accurately in at least outline form:

> Along the northwestern axis, the *Stavka* intended to employ the Leningrad, Volkhov, and Northwestern Fronts to destroy Army Group "North." According to the plan for Operation "Polar Star," the Northwestern Front's left wing would deliver the main attack in the general direction of Pskov and Narva. Initially, the intention was to sever the so-called Ramushevo corridor by concentric attacks from the north and south and destroy the enemy Demiansk grouping. At the same time, the forces of the Leningrad and Volkhov Fronts were to liquidate the Mga salient. General M. S. Khozin's Special Group, which consisted of the 1st Tank and 68th Armies and also a number of other formations and units, was entrusted with a very crucial mission. It was to be committed into the penetration in the 1st Shock Army's sector with the mission of advancing rapidly to the northwest, severing the enemy Leningrad-Volkhov grouping's communications by reaching the Luga, Strugi Krasnye, Porkhov, and Dno regions, and preventing the approach of enemy units to assist the enemy's Demiansk and Leningrad-Volkhov groupings. Subsequently, reinforced by the Northwestern Front's formations, this group was to exploit success to Kingisepp and Narva with part of its forces, while the main force encircled and destroyed the enemy Volkhov and Leningrad grouping in cooperation with the Volkhov and Leningrad Fronts. Marshal of the Soviet Union G. K. Zhukov was entrusted with coordinating the operations of the *fronts* operating along the northwestern axis.[304]

However, Zhukov is singularly silent about the operation in his memoirs, devoting just two paragraphs to his role in the operation, and saying nothing about either Operation "Polar Star" or the operation's grand intent:

> A representative of the *Stavka* at that time, I was on the North-Western Front, which was under the command of Marshal Timoshenko. Having reached the Lovat River, our forces were preparing to cross.
>
> Stalin rang the command post of the North-Western Front on either the 13th or 14th of March.
>
> I described to the Supreme High Commander the situation on the River Lovat and told him that the river had become impassable owing to the early thaw and that the troops of the North-Western Front would evidently have to cease their offensive operations for a while.[305]

In reality, Zhukov spent all of February and half of March actively involved in planning and supervising the Northwestern Front's offensive operations.

Despite the dearth of detailed information about Operation Polar Star in previous Soviet (and Russian) histories of the war, recent archival releases now enable us to describe the genesis, course, outcome, and consequences of the operation in far greater detail.

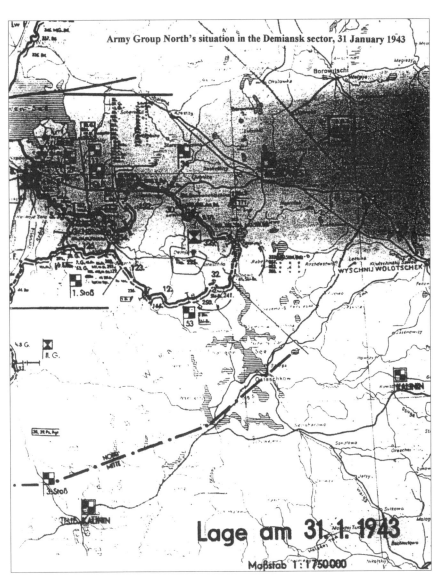

Map 105. Army Group North's situation in the Demiansk sector, 31 January 1943

Planning

Strategic Plans

Although the Northwestern Front never entirely ceased its offensive operations in the Demiansk region during December 1942 and January 1943, by early January its assaults on the salients dwindled in number and intensity to random but vicious local struggles that produced no appreciable gains (see Map 105). Despite his increasing frustration, in mid-January Marshal of the Soviet Union S. K. Timoshenko, the commander of the Northwestern Front, requested the *Stavka* approve an even greater effort by his forces to crush German resistance in the salient once and for all. Unwittingly, the *front* commander's proposal provided a solution to the *Stavka's* dilemma regarding the stalemate in the Leningrad region.

Timoshenko, who had commanded the Northwestern Front since August 1942, submitted his proposal for a new offensive operation to the *Stavka* on 14 January:

I. The 11th and 1st Shock Armies are continuing bitter fighting with the objective of cutting the Ramushevo corridor and encircling the enemy's Demiansk grouping.

The 11th Army penetrated to the entire depth of the enemy's main defensive line along the Viazovka River and, having advanced 6–7 kilometers into the depth of the defensive belt, reached the strong points of Fedorovo and Savkino.

The units of the 1st Shock Army are fighting along the eastern bank of the Korpovka River.

II. The enemy, striving to prevent the 11th and 1st Shock Armies from linking up and hereby seeking to escape the threat of a second encirclement of his Demiansk grouping, is transferring new forces into the Ramushevo corridor both from other fronts and from passive defensive sectors in the sector of the Northwestern Front.

The forces of the *front*, by the fighting to sever the Ramushevo corridor, have forced the enemy to transfer hastily: from the Leningrad Front — the 225th Infantry Division, from the Kalinin Front — the 58th Infantry Division, and from the Volkhov Front — the 254th Infantry Division, which was noted in documents seized from dead soldiers in the Levoshkino region on 12–13 January.

In addition, the enemy has been forced to transfer and commit into combat in the Ramushevo corridor up to 15 separate battalions and detachments from various divisions, chiefly from the Demiansk [encirclement] ring, [including]: a forward detachment from the 12th Infantry Division and a forward detachment and the 1st Battalion from the 154th Infantry Regiment, 58th Infantry Division; and 13 forward detachments from the 75th Infantry Regiment, 5th Light Infantry [Jäger] Division, the 1st Battalion, 30th Motorized Regiment, the 1st Battalion, 426th Infantry Regiment, and the 32nd Antitank Battalion of the 32nd Infantry Division, the 1st Battalion, 28th Infantry Regiment, 8th Light Infantry

Division, the 1st Battalion, 44th Infantry Regiment, a mixed detachment from the 30th Infantry Division, the 551st Infantry Regiment, and an assault battalion from the 553rd Infantry Regiment, 329th Infantry Division, the 89th Infantry Regiment, 12th Infantry Division; the antitank battalion of the 18th Motorized Division; the 1st Battalion, 502nd Infantry Regiment, 290th Infantry Division, and the 2nd Battalion, 94th Infantry Regiment and the 3rd Battalion, 96th Infantry Regiment, 32nd Infantry Division – for a total strength of more than two infantry divisions.

Thus, in addition to the three infantry division previously operating here, the enemy has thrown more than five infantry divisions into the regions of the 11th and 1st Shock Armies' active operations in the Ramushevo corridor,.

III. The chief results of the fighting:

The 81st Infantry Division, the 225th Infantry Division, and up to 10 separate battalions have been completely destroyed during the period from 23 December 1942 through 12 January 1943, and the 58th, 123rd, and 290th Infantry Divisions have suffered heavy losses. The remnants of the 81st Infantry Division, the 89th Infantry Regiment of the 12th Infantry Division, and the 660th Sapper Battalion are being withdrawn to the rear by the enemy.

The enemy's personnel losses during this period amount to roughly 20,000 soldiers and officers.

In spite of his heavy losses, the enemy is continuing to defend his positions protecting the Ramushevo corridor stubbornly, according to prisoner reports "to the last soldier," while clinging to the forested mass and the strong points at Sorokino, Sofronkovo, and Savkino. Massed artillery and mortar fire continues to remain the basis of his defense, and the enemy's artillery fire regime leads us to conclude that he still possesses sufficient quantities of ammunition.

IV. The forces of the Northwestern Front have still not fulfilled their assigned mission – to cut the Ramushevo corridor – as of 13 January 1943. The operations for the resolution of this mission have taken on a bitter and prolonged nature. The combat operations of the forces have been reduced to a slow gnawing through and wedging into the enemy's defense and the successive capture of his strong points.

The average tempo of operations of the 11th Army – is 1 kilometer over 2–3 days.

Such a low tempo of the offensive tempo makes it clear that:

1. The enemy, which has been attacking during this period, has been opposing the nine divisions of the 11th Army with more than six infantry divisions, with powerful artillery and mortar reinforcements (up to 490 guns and 430 mortars).

2. During the course of this fighting, the front of the shock group of the 11th Army has widened from 5 kilometers at the beginning of the offen-

sive to 17 kilometers by 12 January 1943, and, hence, the tactical density of the shock group of the 11th Army has decreased significantly.

As far as the 1st Shock Army is concerned, even though it possessed two-fold superiority in combat personnel and artillery, in essence, to date it has achieved no success. The main reason for this lack of success – the army does not have a sufficient quantity of heavy artillery for the struggle with artillery of the enemy, first and foremost, howitzer artillery necessary to destroy the works [fortifications] and obstacles (pillboxes, wooden walls, etc.) created by the enemy's engineers.

V. Conclusions and Decisions

1. With the objective of holding on to the Ramushevo corridor, the enemy will continue to reinforce the forces which are defending the Ramushevo corridor, while throwing in fresh forces:

a) At the expense of taking them from other fronts, where possible, and subsequently;

b) At the expense of taking part of his forces from passive sectors of our front, chiefly from the Demiansk ring.

2. The Northwestern Front has every opportunity to continue and complete the operation conducted by the 11th and 1st Shock Armies to encircle the Demiansk grouping at the expense of its own internal resources.

As of 13 January 1943, the *front* has six rifle divisions, one rifle brigade, and one tank regiment in its own and the armies' reserves.

3. It would be extremely advantageous to begin offensive operations in the sectors of the 34th and 53rd Armies sooner in order to deprive the enemy of the opportunity to maneuver his forces.

4. Based on the assessment of the enemy and the internal capabilities of the *front* put forth above, I have decided — to continue the operation being conducted by the 11th and 1st Shock Armies with the objective of cutting the Ramushevo corridor.

Simultaneous with this, in order to deprive the enemy of the opportunity to maneuver his forces and weapons and, by this, to provide help to the attacking forces of the 11th and 1st Shock Armies, I request approval to begin resolving the missions of the second stage of the operation for the destruction of the enemy's Demiansk grouping itself.

I am establishing the immediate mission of this stage — to capture the Demiansk region, and by this to create favorable conditions for the subsequent destruction of the Demiansk grouping.

The intent is to employ the free forces presently in the composition of the *front* to resolve this mission and to create two shock groups:

In the 34th Army – consisting of two rifle divisions (the 175th and 245th), one rifle brigade (the 161st), one tank brigade (the 60th), one gun and one howitzer artillery brigade (from the composition of the 11th

Army's artillery), two antitank artillery regiments, two high-powered artillery regiments, and three battalions of multiple rocket launchers.

In the 53rd Army – consisting of three rifle divisions (the 235th, 241st, and 250th), two ski brigades (the 41st and 42nd), one tank brigade (the 177th), one tank regiment (the 57th), one gun artillery regiment, one antitank artillery regiment, two RGK mortar regiments, and two battalions of multiple rocket launchers.

The concentration [areas] and the missions of these groupings are shown on the attached map.

The time of the beginning of the operation for resolution of the missions of the second stage of the operations is ____ [not indicated].

The requirements in ammunition for resolving the missions of the second stage of the operation:

50-mm mines [mortar shells]	60,000 (0.75 combat load)
82-mm mines [mortar shells]	60,000 (0.75 combat loads)
120-mm mines [mortar shells]	42,000 (1.6 combat loads)
45-mm antipersonnel shells	25,000 (0.1 combat loads)
76-mm field [gun shells]	25,000 (1.5 combat loads)
76-mm divisional [gun shells]	40,000 (1.3 combat loads)
120-mm howitzer	25,000 (3.0 combat loads)
152-mm 1937	8.000 (3.0 combat loads)
107-mm 1910/1930	4,500 (2.25 combat loads)
203-mm 1931	1,500 (1.5 combat loads)

In addition to this, I request you provide assistance in the replenishment of the tank units of the *front* with a scattering of tanks.

I request your approval of this proposal.

Attachments: 1:100,000-scale map with the concept for the resolution of the immediate mission of the second stage of the operation.

The commander of the Northwestern Front, Marshal of the Soviet Union Timoshenko,

The member of the Military Council of the Northwestern Front, Lieutenant General Bogatkin,

The chief of staff of the Northwestern Front, Lieutenant General Zlobin[306]

Although his *front* had suffered significant losses in its previous assaults, this time Timoshenko was adamant his forces could reduce the Demiansk salient and the associated Ramushevo corridor, which connected into Army Group North's main lines without receiving significant *Stavka* reinforcements. Three days later, at 1550 hours on 17 January, Stalin approved Timoshenko's proposal with the cryptic statement, "The *Stavka* of the Supreme High Command approves your proposals for the further conduct of the operation."[307]

Reinforcenments and Regroupings

However, even though the *Stavka* accepted Timoshenko's proposed plan, it clearly had more in mind in terms of the scope and scale of the offensive operations it intended to conduct along the northwestern strategic axis. Consequently, throughout the remainder of January, it dispatched a steady stream of reinforcements to the region, ranging from rifle divisions and brigades, separate tank regiments, and numerous artillery and engineer units, up to complete armies. Recently published *Stavka* directives reveal the massive scale of this reinforcement effort (see Figure 3).

Figure 3. Reinforcements Dispatched by the *Stavka* to the Northwestern Front during January and February 1943.

	Stavka Order		
Force	*No./Date*	*Location/Date*	*Notes*
33rd and 137th Rifle Brigade	No. 46008/26.1	Torzhok/Kineshma/1.2	To the 68th Army
24th Army, 157th, 169th, 49th, 277th, and 64th Rifle Divisions, and 66th and 154th Naval and 124th Rifle Brigades	No. 46004/26.1	Ostashkov and west/7.2	Within and to the Northwestern Front. 24th Army diverted to Voronezh on 5.2.
57th Army	No. 46013/29.1	Ostashkov/7–10.2.	To the Northwestern Front as the new 68th Army
1st and 11th Artillery Divisions, 266th, 1103rd, and 1114th Gun Artillery Regiments, and 184th, 186th, 397th, and 500th Antitank Artillery Regiments	No. 46014/29.1 No. 46042/3.2	Ostashkov via Gumrak and Voroponovo/NA	To the Northwestern Front
24,000 personnel replacements	No. 46018/30.1	Northwestern Front/7.2	To the Northwestern Front
Ten tank regiments	No. 46020/30.1	Four at Kresttsy/6.2 and six at Ostashkov/4.2	To the Northwestern Front
1st Tank Army (3rd Mechanized and 6th Tank Corps, and 112th Tank Brigade (formed on the base of the headquarters, 29th Army)	No. 46021/30.1	Ostashkov (Soblago)/5.2	To the Northwestern Front
29th Army (hqs.)	No. 46028/31.1	Soblago/7.2	To the Northwestern Front to form the 1st Tank Army
3rd Mechanized Corps	No. 46029/31.1	Soblago/5.2	To the Northwestern Front's 1st Tank Army

6th Tank Corps	No. 46030/31.1	Ostashkov/7.2	To the Northwestern Front's 1st Tank Army
1st Light Air Assault (Airborne) Division	No. 46023/30.1	Ostashkov/5.2	To the Northwestern Front
Special Group of Forces Khozin (2nd Reserve Army)	No. 46025/30.1	Ostashkov/3.2	
Eleven ski brigades	No. 46022/31.1	Two at Kresttsy and nine at Ostashkov/2–11.2	To the Northwestern Front
10 rifle divisions (50th, 53rd, 69th, 113th, 149th, 194th, 246th, 325th, 354th, and 375th)	No. 46026/31.1	Ostashkov/4.2	To the Northwestern Front
54th Engineer Sapper Brigade	No. 46027/31.1	Marevo (60 kms NW of Peno St.)/7.2	To the Northwestern Front
10th Engineer-Miner Brigade	No. 46032/2.2	Pochinka (10 kms N of Peno St.)/12.2	To the Northwestern Front
538th, 552nd, and 578th Antitank Artillery Regiments, 989th and 395th Gun Artillery Regiments, 11th Antiaircraft Artillery Division, and 283rd, 288th, 293rd, 268th, 265th, 270th, and 263rd Mortar Regiments	No. 46043/3.2	Bologoe, Ostashkov, and Soblago/5–11.2	To the Northwestern Front and its armies

Source: Zolotarev, V. A., ed., "Stavka Verkhovnogo Glavnokomandovaniia: Dokumenty i materialy 1943 g." [The *Stavka* of the Supreme High Command: Documents and materials 1943] in *Russkii arkhiv: Velikaia Otechestvennaia 16–5 (3)* [The Russian archive: The Great Patriotic [War] 16–5 (3)] (Moscow: "TERRA," 1999), 36–46.

The most important of these reinforcements was Special Group of Forces Khozin, an operational group formed within the Northwestern Front, which consisted of one tank and one field army (the 1st Tank and 68th Armies), whose mission would be to exploit the *front's* offensive by leading the advance to Pskov and the southern shore of the Baltic Sea. The *Stavka* formed Khozin's Special Group in a directive it issued at 2300 hours on 30 January:

The *Stavka* of the Supreme High Command orders:

1. Form the headquarters of a Special Group of Forces by 3 February on the basis of a *shtat* numbering 226 military personnel and 19 civilians.

Name the Special Group of Forces "Special Group of Forces of Colonel General Khozin."

2. Turn to the headquarters of the 2nd Reserve Army in the formation of the headquarters of the Special Group.

3. Transfer to the headquarters of the Special Group all of the support units and installations serving the 2nd Reserve Army in their existing *shtats*.

4. Appoint:

As commander of the Special Group – Colonel General M. S. Khozin, as deputy commander of the group – Major General N. N. Klement'ev, and as chief of staff of the group – Major General Iu. L. Gorodinsky.

Report fulfillment.

The *Stavka* of the Supreme High Command

I. Stalin

G. Zhukov[308]

Formed around the nucleus of the former 2nd Reserve Army's headquarters, Khozin's group of forces consisted of the new 1st Tank and 68th Armies, commanded by Lieutenant General of Tank Forces M. E. Katukov and Lieutenant General F. I. Tolbukhin, respectively, and reinforced by a wide range of supporting units of various types. Designated as a powerful shock force to conduct deep operations along the Northwestern axis, the Special Group of Forces was commanded by Colonel General M. S. Khozin, with Lieutenant General N. N. Klement'ev as his member of the Military Council and Major General Iu. L. Gorodinsky as his chief of staff.[309] The *Stavka*, as was its practice, cobbled together Katukov's tank army and Tolbukhin's field army from other existing forces in late January and early February.

The *Stavka* issued its directive forming the 1st Tank Army on 30 January:

In fulfillment of GKO decree No. 2791 of 28 January 1943, the *Stavka* of the Supreme High Command orders:

1. Form the 1st Tank Army in composition and strength in accordance with attached list No. 1 [not available].

2. Appoint:

As the commander of the 1st Tank Army — Guards Lieutenant General of Tank Forces M. E. Katukov; as member of the army's Military Council, Major General N. K. Popel'; and as the chief of staff of the army, Major General N. S. Dronov.

3. Turn to the field headquarters of the 29th Army, with its supporting units and rear service installations, to fill out the 1st Tank Army, renaming the headquarters of the 29th Army the headquarters the 1st Tank Army.

4. Include in the composition of the 1st Tank Army:

The 3rd Mechanized Corps, having filled it out in accordance with the establishment list at attachment No. 2;

The 6th Tank Corps, having filled it out in accordance with the establishment list at attachment No. 3;

The 112th Tank Brigade;

Two rifle divisions and four ski brigades – according to the instructions of the General Staff; and

The 62nd, 63rd, 64th, and 7th Separate Tank Regiments.

5. The commander of the Red Army's Armored and Mechanized Forces will immediately replenish the 3rd Mechanized and 6th Tank Corps with tanks and missing *tankist* [tank crew] personnel up to full establishment strength.

6. The chief of the Main Directorate for the Formation and Manning of Red Army Forces will assign and dispatch 7,500 personnel to the Ostashkov region to fill out the units of the 3rd Mechanized and 6th Tank Corps by 5 February 1943, and will also send by 5 February:

a) For the 3rd Mechanized Corps — a separate communications battalion under *shtat* [establishment] No. 010/561, and for the 6th Tank Corps — a separate communications battalion under *shtat* No. 010/419; and

b) For the 6th Tank Corps — a sapper battalion under *shtat* No. 010/562.
    Dispatch these units to the corps so that they arrive in the Ostashkov region by 7 February.

7. The commander of Red Army Artillery will place the following units at the disposal of Lieutenant General Katukov so as to arrive in the Ostashkov region by 7 February:

a) For the 6th Tank Corps — a motorcycle regiment under *shtat* No. 08/106 and a tank destroyer [antitank] artillery regiment under *shtat* No. 08/100; and

b) For the 3rd Mechanized Corps — a mortar regiment under *shtat* No. 08/106.

8. The commander of Guards-Mortar Units will dispatch two guards-mortar regiments and a separate guards-mortar battalion for the 6th Tank Corps to the Ostashkov region by 7 February 1943.

9. The chief of the Red Army Rear will assign 550 vehicles to fill out the 3rd Mechanized and 6th Tank Corps within a period of four days.

10. The chiefs of the main directorates of the NKO will provide the units forming for the 3rd Mechanized and 6th Tank Corps with weaponry, material, and all types of equipment and will assign specialized personnel from all types of forces in accordance with requests prepared by the commander of the Red Army's Armored and Mechanized Forces.

11. The commander of the Red Army Air Force will place one U–2 aviation communications regiment at the disposal of Lieutenant General Katukov and dispatch it to arrive in the Ostashkov region by 5 February of this year.

12. I am entrusting control over the formation of the 1st Tank Army to the chief of the Red Army General Staff and the commander of the Red Army's Armored and Mechanized Forces.

13. Complete the formation of the 1st Tank Army by 8 February 1943 and report on its readiness.

The *Stavka* of the Supreme High Command
I. Stalin
G. Zhukov[310]

As for Tolbukhin's new 68th Army, the *Stavka* ordered its formation on 9 February 1943, with the headquarters of the former 57th Army, transferred to the Ostashkov region on 29 January, as its nucleus.[311] Made up largely of elite forces, the 68th Army consisted initially of the 1st, 5th, 7th, 8th, and 10th Guards Airborne Divisions, the 32nd, 33rd, 37th, and 137th Rifle Divisions, the 26th Ski Brigade, and various supporting units.

Despite the *Stavka's* strict timetable for the formation and assembly of Katukov's and Tolbukhin's armies, deteriorating weather conditions, the difficult terrain, and the immense challenge associated with of transporting so large a force over such long distances to so remote a region inevitably resulted in delays. Although the tank army's most important formations reached their assigned assembly areas by 8 February, many of its supporting units did not and continued to dribble into the Ostashkov region as late as 23 February. Tolbukhin's army was to complete its concentration by 10 February, but its units were also still arriving in mid-February.

When it finally completed its assembly and concentration, Katukov's army included:

— The 6th Tank and 3rd Mechanized Corps;
— The 112th Separate Tank Brigade;
— The 7th Guards, 62nd, 63rd, and 64th Tank Regiments;
— The 6th and 9th Guards Airborne Divisions;
— The 14th, 15th, 20th, 21st, 22nd, and 23rd Ski Rifle Brigades;
— The 395th and 989th Howitzer Artillery Regiments;
— The 79th and 316th Guards-mortar Regiments;
— The 552nd, 1008th, and 1186th Tank Destroyer [Antitank] Artillery Regiments;
— The 11th Antiaircraft Artillery Regiment;
— The 59th Engineer-Sapper Brigade;
— The 71st and 267th Motorcycle Battalions;
— The 83rd Signal Regiment; and
— Rear service units and installations.[312]

To prepare the Northwestern Front for its forthcoming offensive operations, the *Stavka* also reshuffled the Northwestern Front's senior command cadre to place what it perceived as the most capable commanders in key positions. For example, on 29 January it replaced Major General F. P. Ozerov, the commander of the 27th Army, with Lieutenant General S. G. Trofimenko, the former commander of the 7th Separate Army, who had been successful in holding Finnish forces at bay along the Svir River northeast of Leningrad.[313] The next day it appointed Major General G. P. Korotkov, the former commander of the 53rd Army, to command the 1st Shock Army in place of Lieutenant General V. I. Morozov, who had led the army's unsuccessful assaults on the Ramushevo corridor the previous November.[314] Major General Zhuravlev, the former commander of the disbanded 29th Army, then took command of the 53rd Army. Completing this round of command changes, on 1

February the *Stavka* assigned Morozov as deputy to Colonel General M. S. Khozin, the commander of the Special Group that assumed its commander's name.[315]

In the wake of Timoshenko's proposal for a new offensive from the Staraia Russa and Demiansk regions, Zhukov immediately perceived an opportunity to exploit the Red Army's successes in southern Russia and defeat Army Group North as a whole and raise the Leningrad blockade by conducting a broad envelopment of Army Group North with offensives from both the Demiansk and Staraia Russa regions and Leningrad proper. Therefore, on Zhukov's recommendation, the *Stavka* decided to broaden the scope of the offensive to destroy completely Army Group North and liberate the entire Leningrad region. Under Zhukov's direction and close supervision, by early February the *Stavka* had developed plans for Operation Polar Star, a multi-*front* offensive whose objective was nothing short of the complete destruction of Army Group North (see Map 106).

The *Stavka* timed the operation to coincide with a major offensive by the Red Army's Kalinin, Western, Briansk, and Central Fronts toward Briansk and Smolensk and by the Voronezh, Southwestern, and Southern Fronts to the Dnepr River line. Operation Polar Star required the Northwestern Front to attack from the Demiansk region though Dno and Luga to Pskov and Narva on the Gulf of Finland. Simultaneously, the Leningrad and Volkhov Fronts were to attack the Eighteenth Army around Leningrad and, ultimately, link up with the Northwestern Front's forces to encircle almost all of Army Group North south of Leningrad.

Operational Plans

According to Zhukov's plan, the Leningrad and Volkhov Fronts, commanded by Colonel General L. A. Govorov and Army General K. A. Meretskov, respectively, were to begin Operation Polar Star in early February to distract German attention northward to Leningrad and away from the Demiansk region. Then, in mid-February Timoshenko's Northwestern Front was to commence its assaults to cut the Ramushevo corridor, and, shortly thereafter, Special Group Khozin would conduct an exploitation operation to capture Pskov and Narva. The combined forces of the three *fronts* would then destroy German Army Group North and raise the Leningrad blockade.

Once it developed, Operation Polar Star included four distinct offensive operations, including three initiated by the Leningrad and Volkhov Fronts in separate sectors from 10 and 12 February and an even larger operation begun by the Northwestern Front on 15 February:

- The Leningrad Front's (55th Army) Krasnyi Bor-Tosno operation (10–23 February)
- The Volkhov Front's (54th Army) Chudovo-Tosno operation (10–23 February)
- The Volkhov Front's (67th and 2nd Shock Armies) Siniavino operation (12–23 February)
- The Northwestern Front's (27th, 11th, 1st Shock, 34th, and 53rd Armies) Demiansk operation (15–28 February)

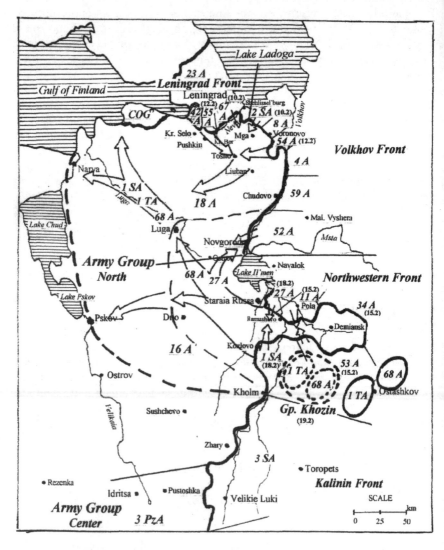

Map 106. Marshal Zhukov's plan for Operation "Polar Star"

Although all of these operations have languished in near total obscurity, recently released *Stavka* documents now permit a more detailed reconstruction of their progress and interrelationship.

The *Stavka* issued the Leningrad and Volkhov Fronts their attack orders at 2355 hours on 1 February:

[Copy to the representative of the *Stavka* [K. E. Voroshilov]]

In view of the fact that, up to this time, the frontal blows in the Siniavino region have not produced the proper results, it will be necessary to organize additional blows from the flanks by the forces of the Volkhov and Leningrad Fronts.

The *Stavka* of the Supreme High Command orders:

1. The Volkhov Front will penetrate the enemy's defenses in the Makar'evskaia Pustyn', Smerdynia, and Korodynia region on 8 February 1943 with the forces of six rifle divisions with reinforcements from the *front* and will attack toward Vas'kiny Nivy and Shapki to arrive in the rear of his Siniavino grouping.

Cut the highway and railroad line in the Liuban' region with part of your forces.

2. The Leningrad Front will attack from the Ivanovskoe and Rozhdestveno region toward Mga Station on 8 February with a force of five to six rifle divisions with reinforcements from the *front* with the objective of arriving in the rear of the enemy's Mga-Mstolovsk grouping.

3. Without waiting for these flank attacks, the Volkhov and Leningrad Fronts will continue to destroy the enemy and seize the Siniavino and Gorodok No. 1 and 2 regions by means of an envelopment of Siniavino Heights and the Gorodok No. 1 and 2 regions.

4. Upon the fulfillment of these missions, destroy the enemy's Mga-Siniavino-Shapki grouping in cooperating with the flank attacks and reach the Ul'ianovka, Tosno, and Liuban' line.

5. The boundary lines are as before. Confirm receipt. Report on the beginning of the operation.

I. Stalin, G. Zhukov[316]

In the Leningrad Front's sector, the 55th Army, commanded by Major General of Artillery Sviridov, was to attack southeastward along the Oktiabr' railroad line from the Kolpino region through Krasnyi Bor to Tosno, wheel its forces east across the Tosno River, and link up with the Volkhov Front's 54th Army (see Map 107). Simultaneously, the 54th Army, commanded by Lieutenant General A. V. Sukhomlin, was to attack westward from the Smerdynia region through Shapki and, subsequently, advance toward Tosno to link up with Sviridov's army. The twin pincers were to encircle all German forces in the Mga-Siniavino region, widen the narrow land corridor to Leningrad, and, subsequently, serve as a hammer to smash the bulk of Army Group North against an anvil formed by the Northwestern Front advancing in the south. In addition, part of the 54th Army was to attack Liuban' both to distract the Eighteenth Army and to tie down its forces.

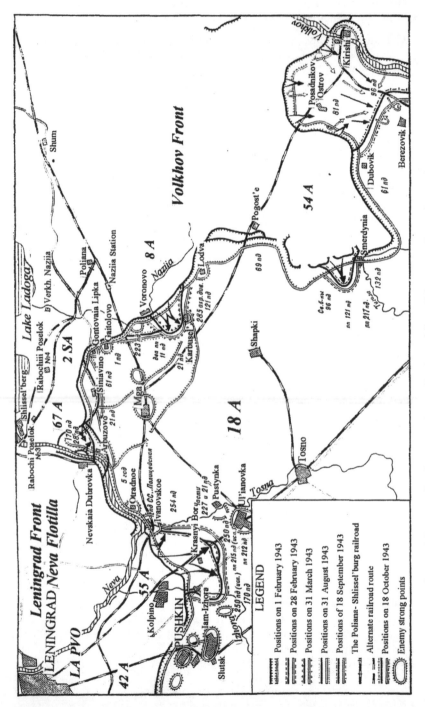

Map 107. Combat operations at Leningrad from February to December 1943

While the 55th and 54th Armies were conducting their pincer maneuver toward Tosno, the Leningrad Front's 67th and the Volkhov Front's 2nd Shock Armies, commanded by Lieutenant Generals V. P. Sviridov and V. Z. Romanovsky, respectively, were to attack Gorodok Nos. 1 and 2 and Siniavino and capture Mga and the Leningrad-Volkhov railroad. Before beginning the operation, the *Stavka* transferred the 2nd Shock Army and its sector north of Siniavino to the Volkhov Front to provide for more unified command and control.[317] The Leningrad and Volkhov Fronts were to begin their offensive on 8 February, one week before the Northwestern Front, to draw Army Group North's reserves northward to Leningrad and away from the Northwestern Front's main attack sector.

Sviridov's 55th Army, which formed the Leningrad Front's arm of the pincer, consisted of eight rifle divisions, two rifle and two ski brigades, and one separate tank regiment.[318] Sviridov planned to lead the assault with his 45th and 63rd Guards and 43rd Rifle Divisions and 34th Ski Brigade in first echelon, supported by the 31st Tank Regiment, a force numbering roughly 33,000 men and 30 tanks. Once his first echelon forces had smashed German defenses at Krasnyi Bor, a mobile group consisting of the 35th Ski and 122nd Tank Brigades under the command of Major General I. M. Liubovtsev was to advance along the Oktiabr' railroad, capture Ul'ianovka Station, and lead the advance on Tosno. Sviridov's forces faced the 250th Spanish "Blue" Infantry Division and the 4th SS Police Division of the Eighteenth Army's L Army Corps, which defended the 32-kilometer wide sector from Krasnyi Bor to the Neva River east of Kolpino. General Esteban-Infantes' Spanish division had a reinforced regiment and 3 infantry battalions totaling 4,500 men with no tanks facing the 55th Army's main attack.[319]

The Volkhov Front's arm of the pincer, Sukhomlin's 54th Army, consisted of 10 rifle divisions, 3 rifle brigades, and 2 tank brigades, with a strength of over 70,000 men and 60 tanks.[320] Sukhomlin's forces were to assault a sector defended by the 96th Infantry Division of the Eighteenth Army's XXVIII Army Corps, flanked on the left by the 69th Infantry Division and on the right by the 132nd Infantry Division. The 96th Infantry had been assigned this "quiet" sector after being decimated in the previous fighting at Siniavino Heights.

Although imposing on paper, the Leningrad Front's 67th and 2nd Shock Armies, which were designated to attack at Gorodok Nos. 1 and 2 and Siniavino, were still woefully under-strength after the intense fighting in January. Nevertheless, they were to join the offensive, based on the assumption that the fighting in the 55th and 54th Armies' sectors would draw German reserves away from the Siniavino region. Romanovsky's 2nd Shock Army consisted of 12 under-strength rifle divisions, 1 rifle, 1 ski, and 2 tank brigades, 1 tank regiment, and 4 separate tank battalions, with an overall strength of roughly 60,000 men and 50 tanks. Dukhanov's 67th Army consisted of 6 rifle divisions, 8 rifle, 2 ski, and 4 tank brigades, 2 tank regiments, 2 separate tank battalions, and 1 fortified region, with about 40,000 men and 30 tanks strong.[321] The German XXVI Army Corps (Group Hilpert) defended the salient around Gorodok Nos. 1 and 2 with its 28th Jäger and 21st Infantry Divisions and the Siniavino region with the 11th and 61st Infantry Divisions, with a combined strength of roughly 35,000 men.

Timoshenko's Northwestern Front was to play the major role in Polar Star by destroying the German Sixteenth Army's II Army Corps lodged in the Demiansk salient and advancing through Staraia Russa and Dno to Pskov and Narva. The *Stavka* issued its final order for the offensive to Timoshenko at 0140 hours on 6 February:

[Copy to the commander of the Special Group of Forces]

To destroy the enemy's Demiansk grouping, the *Stavka* of the Supreme High Command orders:

1. The 1st Shock Army, consisting of eight rifle divisions, one tank brigade, four tank regiments, one artillery division, seven RGK artillery regiments, five mortar regiments, and the 1st Guards-Mortar Division, will penetrate the enemy's defense in the Shotovo and Ovchinnikovo sector on 19 February 1943 and, attacking toward the north and northeast, will reach the Onufrievo and Sokolovo region.

2. The 27th Army, consisting of seven rifle divisions, five rifle brigades, four tank regiments, three ski brigades, two tank brigades, one artillery division, two RGK artillery regiments, two mortar regiments, and one guards-mortar brigade, will penetrate the enemy defense in the Penno and Borisovo sector on 19 February 1943 and, attacking toward the south and southeast, will reach the Onufrievo and Sokolovo region, where it will close the encirclement ring around the enemy's Demiansk grouping.

3. After closing the encirclement ring, the 1st Shock Army, together with two rifle divisions from the 27th Army subordinate to it, will attack toward the east with the mission to destroy the enemy deployed in the Ramushevo corridor.

4. The 27th Army, after the penetration of the enemy's defense and while attacking toward the south and southeast with part of its forces, will wheel its main forces toward to the west to envelop Staraia Russa with the mission of encircling and destroying the enemy's Staraia Russa grouping. After destroying the enemy in the Staraia Russa region, the 27th Army will become subordinate to Colonel General Khozin, the commander of the Special Group of Forces.

5. After the destruction of the enemy in the Ramushevo corridor, the commander of the *front,* having quickly regrouped the *front's* forces and weapons, will destroy the encircled Demiansk grouping.

6. After the penetration of the enemy's defenses by the 1st Shock Army, support the passage of Group Khozin toward Dno Station.

7. The Northwestern Front is entrusted with the material support of Khozin's group of forces.

8. Confirm receipt and report your decision on 10 February 1943.

The *Stavka* of the Supreme High Command
I. Stalin
G. Zhukov[322]

The Northwestern Front's left wing, consisting of the 27th, 11th, 34th, 1st Shock, and 53rd Armies, was to launch Timoshenko's main attack through Staraia

Russa toward Luga and Dno. During the first stage of the operation, these armies were to sever the Ramushevo corridor, which connected German II Army Corps with its parent Sixteenth Army, and destroy German forces at Demiansk. Subsequently, Khozin's Special Group of Forces was to advance northwest, capture Pskov and Narva, and cut off and destroy the German Eighteenth Army in cooperation with the Leningrad and Volkhov Fronts.

A second directive, also dispatched at 0140 hours on 6 February, described the missions of Khozin's Special Group of Forces:

The *Stavka* of the Supreme High Command orders:

1. Complete the concentrating of the group of forces, consisting of the 1st Tank and 68th Armies and the reserve group, in the Marevo, Usad'ba, and Slautino region by day's end on 16 February 1943 and deploy the group for commitment into the penetration in the Ryto, Nikulino 2, Kursko, and Bol'shoi Ostrov region by day's end on 18 February 1943. Be in complete readiness to commit the group into the penetration in the Khodyki and Sluchino sector beginning on the morning of 19 February 1943.

2. The main mission of the group — to cut the communications of the enemy's Leningrad-Volkhov grouping by reaching the Luga, Strugi Krasnye, Porkhov, and Dno regions and to prevent the approach of enemy units to assist his Demiansk and Leningrad-Volkhov groupings.

Seize and hold the city of Pskov with a group of forces consisting of two rifle divisions, two ski brigades, two tank regiments, two RGK artillery regiments, and one engineer brigade.

3. After the destruction of the enemy in the Staraia Russa region, the 27th Army will become subordinate to the commander of the Special Group of Forces for an attack on Luga together with the 68th Army, however, so that part of the forces of the 27th Army will be used to seize Novgorod in cooperation with the 52nd Army of the Volkhov Front.

4. After the seizure of the Luga and Strugi Krasnye [region], seize the Kingisepp and Narva line with part of the group's forces, having cut off the routes of withdrawal of the enemy into Estonia.

Encircle and destroy the enemy's Volkhov and Leningrad groupings with the main forces in cooperation with the Volkhov and Leningrad Fronts.

5. Confirm receipt and report fulfillment by 16 February 1943.

The *Stavka* of the Supreme High Command

I. Stalin

G. Zhukov[323]

The Northwestern Front was to begin its offensive on 15 February, and Khozin's Special Group of Forces would commence its exploitation operation as soon as the *front's* forward shock groups captured the Staraia Russa region. It was not coincidental that, at precisely the same moment it issued the Leningrad and Volkhov Fronts with their attack orders for Polar Star, the *Stavka* issued similar offensive directives to all of its *fronts* operating along the western strategic axis as well (see Figure 4).

Figure 4. The Missions of Red Army *Fronts* Operating along the Northwestern and Western Axes.

Stavka Order	Date	Front	Objectives	Forces
No. 30039	0140 hours on 6 Feb 43	Northwestern (Special group of forces)	Immediate: Luga, Strugy Krasnoe Subsequent: Kingisepp, Narva	1st Tank and 68th Armies
No. 30040	0140 hours on 6 Feb 43	Western	Immediate: Briansk Subsequent: Roslavl', El'nia	16th, 50th, and 10th Armies
No. 30041	0140 hours on 6 Feb 43	Briansk	Immediate: Orel Subsequent: Briansk, Karachev	48th, 13th, 3rd, and 61st Armies
No. 30042	0140 hours on 6 Feb 43	Northwestern	Immediate: Staraia Russa Subsequent: Demiansk, Novgorod	1st Shock and 27th Armies
No. 30043	0140 hours on 6 Feb 43	Central	Immediate: Briansk, Gomel' Subsequent: Orsha, Smolensk	2nd Tank, 65th, 21st, and 70th Armies
No. 30043	0140 hours on 6 Feb 43	Western	Immediate: Roslavl' Subsequent: Smolensk	All armies
No. 30034	0140 hours on 6 Feb 43	Kalinin	Immediate: Vitebsk, Orsha, Smolensk	All armies

Source: Zolotarev, V. A., ed., "Stavka Verkhovnogo Glavnokomandovaniia: Dokumenty i materialy 1943 g." [The *Stavka* of the Supreme High Command: Documents and materials 1943] in *Russkii arkhiv: Velikaia Otechestvennaia 16–5 (3)* [The Russian archive: The Great Patriotic [War] 16–5 (3)] (Moscow: "TERRA," 1999).

Considered collectively, these *Stavka* directives required the all of the Red Army's *fronts* operating along the northwestern and western axes to expel German forces from the entire region east of the Narva, Pskov, Vitebsk, Orsha and Dnepr River line. Furthermore, the final objectives assigned to these *fronts* lined up with those the Voronezh, Southwestern, and Southern Fronts were to seize southward along the lower reaches of the Dnepr River to the Sea of Azov. Together, these objectives indeed underscored the *Stavka's* ambitiousness as it planned the culminating stage of its winter offensive.

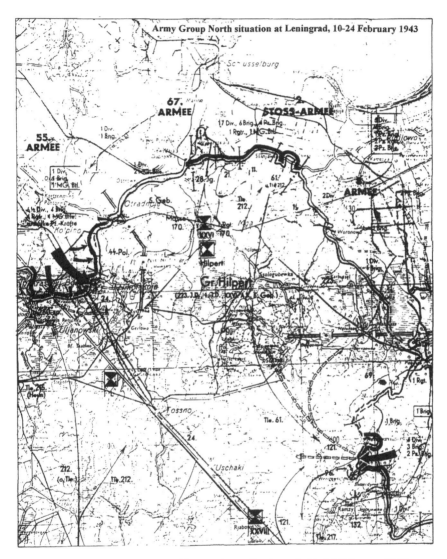

Map 108. Army Group North's situation at Leningrad, 10–24 February 1943

The Offensive

The Leningrad and Volkhov Fronts' Attacks

In accordance with Zhukov's orders, the Leningrad and Volkhov Fronts began their offensive operations in the Leningrad region on 10 February 1943 (see Map 108). As described in the Soviet official history of the war:

> The offensive by the Volkhov and Leningrad Fronts with the objective of liquidating the Mga salient did not develop further. From 10 through 23 February, the Soviet forces managed to wedge only 10–15 kilometers toward Tosno. The enemy threw operational reserves into the threatened sectors and halted the *fronts'* offensives by artillery fire and counterattacks supported by aviation. The fighting took on a prolonged nature. Attempts to continue the offensive during the second half of March were also not crowned with success, since fire superiority could not be achieved over the defending enemy because of shortages in ammunition.[324]

Sviridov's 55th Army of the Leningrad Front attacked early on 10 February along the Kolpino, Krasnyi Bor, and Tosno axis after a two-hour artillery preparation by about 1,000 guns and mortars. Catching the defending forces of the Spanish 250th Infantry Division by surprise, its 63rd Guards Rifle Division captured Krasnyi Bor by 1200 hours, and its 45th Guards Rifle Division captured Mishkino later in the day. By day's end, but against intensifying Spanish resistance, Sviridov's first-echelon forces had advanced 4–5 kilometers and captured Krasnyi Bor, Mishkino, and several nearby villages. Satisfied by the progress, Sviridov then committed Liubovtsev's mobile group into action late on 10 February to exploit the 45th Guards Rifle Division's success. However, heavy enemy resistance coupled with an unexpected thaw, which prevented the ski brigades from operating off the road, halted the mobile group's advance short of its objective, the town of Ul'ianovka, a key node in the German Eighteenth Army's communications network on the main railroad line from Leningrad to the southeast. Sviridov's tanks and infantry bogged down in hand-to-hand fighting with Spanish forces and redeployed German reserves defending the Izhora River and the narrow roads south of Krasnyi Bor.[325] During the later stages of the operation, the Germans reinforced the Spaniards' defenses with regimental *kampfgruppen* from the 212th and 215th Infantry Divisions transferred from Chudovo and Uritsk.

The forces on Sviridov's left wing fared little better. The 43rd Rifle Division and 34th Ski Brigade advanced 3–4 kilometers in two days of heavy fighting, driving the forces of the SS Police Division back toward the Tosno River. Once again, however, the Germans reinforced their defenses with the 24th Infantry Division, portions of the 2nd SS Motorized Infantry Brigade, the Flanders legion, and remnants of the 11th, 21st, and 227th Infantry Divisions that had been heavily damaged in the earlier fighting at Siniavino. The reinforcements stopped the Soviet advance far short of its objectives. Sviridov's forces had advanced 4–5 kilometers along a front of 14 kilometers by 13 February but could advance no more, having lost an estimated 10,000 casualties and most of their tanks in the heavy fighting.

While the 55th Army's forces were conducting their futile attacks at Krasnyi Bor, Sukhomlin's 54th Army of the Volkhov Front went into action early on 10 February in the sector north of Smerdynia and the Tigoda River, aiming its thrust at the railroad line south of Tosno. Sukhomlin ultimately attacked the German 96th Infantry Division's defenses with his 166th, 198th, 311th, and 378th Rifle Divisions, the 14th and 140th Rifle Brigades, the 6th Naval Rifle Brigade, and the 124th Tank Brigade. Despite employing overwhelming force, Sukhomlin's shock group penetrated only 3–4 kilometers into the German defense along a 5-kilometer front in three days of heavy fighting. The Germans halted the assault by reinforcing the 96th Infantry Division with regrouped battalion-size *kampfgruppen* from the 61st Infantry Division at Siniavino, from the 121st and 217th Infantry Divisions, transferred from the Volkhov River front, and from the adjacent 132nd Infantry Division.

The 67th and 2nd Shock Armies joined the assault early on 12 February, capitalizing on the fact that the Eighteenth Army had transferred forces from the Siniavino region to reinforce the defensive sectors which were already under assault, the shock group of Lieutenant General M. P. Dukhanov's 67th Army struck the German 28th Jäger and 21st Infantry Divisions' forces dug in around Gorodok No. 1 and Gorodok no. 2 at the same time that Romanovsky's shock group struck German defenses east and west of Siniavino proper. After six days of heavy fighting, Dukhanov's forces finally succeeded in capturing the smashed ruins of Gorodok No. 1 and Gorodok No. 2 and advanced several kilometers southward to the outskirts of Arbuzovo. Although they had finally pinched off the small German salient on the eastern bank of the Neva River that pointed menacingly toward Shlissel'burg, Dukhanov's forces were too exhausted to accomplish anything more. To the east, however, the assault by Romanovsky's forces on Siniavino and the adjacent Siniavino Heights faltered immediately with heavy losses. The Soviet assault on Siniavino, the fourth in about six months, ended with the strong point still firmly in German hands.

The Leningrad and Volkhov Fronts' offensives at Krasnyi Bor, Tosno, and Siniavino failed for a variety of familiar reasons. Meretskov, the commander of the Volkhov Front, later provided his views of the matter:

> The Volkhov Front came up against strong enemy defenses. The Germans had more than enough troops at their disposal, and their defensive installations were far superior to those which we surmounted in January. To reduce losses in manpower, we decreased pressure and waited for the Northwestern Front to strike at the rear of Kuechler's [Army Group North] troops. But the blow was never delivered. GHQ [the *Stavka*] postponed the attack of our mobile group [Group Khozin] several times in March, and finally we were informed that it had been cancelled altogether. This led me to the conclusion that, despite the considerable successes scored by the Red Army, our commanders still had something to learn in the difficult art of modern warfare.[326]

Meretskov's comments were a bit disingenuous, however, because his armies did indeed attack, as did many of the Northwestern Front's armies poised around Demiansk.

The history of the Volkhov Front, quoting in part from a *Stavka* assessment of the defeat, was far more candid in its assessments as to why the offensives faltered:

The Soviet forces were not able to destroy the enemy's Siniavino-Mga grouping. The main reason for this was the most stubborn German resistance. Several deficiencies also had a negative effect, including those in the organization and conduct of the operation. The forested-swampy and roadless nature of the terrain complicated the offensive, as did the early arrival of the thaw. The chief shortcoming in the offensive was the fact that the 2nd Shock and 67th Armies were operating separately, they dispersed their forces, and, therefore, suffered unwarranted losses. Considering the increased German resistance and the great losses suffered by our forces, the Volkhov and Leningrad Fronts were forced to halt their offensives temporarily and set about preparing a new offensive operation. The overall strategic offensive along the Northwestern axis was cancelled. General M. S. Khozin's Special Group of Forces was disbanded.[327]

The most revealing critique of all is contained in a directive which the *Stavka* issued to Govorov and Meretskov at 2200 hours on 27 February 1943, after the initial offensives in both the Leningrad and Demiansk regions had failed:

[Copy to the representative of the *Stavka*, Marshal of the Soviet Union G. K. Zhukov]

The operations being conducted by the Leningrad and Volkhov Fronts are not producing the expected results. The main shortcoming in the offensive operations of the *fronts* is the fact that the 67th and 2nd Shock Armies are operating separately, and each has been required to penetrate a strongly fortified enemy defense in its sector. This has led to a dissipation of forces and weaponry and to pointlessly heavy casualties in personnel and equipment. It is necessary to put an end to these shortcomings.

The *Stavka* of the Supreme High Command orders:

1. Cease the offensive by the 55th and 67th Armies of the Leningrad Front and by the 2nd Shock and 54th Armies of the Volkhov Front temporarily.

2. The forces of the Leningrad and Volkhov Fronts will consolidate along the lines they occupy and conduct active reconnaissance with the objective of detecting weak places in the enemy's defenses.

3. Transfer the 2nd Shock Army, in full complement and with part of the *front's* reinforcements, to the forces of the Leningrad Front effective at 2400 hours on 28 February 1943. Carry out the transfer of reinforcing weapons based on the instructions of Marshal Voroshilov.

4. Establish a boundary line between the Leningrad and Volkhov Fronts: the Naziia River, Apraksin Gorodok, Gaitolovo, Sigolovo, Sologubovka, and Necheprt' (all inclusive for the Leningrad Front) effective at 2400 hours on 28 February 1943.

5. The commander of the forces of the Leningrad Front will submit to the *Stavka* a plan for an offensive operation with an assessment of the weak places in the enemy defense no later than 3 March 1943 so that the forces and weapons of the 67th and 2nd Shock Armies can be concentrated along a single axis in the future.

6. The commander of the Volkhov Front will submit his views regarding the conduct of an offensive operation in cooperation with the Leningrad Front no later than 3 March 1943.

7. Marshal Voroshilov will prepare his conclusions regarding the plan for joint operations by both *fronts* and present them to the *Stavka*.

The *Stavka* of the Supreme High Command
I. Stalin[328]

In reality, however, the forces of Govorov's Leningrad Front and Meretskov's Volkhov Front were so exhausted by previous fighting that they lacked the strength and endurance necessary to fulfill the *Stavka*'s overly ambitious objectives.

The Northwestern Front's Attack

Despite the obvious failure of the secondary attacks to the north, nonetheless, Zhukov decided to capitalize on their diversionary effect and unleashed the Northwestern Front's main attack (see Map 109). Among the few existing accounts of the ensuing fighting, the Soviet official history of the war provides only a brief summary of the action:

The offensive by the forces of the Northwestern Front began at various times. The formations of the 11th and 53rd Armies launched active operations on 15 February 1943, at a time when the remaining armies were still not prepared to conduct the operation. Although the Soviet attacks did not lead to any essential changes in the situation, however, the German-Fascist command felt a real threat to its grouping. Fearing a new cauldron, it began to withdraw its forces from the Demiansk salient (Operation "Tsiten") on 19 February. Simultaneously, he undertook measures to strengthen the defense of the Ramushevo corridor.[329]

The second account, contained in the 1st Shock Army's history, provides far more detail about the offensive, in particular, regarding the genesis, planning, and course of the operation:

At the end of January, it [the *Stavka*] decided to prepare a strategic offensive operation on the Northwestern Front. The operation, which was given the name "Polar Star," would be conducted with the decisive aim not only to finish off the Demiansk grouping within the shortest period but also to alter fundamentally the situation in the northwest. [The *Stavka*] planned to penetrate the enemy's defense in the western part of the Ramushevo corridor and encircle and destroy the Demiansk grouping with the forces of the Northwestern Front. Simultaneously, [it] would exploit the offensive with the formations of Colonel General M. S. Khozin's mobile group (the 1st Tank and 68th Armies and artillery and

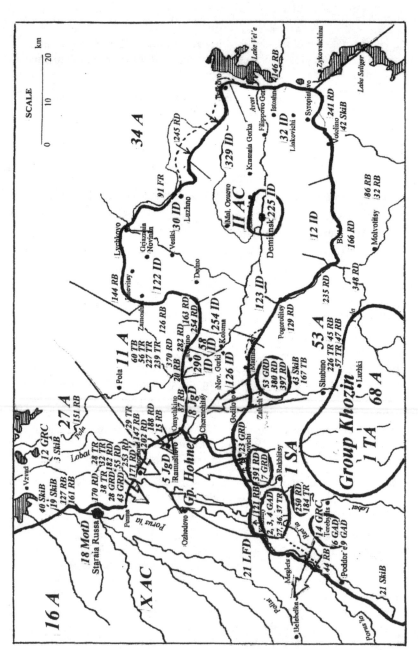

Map 109. The Northwestern Front's operational plan, 14 February 1943

guards-mortar units) and, with part of the forces of the *front*, along the Staraia Russa and Pskov axis. The operation was to begin on 19 February.

In accordance with the *Stavka's* concept, the commander of the *front* decided to create two shock groups, each consisting of one reinforced combined-arms army, north and south of the Ramushevo corridor. They were to launch meeting attacks simultaneously and form an internal encirclement ring along the western bank of the Lovat' River. Thereafter, the northern group (the 27th Army) was to exploit the offensive toward the northwest to envelop Staraia Russa from the south and the southern group (the 1st Shock Army) – from the east to destroy the enemy in the Ramushevo corridor and support the commitment of General Khozin's Group into battle. Thus, as it pointed out in its report about the army's offensive operation, "The role of the forces of the 1st Shock Army in the fulfillment of the mission assigned to it by the *front* was enormous and paramount."[330]

Zhukov finalized his plan for conducting Operation Polar Star during the week preceding the planned attack date of 15 February. On 8 February he met with Marshal of Artillery N. N. Voronov, Marshal of Aviation A. A. Novikov, and General Korotkov, the 1st Shock Army's new commander, at the latter's command post in the village of Khmeli where they coordinated artillery and air support for the army's shock groups. Then on 10 February, Zhukov conducted a planning conference at the Northwestern Front's headquarters, where Timoshenko, Korotkov, Zhuravlev, the commander of the 53rd Army, and all of the 1st Shock and 53rd Armies' division commanders finalized their offensive plans and arranged for cooperation among the attacking forces. During this conference, Zhukov directed Korotkov to transfer the forces on his 1st Shock Army's right wing (the 53rd Guards, 129th, 166th, 235th, 245th, and 380th Rifle Divisions and the 45th and 86th Rifle Brigades) and their tactical sectors to the neighboring 53rd Army so that Zhuravlev could use them to form his army's shock group. The representative of the *Stavka* also ordered Timoshenko to transfer the 13th and 27th Artillery Divisions and the 75th and 226th Tank Regiments, which had previously been supporting the 1st Shock Army, to the 53rd Army to provide Zhuravlev's army with requisite artillery and armor support. Completing the revised plan, Zhukov ordered Korotkov to shift the bulk of his army's forces to his left wing, where, in a sector previously occupied by the 44th and 121st Rifle Brigades, they would form several new shock groups to conduct his army's main attack.

Once finalized, the new offensive plan required the 11th, 34th, and 53rd Armies to begin the operation by assaulting the defenses of the German II Army Corps around the Demiansk salient proper. While shock groups from the 11th and 53rd Armies conducted converging assaults from the north and south against the eastern end of the Ramushevo corridor at the salient's western base to cut off the Germans' withdrawal routes from the salient, the 34th Army was to tie the II Army Corps' forces down by launching multiple local attacks around the salient's entire periphery. Once the II Army Corps was pinned down in the salient, the shock groups of the 27th and 1st Shock Armies were to strike the western end of the Ramushevo corridor from the north and south to complete the isolation and destruction of the II Army Corps, prevent its reinforcement, and then advance westward to capture Staraia Russia and crossings over the Polist' River south of the city. Then the 1st Tank and 68th Armies of Khozin's Special Group of Forces were to go into action to complete the capture of the Staraia Russa region and begin their exploitation toward the northwest. Zhukov ordered Timoshenko to begin his offensive on 15 February with the forces of his *front's* 11th, 34th, and 53rd Armies and then expand the offensive on 18 February with the forces of the 27th and 1st Shock Armies. The two armies of Khozin's Special Group of Forces (1st Tank and 68th) were to begin their exploitation on 19 February.[331]

With the planning completed, the 1st Shock and 53rd Armies began regrouping their forces and concentrating them in their assigned jumping-off positions on 11 February under the protective cover of the 1st Shock Army's 121st and 44th Rifle Brigades. In accordance with Zhukov's instructions, Timoshenko assigned the 2nd, 3rd, and 4th Guards Airborne Divisions, the 250th Rifle Division, and the 27th, 36th, 37th, and 184th Separate Tank Regiments to the 1st Shock Army to replace the forces transferred to the 53rd Army and to form its new shock groups. It also reinforced Korotkov's shock army with the 16th and 27th Artillery Divisions and the 1st and 6th Guards-mortar Divisions to participate in the elaborate artillery offensive. Zhukov's plan required Major General V. G. Riazanov's 1st Assault Aviation Corps to support the 1st Shock Army's assault with 186 aircraft sorties per day and Major General E. M. Beletsky's 1st Fighter Aviation Corps to support the advance with 184 aircraft sorties per day.[332] As the other attacking armies, Korotkov also formed an antiaircraft artillery group within his army consisting of the 707th and 714th Antiaircraft Artillery Regiments, the 242nd Separate Antiaircraft Artillery Battalion from the RVK (*Stavka's* artillery reserve), and four separate antiaircraft machine gun batteries under the 42nd Antiaircraft Artillery Division's control. All of these measures provided the 1st Shock Army with an unprecedented quantity of artillery support.

The Northwestern Front dispatched its final attack orders to its subordinate armies early on 14 February and approved the armies' revised plans the following day. The 1st Shock Army's plan required its shock groups to penetrate the enemy's defenses in several sectors, to cut the Ramushevo corridor in cooperation with the 27th Army's shock groups, and to complete the encirclement of the enemy's Demiansk grouping. Korotkov's main shock group consisted of the 2nd, 3rd, and 4th Airborne Divisions, supported by the 27th, 36th, and 37th Tank Regiments. It was to conduct the army's main attack northward and northeastward from the 10 kilometer sector between the villages of Viazki and Krivavitsy, east of the Red'ia River, capture bridgeheads across the Red'ia and Polist' Rivers, and advance on Staraia Russa from the south. Simultaneously, cooperating with the shock group on the 53rd Army's left wing, the army's second shock group, consisting of the 7th Guards and 391st Rifle Divisions, was to launch a secondary attack northward from the 5 kilometer sector between Shotovo and Viazki on the army's right wing to capture Ramushevo.[333]

Korotkov's ambitious plan required his army's main shock group to advance roughly 20 kilometers in two days, 11 kilometers on the first day and 9 kilometers on the second. Once it crossed the Polist' River, the shock group was to support the commitment of Khozin's Special Group of Forces in its exploitation to the northwest. Farther east, by advancing roughly 7 kilometers in two days, the shock group on the army's right wing was to link up with the 27th Army's shock group attacking from the north and then wheel eastward to reach the western bank of the Lovat' River in the sector between Ramushevo and Shotovo and close the encirclement ring around the German Demiansk grouping. Finally, on the 1st Shock Army's left wing, a third shock group consisting of the 14th Guards Rifle Corps' 6th and 9th Guards Airborne Divisions was to attack westward across the Red'ia River to cut the Staraia Russa-Kholm road and protect the left flank of the army's main shock group and Khozin's Special Group of Forces as they developed their attacks.

Despite Zhukov's and Timoshenko's careful planning and preparations, nothing went as planned. In fact, neither the Germans nor the weather cooperated with their ambitious and meticulous plans. The 1st Shock Army's history described how things went awry:

> The unloading of the units of the airborne divisions and Group Khozin the Ostashkov and Soblago region and their movement to the front did not go unnoticed by the enemy. Frightened by the recent catastrophe at Stalingrad, the High Command of Hitler decided to withdraw the formations of the Sixteenth Army from the Demiansk bridgehead. The Demiansk grouping began its withdrawal on 17 February under the protection of strong rear guards. The weather also sharply worsened in mid-February. Intense cold was replaced by continuous rain. A strong northwest wind blew for two-three days running, and rains came with the snow. This circumstance permitted the Germans to withdraw rapidly along timely prepared roads. At the same time, the thaw put out of commission both winter roads leading from the Ostashkov region to the front lines. The divisions' columns became bogged down for many tens of kilometers, and most of the artillery and vehicles with ammunition, food-stuffs, and fuel became stuck in the deep mud of the stretched-out roads.
>
> On the instructions of Marshal G. K. Zhukov, the 54th Engi-neer-Sapper Brigade was hurriedly transferred from the Kalinin Front, the 59th Brigade from Group Khozin, and the 10th Engineer-Mine Brigade from the 1st Tank Army.
>
> The personnel of the deploying divisions found themselves in extremely difficult conditions. It was assumed that the soldiers would traverse the 150 kilometers from the unloading station to the concentra-tion region on skis, but, because of the thaw, this turned out to be impos-sible. They arrived with their skis on their shoulders and came through the puddles and mud in their felt boots. As a result, the units arrived in the concentration region totally exhausted.
>
> The preparation of the jumping-off positions for the offensive, which were characterized by continuous swamps, went very slowly. The mild winter with continuous thaws in December, January, and February, with snow cover of 50–70 centimeters, made for negligible freezing of the swamps (6–9 centimeters). In that regard Chief Marshal of Artillery N. N. Voronov recalled:
>
> "There were numerous swamps in the region of forthcoming opera-tions, and, where they did not exist, there were dirt roads. Building roads

there was hugely difficult. It was especially difficult for the artillerymen. They had to build solid wood flooring for the majority of firing positions so that the guns would not sink into the quagmire while firing."

The accumulation of material supplies was also difficult. In spite of the increased transportation by narrow-gauge railroad and auto-transport and the use of the 674th Army Aviation Regiment for transport, [the supply effort] managed to cover only routine expenditures. Individual auto-columns overcame the distance from Ostashkov to Marevo (103 kilometers) in two-three days.[334]

Coupled with the deteriorating weather conditions, which disrupted the *front's* preparations for the offensive and forced Zhukov to postpone the start date of the offensive by at least a week, if not more, the numerous intelligence reports concerning an imminent German withdrawal from Demiansk frustrated Zhukov but created a new sense of urgency within the *Stavka*. Despite Zhukov's protestations, at 0200 hours on 20 February, the *Stavka* demanded he begin the offensive as soon as possible:

> The enemy in the Demiansk region has begun to withdraw its units to the west. There is a danger that he will succeed in withdrawing his divisions across the Lovat' River, and our planned operation "Polar Star" will be threatened with disruption.
>
> I think it is absolutely necessary to begin the operations of Trofimenko [27th Army], Korotkov [1st Shock Army], and Khozin [Special Group of Forces] three to four days earlier then originally planned. I await your urgent report.
>
> Vasil'ev [Stalin][335]

However, as the 1st Shock Army's history admitted, "But even the inexhaustible energy of Zhukov and his distinguished organizational capabilities could not save the situation. Neither the 27th Army nor the 1st Shock Army nor Group Khozin were ready for the offensive."[336]

In addition to the unforeseen delays in regrouping and concentrating his forces, Zhukov was also faced with the daunting problem of determining precisely what the Germans intended to do and when they planned to do it. Unknown to Zhukov, as early as 31 January 1943, Hitler had authorized General Küchler, the commander of Army Group North, to withdraw the Sixteenth Army's forces from the Demiansk salient and man new and even stronger defenses protecting the city of Staraia Russa:

> On the night of 31 January, after a week-long debate, Hitler finally gave way to Zeitzler's arguments. The Operations Section, OKH, informed Kuechler that the struggle to get the decision had been unprecedentedly difficult and asked him to get the troops out fast in order not to give Hitler a chance to change his mind. Kuechler, however, refused to risk losing the vast quantity of equipment and supplies poured into the pocket during the past thirteen months. He began pulling back the line on 20 February, after three weeks preparation, and then collapsed the pocket by stages, completing the last on 18 March 1943.[337]

Thus, what Soviet intelligence detected on 17 February that prompted the sharp *Stavka* message were the final German preparations to pull their forces out of the Demiansk salient. In a situation strikingly reminiscent of what was happening in the Rzhev-Viaz'ma salient to the south, the time-phased German withdrawal from the Demiansk salient began occurring only days before Zhukov intended to launch his offensive (see Map 110). In these circumstances, pressed by the *Stavka*, Zhukov had no choice but to commence his offensive prematurely and in piecemeal fashion, before his armies were able to concentrate all of their forces in accordance with his original offensive plan. Anticipating these problems, Zhukov had already ordered the 11th and 53rd Armies to begin their attacks against the northern and southern flanks of the Ramushevo corridor on 15 February, but these attacks achieved only negligible success against well-prepared German defenses. Thereafter, while these armies strove to resume their assaults but in vain, the weaker 34th Army began probing and harassing attacks against the forces of the II Army Corps as they began their phased withdrawal.

With the *Stavka's* approval, Zhukov unleashed his other armies to combat beginning on 23 February, with the 27th Army's shock groups striking the German defenses southeast of Staraia Russa on 23 February and the 1st Shock Army's shock group attacking the German positions along the base of the Ramushevo corridor on 26 February (see Map 111). By the 26th, however, the Sixteenth Army had already withdrawn the forces of the II Army Corps from their exposed positions around the salient westward to a new and far shorter defense line along the Lovat' River south of Ramushevo (see Map 112). Therefore, when the 1st Shock Army attacked, instead of facing the defenses of the single 21st *Luftwaffe* Field Division, it encountered the three German infantry divisions (the 32nd, 329th, and 30th) of *Gruppe* [Group] Höhne, which manned formidable defensive positions along the southern face of the shrunken Ramushevo corridor. The results were predictable.

Korotkov's 1st Shock Army began its assault early on 26 February, attacking through deep snow after an intense three-hour artillery preparation. Despite Zhukov's and Korotkov's careful preparations, however, an immediate shortage of ammunition prevented Korotkov's artillery from suppress the opposing German artillery and smashing the dense network of bunkers, pillboxes, and trenches constituting the German defenses:

> The tanks, a majority of which were American [models], which were cumbersome and had weak armor, narrow tracks, and gasoline engines, began to get struck even before their approach to the forward edge of the enemy defense and, having encountered thawed swampy sectors, halted and searched for ways around. In these circumstances the *desantniki* [assault troops] managed to advance 1–3 kilometers with great difficulty. Having reached the eastern bank of the Polist' River in several sectors, here they were forced to dig in.[338]

Korotkov's shock army tried to resume its offensive on 27 February but once again immediately faltered in the face of the strong German defenses. Meanwhile, to the north, the shock groups of Trofimenko's 27th Army managed to force their way forward in the Penno and Borisovo sectors but could advance no further. As

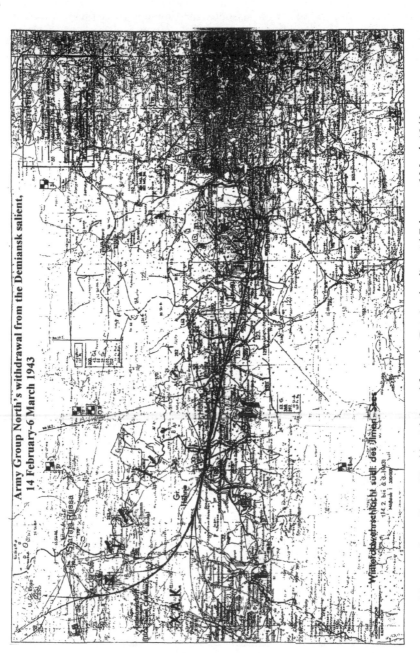

Map 110. Army Group North's withdrawal from the Demiansk salient 14 February–6 March 1943

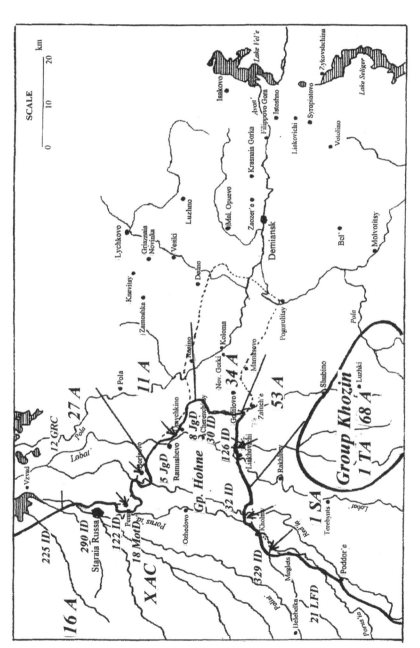

Map 111. The Northwestern Front's situation, 28 February 1943

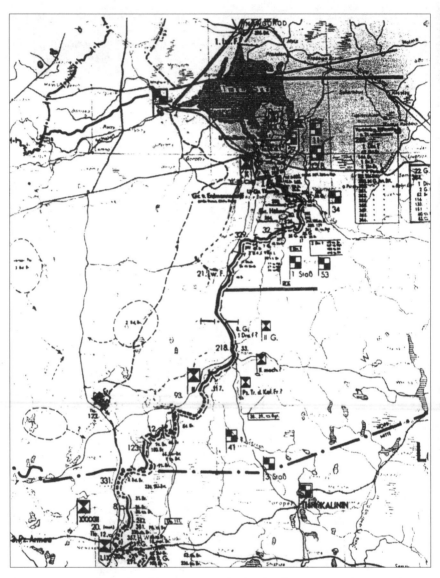

Map 112. Army Group North's situation in the Demiansk sector, 28 February 1943

indicated by the 1st Shock Army's history, Zhukov's attacking forces paid a high price for these failures:

> The forces of the army suffered heavy losses in the stubborn combat, and the medics carried out their work with great intensity. A detachment of medical sledge-dog teams attached to the army played a great role in transporting the wounded from the battlefield to medical points. Seventy-five percent of the wounded that required evacuation during the operation were evacuated by its efforts. In the 391st Rifle Division, Medical Assistant Tartkov provided initial assistance to and removed 98 wounded from the battlefield, for which he was awarded with the Order of Lenin ....[339]

Late on 27 February, Zhukov reported to the *Stavka* that, in two days of fighting, his southern grouping [the 1st Shock Army] was unable to penetrate the enemy defense "because of insufficient amounts of ammunition and the limited quota of ammunition." Nevertheless, he added, "after bringing up several artillery regiments from neighboring sectors to increase the artillery density up to 13–140 guns per 1 kilometer of front, he would once again prepare to penetrate the defense," after halting the operation for three days.[340]

Conclusions

When the forces of Northwestern Front's 34th and 53rd Armies reached the Lovat' River at day's end on 28 February, the saga of long and bloody struggle for possession of the Demiansk salient abruptly ended. Although Zhukov's forces failed to destroy the German II Army Corps before it withdrew from the Demiansk region, the 1st Shock Army's history refused to admit this failure ended Operation Polar Star:

> Thus the enemy's Demiansk grouping ceased its existence, and the Ramushevo corridor was liquidated. The forces of the Northwestern Front had not succeeded in destroying this grouping. However, over the course of a year and a half, around 100,000 German-Fascist forces were tied down [at Demiansk]. The enemy lost around 90,000 men killed in the battles alone, and this prompted the former chief of staff of the Sixteenth Army to describe the battle for the Ramushevo corridor as "a miniature 'Verdun' of the First World War." In addition to liquidating the Demiansk bridgehead, prerequisites were created for developing the offensive along the Pskov axis. And this was precisely what the *Stavka* of the Supreme High Command was planning.[341]

The *Stavka* and Zhukov were indeed undeterred by the successful German withdrawal from their exposed positions around Demiansk. No sooner was the withdrawal a fact than Zhukov and the *Stavka* attempted to implement Operation Polar Star from new starting positions east of Staraia Russa. First, however, on 27 February the *Stavka* ended the fruitless attacks in the Leningrad region to the north by ordering the Leningrad and Volkhov Fronts to postpone any further offensive operations until the Northwestern Front achieved some offensive success in the Staraia Russa region (see above). Zhukov dispatched his new proposal for reviving

Operation Polar Star, albeit in truncated form, to the *Stavka* at 1557 hours on 28 February:

> 1. Our plan for the penetration of the enemy's defense was designed to penetrate a weak defense and, by introducing Group Khozin into the affair, to arrive in the rear of his Leningrad-Volkhov grouping quickly. While doing so, we had in mind that the Demiansk grouping would be encircled by the 1st Shock, 27th, 53rd, and 34th Armies.
>
>> Now the situation has drastically changed.
>
>> The enemy, having noticed the concentration of the 1st Shock and 27th Armies and Group Khozin, is withdrawing behind the Lovat' River, apparently with the intention to settle for a defense along the Lovat' River, with his forward defensive positions along the Red'ia River and, possibly, along the Lovat' River.
>
> 2. The roads have become untraffickable during the last 15 days because of the rain and the thaw. The swamps where the forces are now operating are beginning to become clear of ice, have become a mess, and are covered by continuous water.
>
>> The [weather] forecast is for warm weather beginning on 15 March 1943.
>
> 3. Considering the sharply altered situation and the weather, I am very afraid that we are sitting with our groupings in the local swamps and untraffickable places, having failed to achieve our aims in "Polar Star."
>
>> I think:
>
> 1. Now we now need to limit the advance of the Northwestern Front to the Polist' River, relinquish [the idea] of committing Group Khozin into the affair, seize Staraia Russa, and prepare a jumping-off region for a spring offensive; and
>
> 2. Prepare Group Khozin for the spring [offensive] by reinforcing it with the 34th and 53rd Armies of the Northwestern Front.
>
> We can bring these two armies, which consist of approximately 10–12 divisions, forward by 15 March and take three airborne divisions away from Korotkov [1st Shock Army].
>
> Group Khozin can consist of the 34th, 53rd, 68th, and 1st Tank Armies, for a total of up to 20 rifle divisions and up to 18 rifle brigades plus the tank army.
>
>> I consider that such a grouping can play a very large role in the spring.
>
>> I am reporting my opinion on your decision.
>
>> Konstantinov [Zhukov][342]

The *Stavka* approved Zhukov's recommendation, thus ending his attempt to conduct Operation Polar Star to its full extent. However, having invested so much time and effort into preparing the operation, neither Zhukov nor his colleagues in Moscow were prepared to abandon the offensive, especially since the Red Army's forces in central and southern Russia were still advancing successfully. Therefore, on Zhukov's recommendations, the *Stavka* ordered the Northwestern, Leningrad, and Volkhov Fronts to conduct a truncated version of Operation Polar Star in early March against the same objectives designated in the original operation. This time, however, the offensive would begin staggered fashion, with the Northwestern Front attacking on 4 March and the Leningrad and Volkhov Fronts on 14 March.

Chapter 10

The Leningrad, Volkhov, and Northwestern Fronts' Truncated Operation Polar Star (Staraia Russa) (4 March–2 April 1943)

Planning

With Zhukov's approval, on 1 March Timoshenko ordered the armies of his Northwestern Front to halt their attacks, regroup their forces, and prepare to resume the offensive on 4 March. This time, however, Zhukov subordinated the 34th 53rd, and 68th Armies and the 1st Tank Army to Khozin's Special Group of Forces and ordered the 27th and 1st Shock Armies to capture Staraia Russa and reach the Polist' River. If the latter two armies captured the town, Khozin's entire force was to exploit toward Pskov and Narva. Once again, the *Stavka* ordered the Leningrad and Volkhov Fronts to conduct supporting attacks in the Leningrad region, this time a shallower envelopment of German forces north of Mga without a frontal assault on Siniavino, but to begin these operations on 14 March to exploit the Northwestern Front's 7 March offensive.

The Northwestern Front's new offensive plan required Trofimenko's 27th Army to attack the German defenses north and south of Staraia Russa and Kurochkin's 11th Army, supported by the 34th and 53rd Armies in the vanguard of Khozin's group, to penetrate German positions along the western extremity of the former Ramushevo corridor. Delivering the *front's* main attack, Korotkov's 1st Shock Army was to strike southwest of the Polist' River toward the village of Belousova Bora, 20 kilometers southwest of Staraia Russa, to sever German communications lines to the city from the south. So that it could conduct the *front's* main attack, Timoshenko reinforced Korotkov's army with the 380th Rifle Division, the 20th and 21st Rifle Brigades, the 13th Artillery Division, the 151st Gun Artillery, 987th and 996th Antiaircraft Artillery, and the 184th Tank Regiments and the 55th Engineer-Sapper Brigade, and similarly reinforced the other armies taking part in the penetration operation.

Although the 1st Shock Army was supposed begin its attack at dawn on 5 March after a thorough artillery preparation, once it did, its assaults stalled shortly after they began because, "Once again, much was not done during the preparation for the offensive, especially in transporting ammunition for the artillery in the units."[343] Despite capturing several German strong points on the army's right wing, the 137th Rifle Brigade and 37th Tank Regiment advanced 3 kilometers before becoming bogged down in the face of determined German resistance. The assaults by the *front's* other armies similarly faltered after only negligible gains.

At this juncture, events unfolding far to the south rendered any further attempt to implement Operation Polar Star utterly superfluous. The collapse of both the Southwestern and Voronezh Fronts under the hammer blows of Manstein's counteroffensive and the fall of Khar'kov to the Germans caused alarm bells to ring in the *Stavka*. Heavy armor was needed in the south, and the Red Army's only uncommitted combat-ready tank army was Katukov's 1st Tank Army in Khozin's Special Group of Forces:

> However, an early spring arrived in 1943, and the terrain became untraffickable. For this reason and also because of the counteroffensive by the enemy in the Khar'kov region, the 1st Tank Army, without its airborne divisions, ski rifle brigades, and some other formations and units, was transferred by railroad to the Kursk region during the period from 9 March–4 April.[344]

The *Stavka*, by ordering the transfer of Katukov's tank army southward on about 7 March, effectively abandoned any notion of carrying out as grand an offensive as Operation Polar Star. However, given the precarious situation elsewhere along the front, in characteristic fashion, it deemed it necessary to continue applying pressure against German forces operating along the northwestern axis:

> Because of the exacerbated situation in the Khar'kov region, the beginning of the *rasputitsa*, and the unsuccessful development of Operation "Polar Star," the *Stavka* recognized the inexpedience of continuing it. In order to conceal its operational maneuver — the departure of the 1st Tank Army – the *Stavka* limited the objectives of the offensive, which now involved the liberation of Staraia Russa and reaching the Polist' River.[345]

Zhukov, adjusting to these new realities, insisted the Northwestern Front continue its offensive toward Staraia Russa, this time supported by more limited operations by the Leningrad Front's 55th Army and the Volkhov Front's 8th Army to pinch off the German Mga salient, with the former attacking southeastward from the Krasnyi Bor region and the latter westward from the Voronovo region. The *Stavka* then issued two new directives at 0400 hours on 7 March, the first transferring the 2nd Shock Army from the Leningrad to the Volkhov Front and the second ordering the two *fronts* to conduct the new more limited offensive operations:

[Directive 30065]
　The *Stavka* orders:

1. In a change to *Stavka* directive No. 30057 of 28 February 1943, transfer the 2nd Shock Army in its complete composition and with all of its reinforcements to the Volkhov Front effective at 2400 hours on 8 March 1943.

2. Establish a boundary line between the Leningrad and Volkhov Fronts effective at 2400 hours on 8 March 1943: Rabochii Poselok [Workers'

Settlement] No. 1, Rabochii Poselok No. 6, Mga, and Tosno (all points except Tosno are inclusive for the Volkhov Front).

3. Assign responsibility for protecting the junction between the Leningrad and Volkhov Fronts to the commander of the Volkhov Front.

4. Report fulfillment by 1000 hours on 9 March 1943.

I. Stalin[346]

[Directive 30066]

For the conduct of an operation for the destruction of the enemy's Mga-Siniavino grouping, the *Stavka* of the Supreme High Command orders:

1. The commander of the Volkhov Front will penetrate the enemy's defense along the Voronovo and Lodva front with a force of ten rifle divisions and four rifle brigades with appropriate means of reinforcement and, having cut the enemy dirt road communications in that region, will capture the Sologubovka and Muia regions with a subsequent development of the attack into the rear of the enemy's Mga-Siniavino grouping. Link up with the forces of the Leningrad Front in the Voitolovo region in order to move northward to the Mga region, encircle the enemy's Mga-Siniavino grouping, and destroy or capture it.

Go over to the defense temporarily along the front of the 2nd Shock Army.

2. The commander of the Leningrad Front will penetrate the enemy's defense along the Krasnyi Bor and Poselok Peschanka front with a force of eight rifle divisions and three rifle brigades, attack toward Ul'ianovka, and, having cut the railroad and highway communications in the Ul'ianovka—Mga sector, capture the railroad center at Sablino, with subsequent development of the attack toward Voitolovo, in the rear of the enemy's Mga-Siniavino grouping.

Link up with the forces of the Volkhov Front in the Voitolovo region and, together with the Volkhov Front, encircle the enemy's Mga-Siniavino grouping and destroy or capture it.

Go over to the defense temporarily along the front of the 67th Army.

3. The beginning of the operation for both *fronts* will be on 14 March 1943. Complete the operation for the liquidation of the enemy's Mga-Siniavino grouping no later than 25 March 1943.

4. Entrust the direction of the operation on the Volkhov Front to the commander of the *front*, Comrade Meretskov, and on the Leningrad Front – to the commander of the *front*, Comrade Govorov.

5. Entrust the representative of the *Stavka*, Comrade Voroshilov, with organizing cooperation between the Volkhov and Leningrad Fronts and also coordinating their actions during the course of the operations.

I. Stalin[347]

When he developed the offensive plan for his Volkhov Front, in addition to the 8th Army's assault in the Voronovo region, Meretskov ordered his 52nd Army to conduct a limited-objective offensive against Novgorod to assist the Northwestern Front's assault on Staraia Russa and also to draw some of the Eighteenth Army's forces away from Leningrad.

Zhukov intentionally established 14 March as the start date of the Leningrad and Volkhov Fronts' offensives to coincide with the Northwestern Front's planned offensive on Staraia Russa. Zhukov revealed his plan for Timoshenko's more limited operation against German positions around Staraia Russa to the *Stavka* on 8 March:

1. In view of the fact that we conducted the main attacks with Korotkov's [1st Shock] army from the south in the Verevkino and Liakhnovo regions and from the north with the armies of Lopatin and Trofimenko [the 11th and 27th] in the Staraia Russa region, the enemy has involved his main groupings in the fighting and is keeping them against Korotkov and Staraia Russa. The enemy is keeping a considerably weaker grouping in the center, that is, in the sector of the left wing of the 11th Army and the right wing of the 53rd Army in the Ramushevo, Cherenchitsy, and Onufrievo region, and, apparently, this region is the junction between his northern and the southern groupings.

2. Considering the presence of dirt roads, the closeness of the railroad line, and the difficulty of operating because of the nature of the terrain, I have decided:

To bring the army of Tolbukhin [the 68th] rapidly forward to the north in the Vasil'evshina, Godilovo, and Koloma region and to conduct with it a wedge attack against the enemy in the Ramushevo and Cherenchitsy sector in the general direction through Onufrievo and Sokolovo toward Rechnye Kottsy for cutting off Staraia Russa from the west.

Four days are required for the regrouping and preparation of the offensive, consequently, we can attack beginning on the morning of 13 March 1943.

3. We will completely regroup the army of Kurochkin [the 34th] into the Malye Gorby and Borisovo regions west of the Lovat' River during this period, from which it will attack westward in the general direction of Ozhedovo and, subsequently, toward Ivanovskoe and Velikoe Selo.

The 27th Army will concentrate all of its forces and weapons in the Penno region for an attack to envelop Staraia Russa from the south and southwest in full cooperation with the 34th Army.

I am ordering the commander of the *front* to reinforce the 34th Army with two rifle divisions.

Korotkov and Zhuravlev [the 1st Shock and 53rd Armies] will operate along their previous axes with their previous missions.

The protection of the axes toward Kholm and Poddor'e will be entrusted to the 14th Guards Rifle Corps.

4. If you have no objections, I will now begin to prepare the offensive. Tolbukhin will begin to move to his new region this evening. I have given him a preliminary order.

Konstantinov [Zhukov][348]

Stalin approved Zhukov's new plan without hesitation, issuing an implementing directive of his own at 2150 hours on 8 March which read, "I approve your plan of operations. Proceed immediately with the appropriate regrouping of your forces. During your regrouping, do not cease the artillery fire by the 1st Shock and 27th Armies in order to conceal our maneuver."[349]

However, later that evening and over the next few days, the *Stavka* issued a new series of directives which began stripping Timoshenko's Northwestern Front of the forces necessary to conduct effective offensive operations. The first of these directives, issued at 2340 hours on 8 March, acknowledged the transfer southward of the 1st Tank Army and disbanded Group Khozin, integrating its forces into Timoshenko's Northwestern Front:

[Copy to the chief of the Organizational Directorate of the General Staff]

1. In connection with the transfer of the tank army of Katukov to another axis, disband the Special Group of Colonel General Khozin effective at 1200 hours on 9 March 1943.

2. Transfer the 68th Army of the Special Group to the forces of the Northwestern Front effective at 1200 hours on 9 March 1943.

3. Appoint Colonel General Khozin as deputy commander of the forces of the Northwestern Front.

4. Rename the headquarters of the Special Group, with all of its rear service units and installation and communications units, as the headquarters of the 2nd Reserve Army. Station the army in the Soblago region, with its headquarters in Soblago.

5. Appoint Lieutenant General V. I. Morozov as the commander of the 2nd Reserve Army.

6. Include the rifle divisions brought into the reserve of the *Stavka* from the Northwestern Front, a list of which the General Staff will determine, together with the commander of the Northwestern Front, in the 2nd Reserve Army.

The *Stavka* of the Supreme High Command
I. Stalin[350]

Thereafter, beginning on 11 March, the *Stavka* issued a series of directives ultimately transferring many forces from the Northwestern and other *fronts* to the Kursk region (see Figure 5). These transfers, which were largely designed to thwart Manstein's counteroffensive in the Khar'kov and Belgorod regions, ended the *Stavka's* hopes of conducting a successful theater-wide strategic offensive during February and March 1943. The transfers also signified the shift in the *Stavka's* strategic focus to the Kursk region, where it would remain until early August 1943.

Figure 5. Red Army Forces Transferred to the Kursk Region, March 1943

Stavka Order	Date	Origin	Force	Destination
No. 30071	0135 hours on 11 Mar 43	Northwestern Front	129th, 235th, 348th, 380th, and 397th Rifle Divisions (2nd Reserve Army)	Elets, Lipetsk, and Lebedian' (Reserve Front)
No. 46070	0330 hours on 11 Mar 43	Western Front	9th Tank Corps	Kursk (Central Front)
No. 46075	0330 hours on 11 Mar 43	Kalinin Front	362nd, 238th, and 186th Rifle Divisions (25th Rifle Corps)	Plavsk (Stavka reserve)
No. 46071	0330 hours on 11 Mar 43	Kalinin Front	1st Mechanized Corps	Novyi Oskol (Stavka reserve)
No. 46077	0630 hours on 19 Mar 43	Western Front	70th and 75th Guards Rifle Divisions	Kursk (Central Front)
No. 46078	0630 hours on 19 Mar 43	Northwestern Front	129th, 235th, 380th, 348th, 250th, and 397th Rifle Divisions (2nd Reserve Army)	Livny, Elets (Reserve Front)
No. 46079	0300 hours on 20 Mar 43	Northwestern Front	2nd, 3rd, 4th Airborne Divisions, 28th Guards Rifle Division, 55th, 170th, and 202nd Rifle Divisions, and 15th, 44th, 47th, 121st, 146th, and 161st Rifle Brigades (53rd Army)	Livny (Stavka reserve)
No. 46080	0330 hours on 20 Mar 43	Kalinin Front	41st Army headquarters	Stavka reserve
No. 46082	0300 hours on 20 Mar 43	Kalinin Front	77th and 80th Guards Rifle Divisions and 31st, 236th, 260th, and 273rd Rifle Divisions (41st Army)	Millerovo (Stavka reserve)
No. 30079	0115 hours on 21 Mar 43	Stavka Reserve	1st Tank Army	Voronezh Front
No. 46088	0210 29 March	Northwestern Front	6th Guards Airborne Division and 163rd, 166th, and 241st Rifle Divisions	Stavka reserve
No. 46092 and No. 46095	0130 hours on 31 Mar 43	Northwestern Front	77th and 80th Guards Rifle Divisions, 260th, 273rd, and 308th Rifle Divisions, and 160th Rifle Brigade (11th Army); 6th Guards Airborne Division and 163rd, 166th, and 241st Rifle Divisions (27th Army)	Tula (11th Army) and Gzhatsk (27th Army) (Stavka reserve)

Source: Zolotarev, V. A., ed., "Stavka Verkhovnogo Glavnokomandovaniia: Dokumenty i materialy 1943 g." [The *Stavka* of the Supreme High Command: Documents and materials 1943] in *Russkii arkhiv: Velikaia Otechestvennaia 16–5 (3)* [The Russian archive: The Great Patriotic [War] 16–5 (3)] (Moscow: "TERRA," 1999).

Despite the transfer of these forces to the south, Zhukov insisted the Northwestern, Leningrad, and Volkhov Fronts conduct their offensives on 14 March as planned, if only to remind the Germans that their ordeal along the northwestern axis had not ended. Despite the departure of the 1st Tank Army, the final chapter in the prolonged Soviet struggle to seize Staraia Russa opened under Zhukov's watchful eyes.

The Offensive

The Leningrad and Volkhov Fronts' Mga Offensive

True to the offensive plan of 8 March, the Northwestern Front indeed renewed its attacks at dawn on 14 March after a heavy artillery preparation (see Map 113). Trofimenko's 27th Army assaulted the German X Army Corps' defenses east of Staraia Russa but registered only minor gains in the Penno sector, 8 kilometers south of the city. At the same time, Kurochkin's 11th, Lopatin's 34th, and Zhuravlev's 53rd Armies pounded the German defenses along the Lovat' River and, by penetrating Gruppe Höhne's defenses south of Ramushevo, eventually forced the defending 8th Jäger and 126th Infantry Divisions to fall back to their second defensive belt along the Red'ia River, several kilometers to the west.

Further to the south, although reinforced by the 6th and 9th Guards Airborne Divisions from the now departed 1st Tank Army and the 33rd and 137th Rifle Brigades from the *front's* reserve, the assault by Korotkov's 1st Shock Army northward along the eastern bank of the Red'ia River toward Staraia Russa failed miserably after only meager gains (see Map 114).[351] After further intense but futile fighting, the front stabilized late on 17 March, and the same day the *Stavka* ordered Zhukov to end the offensive and fly to Kursk to restore some order to the Red Army's deteriorating situation in that region. Three days later, Timoshenko ordered his frazzled forces to go over to the defense. The long Soviet agony at Demiansk was finally at an end.

The Leningrad and Volkhov Fronts' MGA Offensive

While these dramatic events were unfolding in the Northwestern Front's sector to the south, the forces of Govorov's Leningrad and Meretskov's Volkhov Fronts struck in the Leningrad region, once again trying to eliminate German forces defending the Mga salient (see Map 115). As before, *Stavka* representative Voroshilov coordinated both offensives. The Volkhov Front's 52nd Army, commanded by Lieutenant General V. F. Iakovlev, began diversionary operations in the Novgorod region on 14 March. His small army consisted of four rifle divisions, one ski brigade, two aerosleigh battalions, and one fortified region, but no tanks, and, just prior to the attack, Meretskov reinforced his army with two more rifle divisions.[352] Iakovlev's assault across the Volkhov River south of Novgorod

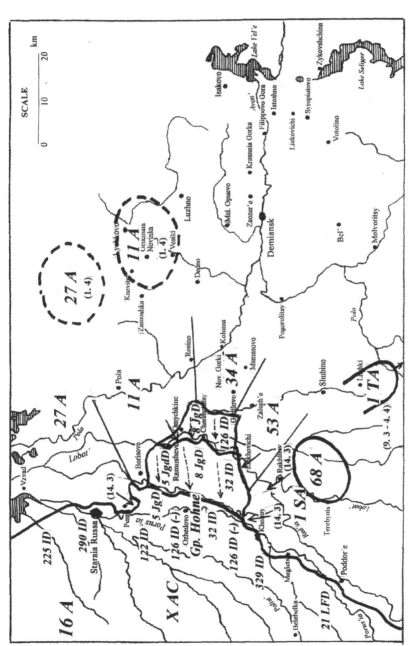

Map 113. The Northwestern Front's operations, 7–18 March 1943

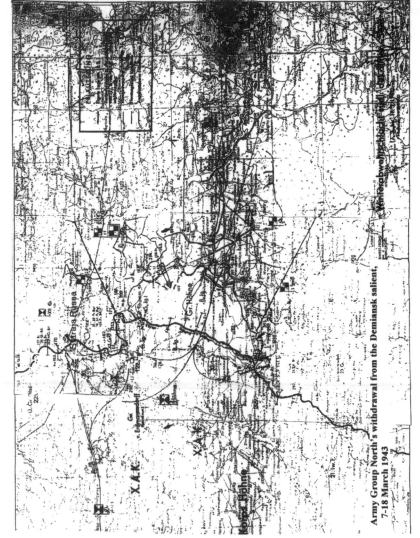

Map 114. Army Group North's withdrawal from the Demiansk salient, 7–18 March 1943

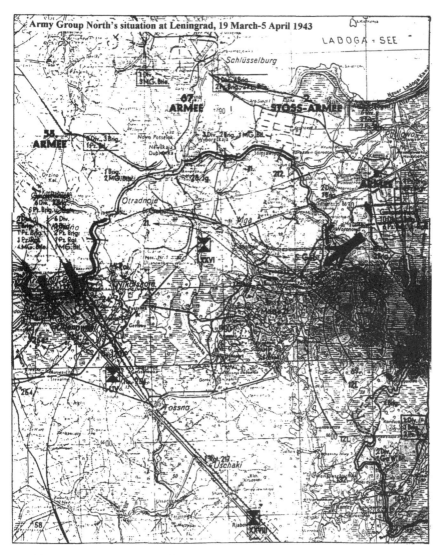

Map 115. Army Group North's situation at Leningrad, 19 March–5 April 1943

struck the defenses of the XXXVIII Army Corps' 1st *Luftwaffe* Field Division but achieved only limited gains in fighting that lasted until 27 March. Nevertheless, the fighting achieved its ends, since the Eighteenth Army had no choice but to reinforce the Novgorod sector with the 217th and 58th Infantry Divisions from the Kirishi region and Demiansk.

Sviridov's 55th Army began the Leningrad Front's offensive south of Krasnyi Bor on 19 March, after a delay of two days to complete offensive preparations. Assaulting southward along the Ul'ianovka road, Sviridov's forces struck the positions of the German L Army Corps' *Gruppe* Plaun (which included the Flanders Legion) and the LIV Army Corps' 24th Infantry Division astride the Ul'ianovka road. The 268th Rifle Division and 55th Rifle Brigade, in Sviridov's first echelon, penetrated the German defenses at the junction between the two German forces and advanced 3 kilometers to the outskirts of Sablino by day's end. However, the Flanders Legion, supported by 88-mm Flak (antiaircraft) guns and several Tiger tanks from the 502nd Panzer *Abteilung* (Detachment), counterattacked and drove Sviridov's forces back to their jumping-off positions. Sviridov tried in vain for eight days to rekindle his offensive but failed. The bitter and fruitless fighting continued until 2 April, when the *Stavka* ordered Govorov's *front* to abandon further offensive operations. By this time, the Germans had reinforced their defenses astride the Ul'ianovka road with the 170th and 254th Infantry Divisions and assigned both to the LIV Army Corps' control. Both sides suffered heavy losses in the fighting, with the Flanders Legion counting only 45 survivors out of its initial strength of 500 men.[353]

Further east, Meretskov's Volkhov Front began the offensive with Lieutenant General F. I. Starikov's 8th Army attacking toward Mga from its sector south of Voronovo at the precise hour that the 55th Army attacked from Krasnyi Bor toward Mga. Starikov's army consisted of nine rifle divisions, two rifle and two separate tank brigades, and four separate tank regiments. He concentrated his 286th, 256th, 378th, 374th, and 265th Rifle Divisions in first echelon supported by the 35th, 25th, 33rd, and 50th Tank Regiments. The 239th, 64th Guards, and 364th Rifle Divisions and the 122nd and 185th Tank Brigades were in second echelon, and the 372nd Rifle Division and 58th Rifle Brigade were in reserve north of the army's penetration sector. Meretskov supported Starikov's army with most of his *front's* artillery. The 8th Army faced the German 1st, 223rd, and 69th Infantry Divisions of the Eighteenth Army's XXVI Army Corps, which occupied defenses extending from Gontovaia Lipka, north of the Mga railroad line to Pogost'e, and were backed up by the 385th Security Division.[354]

As was the case with the Leningrad Front's 55th Army, the 8th Army's preparations were delayed and the attack had to be postponed until 19 March:

> The headquarters of the 8th Army (chief of staff Colonel B. M. Golovchiner) carefully planned the preparation and conduct of the operation under the chief of staff of the *front*, Major General F. P. Ozerov. However, the forested swampy terrain spring conditions, the absence of roads, inadequate intelligence data about the enemy, especially concerning his system of fires in the depths of the first defensive belt, created definite difficulties in planning the employment of artillery, tanks, and aviation. Greater difficulties were encountered with organizing

supply of ammunition and other material and also with the creation of the required force grouping. All of this led to the fact that the commencement of the offensive had to be delayed from 8 to 19 March.[355]

Starikov's army began its assault early on 19 March after a 135-minute artillery preparation. During the first three days of intense fighting, the army's first echelon divisions penetrated 3–4 kilometers along a 7-kilometer front at the junction of the defending 1st and 223rd Infantry Divisions. Starikov then committed a small mobile group, which consisted of the 64th Guards Rifle Division's 191st Guards Rifle Regiment and a battalion of the 122nd Tank Brigade, whose orders were to cut the Mga-Kirishi railroad line and wheel northward toward Mga Station. Advancing in heavy rain, which prevented the 14th Air Army from providing any air support, the mobile group managed to reach the Mga-Kirishi rail line east of Turyshkino Station before being halted by German reinforcements. In haste and despite the bad weather, the Eighteenth Army managed to transfer *kampfgruppen* from the 21st, 61st, and 121st Infantry Divisions to the threatened sector, where they were able to contain Starikov's thrust, but only barely.

Despite the initial failure, Zhukov insisted that Starikov continued his attacks throughout the remainder of March. After almost two weeks of heavy but fruitless fighting, on 1 April Zhukov ordered him to commit his 14th Rifle Division and 1st Separate Rifle Brigade from reserve to support another assault by the 64th Guards Rifle Division on German defenses around Karbusel', just east of the Mga-Kirishi railroad. The German 121st Infantry Division repelled the assault, inflicting heavy losses on the attackers. Finally, at 0140 hours on 2 April, the *Stavka* issued identical directives permitting Starikov's 8th and Sviridov's 55th Armies to halt their attacks and go over to the defense (see Map 116):

> The *Stavka* of the Supreme High Command is permitting you to halt the offensive by the forces of the 8th Army [55th Army] temporarily, consolidate your hold on the positions you have achieved, and do not begin an offensive attack without the special permission of the *Stavka* to do so.
>
> Vasil'ev [Stalin][356]

Relative calm then descended over the front in the Leningrad region on 3 April, just as it did in the Staraia Russa region to the south. In the wake of this calm, Operation Polar Star would become only a memory worthy of nothing more than an occasional footnote in subsequent Soviet military histories.

In part, the *Stavka* ordered the Leningrad and Volkhov Fronts to end their Mga offensive because their forces failed even to dent the German defenses south of Leningrad, and the spring thaw had begun. In reality, however, it halted the Mga operation because Operation Polar Star, which gave meaning and context to the offensive at Leningrad, had failed. In addition, even the *Stavka* could no longer permit the immense waste of manpower in continued futile offensives in the region. Despite its failure, however, the offensive contributed significantly to the *Stavka's* overall efforts by ending, once and for all, any German thoughts about capturing Leningrad. The Mga offensive also pinned down 30 German divisions, some of which could have helped the OKH stabilize the situation along the western and southwestern axes.

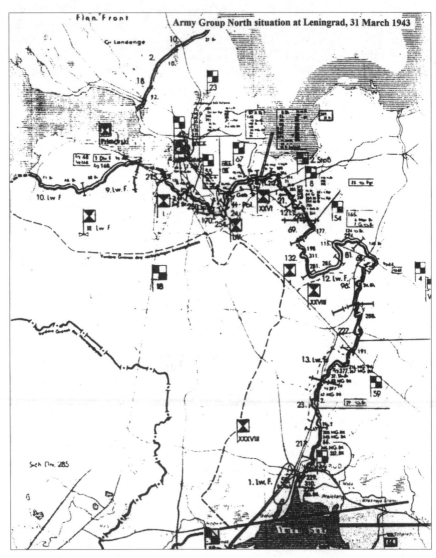

Map 116. Army Group North's situation at Leningrad, 31 March 1943

Conclusions

Given the *Stavka's* ambitious strategic aims in the winter of 1942–1943, Operation Polar Star and its counterpart offensives in the Leningrad region represented the logical culmination to the prolonged series of Red Army offensives that spread from south to north across the entire Soviet-German front. Given the Red Army's capabilities, however, like the other offensives, Polar Star failed. It did so because the Red Army was not yet capable of winning such victories, certainly not in the difficult terrain of the Demiansk, Staraia Russa, and Leningrad regions, where large tank forces could not be brought to bear. Thereafter, a more sober and realistic *Stavka* chose more carefully when and where to fight, attacking only when victory seemed achievable.

Like previous operations, Operation Polar Star proved costly to the many hundreds of thousands of Red Army soldiers who fought in it and tried to overcome the most trying of terrain and weather conditions. Although complete Soviet casualty figures for the first quarter of 1943 are not yet available, those that have been released and estimated figures vividly underscore how costly this operation actually was.

According to official Soviet count, the Northwestern Front began Operation Polar Star with a force of 327,600 men facing roughly 100,000 German troops. During the period from 15 to 28 February, the *front* lost 33,663 men, including 10,016 killed, captured, or missing and 23,647 wounded or sick.[357] After assembling all of the forces designated to participate in Operation Polar Star, the Northwestern Front's strength rose to 401,190 men on 1 March 1943. It then lost another 103,108 men, including 31,789 killed, captured, and missing and 71,319 wounded or sick, during its March offensive.[358] This brought the gruesome toll to over 130,000 men, including over 40,000 irrecoverable losses, out of a force of just over 400,000 men. These losses are even more staggering when considered within the context of the cumulative losses the Northwestern Front suffered during its entire 26-month-long struggle for the Demiansk salient (see Figure 6).

Figure 6. Red Army losses at Demiansk, January 1942–March 1943

		Losses		
Period	*Initial strength*	*Irrecoverable*	*Wounded or ill*	*Total*
7 January 41- 20 May 42	105,700 (+ 300,000)	88,908	156,603	245,511
20 May 42- 4 Oct 42	300,000 est.	90,000 est.	210,000 est.	300,000
15 Feb 43- 19 Mar 43	327,600 – 401,190	41,805	94,966	136,771
TOTAL		220,713	461,569	682,282

Source: G. F. Krivosheev, ed., *Grif sekretnosti sniat': Poteri Vooruzhennykh Sil SSSR v voinakh, boevykh deistviiakh i voennykh konfliktakh: Statisticheskoe issledovanie* [The secret classification is removed: The losses of the Armed Forces of the USSR in wars, combat operations and military conflicts: A statistical analysis] (Moscow: Voenizdat 1993), 224–226.

Nor did the Red Army's forces fighting in the Leningrad region fare any better. The Leningrad and Volkhov Fronts initially committed a force of over 250,000 troops to combat in Operation Polar Star against a German force numbering roughly one third of that number. The two *fronts* then suffered roughly 150,000 casualties, including about 35,000 dead, during its offensives in February and March.[359]

Chapter 11

Conclusions

Depending on their sources or political viewpoint, until quite recently Soviet (Russian) and most Western historians have consistently ignored, overlooked, or understated the *Stavka's* strategic intentions as it planned the Red Army's offensive operations during the fall of 1942 and the winter of 1942–1943 and the full scope and scale of the operations the Red Army conducted during these periods. This is particularly the case in regard to the offensive operations conducted along the western (Moscow-Smolensk), central (Kursk-Orel-Briansk), and northwestern (Leningrad and Staraia Russa) axes.

For example, the official Soviet six-volume *History of the Great Patriotic War of the Soviet Union 1941–1945* [*Istoriia Velikoi Otechestvennoi voiny Sovetskogo Soiuza* 1941–1945] published in 1961 remains totally silent about the Red Army's offensive operations along the western axis during the period of its counteroffensive at Stalingrad, in particular, Operation Mars.[360] Its sequel, the official Soviet eight-volume *History of the Second World War 1939–1945* [*Istoriia Vtoroi Mirovoi voiny 1939–1945*] published in 1976, dismisses the offensive operations the Red Army launched against the Demiansk and Rzhev-Viaz'ma salients in November and December 1942 (Operation Mars) as mere diversionary operations:

> While planning and organizing the counteroffensive at Stalingrad, the *Stavka* envisioned tying the forces of the enemy down with active operations of forces along the western and northwestern axes and in the North Caucasus. It thought that, as soon as the enemy found himself in a difficult situation at Stalingrad and in the North Caucasus, the High Command of the Wehrmacht would try to transfer part of its forces from other regions, in particular, from the Rzhev and Viaz'ma regions, to help its southern grouping. For this reason, it had to begin the offensive operation "Mars." Its [the *Stavka's*] aim was not only to tie down the forces of the enemy and inflict a defeat on them in the region of the Rzhev-Viaz'ma salient but, additionally, also to attract enemy reserves to this axis. The counterstroke by the forces of the Trans-Caucasus Front in the Mozdok region during the Stalingrad offensive operation was assigned the very same role.[361]

More recent Russian accounts of Operation Mars, while providing a bit more detail about the offensive, continue to claim this offensive was part of an elaborate Soviet deception plan designed to draw German attentions and forces away from the Stalingrad region. However, other Soviet studies published internally for Soviet Army use or commercially about Red Army deception operations during wartime make little or no mention of Operation Mars.

Soviet accounts of the offensives the *Stavka* organized along the western and northwestern axes during February and March 1943 have been more candid as evidenced by its 1961 history of the war:

During the winter offensive of the Red Army, intense fighting raged in both the central and northwestern sectors of the Soviet-German front.

At the end of January, the *Stavka* of the Supreme High Command worked out a plan for a series of operations associated with a single strategic concept. Five *fronts* were to participate in them: the Northwestern, Kalinin, Western, Briansk and Central. The concept of the *Stavka* was to destroy the 2nd German Tank [Panzer] Army in the Orel region with the forces of the Briansk and left wing of the Western Fronts and then, with the arrival of the armies of the Central Front, to develop the offensive through Briansk toward Smolensk to reach the rear of the enemy's Rzhev-Viaz'ma grouping and, in cooperation with the Kalinin and Western Fronts, encircle and destroy the main forces of Army Group "Center." At the same time, the Northwestern Front was assigned the mission to smash the enemy in the Demiansk region and support the arrival of a strong mobile group in the rear of German forces operating against the Leningrad and Volkhov Fronts. Simultaneous implementation of these operations should have deprived the Hitlerite command of freedom to maneuver his reserves and prevent it from transferring forces to more threatened *front* sectors.[362]

This history then allocates three pages to describe the course and outcome of the operations along these critical axes.

The official history of World War II published in 1976 paid even less attention to these operations. It stated categorically that the vast panoply of strategic operations the *Stavka* planned and the Red Army conducted during February and March 1943 along the western, central, and northwestern axes were clearly subordinate to and in the interests of the major operations in southern Russia:

> The operations of Soviet forces along the western and northwestern axis, conducted in the beginning of 1943, were closely associated with the strategic offensive in the south. Although they did not achieve their assigned aims, the enemy was deprived of the opportunity to reinforce his groupings on the southern wing of the Soviet-German front at the expense of Army Groups "Center" and "North." This made it considerably easier for the Soviet Army to not only successfully carry out the operations at Stalingrad, on the upper Don River, and along the Khar'kov and Donbas axes but also to repel attempted enemy counteroffensives. The liquidation of the bridgeheads in the Rzhev and Demiansk regions practically removed the threat of an offensive of the enemy along the Moscow axis. Prerequisites were created for the development of operations along the Pskov, Vitebsk, and Smolensk axes.[363]

The first substantial post-Soviet treatment of the war, the four volume Great Patriotic War 1941–1945, which was published in 1998, seven years after the fall of the Soviet Union, represented a genuine and constructive effort to cover these forgotten battles in greater detail, although still insisting they were secondary in nature. An example is this history's treatment of Operation Mars within the context of the counteroffensive at Stalingrad:

The strategic plan for the actions of the armed forces along the southern wing of the Soviet-German front began to be formulated in the *Stavka* of the Soviet Supreme High Command in mid-September, and the winter campaign of 1942/43 as a whole – in November and December ....

Such a plan, however, did not take shape immediately but was formulated gradually. The overall decision was determined only at the end of September and beginning of October, but it was not then formulated in any sort of unified document. Furthermore, in the beginning the General Staff and *Stavka* VGK did not even contemplate further perspectives. The question was only about immediate missions. Therefore, the main attention was paid chiefly to concentrating on the main operation – in the Stalingrad region – and the secondary — at Mozdok (in the northern Caucasus). In addition, it was intended to de-blockade Leningrad (Operation "Iskra") and to liquidate the Rzhev-Viaz'ma salient (Operation "Mars"). The directive about the preparation of these operations was issued in October. The concept of an attack on Rostov (operation "Saturn") also ripened in its most general form but was not worked out in detail. The concepts of the subsequent operations appeared during the course of the developing battles, as favorable conditions were created for them ....

[The *Stavka*] intended to deliver its main attack along the Stalingrad and Rostov axes. Having gone over to the counteroffensive here, the *Stavka* VGK expected to encircle and destroy the main grouping of Army Group "B," thereafter cut off the routes of withdrawal of Army Group "A" from the northern Caucasus into the Donbas, and, subsequently, not only liquidate the most dangerous enemy penetration in the south but also deprive him of the main shock groups of his forces. Subsequently, [the *Stavka*] planned, while broadening the front of the strategic offensive to the north, to crush successively the forces of the enemy along the middle and upper Don [River], develop the offensive along the Khar'kov and Kursk axes and into the Donbas, and penetrate the Leningrad blockade in the north. Along the remainder of the front, the intention was to conduct local, but no less important offensive operations in the Demiansk, Velikie Luki, Rzhev, and Viaz'ma regions with the objective to tie down the forces of the enemy, liquidate the threat to Moscow, and inflict a defeat on the forces of Army Groups "Center" and "North."

The first and most important operation of the winter campaign – the strategic counteroffensive of Soviet forces at Stalingrad – was planned to begin the first ten days of November. The subsequent operations were intended to begin later, based on the concrete situation that existed as operations "Uranus" and "Saturn" developed. Overall, [the *Stavka*] intended to employ 11 of the 12 [existing] *fronts* in active operations during the winter campaign. Their operations would unfold in a 1,500–1,600-kilometer-wide sector to a depth of from 200–600 kilometers. The scale of the operations and the *fronts'* missions were determined accordingly ....

Along the western axis, the Kalinin and Western Fronts were ordered to conduct the offensive operation "Mars" with the objective of the destruction of the enemy's 9th [Army] and 3rd Tank Army in the Rzhev, Sychevka, and Olenino region and to capture Velikie Luki and Novosokol'niki with part of their forces. Along the central axis, the Briansk and Voronezh Fronts were assigned the mission to defend the positions they occupied and prepare to go over to the offensives along their axes "as soon as favorable conditions have been created."[364]

A striking improvement over its predecessors, this account is not only the first officially sanctioned work to mention more than just the name Operation Mars, but it also provides a brief, albeit only partially accurate, description of the operation nestled deep within a more lengthy description of the fighting in the Velikie Luki region:

At the same time [the fall of 1942], the Soviet command intended to conduct a large-scale operation, under the code name Operation "Mars," to liquidate the Rzhev-Viaz'ma salient with the main forces of the Western and Kalinin Fronts. In the Western Front, four armies were enlisted in it, which were supposed to deliver blows toward Rzhev and Sychevka. Four armies from the Kalinin Front were also to participate in the operation with the mission of conducting attacks toward Belyi and Olenino and subsequently to develop the offensive to Smolensk. Deployed on the right wing of this *front*, the 3rd and 4th Shock Armies were initially not employed in active operations. They were at hand to protect the main grouping against possible enemy attack from the northwest for which they were to occupy a defense along the 50 kilometer front from Kholm to Nelidovo. However, the plan was altered because intelligence detected the approach of enemy reserves from the Smolensk and Vitebsk regions. The decision was made to conduct a preventative attack along the Velikie Luki axis with the forces of the 3rd Shock Army, reinforced by units freed up from the 43rd Army.

Thus, in a word, both sides began preparing for active offensive operations in the Velikie Luki region. The only question was which side would be the first to attack and achieve decisive results along this axis. Soviet forces were the first to attack and did so on 24–25 November. But, unfortunately, [the offensive] was not developed in most of the sectors. We achieved success only in the Belyi region. The Kalinin Front's 41st Army, under the command of General G. F. Tarasov, penetrated the enemy defense southwest of Rzhev with its shock group consisting of General S. I. Povetkin's 6th Siberian Rifle Corps and General Solomatin's 1st Mechanized Corps and reached the approaches to the city of Belyi.

However, the situation for the Soviet forces changed abruptly by the beginning of December. This was because Field Marshal G. Kluge, the commander of Army Group "Center," transferred there four panzer divisions, which conducted a powerful counterattack against the 41st Army's weakly protected flank. As a result, it [the 41st Army] was first halted and then encircled. Its formations and units fought in a "sack" for eight days.

By order of the *Stavka*, the encircled grouping under the command of General M. D. Solomatin broke through to the main forces on the night of 16 December. However, all of the formations suffered heavy losses, lost almost all of their heavy equipment, and lost their combat capability. Attempts to revive the offensive were unsuccessful. The penetration of the Western Front's 20th Army to the Rzhev-Sychevka railroad did not help. As a result, the offensive along that axis was halted. At the same time, the most important events were developing on the right flank and in the center of the Kalinin Front's operational formation [in the Velikie Luki region].[365]

Far more candid than previous accounts, the new history's description of what actually took place in Operation Mars is still only a pale reflection of what actually occurred. Although it acknowledges the gruesome fate of one army that participated in the offensive (the 41st Army), it fails to even mention the contributions and fates of five other armies that took part in the operation. Nor does it mention the Western Front's major offensive in the Sychevka sector or the heavy fighting conducted by the *front's* 20th Army during the November phase of the operation. Finally, it blatantly conceals the role Marshal Zhukov played in planning and coordinating the offensive and also says nothing about the role of other commanders, such as Konev and Katukov, who also played significant roles in the failed operation.

On the other hand, this new Russian history of the war pays far more attention to the *Stavka's* ambitious strategic offensive in February-March 1943 along the western, central, and northwestern axes than previous Soviet accounts:

In February 1943 forces along the western and central axes were associated with the general strategic offensive of Soviet forces, begun in the southern, southwestern, and northwestern sectors of the Soviet-German front. While preparing it, the Supreme High Command assessed the existing situation rather optimistically. It presumed that the enemy in the south was beaten and, having abandoned Kursk, Khar'kov, and Belgorod, was withdrawing behind the Dnepr River and was essentially weakened along the remaining axes. Therefore, despite the serious situation in which the forces of the Briansk and Voronezh Fronts found themselves as a result of the long winter offensive, the *Stavka* VGK decided not only to continue it but also to conduct new offensive operations in the sectors of these *fronts* ....

The main characteristic of the planned operations was the fact that, for the achievement of its final objectives, the *fronts* had to fulfill a series of consecutive missions: at first to defeat the enemy in the Orel region, then in the Briansk and Rzhev regions, and, finally, east of Smolensk. Furthermore, if there were insufficient forces for the first stage, then large reserves were required for the subsequent operations. The possibility of their creation appeared only after the capitulation of German forces at Stalingrad, when seven armies were immediately freed up ....

Overall, the concept of the operation was rather complicated. The operations of all of the *fronts* were so closely interwoven and interconnected that any disruption of cooperation between them could lead to the disruption of the entire concept. Not only the efforts of the forces that were operating along the mixed — central and western — axes had to be coordinated carefully but also the attacks of the *fronts* in each of them.[366]

Despite revealing in full the *Stavka's* ambitious offensive plans for operations during the late winter of 1942–1943 and describing these operations in unprecedented detail and with a degree of candor absent in previous Soviet studies of the war, the fact remains that comprehensive studies of these operations have yet to be written.

By consistently ignoring, overlooking, or minimizing the importance these operations during the Red Army's winter campaign of 1942–1943, Soviet as well as Russian historians have perpetuated certain enduring myths regarding the nature of Soviet military strategy during the war, the role played by Stalin and other members of the *Stavka* in its formulation, and how this strategy governed the operations of the Red Army.

The most enduring of these myths is the proposition that, having failed to master the art of strategic concentration when organizing the Red Army's offensive operations during 1941 and most of 1942, Stalin and the *Stavka* finally began concentrating their forces properly during the fall of 1942 and to an even greater extent as the war proceeded. According to this myth, when the dictator and his key advisers planned the Red Army's offensives in the Leningrad (Tikhvin), Moscow, and Rostov regions during November and December 1941, the expanded offensive during the winter of 1941–1942, the offensives during the spring of 1942 to pre-empt the planned German offensive in the summer of 1942, and, finally, the counteroffensives, counterstrokes, and counterattacks during the summer and early fall of 1942 to thwart the German advance toward Stalingrad, they frequently planned and conducted offensive actions along too many strategic and operational axes. As a result, by requiring the Red Army to achieve too much with too few forces, they dispersed its forces, dissipated its strength, and sharply curtailed its ultimate offensive success.

This myth goes on to assert that, beginning in November 1942, throughout the course of the winter campaign of 1942–1943, and to an ever-increasing extent during the war's subsequent campaigns, Stalin and his *Stavka* routinely concentrated the Red Army's offensive efforts along the most critical strategic axes, thus avoiding the mistakes they made earlier in the war and materially improving the army's combat performance. Thus, by concentrating their forces along the southwestern strategic axis in the fall of 1942 and the winter of 1942–1943, they were able to achieve signal victory in the Stalingrad region and drive German forces westward to the Kursk region and the line of the Northern Donets and Mius Rivers. Similarly, by concentrating their forces along the central axis in the summer of 1943, they were able to emerge victorious in the decisive battle for Kursk and subsequently drive German forces back to the Dnepr River. According to this myth, by skillfully concentrating the Red Army's forces along the most decisive strategic axes during each subsequent wartime campaign, Stalin and his *Stavka* were able to achieve victory after strategic victory throughout 1944 and 1945, culminating in the Red Army's victorious march on Berlin April 1945.[367]

Supplementing this myth are two closely associated corollaries. The first maintains that virtually all of the offensive operations the Red Army conducted elsewhere along the front during these campaigns were only secondary and diversionary in nature. The second argues that Stalin, who strictly followed his own strategic counsel in 1942 and the eight months of 1942, began heeding the advice of his chief military advisers as he prepared the Red Army for the offensives it conducted during November 1942 and its winter offensive of 1942–1943. Thereafter, according to this corollary, Stalin gave his senior military advisers, in particular, Marshals Zhukov and Vasilevsky, an ever-increasing role formulating the strategy governing the Red Army's offensive operations to war's end.

Close examination of the offensive operations the Red Army conducted during the winter campaign of 1942–1942, as well as during subsequent campaigns in the war, explodes this myth and its two associated corollaries. It is now abundantly clear that, as had been the case in previous wartime campaigns, during the winter of 1942–1943 and throughout the remainder of the war, Stalin remained convinced the most useful military strategy the Red Army could pursue was to apply maximum pressure against the Germans' strategic defenses by conducting simultaneous offensive operations along as many strategic axes of the front as possible. The dictator did so because, appreciating the numerical superiority of the Red Army over the *Wehrmacht*, he was certain that, if attacked everywhere, the German defense was likely to crack and break somewhere. This is precisely the strategy Stalin adopted when he launched Operations Mars and Uranus in November 1942 and, once again, when he unleashed offensive operations by multiple *fronts* simultaneously along all three strategic axes spanning the entire breadth of the Soviet-German front in February and March 1943 (see Map 117).

Although the employment of this strategy had proven ill-founded during previous wartime campaigns, it began yielding noticeably greater successes beginning in the late 1942. First it produced victory in the Stalingrad region during November and December 1942. Later, it projected the Red Army's forces forward into the Kursk and Viaz'ma regions and to the Northern Donets and Mius Rivers by early March 1943, despite the setbacks they experienced in the Donbas, Khar'kov, and Belgorod regions. Even though the Red Army failed to achieve the ambitious objectives Stalin and his *Stavka* assigned to it during the winter campaign of 1942–1943, the experience it derived from these operations would pay immense dividends in the summer of 1943. Then, after thwarting the last German offensive of the war at Kursk, it embarked on a strategic offensive of its own that drove German forces back to the Dnepr River. Thereafter, as subsequent volumes in this series will demonstrate, contrary to previous assertions, whenever possible, Stalin would continue to maintain maximum pressure on German defenses by ordering the Red Army to conduct offensive operations along multiple strategic axes.[368]

In regard to the two corollaries, first, examination of the offensive operations the Red Army conducted during the winter campaign of 1942–1942 and thereafter demonstrates that many if not most of the offensives it conducted along so-called secondary axes, which have been described as diversionary in nature, were in fact part and parcel of Stalin's deliberate strategy to maintain maximum pressure

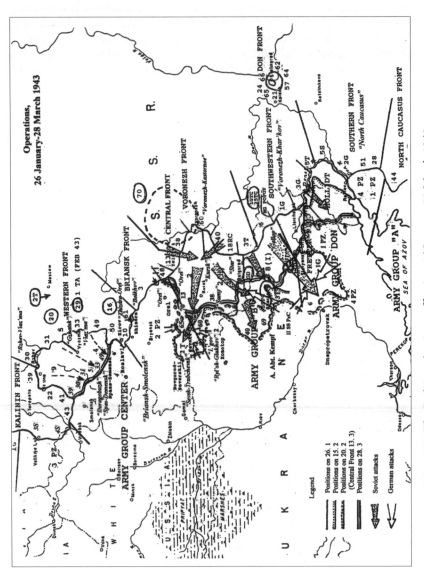

Map 117. The Red Army's winter offensive, 26 January–28 March 1943

on German defenses. It is also clear that Soviet historians have concealed or at least deemphasized these offensives either because they failed or to protect the reputations of those senior commanders who planned and conducted them. Second, there is also no evidence indicating that Stalin ever relinquished his role as chief architect of the military strategy the Soviet Union and its Red Army pursued during the war. On the contrary, close examination of key wartime documents (*Stavka*, NKO, and General Staff) show that the dictator dominated military decision-making as much in the spring of 1945 as he had during the initial period of the war, often on matters tactical and operational as well as strategic.

Regardless of who formulated Soviet military strategy, what that strategy was, and how effective it proved to be, Stalin and his *Stavka*, like the Red Army as a whole, derived valuable lessons from the operations they conducted during the winter campaign of 1942–1943. Even though they displayed far greater skill in planning strategic operations during this campaign than before, the rapidly changing military situation often compelled them to reach hasty decisions without sound consideration of such factors as the actual correlation of opposing forces, necessary logistical support, the fatigue of their troops, and the deleterious effects of deteriorating weather conditions. As a result, their forces regrouped, moved, and concentrated at glacially slow speeds, and, when organizing their assaults, the *fronts* conducted these offensive operations without achieving the mix of combined-arms forces necessary to launch and sustain these operations successfully. In particular, tank, artillery, and air support frequently proved inadequate, and logistical support often utterly failed. In short, these experiences indicated that Stalin and his *Stavka* still had to master the art of the possible in terms of formulating realistic objectives for their forces and in planning and conducting large-scale offensive operations.[369]

Compounding these problems, Stalin and his *Stavka* were also victimized by their own over-optimism and ambitions during the Red Army's winter campaign of 1942–1943. Energized by the Red Army's signal victory at Stalingrad, as had been the case the year before when they planned the Red Army's offensive during the winter of 1941–1942 in the wake of the Red Army's victory at Moscow, they concluded the *Wehrmacht* was ripe for complete collapse and planned accordingly. However, by planning offensive operations spanning the entire front with abandon but without accurately assessing the real capabilities of their own forces, Stalin set the Red Army up for the defeats it suffered in late February and March 1943. Unfortunately but inevitably, the Red Army's soldiers paid for Stalin's excessive optimism with their blood. Largely as a result of these sobering experiences, however, when Stalin and his *Stavka* formulated a strategy governing the Red Army's operations during the summer of 1943, it did so based on the lessons it learned during the winter campaign of 1942–1943, lessons that would first bear fruit during the titanic struggle around the periphery of the famous Kursk Bulge in the summer of 1943.

Photographs

General Vatutin and Nikita Khrushchev. (RGAKFD Moscow)

General Vasilevsky and Marshal Voroshilov.
(Photo archive of the Bulgarian Ministry of Defence)

General Moskalenko. (Photo archive of the Bulgarian Ministry of Defence)

Marshal Timoshenko. (Photo archive of the Bulgarian Ministry of Defence)

General Zhukov. (Photo archive of the Bulgarian Ministry of Defence)

General Malinovsky. (Photo archive of the Bulgarian Ministry of Defence)

General Bagramyan. (Photo archive of the Bulgarian Ministry of Defence)

General Lelyushenko, the commander of the 3rd Guards Army. (RGAKFD Moscow)

General Tolbukhin, the commander of the 68th Army.
(Photo archive of the Bulgarian Ministry of Defence)

General Kazakov, the commander of the 69th Army.
(Photo archive of the Bulgarian Ministry of Defence)

General Batov, the commander of the 65th Army.
(Photo archive of the Bulgarian Ministry of Defence)

Kursk, 1943, shortly after the liberation of the city. A knocked-out German StuG III
assault gun on Lenin Street. (RGAKFD Moscow)

Soviet Central Front, 1943. The inhabitants of Ol'khovatka village chat with their
liberators – Soviet tank men. (RGAKFD Moscow)

Rzhev, 1943. Soviet anti-tank troops move through the city. (RGAKFD Moscow)

Rzhev, 1943. Another shot of Soviet anti-tank troops moving through the city.
(RGAKFD Moscow)

Rzhev region, 1942. Soviet submachinegunners during the battle for Rzhev.
(RGAKFD Moscow)

Rzhev, 1943. Streets of the liberated city are cleared of mines. (RGAKFD Moscow)

Gzhatsk, March 1943, Soviet infantry marching through the city streets.
(RGAKFD Moscow)

Gzhatsk, 1943. A school destroyed by the retreating German troops with an improvised
German cemetery in front of it. (RGAKFD Moscow)

Gzhatsk, March 1943. Soviet military aerosledge (Aerosan) on the streets of the city shortly after its liberation. (RGAKFD Moscow)

Demiansk, March 1943. A school destroyed by the retreating German troops; German artillery equipment is in the foreground. (RGAKFD Moscow)

Leningrad Front, 1943. A liberated settlement held by Soviet armoured forces.
(RGAKFD Moscow)

A formation commanded by General Guriev is taking the oath of the Soviet Guards.
(Photo archive of the Bulgarian Ministry of Defence)

Northwestern Front, 1942. General Kurochkin at a meeting with young commanders shortly before their departure to the frontline. (RGAKFD Moscow)

Khar'kov, 1943. Children play near the former HQ of the German commandant of Khar'kov. (RGAKFD Moscow)

Khar'kov, 1943. A group of volunteers from the liberated city travel to the front.
(RGAKFD Moscow)

Khar'kov, 1943. (Photo archive of the Bulgarian Ministry of Defence)

Khar'kov, February 1943. Soviet anti-aircraft gun on Dzerzhinsky square. (RGAKFD Moscow)

Khar'kov, March 1943. A Soviet tank unit moves through the city. (RGAKFD Moscow)

Khar'kov, February 1943 – Soviet artillery passes through the city. (RGAKFD Moscow)

The Czechoslovak Battalion. It participated in the defensive battles at Khar'kov.
(Photo archive of the Bulgarian Ministry of Defence)

Soviet T-34 tanks used in support of the Czechoslovakian Battalion.
(Photo archive of the Bulgarian Ministry of Defence)

Southwestern Front, 1943. A Soviet solder is destroying German road signs.
(RGAKFD Moscow)

Demiansk region, 1943. A village that had been razed to the ground by the retreating German troops. (RGAKFD Moscow)

Viaz'ma, 1943. Soviet troops. (RGAKFD Moscow)

V'az'ma, 1943. Soviet soldier holding a small child. (RGAKFD Moscow)

Viaz'ma, 13 March 1943. Soviet troops move through the city streets.
(RGAKFD Moscow)

Kalinin Front, January 1943. Soviet infantry overcome German barbed wire obstacles.
(RGAKFD Moscow)

Notes

Notes to Preface

i   The most significant "forgotten battles" which took place during the first two years of the war, that is, from the German invasion of the Soviet Union on 22 June 1941 through the battle of Kursk in July-August 1943, include important aspects of the strategic defensive operations the Red Army conducted to contain the *Wehrmacht's* advances during Operations Barbarossa and *Blau* in 1941 and 1942, the counteroffensive operations the Red Army orchestrated in the Moscow region during December 1941 and the Moscow and Stalingrad regions during November and December 1942, and the strategic offensive operations the Red Army conducted during the winters of 1941–42 and 1942–43. After the battle of Kursk in the summer of 1943, the most important "forgotten battles" include the Kalinin (1st Baltic), Western, and Central (Belorussian) Fronts' 1st Belorussian offensive during the fall of 1943 and the winter of 1943–44, the 2nd and 3rd Ukrainian Fronts' 1st Iasi-Kishinev offensive during late April and May 1944, the 3rd Belorussian Front's Gumbinnen-Goldap offensive into East Prussia during late October 1944, the 1st, 4th, and 2nd Ukrainian Fronts' offensive into eastern Hungary during late September and October 1944, and the 1st, 4th, and 2nd Ukrainian Fronts' Olomouc offensive during March and April 1945.

ii   These include such generals as G. K. Zhukov, I. S. Konev, A. I. Eremenko, K. A. Meretskov, and V. D. Sokolovsky.

iii The most important of these memoir writers were Generals Erich von Manstein, Heinz Guderian, and F. W. von Mellenthin.

iv   The "TERRA" Press published collections of NKO, *Stavka*, and General Staff documents in a series edited by V. A. Zolotarev under the rubric of *Russkii arkhiv: Velikaia Otechestvennaia* [The Russian archives: The Great Patriotic [War]]. While these collections provide extensive coverage of directives, orders, and reports prepared prior to the spring of 1943, major gaps exist in these collections after that date. Although far more selective, a collection of wartime GKO documents is contained in Iurii Gor'kov, ed., *Gosudarstvennyi Komitet postanovliaet* [The State Defense Committee decrees] (Moscow: "Olma," 2002).

Notes to Chapter 1

5   See Anton Detlev von Plato, *Die Geschichte der 5. Panzerdivision 1938 bis 1945*, (Regensburg: Walhalla u. Praetoria Verlag KG Geog Zwickenpflug, 1978), 260.

6   See David M. Glantz, *From the Don to the Dnepr: Soviet Offensive Operations, December 1942-August 1943* (London: Frank Cass, 1991).

7   In some instances, Soviet (Russian) historians have provided some information about the Red Army's failed operations, such as their defeats in the Donbas and Khar'kov regions, in short articles in their military encyclopedias. In addition, the Red Army General Staff published classified studies about many of these other offensive operations, including, the Ostrogozhsk-Rossosh', Voronezh-Kastornoe, and Rostov offensives.

8   Although Russian "official" military historians now admit that Operation Mars actually took place, they insist the offensive was simply a diversionary operation designed

to draw the Germans' attentions and forces away from the far more important struggle in the Stalingrad region. On the other hand, although they have yet to write a detailed history of the Orel, Briansk, Smolensk operation or Operation Polar Star, they recently released a collection of documents related to former under the rubric, *Prelude to Kursk.*

Notes to Chapter 2

9   G. Zhukov, *Reminiscences and Reflections, Vol. 2* (Moscow: Progress Publishers, 1985), 86.

10   V. A. Zolotarev, ed., "Stavki VGK: Dokumenty i materialy 1942" [The *Stavka* VGK: Documents and materials], in *Russki arkhiv: Velikaia Otechestvennaia, 16, 5 (2)* [The Russian archives: The Great Patriotic [War], 16, 5 (2)] (Moscow: "Terra," 1996), 426. Hereafter cited as Zolotarev, "*Stavka* 1942," with appropriate page(s).

11   See David M. Glantz, *Zhukov's Greatest Defeat: The Red Army's Epic Disaster in Operation Mars, 1942* (Lawrence, KS,: The University Press of Kansas, 1999).

12   Soviet accounts of the battle for Stalingrad and associated offensive operations in the fall of 1942, including Zhukov's memoirs, obfuscate precisely when the *Stavka* planned to conduct Operation Uranus but assert it was planned in late October and early November. It is now clear, however, that both Operation Mars and Uranus were planned in late September but postponed several times before they were actually conducted on 19 and 25 November, respectively.

13   Zhukov's memoirs, in which he mentions Operation Mars but confuses the date of its conduct as well as the offensive's purpose and course, distort both the calendar of events in the fall of 1942 and the role he played in planning and conducting the operation. For a more precise account of Zhukov's wartime itinerary, see S. I. Isaev, *Vekhi frontovogo puti* [Landmarks of a front path], *Voenno-istoricheskii zhurnal* [Military-historical journal], No. 10 (October 1991), 22–25. Hereafter cited as *VIZh* with appropriate issue and date. This calendar indicates that Zhukov spent the bulk of this critical fall period with the Western and Kalinin Fronts. All subsequent references to Zhukov's activities accord with this calendar.

14   At the beginning of the war, Zhukov had advocated a "southern" strategy, meaning placing primary emphasis on the defense of the Ukraine. This accorded with his prior service in the Kiev Special Military District and his role in drafting prewar Soviet defense plans while he was serving as chief of the General Staff. Zhukov converted to a "northern" strategy, which assigned highest priority to the defense of Moscow, after his experiences during the battle for the Soviet capital city during the winter of 1941–1942. Thereafter, he strenuously argued that point of view throughout the spring, summer, and fall of 1942. See David M. Glantz, *Khar'kov, May 1942: The Anatomy of a Military Disaster* (London: Ian Allen, 1999).

15   The forces of the Kalinin and Western Fronts, together with those assigned to the Moscow Defense Zone, comprised 31 percent of the manpower, 32 percent of the artillery, almost 50 percent of the armor, and over 35 percent of the total strength of the Soviet Armed Forces. These forces were concentrated along only 17 percent of the overall front.

16   See overall Soviet strength figures in A. A. Grechko, chief ed., *Istoriia Vtoroi Mirovoi voiny 1939–1945, tom shestoi* [A history of the Second World War, volume six] (Moscow: Voenizdat, 1976), 34–35. German intelligence records generally substantiate these relative strengths.

17   As was the custom, all *Stavka* members took part in planning both offensive operations. As deputy Supreme Commander, Zhukov did so as well, which later permitted

him to share in the glory of the Stalingrad victory. Colonel General A. I. Eremenko, the commander of the Stalingrad Front, who thought it futile to continue efforts to rescue the 62nd Army in Stalingrad by conducting counterstrokes in the regions immediately north and south of the city, first proposed a broader counteroffensive to envelop all German and Rumanian forces in the Stalingrad region in late September 1942. Eremenko's plan ultimately became the basis of the *Stavka's* plan for Operation Uranus.

18 Since no documents released to date indicate the actual name of this operation, this is an assumption on the part of the author. In early November 1942, the Kalinin Front's 43rd Army consisted of the 9th and 21st Guards and 32nd, 145th, 279th, and 306th Rifle Divisions, supported by the 2nd Mechanized Corps and 154th Tank Brigade, and the *front's* 4th Shock Army included the 47th, 332nd, 334th, 358th, and 360th Rifle Divisions, the 24th Cavalry Division, and the 26th Destroyer and 45th Ski Brigades, supported by the 78th, 143rd, and 236th Tank Brigades and the 136th Separate Tank Battalion. The Western Front's 5th Army consisted of the 3rd Guards Motorized, 29th Guards and 19th, 108th, 144th, and 352nd Rifle Divisions and the 28th, 35th, 40th, and 49th Rifle Brigades, supported by the 120th and 161st Tank Brigades, and its 33rd Army included the 7th Guards Rifle Corps's 5th Guards Rifle Division and 112th, 125th, and 128th Rifle Brigades, the 17th, 50th, 53rd, 110th, 113th, 160th, and 222nd Rifle Divisions, and the 36th Rifle and 50th Ski Brigades, supported by the 213th, 248th, and 256th Tank Brigades and the 520th Separate Tank Battalion. Thus, the Western Front's 5th and 33rd Armies were far stronger than the *front's* other armies, except for those delivering the main attack in Operation Mars. See *Boevoi sostav Sovetskoi Armii, chast' 2 (Ianvar'-dekabr' 1942 goda* [The combat composition of the Soviet Army, part 2, January-December 1942] (Moscow: Voenizdat, 1968), 211–212. Prepared by the Red Army General Staff's Military-Scientific Directorate and classified secret. Hereafter cited as *Boevoi sostav*, with appropriate part and page(s).

19 The *Stavka* realized that the Romanian Third Army was defending the German Sixth Army's left flank along the Don River northwest of Stalingrad, and a portion of the German Fourth Panzer Army and the Romanian Fourth Army were protecting the Sixth Army's right flank south of Stalingrad.

20 Ultimately, because German resistance in the Stalingrad region proved stronger than anticipated, the *Stavka* decided to truncate Operation Saturn into Operation Little Saturn. Instead of propelling Vasilevsky's forces to Rostov, Operation Little Saturn sought to destroy Italian and German forces defending along the middle reaches of the Don River.

21 For the contents of the Western Front directive, see *Tsentral'nyi Arkhiv Ministerstva Oborony* [Central Archives of the Ministry of Defense], abbreviated *TsAMO*, fond 386, opis' 8583, ed. khr. [individual custody] 144, list [page] 8. All archival references hereafter cited as *TsAMO*, with appropriate fond (f.), opis (op.), delo (d.), and page (l.) or pages (ll.).

22 "Sychevsko-Rzhevskai oper. 31 A" [The Sychevka-Rzhev operation of the 31st Army], in *TsAMO*, f. 386, op. 8583, ed. khr. 144, ll. 7–8.

23 "Opisanie boevykh deistvii na rubezhe r. Vazuza za 25 noiabria–18 dekabria 1942 goda" [An account of combat operations along the Vazuza River line from 25 November–18 December 1942], Polevoe upravlenie 20 Armii [The field headquarters of the 20th Army], in *TsAMO RF* [Central Archives of the Ministry of Defense of the Russian Federation], f. 373, op. 6631, d. 65, l. 2.

24 The *Stavka* planners adjourned their sessions late on 26 September and returned to their respective *front* sectors to coordinate planning with *front* commanders and

staffs. After surveying the latest conditions in the south, Zhukov intended to rejoin his Western and Kalinin Fronts on 12 October, the initial date set for the launch of Operation Mars. However, bad weather delayed the preparations for Mars, and, instead of rejoining his *fronts*, on 12 October Zhukov returned to Moscow to finalize plans for the operation's first phase, now rescheduled for 28 October. On 21 October, while Zhukov traveled to the Kalinin Front to finalize attack preparations, the General Staff prepared final orders and dispatched them to the respective *fronts*.

25 For a full explanation of the operational concept, see "Vvod v proryv konno-mekhanizirovannykh grupp" [Introduction into the penetration of a cavalry-mechanized group], *Sbornik materialov po izucheniiu opyta voiny, No. 9 (Noiabr'-dekabr' 1943 g.)* [Collections of materials for the study of war experience, No. 9 (November-December 1943)] (Moscow: Voenizdat, 1944), 135–139. This classified study of the operations of 20th Army's mobile group was prepared by the Red Army General Staff's Section for the Exploitation of War Experience. Hereafter cited as *SMPIOV*, with appropriate page (s).

26 "Sychevsko-Rzhevskaia oper.," in *TsAMO*, f. 386, op. 8583, ed. khr. 144, l. 10.

27 For a description of the 41st Army's mission within the context of the Kalinin Front's operations, see M. D. Solomatin, *Krasnogradtsy* [The men of Krasnograd] (Moscow: Voenizdat, 1963), 11–13, and "Boevye doneseniia i operativnye svodki shtaba 1 mekhkorpusa" [Combat reports and operational summaries of the 1st Mechanized Corps], in *TsAMO*, f. 3424, op. 1. d. 2, l. 31. Solomatin's memoir contains a thorough and generally accurate account of the 1st Mechanized and 6th Rifle Corps' operations. Less detailed descriptions of the 22nd and 39th Armies' missions and operations are found in M. E. Katukov, *Na ostrie glavnogo udara* [On the point of the main attack] (Moscow: Voenizdat, 1976), 182–183, and K. A. Malygin, *V tsentre boevogo poriadka* [In the center of the combat formation] (Moscow: Voenizdat, 1986), 69–70.

28 Army Group Center's Third Panzer and Fourth Armies defended the eastern face of the Rzhev-Viaz'ma salient, its Third Panzer Army the sector east of Viaz'ma, and its Fourth Army the sector southward to the Kirov region.

29 Although few if any Soviet archival sources, open or classified, mention specific plans for conducting Operations Neptune or Jupiter, the German Ninth Army's records document a major build-up in the sectors of the Western Front's 5th and 33rd Armies during October and November 1942. Soviet archival sources confirm this build-up. In addition to assigning the 3rd Tank Army to the Western Front in October and positioning it east of Viaz'ma, the *Stavka* also concentrated the 9th and 10th Tank Corps in the 5th and 33rd Armies' rear area. According to "Prikazy 10-mu TK s 13.5 po 27.12.42" [Orders to the 10th Tank Corps from 13 May through 27 December 1942], in *TsAMO*, f. 3404, op. 1, d. 1, l. 225, the *Stavka* assigned the 10th Tank Corps from its reserve to the Western Front's control at 1800 hours on 13 November 1942. Subsequent documents track the corps' redeployment into the 5th Army's sector. *Boevoi sostav, chast 2*, 190–91, 211–12, 235–36, also records the subsequent reinforcement of the 5th Army with the 30th Guards, 78th, 194th, and 379th Rifle Divisions and both the 5th and the 33rd Armies with heavy amounts of supporting artillery.

30 The *Stavka* support for the Western and Kalinin Fronts included 31 tank brigades and 12 tank regiments, totaling 2,352 tanks, over 54 artillery regiments, 30 guards mortar battalions, and 23 antitank regiments with almost 10,000 guns and mortars, and 20 separate engineer and sapper battalions. This support included one of the newly fielded separate heavy guards-mortar regiments (heavy *Katiushas* or "Stalin

organ" multiple-rocket launchers) and 18 separate heavy guards-mortar battalions. See *Boevoi sostav, chast 2*, 211–212.

31   *TsAMO RF*, f- 398, op. 3908, ed. khr. 366. Few documents related to the 4th Shock Army's role in Operation Mars have been released.

32   "Direktiva Stavki VGK No. 170651 komanduiushchemu voiskami Kalininskogo Fronta ob usileni voisk fronta" [*Stavka* VGK directive no. 170651 to the commander of the forces of the Kalinin Front about the reinforcement of the front], in Zolotarev "*Stavka* 1942," 426.

33   Ibid.

34   For offensive details, see *SMPIOV*, No. 9, 141–150, A. L. Getman, *Tanki idut na Berlin (1941–1945)* [Tanks advance on Berlin], (Moscow: "Nauka," 1973), 70–76, and P. G. Kuznetsov, *Gvardeitsy-moskvichi* [Moscow guardsmen], (Moscow: Voenizdat, 1962), 185–190. The latter are the histories of 6th Tank Corps and the 1st Guards Motorized Division.

35   For German accounts of the operation along the Vazuza River, see H. Grossman, *Rzhev: The Cornerstone of the Eastern Front*, translated from the German *Rshew: Eckpfeiler der Ostefront*, (Freidberg, 1980), and Anton Detlev von Plato, *Die Geschichte der 5. Panzerdivision 1938 bis 1945*, (Regensburg: Walhalla u. Praetoria Verlag KG Geog Zwickenpflug, 1978), 23–257.

36   The 31st Army's shock group consisted of the 88th, 336th, and 239th Rifle Divisions, supported by the 332nd and 145th Tank Brigades. The defending Germans decimated both tank brigades in three days of battle and inflicted heavy losses on the rifle divisions. The story of the 102nd Infantry Division's defense and, in particular, the intelligence situation before the operation is found in David Kahn, "An Intelligence Case History: The Defense of Osuga, 1942," *Aerospace Historian*, Vol. 28, No. 4 (Winter/December 1981), 242–251.

37   In the sector between the Osuga and Vazuza Rivers, the German 102nd Infantry Division's 195th Infantry Regiment defended against a shock group made up of the 20th Army's 326th, 42nd Guards, and 251st Rifle Divisions, supported by the 25th and 93rd Tank Brigades.

38   This shock group included the 80th and 240th Tank Brigades, supporting the 247th and 331st Rifle Division. The 8th Guards Rifle Corps, which constituted the shock group's second echelon, consisted of the 26th Guards Rifle Division and the 148th and 150th Rifle and 11th and 18th Tank Brigades. The corps' mission was to expand the bridgehead after its initial seizure and pave the way for the commitment of the mobile group into the penetration. In addition, 20th Army held the 1st Guards Motorized Rifle Division and 31st Tank Brigade in its own army reserve

39   A combination of ice on the river and the limited size of the bridgehead prevented the supporting tank brigades from crossing the river.

40   The 22nd and 20th Tank and 6th Motorized Rifle Brigades of Colonel Arman's 6th Tank Corps made it across the Rzhev-Sychevka road, but only after suffering heavy losses. The corps' 100th Tank Brigade remained in the bridgehead, halted by fire from the interlocking German strong points.

41   Elements of the 2nd and 3rd Guards Cavalry Divisions of Kriukov's 2nd Guards Cavalry Corps, plus the corps' entire 20th Cavalry Division, made it across the road. However, the corps' headquarters and 4th Guards Cavalry Division remained behind in the bridgehead.

42   The immense traffic jam along the Vazuza River also delayed the forward deployment of supporting artillery.

43   For details on the Soviet offensive in the Belyi sector, see M. D. Solomatin, *Krasnogradtsy* [The men of Krasnograd], (Moscow: Voenizdat, 1963), "Report by the

representative of the 3rd Air Army with the 1st MC during Operation "Mars," in *TsAMO*, f. 311, op. 311, d. 24, ll. 86–87. Original document from the archives (translator unknown), and *"Boevye doneseniia i operativnye svodki shataba i mekhkorpua"* [Combat reports and operational summaries of the headquarters of the 1st Mechanized Corps], in *TsAMO*, f. 3404, op. 1, d. 2, ll. 2–36.

44 Povetkin's rifle corps consisted of the 150th Rifle Division and the 74th, 75th, 78th, and 91st Rifle Brigades, and Solomatin's corps, the 65th and 219th Tank and the 19th, 35th, and 37th Mechanized Brigades.

45 Solomatin's corps numbered 10 KV heavy, 119 T–34 medium, and 95 T–70 light tanks. See the corps' after-action report in *TsAMO*, f. 3424, op. 1. d. 2. ll. 2–36.

46 Povetkin's infantry accompanied Solomatin's advance, but, since it lagged behind the armor, it made seizure of the Belyi-Vladimirskoe road more difficult.

47 The 41st Army's initial assault south of Belyi routed the 246th Infantry Division's 352nd Infantry Regiment, and Tarasov believed few German reserves were available to defend the town. Furthermore, Belyi was an enticing target because the Germans had defended it successfully against numerous Soviet attacks during the Red Army's offensive in the winter of 1941–1942 and on several occasions thereafter.

48 Tarasov reinforced Gruz's division with the 19th Mechanized Brigade from Solomatin's mechanized corps and, subsequently, by the 6th Rifle Corps' 91st Rifle Brigade.

49 For details on German actions in the Belyi sector, see Grossman, *Rzhev*, and Rolf Stoves, *1. Panzer-Division 1935–1945*, (Bad Neuheim: Verlag Hans-Henning Podzun, 1961), 375–409.

50 The 1st Panzer Division's *Kampfgruppe* von Wietersheim consisted of the panzer division's 113th Panzer Grenadier Regiment, and the *Grossdeutschland* Panzer Grenadier Division's *Kampfgruppe* Kassnitz was made up of the panzer grenadier division's Fusilier Regiment.

51 The Belyi-Vladimirskoe road was the only German supply route into Belyi.

52 The 47th and 48th Separate Mechanized Brigades, each of which fielded a tank regiment with 39 tanks, were in army reserve.

53 In his memoirs, *Nastupala grozhaia bronia* [Threatening armor attacks], (Kiev: Politicheskoi literatury Ukrainy, 1981), 38, Dremov notes only that his brigade took part in "an unsuccessful operation near Belyi."

54 For additional details on Ninth Army's defense and detailed intelligence information on Soviet forces throughout the operation, see "Tatigkeitsbericht der Abteilung Ic/A.O." dated 1 July–3 Dec 1942, *AOK 9, 27970/6*, in National Archives (NAM) microfilm series NAM T–312, Roll 304. Daily operational and intelligence maps accompany these reports.

55 The *Grossdeutschland* Division's Grenadier Regiment regrouped into the Luchesa valley region one battalion at a time, only after it helped repulse Soviet assault further north. Details on the 22nd Army's operations in the Luchesa valley are indeed quite sketchy. Among the few sources on the fighting, see M. E. Katukov, *Na ostrie glavnogo udara* [At the point of the main attack], (Moscow: Voenizdat, 1976, which, although admitting the offensive took place, says little about its conduct or consequences. Postwar memoirs written by Colonels A. Kh. Babadzhanian and D. A. Dragunsky, both of whom served as brigade commanders in Katukov's mechanized corps during this operation offer few details about the fighting. Therefore, the archival records of the Ninth Army and the *Grossdeutschland* Division remain the most thorough accounts and also confirm identity of the Soviet units that participated in the 22nd Army's offensive.

56   During this period Iushkevich committed the 114th Rifle Brigade and the 39th Tank Regiment into combat from his army's reserve. When these forces proved inadequate to the task, he began shifting rifle regiments into battle from divisions operating in other (inactive) army sectors. The Germans, however, matched these piecemeal reinforcements with just enough strength to hold Iushkevich's army at bay, although not enough to close the breech.

57   Zygin's 39th Army conducted its main attack against the XXIII Army Corps' 206th Infantry Division, which was defending a broad sector along the Molodoi Tud River east of the town of Molodoi Tud, with his army's 373rd, 135th, and 158th Rifle Divisions, supported by the 28th and 81st Tank Brigades. At the same time, he also launched smaller attacks against the 206th Infantry Division's flanks, with the 100th and 117th Rifle Brigades striking the German division's left wing and the 136th and 101st Rifle Brigades, supported by the 28th and 29th Tank Regiments, striking the same division's right wing. The only Soviet sources providing details of this fighting are, V. P. Boiko, *S dumoi o Rodine* [With thoughts about the Homeland], (Moscow: Voenizdat, 1979) and N. M. Khlebnikov, *Pod grokhot soten baterei* [Under the thunder of hundreds of batteries], (Moscow: Voenizdat, 1979). The former was the commander of 28th Tank Brigade, and the latter was the chief of the 39th Army's artillery.

58   In the most dramatic of these successes, the 39th Army's 100th Rifle Brigade broke through the defenses of the XXIII Army Corps' 253rd Infantry Division southwest of the town of Molodoi Tud and advanced 5 kilometers into the German rear area. However, Zygin was unable to reinforce this success before two battalions from the *Grossdeutschland* Division's Grenadier Regiment skillfully conducted a counterattack that thwarted the 100th Brigade's advance. Thereafter, the *Grossdeutschland* Division's two battalions quickly regrouped southward to help halt the 22nd Army's offensive in the Luchesa valley.

59   Getman, *Tanki idut na Berline*, 73–74, and *SMPIOV*, No. 9, 148–149. All of the brigades in Arman's tank corps were decimated in the breakout attempt except for the corps' 100th Tank Brigade, which had not been able to accompany the corps in its advance across the Rzhev-Sychevka road.

60   For additional details about the 20th Cavalry Division's "raid" through the German rear, see A. I. Sekretov, *Gvardeiskaia postup' (boevoi put' 17-i Mozyrskoi Krasnoznamennoi ordena Lenina, Suvorova i Kutuzova kavaleriiskoi divizii, podwhefnoi Tadzhikistnu, v gody Velikoi Otechestvennoi voiny 1941–1945 gg.)* [Guards gait (the combat path of the Mozyr, Red Banner, Orders of Lenin, Suvorov, and Kutuzov 17th Guards Cavalry Division, raised by Tadzhikistan in the Great Patriotic War, 1941–1945)], (Dushanbe: "Donish, " 1985), 40–48.

61   Solomatin, *Krasnogradtsy*, 28–29. Solomatin had already withdrawn his corps' 37th Mechanized Brigade from the outskirts of Vladimirskoe, where it had severed the critical German rail line and road to Belyi.

62   The Ninth Army's records confirm the extensive interdiction efforts conducted by Soviet partisans, which significantly slowed the 20th Panzer Division's advance into the region south of Belyi.

63   See Solomatin, *Krasnogradtsy*, 30–35, and the 1st Mechanized Corps' official after-action report on the operation, which are remarkably congruous.

64   See Getman, *Tank idut na Berline*, 74, which states that the 6th Tank Corps' armor strength increased to 100 tanks by 11 December and A. D. Kochetkov, *Dvinskiii tankovyi:Boevoi put'5-go tankovogo dvinskogo korpusa* [The Dvina Tank: The combat path of the 5th Dvina Tank Corps], (Moscow: Voenizdat, 1989). The latter, which coincides closely with the 5th Tank Crops' archival records, provides significant

information about the tank corps' strength and its role in the December operation. Between 2 and 10 December, Zhukov and Konev reinforced the 20th Army with the fresh 5th Tank Corps and several divisions transferred from the neighboring 31st Army, hastily re-formed and reorganized Arman's 6th Tank Corps, and dispatched reinforcements to the 29th Army as well. These reinforcements almost doubled the 20th Army's strength and significantly increased the 29th Army's strength.

65 "Rasporiazhenie Verkhovnogo Glavnokomanduiushchego predstaviteliu Stavki ob usilenii 20-i armii" [Instructions from the Supreme High Commander to the representative of the *Stavka* about the reinforcement of the 20th Army], in Zolotarev, "*Stavka* 1942," 460.

66 "Direktiva Stavki VGK No. 170700 komanduiushchim voiskami Zapadnogo i Kalininskogo frontov o zadachakh po razgromu Rzhevsko-Sychevsko-Olenino-Belyiskoi gruppirovka protivnika" [*Stavka* VGK directive no.170700 to the commanders of the forces of the Western and Kalinin Fronts about the missions for the destruction of the enemy's Rzhev-Sychevka-Olenino-Belyi grouping], in Zolotarev, "*Stavka* 1942," 462–463.

67 See the 5th Tank Corps' combat reports in *TsAMO*, f. 3404, op. 1, d. 9, 10, and 259. These reports include an account of the corps' daily actions and losses from 11–15 December.

68 *TsAMO*, f. 3424, op. 1, d. 2, l. 36.

69 Red Army archival documents indicate that 545,070 Red Army soldiers actively participated in Operation Mars, and the attacking forces lost 215,674 soldiers, including 70,373 irrecoverable losses (killed, wounded, and missing-in-action) and 145,301 medical losses (wounded and sick). These figures include the Kalinin Front's 22nd, 39th, and 41st Armies and 3rd Air Army and the Western Front's 20th, 30th, and 31st Armies and 1st Air Army. However, they do not include the 29th Army's losses. See "Liudskie poteri Sovetskikh Vooruzhennykh Sil v 1941–1945 gg.: Novye aspekty" [Personnel losses of the Soviet Armed Forces 1941–1945: New aspects], *VIZh*, No. 2 (March-April 1999), 6.

70 The casualty toll in specific Western and Kalinin Front formations was equally shocking. For example, in its after-action-report, Khozin's 20th Army admitted to losing 58,524 soldiers out of the 114,176 soldiers it initially committed into combat. The same army's 8th Guards Rifle Corps reported losing 6.058 soldiers during the first five days of combat, and the corps' 26th Guards Rifle Division had just over 400 "fighters" remaining on 7 December. The same corps' 148th Separate Rifle Brigade emerged from combat with only 47 riflemen remaining and its 150th Rifle Brigade with only 110 riflemen. Equally decimated, the 6th Tank Corps lost virtually its entire strength twice over, the 1st Mechanized Corps was essentially destroyed, and the 5th Tank Corps, whose tanks went into combat without their white camouflage paint, lost its entire complement of tanks in just three days of combat, while the 5th Tank Corps' 5th Motorized Rifle Brigade suffered more than 1,500 dead, 70 percent of its total combat strength. By 15 December the 5th Tank Corps was able to muster only one composite rifle battalion. These losses were but a microcosm of the price the Red Army paid for its defeat in Operation Mars.

Notes to Chapter 3

71 Earl F. Ziemke, *Stalingrad to Berlin: The German Defeat in the East* (Washington, DC: Office of the Chief of Military History United States Army, 1968), 112.

72 P. A. Zhilin, ed., *Na severo-zapadnom fronte 1941–1943* [On the Northwestern Front 1941–1943] (Moscow: "Nauka," 1969), 323–324.

73   "Doklad komanduiushchego voiskami Severo-Zapadnogo fronta No. 33/nsh Verkhovnomu Glavnokomanduiushchemu plana operatsii po okruzheniiu Demianskoi gruppirovki protivnika" [Report of the commander of the forces of the Northwestern Front No. 33/nsh to the Supreme High Commander on an operational plan for the encirclement of the enemy Demiansk grouping], in Zolotarev, "*Stavka 1942*," 553–555.

74   "Direktiva Stavki VGK No. 05 komanduiushchemu Severo-Zapadnogo fronta ob utochnenii plana operatsii fronta" [*Stavka* VGK directive no. 05 to the commander of the Northwestern Front concerning the elaboration of the *front's* operational plan], in Ibid., 439.

75   "Prikaz Stavki VGK No. 994280 o naznachenii komanduiushchikh 11-i i 1-i udarnoi armiiami" [*Stavka* VGK order no. 994280 concerning the appointment of commanders of the 11th and 1st Shock Armies], in Ibid., 450.

76   G. I. Berdnikov, *Pervaia udarnaia: Boevoi put' 1-i udarnoi armii v Velikoi Otechestvennoi voine* [1st Shock: The combat path of the 1st Shock Army in the Great Patriotic War] (Moscow: Voenizdat, 1985), 118–119.

77   Ibid. See also *Boevoi sostav, chast 2*, 209, 233.

78   See Berdnikov, *Pervaia udarnaia*, 120–121 for a description of the 1st Shock Army's assault.

79   Ibid., 120.

80   Ibid., 121.

81   "Direktiva Stavki VGK No. 170702 komanduiushchemu voiskami Severo-zapadnogo fronta na razgrom Demianskoi gruppirovki protivnika" [*Stavka* VGK directive no. 170702 to the commander of the forces of the Northwestern Front on the destruction of the enemy's Demiansk grouping], in Zolotarev, "*Stavka 1942*," 463–464.

82   Berdnikov, *Pervaia udarnaia*, 122.

83   Ibid.

84   "Direktiva Stavki VGK No. 170716 komanduiushchemu voiskami Severo-zapadnogo fronta ob usilenii fronta" [*Stavka* VGK directive no. 170716 to the commander of the forces of the Northwestern Front about reinforcement of the *front*], in Zolotarev, "*Stavka 1942*," 474.

85   "Direktiva Stavki VGK No. 170717 komanduiushchemu voiskami Severo-zapadnogo fronta ob uskorenii perekrytiia Ramushevskogo koridora" [*Stavka* VGK directive no. 170717 to the commander of the forces of the Northwestern Front about the acceleration of the damming up of the Ramushevo corridor], in Ibid., 474.

86   Berdnikov, *Pervaia udarnaia*, 122–123.

Notes to Chapter 4

87   See V. Morozov, "Pochemu ne zavershilos' nastuplenie v Donbasse vesnoi 1943 goda" [Why was the offensive in the Donbas in the spring of 1943 not completed], *VIZh*, No. 3 (March 1963), 14–34.

88   David M. Glantz, *From the Don to the Dnepr: Soviet Offensive Operations, December 1942-August 1943* (London: Frank Cass, 1991), 82–151.

89   "Doklad komanduiushchego voiskami Iugo-zapadnogo fronta No. 15 Verkhovnomu Glavnokomanduiushchemu plana operatsii po razgromu protivnika v Donbassa" [Report no. 15 of the commander of the forces of the Southwestern Front to the Supreme High Commander concerning an operational plan for the destruc-

tion of the enemy in the Donbas], in V. A. Zolotarev, ed., "Stavka Verkhovnogo Glavnokomandovaniia: Dokumenty i materialy, 1943 god." [The *Stavka* of the Supreme High Command: Documents and materials, 1943], *Russkii arkhiv: Velikaia Otechestvennaia, 16, 5 (3)* [The Russian archives: The Great Patriotic [War], 16, 5 (3)] (Moscow: "TERRA," 1999), 271–272. Hereafter cited as Zolotarev, "*Stavka* 1943," with appropriate page(s).

90 "Direktiva Stavki VGK No. 30020 komanduiushchemu voiskami Iugo-zapadnogo fronta ob utvershdenii plana operatsii po razgromu protivnika v Donbasse" [*Stavka* VGK directive no. 30020 to the commander of the forces of the Southwestern Front about the approval of an operational plan for the destruction of the enemy in the Donbas], in Ibid., 32.

91 "Direktiva komanduiushchego voiskami Iugo-zapadnogo No. 0078 komanduiushchim 3-i gv., 5-i tankovoi i 17-i vozdushnoi armiami na okruzhenie i unichtozhenie Donbasskoi gruppirovki protivnika" [Directive no. 0078 of the commander of the forces of the Southwestern Front to the commanders of the 3rd Guards, 5th Tank, and 17th Air Armies on the encirclement and destruction of the enemy's Donbas grouping], in V. A. Zolotarev, "Preliudiia Kurskoi bitvy: Dokumenty i materially, 6 dekabria 1942 g.–25 aprelia 1943 g," [Prelude to the Battle of Kursk: Documents and materials, 6 December 1942–25 April 1943], *Russkii arkhiv: Velikaia Otechestvennaia, 15, 4 (3)* [Russian archives; The Great Patriotic [War], 15, 4 (3)] (Moscow: "TERRA," 1997), 271–272 193–195. Hereafter cited as Zolotarev, "Prelude to Kursk," with appropriate page(s).

92 "Doklad komanduiushchego 1-i gv. armiei komanduiushchemu voiskami Iugo-zapadnogo fronta plana Donbasskoi nastupatel'noi operatsii armii" [A report of the commander of the 1st Guards Army to the commander of the forces of the Southwestern Front on the army's plan for the Donbas offensive operation], in Ibid., 196–197.

93 "Direktiva Stavki VGK No. 30031 komanduiushchemu voiskami Iuzhnogo fronta ob uluchshenii upravelnii i uskorenii tempov nastupleniia [*Stavka* VGK directive no. 30031 to the commander of the forces of the Southern Front about the improvement of command and control and the acceleration of the tempos of the offensive], in Ibid., 23.

94 "Boevoe donesenie komanduiushchego voiskami Iugo-zapadnom fronta No. 030 Verkhovnomu Glavnokomanduiushchemu o perekhod voisk fronta v nastuplenie" [Combat report no. 030 of the commander of the forces of the Southwestern Front to the Supreme High Commander concerning the transition of the forces of the *front* to the offensive], in Ibid., 198–199.

95 "Boevoe rasporiazhenie komanduiushchego voiskami Iugo-zapadnogo fronta komanduiushchim 3-i i 1-i gv. armiami na okruzhenie i unichtozhenie Voroshilovgradskoi gruppirovki protivnika" [A combat order of the commander of the forces of the Southwestern Front to the commanders of the 3rd and 1st Guards Armies on the encirclement and destruction of the enemy's Voroshilovgrad grouping], in Ibid., 202.

96 "Boevoe rasporiazhenie komanduiushchego voiskami Iugo-zapadnogo fronta komanduiushchemu 1-i gv. armiei o prodolzhenii nastupleniia" [Combat order of the commander of the forces of the Southwestern Front to the commander of the 1st Guards Army about the continuation of the offensive], in Ibid., 202.

97 "Doklad komanduiushchego voiskami Iugo-zapadnogo fronta No. 01584 Verkhovnomu Glavnokomanduiushchemu plana operatsii po zakhvatu platsdarmov na Dnepre" [Report no. 01583 of the commander of the forces of the Southwestern

Front to the Supreme High Commander on an operational plan for the seizure of bridgeheads on the Dnepr], in Ibid., 204–205.

98   "Direktiva Stavki VGK No. 30044 komanduiushchemu voiskami Iugo-zapadnogo fronta na provedenie nastupatel'noi operatsii" [*Stavka* VGK directive no. 30044 to the commander of the forces of the Southwestern Front on the conduct of the offensive operation], in Ibid., 34.

99   "Boevoe donesenie komanduiushchego voiskami Iugo-zapadnogo fronta No. 044 Verkhovnomu Glavnokomanduiushchemu o prodolzhenii nastupleniia voisk fronta" [Combat report no. 044 of the commander of the forces of the Southwestern Front to the Supreme High Commander about the continuation of the offensive of the forces of the *front*], in Ibid., 206–208.

100   For details on the 8th Cavalry Corps' operations from the Soviet perspective, see M. S. Dokuchaev, *V boi shli eskadrony* [The squadrons went into battle] (Moscow: Voenizdat, 1984), 35–59, and from the German perspective Kent A. Larson, "The Debal'tsevo Raid, February 1943: A Case Study in the Role of Initiative in Soviet Operational Art," *The Journal of Soviet Military Studies*, vol. 5, no. 3 (September 1992), 426–450.

101   Larson, "The Debal'tsevo Raid," 440. The perimeter included only the eastern outskirts of Debal'tsevo.

102   "Prikaz komanduiushchego voiskami Iugo-zapadnogo fronta No. 0011 komanduiushchemu 3-i gv. armiei o prodolzhenii nastupleniia v napravlenii g. Stalino" [Order no. 0011 of the commander of the forces of the Southwestern Front to the commander of the 3rd Guards Army about the continuation of the offensive toward Stalino], in Zolotarev, "Prelude to Kursk," 209–210.

103   "Doklad komanduiushchego voiskami Iugo-zapadnom fronta Verkhovnomu Glavnokomanduiushchemu predlozhenii po provedeniiu operatsii s tsel'iu vykhoda voisk fronta k r. Dnepr i zakhvata platsdarma" [A report of the commander of the forces of the Southwestern Front to the Supreme High Commander concerning a proposal for the conduct of an operation with the aim of the arrival of the forces of the *front* at the Dnepr River and the seizure of bridgeheads], in Ibid., 210–212.

104   "Gallop" was the code name the *Stavka* assigned to the Donbas offensive operation of January-February 1943.

105   "Direktiva Stavki VGK No. 30048 komanduiushchemu voiskami Iugo-zapadnogo fronta ob utverzhdenii plana Voroshilovgradskoi nastupatel'noi operatsii" [*Stavka* VGK directive no. 30048 to the commander of the forces of the Southwestern Front about approval of the plan for the Voroshilovgrad offensive operation], in Zolotarev, "Prelude to Kursk," 36.

106   "Boevoe donesenie shtaba Iugo-zapadnogo fronta No. 049 Verkhovnomu Glavnokomanduiushchemu o khode nastupleniia" [Combat report No. 049 of the headquarters of the Southwestern Front to the Supreme High Commander about the course of the offensive], in Ibid., 214–215.

107   "Prikaz komanduiushchego voiskami Iugo-zapadnom fronta komandiram 4-go gv. i 10-go tankovykh korpusov ob okruzhenii i unichtozhenii gruppirovki protivnika v raione Krasnoarmeiskogo" [Order of the commander of the forces of the Southwestern Front to the commanders of the 4th Guards and 10th Tank Corps about the encirclement and destruction of the enemy's grouping in the Krasnoarmeiskoe region], in Ibid., 215.

108   "Boevoe rasporiazhenie komanduiushchego voiskami Iugo-zapadnogo fronta komanduiushchemu podvizhnoi gruppoi voisk General-Leitenantu Popovu M. M. o vostanovlenii polozheniia v raione Krasnoarmeiskogo" [Combat order of the commander of the forces of the Southwestern Front to the commander of the Mobile

Group, Lieutenant General M. M. Popov, about restoration of the situation in the Krasnoarmeiskoe region], in Ibid., 216.

109 "Boevoe rasporiazhenie komanduiushchego voiskami Iugo-zapadnogo fronta komanduiushchemu 6-i armiei ob unichtozhenii chastei protivnika, otkhodiashchikh k r. Dnepr" [Combat order of the commander of the forces of the Southwestern Front to the commander of the 6th Army about the destruction of the units of the enemy withdrawing to the Dnepr River], in Ibid., 216.

110 "Itogovaia pazvedsvodka shtaba Iugo-zapadnogo fronta No. 90 za period s 10 po 20 fevralia 1943 g." [Summary intelligence report of the headquarters of the Southwestern Front no. 90 for the period from 10 through 20 February 1943], in Ibid., 216–222.

111 Prikaz komanduiushchego voiskami Iugo-zapadnogo fronta komanduiushchim armiami i podvizhnoi gruppoi voisk o novykh razgranliniiakh, bystroi i polnoi likvidatsii protivnika v Donbasse" [Order of the commander of the forces of the Southwestern Front to the commanders of the armies and the mobile group about new boundary lines and the rapid and complete liquidation of the enemy in the Donbas], in Ibid., 222.

112 "Boevoe rasporiazhenie komanduiushchego voiskami Iugo-zapadnogo fronta komanduiushchemu podvizhnoi gruppoi voisk General-Lieutenantu Popovu M. M. o nemedlennom doklade obstanovki v raione Krasnoarmeiskogo" [Combat order of the commander of the forces of the Southwestern Front to the commander of the mobile group of forces, Lieutenant General M. M. Popov, about an immediate report on the situation in the Krasnoarmeiskoe region], in Ibid., 223.

113 "Boevoe donesenie komanduiushchego voiskami Iugo-zapadnogo fronta No. 051 Verkhovnomu Glavnokomanduiushchemu ob obstanovke v polose fronta" [Combat report of the commander of the forces of the Southwestern Front no. 051 to the Supreme High Commander about the situation in the sector of the *front*], in Ibid., 223–225.

114 "Prikaz komanduiushchego voiskami Iugo-zapadnogo fronta komanduiushchemu podvizhnoi gruppoi ob ovladenii raionom Grishino, Krasnoarmeiskoe, Novo-Aleksandrovka i perekhvate putei otkhoda protivnika na Dnepropetrovsk i Zaporozh'e" [Order of the commander of the forces of the Southwestern Front to the commander of the mobile group about the capture of the Grishino, Krasnoarmeiskoe, and Novo-Aleksandrovka regions and the severing of the withdrawal routes of the enemy to Dnepropetrovsk and Zaporozh'e], in Ibid., 225.

115 "Doklad komandira 4-go gv. tankovogo korpusa komanduiushchemu voiskami Iugo-zapadnogo fronta o boevykh deistviiakh i sostoianii podchinennykh chastei" [A report by the commander of the 4th Guards Tank Corps to the commander of the forces of the Southwestern Front about combat operations and the state of subordinate units], in Ibid., 226.

116 Dokuchaev, *V boi shli eskadrony*, 44.

117 Ibid., 48.

118 For details on the senior officers killed and captured, see A. A. Maslov, "The Unknown Pages of a Heroic Raid," *The Journal of Slavic Military Studies*, vol. 10, no. 2 (June 1997), 176–180.

119 Ibid., 176–17. Formerly classified Soviet General Staff assessments of the cavalry corps' operation admit to the loss of 2,519 men killed, wounded, and missing in action and 2,906 horses. This figure is clearly understated. For details on the operation, see also, *Sbornik materialov po izucheniiu opyta voiny No. 7, iiun'-iiul' 1943 g.* [Collection of materials for the study of war experience, No. 7, June-July 1943]

(Moscow: Voenizdat, 1943), 83–94. Classified secret and prepared by the General Staff's Department for the Exploitation of War Experience.

120 "Boevoe donesenie komanduiushchego voiskami Iugo-zapadnogo fronta No. 054 Verkhovnomu Glavnokomanduiushchemu o rezul'tatakh vypolneniia boevykh zadach na Iziumskom i Slavianskom napravleniakh" [Combat report no. 054 of the commander of the forces of the Southwestern Front to the Supreme High Commander about the results of the fulfillment of combat missions along the Izium and Slaviansk axes], in Zolotarev, "Prelude to Kursk," 226–228.

121 "Prikaz komanduiushchego voiskami Iugo-zapadnogo fronta komanduiushchemu podvizhnoi gruppoi voisk General-Leitenantu Popovu M. M. i komanduiushchemu 1-i gv. armiei o rasformirovanii gruppy voisk [Order of the commander of the forces of the Southwestern Front to the commander of the mobile group, Lieutenant General M. M. Popov, and the commander of the 1st Guards Army about the disbanding of the group of forces], in Ibid., 228–229.

122 "Boevoe rasporiazhenie komanduiushchego voiskami Iugo-zapadnogo fronta komanduiushchemu podvizhnoi gruppy voisk General-Leitenantu Popovu M. M. ob uderzhenii raiona Barvenkovo i nedopushenii vykhoda protivnika v tyl voisk fronta" [Combat order of the commander of the forces of the Southwestern Front to the commander of mobile group of forces, Lieutenant General M. M. Popov, about retention of the Barvenkovo region and the intolerable arrival of the enemy in the rear of the forces of the *front*], in Ibid., 229.

123 "Boevoe donesenie komanduiushchego voiskami Iugo-zapadnogo fronta No. 056 Verkhovnomu Glavnokomanduiushchemu ob oboronitel'nykh boiakh na pravom flange i tsentral'nom uchaske fronta" [Combat report no. 056 of the commander of the forces of the Southwestern Front to the Supreme High Commander about the defensive battles on the right wing and central sector of the *front*], in Ibid., 230–232.

124 "Boevoe rasporiazhenie komanduiushchego voiskami Iugo-zapadnogo fronta General-Leitenantu Popovu M. M. ob otvode chasti voisk fronta i organizatsii aktivnoi oborony na novom rubezhe" [Combat order of commander of the forces of the Southwestern Front to Lieutenant General M. M. Popov about the withdrawal of units of the forces of the *front* and the organization of an active defense along a new line], in Ibid., 232.

125 "Prikaz komanduiushchego voiskami Iugo-zapadnogo fronta komanduiushchim 6-i i 1-i gv. armiiami, General-Leitenantu Popovu M. M. na perekhod k aktivnym deistviiam" [An order of the commander of the forces of the Southwestern Front to the commanders of the 6th [Army] and 1st Guards Army and to Lieutenant General M. M. Popov on a transition to active operations], in Ibid., 233.

126 "Zapis' peregovorov po priamomu provodu komanduiushchego voiskami Iugo-zapadnogo fronta s komanduiushchim 6-i armiei" [Notes of a conversation by direct line of the commander of the forces of the Southwestern Front with the commander of the 6th Army], in Ibid., 233–234.

127 "Prikaz komanduiushchego voiskami Iugo-zapadnogo fronta komanduiushchim 3-i gv., 5-i tankovoi i 1-i gv. armiiami ob usilenii oborony" [An order of the commander of the forces of the Southwestern Front to the commanders of the 3rd Guards, 5th Tank, and 1st Guards Armies about a strengthening of the defense], in Ibid., 235.

128 "Boevoe donesenie komanduiushchego Iugo-zapadnogo fronta Verkhovnomu Glavnokomanduiushchemu o khode boevykh deistvii v polose fronta" [Combat report of the commander of the forces of the Southwestern Front to the Supreme High Commander about the course of combat operations in the sector of the *front*], in Ibid., 236–237.

129 "Direktiva Stavki VGK No. 30059 komanduiushchim voiskami Voronezhskogo i Iugo-zapadnogo frontov, predstaviteliu Stavki o perepodchinenii 3-i tankovoi armii" [*Stavka* VGK directive no. 30059 to the commanders of the forces of the Voronezh and Southwestern Fronts and the representative of the *Stavka* about the re-subordination of the 3rd Tank Army], in Zolotarev, "*Stavka* 1943," 83. The *Stavka* representative was A. M. Vasilevsky.

130 "Boevoe donesenie komanduiushchego voiskami Iugo-zapadnogo fronta Verkhovnomu Glavnokomanduiushchemu ob ozhestochnnykh oboronitel'nykh boiakh" [Combat report of the commander of the forces of the Southwestern Front to the Supreme High Commander about the fierce defensive fighting], in Zolotarev, "Prelude to Kursk," 237–238.

131 "Prikaz komanduiushchego 6-i armiei No. 0094 o nedopushenii vykhoda protivnika na r. Severnii Donets" [Order no. 0094 of the commander of the 6th Army about the inadmissibility of the arrival of enemy forces at the Northern Donets River], in Ibid., 239–240.

132 "Doklad komanduiushchego voiskami Iugo-zapadnogo fronta Verkhovnomu Glavnokomanduiushchemu zamysla predstoiashchei nastupatel'noi operatsii" [A report of the commander of the forces of the Southwestern Front to the Supreme High Commander on the concept for a forthcoming offensive operation], in Ibid., 243–244.

133 V. V. Gurkhin, "Liudskie poteri Sovetslikh Vooruzhennykh Sil v 1941–1945 gg.: Novye aspekty" [The personnel losses of the Soviet Armed Forces, 1941–1945: New aspects], *Voenno-istoricheskii zhurnal*, no. 2 (March-April 1999), 6.

134 G. F. Krivosheev, ed., *Grif sekretnosti sniat: Poteri Vooruzhennykh Sil SSSR v voinakh, boevykh deistviakh i voennykh konfliktakh: Statisticheskoe issledovanie* [The secret classification is removed: The losses of the USSR's Armed Forces in wars, combat operations, and military conflicts: A statistical study] (Moscow: Voenizdat, 1993, 186–187.

135 "Doklad komanduiushchego voiskami Iugo-zapadnogo fronta Narodnomu Komissaru Oborony o neobkhodimosti doukomplektovaniia chastei i soedinenii fronta lichnym sostavom, vooruzheniem i spetsial'nym imushestvom" [A report of the commander of the forces of the Southwestern Front to the People's Commissar of Defense about the necessity for filling-out the units and formations of the *front* with personnel, weapons, and special equipment], in Zolotarev, "Prelude to Kursk," 245–247.

Notes to Chapter 5

136 "Prikaz komanduiushchego voiskami Iuzhnogo fronta No. 0016 komanduiushchim armiiami, konno-mekhanizirovannoi gruppoi na unichtozhenie Rostovsko-Novocherkasskoi gruppirovki protivnika" [Order no. 0016 of the commander of the forces of the Southern Front to the commanders of the armies and the cavalry-mechanized group on the destruction of the enemy's Rostov-Novocherkassk grouping], in Ibid., 259–260.

137 Kirichenko's CMG consisted of the 4th Guards Cavalry Corps' 9th and 10th Guards and 30th Cavalry Divisions and the 5th Guards Cavalry Corps' 11th and 12th Guards and 63rd Cavalry Divisions.

138 "Prikaz komanduiushchego voiskami Iuzhnogo fronta No. 0018 komanduiushchim armiiami i konno-mekhanizirovannoi gruppoi na presledovanie protivnika i vykhod na r. Mius" [Order no. 0018 of the commander of the forces of the Southern Front to

the commanders of the armies and mobile group on the pursuit of the enemy and arrival at the Mius River], in Ibid., 264–265.

139 "Boevoe donesenie komanduiushchego voiskami Iuzhnogo fronta No. 0046 Verkhovnomu Glavnokomanduiushchemu ob osvobozhdenii g. Rostov-na-Donu" [Combat report no. 0046 of the commander of the forces of the Southern Front to the Supreme High Commander about the liberation of Rostov-on-the-Don], in Ibid., 266.

140 "Boevoe rasporiazhenie komanduiushchego voiskami Iuzhnogo fronta komanduiushchim armiiami i konno-mekhanizirovannoi gruppoi na presledovanie protivnika i vkhod na r. Mius" [Combat order of the commander of the forces of the Southern Front to the commanders of the armies and the Cavalry-Mechanized Group on the pursuit of the enemy and arrival at the Mius River], in Ibid., 266.

141 "Boevoe rasporiazhenie komanduiushchego voiskami Iuzhnogo fronta komanduiushchim armiiami i konno-mekhanizirovannoi gruppoi na prizhatie k moriu gruppirovki protivnika" [Combat order of the commander of the forces of the Southern Front to the commanders of the armies and the Cavalry-Mechanized Group on pinning the enemy's grouping to the sea], in Ibid., 266–267.

142 For details on the 4th Mechanized Corps' operations, see V. F. Tolubko, N. I. Baryshev, *Na uizhnom flange: Boevoi put' 4-go gvardeiskogo mekhanizirovannogo korpusa (1942–1944 gg.)* [On the southern flank: The Combat path of the 4th Guards Mechanized Corps (1942–1945)] (Moscow: "Nauka," 1973), 84.

143 "Boevoe donesenie komanduiushchego voiskami Iuzhnogo fronta No. 0052 Verkhovnomu Glavnokomanduiushchemu o khode boev na r. Mius" [Combat report no. 0052 of the commander of the forces of the Southern Front to the Supreme High Commander about the course of the fighting along the Mius River], in Ibid., 268. Dated 18 February, this order was addressed to the commanders of the 5th Shock, 2nd Guards, 51st, 28th, and 44th Armies and the Cavalry-Mechanized Group and directed them to reach the Mokryi Elanchik River by the end of 19 February and the Tel'manovo and Budennovka line with their forward units the same time.

144 "Boevoe donesenie komanduiushchego voiskami Iuzhnogo Fronta No. 0051 Verkhovnomu Glavnokomanduiushchemu o vykhode voisk fronta k r. Mius" [Combat report no. 0051 of the commander of the forces of the Southern Front to the Supreme High Commander about the arrival of the forces of the front at the Mius River], in Ibid., 267–268.

145 Ibid., 84.

146 V. M. Domnikov. ed., *V nastuplenii gvardiia: Ocherk boevom puti 2-i Gvardeiskoi armii* [Guards on the offensive: A survey of the combat path of the 2nd Guards Army] Moscow: Voenizdat, 1971), 100.

147 "Boevoe donesenie komanduiushchego voiskami Iuzhnogo fronta No. 0052 Verkhovnomu Glavnokomanduiushchemu o khode boev nap. Mius" [Combat report no. 0052 of the commander of the forces of the Southern Front to the Supreme High Commander concerning the course of battle on the Mius River], in Zolotarev, "Prelude to Kursk," 268–269.

148 Domnikov, *V nastuplenii gvardiia,* 102.

149 "Zapis' peregovorov po priamomu provodu zamestitelia nachal'nika operativnogo upravleniia General'nogo Shtaba s nachal'nikom shtaba Iuzhnogo fronta" [Notes of a telephone conversation by direct line between the deputy chief of the Operations Directorate of the General Staff and the chief of staff of the Southern Front], in Zolotarev, "Stavka 1943," 77–79.

150 "Boevoe prikaz komanduiushchego voiskami Iuzhnogo fronta No. 0020 komanduiushchim armiiami na nastuplenie s tsel'iu osvobozhdeniia Donbassa" [Combat order no. 0020 of the commander of the forces of the Southern Front to the commanders of the armies on an offensive with the aim of liberating the Donbas], in Zolotarev, "Prelude to Kursk," 269–270.

151 Domnikov, *V nastuplenii gvardiia,* 103–104.

152 "Prikaz komanduiushchego voiskami Iuzhnogo fronta No. 0021 komanduiushchim armiiami na proryv oborony protivnika na r. Mius" [Order no. 0021 of the commander of the forces of the Southern Front to the commanders of the armies on the penetration of the enemy's defense along the Mius River], in Zolotarev, "Prelude to Kursk," 271–272.

153 "Boevoe donesenie komanduiushchego voiskami Iuzhnogo fronta No. 0058 Verkhovnomu Glavnokomanduiushchemu o peregruppirovke voisk fronta i reshenii na prodolzhenie nastupleniia" [Combat report no. 0058 of the commander of the forces of the Southern Front to the Supreme High Commander about the regrouping of forces of the front and a decision on the continuation of the offensive], in Ibid., 272–273.

154 "Prikaz komanduiushchego voiskami Iuzhnogo fronta No. 0026 komanduiushchim 5 ud., 2 gv. i 51-i armiiami na zakhvat i rasshirenie platsdarmov na r. Mius" [Order no. 0026 of the commander of the forces of the Southern Front to the commanders of the 5th Shock, 2nd Guards, and 51st Armies on the seizure and widening of bridgeheads on the Mius River], in Ibid., 273.

155 Krivosheev, *Grif sekretnosti sniat,* 183.

156 Gurkhin, "Liudskie poteri Sovetskikh Vooruzhennykh sil," 6.

157 See Zolotarev, "Prelude to Kursk," 364–366.

Notes to Chapter 6

158 Among these many histories, only that of John Erickson (*The Road to Berlin*) mentions Soviet plans for an expanded offensive against Army Group Center. A particularly perceptive German account also detected the ultimate Soviet plan for an expanded strategic offensive in February 1943. See Generalleutnant a. D. A.D. von Plato, *Die Geschichte der 5. Panzerdivision 1938 bis 1945* [The History of 5th Panzer Division from 1938 to 1945], (Regensburg: Walhalla u, Praetoria Verlag KG Georg Zwickenpflug, 1978).

159 For details about the Donbas and Khar'kov operations, see David M. Glantz, *From the Don to the Dnepr: Soviet Offensive Operations, December 1942-August 1943,* (London: Frank Cass and Co., Ltd, 1991). Among the few complete and candid Soviet accounts of the Khar'kov and Donbas operations are V. P. Morozov, *Zapadnee Voronezha* [West of Voronezh], (Moscow: Voenizdat, 1956), and A. G. Ershov, *Osvobozhdenie Donbassa* [The liberation of the Donbas], (Moscow: Voenizdat, 1973). The extensive, recently released Soviet archival collections prepared during and after the war by the Soviet General Staff mention neither of the operations. Nor does this material cover the expanded February offensive in any detail.

160 For details on these counterstrokes, see David M. Glantz, *Forgotten Battles of the German-Soviet War (1941–45): Volume III, The Summer Campaign (12 May–18 November 1942)* (Carlisle, PA: Self-published, 1999). The 5th Tank Army, operating under the Briansk Front's control, conducted its unsuccessful counterstroke from 5–15 July in the region northwest of Voronezh in an attempt to halt the German advance on the city. Although Soviet open source accounts claim this counterstroke took place from 5–12 July, the Briansk Front continued this counterstroke virtually

to month's end. See, for example, "Boevye deistviia voisk Brianskogo i Voronezhskogo frontov letom 1942 na Voronezhkom napravlenii" [Combat operations of the forces of the Briansk and Voronezh Front in the summer of 1942 along the Voronezh axis], in the formerly classified *Sbornik voenno-istoricheskikh materialov Velikoi Otechestvennoi voiny* [Collection of military-historical materials of the Great Patriotic War], Vol. 15 (Moscow: Voenizdat, 1955), 115–46. On 17 July the *Stavka* once again directed the Briansk Front, together with the newly-formed Voronezh Front, to conduct yet another counterstroke. This time, the Briansk Front employed Group Chibisov and the tank corps formerly assigned to the now disbanded 5th Tank Army to conduct the attack. Although this counterstroke also failed, the *Stavka* issued new attack orders to the Briansk and Voronezh Fronts in early August, this time to advance against the left wing of Army Group "B" in the Voronezh region, while the 1st and 4th Tank Armies of the Stalingrad Front assaulted Army Group "B's" right wing, then was advancing into the "great bend" of the Don River. For sketchy details about these coordinated counterstrokes, see S. Mikhalev, "O razrabotke zamysla i planirovanii kontrnastuleniia pod Stalingradom" [About working out the concept and planning of the counteroffensive at Stalingrad], *Vestnik voennoi informatsii* [Herald of military information], No. 8 (August 1992), 7. The records of Army Group "B's" German Second Army reveal the massive nature of the Briansk Front's and 5th Tank Army's attacks, which were conducted by such future luminaries as Generals Katukov, Rotmistrov, and Solomatin.

161 Although we know that Operation Saturn was to follow Operation Uranus, the precise code-name for the follow-on operation to Operation Mars remains obscure.

162 The encircled Axis forces included Paulus' German Sixth Army, the bulk of Hoth's German Fourth Panzer Army, and portions of the Romanian Third and Fourth Armies.

163 For an account of the Voronezh-Kastornoe operation, see Ershov, *Osvobozhdenie Donbassa*, and the formerly classified Soviet General Staff study, "Voronezhsko-kastornenskaia nastupatel'naia operatsiia voisk Voronezhskogo i levogo kryla Brianskogo frontov" [The Voronezh-Kastornoe offensive operation of the forces of the Voronezh and left wing of the Briansk Fronts], *Sbornik voenno-istoricheskikh materialov Velikoi Otechestvennoi voiny, vypusk 13* [Collection of military-historical materials of the Great Patriotic War, Issue 13], (Moscow: Military-historical Directorate of the Soviet Armed Forces General Staff, 1954). Classified secret. Declassified 1964. As a result of the German Second Army's defeat, its commander, Colonel General Hans von Salmuth, was replaced by Colonel General Walter Weiss.

164 The First Panzer Army was transferred from the Caucasus to Army Group Don beginning on 27 January, and the Fourth Panzer Army withdrew from Rostov to the Mius River line from 8–18 February. See Earl F. Ziemke, *Stalingrad to Berlin: The German Defeat in the East* (Washington, DC: US Army Office of the Chief of Military History, 1968), 85, 88.

165 "Prikaz Stavki VGK komanduiushchim voiskami Brianskogo i Voronezhskogo frontov, predstaviteliu Stavki na ovladenie raionami Maloarkhangel'ska i Kurska" [*Stavka* VGK order to the commanders of the forces of the Briansk and Voronezh Fronts on the capture of the Maloarkhangel'sk and Kursk regions], in Zolotarev, "Preliudiia Kurskoi bitvy," 22.

166 "Boevoe donesenie komanduiushchego voiskami Brianskogo fronta No. 0020 Verkhovnomu Glavnokomanduiushchemu o khode nastupleniia" [Combat report no. 0020 of the commander of the forces of the Briansk Front to the Supreme High Commander about the offensive], in Ibid., 157–158.

167 "Operativnaia svodka shtaba Brianskogo fronta No. 0068" [Operational summary no. 0068 of the headquarters of the Briansk Front], in Ibid., 158–159.

168 "Boevoe donesenie komanduiushchego voiskami Brianskogo fronta No. 0036 Verkhovnomu Glavnokomanduiushchemu o khoda nastupleniia" [Combat report no. 0036 of the commander of the forces of the Briansk Front to the Supreme High Commander about the course of the offensive], in Ibid., 160–161.

169 "Direktiva Stavki VGK No. 30041 komanduiushchemu voiskami Brianskogo fronta na razgrom Orlovsko-Brianskoi gruppirovki protivnika" [Stavka VGK directive no. 30041 to the commander of the forces of the Briansk Front on the destruction of the enemy's Orel-Briansk grouping], in Ibid., 26. The BODO was a letter-printing telegraph apparatus, which has since been replaced by teletype.

170 "Boevoe donesenie komanduiushchego voiskami Voronezhskogo fronta No. 0048 Verkhovnomu Glavnokomanduiushchemu o boiakh po ovladeniiu Kurskom i Belgorodom" [Combat report no. 0048 of the commander of the forces of the Voronezh Front to the Supreme High Commander about the fighting for the capture of Kursk and Belgorod], in Ibid., 90–91.

171 "Boevoe donesenie komanduiushchego voiskami Brianskogo fronta No. 0040 Verkhovnomu Glavnokomanduiushchemu o khoda nastupleniia" [Combat report no. 0040 of the commander of the forces of the Briansk Front to the Supreme High Commander about the course of the offensive], in Ibid., 162.

172 "Donesenie komanduiushchego 61-i armiei No. 4 komanduiushchemu voiskami Brianskogo fronta o prichinakh neudachnoi ataki" [Report no. 4 of the commander of the 61st Army to the commander of the forces of the Briansk Front about the reasons for the unsuccessful attack], in Ibid., 164.

173 "Donesenie komanduiushchego 61-i armiei No. 5 komanduiushchemu voiskami Brianskogo fronta o neudachnoi povtornoi atake" [Report no. 5 of the commander of the 61st Army to the commander of the forces of the Briansk Front about the unsuccessful repeated attack], in Ibid., 164.

174 "Boevoe donesenie komanduiushchego voiskami Brianskogo fronta No. 0043 Verkhovnomu Glavnokomanduiushchemu o khoda nastupleniia" [Combat report no. 0043 of the commander of the forces of the Briansk Front to the Supreme High Commander about the course of the offensive], in Ibid., 165.

175 "Prikazanie komanduiushchego voiskami Brianskogo fronta komanduiushchim, chlenam Voennykh Sovetov i nachal'nikam politicheskikh otdelov armii o bespereboinom snabzhenii voisk produktami pitaniia, boeprepasami i goriuchim" [An order of the commander of the forces of the Briansk Front to the commanders, members of the Military Council, and chiefs of the political departments of the armies about the uninterrupted supply of forces with foodstuffs, ammunition, and fuel], in Ibid., 166.

176 "Boevoe donesenie komanduiushchego voiskami Brianskogo fronta No. 0044 Verkhovnomu Glavnokomanduiushchemu o sosredotochenii protivnika" [Combat report no. 0044 of the commander of the forces of the Briansk Front to the Supreme High Commander about the concentration of the enemy], in Ibid., 166.

Notes to Chapter 7

177 The Stavka reorganized the headquarters of the Don Front's 57th Army into the headquarters of the new 68th Army, assigned the 68th Army to the Northwestern Front, and distributed the former 57th Army's forces to other armies.

178 A. M. Vasilevsky, Delo vsei zhizni [A lifelong cause], (Moscow: Politizdat, 1983), 279–80. Detailed Stavka records on the planning of this operation have yet to be

released from the Russian archives. Based on materials already released, this account by Vasilevsky is correct, as far as it goes.

179 Direktiva Stavki VGK No. 46038 komanduiushchemu voiskami Donskogo fronta o vyvode v rezerv Verkhovnogo Glavnokomandovaniia upravlenii 21-i i 64-i armii" [*Stavka* VGK directive no. 46038 to the commander of the forces of the Don Front about the withdrawal into the reserve of the Supreme High Command the headquarters of the 21st and 64th Armies], in Zolotarev, "*Stavka* 1943," 58.

180 "Direktiva Stavki VGK No. 46039 komanduiushchim voiskami Donskogo i Brianskogo frontov o peredislokatsii upravleniia, frontovykh chastei i uchrezhdenii Donskogo fronta" [*Stavka* VGK directive no. 46039 to the commanders of the forces of the Don and Briansk Fronts about the relocation of the headquarters, *front* units, and installations of the Don Front], in Ibid., 61.

181 "Direktiva Stavki VGK No. 46046 komanduiushchemu voiskami Donskogo fronta o vyvode upravleniia, armeiskikh chastei i uchrezdenii 65-i armii v rezerv Verkhovnogo Glavnokomandovaniia" [*Stavka* VGK directive no. 46046 to the commander of the forces of the Don Front about the withdrawal of the headquarters, army units, and installations of the 65th Army into the reserve of the Supreme High Command], in Ibid., 64.

182 "Direktiva Stavki VGK No. 46053 komanduiushchemu voiskami Donskogo fronta ob organizatsii rukovodstva ostaiushchimisia v raione Stalingrada voiskami" [*Stavka* VGK directive no. 46053 to the commander of the forces of the Don Front about the organization of control of the forces remaining in the Stalingrad region], in Ibid., 66.

183 "Direktiva Stavki VGK No. 46051 komanduiushchemu otdel'noi armiei o peredislokatsii armii" [*Stavka* directive no. 46051 to the commander of the Separate Army about the relocation of the army], in Ibid., 68.

184 "Direktiva Stavki VGK No. 46052 zamestiteliu Narodnogo Komissara Vnutrennikh Del, nachal'niku Glavnogo Upraveleniia Formirovaniia i Ukomplektovaniia Voisk o vkliuchenii v sostav voisk Krasnoi Armii 70-i armii" [*Stavka* directive no. 46052 to the deputy People's Commissar of Internal Affairs and the chief of the Main Directorate for the Formation and Manning of Forces about the inclusion of the 70th Army in the composition of the forces of the Red Army], in Ibid., 69.

185 "Direktiva Stavki VGK No. 46056 komanduiushchemu voiskami Donskogo fronta ob obrazovanii Tsentral'nogo Fronta" [*Stavka* VGK directive no. 46056 to the commander of the forces of the Don Front about the formation of the Central Front], in Ibid, 70. See also K. Rokossovsky, *A Soldier's Duty*, (Moscow: Progress Publishers, 1985), 174.

186 Vasilevsky, *Delo vsei zhizhi*, 283–284, S. M. Shtemenko, *General'nyi shtab v gody voiny* [The General Staff at War], (Moscow: Voenizdat, 1968), 107–08, and K. F. Telegin, *Voiny neschitannye versty* [The countless versts of war], (Moscow: Voenizdat, 1988), 173.

187 "Direktiva Stavki VGK No. 30043 komanduiushchemu voiskami Tsentral'nogo Fronta na nastuplenie s tsel'iu vykhoda v tyl Rzhevsko-Viazemsko-Brianskoi gruppirovki protivnika" [*Stavka* VGK directive no. 30043 to the commander of the forces of the Central Front on an offensive with the aim of arriving in the rear area of the enemy's Rzhev-Viaz'ma, and Briansk grouping], in Zolotarev, "*Stavka* 1943," 73–74. See also Vasilevsky, *Delo vsei zhizni*, 283–84.

188 Rokossovsky, *A Soldier's Duty*, 175–76. See also, P. I. Batov, *V pokhodakh i boiakh* [In marches and battles], (Moscow: Voenizdat, 1966), 289–90.

189 "Plan nastupatel'noi operatsii voisk Tsentral'nogo fronta na Smolenskom napravelenii" [A plan for an offensive operation of the forces of the Central Front

along the Smolensk axis], in Zolotarev, "Preliudiia Kurskoi bitvy," 280–283. The precise numbers of aircraft were not indicated.

190 "Direktiva Stavki VGK No. 30049 komanduiushchim voiskami Brianskogo, Tsentral'nogo i Voronezhkogo frontov ob izmenenii razgranitel'nykh linii" [*Stavka* VGK directive no. 30049 to the commanders of the forces of the Briansk, Central, and Voronezh Fronts about changes in the boundary lines], in Ibid., 37.

191 "Rasporiazhenie shtaba Brianskogo fronta komanduiushchemu operativnoi gruppoi General-leitenantu Novosel'skomu ob uskorenii tempov nastupleniia" [Instructions of the headquarters of the Briansk Front to the commander of the operational group, Lieutenant General Novosel'sky, about an acceleration of the tempo of the offensive], in Ibid., 186.

192 "Iz operativnoi svodki shtaba Brianskogo Fronta No. 095" [From operational summary no. 095 of the headquarters of the Briansk Front], in Ibid., 168–169.

193 "Rasporiazhenie shtaba Brianskogo Fronta komanduiushchemu operativnoi gruppoi General-leitenantu Novosel'skomu s trebovaniiami ob'iasnit' prichiny medlennogo vypolneniia boevoi zadachi" [Instructions of the headquarters of the Briansk Front to the commander of the operational group, Lieutenant General Novosel'sky, with demands he clarify the reasons for the slow fulfillment of his combat mission], in Ibid., 169.

194 "Donesenie komanduiushchego operativnoi gruppoi General-leitenanta Novosel'skogo komanduiushchemu voiskami Brianskogo Fronta ob obstanovke" [A report by the commander of the operational group, Lieutenant General Novosel'sky, to the commander of the forces of the Briansk Front about the situation], in Ibid., 170.

195 "Donesenie komanduiushchego operativnoi gruppoi General-leitenanta Novosel'skogo nachal'niku shtabu Brianskogo fronta o dorozhnykh usloviakh v poloce deistvii gruppy [A report by the commander of the operational group, Lieutenant General Novosel'sky, to the chief of staff of the Briansk Front about road conditions in the sector of operations of the group], in Ibid.

196 "Dokladnaia zapiska General-maiora Popova Voennomu Sovetu Brianskogo Fronta po povodu prisvoeniia gvardeiskogo zvaniia 307-i strelkovoi divisii 13-i armii" [Memorandum of Major General Popov to the Military Council of the Briansk Front concerning the award of a guards' banner to the 307th Rifle Division of the 13th Army], in Ibid., 170–172. Despite this message, Colonel Laz'ko was promoted to the rank of Major General on 22 February 1943.

197 For a sketchy account of the 13th, 60th, and 38th Armies' operations during this and subsequent periods, see *V plameni srazhenii:Boevoi put' 13-i armii* [In the flames of battle: The combat path of 13th Army], (Moscow: Voenizdat, 1973), 84–88, A. Sharipov, *Cherniakhovskii*, (Moscow: Voenizdat, 1971), 185–195, and K. S. Moskalenko, *Na iugo-zapadnom napravlenii*, *T.2* [On the southwestern direction, Vol. 2], (Moscow: Izdatel'stvo "Nauka," 1969), 397–451.

198 "Boevoe donesenie komanduiushchego voiskami Voronezhskogo fronta No. 0054 Verkhovnomu Glavnokomaduiushchemu o khode nastupleniia chastei fronta na Khar'kovskom i drugikh napravelniiakh" [Combat report no. 0054 of the commander of the forces of the Voronezh Front to the Supreme High Command about the course of the offensive of the units of the *front* offensive along the Khar'kov and other axes], in Zolotarev, "Preliudiia Kurskoi bitvy," 95–96.

199 See "Considerations concerning the conduct of the 60th Army's L'gov-Ryl'sk opera-tion," classified top secret, from, "Materialy po planirovaniiu i provedeniiu Voronezhskoi i L'govsko-Ryl'skoi nastupatel'noi operatsii 2. 1–18. 3. 43g" [Mate-rials concerning the planning and conduct of the Voronezh and L'gov-Ryl'sk offen-

sive operations, 2 January–18 March 1943], in *TsAMO*, f. 417, op. 10564, d. 256, ll. 63–65.

200 "Doklad komanduiushchego voiskami Tsentral'nogo fronta Verkhovnomu Glavnokomanduiushchemu dopolnenii k planu nastupatel'noi operatsii fronta" [Report of the commander of the forces of the Central Front to the Supreme High Commander on additions to the plan of the *front's* offensive operation], in Zolotarev, "Preliudiia Kurskoi bitvy," 283–284.

201 "Boevoe rasporiazhenie komanduiushchego voiskami Tsentral'nogo Fronta No. 0022 komanduiushchemu 2-i tankovoi armiei na zaniatie iskhodnogo polozheniia dlia nastupleniia" [Combat instructions no. 0022 of the commander of the forces of the Central Front to the commander of the 2nd Tank Army on the occupation of the jumping-off position for the offensive], in Ibid., 284.

202 "Boevoe rasporiazhenie komanduiushchego voiskami Tsentral'nogo fronta No. 0023 komanduiushchemu 65-i armiei na zaniatie iskhodnogo polozheniia dlia nastupleniia" [Combat instructions no. 0023 of the commander of the forces of the Central Front to the commander of the 65th Army on the occupation of the jumping-off position for the offensive], in Ibid., 285.

203 "Boevoe rasporiazhenie komanduiushchego voiskami Tsentral'nogo fronta No. 0024 komanduiushchemu konno-strelkovoi gruppoi na zaniatie iskhodnogo polozheniia dlia nastupleniia" [Combat instructions no. 0024 of the commander of the forces of the Central Front to the commander of the Cavalry-Rifle Group on the occupation of the jumping-off position for the offensive], in Ibid., 285–286.

204 For details of the 2nd Tank Army's difficult march, see "Operativnoe marshi tankovykh i mekhaninizirovannykh soedinenii" [The operational marches of tank and mechanized formations], in *Sbornik materialov po izucheniiu opyta voiny, No. 9 noiabr'-dekabr' 1943 g.* [Collection of Materials for the Exploitation of War Experience, No. 9, November-December 1943], (Moscow: Voenizdat, 1944), 59–63.

205 For a detailed account of the 2nd Tank Army's operations, see F. I. Vysotsky, M. E. Makukhin, F. M. Sarychev, M. K. Shaposhynikov, *Gvardeiskaia tankovaia* [Guards tank], (Moscow: Voenizdat, 1963), 15–23. Some Russian sources claim that the offensive began on 26 February. This disparity results from the fragmented nature of the attack.

206 "Direktiva Stavki VGK No. 30055 predstaviteliu Stavki A. M. Vasilevskomu, komanduiushchemu voiskami Brianskogo fronta na razgrom Orlovsko-Kromskoi gruppirovki protivnika" [*Stavka* VGK directive no. 30055 to the representative of the *Stavka*, A. M. Vasilevsky, and the commander of the forces of the Briansk Front on the destruction of the enemy's Orel-Kromy grouping], in Zolotarev, "Preliudiia Kurskoi bitvy," 38.

207 Colonel V. E. Grigor'ev replaced Major General of Technical Forces A. G. Maslov as commander of the 16th Tank Corps temporarily on 24 February and permanently on 8 March.

208 "Spravka o polozhenii i sostoianii voisk Tsentral'nogo fronta k utru 24. 2. 1943 g." [Information about the situation and state of the forces of the Central Front by the morning of 24 February 1943], in Zolotarev, "Preliudiia Kurskoi bitvy," 286–288.

209 "Plan nastupatel'noi operatsii 2-i Tankovoi armii po proryvu oborony protivnika i ovladeniiu gorodom Trubchevsk v period s 23 po 28. 2. 1943 g." [The plan of an offensive operation by the 2nd Tank Army for the penetration of the enemy's defense and the capture of the city of Trubchevsk in the period from 23 through 28 February 1943], in Ibid., 288–290.

210 See I. Kh. Bagramian, *Tak shli my k pobede* [As we went on to victory], (Moscow: Voenizdat, 1988), 371–78, which provides greater detail about the 16th Army's

operations from 22 February through late March and contains Bagramian's criticism of his *front* commanders. For additional details about the fighting at the division level, see V. Lobanov, *Vosemnadtsataia gvardeiskaia* [The 18th Guards], (Kaliningrad: Kaliningradskoe knizhnoe izdatel'stvo, 1975), 74–77, and P. G. Kuznetsov, *Gvardeitsy-Moskvichi* [Guards-Muscovites], (Moscow: Voenizdat, 1962), 190–93. The Second Panzer Army's records fully document the scope and intensity of Bagramian's assaults. General Sokolovsky replaced Konev as commander of the Western Front on 28 February.

211 See, D. K. Mal'kov, *Skvoz' dym i plamia* [Through smoke and flames], (Moscow: Voenizdat, 1970), 61–62, a history of the 12th Guards Rifle Division, which provides a detailed assessment of why the division's assault failed.

212 See, for example, I. M. Tret'iak, *Khrabrye serdtsa odnopolchan* [The brave hearts of the peoples' militia] (Moscow: Voenizdat, 1987), 38–42, and "Lagenkarten Anl. Z. Taetigkeitsbericht d, Abt. Ic d. AOK 4, Sep 1942-Mar 1943," *AOK 4, 32542/8*, in NAM, T–312 Roll 1242.

213 "Prikaz Stavki VGK No. 0045 o smene komanduiushchego voiskami i nachal'nika shtaba Zapadnogo fronta" [*Stavka* VGK order no. 0045 about a change in the commander of the forces and the chief of staff of the Western Front], in Zolotarev, "*Stavka* 1943," 81.

214 "Prikaz Stavki VGK No. 0046 o smene komanduiushchikh armiiami Zapadnogo fronta" [*Stavka* VGK order no. 0046 about a change in the commanders of the armies of the Western Front], in Ibid., 81.

215 "Direktiva Stavki VGK No. 30058 komanduiushchemu voiskami Zapadnogo fronta o merakh po razvitiiu uspekha 16-i armii" [*Stavka* VGK directive no. 30058 to the commander of the forces of the Western Front about measures for the development of the success of the 16th Army], in Ibid., 82.

216 "Direktiva Stavki VGK No. 46058 upolnomochennomu Stavki, komanduiushchemu voiskami Zapadnogo fronta o perepodchinenii chetyrekh strelkovykh divizii" [*Stavka* VGK directive no. 46058 to the representative of the *Stavka* and the commander of the forces of the Western Front about the re-subordination of four rifle divisions], in Ibid., 83–84.

217 For details about Soviet conduct of the Donbas and Khar'kov operations, see David M. Glantz, *From the Don to the Dnepr*, (London: Frank Cass, 1991).

218 Here and elsewhere, I use the standard German Army Roman numeral designations for German panzer corps, that is, XXXX through XXXIX instead of XL through XLVI. The Germans used the former in their operational maps and records to avoid confusing the designations of these corps.

219 For operational and tactical detail regarding the disposition and actions of German forces throughout the operation, see, "Chefkarten, 28 Anlagen, Anlagenband 33, Pz AOK 2," " Ia, Lagenkarten 1.2.1943 – 28. 2. 1943," *Pz AOK 2, 37075/46*, in NAM T–313, Roll 171; "Chefkarten, 14 Anlagen, Pz AOK 2," " Ia, Lagenkarten 18. 3.1943 – 31. 3. 1943," *Pz AOK 2, 37075/47*, in NAM T–313, Roll 171; and, "Anlage zum Kriegstagebuch A. O. K. 2 – Ia, Russland Teil 9, Lagenkarten 1. Januar 1943 bis 31. Marz 1943," *AOK 2, 31811/2*, in NAM T–312, Roll 1213. For the German intelligence appreciation, see, "Situation maps and overlays (1:300,000), prepared by the Second Army, Counter-intelligence Officer (Ic/AO), December 1942-July 1943 [no German title]," *AOK 2, 31811/123*, in NAM T–312, Roll 1223. This intelligence material verifies the Soviet accounts of the operation and clearly indicates Soviet offensive intent.

220 For additional details about the 65th Army's operations throughout the entire period, see G. S. Nagysev, *Na sluzhbe shtabnoi* [In staff service], (Riga: Izdatel'stbo

"Pissma", 1972), 110–13; and I. N. Pavlov, *Ot Moskby do Shtrol'zunda* [From Moscow to Strasland], (Moscow: Voenizdat, 1985), 45–47. The latter is a history of the 65th Army's 354th Rifle Division.

221 Batov, *V pokhodakh i boiakh*, 295–98. For details about the coordination problems between the 65th Army and 70th Armies and the operations of the 69th Rifle Division, see A. A. Andreev, *Po voennym dorogam* [Along military roads], (Moscow: Voenizdat, 1971), 36–57. One of the few existing accounts of the 70th Army's operations during this period is from the perspective of the 102nd Rifle Division found in A. M. Andreev, *Ot pervogo mgnoveniia do poslednego* [From the first moment to the last], (Moscow: Voenizdat, 1984), 70–76, and in the records of opposing German forces.

222 An account of the 194th Rifle Division's role in the operation is found in K. K. Shilov, *Rechitskaia krasnoznamennaia* [Rechitsa red banner], (Moscow: Voenizdat, 1984), 63–73.

223 The 6th Guards and 137th Rifle Divisions were under the Briansk Front's direct control. Apparently, Reiter's intent was to reinforce the 48th Army's shock group along the Neruch River north of Maloarkhangel'sk with the 19th Tank Corps and then resume the advance on Orel from the southeast.

224 "Donesenie komanduiushchego voiskami Brianskogo fronta No. 0058 Verkhovnomu Glavnokomanduiushchemu ob obstanovke" [Report no. 0058 of the commander of the forces of the Briansk Front the Supreme High Commander about the situation], in Zolotarev, "Preliudiia Kurskoi bitvy," 173–174.

225 "Donesenie komanduiushchego voiskami Brianskogo fronta No. 0059 Verkhovnomu Glavnokomanduiushchemu ob obstanovke" [Report no. 0059 of the commander of the forces of the Briansk Front to the Supreme High Commander about the situation], in Ibid., 174.

226 "Boevoe donesenie komanduiushchego voiskami Brianskogo fronta Verkhovnomu Glavnokomanduiushchemu o boevykh deistviiakh s 26 ianvaria po 26 fevralia 1943 g." [Combat report of the commander of the forces of the Briansk Front to the Supreme High Commander about combat operations from 26 January through 26 February 1943], in Ibid., 175.

227 "Boevoe donesenie komanduiushchego voiskami Brianskogo fronta No. 0060 Verkhovnomu Glavnokomanduiushchemu ob obstanovke" [Combat report no. 0060 of the commander of the forces of the Briansk Front to the Supreme High Commander about the situation], in Ibid., 176.

228 "Prikazanie shtaba Brianskogo fronta komanduiushchemu 61-i armiei o provedenii meropriatii po dezinformatsii protivnika" [Order of the headquarters of the Briansk Front to the commander of the 61st Army about the conduct of measures for misinforming the enemy], in Ibid., 176.

229 For details of the 11th Tank Corps operations, see I. I. Iushchuk, *Odinnadtsatyi tankovyi korpus v boiakh za rodinu* [The 11th Tank Corps in battles for the fatherland], (Moscow: Voenizdat, 1962), 18–27.

230 "Plan shtaba partizanskogo dvizheniia na Brianskom fronte po vzaimodeistviiu partizanskikh brigade s voiskami Tsentral'nogo fronta" [Plan of the headquarters of the Partisan Movement in the Briansk Front for cooperation of the partisan brigades with the forces of the Central Front], in Ibid., 290–291.

231 "Boevoe donesenie komanduiushchego voiskami Brianskogo fronta No. 0067 Verkhovnomu Glavnokomanduiushchemu o perekhode v nastuplenie 48-i i 13-i armii" [Combat report no. 0067 of the commander of the forces of the Briansk Front to the Supreme High Commander about the transition to the offensive of the 48th and 13th Armies], in Ibid., 179.

232 Originally, the only forces opposing Lazarov's exploiting 11th Tank Corps and Kriukov's Cavalry-Rifle Group were the Hungarian 104th and 108th Light [Jäger] Divisions, which had been deployed into this region to provide rear area security, primarily against partisans. When Rodin's tank army marched westward, the two Hungarian divisions conducted a light delaying action from Sevsk westward toward the Desna River.

233 For details about the 21st Army's intended role in the offensive, see *Po prukazu Rodiny* [By order of the Fatherland], (Moscow: Voenizdat, 1971), pp. 68–75, and I. M. Chistiakov, *Sluzhim otchizne* [In the service of the Fatherland], (Moscow: Voenizdat, 1975), pp. 130–37.

Notes to Chapter 8

234 "Direktiva Stavki VGK No. 46059 upolnomochennomu Stavki, komanduiushchim voiskami Kalininskogo fronta i 66-i armii o perepodchinenii armii" [*Stavka* VGK directive No. 46059 to the representative of the *Stavka* and the commanders of the forces of the Kalinin Front and the 66th Army about the re-subordination of the army], in Zolotarev, "*Stavka* 1943," 84. The representative of the *Stavka* [in this case referred to as the "plenipotentiary"] was Lieutenant General V. V. Kosiakin. See the *Stavka* implementing directive no. 36832 in Zolotarev, "Preliudiia Kurskoi bitvy," 44–45.

235 "Direktiva Stavki VGK No. 46060 upolnomochennomu Stavki, komanduiushchemu 24-i armii o vkliuchenii v sostav armii shesti strelkovykh divizii" [*Stavka* VGK directive no. 46060 to the representative of the *Stavka* and the commander of the 24th Army about the inclusion of six rifle divisions in the composition of the army], in Zolotarev, "*Stavka* 1943," 84–85.

236 "Direktiva Stavki VGK No. 46061 upolnomochennomu Stavki, komanduiushchim voiskami Iugo-zapadnogo fronta i 62-i armiei o perepodchinenii armii" [*Stavka* VGK directive no. 46061 to the representative of the *Stavka*, the commanders of the forces of the Southwestern Front and the 62nd Army concerning the re-subordination of the army], in Ibid., 85. The representative of the *Stavka* was Lieutenant General V. V. Kosiakin. See the *Stavka* implementing directive no. 36883 in Zolotarev, "Preliudiia Kurskoi bitvy," 45–46. *Stavka* VGK directive No. 46062 dispatched the 7th Rifle Corps to the Southwestern Front in the same fashion

237 "Direktiva Stavki VGK No. 46063 upolnomochennomu Stavki, komanduiushchim voiskami Voronezhskogo fronta i 64-i armiei o perepodchinenii armii" [*Stavka* VGK directive no. 46063 to the representative of the *Stavka* and the commanders of the forces of the Voronezh Front and the 64th Army about the re-subordination of the army], in Zolotarev, "*Stavka* 1943," 86. The representative of the *Stavka* was Lieutenant General V. V. Kosiakin. See the *Stavka* implementing directive no. 36885 in Zolotarev, "Preliudiia Kurskoi bitvy," 47.

238 "Direktiva Stavki VGK No. 46064 upolnomochennomu Stavki VGK general-leitenantu Kosiakinu o peredache v Iugo-zapadnyi front i sosredotechivanie v raione Starobel'sk 66-i armii" [*Stavka* VGK directive no. 46064 to the representative of the *Stavka* VGK, Lieutenant General Kosiakin, about the transfer of the 66th Army to the Southwestern Front and its concentration in the Starobel'sk region], in Zolotarev, "Preliudiia Kurskoi bitvy," 42

239 Originally, both the 62nd and 64th Armies had probably been designated to reinforce the Soviet's expanded winter offensive after they completed their refitting, either in the Central Front's sector or elsewhere. They began their movements forward in late February and completed their assembly by mid-March.

240 "Direktiva Stavki VGK No. 30067 komanduiushchemu voiskami Tsentral'nogo fronta na razgrom Dmitrovsko-Orlovskoi gruppirovki protivnika" [*Stavka* VGK directive no. 30067 to the commander of the forces of the Central Front on the destruction of the enemy's Dmitrovsk-Orlovskii grouping], in Zolotarev, "Preliudiia Kurskoi bitvy," 47–48.

241 Ziemke, *Stalingrad to Berlin*, 115–116.

242 Horst Grossman, *Rzhev: The Cornerstone of the Eastern Front* Unpublished manuscript translated by Joseph Welch from the German *Rshew: Eckpfeiler der Ostfront* (Friedberg, 1980), 65.

243 For details, see N. I. Krylov, I. I. Alekseev, and I. G. Dragon, *Navstrechu pobede: Boevoi put's 5-i armii* [Meeting victory: The combat path of the 5th Army] (Moscow: "Nauka," 1970), 133–135. This account is confirmed by Hans Baumann, *Die 35. Infantrie-division im 2. Wletkrig 1939–1945* (Karlsruhe: Verlag G. Braun GMBH, 1964), 173–182.

244 "Direktiva Stavki VGK No. 30062 komanduiushchim voiskami Kalininskogo i Zapadnogo frontov na presledovanie otkhodiashchego protivnika" [*Stavka* VGK directive no. 30062 to the commanders of the forces of the Kalinin and Western Fronts on the pursuit of the withdrawing enemy], in Zolotarev, "*Stavka* 1943," 87.

245 Grossman, *Rzhev*, 65.

246 Ibid., 66–67.

247 Ibid., 67–68.

248 Krylov, Alekseev, Dragon, *Navstrechu pobede*, 39–141.

249 Ibid., 144.

250 N. M. Afanas'ev, N. K. Glazunov, P. A. Kazanskii, and N. A. Fifonov, *Dorogami ispytanii i pobed: Boevoi put' 31-i armii* [The roads to experience and victory] (Moscow: Voenizdat, 1986), 83–84.

251 F. D. Pankov, *Ognennye rubezhi* [Firing positions] (Moscow: Voenizdat, 1964), 128.

252 Gurkin, "Liudskie poteri," 7.

253 Afanas'ev et al., *Dorogami ispytanii i pobed*, 77.

254 "Prikaz komanduiushchego voiskami Tsentral'nogo fronta No. 0072 komanduiushchemu 21-i armiei na perekhode v nastuplcnie" [Order no. 0072 of the commander of the forces of the Central Front to the commander of the 21st Army on the conduct of the offensive], in Zolotarev, "Preliudiia Kurskoi bitvy," 293.

255 "Prikaz komanduiushchego voiskami Tsentral'nogo fronta No. 0073 komanduiushchemu 70-i armiei na razvitie nastuplenie" [Order no. 0073 of the commander of the forces of the Central Front to the commander of the 70th Army on the development of the offensive], in Ibid., 293–294.

256 "Prikaz komanduiushchego voiskami Tsentral'nogo Fronta No. 0074 komanduiushchim 65-i i 2-i tankovoi armiiami na razvitie nastuplenie" [Order no. 0074 of the commander of the forces of the Central Front to the commanders of the 65th and 2nd Tank Armies on the development of the offensive], in Ibid., 294–295.

257 "Boevoe donesenie komanduiushchego voiskami Brianskogo Fronta No. 0069 Verkhovnomu Glavnokomanduiushchemu ob obstanovke" [Combat report no. 0069 of the commander of the forces of the Briansk Front to the Supreme High Commander about the situation], in Ibid., 180.

258 "Donesenie komanduiushchego voiskami Brianskogo fronta chlenu GKO G. M. Malenkovu o trudnostiakh v snabzhenii voisk" [Report of the commander of the forces of the Briansk Front to the member of the State Defense Committee (GKO), G. M. Malenkov, about difficulties in supplying the forces], in Ibid., 182.

259 "Donesenie shtaba Brianskogo fronta komanduiushchemu BT i MV Krasnoi Armii o bezvozvratnykh poteriakh tankov za fevral' 1943 g." [Report of the headquarters of the Briansk Front to the commander of the Armored and Mechanized Forces of the Red Army about the irreplaceable losses of tanks for February 1943], in Ibid., 183.

260 "Boevoe donesenie komanduiushchego voiskami Brianskogo fronta No. 0072 Verkhovnomu Glavnokomanduiushchemu ob obstanovke" [Combat report no. 0072 of the commander of the forces of the Briansk Front to the Supreme High Commander about the situation], in Ibid., 183.

261 "Direktiva Stavki VGK No. 30070 chlenu GKO G. M. Malenkovu, predstaviteliu Stavki A. I. Antonovu, komanduiushchim voiskami Zapadnogo, Brianskogo i Tsentral'nogo frontov o rasformirovanii Brianskogo fronta" [Stavka VGK directive no. 30070 to the member of the State Defense Committee GKO, G. M. Malenkov, representative of the Stavka, A. I. Antonov, and to the commanders of the forces of the Western, Briansk, and Central Fronts about the disbanding of the Briansk Front], in Ibid., 50.

262 "Direktiva Stavki VGK No. 30071 komanduiushchemu voiskami Brianskogo fronta o sformirovanii Rezervnogo fronta" [Stavka VGK directive no. 30071 to the commander of the forces of the Briansk Front about the formation of the Reserve Front], in Ibid., 183.

263 "Prikaz komanduiushchego voiskami Tsentral'nogo fronta No. 00548 o vkliuchenii voisk Brianskogo fronta v sostav Tsentral'nogo fronta" [Order no. 00548 of the commander of the forces of the Central Front about the inclusion of the forces of the Briansk Front in the composition of the Central Front], in Ibid., 296.

264 "Boevoe donesenie komanduiushchego 2-i tankovoi armiei komanduiushchemu voiskami Tsentral'nogo fronta o khode nastupleniia" [Combat report of the commander of the 2nd Tank Army to the commander of the forces of the Central Front about the course of the offensive], in Ibid., 296–298.

265 "Direktiva Stavki VGK No. 30072 komanduiushchemu voiskami Tsentral'nogo fronta o razgrome protivnika iuzhnee Kurska" [Stavka VGK directive no. 30072 to the commander of the forces of the Central Front about the destruction of the enemy south of Kursk], in Zolotarev, "Stavka 1943," 93.

266 See "Direktiva Stavki VGK No. 46070 komanduiushchego voiskami Zapadnogo i Tsentral'nogo frontov o perepodchinenii 9-go tankovogo korpusa" [Stavka VGK directive no. 46070 to the commanders of the forces of the Western and Central Fronts about the re-subordination of the 9th Tank Corps], in Ibid., 94. This directive accompanied four others ordering the re-deployments of other tank corps (the 4th Guards, 25th, 10th, and 3rd) across the entire front.

267 The NKO had formed the 1st Tank Army in the Ostashkov region in the Northwestern Front's sector between 30 January and 23 February 1943. Created on the base of the headquarters of the Western Front's 29th Army, initially the tank army consisted of the 6th Tank Corps, the 3rd Mechanized Corps, the 112th Separate Tank Brigade, the 6th and 9th Guards Airborne Divisions, six ski brigades, and several separate tank regiments. In mid-February the 1st Tank Army joined Lieutenant General F. I. Tolbukhin's 68th Army, itself a special assault army made up primarily of airborne divisions, to form special Operational Group Khozin, commanded by Lieutenant General M. S. Khozin. Khozin's group was designated as the exploitation force for a major offensive by the Northwestern Front, which was planned for late February against Army Group North's Sixteenth Army. Group Khozin, after exploiting the attack of the 1st Shock Army, was to advance to capture Dno and then exploit through Luga to the southern coast of the Gulf of Finland to isolate German Army Group North's forces in the Leningrad region. However, on 23

February (9 March according to other sources), the *Stavka* ordered the 1st Tank Army to move south, either to participate in offensive operations against the Rzhev-Viaz'ma salient under the Western Front's control or against the Orel salient under the Central Front's control or to help thwart Manstein's counterstroke. The tank army's main combat elements reached the Oboian region by 23 March. The fact that the *Stavka* had previously intended to employ this powerful armored force in a major offensive code-named "Polar Star," south of Leningrad, provides additional evidence of the ambitiousness of the *Stavka's* offensive planning in February 1943. For further details, see M. E. Katukov, *Na ostrie glavnogo udara* [On the point of the main attack], (Moscow: Voenizdat, 1976), 193–197, and A. Kh. Babadzhanian, N. K. Popol', M. A. Shalin, I. M. Kravchenko, *Liuki otkryli v berline* [They opened the hatchway to Berlin], (Moscow: Voenizdat, 1973), 7–13.

See details about the deployment of the 24th and 66th Armies to the Voronezh region in *Ot volzhskikh stepei do avstrilskikh al'p* [From the Volga steppes to the Austrian Alps], (Moscow: Voenizdat, 1971), 26-27, and I. A. Samchuk, P. G. Skachko, Iu. N. Babikov, I. L. Ghedoi, *Ot Volgi do El'by i Pragi* [From the Volga to the Elbe and Prague], (Moscow: Voenizdat, 1970), 45-49. The 66th Army received its movement order on 23 March.

268 "Direktiva Stavki VGK No. 46076 komanduiushchemu 5-i gvardeiskoi tankovoi armiei na smenu raione sosredotocheniia" [*Stavka* VGK directive no. 46076 to the commander of the 5th Guards Tank Army on a change in its concentration region], in Zolotarev, "*Stavka* 1943," 96. The *Stavka* had begun forming the 5th Guards Tank Army in the Southern Front during mid-February 1943 as the first of its new tank armies formed under the new unified establishment adopted on 29 January 1943, which mandated the formation of fully mechanized tank armies to replace the older mixed-composition (tanks, infantry, and cavalry) tank armies. Although it had initially planned to employ the tank army as an exploitation force during the ongoing winter offensive, after Manstein launched his devastating counterstroke in the Donbas region, at 0015 hours on 27 February, the *Stavka* had instead ordered the tank army to assemble in the Millerovo region in readiness to back up the Southwestern and Voronezh Fronts' sagging defenses:

[To the commander of the forces of the Southern Front, the commander of Red Army Armored and Mechanized Forces, the chief of the Organizational Directorate of the General Staff, and the commander of the 5th Guards Tank Army]

1. The 5th Guards Tank Army is formed in the Millerovo region by Directive No. 1124821ss of the NKO, dated 22 February 1943. Date of readiness — 25 March 1943.

2. [The following are] included in the composition of the army:
— The 3rd Guards Kotel'nikovskii Tank Corp;
— The 5th Guards Zimovnikovskii Mechanized Corps; and
— The 29th Tank Corps and army reinforcing units.

3. Concentrate the 3rd Guards Tank Corps and 5th Guards Mechanized Corps in the Millerovo region at the disposal of the military council of the Southern Front by 5 March 1943.

4. The field headquarters of the 5th Guards Tank Army, with rear service units and installations, and the 29th Tank Corps, with army reinforcing units, will arrive in the Millerovo region in the period from 5 through 12 March 1943.

5. The commander of the Armored and Mechanized Forces of the Red Army [BTMV-KA] and the commander of the 5th Guards Tank Army will send representatives to Millerovo Station to organize the receipt and acceptance of the units joining the army, so that they reach the site no later than 1 March 1943.

6. The commander of the forces of the Southern Front will:

a) Support the stationing of the units and formations of the 5th Guards Tank Army arriving in the Millerovo region and include them [on the list] for all types of supplies

b) Send responsible representatives to Millerovo before the arrival of the field headquarters of the 5th Guards Tank Army in Millerovo and supervise the organization of the receipt, acceptance, and stationing of the units and formations of the 5th Guards Tank Army.

7. Report to the General Staff and the commander of the BTMV KA regarding the course of concentrating the units and formations of the 5th Guards Tank Army in the Millerovo region on even numbered days of the month beginning from 2 March 1943.

8. The combat employment of the 5th Guards Tank Army – only with the special permission of the *Stavka*.

The Deputy Chief of the General Staff
Bokov.

See, Direktiva General'nogo shtaba No. 36786 komanduiushchemu voiskami Iuzhnogo fronta na sosredotochenie formiruiushcheisia 5-i gv. tankovoi armii v raione Millerovo" [General Staff directive no. 36786 to the commander of the forces of the Southern Front on the concentration of the forming 5th Guards Tank Army in the Millerovo region], in Zolotarev, "Preliudiia Kurskoi bitva," 39.

When Manstein's forces began assaulting the Voronezh Front's defensive positions south of Khar'kov, at 2030 hours on 8 March, the *Stavka* had issued a new directive transferring the 5th Guards Army from the Southern Front's control to that of the Southwestern Front:

1. Transfer the 3rd Guards Tank Corps to the disposal of Marshal Vasilevsky for employing it with the objective of the defense of the city of Khar'kov.

2. Subsequently, after the approach of new forces to the Khar'kov region from the reserve of the *Stavka*, transfer Rotmistrov's tank army to the subordination of the commander of the Southwestern Front, Army General Vatutin.

The *Stavka* of the Supreme High Command
I. Stalin
Sent by telephone to Comrade Bokov
Beliusov

See "Rasporiazhenie Stavki VGK predstaviteliu Stavki Marshalu Sovetskogo Soiuza Vasilevskomu komanduiushchemuvoiskami Iugo-zapadnogo fronta o perepodchinenii 3-go gv. tankovoi korpusa i 5-go gv. tankovoi armii" [*Stavka* VGK instructions to representative of the *Stavka*, Marshal of the Soviet Union Vasilevsky, and the commander of the forces of the Southwestern Front about the re-subordination of the 3rd Guards Tank Corps and the 5th Guards Tank Army], in Ibid., 48.

269 See "Boevoi prikaz No. 001 shtaba Kurskogo fronta" [Combat order no. 001 of the headquarters of the Kursk Front]," from "Prikazy NKO i voiskam Voronezhskogo fronta (1943)" [Orders of the NKO and to the forces of the Voronezh Front], in *TsAMO*, f. 417, op. 10564, d. 243, l. 12, and Ibid., 52–53.

270 "Direktiva Stavki VGK No. 30077 General-polkovniku Reiteru, komanduiushchim voiskami Tsentral'nogo i Voronezhskogo frontov ob obrazovanii Kurskogo fronta" [*Stavka* VGK directive no. 30077 to Colonel General Reiter and the commanders of the forces of the Central and Voronezh Fronts about the formation of the Kursk Front], in Zolotarev, "Preliudiia Kurskoi bitvy," 52–53.

271 "Direktiva Stavki VGK No. 30081 Marshalam Sovetskogo Soiuza Zhukovy i Vasilevskomu, General-polkovniku Reiteru, komanduiushchim voiskami Zapadnogo i Tsentral'nogo frontov ob obrazovanii Orlovskogo fronta" [*Stavka* VGK directive no. 30081 to Marshals of the Soviet Union Zhukov and Vasilevsky, Colonel General Reiter, and the commanders of the forces of the Western and Briansk Fronts about the formation of the Orel Front], in Ibid., 54.

272 "Direktiva Stavki VGK No. 30082 Marshalam Sovetskogo Soiuza Zhukovy i Vasilevskomu, General-polkovniku Reiteru, komanduiushchim voiskami Tsentral'nogo i Voronezhskogo frontov o peredache 60-i i 38-i armii i ustanovlenii novoi razgranichitel'noi linii mezhdu frontami" [*Stavka* VGK directive no. 30082 to Marshals of the Soviet Union Zhukov and Vasilevsky, Colonel General Reiter, and the commanders of the forces of the Central and Voronezh Fronts about the transfer of the 60th and 38th Armies and the establishment of a new boundary line between the *fronts*], in Ibid.,.55.

273 See *V srazheniiakh za Pobedy: Boevoi put' 38-i armii v gody Velikoi Otechestvennoi voiny 1941–1945* [The battles for the Homeland: the combat path of the 38th Army in the Great Patriotic War 1941–1945] (Moscow: "Nauka," 1974), 220.

274 "Direktiva Stavki VGK No. 30085 Marshalu Sovetskogo Soiuza Zhukovu, komanduiushchim voiskami Orlovskogo, Zapadnogo i Tsentral'nogo frontov o pereimenovanii Orlovskogo fronta v Brianskii" [*Stavka* directive no. 30085 to Marshal of the Soviet Union Zhukov and the commanders of the forces of the Orel, Western, and Central Fronts about renaming the Orel Front the Briansk Front], in Zolotarev, "Preliudiia Kurskoi bitvy," 55.

275 For details see, "Perepiski operativnogo otdela shtaba 13A co shtabom 15sd" [Correspondence of the operational department of the headquarters of the 13th Army with the headquarters of the 15th Rifle Division], in *TsAMO*, f. 361, op. 6079, d. 183, ll. 193, 204, 206, and 285.

276 These figures are taken from Krivosheev, *Grif sekretnosti sniat'*, 186–227.

277 See "Postanovlenie Voennogo Soveta Tsentral'nogo fr. No. 00116, 4 Aprelia 1943 g. [Decree of the Military Council of the Central Front no. 00116, 4 April 1943]," from "Direktivy SVGK, GSh, KA voiskam Brianskogo fronta, 13A, 2. 1–20. 7. 43" [Directives of the *Stavka* of the Supreme High Command to the forces of the Briansk Front and the 13th Army, 2 January–20 July 1943], in *TsAMO*, f. 361, op. 6079, d. 173, ll. 142–144.

278 Krivosheev, *Grif sekretnosti sniat*, 226.

279 For the full report, see "Boevaia kharakteristika 38 gv RD" [The combat characteristics of the 38th Guards Rifle Division], in *TsAMO*, f. 1131, op. 1, d. 3, ll. 7–8.

280 See "Operativnoe svodki i boevye donesenii 350 sd" [Operational summaries and combat reports of the 350th Rifle Division], in *TsAMO*, f. 1669, op. 1, d. 24, l. 165.

281 See "Otchety shtaba 184 rd o boevykh deistviiakh" [An account by the headquarters of the 184th Rifle Division about its combat operations], in *TsAMO*, f. 1435, op. 1, d. 8, l. 31.

282 "Boevaia kharakteristika na 121 sd" [The combat characteristics in the 121st Rifle Division]," from "Boevye rasporiazheniia shtaba Voronezhskogo fronta" [Combat orders of the headquarters of the Voronezh Front], in *TsAMO*, f. 417, op. 10564, d. 252, l. 12.

283 "Boevaia kharakteristika na 248 otdel'nuiu kursantskuiu strelkovuiu brigadu" [Combat characteristics in the 248th Student Rifle Brigade]," from "Boevye rasporiazheniia shtaba Voronezhskogo fronta" [Combat orders of the headquarters of the Voronezh Front], in *TsAMO*, f. 417, op. 10564, d. 252, l. 13.

284 Ibid.

285 "Komandiram 1, 2, 3 armeiskikh zagradotriadov, 16. 3. 43g. No. 0224" [Order no. 0224, 6 March 1943, to the commanders of the 1st, 2nd, and 3rd Army Blocking Detachments]," from "Direktivy SVGK, GSh, KA voiskam Brianskogo fronta, 13A, 2. 1–20. 7. 43" [Directives of the *Stavka* of the Supreme High Command to the forces of the Briansk Front and the 13th Army, 2 January–20 July 1943], in *TsAMO*, f. 361, op. 6079, d. 173, l. 105.

286 See "Prikaz chastiam 121sd No. 0045, 12. 3. 43. [Order No. 0044 to the units of the 121st Rifle Division, dated 12 March 1943]," from "Boevye prikazy i pazporiazheniia soedinenii 60A (1942–1943 gg.)" [Combat orders and instructions of the formations of the 60th Army (1942–1943)], in *TsAMO*, f. 417, op. 10564, d. 215, l. 67.

287 "Prikaz chastiam 121sd No. 074. 31. 3. 43g. [Order no. 074 to the units of the 121st Rifle Division, dated 31 March 1943]," from "Boevye prikazy soedinenii 60A (1943g.)" [Combat orders to the formations of the 60th Army (1943)], in *TsAMO*, f. 417, op. 10564, d. 251, l. 6.

288 From "Prikaz 65A. 25. 3. 43g. [65th Army Order No. 4, dated 25 March 1943]," from "Dokumenty iz fondov 65A" [Documents from the archives of the 65th Army], in *TsAMO*, f. 422, op. 10496, d. 81, l. 12.

289 See "Komandirom divizii 13A, No. 0144. 11. 3. 43g. [Order No. 0144, dated 11 March 1943, to the commanders of the divisions of the 13th Army], in *TsAMO*, f. 361, op. 6079, d. 173, l. 80.

290 "Politupravlenie Brianskogo fronta, 3. 2. 34g., No. 0523 Komanduiushchim 13 i 48 armii. Sovershenno sekretno"[Order No. 0523, dated 3 February 1943, of the Political Directorate of the Briansk Front to the commanders of the 13th and 48th Armies. Top secret]," from Direktivy SVGK, GSh, KA voiskam Brianskogo fronta, 13A (2. 1–20. 7. 43g.) [Directives of the *Stavka* of the Supreme High Command and Red Army General Staff to the forces of the Briansk Front and the 13th Army (2 January–20 July 1943)], in *TsAMO*, f. 361, op. 6079, d. 173, l. 76.

291 "Iz direktivy Voennogo Soveta Brianskogo fronta komanduiushchemu 13 armii (kopiia komanduuishchemu 3 armii), 4. 2. 43g." [From a directive of the Military Council of the Briansk Front to the commander of the 13th Army, dated 4 February 1943 (a copy to the commander of the 3rd Army], from "Direktivy SVGK" [Directives of the *Stavka* of the Supreme High Command], in *TsAMO*, f. 361, op. 6079, d. 173, l 74.

292 "Prikaz voiskam Brianskogo fronta No. 31/2, 1. 2. 43g. Sekretno" [Order No. 31/2 to the forces of the Briansk Front, dated 1 February 1943. Secret], from "Direktivy SVGK" [Directives of the *Stavka* of the Supreme High Command], in *TsAMO*, f. 361, op. 6079, d. 174, l. 70.

293 "Iz direktivy Voennogo Soveta Brianskogo fronta ot 6.2 43g. komanduiushchim, chlennam Voennykh Sovetov, nachal'nikam politotdelov armii [From a 6 February directorate of the Military Council of the Briansk Front to the commanders, members of the Military Councils, and political workers of the armies]," from "Direktivy SVGK" [Directives of the *Stavka* of the Supreme High Command], in *TsAMO*, f. 361, op. 6079, d. 174, l. 79.

294 "Iz direktivy Voennogo Soveta Brianskogo fronta ot 17. 2. 43g. [From a directive of the Military Council of the Briansk Front of 17 February 1943]," from "Direktivy

SVGK" [Directives of the *Stavka* of the Supreme High Command], in *TsAMO*, f. 361, op. 6079, d. 174, I. 87.

295 "Direktivy i prikazy SVGK. Genshtaba Kr. Ar. Brianskogo fronta voiskam [Directives and orders of the *Stavka* of the Supreme High Command to the forces of the Briansk Front]," in *TsAMO*, f. 361, op. 6079, d. 174. l. 35.

296 "Direktivy SVGK, GSh, KA voiskam Brianskogo fronta, 13A, 2. 1–20. 7. 43" [Directives of the *Stavka* of the Supreme High Command to the forces of the Briansk Front and 13th Army, 2 January–20 July 1943]," in *TsAMO*, f. 361, op. 6079, d. 173, ll. 138–140.

297 Ibid., l. 164.

298 "Direktiva Voennogo Soveta Tsentral'nogo fronta No. 027 ot 18. 4. 43g. [Directive no. 027 of the Military Council of the Central Front of 18 March 1943]": l. 166.

299 "Postanovlenie Voennogo Soveta Tsentral'nogo fronta No. 00116, 4 aprelia 1943g. Deistvuiushchaia Armiia [Decree no. 00116 of the Military Council of the Central Front, 4 April 1943. Field Army]," ll. 142–144.

300 Tarasov, who later served as the commander of the 53rd Army from December 1943 to January 1944 and deputy commander of the same army from January to October 1944, was killed in action in Hungary on 19 October 1944.

301 E.g., planning time for the Stalingrad operation lasted more than one month. Thus, offensive preparations were extensive. Planning time for other operations was as follows: Little Saturn – over three weeks; Ostrogozhsk-Rossosh' – about 20 days; and about one week for the Voronezh-Kastornoe and subsequent operations.

Notes to Chapter 9

302 See "Direktiva Stavki VGK No. 170696 komanduiushchim voiskami Volkhovskogo i Leningradskogo frontov ob utvershdenii plana operatsii "Iskra" [*Stavka* directive no. 170696 to the commander of the forces of the Bolkhov and Leningrad Fronts about the approval of a plan for operation "Iskra"], in Zolotarev, "*Stavka* 1942," 458. See the Leningrad Front's original proposals for such an offensive in Ibid., 560–564.

303 For details on Operation Spark [*Iskra*], see David M. Glantz, *The Battle for Leningrad, 1941–1944* (Lawrence, KS: The University Press of Kansas, 2002), 259–287.

304 A. A. Grechko, ed., *Istoriia vtoroi mirovoi voiny 1939–1945 v 12 tomakh, T. 6* [A history of the Second World War 1939–1945 in 12 volumes, vol. 6] (Moscow: Voenizdat, 1976), 142.

305 G. K. Zhukov, *Reminiscences and Reflections, Volume 2* (Moscow: Progress Publishers, 1985), 145.

306 "Doklad komanduiushchego voiskami Severo-zapadnogo fronta No. 0080 Verkhovnomu Glavnokomanduiushchemu plana operatsii po zaversheniiu okruzheniia i razgromu Demianskoi gruppirovki protivnika" [Report no. 0089 of the commander of the forces of the Northwestern Front to the Supreme High Commander concerning an operational plan to complete the encirclement and destruction of the enemy Demiansk grouping], in Zolotarev, "*Stavka* 1943," 268–270.

307 "Direktiva Stavki VGK No. 30018 komanduiushchemu voiskami Severo-zapadnogo fronta ob utvershdenii plana operatsii po zaversheniu razgroma Demianskoi gruppirovki protivnika" [*Stavka* VGK directive no. 30018 to the commander of the forces of the Northwestern Front about the approval of a plan for the destruction of the enemy Demiansk grouping], in Ibid., 31.

308 See "Direktiva Stavki VGK No. 46025 General-polkovniku Khozinu M. S. o formirovanii osoboi gruppy voisk" [Stavka directive no. 46025 to Colonel General Khozin about the formation of a Special Group of Forces], in Ibid., 49.

309 See V. A. Belaivsky, *Strely skrestilis' na Shpree* [Shots crisscrossed along the Spree] (Moscow: Voenizdat, 1973), 68–71.

310 "Direktiva Stavki VGK No. 46021 nachal'niku General'nogo Shtaba, komanduiushchim voiskami Severo-zapadnogo fronta, bronetankovymi i mekhanizirovannymi voiskami Krasnoi Armii, osoboi gruppoi o formirovanii 1-i tankovoi armii" [Stavka VGK directive no. 46021 to the chief of the General Staff, the commanders of the forces of the Northwestern Front, the Armored and Mechanized Forces of the Red Army, and the Special Group about the formation of the 1st Tank Army], in Zolotarev, *Stavka 1943*, 47–48.

311 See "Direktiva Stavki VGK No. 46013 komanduiushchim voiskami Donskogo i Severo-Zapadnogo frontov o vyvode upravleniia, armeiskikh chastei i uchrezhdenii 57-i armii v rezerv Verkhovnogo Glavnokomandovaniia" [Stavka VGK directive no. 46013 to the commanders of the forces of the Don and Northwestern Fronts about the withdrawal of the headquarters and the army units and installations of the 57th Army into the reserve of the Supreme High Command], in Ibid., 42–43.

312 A. Kh. Babadzhanian, N. K. Popol', M. A. Shalin, I. M. Kravchenko, *Liuki otkryli v berline* [They opened the hatchway to Berlin], (Moscow: Voenizdat, 1973), 7–13.

313 See "Prikaz Stavki VGK No. 073 o naznacheniiakh i peremeshcheniiakh komanduiushchikh armiiami Severo-Zapadnogo fronta i 7-i otdel'noi armii" [Stavka order no. 073 about the appointment and shift of the commanders of the armies of the Northwestern Front and 7th Separate Army], in Zolotarev, *Stavka 1943*, 44.

314 See "Direktiva Stavki VGK No. 46019 o naznacheniiakh komanduiushchikh armiiami" [Stavka directive no. 46019 about the appointment of army commanders], in Ibid., 46.

315 See "Prikaz Stavki VGK No. 0015 o naznachenii zamestitelia komanduiushchego Osoboi gruppoi voisk" [Stavka order no, 0015 about the appointment of a deputy commander of the Special group of forces], in Ibid., 56.

316 "Direktiva Stavki VGK No. 30034 komanduiushchim voiskami Leningradskogo i Volkhovskogo frontov o nanesenii udarov po Siniavinskoi gruppirovke protivnika" [Stavka VGK directive no. 30034 to the commanders of the forces of the Leningrad and Volkhov Fronts about the delivery of attacks against the enemy's Siniavino grouping], in Ibid., 56–57.

317 S. P. Platonov, ed., *Bitva za Leningrad* [The battle for Leningrad] (Moscow: Voenizdat, 1964), 276.

318 The 55th Army consisted of the 45th and 63rd Guards, 43rd, 46th, 56th, 72nd, 131st, and 268th Rifle Divisions, the 56th and 250th Rifle, 34th and 35th Ski, and 222nd Tank Brigades, and the 31st Tank Regiment. See *Boevoi sostav, chast' 3*, 57.

319 Paul Carell, *Scorched Earth: The Russian-German War, 1943–1944* (New York: Ballantine Books, 1966), 246.

320 The 54th Army consisted of the 115th, 166th, 177th, 198th, 281st, 285th, 294th, 311th, 374th, and 378th Rifle Divisions and the 14th and 140th Rifle, 6th Naval Rifle, and 122nd and 124th Tank Brigades. See *Boevoi sostav, chast' 3*, 58.

321 On 1 February 1943, the 2nd Shock Army consisted of the 64th Guards, 11th, 18th, 71st, 128th, 147th, 314th, 364th, 376th, and 379th Rifle Divisions, the 72nd Rifle, 73rd Naval Rifle, and 16th and 98th Tank Brigades, the 32nd Guards Tank Regiment, and the 501st, 503rd, and 507th Separate Tank Battalions. The 67th Army consisted of the 13th, 46th, 90th, 142nd, 189th, and 224th Rifle Divisions, the 11th, 55th, 56th, 102nd, 123rd, 138th, 142nd, and 250th Rifle and 1st, 61st, 152nd, and

220th Tank Brigades, the 31st and 46th Guards Tank Regiments, the 86th and 118th Separate Tank Battalions, and the 16th Fortified Region. See *Boevoi sostav, chast' 3*, 32.

322 "Direktiva Stavki VGK No. 30042 komanduiushchemu voiskami Severo-zapadnogo fronta o poriadke razgroma Demianskoi gruppirovki protivnika" [Stavka directive no. 30042 to the commander of the forces of the Northwestern Front about the sequencing of the destruction of the enemy's Demiansk grouping], in Zolotarev, "*Stavka* 1943," 72–73.

323 "Direktiva *Stavka* VGK No. 30039 komanduiushchemu osoboi gruppoi voisk na razgrom Leningradsko-Volkhovskoi gruppirovki protivnika" [Stavka VGK Directive no. 30039 to the commander of the Special Group of Forces on the destruction of the enemy's Leningrad-Volkhov grouping], in Ibid., 70–71.

324 Grechko, *Istoriia Vtoroi Mirovoi voiny 1939–1945*, vol. 6, 146.

325 See A. I. Gribkov, ed., *Istoriia ordena Lenina Leningradskogo Voennogo Okruga* [A history of the Order of Lenin Leningrad Military District] (Moscow: Voenizdat, 1974), 328–329.

326 K. A. Meretskov, *Serving the People* (Moscow: Progress, 1971), 255–256.

327 *Na Volkhovskom Fronte 1941–1944 gg.* [On the Volkhov Front 1941–1944] (Moscow: "Nauka," 1982), 56.

328 See "Direktiva Stavki VGK NO. 30057 komanduiushchim voiskami Leningradskogo i Volkhovskogo frontov o zakreplenii na dostignutykh rubezhakh i podgotovke nastupleniia" [Stavka VGK directive no. 30057 to the commanders of the forces of the Leningrad and Volkhov Fronts about the consolidation in achieved positions and preparations for an offensive], in Zolotarev, "Stavka 1943," 82–83.

329 Grechko, *Istoriia Vtoroi Mirovoi voiny*, vol. 6, 146.

330 E. I. Berdnikov, *Pervaia udarnaia: Boevoi put'1-i udarnoi armii v Velikoi Otechestvennoi voine* [The 1st Shock: The combat path of the 1st Shock Army in the Great Patriotic War] (Moscow: Voenizdat, 1985), 124.

331 Ibid., 124–125.

332 Ibid., 125.

333 Ibid., 125–126.

334 Ibid., 126–127.

335 Direktiva Stavki VGK No. 30052 predstaviteliu Stavki o srokakh nachala operatsii "Poliarnaia zvezda" [Stavka VGK directive no. 30052 to the representative of the *Stavka* about the dates for the beginning of operation "Polar Star"], in Zolotarev, "*Stavka* 1943," 76.

336 Berdnikov, *Pervaia udarnaia*, 127.

337 Earl F. Ziemke, *Stalingrad to Berlin: The German Defeat in the East* (Washington, D.C.: The Office of the Chief of Military History, United States Army, 1968), 112.

338 Berdnikov, *Pervaia udarnaia*, 128.

339 Ibid., 129.

340 Ibid., 130.

341 Ibid., 128.

342 "Doklad predstavitelia Stavki No. 43 Verkhovnemu Glavnokomanduiushchemu predlozhenii o perenose srokov nachala operatsii "Poliarnaia zvezda" [Report no. 43 of the representative of the *Stavka* to the Supreme High Commander about a proposal for shifting the timing of the beginning of operation "Polar Star"], in Zolotarev, "*Stavka* 1943," 282–283.

AFTER STALINGRAD

Notes to Chapter 10

343 Berdnikov, *Pervaia udarnaia*, 130.

344 A. Kh. Babadzhanian, N. K. Popel', M. A. Shalin, I. M. Kravchenko, *Liuki otkryli v Berline; Boevoi put' 1-i gvardeiskoi tankovoi armii* [They opened the hatchway to Berlin; The combat path of the 1st Guards Tank Army] (Moscow: Voenizdat, 1973), 12–13.

345 Berdnikov, *Pervaia udarnaia*, 130–131.

346 "Direktiva Stavki VGK No. 30056 komanduiushchim voiskami Leningradskogo i Volkhovskogo frontov, predstavitel'iu Stavki o perepodchinenii 2-i udarnoi Armii" [Stavka VGK directive no. 30065 to the commanders of the forces of the Leningrad and Volkhov Fronts and the representative of the *Stavka* about the re-subordination of the 2nd Shock Army], in Zolotarev, "*Stavka* 1943," 89.

347 "Direktiva Stavki VGK No. 30066 komanduiushchim voiskami Leningradskogo i Volkhovskogo frontov, predstaviteliu Stavki na razgrom Mginsko-Siniavinskoi gruppirovki protivnika" [Stavka VGK directive no. 30066 to the commanders of the forces of the Leningrad and Volkhov Fronts and the representative of the *Stavka* on the destruction of the enemy's Mga-Siniavino grouping], in Ibid., 89–90.

348 "Doklad zamestitelia Verkhovnogo Glavnokomanduiushchego No. 1496 Verkhovnomu Glavnokomanduiushchemu ob izmeneniiakh v plane razgroma protivnika v raione Staroi Russy" [Report No. 1496 of the deputy Supreme High Commander to the Supreme High Commander about changes in the plan for the destruction of the enemy in the Staraia Russa region], in Ibid., 283–284.

349 "Direktiva Stavki VGK predstaviteliu Stavki ob utvershdenii plana razgroma protivnika v raione Staroi Russy" [Stavka VGK directive to the representative of the *Stavka* about the approval of a plan for the destruction of the enemy in the Staraia Russa region], in Ibid., 91.

350 "Direktiva Stavki VGK No. 46068 predstaviteliu Stavku, komanduiushchim voiskami Severo-zapadnogo fronta, osoboi gruppoi voisk o formirovanii na base gruppy reservnoi armii" [Stavka VGK directive no. 46068 to the representative of the *Stavka* and the commanders of the forces of the Northwestern Front and the Special Group of Forces about the formation of a reserve army on the basis of the Special Group], in Ibid., 91.

351 Berdnikov, *Pervaia udarnaia*, 130–132. The reinforcing 6th and 9th Guards Airborne Divisions had been transferred to the 1st Tank Army after the February assaults failed. Zhukov then reassigned them to the 1st Shock Army to replace the 3rd Guards and 391st Rifle Divisions, which had been decimated in the previous fighting.

352 The 52nd Army consisted of the 65th, 225th, 229th, and 310th Rifle Divisions, the 38th Ski Brigade, the 34th, and 53rd Aerosleigh Battalions, and the 150th Fortified Region. The 229th and 310th Rifle Divisions reinforced Iakovlev's army just prior to the attack. See *Boevoi sostav, chast' 3*, 58.

353 Platonov, *Bitva za Leningrad, 187, and* Gribkov, *Istoriia Leningradskogo voenogo okruga*, 329.

354 Ibid., 119, and *Na Volkhovskom fronte*, 56–57.

355 *Na Volkhovskom fronte*, 57.

356 See "Direktiva Stavki VGK No. 30086 komanduiushchemu voiskami Volkhovskogo fronta o zakreplenii 8-i armii na dostignutom rubezhe" [*Stavka* VGK directive no. 30086 to the commander of the forces of the Volkhov Front about the consolidation of the 8th Army in its achieved positions], in Zolotarev, "*Stavka* 1943," 113, and "Direktiva Stavki VGK No. 30087 komanduiushchemu voiskami Leningradskogo

fronta o zakreplenii 55-i armii na dostignutom rubezhe" [*Stavka* VGK directive no. 30087 to the commander of the forces of the Leningrad Front about the consolidation of the 55th Army its achieved positions], in Ibid., 114.

357 Krivosheev, *Grif sekretnosti sniat*, 226.

358 Gurkin, "*Liudskie poteri*," 7.

359 Krivosheev, *Grif sekretnosti sniat*', 224, and Gurkin, "*Liudskie poteri*," 4.

Notes to Chapter 11

360 See, P. N. Pospelov, ed., *Istoriia Velikoi Otechevesnnoi voiny Sovetskogo Soiuza 1941–1945 v shesti tomakh, tom tretii* [A History of the Great Patriotic War of the Soviet Union 1941–1945 in six volumes, volume 3] (Moscow: Voenizdat, 1961), 142–143.

361 Grechko, *Istoriia Vtoroi Mirovoi voiny*, Vol. 6, 30.

362 Pospelov, *Istoriia Velikoi Otechevesnnoi voiny Sovetskogo Soiuz*, Vol. 3, 142–143.

363 Grechko, *Istoriia Vtoroi Mirovoi voiny*, Vol. 6, 146–147.

364 V. A. Zolotarev, ed., *Velikaia Otechestvennia voina 1941–1945 v chetyrekh tomakh, kniga 2 Perelom* [The Great Patriotic War 1941–1945 in four volumes, book 2 The turning point] (Moscow: "Nauka," 1998), 37–39.

365 Ibid., 213–214.

366 Ibid., 229–231.

367 According to this myth, Stalin and the *Stavka* concentrated the Red Army's forces along the southwestern and southern axes (in the Ukraine and the Crimea) during the winter campaign of 1943–1944, along the western axis (in Belorussia) during the mid-summer of 1944, along the northwestern axis (the Baltic region) and the southern axis (Romania and the Balkans) during the late summer and fall of 1944, along the western axis (in East Prussia and Poland) during the winter of 1944–1945, and along the western axis (toward Berlin) during the spring of 1945.

368 For example, while the Red Army was conducting its offensives in the Ukraine and the Crimea during the winter campaign of 1943–1944, it also launched a major offensive against German forces in Belorussia. When it conducted its offensive in Belorussia during the summer of 1944, it also launched offensives into the Baltic region, southern Poland and Rumania. As it conducted its offensive into the Baltic region and the Balkans during the late summer and fall of 1944, it also attempted to invade East Prussia and conduct a major envelopment of Axis forces in eastern Hungary. When it launched its offensives into East Prussia and Poland during January 1945, it also conducted important offensive operations in central Hungary, and, finally, before advancing to Berlin April 1945, it conducted a major thrust to Vienna and eastern Austria.

369 For example, planning time for the Stalingrad operation lasted more than one month. Thus, offensive preparations were extensive. Planning time for other operations was as follows: Little Saturn — over three weeks; Ostrogozhsk-Rossosh' — about 20 days; and about one week for the Voronezh-Kastornoe and subsequent operations.

Bibliography

Abbreviations

JSMS — *The Journal of Soviet Military Studies*

NAM — National Archives microfilm series

SMPIOV — *Sbornik materialov po izucheniiu opyta voiny* [Collection of materials for the study of war experience]

SVIMVOV — *Sbornik voenno-istoricheskikh materialov Velikoi Otechestvennoi voiny* [Collection of military-historical materials on the Great Patriotic War]

TsAMO RF — *Tsentral'nyi arkhiv ministerstva oborony RF* [Central Archives of the Russian Federation's Ministry of Defense. All archival references cited as *TsAMO*, with appropriate fond (f.), opis (op.), delo (d.), page (l.), and, if present, specific title.

VIZh — *Voenno-istoricheskii zhurnal* [Military-historical journal]

Primary Sources

"Anlage zum Kriegstagebuch A. O. K. 2 – Ia, Russland, Teil 9, Lagenkarten 1. January 1943 bis 31. Marz 1943," *AOK 2, 31811/2*, in NAM T–312, Roll 1213.

"Boevaia kharakteristika na 38 gv. RD" [The combat characteristics of 38th Guards Rifle Division], in *TsAMO RF*, f. 1131, op. 1, d. 3, ll. 7–8.

"Boevaia kharakteristika na 121 sd" [Combat Characteristics of 121st Rifle Division], from "Boevye rasporiazheniia shtaba Voronezhskogo fronta" [Combat orders of Voronezh Front], in *TsAMO RF*, f. 417, op. 10564, d. 252, l. 12.

"Boevaia kharakteristika na 248 otdel'nuiu kursantskuiu strelkovuiu brigadu" [Combat characteristics of 248th Student Rifle Brigade], from "Boevye rasporiazheniia shtaba Voronezhskogo fronta" [Combat orders of Voronezh Front], in *TsAMO RF*, f. 417, op. 10564, d. 252, l. 13.

"Boevoi prikaz No. 001 shtaba Kurskogo fronta" [Combat order No. 001 of Kursk Front's headquarters], from "Prikazy NKO i voiskam Voronezhskogo fronta (1943)" [Orders of the NKO and to the Voronezh Front's forces (1943)], in *TsAMO RF*, f. 417, op. 10564, d. 243, l. 12.

Boevoi sostav Sovetskoi armii, Chast' 2 (Ianvar'-dekabr' 1942 goda) [Combat composition of the Soviet Army, Part 2 (January-December 1942)]. Moscow: Voenizdat, 1966. Prepared by the Military-Scientific Directorate of the General Staff.

"Boevye deistviia voisk Brianskogo i Voronezhskogo frontov letom 1942 na voronezhkom napravlenii" [Combat actions of Briansk and Voronezh Front forces in the summer of 1942 along the Voronezh direction], in *SVIMVOV*, *vypusk 15* [Issue 15]. Moscow: Voenizdat, 1955.

"Boevye doneseniia i operativnye svodki shtaba 1 mekhkorpusa" [Combat reports and operational summaries of 1st Mechanized Corps' headquarters], in *TsAMO RF*, f. 3404, op. 1, d. 2, ll. 2–36.

"Chefkarten, 14 Anlagen, Pz AOK 2, Is, Lagenkarten 18. 3.1943 – 31. 3. 1943, *Pz AOK 2 237075/47, in NAM T–313, Roll 171.*

"Chefkarten, 28 Anlagen, Anlagenband 33, Pz AOK 2, Ia, Lagenkarten 1.2.1943-28.2.1943," *Pz AOK 2, 37075/46*, in NAM T–313, Roll 171.

"Direktivy i prikazy SVGK. Genshtaba Kr. Ar. Brianskogo fronta voiskam" [Directives and orders of the *Stavka* of the Supreme High Command and the Red Army General Staff to the forces of Briansk Front], in *TsAMO*, f. 361, op. 6079, d. 174. l. 35.

"Direktivy SVGK, GSh, KA voiskam brianskogo fronta, 3A, 2. 1–20. 7. 43" [Directives of the *Stavka* of the Supreme High Command to the forces of Briansk Front and 13th Army, 2 January–20 July 1943], in *TsAMO RF*, f. 361, op. 6079, d. 173, ll. 138–144.

"Iz direktivy Voennogo Soveta Brianskogo fronta komanduiushchemu 13 armii (kopiia komanduuishchemu 3 armii. 4. 2. 43g." [From a directive of Briansk Front's Military Council to 13th Army commander, dated 4 February 1943, with a copy to the commander of 3rd Army], from "Direktivy SVGK" [Directives of the *Stavka* of the Supreme High Command], in *TsAMO RF*, f. 361, op. 6079, d. 173, l 74.

"Iz direktivy Voennogo Soveta Brianskogo fronta ot 6.2 43g. komanduiushchim, chlennam Voennykh Sovetov, nachal'nikam politotdelov armii [From a 6 February directive of Briansk Front's Military Council to the commanders, members of the Military Councils, and chiefs of the armies' political departments], from "Direktivy SVGK" [Directives of the *Stavka* of the Supreme High Command], in *TsAMO*, f. 361, op. 6079, d. 174, l. 79, 87.

"Komandiram 1, 2, 3 armeiskikh zagradotriadov. 16. 3. 43g. No. 0224" [Order No. 0224, dated 16 March 1943, to the commanders of 1st, 2nd, and 3rd Army Blocking Detachments], from "Direktivy SVGK, GSh, KA voiskam Brianskogo fronta, 13A, 2. 1–20. 7. 43" [Directives of the *Stavka* of the Supreme High Command to the forces of Briansk Front and 13th Army, 2 January–20 July 1943], in *TsAMO RF*, f. 361, op. 6079, d. 173, l. 105.

"Komandiram divizii 13A. No. 0144. 11. 3. 43g. [Order No. 0144, dated 11 March 1943, to the commanders of 13th Army's divisions], in *TsAMO RF*, f. 361, op. 6079, d. 173, l. 80.

"Materialy po planirovaniiu i provedeniiu Voronezhskoi i L'govsko-Ryl'skoi nastupatel'noi operatsii 2. 1–18. 3. 43g" [Materials concerning the planning and conduct of the Voronezh and L'gov-Ryl'sk offensive operations, 2 January–18 March 1943], in *TsAMO RF*, f. 417, op. 10564, d. 256, ll. 63–65.

"Operativnoe marshi tankovykh i mekhaninizirovannykh soedinenii" [The operational marches of tank and mechanized formations], in *SMPIOV, No. 9 noiabr'-dekabr' 1943 g.* [No. 9, November-December 1943]. Moscow: Voenizdat, 1944.

"Operativnye svodki i boevye donesenii 350 sd" [Operational summaries and combat reports of 350th Rifle Division], in *TsAMO RF*, f. 1669, op. 1, d. 24, l. 165.

"Opisanie boevykh deistvii na rubezhe r. Vazuza za 25 noiabria–18 dekabria 1942 goda" [An account of combat operations along the Vazuza River line from 25 November–18 December 1942], Polevoe upravlenie 20 Armii [20th Army's field headquarters], in *TsAMO RF*, f. 373, op. 6631, d. 65, l. 2.

"Otchety shtaba 184 rd o boevykh desistviiakh" [An account by the headquarters, 184th Rifle Division, of its combat operations], in *TsAMO RF*, f. 1435, op. 1, d. 8, l. 31.

"Perepiski operativnogo otdela shtaba 13A co shtabom 15sd" [Correspondence of the operational department of 13th Army's headquarters with 15th Rifle Division's headquarters], in *TsAMO RF*, f. 361, op. 6079, d. 183, ll. 193, 204, 206, and 285.

"Politupravlenie Brianskogo fronta. 3. 2. 34g. No. 0523. Komanduiushchim 13 i 48 armii. Sovershenno sekretno"[Order No. 0523, dated 3 February 1943, of Briansk Front's Political Directorate. To the commanders of 13th and 48th Armies. Top secret], from "Direktivy SVGK, GSh, KA voiskam Brianskogo fronta, 13A (2. 1–20. 7. 43g.)" [Directives of the *Stavka* of the Supreme High Command and Red Army General Staff to the forces of Briansk Front and 13th Army (2 January–20 July 1943)], in *TsAMO RF*, f. 361, op. 6079, d. 173, l. 76.

"Prikaz chastiam 121sd No. 0045. 12. 3. 43." [Order No. 0044 to 121st Rifle Division's units, dated 12 March 1943], from "Boevye prikazy i pazporiazheniia soedinenii 60A (1942–1943 gg.)" [Combat orders and instructions of 60th Army's formations (1942–1943)], in *TsAMO RF*, f. 417, op. 10564, d. 215, l. 67.

"Prikaz chastiam 121 sd No. 074. 31. 3. 43g. [Order No. 074 to 121st Rifle Division's units, dated 31 March 1943] from "Boevye prikazy soedinenii 60A (1943g.)" [Combat orders to 60th Army's formations (1943)], in *TsAMO RF*, f. 417, op. 10564, d. 251, l. 6.

"Prikaz voiskam Brianskogo fronta No. 31/2. 1. 2. 43g. Sekretno" [Order No. 31/2 to Briansk Front's forces, dated 1 February 1943. Secret], from "Direktivy SVGK" [Directives of the *Stavka* of the Supreme High Command], in *TsAMO*, f. 361, op. 6079, d. 174, l. 70.

"Prikaz 65A. 25. 3. 43g." [65th Army's Order No. 4, dated 25 March 1943] from "Dokumenty iz fondov 65A" [Documents from the archives of 65th Army], in *TsAMO RF*, f. 422, op. 10496, d. 81, l. 12.

"Prikazy 10-mu TK s 13.5 po 27.12.42" [Orders to 10th Tank Corps from 13 May through 27 December 1942], in *TsAMO RF*, f. 3404, op. 1, d. 1, l. 225.

"Report by 3rd Air Army's representative with 1st MC during Operation "Mars" (Russian title unknown), in *TsAMO RF*, f. 311, op. 311, d. 24, ll. 86–87.

"Situation maps and overlays (1:300,000), prepared by the Second Army, Counter-intelligence Officer (Ic/AO) (no German title), December 1942-July 1943, *AOK 2, 31811/123*, in NAM T–312, Roll 1223.

SMPIOV, No. 7, iiun'-iiul' 1943 g. [No. 7, June-July 1943]. Moscow: Voenizdat, 1943.

"Sychevsko-Rzhevskaia oper. 31 A" [Sychevka-Rzhev operation of 31st Army], in *TsAMO RF, f. 386, op. 8583, ed. khr. 144, ll. 7–10.*

"Tatigkeitsbericht der Abteilung Ic/A.O." dated 1 July–3 Dec 1942. *AOK 9, 27970/6*, in NAM T–312, Roll 304.

"Voronezhsko-kastornenskaia nastupatel'naia operatsiia voisk Voronezhskogo i levogo kryla Brianskogo frontov" [The Voronezh-Kastornoe offensive operation of forces of the Voronezh and left wing of the Briansk Fronts], in *SVIMVOV, vypusk 13* [Issue 13]. Moscow: Military-historical Directorate of the Soviet Armed Forces General Staff, 1954.

"Vvod v proryv konno-mekhanizirovannykh grupp" [The commitment of a cavalry-mechanized group into the penetration], *SMPIOV, No. 9 (noiabr'-dekabr' 1943 g.)* [No. 9 (November-December 1943)]. Moscow: Voenizdat, 1944.

Zolotarev, V. A., ed. "Preliudiia Kurskoi bitvy: Dokumenty i materily, 6 dekabria 1942 g.25 aprelia 1943 g." [Prelude to the battle of Kursk, 6 December 1942–25 April 1943], in *Russkii arkhiv: Velikaia Otechestvennaia*, 15, 4 (3) [The Russian archives: Great Patriotic, 15, 4 (3)]. Moscow: TERRA, 1997.

——————. "Stavka VGK: Dokumenty i materialy 1942" [The *Stavka* VGK: Documents and materials], in *Russki arkhiv, 16, 5 (2)* [The Russian archives, 16, 5 (2)]. Moscow: "Terra," 1996.

——————. "*Stavka* Verkhovnogo Glavnokomandovaniia: Dokumenty i materialy, 1943 god." [The *Stavka* of the Supreme High Command: Documents and materials, 1943], in *Russkii arkhiv, 16, 5 (3)* [Russian archives, 16, 5 (3)]. Moscow: TERRA, 1999.

"5th Tank Corps combat reports from 11–15 December," in *TsAMO RF*, f. 3404, op. 1, d. 9, 10, l. 259.

Secondary Sources: Books

Afanas'ev, N. M., N. K. Glazunov, P. A. Kazanskii, and N. A. Fifonov. *Dorogami ispytanii i pobed: Boevoi put' 31-i armii* [The roads to experience and victory: The combat path of 31st Army]. Moscow: Voenizdat, 1986.

Andreev, A. A. *Po voennym dorogam* [Along military roads]. Moscow: Voenizdat, 1971.

Andreev, A. M. *Ot pervogo mgnoveniia do poslednego* [From the first moment to the last]. Moscow: Voenizdat, 1984.

Babadzhanian, A. Kh., N. K. Popol', M. A. Shalin, and I. M. Kravchenko. *Liuki otkryli v Berline* [They opened the hatchway to Berlin]. Moscow: Voenizdat, 1973.

Bagramian, I. Kh. *Tak shli my k pobede* [As we went on to victory]. Moscow: Voenizdat, 1988.

Batov, P. I. *V pokhodakh i boiakh* [In marches and battles]. Moscow: Voenizdat, 1966.

Baumann, Hans. *Die 35. Infantrie-division im 2. Weltkrig 1939–1945*. Karlsruhe, Germany: Verlag G. Braun GMBH, 1964.

Belaivsky, V. A. *Strely skrestilis' na Shpree* [Shots crisscrossed along the Spree]. Moscow: Voenizdat, 1973).

Berdnikov, G. I. *Pervaia udarnaia: Boevoi put' 1-i udarnoi armii v Velikoi Otechestvennoi voine* [1st Shock: The combat path of 1st Shock Army in the Great Patriotic War. Moscow: Voenizdat, 1985.

Boiko, V. P. *S dumoi o Rodine* [With thoughts about the Homeland. Moscow: Voenizdat, 1979.

Chistiakov, I. M. *Sluzhim otchizne* [In the service of the fatherland]. Moscow: Voenizdat, 1975.

Dokuchaev, M. S. *V boi shli eskadrony* [The squadrons went into battle]. Moscow: Voenizdat, 1984.

Domnikov, V. M., ed. *V nastuplenii gvardiia: Ocherk boevom puti 2-i gvardeiskoi armii* [Guards on the offensive: A survey of the combat path of 2nd Guards Army]. Moscow: Voenizdat, 1971.

Dremov, I. F. *Nastupala grozhaia bronia* [Threatening armor attacks]. Kiev: Politicheskoi literatury Ukrainy, 1981.

Ershov, A. G. *Osvobozhdenie donbassa* [The liberation of the Donbas]. Moscow: Voenizdat, 1973.

Getman, A. L. *Tanki idut na Berlin (1941–1945)* [Tanks advance on Berlin (1941–1945]. Moscow: Nauka, 1973.

Glantz, David M. *From the Don to the Dnepr: Soviet Offensive Operations, December 1942-August 1943*. London: Frank Cass, 1991.

——————. *Khar'kov, May 1942: The Anatomy of a Military Disaster*. London: Ian Allen, 1999.

Grechko, A. A. ed., *Istoriia vtoroi mirovoi voiny 1939–1945 v 12 tomakh, T. 6* [A history of the Second World War 1939–1945 in 12 volumes, vol. 6]. Moscow: Voenizdat, 1976.

Gribkov, A. I., ed. *Istoriia ordena Lenina Leningradskogo Voennogo Okruga* [A history of the Order of Lenin Leningrad Military District]. Moscow: Voenizdat, 1974.

Grossman, H. *Rzhev: The Cornerstone of the Eastern Front*, unpublished manuscript translated by Joseph Welch from the German, *Rshew: Eckpfeiler der Ostefront*. Freidberg, Germany, 1980.

Iushchuk, I. I. *Odinnadtsatyi tankovyi korpus v boiakh za rodinu* [The 11th Tank Corps in battles for the Homeland]. Moscow: Voenizdat, 1962.

Katukov, M. E. *Na ostrie glavnogo udara* [On the point of the main attack]. Moscow: Voenizdat, 1976.

Khlebnikov, N. M. *Pod grokhot soten baterei* [Under the thunder of hundreds of batteries]. Moscow: Voenizdat, 1979.

Kochetkov, A. D. *Dvinskiii tankovyi: boevoi put'5-go tankovogo dvinskogo korpusa* [The Dvina Tank: The combat path of 5th Dvina Tank Corps. Moscow: Voenizdat, 1989.

Krivosheev, G. F., ed. *Grif sekretnosti sniat: Poteri Vooruzhennykh Sil SSSR v voinakh, boevykh deistviakh i voennykh konfliktakh: Statisticheskoe issledovanie* [The secret classification is removed: The losses of the USSR's Armed Forces in wars, combat operations, and military conflicts: A statistical study]. Moscow: Voenizdat, 1993.

Krylov, N. I, I. I. Alekseev, and I. G. Dragon. *Navstrechu pobede: Boevoi put's 5-i armii* [Meeting victory: The combat path of 5th Army]. Moscow: Nauka, 1970.

Kuznetsov, P. G. *Gvardeitsy-moskvichi* [Guards-Muscovites]. Moscow: Voenizdat, 1962.

Lobanov, V. *Vosemnadtsataia gvardeiskaia* [The 18th Guards]. Kaliningrad: Kaliningradskoe knizhnoe izdatel'stvo, 1975.

Mal'kov, D. K. *Skvoz' dym i plamia* [Through smoke and flames]. Moscow: Voenizdat, 1970.

Malygin, K. A. *V tsentre boevogo poriadka* [In the center of the combat formation]. Moscow: Voenizdat, 1986.

Meretskov, K. A. *Serving the People*. Moscow: Progress Publishers, 1971.

Morozov, V. P. *Zapadnee voronezha* [West of Voronezh]. Moscow: Voenizdat, 1956.

Moskalenko, K. S. *Na iugo-zapadnom napravlenii, Tom. 2* [Along the southwestern axis, Vol. 2]. Moscow: Izdatel'stvo Nauka, 1969.

Nagysev, G. S. *Na sluzhbe shtabnoi* [In staff service]. Riga: Izdatel'stbo Pissma, 1972.

Na Volkhovskom Fronte 1941–1944 gg. [On the Volkhov Front 1941–1944]. Moscow: Nauka, 1982.

Ot volzhskikh stepei do avstrilskikh al'p [From the Volga steppes to the Austrian Alps]. Moscow: Voenizdat, 1971.

Pankov, F. D. *Ognennye rubezhi* [Firing positions]. Moscow: Voenizdat, 1964.

Pavlov, I. N. *Ot Moskby do Shtrol'zunda* [From Moscow to Straslund]. Moscow: Voenizdat, 1985.

Plato, Anton Detlev von. *Die Geschichte der 5. Panzerdivision 1938 bis 1945.* Regensburg: Walhalla u. Praetoria Verlag KG Geog Zwickenpflug, 1978.

Po prukazu Rodiny [By order of the fatherland]. Moscow: Voenizdat, 1971.

Pospelov, P. N., ed. *Istoriia Velikoi Otechevesnnoi voiny Sovetskogo Soiuz 1941–1945 v shesti tomakh, tom tretii* [A History of the Great Patriotic War of the Soviet Union 1941–1945 in six volumes, vol. 3]. Moscow: Voenizdat, 1961.

Rokossovsky, K. *A Soldier's Duty*. Moscow: Progress Publishers, 1985.
Samchuk, A. I., P. G. Skachko, Iu. N. Babikov, and I. L. Ghedoi. *Ot Volgi do El'by i Pragi* [From the Volga to the Elbe and Prague]. Moscow: Voenizdat, 1970.
Sekretov, A. I. *Gvardeiskaia postup' (boevoi put' 17-i Mozyrskoi Krasnoznamennoi ordena Lenina, Suvorova i Kutuzova kavaleriiskoi divizii, podwhefnoi Tadzhikistnu, v gody Velikoi Otechestvennoi voiny 1941–1945 gg.)* [Guards gait (the combat path of the Mozyr, Red Banner, Orders of Lenin, Suvorov, and Kutuzov 17th Guards Cavalry Division, sponsored by Tadzhikistan in the Great Patriotic War, 1941–1945)]. Dushanbe: Donish, 1985.
Sharipov, A. *Cherniakhovskii*. Moscow: Voenizdat, 1971.
Shilov, K. K. *Rechitskaia krasnoznamennaia* [Rechitsa red banner]. Moscow: Voenizdat, 1984.
Shtemenko, S. M. *General'nyi shtab v gody voiny* [The General Staff in the war years]. Moscow: Voenizdat, 1968.
Solomatin, M. D. *Krasnogradtsy* [The men of Krasnograd]. Moscow: Voenizdat, 1963).
Stoves, Rolf O. G. *1. Panzer-Division 1935–1945*, (Bad Neuheim, Germany: Verlag Hans-Henning Podzun, 1961.
Telegin, K. F. *Voiny neschitannye versty* [Uncounted versts of war]. Moscow: Voenizdat, 1988.
Tolubko, V. F and N. I. Baryshev. *Na Uizhnom flange: Boevoi put' 4-go gvardeiskogo mekhanizirovannogo korpusa (1942–1944 gg.)* [On the southern flank: The combat path of 4th Guards Mechanized Corps (1942–1945)]. Moscow: Nauka, 1973.
Vasilevsky, A. M. *Delo vsei zhizni* [A lifelong cause]. Moscow: Politizdat, 1983.
V plameni srazhenii: Boevoi put' 13-i armii [In the flames of battle: The combat path of 13th Army]. Moscow: Voenizdat, 1973.
V srazheniiakh za Pobedy: Boevoi put' 38-i armii v gody Velikoi Otechestvennoi voiny 1941–1945 [The battles for the Homeland: The combat path of 38th Army in the Great Patriotic War 1941–1945]. Moscow: Nauka, 1974.
Vysotsky, F. I. M. F. Makukhin, F. M. Sarychev, and M. K. Shaposhynikov. *Gvardeiskaia tankovaia* [Guards tank]. Moscow: Voenizdat, 1963.
Zhilin, P. A. ed. *Na severo-zapadnom fronte 1941–1943* [On the Northwestern Front 1941–1943]. Moscow: Nauka, 1969.
Zhukov, G. *Reminiscences and Reflections, Vol. 2*. Moscow: Progress Publishers, 1985.
Ziemke, Earl F. *Stalingrad to Berlin: The German Defeat in the East*. Washington, DC: Office of the Chief of Military History United States Army, 1968.
Zolotarev, V. A., ed. *Velikaia Otechestvennia voina 1941–1945 v chetyrekh tomakh, kniga 2 Perelom* [The Great Patriotic War 1941–1945 in four volumes, book 2 The turning point]. Moscow: Nauka, 1998).

Secondary Sources: Articles

Gurkhin, V. V. "Liudskie poteri Sovetskikh Vooruzhennykh Sil v 1941–1945 gg.: Novye aspekty" [Personnel losses of the Soviet Armed Forces 1941–1945: New aspects], in *VIZh*, No. 2 (March-April 1999).
Isaev, S. I. *"Vekhi frontovogo puti"* [Landmarks of a front path], in *VIZh*, No. 10 (October 1991).
Kahn, David. "An Intelligence Case History: The Defense of Osuga, 1942," in *Aerospace Historian*, Vol. 28, No. 4 (Winter/December 1981), 242–251.

Larson, Kent A. "The Debal'tsevo Raid, February 1943: A Case Study in the Role of Initiative in Soviet Operational Art," in *JSMS*, Vol. 5, No. 3 (September 1992).

Maslov, A. A. "The Unknown Pages of a Heroic Raid," in *JSMS*, Vol. 10, No. 2 (June 1997.

Mikhalev, S. "O razrabotke zamysla i planirovanii kontrnastuleniia pod stalingradom" [About working out the concept and planning of the Stalingrad counteroffensive], in *Vestnik voennnoi informatsii* [Herald of military information], No. 8 (August 1992).

Morozov, V. "Pochemu ne zavershilos' nastuplenie v Donbasse vesnoi 1943 goda" [Why was the offensive in the Donbas in the spring of 1943 not completed], in *VIZh*, No. 3 (March 1963).

Index

Related titles published by Helion & Company

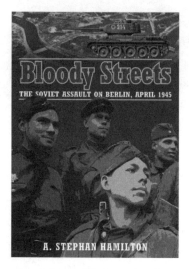

Bloody Streets: The Soviet Assault on
Berlin, April 1945
A.S. Hamilton
424pp, 325 photos, 8pp colour
AFV profiles, c.60 maps, 12 tables
ISBN 978 1 906033 12 5

Road to Destruction: Operation Blue and
the Battle of Stalingrad 1942–43,
A Photographic History
Ian Baxter
128pp, c.200 photos, maps
ISBN 978 1 906033 15 6

A selection of forthcoming titles

Battle in the Baltics 1944–45. The Fighting for Latvia, Lithuania and Estonia,
A Photographic History
Ian Baxter   ISBN 978 1 906033 33 0

A Flawed Genius: Field Marshall Walter Model, A Critical Biography
Marcel Stein   ISBN 978 1 906033 30 9

Over Fields of Fire: Flying the Sturmovik in Action on the Eastern Front 1942–45
Anna Timofeeva-Egorova   ISBN 978 1 906033 27 9

HELION & COMPANY LIMITED
26 Willow Road, Solihull, West Midlands, B91 1UE, England
Tel 0121 705 3393   Fax 0121 711 4075
Website: http://www.helion.co.uk